ADMINISTRATIVE LAW

Other books in *Essentials of Canadian Law* Series

ESSENTIALS OF CANADIAN LAW

ADMINISTRATIVE LAW

DAVID J. MULLAN

IRWIN
LAW

A Quicklaw Company

Published in 2001 by
Irwin Law
Suite 930, Box 235
One First Canadian Place
Toronto, Ontario
M5X 1C8

ISBN: 1-55221-009-X

Canadian Cataloguing in Publication Data

Mullan, David J.
    Administrative law

(Essentials of Canadian law)
Includes bibliographical references and index.
ISBN 1-55221-009-X

1. Administrative law – Canada.   I. Title.   II. Series.

KE5015.M84 2000   342.71'066   C00-930148-8
KF5402.M84 2000

Printed and bound in Canada.

1   2   3   4   5   04   03   02   01   00

SUMMARY
TABLE OF CONTENTS

DETAILED
TABLE OF CONTENTS

To the memory of David Cox, Martha Reid,
and Agnès Lefas

PREFACE

This contribution to the Essentials of Canadian Law series has been in the works for a long time — indeed far, far longer than either the publishers or I ever wanted. The fault for that lies almost entirely with me, and I thank William Kaplan, Jeff Miller, and, latterly, Hugh Lawford, and Lillian Simkins for their forbearance and the patience with which they tolerated my many postponements of the delivery of the manuscript and corrected page proofs.

In writing this monograph, I had the benefit of research assistance from Shannon Chace-Hall, Queen's Law '01, for the section on the authority of tribunals to deal with Charter issues, while David Stratas and Garry Watson were kind enough to comment on the material on issue estoppel. My thanks go out to them. As the book largely reflects the content of the administrative law course that I have taught on and off over the past thirty years, I also owe a special debt to my students. They have both stimulated my thinking and provided ideas and perspectives that have added to my understanding of the subject area. In particular, the material on remedies was influenced for the better in many ways by the discussions that took place in a seminar that I led in 1997 as part of the Osgoode Hall Law School's part-time LL.M. program in administrative law. As well, I have benefited from interactions with a number of very talented students who have been members of the Laskin Constitutional and Administrative Law Moot teams of the Queen's Faculty of Law in the last few years. Also, since 1980, I have used as the teaching materials for my course in Administrative Law successive editions of Evans, Janisch, Mullan, & Risk, *Administrative Law: Cases, Text & Materials*. As a result, the current work is based in many parts both in its form and its content on that casebook. It has also been enhanced significantly by the talents, endeavours, and views of my partners in that enterprise: John Evans (now a Justice of the Federal Court of Appeal), Hudson Janisch, and Dick Risk. I am also particularly grateful to the anonymous reviewer selected by the publishers and whose detailed comments have made this a better work and saved me from some embarrassment. To these, as well as my various teachers and many other fans of administrative law with whom I have interacted over the years, my warmest thanks.

Inevitably, the content of this book relies a great deal on my previous work in the area of administrative law, and particularly the casebook and the administrative law title in the *Canadian Encyclopedic Digest*, published by Carswell. However, with two exceptions, all the material drawn from my previous work has been rewritten and in many instances reflects evolutions in both the jurisprudence and my own ideas. The first exception is some of the discussion of the impact of the judgment of the Supreme Court of Canada in *Baker* v. *Canada (Minister of Citizenship and Immigration)*, [1999] 2 S.C.R. 817. Parts of that are lifted directly from my case comment on the judgment, which appeared in (1999), 7 *Reid's Administrative Law* 145. As well, I have drawn on two conference presentations for the material on the impact of *Blencoe* v. *Canadian Human Rights Commission*, [2000] SCC 44 (October 5, 2000) on the scope of section 7 of the *Canadian Charter of Rights and Freedoms*.

Finally, I would be extremely remiss if I did not thank my secretary, Phyllis Reid, for all her work in preparing the manuscript for submission, and my spouse, Liz, for her support and continuing good humour and calm during what was often for me a very frustrating exercise.

To the extent that it has proved feasible, the law as stated is current to the end of 1999, with some adjustments made for cases decided in the first ten months of 2000.

PART ONE

BACKGROUND

CHAPTER 1

THE REACH OF ADMINISTRATIVE LAW

A. INTRODUCTION

Providing a satisfactory definition of administrative law is not an easy task. At its most general, it is the field of law that has as its concern the statutes (other than the Constitution), principles, and the rules that govern the operations of government and its various emanations. It embraces not only the relationships that exist among various branches of government but, perhaps more important, the relationship between those same agencies of governance and the constituencies with which they deal — individuals, groups, and other entities that possess legal personality. It comprises the operational principles and rules by which public decision makers function.

Another way of defining administrative law is that it constitutes the body of law that establishes or describes the legal parameters of powers that exist by virtue of statute or residual Royal prerogative.[1] In terms of the relation between the administrative process and the regular courts, administrative law embodies the principles by which the courts supervise the functioning of persons and bodies that derive their powers from either statute or the Royal prerogative. In this negative guise, which will figure prominently throughout this book, it involves the

---

1   Those residual powers not formally removed from the monarchy by Parliament and now for the most part exercised by the executive in the name of the Crown, such as the bestowing of honours and the declaration of war.

principles by which the courts ensure that statutory or prerogative decision-makers observe the limits on the authority which they exercise; that they do not act invalidly or without authority.

However, those two conceptions of the scope of administrative law immediately encounter a number of difficulties. At one level, these definitions are probably over-inclusive. They embrace statutory forms of empowerment that most would not treat as part of administrative law and, most notably, all corporations and other artificial legal persons that owe their existence to statute. To avoid including such bodies within the domain of administrative law, those who engage in such demarcation exercises generally limit the scope of the definition by making some reference to the "public" nature of the powers being exercised. Yet, the moment that concept is insinuated into the description of administrative law, the spectre of the controversy surrounding the delineation of the public from the private sphere immediately presents itself.

This definitional conundrum is further complicated when one starts conceiving of administrative law as involving a distinct set of legal principles that applies to the exercises of public power and not elsewhere. Many of the constraints on the exercise of various forms of statutory or public power are replicated or paralleled in domains normally regarded as private. For example, there is a long history of the courts' imposing procedural obligations — commonly known as the rules of natural justice or procedural fairness — on clubs, trade organizations, and even religions, particularly when these bodies are dealing with rights pertaining to membership. Similarly, traditional corporate law was built on principles of authority, jurisdiction, or *ultra vires*; a corporation could not act in a manner that was beyond the reach of the objects set out in its articles of incorporation. Yet, these two concepts, procedural fairness and jurisdiction, form the bedrock of administrative law, at least as reflected in the grounds on which the courts evaluate or review administrative action.

Conversely, it is also clear that the courts subject many exercises of state or governmental power to the ordinary common law applicable to the private sector with separate principles of administrative or public law seldom, if ever, intruding. In so doing, the courts, in part, continue to recognize one of the three meanings or aspects that the eminent jurist A.V. Dicey ascribed to the concept of the "rule of law" in 1885: the equality of all before the law including the subjection of administrative officials "to the ordinary law of land administered by the ordinary law courts."[2] Thus, for example, any modern text or casebook on

---

2   A.V. Dicey, *Introduction to the Study of the Law of the Constitution*, 10th ed. by E.C.S. Wade (London: Macmillan, 1959) at 202.

the law of contracts will frequently illustrate the general principles of the common law of contracts by reference to precedents that involve a public body as either plaintiff or defendant with no suggestion that its public nature matters to the outcome or the principles being applied.

Adding further to the dilemma of elucidating the scope of administrative law is a problem that has magnified enormously as a consequence of the current tendency of Canadian governments of all political stripes to engage in the restructuring of a broad range of government services and programs. The phenomena of privatization, corporatization, and outsourcing have each brought with them issues regarding the continued applicability of traditional principles of administrative law and judicial review. When a province decides to hand over the running of juvenile correctional facilities to the private sector, to what extent do the rules of procedural fairness — indeed the *Canadian Charter of Rights and Freedoms* — still avail the inmates of those facilities?

What these definitional challenges demonstrate, of course, is that administrative law is like every other category of law. Complete self-containment is not possible. Overlap is inevitable. Indeed, borrowing or cross-fertilization may often be a virtue. Just as the law of contracts interacts increasingly and revealingly with tort law and the law of restitution, so too do the spheres of public and private law interconnect and feed off one another in informative and productive ways.

I will therefore eschew the task of attempting a more precise or complete definition of administrative law. However, later in this chapter, I will provide examples of and discuss some important areas in which the limits of administrative law remain fudged or are currently evolving. I will be looking particularly at situations where administrative law is either extending its tentacles or, conversely, is being influenced by principles previously considered the preserve of private law. First, however, I will provide an overview or map of the administrative state and the role that administrative law plays in its functioning.

B. THE PLAYERS, THEIR ROLES, AND THEIR LIMITS

1) The Players

In providing a more concrete sense of the types of authority that are the subject of administrative law principles, it is easiest to start with government.

At the formal apex of those possessing prerogative or statutory powers is the head of state — in Canada, the Queen in right of Canada and the various provinces almost invariably functioning through her royal representatives, the governor general or the lieutenant governors of the provinces. However, the powers, vested even theoretically in the monarch or the Royal representatives in their own right, are nowadays remarkably few in number and exercised infrequently. Rather, the effective apex of executive power is the prime minister or the premiers, and her or his Cabinet, most commonly operating through statutory powers conferred on the governor general or the lieutenant governors in council. Frequently, statutes will confer powers on individual members of Cabinet or ministers of the Crown either specifically or implicitly through the creation of departments of state and the designation of a particular minister as the head or chief executive officer of those departments. Also, particular members of Cabinet, most notably the prime minister or the premiers as well as the attorneys general, are the recognized repositories of certain categories of residual prerogative power.

Within the departmental structure, there is a presumption that ministers are entitled to act through their responsible officers so that, in most instances, the real decision makers are civil servants performing their functions within a department's organizational plan. Statutes will often confer authority directly on a particular category of civil servant, such as the following power of immigration officers under the *Immigration Act*[3]:

> 6. (1) Subject to this Act and the regulations, any immigrant, including a Convention refugee, and all dependants, if any, may be granted landing if it is established to the satisfaction of an immigration officer that the immigrant meets the selection standards established by the regulations for the purpose of determining whether or not and the degree to which the immigrant will be able to become successfully established in Canada, as determined in accordance with the regulations.

It should, however, be noted that not all of the business conducted by government departments (or agencies or tribunals, for that matter) implicates the principles of public law. In many respects, government departments largely function subject to the same rules as those in the private sector. This is true particularly in matters such as liability in contract or tort in the infrastructural operations of the department, such as purchasing equipment and operating motor vehicles. Nonetheless, as

---

3   R.S.C. 1985, c. I–2.

will be shown later in this section, even in domains such as government procurement, special public principles or rules may intrude.

Operating outside departmental frameworks but generally treated as part of the apparatus of government are various tribunals, regulatory agencies, and Crown corporations charged with a variety of tasks from resolving disputes in a truly judicial manner through granting licences, permits, and authorizations of various kinds to doing business very much in the manner of a private entrepreneur. In most instances, bodies such as this are linked to government directly through the agency of a minister to whom they must report and who, on occasion, may have authority to give directions regarding the exercise of their functions. However, there also exist many examples, particularly in the provincial domain, of bodies that owe their existence to statute and which, while structurally independent of government, nonetheless perform functions that are sufficiently governmental or public in their nature as to attract the attention of public law. Among the most prominent of these agencies of public policy are universities, hospital boards, and professional organizations. Despite their historic status as autonomous, self-governing bodies, they have been transformed over the years, largely through legislative appropriation and, in many instances, government funding, into bodies that possess an array of regulatory powers in matters of great significance to the polity at large. Finally, account also has to be taken of other tiers of government, such as the various territorial governments, Indian band councils, and municipalities, all of which are public bodies subject to the principles and remedies of public law in the exercise of their statutory powers.

The other group of players that needs to be identified are the constituencies of, or those affected by, these various exercises of government power or authority. Administrative law is often conceived of as the non-constitutional aspects of the law governing the relationship between the individual and the state. However, it is necessary to emphasize that the subjects of administrative law are not just individual Canadians. In many instances, our administrative law affects foreign nationals — indeed, increasingly so. It also involves corporations and other forms of artificial legal personality, and on occasion other informal groups or associations of people. In many situations, administrative law is also about the relations among various levels of government. These include details of the association between the federal government and the provinces under statutes and agreements dealing with cost-sharing in areas such as health, education, and welfare. Also, various government departments and agencies are subject to the jurisdiction of administrative tribunals such as those that hear complaints about environmental depredation or discriminatory conduct.

2) Their Roles

The statutory and prerogative authorities that form the administrative state are engaged in an extremely wide range of functions. Theoretically, they legislate, exercise discretion or make various kinds of choice, and adjudicate disputes.

Primary examples of legislative power are found in the regulation-making capacities of the governor general and the lieutenant governors in council — to promulgate subordinate legislation that expands the scope of and fills in the details of the statutes or primary legislation that are enacted by Parliament or the legislative assemblies. Municipalities possess significant legislative capacities of their own in the form of their by-law-making powers. Nowadays, it is also more and more common to find tribunals and other government agencies with the authority to make binding rules, by-laws, and regulations, in some cases, but not always, with the approval of the governor general or the lieutenant governor in council.

Discretionary executive powers are the heart and soul of modern legislation, and indeed of the modern state itself. A full account of the substantive scope of statutory discretion would require a complete list of all the various activities in which government is involved. In other words, statutory discretion is the pre-eminent tool of government regulation of all kinds, be it the setting of rates, the granting of permissions, the distribution of various forms of government largesse, and the subjecting of individuals and groups to all sorts of demands by the state — providing information, paying levies, fees, and taxes, engaging in certain activities. Discretionary power comes in many forms and is exercised in all kinds of settings.

Discretion involves the making of choice though almost invariably one constrained by the policies and purposes of the statutory regime under which the decision maker is operating. Typically, it is expressed in permissive rather than mandatory language: "The Minister may . . .", rather than "The Minister shall. . . ." Thereafter, many variations exist. Sometimes discretion is conferred in completely, open-ended statutory language with the subjective opinion of the person on whom the discretion is conferred the express touchstone for its exercise. On other occasions, it is structured closely or confined, in that it is conferred in objective rather than subjective language, and is hedged in by references to limiting considerations or factors and sometimes even the requirement of a hearing or some other procedural requirement.

A large part of administrative law is also concerned with various forms of administrative adjudication, frequently performed by specially set-up administrative tribunals, though also, on occasion, carried out by adjudicators or other officials within government departments. In many instances, these adjudications will be in areas of civil dispute that have been conferred by legislation on tribunals rather than, or in place of, the regular courts (as typified by the domains of workers' compensation, labour relations, and human rights). In other cases, the nature of the adjudication will be more akin to criminal law; tribunals are charged with determining whether or not someone has lived up to a statutory standard, as in the case of proceedings taken against someone for the removal for cause of a licence or permission.

As already noted, we live in an age in which, for some time now, there have been many examples of government withdrawing from areas of regulation — of privatization of previous government activities. Even so, the range of governmental and public activities that forms the backdrop to the development and operation of administrative law principles remains vast and, indeed, almost perforce will continue to be so, leaving much fodder for the further refinement of what follows in this work.

3) Their Limits

In performing their various roles, public authorities must respect the legal limits of their mandates. The sources of those limits are many and constitute the basis of this work.

Pre-eminent among these legal limits are those imposed by the *Constitution Acts* and, most commonly, the division of powers between the federal Parliament and the provincial legislatures, provided for in sections 91 and 92 of the *Constitution Act, 1867*, the guaranteed role of the superior court judiciary as found in sections 96 to 101 of the same Act, and those resulting from the rights and freedoms recognized by the 1982 *Canadian Charter of Rights and Freedoms*. In their functioning, statutory and prerogative authories must observe the federal–provincial division of powers, they must not trespass in domains reserved for the exclusive jurisdiction of section 96 court judges, and they must respect constitutional entitlements arising from the individual rights and freedoms enshrined in the *Charter*.

Far more frequently, however, the issues of administrative law concern the limits resulting from the terms of the statutory regime under which the decision maker is operating and the various common law restrictions or obligations that the courts have historically been ready to graft onto those statutory regimes. Theoretically, the most significant of the legal limitations arising from the statutory regime itself is the obligation on statutory authorities to adhere to the confines of their statutory authority or "jurisdiction." They cannot trespass in areas where the legislature has not assigned them authority. To give an extreme example, the Law Society of British Columbia could not rezone a piece of land in Newfoundland without a justified complaint that it had exceeded its jurisdiction, acted without authority, or, to use the Latin term still in currency in this and the constitutional domain, behaved in an *ultra vires* manner. However, as we will see shortly, what constitute the limits of a statutory authority's jurisdiction or what characteristics denote a question or issue that affects its jurisdiction has been one of the most contentious issues in the whole of Canadian administrative law. This will occupy much of our attention.

Within the rubric of abuse of authority, the law constrains more than the incorrect determination of purely legal issues pertaining to the scope of a public authority's mandate. It also defines the limits on those situations where a decision maker is given discretion or choice in exercising a statutory or prerogative authority. Seldom if ever does this represent an opportunity for completely unbridled uses of power. Even discretion in the broadest sense is reined in by the objectives or purposes of the empowering legislation generally and the relevant legislative provision in particular, as well as limitations derived from sources external to the statute, such as underlying constitutional norms and the dictates of international law.

While it might seem self-evident that statutory authorities should always observe or adhere to the law, the fact is that there are situations where statutory authorities define or set the law; where, in a sense, they are a law unto themselves. On issues that do not affect the jurisdiction or authority of the decision maker, the statutorily designated body will frequently be responsible for determining questions of law and in that domain be subject to very limited policing by other authorities. What is true of questions of law is even more frequently so of the determination of matters of fact. Obviously the extent to which this "independence" exists is another very important aspect of Canadian administrative law.

In a great many instances, the limits that administrative law places on the exercise of statutory power or authority are procedural, not substantive. Those limits are sometimes found in constitutional or near constitutional provisions, such as certain sections in the *Canadian Charter of Rights and Freedoms* and the federally enacted and applicable *Canadian Bill of Rights*. Both of these provide guarantees of adherence to the principles of fundamental justice, a notion that encompasses entitlement to a hearing before certain rights or interests are affected.

More frequently, these procedural rights or entitlements are located in either the statute conferring the relevant power or, in some provinces, in a general procedures statute that applies to many of that jurisdiction's statutory authorities. They are also found in subordinate legislation of various kinds — regulations, rules, and by-laws promulgated under the authority granted by primary legislation for the crafting of procedures to be followed in the exercise of the substantive powers granted in that primary legislation. On still other occasions, the procedures will be those derived from the principles of the common law and its general prescription that certain kinds of statutory and prerogative power must be exercised in accordance with the dictates of what are called generally but not always interchangeably the rules of natural justice or the rules of procedural fairness. The delineation of the circumstances to which those principles apply and their actual content in particular cases constitutes much of the work of Canadian administrative law. What does a fair hearing entail in a particular situation and what defines an entitlement to a decision maker who is both independent and unbiased?

C. PATROLLING THE LIMITS: AVENUES OF RECOURSE WHEN STATUTORY AND PREROGATIVE AUTHORITIES "BEHAVE BADLY"

Many mature administrative structures contain or provide internal mechanisms for the correction of error. Sometimes these mechanisms are provided for specifically in the relevant empowering legislation, such as an internal right of appeal or the conferral of authority on the decision maker to itself rehear, review, or reconsider a matter it has already decided. It is important to take account of this possibility in any situation where there is concern about the correctness or legality of an exercise of statutory or prerogative power. For the most part, however, this work is concerned with the various external modes of control and, in particular, those provided by the ordinary courts of the land.

Quantitatively, the most significant avenue of recourse to those ordinary courts is by way of a right of appeal provided for in the legislation creating the statutory power in question or some related or connected statute. (With the limited exception of the province of Québec — and as opposed to the situation in some other countries — there are no general administrative appeal tribunals in Canada.) Within the world of statutory appeals, there are enormous variations, ranging from *de novo* or completely from-scratch hearings to those carefully limited to questions of law and jurisdiction. Therefore it is always vital to be attentive to the precise language of the provision that creates the statutory right of appeal.

Historically, the common law also provided a range of remedies for those discontented with actions taken under statute or prerogative power and affecting them in some way or other. These remedies, called the *prerogative writs*, presumably because they were issued by the Royal courts in the name of the Crown, formed the basis for the evolution of most of the principles of today's largely jurisdiction-based regime of judicial review. In time, they were also supplemented by remedies originally developed in a private law setting: the declaration and the equitable remedy of injunction. Today, in a number of jurisdictions, these common law modes of judicial review have been simplified statutorily and codified in the form of a single application for judicial review to be used when there is no effective statutory right of appeal.

Not all judicial scrutiny of administrative action is the response to a direct attack on a particular decision or action. Sometimes, though infrequently, these attacks will be made in the context of other proceedings or collaterally, such as where the invalidity of administrative action is raised as a defence to a charge of violation of a municipal by-law. We will consider this species of judicial review as well as the limited range of situations in which financial relief is available for unlawful administrative action.

The regular courts are not the only external control on the functioning of the administrative process. While, as already mentioned, there is only one broadly-based administrative appeal tribunal in Canada, in most provinces, an officer of the legislature — generally called the *ombudsman* — provides an avenue of access for making complaints against the exercise of statutory power on the merits as well as on the basis of legal infirmity. Such a potentially broad basis for providing relief clearly merits attention.

D. THE DISPUTED TERRITORY: SOME ILLUSTRATIVE EXAMPLES

As foreshadowed earlier in the chapter, I turn now to providing examples of domains or areas where there are no clear delineation or demarcation points between the reach of administrative law and that of private law. As might be expected, this is a terrain of shifting sands as concepts of the public and the private and expectations regarding the proper role of the state change, and also as institutions evolve, contracting and expanding — sometimes incrementally, sometimes dramatically. It is a hybrid world in which there is much cross-fertilization of concepts and rules. At its best, it is an aspect of the law where ideas about the proper role of the state and the appropriate instruments of control are the subject of informed and ultimately profitable debate. At its worst, it is a veritable minefield for those who become embroiled in its intricacies, one in which technicality and formalism can triumph over policy-based analysis and a clear-sighted focus on just outcomes.

1) The Reach of the Rules of Procedural Fairness: Office Holders and Mere Statutory Employees

Under traditional common law principles, an employer may dismiss an employee without providing that employee with a hearing unless the contract of employment specifies such a requirement as a precondition of termination. Without such an express provision, a dismissal does not become wrongful merely because it was not preceded by a hearing. Moreover, even where a dismissal is wrongful, the only recourse available to the employee is an action in damages; there is no entitlement to reinstatement or specific performance.

In contrast, those whom the law classifies as statutory office holders are entitled to procedural fairness as a prelude to any dismissal, and any failure to afford procedural fairness nullifies the dismissal. In these circumstances, the affected person is entitled to apply to a court for judicial review or scrutiny of the decision. Success in making such an application will lead, in some instances, to effective reinstatement, at least until such time as there has been the requisite hearing. Moreover, effective reinstatement may also be the outcome of an application for judicial review of a decision dismissing a statutory officer holder which is substantively flawed.

Given these significant differences in the terms of legal entitlements between mere employees and statutory office holders, it seems important to be able to identify precisely the badges or indicia of an office holder. At what point does someone who is employed by or under a power conferred by statute cease to be a mere employee and become an office holder? Or, is that the status of everyone employed under a statutory power?

Until quite recently, the courts were quite circumspect in attributing the status of office holder. Indeed, even within that category, those who held their offices "at pleasure" or from which they could be dismissed for any reason or without cause, were not entitled to procedural fairness. This was an entitlement restricted to those who by virtue of provision in the relevant statute could be dismissed only for cause. More generally, the designation of office holder seemed reserved to persons whose offices and functions were created with some degree of precision by statute. It did not apply to those hired under a general statutory power to appoint staff for the furtherance of the activities of a department, a tribunal, or an agency.

However, there was a major shift in at least one aspect of this jurisprudence with the 1990 judgment of the Supreme Court of Canada in *Board of Education of Indian Head School Division No. 19 of Saskatchewan* v. *Knight*.[4] There, the Supreme Court of Canada not only extended the benefit of the rules of procedural fairness to office holders at pleasure but also held that the Director of Education, one of the administrative personnel of the Board was an office holder for these purposes.

In fact, this latter holding was not all that surprising in so far as the relevant legislation made specific provision for the appointment of a Director to act in the capacity of chief executive officer of the Board and went on to set out at least some of the duties of that official. This corresponded with earlier jurisprudence, such as the judgment of the House of Lords in *Ridge* v. *Baldwin*,[5] in which the Chief Constable of Brighton was held to be an office holder. According to the Court, this gave the position sufficient "statutory flavour" to entitle the plaintiff to the benefits accruing to office holders. At the same time, the judgment clearly implied that there were still categories of statutory employees hired under more general powers who would not fall within that category.

Subsequently, the Ontario Court of Appeal muddied these waters in *Hanis* v. *Teevan*.[6] In this instance, the director of a laboratory at a university was held to be an office holder not on the strength of any statutory provision establishing the position and its duties but on the basis of dictionary definitions of office holder, definitions which included persons in positions of trust in public institutions. As a consequence, the bar has been lowered still further for claims to procedural fairness in statutory employment situations.

Again, this is not surprising. After all, the Canadian courts have now had considerable experience in dealing with situations in the collectively organized sector and under unfair dismissal legislation in three Canadian jurisdictions in which mere employees are entitled to a

---

4   [1990] 1 S.C.R. 653 [*Knight*].
5   [1964] A.C. 40 (H.L., Eng.).
6   (1998), 38 C.C.E.L. (2d) 78 (Ont. C.A.) [*Hanis*].

hearing grieving their dismissal[7] and, in the case of the unionized sector, a range of other employment decisions as well. Moreover, while general wrongful dismissal law has probably not yet reached the stage of reversing the traditional rule that there is no claim to a hearing before dismissal,[8] the judgment of the Supreme Court of Canada in *Wallace v. United Grain Growers Ltd.*[9] suggests strongly that there are at least a number of situations in which it would be unwise for an employer to dismiss an employee without some form of hearing. In that case, the Court adopted the position that the length of the notice period to which any employees dismissed without cause were entitled may be affected by the manner of their dismissal. In situations where serious but ultimately unfounded allegations form the basis for the dismissal, it is easy to see how a failure on the part of the employer to confront the employee and provide an opportunity to refute the allegations could have consequences for the level of damages to which the employee is entitled in any wrongful dismissal action.

It is also significant that, in both *Knight* and *Hanis*, the right of the office holders to procedural fairness was recognized not in the context of an application for public law relief, but as an element in a wrongful dismissal claim for damages. Making a private law claim does not disentitle a plaintiff from the assertion of rights that arise at public law. However, what is not only significant but also problematic is the Court's acceptance, in *Knight*, in a passage in the judgment cited in *Hanis*, that the public law entitlement to procedural fairness is one that an employee can surrender in his or her contract of employment. Given the Court's insistence on the importance of public law values at other points in its judgment in *Knight*, it is surprising that it would thereafter provide statutory employers with an easy way out of their procedural fairness obligations: a clearly expressed and signposted provision in what will, in many instances, be a contract of adhesion with its statutory employees *cum* office holders.

The fact that the plaintiffs in both *Knight* and *Hanis* chose to pursue damages remedies rather than public law relief obviously speaks to a situation in which they did not want reinstatement, believed that a hearing would not make a difference to the outcome, or felt that the particular circumstances diminished or precluded whatever potential normally existed for effective reinstatement in the form of public law relief. Indeed, what has become clear in the domain of public or

---

7   Nova Scotia, Québec, and employees subject to federal regulatory competence.
8   A position accepted by the Court in *Hanis*, above.
9   [1997] 3 S.C.R. 701.

administrative law in recent times is that, in a variety of contexts, the courts have not been prepared to follow the logic of invalidity to its ultimate conclusion. Thus, in the domain of office holders, the invalidity of a dismissal decision does not lead immutably to reinstatement. While that sometimes will be the effect of a judicial quashing or a declaration of invalidity of the decision under attack, pragmatic considerations may persuade a court that such an outcome is unwarranted.

In such cases, problems may arise not just because the successful applicant's term of office has since expired but even more dramatically in situations, where a successor has been appointed.[10] Thus, while the court might declare the applicant's dismissal to have been unlawful, there will be a reluctance to follow through with all of the logical consequences of branding a decision a nullity or *ultra vires*. In particular, there will be a reluctance to require the successor to vacate her or his office in favour of the "true" holder of that office. Even if reinstatement were theoretically possible because no successor had been appointed, questions could still arise as to whether the court had any overriding discretion to deny that form of relief — because, for example, of some of the same considerations that lead courts to deny specific performance of contracts under private employment law. For example, the courts would be reluctant to force the continuation of a working relationship characterized by incompatibility between personalities or, perhaps more commonly in public law situations, between the policy perspectives and positions of a new government and those of the dismissed office holders.

So far, there appears to have been no definitive resolution of that issue in Canadian law. The Supreme Court of Canada[11] has cited with approval Privy Council authority to the effect that the common law rules apply to statutory employment.[12] However, that does not necessarily hold for public office holders. More recently, the Ontario courts were confronted with aspects of this problem in a series of cases involving the incoming Conservative government's dismissal of members of boards and agencies appointed by its predecessor. In one case, because the matter was brought on for hearing before any further busi-

---

10   See, for example, *Brown v. Waterloo Regional Board of Commissioners of Police* (1983), 150 D.L.R. (3d) 729 (Ont. C.A.), in which a new chief of police was well ensconced by the time his predecessor's application for judicial review was ultimately decided.

11   *Emms v. R.*, [1979] 2 S.C.R. 1148 at 1164–65.

12   *Francis v. Municipal Councillors of Kuala Lumpur*, [1962] 1 W.L.R. 1411 (P.C., Mal.) at 1417–18.

ness had been conducted and successors appointed, the Court in effect reinstated members of the Board of Directors of Ontario Hydro.[13] However, in two other cases, the Court of Appeal refused to order that form of relief even in the face of a strong plea that reinstatement was necessary to underscore the importance of the independence of the Ontario Labour Relations Board and a Police Services Board. Instead, the Court left it to the parties to resolve the consequences of the declarations of invalidity.[14] While one of the positions was not due to expire for at least another year, the Court of Appeal simply assumed that it had been filled already. Thus, an important principle has been left unresolved: the tensions between claims based on the need for tribunal independence from the arbitrary dismissal of its members and the effective entitlement of governments to get rid of office holders, provided they are prepared to live with the other consequences of any declaration of invalidity, such as the payment of any salary, fees, or other emoluments that would have accrued in the meantime.

What is also surfacing in these cases is the influence of private law principles and, in particular, the traditional posture of equity that specific performance is not available in aid of the continuation of an employment relationship. Indeed, there is nothing surprising in this. Rather, to the extent that the courts are expanding the scope of who is an office holder, we may logically expect that, in cases where such an office holder is pursuing his or her rights through the remedies of public law, the courts will be keen to assert an increasing degree of remedial discretion over the availability of particular forms of relief.

In this connection, the issue has been raised subsequently of whether it is even appropriate in such cases to award public law relief. This can take the form of either a declaration of invalidity or relief in the nature of *certiorari*.[15] These doubts have arisen principally as a result of the Supreme Court of Canada's judgment in *Wells* v. *Newfoundland*.[16] There, the Court was dealing with a claim for both public law relief and damages for breach of contract brought by a former member of the Newfoundland Public Utilities Board who had lost his position when the Board was restructured legislatively. Under what the Court held was a "contract" with the government of Newfoundland,

---

13   *Murphy v. Ontario (A.G.)* (1996), 28 O.R. (3d) 220 (G.D.).

14   *Hewat v. Ontario* (1998), 37 O.R. (3d) 161 (C.A.) and *Dewar v. Ontario* (1998), 37 O.R. (3d) 170 (C.A.).

15   An historically important remedy by which the courts call upon a statutory authority to file its record so that it can be checked for reviewable error.

16   [1999] 3 S.C.R. 199.

Wells was entitled, subject to good behaviour, to keep his position until age seventy. Notwithstanding the restructuring and Wells's loss of his seat on the Board, in the absence of express provision to the contrary, this obligation subsisted at least to the extent of entitling Wells to compensation for the loss of his position.

More generally, however, the Court in *Wells* moved a considerable distance in merging the contractual rights of "mere" statutory employees and those of persons holding positions with sufficient statutory flavour to entitle them to public law relief in appropriate cases. This is obvious from the following statement by Major J., delivering the judgment of the Court:

> While the terms and conditions of the contract [between the state and its employees] may be dictated in whole or in part, by statute, the employment relationship remains a contract in substance and the general law of contract will apply unless specifically superceded by explicit terms in the statute or the agreement.
>
> This is the case for most senior public officers. Exceptions are necessary for judges, ministers of the Crown and those who fulfill constitutionally defined state roles.[17]

Clearly, this statement presages the possibility that, even in situations where the position still exists, the Court will not treat reinstatement as an available remedy in the case of dismissal from such public law "offices" irrespective of whether the matter arises in the context of a public law remedy or an action for breach of contract. Relief will be conditioned on the normal principles of contract law, and they do not include specific performance.

Given that Wells was not in fact seeking reinstatement, this may, of course, be reading too much into the judgment generally and these statements in particular. Indeed, it leaves wide open the legal rights of those who are simply appointed to a public office and do not have a formal contract as such. Nonetheless, it is not the only indicator of the possibility that the remedial law in this domain will be more and more that applicable to normal contracts of employment.

In one of the Ontario cases, *Hewat*, the relevant legislation provided for appointments at pleasure. However, the Court of Appeal held that the right to dismiss without cause that pertains to offices held at pleasure was lost once an order-in-council appointed the plaintiff vice-chairs of the Ontario Labour Relations Board to their positions for a term of

---

17   *Wells* above, at paras. 30–31.

years. Thereafter, there could be dismissal during that period only for cause, and a declaration of invalidity would follow from any form of arbitrary dismissal. Subsequently, and without reference to *Hewat*, the British Columbia Court of Appeal, in *Ocean Port Hotel Ltd.* v. *British Columbia (General Manager Liquor Control)*,[18] held that appointment to a specified term in such circumstances did not affect the appointing authority's ability to dismiss a member of the Liquor Appeal Board without cause. There could be no public law relief in such circumstances; there could be only a private law action for breach of contract.

More generally, what the example of office holders and statutory forms of employment demonstrates is an evolution of the law in which public law influences are surfacing in cases brought as private law wrongful dismissal claims and where, conversely, private law concerns are being brought to bear in public law applications. Equally significant may be the extent to which legislative developments in the field are also influencing both domains. Given that legislatures are providing vehicles whereby those dismissed from their jobs can assert procedural rights and entitlements to be considered for reinstatement, it becomes even more likely that these same entitlements will be recognized at common law by way of analogy, whether under the rubric of a public or a private law remedy.

2) Government Procurement

On the whole, when governments engage in the procuring of the goods and services that they need in order to conduct their business, the normal principles of the law of contract apply to the transactions that they enter or attempt to enter. However, in recent years, the courts have on occasion applied somewhat more rigorous standards to the conduct of governments engaged in procurement than they do to private sector contractors.

The primary foundation for the application of overriding public law values in the domain of government procurement is the judgment of McLachlin J. in *Shell Canada Products Ltd.* v. *Vancouver (City)*.[19] The city council passed resolutions not to buy Shell products as long as the company continued to do business with South Africa. In Shell's challenge to the validity of that resolution, a preliminary question arose as to whether or not this resolution was subject to challenge on public law principles or whether for these purposes the municipality should be

---

18   (1999), 174 D.L.R. (4th) 498 (B.C.C.A.).
19   [1994] 1 S.C.R. 231 [*Shell*].

treated just like any private sector actor and not be accountable (save under human rights and fair trading statutes) for its choices as to those with whom it would do business. While McLachlin J. ultimately dissented on the merits of the case, her assessment of the special position of public authorities in the domain of procurement decisions, be they general resolutions or particular contracting choices, was accepted by the majority. In sustaining the proposition that the Court could review such exercises of power for impropriety both in its purposes and the manner of its exercise, she advanced the following justifications:

> The most important difference is the fact that municipalities undertake their commercial and contractual activities with the use of public funds. Another consideration justifying different treatment of public contracting is the fact that a municipality's exercise of its contracting power may have consequences for other interests not taken into account by the purely consensual relationship between the council and the contractor. For example, public concerns such as equality of access to government markets, integrity in the conduct of government business, and the promotion and maintenance of community values require that the public procurement function be viewed as distinct from the purely private realm of contract law. Finally, it must be remembered that municipalities, unlike private individuals, are statutory creations, and must always act within the legal bounds conferred on them by statute. In particular, council members cannot act in pursuit of their own private interests, but must exercise their contractual power in the public interest.[20]

Clearly, these special public law dimensions to the way statutory and prerogative authorities exercise procurement powers have procedural and substantive consequences.

In the procedural domain, there is some, though not consistent, authority to the effect that governments owe duties of procedural fairness in some situations where the interests of those wishing to do business with government are affected. The Northwest Territories Court of Appeal in *Volker Stevin NWT (1992) Ltd.* v. *Northwest Territories (Commissioner)*[21] held that the company had an expectation of procedural fairness before its name was removed from the list of those eligible to bid on or having a preferred place among those bidding on government contracts. Moreover, in an earlier case, Strayer J., then of the Federal

---

20   *Ibid.*, at 240–41.
21   (1994), 113 D.L.R. (4th) 639 (N.W.T.C.A.).

Court, Trial Division, had held that there was a reviewable absence of procedural fairness when a company had been denied a government contract on the basis of substantive criteria that had not appeared in the call for tenders.[22]

What is also significant about these cases is that each was brought as an application for judicial review — in both instances relief in the nature of *certiorari*. In *Volker Stevin*, the Court held that its ability to award such relief was not affected by the fact that the regime in issue had not been created directly by statute but represented the government's exercise of its common law or prerogative powers: "The Advisory Committee is a public body exercising a power which affects the status of business enterprises, and their ability to compete effectively in the Northwest Territories."[23] It is, however, also worthy of note that, as opposed to the judgment of Strayer J. in *Thomas Assaly*, the Northwest Territories Court of Appeal distinguished the process at issue in this specific case from a single procurement decision. On this point, it affirmed the position of the first instance judge that such decisions were purely commercial ones that do not normally come within the ambit of judicial review. While that particular position might not withstand scrutiny in the wake of the Supreme Court of Canada's judgment in *Shell Canada*, it does nonetheless reflect a tension still existing in the case law as to whether obligations of procedural fairness do attach to particular tendering exercises.

There is other authority — albeit in the context of a breach of contract action rather than judicial review — in which the way a government conducted a particular tendering process has been held unlawful on substantive grounds. In delivering the judgment of the Newfoundland Court of Appeal in *Health Care Developers Inc.* v. *Newfoundland*,[24] Cameron J.A. held that the government had failed to act in good faith in the conduct of the particular bidding process and that this constituted a breach of contract. This case also raises the important issue of whether the public law values that McLachlin J. identified in *Shell Canada* involve special obligations of good faith conduct in government procurement activities, obligations which extend beyond whatever good faith obligations fall on private individuals involved in the same kind of exercise.

While good faith is a concept that is increasingly accepted in the general law of contracts and while Cameron J.A. makes reference to that emerging body of law, she explicitly refuses to be drawn into the

---

22 *Assaly (Thomas C.) Corp.* v. *Canada*, (1990), 44 Admin. L.R. 89 (F.C.T.D.).
23 *Wells*, note 15 at 645.
24 (1996), 141 Nfld & P.E.I.R. 34 (Nfld. C.A.).

question of whether the particular obligation of good faith that she is applying in this case would also apply in a private sector tendering process. Instead, she relies primarily on cases such as *Thomas Assaly* in which the party calling for tenders was a public body or authority.

On the other hand, her primary policy reference is to the judgment of Estey J. in *R. v. Ron Engineering & Construction (Eastern) Ltd.*[25] While the plaintiff in this case was the Crown seeking to sue on a tender submitted by a private sector company, the public nature of the process appeared to have little or no bearing on the Court's conclusion. It was supported primarily by reference to the need to protect the integrity of the bidding process. As well, Cameron J.A.'s analysis focuses on discerning the intention of the parties and, in this context also, she declines to express any opinion on the controversial issue of whether the Crown could actually contract out of its obligations of good faith.

Obviously, these aspects of this important judgment raise questions about the extent to which the relevant principles applied in cases such as this have any peculiar public law components. The most recent judgment of the Supreme Court of Canada regarding the obligations of government when engaging in a tendering exercise in no way clarifies this issue. In *M.J.B. Enterprises Ltd. v. Defence Construction (1951) Ltd.*,[26] the procurement arm of the federal Department of National Defence was held to have breached its contractual obligations when it awarded a contract to a bidder who did not comply with the terms of the call for tenders. In ruling that the defendant's actions could not be justified even on the basis of a "privilege" clause in the call for tenders, which stated that the contract would not necessarily be awarded to the lowest or indeed to any bidder, the Supreme Court justified its conclusions simply on the construction of the relevant documents and the presumed intention of the parties. Good faith did not enter the picture, let alone any suggestion that the result depended in any way upon the public status of the defendant.

This continues to leave open the question of whether special obligations of general good faith should ever govern the conduct of governments as contracting parties. To the extent that notions of good faith continue to evolve in general contract law, this may, of course, be a question with relatively little practical significance. Save to the extent that the concept of good faith might have a different content for public sector contractors than it does for the private sector, normal, generally applicable private law principles may suffice. In a sense, the law governing public bodies will be fed by evolutions in private law.

---

25   [1981] 1 S.C.R. 111.
26   [1999] 1 S.C.R. 619.

On the other hand, should the courts continue to be very cautious in their extension of obligations of good faith in general contractual settings, there may well be more point to the question. Moreover, if the next time Defence Construction (1951) Ltd. comes before the courts and the privilege clause in the call for tenders now clearly allows it to accept non-conforming bids, should this be a complete defence to a cause of action? Intention analysis would obviously produce a positive answer. However, as hinted in Cameron J.A.'s judgment in *Health Care Developers Inc.*, there may be circumstances in which the courts by reference to the public nature of the defendant should be able to deny efficacy to such a clause.

3) Religion

The judicial review of decision making by religious bodies may seem an unlikely candidate for inclusion within the domain of administrative law. In the absence of a constitutionally established state religion, the relationships that exist within religious organizations would appear to be completely outside the zone of what counts as public and therefore administrative law. Indeed, decision making within religions is, in general, not part of Canadian administrative law. However, there are dimensions to the case law in this domain which serve as a caution against the too-ready transference of the principles of public law review to other, more private relationships and organizations.

Judicial scrutiny of decision making by religions, and particularly review of decisions affecting the clergy of those religions, traces its pedigree to the United Kingdom. This probably resulted from the combination of an established church and the willingness of the courts to apply common law procedural entitlements to "private" organizations of various kinds at least in the domain of membership rights. These common law procedural entitlements have been described as the rules of natural justice and now, more commonly, simply as the rules of procedural fairness.

Some of these authorities and the principles underlying them found a ready home in Canadian case law concerned similarly with the review of decisions affecting the status of clergy. In some instances, statutory recognition of the status of the church in question — such as the federal Act incorporating the United Church of Canada[27] — provided further justification for this form of intervention, as in the case of the "self-regulating" professions. Indeed, in Ontario, the assimilation

---

27 S.C. 1926, c. 100.

has gone as far as the subjection of decision making involving clergy to the regime of public law judicial review found in the *Judicial Review Procedure Act*.[28] This statute allows for applications for relief "in the nature of" various old forms of administrative law remedy. Because the review of decisions affecting clergy was similar to or "in the nature of" that form of remedy, it was held that judicial review of those decisions was sought appropriately under the Act.[29] I will return later in this book to an assessment of the merits of that conclusion. However, for present purposes, my principal concern is with another aspect of assimilation, the subjection of decisions by religious groups on membership issues to the procedural requirements of public law.

The most dramatic manifestation of this and the problems it can create is provided by the judgment of the Supreme Court of Canada in *Lakeside Colony of Hutterian Brethren* v. *Hofer*.[30] There, the Supreme Court of Canada held that the Colony had acted unfairly in the procedures it had employed to expel members of the Hofer family from the congregation and thereby also taking away the property rights attached to membership. In defending itself against this argument and the fact that it had not conducted the kind of hearing that would pass muster at common law in the public law domain, the Colony argued that the Hofers had in effect by their conduct expelled themselves and that they were not only told this but also, as members of the Colony knowledgeable in its ways and laws, would have realised that this would be the consequence of their actions. In such a context, a hearing of the kind that they were now asserting made no sense and was contrary to the norms of this religious group. However, over the solitary dissent of McLachlin J. (as she then was), the Court rejected the Colony's argument and adjudicated the issue by reference to the "external" standard of natural justice.

This approach is troubling in that it seems to accept that, notwithstanding the known processes of the church for dealing with such matters, the Court was perfectly happy, without any apparent deference to or respect for the preferences or informed choices of the church, to impose its own regular standards of procedural fairness on a very closely knit religious community. While this is not meant to suggest that administrative law conceptions of natural justice have no role to play in decision making by religious bodies; there was certainly a case here for the

---

28   R.S.O. 1990, c. J.1, s. 2(1)(a).

29   *Lindenburger* v. *United Church of Canada* (1985), 17 C.C.E.L. 143 (Ont. Div. Ct.), aff'd (1987), 17 C.C.E.L. 172 (Ont. C.A.) and *Davis* v. *United Church of Canada* (1992), 8 O.R. (3d) 75 (Div. Ct.)

30   [1992] 3 S.C.R. 165.

Court to restrict itself to inquiring into whether the colony had adhered faithfully to its own processes and to decline to interfere with the decision if it had. In fact, it was largely within the framework of the Hutterites' own regime that McLachlin J. reasoned in penning her dissent.[31]

4) Professional Discipline

It has long been accepted that decision making that pertains to membership rights in the traditional professions is subject to the regime of public law judicial review. Despite the fact that, for certain purposes, these professions are still regarded as self-governing and self-disciplining, the combination of the appropriation of their affairs by the enactment of public statutes containing ever-increasingly detailed prescriptions and the significance of the role they play in the public life of this country made it virtually inevitable that general administrative law principles would apply to their activities.

At the same time, it is also the case that the courts are less sure about the status of a number of other groups that exercise varying degrees of control over the practice of a profession or the way their members carry on an occupation. For example, in *Ripley* v. *Investment Dealers Association of Canada (No.2)*, the Appeal Division of the Nova Scotia Supreme Court held that Ripley could not challenge, by way of public law remedy, the disciplinary decisions taken by the Investment Dealers Association.[32] A similar conclusion was reached by the Ontario Divisional Court in *Re Pestell and Kitchener-Waterloo Real Estate Board*,[33] in the context of an application for judicial review under the *Judicial Review Procedure Act*. While neither of these judgments necessarily excludes the possibility of the affected members seeking the application of public law principles of procedural fairness from applying for a private, rather than a public law remedy, they obviously do raise questions as to where the line is to be drawn between those occupational groups that are subject to public law judicial remedies and those that are not. Moreover, as demonstrated by the judgment of the Ontario Court of

---

31 There is also considerable irony in the fact that the Court, while prepared to impose public law procedural values on the Hutterites was, some four years later, unwilling to treat a fraternal order operating in a much more public manner than the Hutterites as sufficiently public in nature to apply the Yukon Territory's anti-discrimination laws. Here again, McLachlin J. dissented. *Gould* v. *Yukon Order of Pioneers*, [1996] 1 S.C.R. 571.

32 (1991), 108 N.S.R. (2d) 38 (A.D.), aff'g. (1990), 99 N.S.R. (2d) 338 (T.D.).

33 (1981), 131 D.L.R. (3d) 88 (Ont. Div. Ct.).

Appeal in *Chalmers* v. *Toronto Stock Exchange*,[34] these classifications can have substantive ramifications. There, the Court held that the Exchange had no jurisdiction to discipline a former member, and among the principal justifications offered for this conclusion was the status of the Exchange as a self-governing, private body.

As already mentioned, what tends to be a crucial factor in all of these situations is the nature of the body's status: Is it established by statute? If so, what kind of statute is it — a public or a private act? To what extent does the statute simply empower, as opposed to direct or regulate? Obviously, these are relevant inquiries. Particularly as we move further down the road in the delegation of all manner of public or governmental tasks to "private" bodies, statutory status should not remain the exclusive litmus test. Thus, to the extent that securities commissions delegate a number of their regulatory responsibilities to stock exchanges, for example, it should follow, *Chalmers* notwithstanding, that the exercise of those functions in their new home attracts the principles of administrative law. Indeed, as the example of private prisons emphasizes, these questions have ramifications well beyond the arena of occupational licensing. What will be called for are new conceptions of what makes a body or a task sufficiently "public" in nature to qualify for administrative law treatment. In the particular domain of occupational licensing, it may not be going too far to suggest that an effective monopoly over entry into a field is in itself sufficient.

FURTHER READINGS

General Monographs and Periodicals

BLAKE, S., *Administrative Law in Canada*, 2d ed. (Toronto: Butterworths, 1997)

BROWN, D.J.M. & J.M. EVANS, *Judicial Review of Administrative Action in Canada* (2 volumes) (Toronto: Canvasback, 1998) (a looseleaf service)

Canadian Journal of Administrative Law and Practice

DUSSAULT, R., & L. BORGEAT, *Administrative Law: A Treatise*, 5 vols., 2nd ed. Tr. Breen (Toronto: Carswell, 1985–90)

---

34   (1989), 70 O.R. (2d) 532 (C.A.).

EVANS, J.M., H. JANISH, D. MULLAN, & R. RISK, *Administrative Law: Cases, Text & Materials*, 4th ed. (Toronto: Emond Montgomery, 1995)

GARANT, P., *Droit administratif* (2 volumes), 4th éd. (Cowansville, Qué.: Editions Yvon Blais Inc., 1996)

ISSALYS, P., & D. LEMIEUX, *L'action gouvernementale* (Cowansville, Qué: Les Éditions Yvon Blais Inc., 1997)

JONES, D. PHILLIP, & A. S. DE VILLARS, *Principles of Administrative Law*, 3rd ed. (Toronto: Carswell, 1999)

LEMIEUX, D., *Le contrôle judiciaire de l'action gouvernementale* (Montreal: CEJ, 1981) (an ongoing looseleaf publication)

MACAULAY, R.W., *Practice and Procedure Before Administrative Tribunals* (Toronto: Carswell, 1988–) (a looseleaf service)

MULLAN, D.J., *Administrative Law*, 3rd ed. (Toronto: Carswell, 1996) (also published as the Administrative Law title in the *Canadian Encyclopedic Digest*)

Supreme Court Law Review. (The annual administrative law chapter is a particularly valuable source for other discussions of many of the Supreme Court of Canada judgments that appear in the text. However, as in the case of the standard texts, I have not provided specific references in the Further Readings lists that appear throughout this work.)

SOSSIN, L.M., *Boundaries of Judicial Review: The Law of Justiciability in Canada* (Toronto: Carswell, 1999)

Chapter Specific Readings

ARTHURS, H., "'Mechanical Arts and Merchandise': Canadian Public Administration in the New Economy" (1997), 42 McGill L.J. 29

HARVISON YOUNG, A., "Feminism, Pluralism and Administrative Law." In M. Taggart, ed., *The Province of Administrative Law* (Oxford: Hart Publishing, 1997) 331

LORDON, J.P., "Are Administrative Tribunals Effective in Delivering Justice?" in *Justice to Order: Adjustment to Changing Demands and Co-ordination Issues in the Justice System in Canada* (Montreal: Editions Thémis, 1999) 23

MOLOT, H.L. "Employment During Good Behaviour and at Pleasure" (1989), 2 Canadian Journal of Administrative Law and Practice 238

MULLAN, D., "Administrative Law at the Margins" in M. Taggart, ed., *The Province of Administrative Law* (Oxford: Hart Publishing, 1997) 160

OGILVIE, M.H., "Ecclesiastical Law — Jurisdiction of Civil Courts — Status of Clergy — *McGaw* v. *United Church of Canada*" (1992), 71 Can. Bar Rev. 597

PRIEST, M., "Structure and Accountability of Administrative Agencies," in *Administrative Law: Principles, Practice and Pluralism*, [1992] Special Lectures of the Law Society of Upper Canada 11

TAGGART, M., "The Province of Administrative Law Determined," in M. Taggart, ed., *The Province of Administrative Law* (Oxford: Hart Publishing, 1997) 1

TAGGART, M., "Reinvented Government, Traffic Lights, and the Convergence of Public and Private Law," [1999] Public Law 124

VANCISE, W.J., "Are Administrative Tribunals Effective in Delivering Justice?" in *Justice to Order: Adjustment to Changing Demands and Co-ordination Issues in the Justice System in Canada* (Montréal: Editions Thémis, 1999) 39

CHAPTER 2

CONSTITUTIONAL FOUNDATIONS

A. DIVISION OF POWERS

Both in the creation and the operation of the administrative process, constitutional norms impose constraints. Traditionally, the most prominent of those limitations were those imposed by the federal nature of Canada. Thus, in creating statutory regimes, the federal Parliament and the provincial legislatures are subject to the division of powers created in the *Constitution Act, 1867*, principally as detailed in sections 91 and 92. Agencies and tribunals must adhere to that same delineation of powers. Without a permissible subdelegation or interdelegation of powers, a provincially created agency cannot exercise jurisdiction over matters within the legislative competence of Parliament, and *vice versa*. Accordingly, the Canada Industrial Relations Board cannot deal with an employment relationship that is outside the realm of those sectors that are subject to federal legislative competence under section 91. The precise ambit of the restraints imposed by sections 91 and 92 of the *Constitution Act, 1867*, however, is more a matter for a text on constitutional law[1] and will not, for the most part, be explored further in this monograph.

---

1   See P.W. Hogg, *Constitutional Law of Canada*, 4th ed. (Toronto: Carswell, 1996), and P.J. Monahan, *Constitutional Law* (Toronto: Irwin Law, 1997).

B. IMPLIED BILL OF RIGHTS AND OTHER UNWRITTEN CONSTITUTIONAL NORMS

In addition to the constraints imposed by the federal nature of the Canadian state, other forms of constitutional limitation apply to both the federal and provincial entities within Confederation. Nowadays, the principal focal points are the restrictions on legislative capacity that arise out of the various rights and freedoms protected under the *Canadian Charter of Rights and Freedoms*. However, even before the advent of the *Charter* in 1982, there was always some acceptance of the theory that there is an implied bill of rights in the *Constitution Act, 1867*, which limits the legislative capacities of both Parliament and the provincial legislatures and places operational constraints on those exercising statutory and prerogative powers.

This clearly did not extend as far as allowing the courts to review legislation on the basis of its morality or its conformity with general conceptions of fundamental justice. As exemplified by the advice of the Judicial Committee of the Privy Council in *Liyanage* v. *The Queen*,[2] such overarching concepts were antithetical to any constitution based on the constitutional principles of the United Kingdom, and in particular, on the prerogatives of a sovereign legislature. However, this did not necessarily pre-empt arguments for restrictions on legislative capacities based on rather more concrete and narrow species of allegedly fundamental rights and freedoms. So, for example, in *Saumur* v. *City of Québec*,[3] Rand J. held that the ability of the City and province of Québec to pass by-laws and primary legislation and was limited by implied freedoms of religion and speech emanating from the preamble to the *British North America Act, 1867* and its declaration of an intention that Canada have a constitution "similar in principle" to that of the United Kingdom. From the "fact" that the citizens of the United Kingdom possessed these freedoms in 1867 could be derived a similar guarantee of such rights for Canadians.

In the pre-*Charter* era, the implied bill of rights theory, though remarkably persistent, never achieved support at any one point from a majority of judges in any case before the Supreme Court of Canada. It is even arguable that it had been repudiated explicitly by the majority judgment of Beetz J. in *Canada (A.G.)* v. *Montréal (City)*.[4] In rejecting

---

2   [1967] A.C. 259 (P.C. Cey.).
3   [1953] 2 S.C.R. 299.
4   [1978] 2 S.C.R. 770 (sub nom. *Dupond*).

arguments based on the implied bill of rights, he noted the even more transcendent principle of the unwritten constitution of the United Kingdom, that of the sovereignty of Parliament, a sovereignty that could be exercised to abrogate legislatively any of the common law rights and freedoms of its citizenry.

Whether or not this marked the death knell of the implied bill of rights, there was some reason to believe that, with the adoption of the *Canadian Charter of Rights and Freedoms* in 1982, the whole question would become one of largely academic interest. The principal candidates for inclusion in any implied bill of rights to that point formed the core of the expressly guaranteed rights and freedoms in the *Charter*: freedoms of speech, religion, assembly, and the press. Thereafter, subject to the possibilities for legislative override provided by section 33(1) — "the notwithstanding clause" — and the avenue for justification provided by section 1, the federal, provincial, and territorial legislatures were constrained by the *Charter* as were governmental processes across Canada.

Nonetheless, the implied bill of rights theory has staged a quite remarkable resurgence. Indeed, despite the arrival of the *Charter*, it has even expanded. While he apparently condemned the whole idea in *Dupond*, Beetz J. himself had a change of heart. In the early *Charter* judgment, *OPSEU* v. *Ontario*,[5] quoting with approval from earlier individual judgments in the Court accepting the existence of an implied bill of rights, Beetz J. expressed the view that, quite apart from the *Charter*, legislatures were obliged to "conform to these basic structural imperatives and can in no way override them."[6]

More recently, this theme has been elaborated further by Lamer C.J.C., delivering the judgment of the majority of the Court in *Reference re Remuneration of Judges of Provincial Court of Prince Edward Island*.[7] There, Lamer C.J.C. was prepared[8] to find constitutional justification for the independence and impartiality of provincially appointed judges in the underlying principles of the Canadian Constitution, which were derived in large measure from the Preamble to the *Constitution Act*,

---

5   [1987] 1 S.C.R. 2 at 57. (See also the judgment of Dickson C.J.C. to the same effect at 25.)

6   *Ibid.*

7   [1997] 3 S.C.R. 3 [*Remuneration of Judges*].

8   Technically, this part of the judgment was *obiter dicta*, since, at the conclusion of his discussion of this issue, Lamer C.J.C. expressly noted that the case was actually being decided on the basis of section 11(h) of the *Charter of Rights and Freedoms*.

1867.[9] In so doing, he too relied on earlier individual judgments in the Court that supported the existence of an implied bill of rights, including Beetz J.'s statement in *OPSEU*. He summarized his views:

> In this way, the preamble's recognition of the democratic nature of Parliamentary governance has been used by some members of the Court to fashion an implied bill of rights, in the absence of any express indication to this effect in the constitutional text. This has been done, in my opinion, out of a recognition that political institutions are fundamental to the "basic structure of our Constitution" (*OPSEU, supra*, at p. 57) and for that reason governments cannot undermine the mechanisms of political accountability which give those institutions definition, direction and legitimacy.
>
> The preamble identifies the organizing principles of the *Constitution Act, 1867*, and invites the courts to turn those principles into the premises of a constitutional argument that culminates in the filling of gaps in the express terms of the constitutional text.[10]

Subsequently, in *Reference re Secession of Québec*,[11] the Court was to go even further in articulating the underlying, unwritten fundamental premises of the *Constitution Acts*. There, the Court posited four organizing principles behind the Canadian Constitution: federalism, democracy, constitutionalism and the rule of law, and the protection of minorities. (Under this broader conception, the concept of democracy includes the implied bill of rights.) The Court took pains to make it clear that these organizing principles were the basis of more than those rights, freedoms, and other forms of constitutional protection explicitly articulated in the various *Constitution Acts*. They also had a substantive content of their own, which imposed "substantive limitations upon government action."[12]

What remains to be seen is whether this will have any significant impact on the administrative process. However, if the experience of the implied bill of rights is any indication, there is a strong possibility that,

---

9   The fact that the Preamble can support the independence and impartiality of provincial court judges might open up the further possibility that it provides a constitutional basis for the independence and impartiality of some adjudicative tribunals, particularly those performing functions previously exercised by regular courts or analogous to those exercised by regular courts. I raise this possibility again in chapter 14 dealing independence and impartiality.

10   *Remuneration of Judges*, above note 7 at 75.

11   [1998] 2 S.C.R. 217 [*Session of Quebec*].

12   *Ibid.* at para. 54.

at least in the exercise of certain forms of discretion or choice, statutory authorities will have to take these underlying principles into account. This is a subject that I return to in greater detail in the chapter on judicial control of discretionary powers (chapter 6). For now, suffice it to note that the famous judgment of Rand J. in *Roncarelli* v. *Duplessis*[13] was clearly infused with conceptions of the underlying foundations of our polity. In the operation of a liquor licensing regime, those charged with authority could not act on the basis of the religion of the licensee or the fact that the licensee had been exercising the freedom that all citizens have to post bail for those in custody following the laying of criminal charges.

C. *THE CANADIAN CHARTER OF RIGHTS AND FREEDOMS*

As mentioned, this work is not the place for a detailed examination of all of the rights and the freedoms enshrined in the *Charter*.[14] I will pay specific attention to those *Charter* rights that have had a particular bearing on what up until 1982 had been a largely common law of judicial review administrative action. In particular, I will concentrate on examining the *Charter's* impact on procedural law and especially the section 7 guarantee of the "principles of fundamental justice" whenever a person's right to "life, liberty and security of the person" is threatened. As well, along with the implied bill of rights and the four organizing principles of the Canadian Constitution, I will consider the impact of the *Charter of Rights and Freedoms* on the exercise of statutory and prerogative discretions.

There is, however, one more general point about the reach of the *Charter* that merits specific attention in this chapter. The *Charter's* ambit is not coincident with what is generally conceived of as the full extent of administrative law. This emerged from the 1990 judgment of the Supreme Court of Canada in *McKinney* v. *University of Guelph*.[15] There, the Court held that section 32(1) of the *Charter* was controlling in terms of its direct applicability. The *Charter* operated to constrain only the legislatures and the "government." Moreover, for these purposes, government and those bodies created and empowered by statute were

---

13   [1959] S.C.R. 121 [*Roncarelli*].
14   See R. A. Sharpe and K. E. Swinton, *The Charter of Rights and Freedoms* (Toronto: Irwin Law, 1998).
15   [1990] 3 S.C.R. 229.

not synonymous. Thus, according to a majority of the Court the various university respondents in that case were not government. They were not part of the apparatus of the provincial government of Ontario in that they were not subject to day-to-day direction and control by the provincial government or made effectively so by the presence of a majority of government nominees on their governing bodies.[16]

This did not mean that the Supreme Court was at the same time eliminating universities from the realm of administrative law judicial review. In an earlier precedent, the Court had already assumed that administrative law principles applied to universities,[17] and this was acknowledged explicitly by La Forest J., delivering the judgment of the majority on the point. Indeed, La Forest J. also appeared to suggest that, in some specific contexts, universities might be subject to sections of the *Charter*. What this seemed to imply was that, even without a general reconfiguration of universities across Canada to place them more directly under government direction and control, some functions that universities fulfil under direct government direction would qualify for *Charter* protection.

This idea of non-governmental bodies exercising government functions began to evolve in the subsequent jurisprudence. It reached its culmination in another judgment of La Forest J., when he spoke for the Court in *Eldridge* v. *British Columbia*.[18] At stake here was the failure of the British Columbia healthcare system, through either its hospitals or its Medical Services Commission, to provide sign language services for the deaf in the province's hospitals.

To the extent that the decision under challenge, by reference to the *Charter's* guarantee of equality in section 15, was one that had been made by the hospitals, a threshold issue was raised as to whether the hospital was a body that was even subject to the *Charter*. Indeed, the Supreme Court had already decided in another judgment delivered the same day as *McKinney*, *Stoffman* v. *Vancouver General Hospital*,[19] that in general and for the purposes of mandatory retirement arrangements in particular, British Columbia's hospitals were not part of government and therefore not subject to the *Charter*.

---

16   In other judgments released the same day, the same was held to be the case for British Columbia universities (*Harrison* v. *University of British Columbia*, [1990] 3 S.C.R. 451) and hospital boards (*Stoffman* v. *Vancouver General Hospital*, [1990] 3 S.C.R. 483 [*Stoffman*]), but not community colleges (*Douglas/Kwantlen Faculty Association* v. *Douglas College*, [1990] 3 S.C.R. 570).

17   *Kane* v. *Board of Governors of University of British Columbia*, [1980] 1 S.C.R. 1105.

18   [1997] 3 S.C.R. 624 [*Eldridge*].

19   *Stoffman*, above note 16.

However, in *Eldridge*, La Forest J. developed further the notion that bodies that were not generally part of government for the purposes of the *Charter* could, nonetheless, be bound by the *Charter* when performing inherently governmental functions or "implementing a specific governmental policy or program." The delivery of healthcare services to the general public constituted such an instance. However, it was not enough that the body in question was simply performing a "public function"; the *Charter* would be implicated if it went beyond that to a situation where an otherwise non-governmental body was "implementing a *specific* governmental policy or program."[20] Applying this to the facts, he concluded:

> Unlike *Stoffman*, then, in the present case there is a "direct and . . . precisely-defined connection" between a specific government policy and the hospital's impugned conduct. The alleged discrimination — the failure to provide sign language interpretation — is intimately connected to the medical care delivery system instituted by the legislation. The provision of these services is not simply a matter of internal hospital management; it is an expression of government policy. Thus, while hospitals may be autonomous in their day to day operations, they act as agents for the government in providing the specific medical services set out in the Act.[21]

At the least, this further complicates inquiry into the circumstances in which the very *Charter* applies and leaves much room for argument in future cases as to whether an otherwise non-governmental body is, in certain respects, delivering a government program or service. Indeed, given the extent to which governments now engage frequently in both privatizing and contracting out, or "outsourcing," there will undoubtedly be many situations in which the debate will be as to which of these phenomena has taken place in the particular instance. Has the government genuinely privatized a former area of its responsibilities, or has it secured a private sector or non-governmental actor to carry out what is still essentially a government program or an inherently governmental function?

Difficult line-drawing questions aside, the case does relieve at least some of the concerns that governments could avoid their *Charter* responsibilities by simply finding private sector providers. According to La Forest J.:

> Just as governments are not permitted to escape *Charter* scrutiny by entering into commercial contracts or other "private" arrangements,

---

20 *Eldridge*, above note 18 at 661.
21 *Ibid.* at 665.

they should not be allowed to evade their constitutional responsibilities by delegating the implementation of their policies and programs to private entities.[22]

Thus, for example, in the wake of *Eldridge*, it is difficult to conceive of a credible argument being advanced that the inmates of private prisons have no section 7 entitlements.

However, the status of a range of decision makers that normally are within the ambit of administrative law principles was still left uncertain for *Charter* purposes. Are municipalities "government" or does section 32(1)(b), in referring to the "government of each province," reach only the executive and administrative arms of the central provincial government?[23] What is the status of other bodies, beside universities, that operate in a spirit and tradition of autonomy from government yet that are also generally subjected to review for administrative law errors, bodies such as Law Societies and others among the historically self-governing professions?

Subsequently, the Court clarified the situation considerably, if not entirely by its judgment in *Blencoe* v. *British Columbia (Human Rights Commission)*.[24] It was alleged in that case that the British Columbia Human Rights Commission (as well as adjudicative tribunals resolving allegations of discrimination under the province's human rights legislation) were not caught by the *Charter*. The bases for this claim were that both operated independently of government and exercised judicial power in the manner of the regular courts. The Supreme Court rejected both arguments.

Even though the Commission was meant to operate at arm's length from government, the legislature had established it as part of a specific governmental programme, the combatting of discrimination. For these purposes, it mattered not that the Commission possessed adjudicative characteristics. In so ruling, the Court also made it clear that the *Charter* would apply to any body on which the legislature had conferred powers of compulsion such as the attendance of witnesses and the production of documents. To the extent that professional disciplinary bodies are given such powers, they must now be seen as subject to the *Charter*. Also, later in the judgment, the Court referred with approval to a concurring judgment of La Forest J. in *Godbout* v. *Longueuil (City)*[25]

---

22   *Ibid.* at 660.
23   In *Godbout* v. *Longueuil (City)*, [1997] 3 S.C.R. 844, three judges in a nine-judge Supreme Court of Canada held that municipalities were government for the purposes of applying the *Charter*. The remaining six judges refrained from ruling on the issue.
24   [2000] S.C.J. No. 43 (QL).
25   Above note 23.

where he had treated municipalities as covered by the *Charter*. That too would seem to resolve the issue of whether "municipalities" count as "government" or are sufficiently engaged in the delivery of a government programme as to bring them within the reach of section 32.

Blencoe does perhaps leave one important question unresolved. Bastarache J., in delivering the judgment of the majority, only addresses the status of the Commission, not that of human rights tribunals. Does that suggest that the *Charter* does not apply directly to the tribunals because they act in a purely adjudicative capacity in the manner of the regular courts? That would be a surprising conclusion. However, the judgment appears to undercut this as a possibility when later it refers with obvious approval to the much earlier precedent of *Slaight Communications* v. *Davidson*.[26] There, the Court had applied the *Charter* to an adjudicator appointed to resolve unfair dismissal complaints under the *Canada Labour Code*. In citing *Davidson*, Bastarache J. adopts the following statement by Lamer J. (as he then was): "The adjudicator is a statutory creature; he is appointed pursuant to a legislative provision and derives all his powers from the statute".[27] The same should surely hold for human rights tribunals and other adjudicative regimes established by statute.

It is crucial to appreciate two further dimensions to this debate. To the extent that the powers being exercised in any particular case are powers created expressly by legislation, the fact that the body exercising them is not government in terms of *McKinney* or fulfilling an essentially governmental function in terms of *Eldridge* does not mean that the *Charter* is irrelevant. The relevant legislation itself is always subject to *Charter* scrutiny[28], though, here too, it may be necessary to distinguish between legislation that facilitates or enables and legislation that specifically creates a particular power or function. Second, to the extent that the courts increasingly concede the relevance of the *Charter* to the development and evolution of the common law[29] in the private as well as the public sectors, the distinctions between the direct applicability

---

26   [1989] 1 S.C.R. 1038.

27   *Ibid.* at pp. 1077-78.

28   This was exemplified by *McKinney* itself, where the Court, after holding that the *Charter* did not reach directly the mandatory retirement policies of Ontario universities, proceeded to evaluate the limited protection provided to discrimination on the basis of age in the *Ontario Human Rights Code*. This was the formula under which the universities were operating. There, the Court found that s. 15 had been infringed but that the exempting provisions were saved by reference to s. 1.

29   See, for example, *Young* v. *Young*, [1993] 4 S.C.R. 3, and *Hill* v. *Church of Scientology*, [1995] 2 S.C.R. 1130.

of the *Charter* and its use as a guide to the direction of the common law may be diminishing in practical importance.

D. SECTIONS 96 TO 101 OF *THE CONSTITUTION ACT, 1867*

It is always said that the Canadian Constitution differs from that of the United States in that it does not embody the theory of a separation of powers, one of the cornerstones of the American Constitution. In other words, there is no "strict" separation of the legislative, executive, and judicial functions of the kind that characterizes the United States constitutional design. However, what has now emerged in Canada is a guaranteed role for the superior courts, the existence of which is recognized in sections 96 to 101 of the *Constitution Act, 1867*. It is to the ramifications of this proposition for administrative law that I now turn.

Under section 96 of the *Constitution Act, 1867*, the power to appoint the judges of "superior, county and district courts" is conferred on the Governor General of Canada. This is notwithstanding the fact that, under section 92(14), the administration of justice in the various provinces is a matter of provincial legislative competence. Presumably, this sharing of responsibilities between the federal and provincial units reflected a desire for some sort of stabilizing balance in the way the major courts of the country would operate as well as a desire for federal/provincial co-operation in the dispensing of justice. Irrespective of the motivations behind this section, the courts have always seen the federal appointing power conferred by section 96 as involving something more than a mere appointing power. More specifically, they have accepted that the federal appointing power would be rendered meaningless or devoid of real content if the provincial legislatures, in the name of section 92(14) or some other head of provincial power, could remove all jurisdiction from the "superior, district and county courts" and repose that jurisdiction in courts and agencies created by the provinces and staffed by provincial appointees.

From this premise emerged a very complex body of law that provided a basis upon which provincial legislation establishing administrative tribunals and agencies was subjected to judicial scrutiny for constitutional infirmity. Often that scrutiny would involve the entirety of a provincial statutory body's jurisdiction, but frequently such challenges were confined to particular aspects of provincial grants of power and jurisdiction.

In the context of such challenges, a generally accepted test has now emerged, particularly since the *Nova Scotia Residential Tenancies Act* case.[30] Under that test, the first task involves a characterization of the nature of the function that forms the jurisdiction subject to attack. Once the function has been appropriately identified, the reviewing court must then inquire whether the exercise of that function by a provincially-created body can be justified by reference to any one of three questions. If the function was one that at the time of Confederation in 1867 was being exercised by courts or tribunals other than a section 96 court or was being exercised by both section 96 and non-section 96 courts under a system of meaningful or substantial concurrency, the legislation passes muster. If not, the court must then move on to a second question — whether the function is being performed in a judicial manner. If the answer to that question is negative, the legislation will survive, at this stage. However, if the tribunal's constitutionality has still not been established, the court moves to a third and final possible source of justification. Notwithstanding the fact that the function "broadly conforms with" one that was exercised exclusively or primarily by section 96 courts at the time of Confederation, provincial legislation that has the impact of conferring that same function on a provincially created and appointed body will be *intra vires* if it is "either subsidiary or ancillary to a predominantly administrative function or necessarily incidental to such a function."[31]

Frequently, the initial classification of such functions is relatively easy. In the *Nova Scotia Residential Tenancies Act* case itself, the jurisdiction assigned to the provincial director of residential tenancies and the residential tenancies board was the resolution of disputes between landlords and residential tenants — landlord and tenant law. On other occasions, the exercise will be complicated by the presence of contending visions of the function at issue.

For example, in an earlier Supreme Court of Canada case on appeal from Nova Scotia, *Sobey's Stores Ltd.* v. *Yeomans*,[32] the parties advanced varying characterizations of legislation creating a mechanism for dealing with unfair dismissal complaints by non-unionized sector workers, a process that could potentially lead to reinstatement. Was this employment standards legislation? Was it legislation regulating the

---

30 *Reference re An Act to Amend Chapter 401 of the Revised Statutes 1989, the Residential Tenancies Act, S.N.S. 1992, c.31.*, [1996] 1 S.C.R. 186 [*Nova Scotia Residential Tenancies Act*].

31 *Ibid.*, at 233.

32 [1989] 1 S.C.R. 238 [*Sobey's Stores*].

common law of employment or the "master/servant" relationship? Was it contract law? And what role did the fact that reinstatement was potentially available have in all of this — was it a statutory form of decree of specific performance available from the superior courts yet at the same time a remedy that was not available at common law in the context of employment relationships?

In concluding that it was classified properly as employment law, Wilson J., for a majority of the Court, urged against the use of broad classifications as a way of pre-empting from the outset a genuine section 96 inquiry. Defining the problem away was not appropriate if section 96 was to have any meaningful content. However, she also cautioned against defining the function too narrowly particularly in the context of a jurisdiction-wide challenge. So, to describe the function as a matter of deciding whether or not to award specific performance of an employment contract would be to conceive of what was at stake too narrowly. Once again, the question would be defined away by the process of classification.

The three-part test had its genesis in an earlier case involving residential tenancies legislation in the province of Ontario.[33] Once the focus shifts from classification to the test, the court turns to an historical and empirical inquiry. This involves ascertaining which bodies, if any, were responsible for the function as characterized at the time of or in and around the time of Confederation.[34] In particular, the Court generally considers the extent of the jurisdiction of those courts existing in each of the founding provinces that were not "superior, district and county courts" — and therefore not within the federal appointing authority created by section 96.

For these purposes, it is important to realize that the Supreme Court, after a period of some uncertainty,[35] has accepted that the stan-

33   *Reference re Residential Tenancies Act (Ont.)*, [1981] 1 S.C.R. 714.
34   In delivering the judgment of the majority in *Nova Scotia Residential Tenancies Act* case, above, note 26, McLachlin J. (at para. 79) makes it clear that the inquiry should not confine itself slavishly to the precise state of affairs in 1867:
    The historical inquiry mandated by the first step of the test should be realistic and not arbitrarily swayed by the caprice of history. Results should not turn on technicalities such as the date a particular bill came into force. The concern is to ascertain whether the dispute at issue is broadly conformable to one which fell to be decided exclusively or predominantly by the superior courts at or about the time of Confederation.
35   Earlier in *Québec (A.G.) v. Grondin*, [1983] 2 S.C.R. 364, the Supreme Court had dealt with this issue by reference to the state of affairs in the province that had enacted the impugned legislation.

dard to be applied is a nation-wide one and not one that is specific to the province the legislation of which, is under scrutiny. Such a posture would have involved the potential for certain configurations of jurisdiction to pass muster in some provinces but not in others. Thus, the point of reference is the position in all of the four founding provinces in and around 1867 and, where the answer to the historical and empirical inquiry varies among those provinces, the majority position prevails, with the situation in the United Kingdom providing the basis for breaking a two-two tie.[36]

The second part of the test serves to eliminate the possibility of constitutional challenges in situations where a former section 96 function is now being exercised in a manner distinct from the judicial processes that characterize regular court proceedings. Thus, in *Sobey's Stores* v. *Yeomans*, the first stage of the process of resolving unfair dismissal complaints survived by reference to this consideration. The role of the Director of Labour Standards in receiving and investigating complaints and then attempting to mediate an outcome was seen as a non-judicial function, even though it involved a process aimed at resolving a dispute between private parties. However, at the second stage of the process, the hearing of the matter by the Labour Standards Tribunal, there had not been a sufficient transformation from the traditional adversarial, party-controlled adjudicative model for the Tribunal to survive.

In the event that a tribunal's jurisdiction does not survive scrutiny by reference to the first two stages of the test, the court must determine whether it can be justified by reference to the institutional setting in which the role is being carried out, still in a judicial manner and formerly the domain of the section 96 courts. Here again, *Sobey's Stores Ltd.* v. *Yeomans* provides a good example of the factors that the Supreme Court treats as relevant to this evaluation. First, Wilson J. emphasized that the role of the Labour Standards Tribunal was not confined to questions of law and jurisdiction; its decisions were subject to both review and appeal to the superior courts. This point clearly was relevant in establishing that the Tribunal's function extended beyond a disguised form of judicial review. Thereafter, Wilson J. proceeded to accept that the regime was "necessarily incidental to a broader policy goal of the legislature."[37] She premised this conclusion primarily on the fact that, as well as making changes to the substantive entitlements of

---

36   Indeed, Wilson J. had to visit the situation in the United Kingdom to resolve a tie in *Sobey's Stores Ltd.* v. *Yeomans*, above, note 28.

37   *Sobey's Stores*, above at 278.

non-unionized employees, the legislation consolidated under one umbrella a whole series of statutory protections for non-unionized employees in the province. This indicated "a desire to consolidate, rationalize and unify policy in the area"[38] through the creation of a comprehensive scheme, of which the tribunal was a part. It therefore passed muster as a component of this policy and its broader institutional framework.

Subsequently, however, in delivering the majority judgment in the *Nova Scotia Residential Tenancies Act* case,[39] McLachlin J. cautioned against using the third test as a basis for sustaining regimes simply because they were the product of understandable policy objectives. Nor did the combination and modernization of already existing regimes suffice in and of themselves. It had to go beyond that. The judicial power in question must have been "transformed by the new legislative and administrative context in such a way that it is no longer a s.96 power, but rather a power that is ancillary or necessarily incidental to the new scheme or legislative goal. . . ."[40] She went on to intimate that, had she not sustained the legislation on the basis of a substantial sharing of jurisdiction over landlord and tenant disputes between section 96 and provincial courts at the time of Confederation, she would have struck it down. The way in which these disputes were being handled under the new, provincially appointed regime was essentially the same way the regular courts had been adjudicating them previously, in terms of both substance and procedure.

In sum, the lesson seems to be that, if the judicial functions of the superior courts are going to be removed effectively and vested in a provincial tribunal that exercises them in a judicial manner, the more radical the transformation of the particular regime, the more likely it is that it will survive constitutional scrutiny. However, there are only certain conditions under which the transformation will be acceptable. In the case of the Nova Scotia Labour Standards Tribunal, consolidation of existing related jurisdictions within a much broader administrative structure, along with a process that offered readier access, simpler procedures, and more expeditious justice than the regular courts were undoubtedly crucial elements. Yet, as the Court was to make clear shortly thereafter, the changes in the substantive protections available to non-unionized employees were another necessary component.

---

38   *Ibid.*
39   *Nova Scotia Residential Tenancies Act case*, above, note 26.
40   *Ibid.* at p.251.

1) The Core

Obviously, in situations where a matter previously dealt with exclusively or substantially by the section 96 courts at the time of Confederation is taken away from those courts and survives constitutionally by reference to either of the second or third questions under the now refined *Ontario Residential Tenancies Act* test, there has been an effective diminution in the substantive jurisdiction of the federally appointed courts. The integrity of their processes has been compromised. Indeed, a more accurate statement of the position in this regard is that, if certain tasks are going to be performed in a normal adjudicative manner and framework, they must be performed by section 96 courts. However, if there is sufficient transformation of the way in which they are carried out or in the institutional framework of which they are part, the provincial legislatures can effectively seize jurisdiction over that function.

If this were true of all the functions exercised by section 96 courts, then there would be an academic possibility that they could cease to have any jurisdiction in matters within provincial legislative competence. The question that therefore arises is whether there are any aspects of the competence of section 96 courts that cannot be taken away, that must be exercised by the section 96 courts either alone or at the very least on a shared basis with provincially established bodies? To use a term that is sometimes employed in this domain, is there a constitutionally guaranteed *core* of section 96 court jurisdiction?

In administrative law, there has been at least one positive answer to that question. In *Crevier* v. *Québec (A.G.)*,[41] the Supreme Court held that not only was it impermissible for the provincial legislatures to create a non–section 96 court the central task of which was to act in the manner of section 96 court engaging in judicial review of administrative action but also there was a constitutional guarantee of section 96 court review of provincial statutory authorities for jurisdictional error. In short, there could not be statutory preclusion of such review. In so holding, Laskin C.J.C. equated review for jurisdictional error with review for constitutional infirmity, thereby identifying another domain where section 96 court review is constitutionally assured. While Canada never had a *Marbury* v. *Madison*,[42] which unequivocally proclaimed the supremacy of the courts in the interpretation and application of the Constitution, such jurisdiction was assumed early on by the Judicial

---

41   [1981] 2 S.C.R. 220.
42   (1803), 5 U.S. (1 Cranch) 137.

Committee of the Privy Council on the basis that infringement of the limits laid down by a British statute, the *Constitution Act, 1867*, was *ultra vires* of the power delegated by that Act to the Parliament of Canada and the legislatures of the provinces.

Another variation on the existence of a guaranteed "core" is provided by *MacMillan Bloedel Ltd.* v. *Simpson.*[43] At stake here were provisions in federal legislation that attempted to clothe provincial youth courts with exclusive jurisdiction to try youths for *ex facie* contempt of superior courts. The Supreme Court of Canada agreed that while it was permissible to confer jurisdiction over such matters on courts staffed by provincial appointees, that jurisdiction could not be to the exclusion of the superior courts. As in *Simpson* itself, a superior court had a constitutionally guaranteed entitlement to try youths for flouting an injunction issued by it.

What this indicates, of course, is that there are not just three but four categories of superior court jurisdiction for the purposes of section 96:

- jurisdiction which was shared substantially with provincial courts at the time of Confederation;
- exclusive jurisdiction that can be transferred, if sufficiently transformed;
- exclusive jurisdiction that can be conferred and shared; and
- exclusive jurisdiction that must remain with the section 96 courts, or the true core.

Delineating among the four categories is not, however, always an easy exercise.

2) Application to Federal Parliament

Simpson also established definitively a point that had long been a matter of academic dispute: whether the Judicature provisions of the *Constitution Act, 1867* act as a brake on the federal Parliament as well as the provincial legislatures. Aside from the fact that section 96 was applied in *Simpson* to federal legislation, the *Young Offenders Act*, the Court stated expressly that the Judicature provisions did more than simply protect the power of the federal government to appoint the judges of the superior, district, and county courts. Judicial independence was also part of their objective, and that included at least some guarantee of substantive jurisdiction. According to Lamer C.J.C.,

---

43   [1995] 4 S.C.R. 725 [*Simpson*].

The superior courts have a core or inherent jurisdiction which is integral to their operations. The jurisdiction which forms this core cannot be removed from the superior courts by either level of government, without amending the Constitution. Without this core jurisdiction, section 96 could not be said to either ensure uniformity in the judicial system throughout the country or to protect the independence of the judiciary.[44]

It is unclear at this point what the precise ramifications of this are for the limits on the creation of administrative processes in areas otherwise within federal legislative competence by virtue principally of section 91 of the *Constitution Act, 1867*. Certainly, it would seem to confirm that privative clauses that have the intention and effect of preventing review of federal statutory authorities for jurisdictional error would be unconstitutional. Presumably it also would prevent such exercises as the creation of an administrative tribunal to deal with untransformed tort claims against all entities that come within federal legislative competence unless, of course, that tribunal constituted an "additional" court for the "better administration of the laws of Canada," as set out in of section 101. For those purposes, by implication, if not by express provision, section 101 would presumably require that the members of such an administrative tribunal have all of the guarantees of judicial independence found in the preceding provisions in the Judicature section of the *Constitution Act, 1867*. In other words, as is the case with the judicial review jurisdiction of the Federal Court of Canada under the *Federal Court Act*, the exercise could be accomplished successfully — but only if the authority is conferred on a statutory form of federal superior court.

FURTHER READINGS

CORBETT, S., "Reading the Preamble to the *British North America Act, 1867*" (1998), 9 Constitutional Forum 42

ELLIOT, R., "Rethinking Section 96: From a Question of Power to a Question of Rights" in D. Magnusson and D. Soberman, eds., *Canadian Constitutional Dilemmas Revisited* (Kingston, Ont. Institute of Intergovernmental Relations, 1997) 17

WILLIS, J., "Administrative Law and the *British North America Act*" (1939), 53 Harv. L.R. 251

---

44   *Ibid.* at 741.

PART TWO

SUBSTANTIVE REVIEW

Save in limited circumstances where there is a full right of appeal from a decision taken under statutory authority, judicial scrutiny or review of the administrative process does not involve the courts in a reassessment of the full merits of the decision that is subject to attack. Historically, the courts confined themselves to determining whether the decision maker had in some way acted without or in excess of jurisdiction.

While the dimensions of what constitutes jurisdictional infirmity is one of the most intractable questions in the whole of administrative law, nonetheless, this remains the quintessential species of judicial review under our law. Accordingly, the delineation of its scope is a central concern of this part. I will also consider the limited circumstances under which judicial review is available on grounds other than jurisdictional error and, particularly, for other species of error of law and fact. I will also examine how the scope of the courts' review powers is affected when the exercise of discretion or choice is at stake (as opposed to the determination of narrow legal and factual questions). On what grounds can such discretionary decision making be attacked? What are the links between this as a basis for judicial intervention and a review for lack or excess of jurisdiction?

CHAPTER 3

JURISDICTION

A. INTRODUCTION

The most significant theoretical concept in Anglo-Canadian judicial review of administrative action has been that of jurisdiction. Two inter-related principles make it central to this domain of law.

First, there is the principle derived from a combination of the Constitution, parliamentary sovereignty, and the rule of law: there must be a constitutionally proper statutory source for all exercises of public power or, to put it another way, for the use of the coercive power or authority of the state. This invites inquiry into the legitimacy and scope of the statute that is claimed as the justification for the use of such power. What is the extent of the mandate this legislation establishes and on whom has it been conferred? On occasion, this will also mean asking whether the statute trenches on any norms established by the *Constitution Acts*, including the *Canadian Charter of Rights and Freedoms*.

The only exception to this proposition are those powers and authorities existing or conferred by virtue of residual Royal prerogative. Here, too, however, questions of jurisdiction intrude. Exercises of the Royal prerogative are themselves subject to jurisdictional inquiry. Does the matter in issue come within the limited vestiges of prerogative power? And, where relevant, has that prerogative power been exercised to confer the jurisdiction or authority claimed as justification for a decision or action? Moreover, to the extent that the prerogative powers of the monarch or Crown exist today only by parliamentary sufferance, the seeming exception does not compromise the primacy of Parliament. Indirectly, parliamentary consent is actually implicit in the persistence of prerogative power.

A second order principle supports the foundations for the effective enforcement of jurisdictional limits. The superior courts have always claimed and been recognized as having a superintending authority over all exercises of state power that are justified by reference to a statutory or prerogative source. The delegates of Parliament (including all "inferior" courts and tribunals) are creatures of limited jurisdiction, and among the inherent functions of the Royal or "superior," courts has "always" been the policing of those limits.

In Canada, as we have seen already, this system of superior court review based on the enforcement of jurisdictional limits has become one of the constitutional guarantees implicit in the recognition of independent judiciary by sections 96 to 101 of the *Constitution Act, 1867*. Among the guaranteed powers of Canada's superior courts is that of scrutinizing purported exercises of statutory or prerogative power for jurisdictional infirmity. Neither the provincial legislatures nor the federal Parliament can remove this authority. It is sacrosanct.

Below the level of principle, there are also a number of pragmatic or practical reasons why the concept of jurisdiction is fundamental in Canadian administrative law. The availability and scope of review for jurisdictional error is absolutely critical in situations where standard forms of privative clause protect the decisions and orders of a statutory authority from judicial review:

101(1) Except as provided in this *Act*, every order, award, direction, decision, declaration, or ruling of the Board, the Arbitration Tribunal or an adjudicator is final and shall not be questioned or reviewed in any court.

101(2) No order shall be made or process entered, and no proceedings shall be taken in any court, whether by way of injunction, *certiorari*, prohibition, *quo warranto*, or otherwise, to question, review, prohibit or restrain the Board, the Arbitration Tribunal or an adjudicator in any of its or his proceedings.[1]

Such provisions effectively preclude judicial review for all but jurisdictional infirmity. Sometimes jurisdiction is also deployed in defining the

---

1   These privative clauses were the ones in issue in the leading judgment of *Canadian Union of Public Employees, Local 963 v. New Brunswick Liquor Corporation*, [1979] 2 S.C.R. 227 [*New Brunswick Liquor*]. They appeared in the New Brunswick *Public Service Labour Relations Act*, R.S.N.B. 1973, c. P-25 [*N.B.P.S.L.R.A.*].

scope of a statutory right of appeal. Further, it is commonly accepted that statutory authorities are subject only to preemptive judicial review in the form a prohibition or an injunction where there is an actual or threatened absence or excess of jurisdiction. Finally, an absence of jurisdiction is generally seen as a necessity for mounting a collateral attack on the decision or order of a statutory authority.[2] Thus, only where a decision or order is made without jurisdiction will persons affected by it have any prospect of being able to challenge it in subsequent enforcement proceedings.

At a superficial level, the whole concept of jurisdiction might appear perfectly logical and not susceptible to much controversy either as a matter of principle or as to the general contours of its application. After all, it involves no more than an inquiry into whether a person purporting to exercise power is in fact keeping within the realm or ambit of her or his statutory or prerogative mandate. Certainly, one could envisage considerable debate at times about the meaning and scope of individual manifestations of statutory power and the conduct of jurisdictional review in those specific situations. Just as general statutory interpretation is often a highly contentious exercise, so too might be inquiries as to whether the relevant legislation has conferred a specific power and whether that power is justified constitutionally. That obvious point aside, the rest might at first blush appear self-evident and self-applying.

That such sanguinity is in no sense warranted is manifest at the very outset of any examination of Canadian jurisdictional review jurisprudence. The scope and methodology of jurisdictional review has produced a now immense body of case law, and the terrain on which that litigation has been conducted has changed constantly and often dramatically. It has also been the battleground for the attempted resolution of some of the deepest divisions over what is a constitutionally appropriate relationship among the legislative, executive, and judicial arms of government. More specifically, jurisdictional review has slurred debate about the nature and legitimacy of the administrative state in its various manifestations.

The concept of this form of review has proved both highly malleable and impossible to pin down with any real precision. This has led litigants to engage frequently in cynical attempts to manipulate it in order to resist legitimate exercises of state power. By appealing to jurisdiction

---

2   Situations where the validity of an administrative tribunal's order is being challenged in proceedings other than ones in which the remedy sought attacks that order directly, such as where the validity of the order is called into question in defending or resisting subsequent enforcement proceedings.

as an objective, self-applying concept, both protagonists and the judiciary on a great many occasions have generated a considerable air of unreality in the jurisdictional discourse. In many instances, this has lead to failure in the articulation of the issues that are really at stake.

In this chapter, I will first provide a more detailed framework for both thinking about the concept of jurisdiction and identifying how the tensions just identified arise. I will then describe the current Canadian law on jurisdictional review and then subject that law to critical analysis within this same framework. I will conclude by considering whether continued judicial adherence to the concept of jurisdiction is justified.

B. THE MEANING OF JURISDICTION

When we say that a person has jurisdiction to deal with a particular matter or to exercise a certain power, on first impression, we might seem to be advancing the proposition that, on examinating the terms of the relevant statute, the person in question is exercising an authority that the Act has conferred on her or him. Take the frequently cited example of a tribunal or board of inquiry appointed under a *Human Rights Code* to inquire into a complaint of discrimination:

> 36(1) Where the Commission does not effect a settlement of the complaint and it appears to the Commission that the procedure is appropriate and the evidence warrants an inquiry, the Commission may refer the subject matter of the complaint to the board of inquiry.
>
> 39(1) The Board of Inquiry shall hold a hearing,
>
> (a) to determine whether a right of the complainant under this Act has been infringed;
>
> (b) to determine who infringed the right; and
>
> (c) to decide upon an appropriate order under section 41. . . .[3]

Implicit in these two provisions are a number of assumptions underpinning the status of the inquiry. If brought into question, these assumptions would involve a court in determining whether the board has jurisdiction to proceed at all or in the way the board proposes to proceed. Thus, the following issues might arise: Do the members of the board of inquiry possess whatever statutory qualifications are made

---

3   *Human Rights Code*, R.S.O. 1990, c. H.19 (as amended).

mandatory by the legislation? Have the members been appointed in the manner prescribed by the Act? A court might have to respond to an argument that the complaint has not been launched properly in the sense that prerequisites to the setting up of an inquiry have not been met. For example, perhaps no mandatory investigation of the complaint by the relevant human rights commission was conducted before the appointment of the board of inquiry. In a slightly different vein, questions of jurisdiction might compel a court to consider a challenge to the board of inquiry's attempt to coerce testimony. Does the statute confer this adjectival power or not? There might be a challenge to ultimate remedial orders. Does the *Code* authorize an order that imprisons a respondent or awards punitive damages? All of these questions concern the limits of statutory power or authority and can be legitimately branded as jurisdictional in nature.

Indeed, a purely rule-of-law approach to the concept of jurisdiction might mandate an even broader reach to such inquiries. In this light, everything express or implied in a statute can be viewed as a species of jurisdictional limit. The *Human Rights Code* authorizes the remedying only of that which is defined as discrimination in terms of that *Code*. What constitutes discrimination? The following is a non-exhaustive list: Did the conduct take place within the geographic limits covered by the statutory regime? Was the person whose conduct has been called into question someone within the reach of the statute? Does the alleged conduct fall within the scope and definition of a species of discrimination outlawed by the *Code*? Did the evidence presented support the finding that the board of inquiry made on the facts? If the answer to any one of these questions is negative, then the respondent has not disobeyed *this* law. Therefore, it might be asserted that the board of inquiry has no jurisdiction or authority to make a finding against her or him and, as a consequence, no justification for sanctioning that person. Any such finding is contrary to the law that states that only persons responsible within the terms of the statute are subject to the sanctions that the legislation created.

Let us consider what accepting this broader conception of jurisdictional questions means. All matters of fact and law that a statutory authority deals with or considers would be jurisdictional. These would be subject to review by the courts based on whether the authority has made a correct or incorrect determination (or "correctness" review, as it is referred to commonly in the case law). All matters that have been or should have been considered from the very first to the very last, from the most important to the most trivial, whether they are matters of pure law, mixed fact and law, or pure fact are jurisdictional since the statutory authority's ability to do anything depends on its "getting everything right."

Not only has this sequential theory of jurisdiction never attracted direct support from the English or Canadian courts, but it has also quite recently been expressly repudiated by at least one judge of the Supreme Court of Canada.

Professor Paul P. Craig, in his text *Administrative Law* (London, Sweet & Maxwell, 1983, at pp. 299 *et seq*) also emphasizes that the great weakness of the preliminary questions theory is the absence of any coherent test for distinguishing what is in fact preliminary. To use the writer's words, at p. 302:

> The enabling statute always, explicitly or implicitly, states, if X1, X2, X3 exist, you may or shall do [Y1, Y2, Y3].
>
> It is clear that all the "X" conditions can to some extent be categorized as prerequisites to the exercise of the "Y" powers. In my view, there is no logical reason for distinguishing between condition X1 and condition X2 and concluding that one is a preliminary and the other is not. Thus, if all the "X" conditions are said to be preliminary, the administrative tribunal has lost the capacity to err: it can only exercise the power conferred on it by the law if it is right in its interpretation of what is meant by X1, X2 and X3. Ultimately, the distinction between an appeal and judicial review is somewhat fine. This distinction becomes nonexistent if we also adopt the theory that the administrative tribunal cannot err as to the content of powers Y1, Y2 and Y3, since it is then exercising a power that the law does not confer on it.

In short, it is important not to distort the superintending power of the superior courts, and to use the "theory of prerequisites to the exercise of jurisdiction" with a great deal of caution.[4]

Why is this the case? To answer that question requires a refinement of the discourse and the arguments based on parliamentary sovereignty, the rule of law, and the constitutionally guaranteed jurisdiction of the courts over jurisdictional error. That refinement is provided in the case law. There are at least two recognized classes of issue that confront statutory authorities — those that are seen as coming within the jurisdiction of a statutory authority and those that go to or

---

4   Lamer J. (as he then was) in *Blanchard v. Control Data Canada*, [1984] 2 S.C.R. 476 at 490–91. See also the abortive attempt to resurrect this kind of approach in *Royal Oak Mines Inc. v. Canada (Labour Relations Board)*, [1996] 1 S.C.R. 369 at 400.

affect that statutory authority's jurisdiction. Only the latter are truly questions of jurisdiction.

Justifying this distinction between matters within and matters going to jurisdiction in terms of parliamentary sovereignty, the rule of law, and the constitutional role of the courts requires acceptance of the following proposition: Parliament, in creating statutory powers and apparently conferring those powers on a particular authority, intended to establish a regime where primary, if not exclusive, authority for the delineation, elaboration, and application of certain norms rests with the statutory authority and with no other body even the superior courts. Indeed, to assert the contrary would mean stating the opposite: that Parliament's apparent conferral of a power on a statutory authority implies that ultimate authority for the correctness of everything that statutory authority does resides in the superior courts. While theoretically tenable, this position has never been that of either the English or the Canadian courts. The role of the courts both at common law and under the *Constitution Act* has placed no such severe brake on parliamentary sovereignty; Parliament has autonomy in the assignment or delegation of primary responsibility for the exercise of much, if not all, state power. Moreover, to some extent, the exercise of that power involves resolving questions of law as well as questions of fact. Acceptance of this proposition also involves acceptance of a related argument — that the rule of law under our system does not necessarily involve the primacy of the courts over all issues of law. Rather, the rule of law, when seen through the lens of parliamentary sovereignty, demands acceptance of Parliament's capacity to assign at least certain legal questions to bodies other than the courts.

If this is so, then is no issue necessarily jurisdictional? Can all questions ultimately be assigned elsewhere? There are at least two answers to this question, one pragmatic and one constitutional. The pragmatic answer is that, regardless of whether Parliament could actually make a statutory authority the complete master of its own house and the extent of what it does, no Parliament does that. In creating statutory powers Parliament always intends to assign some powers and to retain others. Dividing tasks in the name of jurisdiction or power responds to parliamentary intention. The constitutional response depends on more than simply accepting that legislation cannot be drafted in a way that defeats the guaranteed judicial review role of the superior courts. Perhaps even more fundamentally, it relies on the proposition that to countenance the spectre of a statutory authority with an at large, unreviewable jurisdiction is to admit the possibility of Parliament could delegate all of its authority to an unrepresentative statutory body.

All of this tends to suggest that neither the extreme of everything being jurisdictional nor its polar opposite, of nothing being jurisdictional, is acceptable. This is the case both as a matter of parliamentary intention and as a constitutional principle. Any argument that the rule of law demands court responsibility for all questions of law also has to yield to this tenet. While, however, this may be seen as justification for a division of matters into those within and those outside or going to jurisdiction, the point provides scant basis for discerning which matters fit into which category in any statutory conferral of power.

This whole question becomes further complicated once it is accepted that there are further refinements of the jurisdictional dilemma. First, the legislation might empower a statutory authority to consider questions bearing upon its own jurisdiction. Indeed, there is not necessarily anything wrong with a statutory authority's being given the power to hear and decide challenges to its jurisdiction. What is not permissible under the Canadian Constitution is a statutory authority's being given the ability to make *unreviewable* determinations of the scope of its own jurisdiction.

Accepting this premise means accepting three, not two, categories of questions. First, there are challenges to a statutory authority's jurisdiction that that authority has no power to even entertain. Second, there are challenges to jurisdiction that the statutory authority is empowered to entertain and determine, albeit tentatively, and subject to after-the-event court review. Finally, there are issues that the statutory authority has not only power to entertain but also to entertain to the exclusion of the courts. These latter questions or matters fall within its jurisdiction in the fullest sense of the word.

Centuries of experience, if not logic, suggest that there may be other species of error by statutory authorities that might also give rise to reviewable jurisdictional error. Frequently, the statutory authority doubtless has power over both the subject matter and the persons as well as the kind of order that it is proposing as a possible outcome of the proceedings or evaluation of a situation. However, perhaps it should not follow automatically that the statutory authority thereafter is immune from challenge in the name of jurisdictional defect. The manner in which material is processed may lead to questions regarding the body's capacity. In particular, there may be species of conduct or behaviour that cause the statutory authority to be infected fatally. Malice, bad faith, bias, lack of independence, failure to adhere to procedural norms can all be advanced as reasons for denying capacity to a statutory authority. Jurisdiction assumed properly might be lost for any of these essentially process reasons. As we shall also see shortly, the notion of exceeding or losing jurisdiction over matters otherwise within the capacity of the statutory authority has not been restricted to adjectival matters such as these. Resolution of questions within the capacity of the statutory body is also subject to substantive limitations on the extent of discretion or choice that is permissible.

Thus, a further dimension has to be added to the picture. Even within the categories of question that have been legislatively assigned to the jurisdiction of a statutory power or those "within jurisdiction," the power of that body is not absolute. Not only in terms of the sanctions that can be imposed or the remedies provided, but also in the way matters are resolved both substantively and procedurally, these are jurisdiction limits on the decision-making autonomy of statutory authorities. Understanding jurisdiction, then, is in no easy matter.

These additional issues aside, a basic question remains central to any clear understanding of jurisdiction. How does one go about delineating those matters that have been left to the statutory authority for determination as opposed to those that are ultimately the province of the courts, whether before or after the statutory authority has arrived at an initial determination? By what standards or tests are these two categories of issue to be segregated from each other?

For these purposes, it is useful to return to a judgment that for many years attracted both judicial and academic attention in this context: *Bell* v. *Ontario Human Rights Commission*.[5] The case arose out of the appointment of a board of inquiry under the *Ontario Human Rights Code* to determine whether there had been racial discrimination by a landlord in refusing to rent to residential accommodation. The owner of the property applied for an order in the nature of prohibition to prevent the board of inquiry proceeding with its hearing. The argument was that the accommodation in question was not a "self-contained dwelling unit" and, as a result, not caught by the *Code*'s prohibitions. Since the remedy of prohibition was available only to prevent wrongful assumptions of jurisdiction, it therefore was imperative that the reviewing court determine whether the status of the premises as a "self-contained dwelling unit" was a matter that went to or affected the jurisdiction of the board of inquiry or was one that was within the jurisdiction of the board.

At one level, and this essentially was the position of the Supreme Court of Canada, it could be argued that the drafters of the *Code* were indeed establishing a jurisdictional limit in determining that not all residential rentings and lettings should be subject to the Act's prohibition against racial discrimination. They also set the limits of that prohibition by

5   [1971] S.C.R. 756.

employing the term "self-contained dwelling" unit. "Only if this pre-condition exists, may you go about your task of determining whether there was discrimination as a matter of law and fact." There is also the consideration that this issue is likely one that will be raised early on and as a prelude to any consideration of conduct that is alleged to constitute discrimination. Moreover, while the term "self-contained" was not defined in the *Code*, it is one that exists outside the human rights domain and has been assigned meaning in other common law and statutory contexts.

In contrast, it might be asserted that the mere fact that an issue tends to arise early on does not carry much weight in determining whether it goes to or affects jurisdiction. The lack of definition of the relevant term may just as easily, if not more so, be interpreted as a legislative conferral of discretion on or reposing of trust in the capacities of human rights boards of inquiry to develop the content or the meaning of that term themselves. This they might do within the framework of objectives and purposes of the relevant legislation, rather than on the basis of some earlier interpretations of its meaning in marginally relevant situations. As the creation of limits to the reach of the statutory prohibition reflects a concern about balancing considerations of individual autonomy and privacy and the objectives of the *Code*, it might also be asserted that this balancing role is one for which a board of inquiry is ideally suited. In a sense, it represents the very kind of issue that the legislature, in removing human rights suits from the regular courts and establishing an administrative regime, intended to entrust to development by the specialized adjudicators constituting boards of inquiry. Further, as various arrangements are feasible within dwellings in which residential accommodation is available, this is also an issue that requires considerable sensitivity to the specific facts in a case and an appreciation of the potential for creative arrangements that may be intended to avoid the legislation's reach. Such issues are best left to experienced adjudicators who will bring an informed perspective to the delineation task. There is also the overall concern that the more issues that are labelled as jurisdictional and thereby subject to judicial review on the basis of correctness, the more opportunities there are for inevitably expensive and delaying judicial review. In many instances, such delays frustrate the objectives of the legislature in creating an alternative, more expeditious, and less expensive way of dealing with societal problems than would be possible within the regular court structures.

Further counterpoints can be advanced to these arguments. First, human rights boards of inquiry under the *Code* are *ad hoc* bodies appointed to hear a particular case. Board members require no legal training. One could suggest, then, that any claims based on the expertise of the adjudicators are necessarily speculative and not a matter of legislative prescription. Second, it might also be argued that, if the issue involves resolving competing policies (the anti-discrimination policy of the *Code* versus sometimes antithetical, autonomy-based claims), the courts are in a better position to weigh the contending arguments than an adjudicator who might have been appointed primarily because of a personal commitment to the primary objectives of the *Code*, the elimination of discrimination. And so the debate about the nature of the issue might and does go on.

What, then, are the lessons to be learned from the issue that confronted the courts in *Bell*? First, it is clear that there will be some, possibly many, occasions on which the classification of an issue as either within or going to jurisdiction will be highly problematic. Resolving that question appropriately will depend on consideration of many factors, a number of which will tug in opposite directions. That in turn suggests the need for a commonly accepted judicial approach to such tasks, an approach that will at least identify at a useful level of generality the relevant components of the inquiry. And, in fact, in the post-*Bell* era, that is just what the Supreme Court of Canada has in large measure achieved.

Before turning to that defining jurisprudence, however, it is appropriate at this point to emphasize that it is not always necessary to engage in a broadly based inquiry into whether an issue or a question is one that goes to or affects a statutory authority's jurisdiction as opposed to being within that body's jurisdiction. Legislatures sometimes speak explicitly on this issue. Infrequently they do so by way of a statement that a matter goes to or affects jurisdiction; far more commonly they do so by way of listing matters that are within a tribunal's jurisdiction and where the tribunal's determination of such issues is stated as final and conclusive (one of a number of forms of "privative clause"):

> 22(1) The board shall have exclusive jurisdiction to examine, hear and determine all matters and questions arising under this Act and any other matter in respect of which a power, authority or discretion is conferred on the board and, without limiting the generality of the foregoing, the board shall have exclusive determination to determine:
>
> (a) whether any condition or death in respect of which compensation is claimed was caused by an injury;
>
> (b) whether any injury has arisen out of or in the course of an employment;
>
> (c) the existence and degree of functional impairment to a worker by reason of an injury;

(d) the permanence of a functional impairment resulting from an injury;

(e) the degree of diminution of earning capacity caused by an injury;

(f) the average earnings;

(g) the existence of the relationship of any member of the family of a worker and the degree of dependency;

(h) whether any industry or any part, branch or department of any industry is within the scope of this Act and the class to which it is assigned;

(i) whether any worker is within the scope of this Act.

(2) The decision and finding of the board under this Act upon all questions of law and fact are final and conclusive and no proceedings by or before the board shall be restrained by injunction, prohibition or other proceeding or removable by *certiorari* or otherwise in any court.[6]

Subject to the constraints imposed by sections 96 to 101 of the *Constitution Act, 1867* and the non-delegation principle, such legislative statements will be decisive.

It is also clear that insofar as constitutional questions have to be decided in the course of tribunal or agency proceedings, they will be treated as jurisdictional and always subject to scrutiny for correctness on judicial review. This position rests on the twin foundations of the constitutional role of section 96 courts as the guardians or interpreters of the Constitution and the pragmatic consideration that such matters do not come within the expected area of expertise or competence of many, if any, statutory authorities. For these purposes, constitutional questions obviously include those arising under the *Constitution Act, 1867*, such as whether, in terms of sections 91 and 92, an enterprise is federal or provincial for collective bargaining purposes. Such a determination will establish the jurisdiction of either the Canada Industrial Relations Board or a provincial labour relations tribunal. *Charter* and perhaps even *Canadian Bill of Rights* issues also come within the reach of this principle. Indeed, as will be seen in more detail later, the Supreme Court has gone so far as to withhold from certain statutory authorities the right to consider even in a tentative or preliminary way *Charter* challenges to their jurisdiction.

---

6   *The Workers' Compensation Act, 1979*, S.S., c.W-17.1. This was the privative clause in issue in *Pasiechnyk v. Saskatchewan (Workers' Compensation Board)*, [1997] 2 S.C.R. 890, [*Pasiechnyk*] discussed below at note 21 and accompanying text.

More generally, it is also to be expected that where the question for determination means drawing a line between the competing and mutually exclusive claims of two regimes, the matter will be treated as a jurisdictional question. Thus, even outside the constitutional domain, questions concerning the geographic boundaries of a statutory body's authority would usually seem to be jurisdictional in nature. In 1995, the Supreme Court also accepted as jurisdictional in this sense the determination by First Nations taxation appeals tribunals of whether land owned by Canadian Pacific was "in the reserve" and could it be taxed by the respective Indian Bands.[7] Similarly, the Court did not need to engage in any sophisticated analysis in *Regina Police Assn. Inc.* v. *Regina (City) Board of Police Commissioners*[8] to enable it to treat as jurisdictional and, as such, subject to correctness review, the issue of whether it came within the authority of a labour arbitrator or the disciplinary structure created by the province's *Police Act*. Other such cases include *Wilder* v. *Ontario (Securities Commission)*[9] in which this question was whether the Commission had any authority over a lawyer providing legal advice to a client in a matter that could affect interests that the provincial *Securities Act* protected. The alternative view was that this was the sole preserve of the disciplinary processes of the Law Society of Upper Canada. Similarly, *Taylor* v. *Canada (A.G.)*[10] considered whether the Canadian Human Rights Commission had any authority to deal with a complaint of discrimination brought against a section 96 judge based on his conduct in court. These kinds of issues are self-evidently jurisdictional. The term can be applied to them usefully and without controversy or apology. While the category of what the courts will treat as truly jurisdictional may have diminished dramatically, and for good reason, there are still obvious instances of such cases.

C. THE MODERN APPROACH OF THE SUPREME COURT OF CANADA

1) The Foundational Jurisprudence

General or theoretical discussion can advance the matter of jurisdiction only so far. At this stage, it is useful to turn to the modern jurispru-

---

7 *Canadian Pacific Ltd.* v. *Matsqui Indian Band*, [1995] 1 S.C.R. 3. Despite this classification, a majority of the Court was prepared to concede to the tribunals the opportunity to have first crack at determining the question.

8 [2000] 1 S.C.R. 360.

9 (2000), 184 D.L.R. (4th) 115 (Ont. S.C.J).

10 [2000] 3 F.C. 298 (C.A.).

dence to elaborate further on of the principles that are applied. The seminal authority remains the judgment of Dickson J., as he then was, for the Supreme Court of Canada in *Canadian Union of Public Employees, Local 963* v. *New Brunswick Liquor Corporation.*[11] The New Brunswick Public Service Staff Relations Board had had to determine the meaning of a badly worded section in its empowering Act dealing with the performance of work by persons other than the regular employees during the course of a lawful strike. In language that bristled with ambiguity, it provided that:

> (a) the employer shall not replace the striking employees or fill their position with any other employee.[12]

The Act went on to protect the actions of the board with two privative clauses.[13] The initial question in the judicial review litigation was whether those clauses applied to this particular determination or whether this question was truly one of jurisdiction and outside the umbrella of the privative provisions.

In the New Brunswick Court of Appeal, the judges in fact had segmented the inquiry confronting the Board. In so doing, they labelled one part of that inquiry as going to or affecting jurisdiction — the meaning of the provision — and the other as being within the jurisdiction of the Board — whether on the facts, prohibited conduct under the assigned meaning had taken place. On behalf of the Supreme Court of Canada, Dickson J. rejected this segmentation of the issues out of hand. Such an approach suggested by implication that questions of law were always for the courts and that questions of fact and law/fact application were for the tribunal. Rather, by reference to the nature of the tribunal, its expected area of expertise, and the fact that it was interpreting its "home" or constitutive statute, Dickson J. readily concluded that delineating the meaning of provisions prescribing the rights and obligations of the parties to a collective agreement during the course of a strike clearly lay at the heart of the board's jurisdiction and competence. The board's conclusions on this issue therefore came within the protective shield of the privative clauses and were not in any respect subject to judicial review on the basis of correctness. In so deciding, Dickson J. also identified, in what was then the rubric of such discourse what he believed should be the courts' approach to deciding

---

11   *New Brunswick Liquor*, above note 1.
12   *N.B.P.S.L.R.A.*, above note 1, s. 102(3).
13   *New Brunswick Liquor*, above note 1 and accompanying text.

whether or not an issue went to or involved a tribunal's jurisdiction. As a "preliminary or collateral"[14] matter:

> The question of what is or is not jurisdictional is often very difficult to determine. The courts, in my view, should not be alert to brand as jurisdictional, and therefore subject to broader curial review, that which may be doubtfully so.[15]

The instruction is clear: in close cases, the lower courts are always to give the benefit of the doubt to the statutory authority's capacity. Even more significantly, *New Brunswick Liquor* presaged a new era, one in which the courts began to pay much more attention to statutory purposes and structures and the sense they conveyed of the relevant tribunal's expected areas of competence or expertise.

Did the legislature intend that the relevant question fall within the purview, or bailiwick, of the tribunal under attack? Here, pragmatism and a genuine purposive assessment supersede formalism. For the first time, the Court shows considerable deference to[16], or respect for, the decision-making instrument chosen by the legislature. Henceforth, the Court was committed to a circumscribed approach to the substantive determinations of many administrative tribunals and agencies.

The Dickson judgment was also responsible for enshrining in the vocabulary of the law of judicial review another concept, that of "patent unreasonableness." Dickson J. condemned the too ready labelling of issues or questions as jurisdictional in a preliminary or collateral sense. He also conceded that, by certain conduct or decision making, tribunals or agencies acting within their jurisdiction or competence could lose jurisdiction and the protection of the otherwise applicable privative

---

14   This term, traditionally used in this context, draws attention to the point that not all "jurisdictional" questions arose at the threshold or outset of a tribunal's inquiry. Issues of authority to order the attendance of witnesses or to grant a particular form of remedy were classified as jurisdictional sometimes even though they arose during the course of or even at the ultimate stage of a tribunal's hearing. Where jurisdictional in nature, such "collateral" or "along the way" questions had to be answered correctly, along with preliminary questions.

15   *New Brunswick Liquor*, above note 1 at 233.

16   While I have not done a thorough search, the incorporation of the term "deference" into the rubric of Canadian judicial review law seems to have started in earnest with the dissenting judgment of Cory J. in *Canada (A.G.) v. Public Service Alliance of Canada*, [1991] 1 S.C.R. 614. There, after quoting from and describing the use of the expression in United States judicial review law, he thereafter used it as a synonym for the philosophy of the Court's approach in *New Brunswick Liquor* and its progeny: at 648 *ff*.

clauses. Species of conduct carrying this consequence included bad faith and breaches of the rules of natural justice or procedural fairness. In the domain of intra-jurisdictional or normally protected decision making, giving a statutory provision an interpretation which "cannot be rationally supported by the relevant legislation" amounted to acting in a "patently unreasonable manner." It also "demands intervention by the court on judicial review."

Later in this chapter, I will return to the term "patent unreasonableness" as a constraint on the jurisdiction or authority of statutory bodies. For now, suffice it to say that, in the context of *New Brunswick Liquor*, Dickson J. was not disposed to label the Board's decision as patently unreasonable. After identifying four possible meanings of the relevant provision, Dickson J. held that the Board's sense of the meaning to be attributed to the language of the relevant section came within the range of permissible readings. He stated that no one interpretation was necessarily correct and, in sustaining the Board, he, in effect, conceded that primary responsibility for delineating the provision's meaning rested in the Board, not in the courts even though that delineation was primarily a question of law.

Two subsequent Supreme Court cases refined this whole approach further. In both, Beetz. J., delivered the judgment: *Syndicat des Employés de production du Québec et de l'Acadie* v. *Canada Labour Relations Board*[17] and *Union des employés de service, Local 298* v. *Bibeault*.[18] First, Beetz J. suggested that using the terminology "preliminary or collateral" to describe jurisdictional questions was not particularly helpful; indeed, it had produced much confusion. It also tended to distract judges from what was the only really relevant inquiry in such cases: identifying legislative intent as to primary responsibility for developing the meaning of the relevant statutory provision. Without completely expunging that terminology from the law, he suggested that a more appropriate approach was to ask whether the provision in question was a jurisdiction-conferring one. This, he further identified, as one that described, limited, or listed the tribunal's powers. On such matters, the standard of review was that of correctness; on all other questions, patent unreasonableness became the touchstone for judicial intervention, at least where the tribunal's functions were protected by privative provisions.

Second, Beetz J. introduced another term that became standard in subsequent jurisprudence. "Courts should use pragmatic and func-

---

17   [1984] 2 S.C.R. 412 [*L'Acadie*].
18   [1988] 2 S.C.R. 1048 [*Bibeault*].

tional analysis" to determine whether an issue was of the jurisdiction-conferring species. This meant examining

> not only the wording of the enactment conferring jurisdiction on the administrative tribunal, but the purpose of the statute creating the tribunal, the reason for its existence, the area of expertise of its members and the nature of the problem before the tribunal.[19]

The actual outcome of this form of analysis in the two cases in which it was developed evoked considerable criticism and concern that Beetz J. was not as committed to a policy of deference towards tribunal decision making as Dickson J.'s seemed to demonstrate in the *New Brunswick Liquor* judgment. Nonetheless, as a result of these three judgments, the basic contours of late twentieth-century Canadian jurisdictional review law were now firmly in place. Indeed, these judgments continue to define the approach that the Supreme Court itself still espouses as well as urges in lower courts.

2) Questions Involving External Statutes and the Civil or Common Law

How does the delineation exercise work in practice? A number of more recent judgments of the Supreme Court itself provide good examples. The first is *Canadian Broadcasting Commission* v. *Canada (Labour Relations Board)*.[20] Here, the Court was confronted with a labour board determination that the CBC had committed an unfair labour practice. In question were actions taken against the president of the union, who was also a broadcast journalist. During the course of a federal election campaign, he had written an article in the union newspaper criticizing free trade when that was one of the issues in the election. The CBC, believing that such writings could impair public perception of the impartiality of its on-air journalists, removed the president from his on-air role until after the election and thereafter forced him to choose between that work and his presidency of the union. He did so, resigning as president.

The majority of the Supreme Court of Canada sustained the ruling of a majority of the panel of the Board that the CBC's actions had violated the relevant provision of the *Code*. The Court deployed a pragmatic and functional approach, classifying the question before the board as one clearly within its expected area of competence; in terms of

---

19   *Ibid.* at 1088.
20   [1995] 1 S.C.R. 157.

Dickson J's judgment in *New Brunswick Liquor*, it lay at the heart of its specialized functions. In so doing, the Court rejected CBC counsel's attempt to reintroduce the concept that the interpretation exercise in which the board had been engaged could be segmented into various steps. The first of these was the Board's characterization of the relevant union activity to determine whether management had interfered in the union's role. This constituted a jurisdictional question on which the board had to be correct. In rejecting this approach, the Court referred to the CBC's approach as an attempt to reinsinuate the test of "preliminary" error into the jurisprudence. Second, the Court dealt with an argument that, because the question before the board involved consideration or attention to the CBC's obligations under the *Broadcasting Act*, the standards of an external statute informed the Board's function. Because of this, the CBC urged that the board's overall determination was subject to a correctness standard of judicial review. This assumed particular significance in light of Beetz J.'s judgment on the merits in *Bibeault*.

In *Bibeault*, one of the factors influencing Beetz J. in applying a correctness standard of review to the relevant determination, was the legislation's use of a term from the civil law and the *Civil Code* of Quebec, the concept of "alienation." Where issues of general law or external statutory standards are in issue, the tribunal's entitlement to deference diminishes or disappears. These are matters on which the reviewing courts will be equally, if not more, adept. An expertise-based claim to respect does not hold up. Indeed, as we will see later, this is always the case when a statutory authority is called upon to determine the meaning of the *Constitution Act, 1867* or the *Canadian Charter of Rights and Freedoms*. Save perhaps in the limited domain of evidential assessment, the statutory authority receives no deference whatsoever in its determination of such constitutional issues. Archetypically, this is the area of expertise of the section 96 courts.

However, in *C.B.C.*, the majority of the Court did not accept the application of that principle. Indeed, two of the judges explicitly repudiated the principle that a tribunal confronted with the interpretation of an external statute was not entitled to deference or respect as reflected in the patent unreasonableness standard of judicial review. For the plurality, the approach was more subtle. First, this group of judges recognized that distinctions might have to be made between various categories of external statute with deference still being in order where the external statute is one that relates to the tribunal's mandate and is encountered by it frequently. While this was not the case with the *Broadcasting Act*, nevertheless, the way in which the *Act* became relevant in this case also gave rise to a deference-based claim. In this situation, the Board was not dealing in isolation with the meaning of a particular provision of that Act; rather, it was concerned with mediating between the potentially conflicting values of that Act and the purposes and provisions of the *Canada Labour Code* given that such a mediation exercise called upon the board's expertise, there was no basis for an assertion that its overall conclusion became subject to correctness analysis simply because the values of an external statutory regime not frequently encountered by the Board had become relevant. Indeed, even an incorrect interpretation of a provision in the external Act might not necessarily infect the board's ultimate conclusion with "patent unreasonableness."

Subsequently, the Court has applied the patent unreasonableness standard of review in sustaining determinations of the Saskatchewan Workers' Compensation Board on issues that presented an even stronger claim for recognition as jurisdiction-conferring ones. In *Pasiechnyk v. Saskatchewan (Workers' Compensation Board)*,[21] the issue was whether or not the exclusivity provisions of the provincial workers' compensation legislation precluded certain kinds of action in tort arising from accidents on a work site. Yet, despite the fact that what was at stake was a question involving the scope, if any, of the residual jurisdiction of section 96 courts over work-related injuries, the Court held that the standard of review was not correctness but patent unreasonableness. All of the statutory provisions indicated that this was one of the very issues that the legislature had entrusted to the expert board for determination.

3) Remedial Authority

A number of other recent judgments involving the scope of the remedial powers of tribunals reaffirm the approach that Dickson J. developed in *New Brunswick Liquor* and that Beetz J. fleshed out at the level of principle in the two subsequent judgments. Once again, these judgments are important as they lessen concerns stemming from Beetz J.'s application of his theories to the facts of the two foundation cases. In *L'Acadie*,[22] Beetz J. analyzed the relevant remedial provisions of the empowering statute and held that the Board's remedial solution should be assessed on the basis of correctness; the remedial powers in question were treated as part of a "jurisdiction-conferring" series of provisions. Some read this as undercutting an earlier judgment of Laskin C.J.C.[23] in which

---

21 *Pasiechnyk*, above note 6.
22 *L'Acadie*, above note 17.
23 *Canada Labour Relations Board v. Halifax Longshoremen's Association*, [1983] 1 S.C.R. 245 at 255.

he had stated that claims to deference could arise in the context of remedial powers in exactly the same way that they did in substantive determinations. In other words, after *L'Acadie*, the fear was expressed that, henceforth, the courts would treat remedial questions as commonly, if not invariably, subject to a correctness standard of scrutiny.

Those fears have now been largely put to rest. In both *Royal Oak Mines Inc.* v. *Canada (Labour Relations Board)*[24] and *Canadian Union of Public Employees, Local 301* v. *Montréal (City)*,[25] the Court applied the standard of patent unreasonableness in sustaining the award of remedies by labour tribunals. In each, the Court emphasized the breadth of the language of the empowering statute and the central nature of flexible remedial tools in the exercise of the overall jurisdiction conferred on the particular decision makers — in one case, the Canada Labour Relations Board, and in the other, the Québec Essential Services Council. L'Heureux-Dubé J. delivered the judgment of a unanimous Court in the latter case. She took pains to distinguish *L'Acadie* as a case involving a statutory regime in which the remedial options were constrained by a list of specific actions that could be taken to deal with an illegal strike. She also noted that in *L'Acadie* the Court was of the view that the Board had gone beyond the specific objectives of the relevant remedial provision and tried through its remedy to remove the underlying cause of continued friction between the parties. Such a response conflicted with the principle of free collective bargaining. It also found no warrant in the jurisdiction-conferring provisions of the Act. In contrast, the remedial powers before the Court in this instance "were much more flexibly and broadly worded and have the further purpose of protecting public services."[26]

Each of these cases presents an example of the Court deferring in situations where previously there had been considerable doubts about the appropriateness of such deference. Both also underscore the predominance of the Court's functional and pragmatic approach. More concretely, the Court continues to treat seriously the admonition in *Bibeault* that in determining the appropriate standard of review, the Court must take into careful account not only the language and purpose of the empowering statute but the decision maker's expected area of competence or expertise. These considerations or factors must then be matched against the dimensions of the particular interpretation exercise which is the target of the judicial review application. Indeed, L'Heureux-

---

24   [1996] 1 S.C.R. 369 [*Royal Oak Mines*].
25   [1997] 1 S.C.R. 793 [*C.U.P.E., Local 301*].
26   *Ibid.* at 826.

Dubé J.'s meticulous examination of the background, purposes, and structure of the Quebec essential services regime and the framework and wording of the relevant remedial provision graphically demonstrate the seriousness with which the Court views this task.

4) Patent Unreasonableness Review

Now that the Court is committed to a philosophy under which jurisdiction-conferring issues are a relatively rare phenomenon, it has become that much more important to understand the dimensions of patent unreasonableness. What will cause a tribunal to exceed or lose its jurisdiction on the basis of that standard?

In *New Brunswick Liquor*, as we have already seen, the Court's approach was characterized by an acceptance that statutory language often admits of more than one possible meaning. Provided the tribunal's meaning does not move outside the bounds of reasonably permissible visions of the appropriate interpretation, there is no justification for court intervention. Elaborating further, Dickson J. stated that the appropriate test to which to subject the Board's interpretation was whether it could be "rationally supported by the relevant legislation."[27] However, he also employed another characterization that poses tremendous difficulties. Quoting from his own earlier judgment in *Service Employees' International Union, Local 333* v. *Nipawin Union Hospital*,[28] the case that is the real genesis of the patent unreasonableness test, he provided examples of errors that crossed that threshold. They included

> acting in bad faith, basing the decision on extraneous matters, failing to take relevant factors into account, breaching the provisions of natural justice or misinterpreting the provision of the Act so as to embark on an inquiry or answer a question not remitted to it.

What is problematic about this list of examples of patent unreasonableness? First, it is interesting to note that it repeats the list of "nullifying" errors that Lord Reid laid out in the landmark House of Lords' judgment in *Anisminic* v. *Foreign Compensation Commission*.[29] This judgment is usually treated as the foundation case in establishing in English law the reviewability of all issues of law on a correctness basis. Indeed, earlier, this Supreme Court had cited with approval this portion of Lord Reid's judgment and deployed it to justify judicial intervention

---

27   *New Brunswick Liquor*, above note 1 at 237.
28   [1975] 1 S.C.R. 382 at 389.
29   [1969] 2 A.C. 147 (H.L. Eng.).

in a case described[30] as the "high water mark of activist" review in Canada: *Metropolitan Life Insurance Co.* v. *International Union of Operating Engineers, Local 796.*[31] More concretely, one version of the last category in the *Anisminic* list constitutes a definition of any error of law: any time a tribunal misinterprets its empowering legislation in applying the incorrect version of the law to the facts thereafter, it is asking a question not remitted to it. Similarly, there are problems with the notion that judicial intervention should take place every time a tribunal takes into account extraneous considerations. This raises the spectre of the tribunal being held to account any time it incorrectly identifies the factors that any provision of its empowering legislation either mandates or empowers it to take into account. In terms of both the history of the particular quotation and the possible interventionist interpretations that it opens up, it is easy to see why Dickson J.'s use of it is problematic.

Nonetheless, one essential fact remains. In this same judgment, Dickson J. reveals himself as a devout apostle of the theory that statutory language does not always admit of only one correct answer or a single interpretation. Thus, in using this terminology, he cannot have conceived of it as a basis on which all questions of law would be reviewable on a correctness basis with no respect for the role and expertise of the tribunal or agency. That interpretation would go against the whole thrust of the judgment. Therefore, it may well be that those parts of the quotation that refer to substantive bases for review — asking the wrong question, taking into account extraneous factors or considerations, and failing to take relevant considerations into account — must themselves be read within the rubric of patent unreasonableness. For example, review will only take place if it would be patently unreasonable for the tribunal or agency not to consider a particular factor, or, as sometimes happens, if the empowering legislation mandates taking into account the particular factor. Indeed, the recent judgment of the Supreme Court of Canada confirms this reading in *Baker* v. *Canada (Minister of Employment and Immigration).*[32] I will return in detail to this subject in chapter on review for abuse of discretion.

---

30   Evans, Janisch, Mullan, & Risk, *Administrative Law: Cases, Text, and Materials*, 3rd ed. (Toronto: Emond Montgomery, 1989) at 565, which in turn is quoted by Wilson J. in *National Corn Growers Association* v. *Canada (Import Tribunal)*, [1990] 2 S.C.R. 1324 at 1335.

31   [1970] S.C.R. 425.

32   [1999] 2 S.C.R. 817.

In other contexts, judges of the Supreme Court have attempted to provide a more expansive sense of the badges of "patent unreasonableness." Cory J., by reference to dictionary definitions, has spoken of the decision being protected from judicial intervention if it "is not clearly irrational, that is to say evidently not in accordance with reason. . . . This is clearly a very strict test."[33] As however, he himself also conceded, there will inevitably be disagreement among judges as to whether that standard has been met in particular cases.

In fact, beyond this, it is only in the domain of remedies that the Court has developed any other, more concrete sense or definition of what patent unreasonableness involves. Once again, the judge was Cory J., delivering the judgment of the Court in *Royal Oak Mines*. In a statement that L'Heureux-Dubé J. endorsed in *C.U.P.E., Local 301 v. Montréal (City)*, he identified four situations in which a remedy might represent a patently unreasonable exercise of power:

- where it is punitive in nature;
- where it infringes the *Charter*;
- where there is no rational connection between the breach, its consequences, and the remedy; and
- where the remedy awarded is inconsistent with the objects and purposes of the Act.

In neither case was any of those thresholds for intervention met.

What, in fact, may be just as important as or more crucial than definition in setting the scope of "patent unreasonableness" review is the methodology by which judges approach their task. In one judgment, Sopinka J. elaborated on an approach under which the reviewing judge first asks whether the tribunal answered the question correctly. If the answer is not, then the court should inquire whether the error in question was a patently unreasonable one.[34] This approach conflicts with the whole notion that Dickson J. espoused in *New Brunswick Liquor* that there is often no single correct answer to statutory interpretation problems. Also, it assumes the primacy of the reviewing court over the agency or tribunal in delineating the meaning of the relevant statute. At a more basic level, it makes judicial review that much more likely. It will frequently be difficult for conscientious judges to rule that an error has been committed but to then do nothing to correct that error on the basis that it was not as big an error as it could have been. Fortunately,

---

33 *Canada (A.G.) v. Public Service Association of Canada*, [1993] 1 S.C.R. 941 at 963–64.
34 See his concurring judgment in *CAIMAW, Local 14 v. Paccar of Canada Ltd.*, [1989] 2 S.C.R. 983 at 1018.

this approach did not commend itself to other members of the Court and it seemed clear that Sopinka J. himself later repudiated it.[35]

In another judgment of the Court, *National Corn Growers Association* v. *Canada (Import Tribunal)*,[36] a lively debate ensued between two judges (who ultimately concurred in the outcome) as to the level of intensity the reviewing court should apply in scrutinizing the tribunal or agency's reasoning processes and its methodology in reaching its decisions. In a judgment which attracted the support of a majority of the Court, Gonthier J. wrote that it was necessary to examine in some detail the tribunal's reasoning processes and to apply to various stages of those processes the test of patent unreasonableness. In its most extreme form in that case, he asked whether it was patently unreasonable for the Canadian Import Tribunal to refer to the provisions of the General Agreement on Tariffs and Trade (GATT) as a guide in interpreting the relevant empowering legislation. More generally, Gonthier J. was of the view that the test involved asking whether the tribunal had "acted outside of its jurisdiction by reason of its conclusions being patently unreasonable."

In her judgment, the other two members of the Court with which concurred, Wilson J. took issue with Gonthier J.'s statement of the test in terms of the tribunal or agency's *conclusion*. This was not what Dickson J. had said in *New Brunswick Liquor*; rather, he had considered whether the tribunal's interpretation of the relevant provision was patently unreasonable and cautioned against the court engaging in thorough re-examination of the reasoning processes that the tribunal deployed to reach the conclusion that it did. Wilson J. then expressed the opinion that to subject every stage of the tribunal's reasoning processes to "patent unreasonableness" scrutiny would increase significantly the possibility of inappropriate judicial intervention. Such an exercise also would entail replicating the tribunal's decision-making processes. This could be very costly.

Subsequent case law has shown that neither position is necessarily the correct one. On occasion, it will simply not be possible to understand and respond to a patent unreasonableness argument without a thorough examination and appreciation of the tribunal's record and reasoning processes. In other cases, where, for example, the contention centres on a relatively narrow issue of straight statutory interpretation — particularly in situations where the tribunal has not articulated fully

---

35   *United Brotherhood of Carpenters and Joiners of America, Local 579* v. *Bradco Construction Ltd.*, [1993] 2 S.C.R. 316 at 341.

36   [1990] 2 S.C.R. 1324.

its reasoning processes — the reviewing court's assessment of the situation will be more in line with the Wilson style of analysis.

Canada Safeway Ltd. v. *R.W.D.S.U., Local 454*[37] provides a good example of the latter. Here, the majority of the Court discerned patent unreasonableness simply on the basis of the board of arbitration's reasoning. It was patently unreasonable for the arbitrator to find that there had been a layoff in terms of the collective agreement when an employee's hours of work were reduced. This patently unreasonable conclusion resulted from the arbitration board's insinuating inappropriately the common law employment doctrine of "constructive dismissal" into the collective agreement in the form of "constructive layoff."

It may, however, be that Gonthier J.'s approach will be more appropriate in most situations. First, to the extent that the Court has held that the issue of patent unreasonableness should also be linked to "functional and pragmatic" considerations, the Court has apparently accepted that delineating patent unreasonableness requires close attention to the context or the circumstances, of each case. Further, the Court has now accepted that the patent unreasonableness approach is relevant to questions of fact as well as to questions of law. This means that the exercise is no longer confined to "interpretations" (Wilson); it also extends to "conclusions" (Gonthier). Also, the assessment of whether there has been a patently unreasonable finding of fact will, of necessity, involve the court in a review of the transcript (if any) to ascertain whether such an error has occurred.

In this latter regard, the Supreme Court's judgment in *Toronto Board of Education* v. *O.S.S.T.F.*[38] is instructive. There, the Court found that one of the fundamental findings in an arbitral award lacked any foundation in the evidence. The Court could only reach that conclusion from a review of the transcript itself and/or the affidavit evidence that the parties filed. In holding that a penalty less than dismissal was justified, the board of arbitration had relied on two facts — that the condition that gave rise to the relevant misconduct was temporary and that the employee was not beyond redemption. Evidence in the record supported neither of those crucial factual conclusions but pointed in exactly the opposite direction. So the arbitrators had made a patently unreasonable finding of fact.

Shortly thereafter, in *Canada (Director of Investigation and Research (Competition Act)* v. *Southam Inc.*,[39] Iacobucci J, delivering the judg-

---

37   [1998] 1 S.C.R. 1079.
38   [1997] 1 S.C.R. 487.
39   [1997] 1 S.C.R. 748 [*Southam*].

ment of the Court, attempted to capture the essence of the Court's role in describing the difference between "reasonableness" review and "patent unreasonableness review":

> The difference between "unreasonable" and "patently unreasonable" lies in the immediacy or obviousness of the defect. If the defect is obvious on the face of the tribunal's reasons, then the tribunal's decision is patently unreasonable. But if it takes some significant searching or testing to find the defect, then the decision is unreasonable but not patently unreasonable. . . . This is not to say, of course, that judges reviewing a decision on the standard of patent unreasonableness may not examine the record. If the decision under review is sufficiently difficult, then perhaps a reading and thinking will be required before the judge will be able to grasp the dimensions of the problem. . . . But, once the lines of the problem have come into focus, if the decision is patently unreasonable, the unreasonableness will be evident.[40]

5) The Relevance of Privative Clauses and Statutory Rights of Appeal

To this point, the discussion of the standard of review has been developed primarily against the backdrop of tribunals, the decisions and orders of which are protected by a standard form of privative clause. The question does arise, however, as to whether there is any room for judicial deference in situations where there is no such privative protection.

Until comparatively recently, the answer to this question would have been relatively straightforward: where there is no privative clause, all errors of law are subject to judicial review on the basis of correctness. In other words, the principal effect of broadly worded or strong privative clauses was to remove what was otherwise the capacity of the courts to review on a correctness basis all errors of law, subject to the one proviso that they appear on the face of the tribunal's record. However, for these purposes, a clause that stated that the decisions of the tribunal were "final" or "final and binding" was not treated as a privative clause; it was merely a legislative statement that there was no right of appeal from the tribunal's decisions. All that has now changed.

First, provisions that purport to make decisions "final and binding" have been recognized as having some privative impact. However, in the context of awards of labour arbitrators, the coalescence of the limited form of privative clause and the Supreme Court's perception of the

---

40   *Ibid.* at 777.

expertise of such adjudicators have led the Court to hold that deference could be expected only in the arbitrator's interpretation of the collective agreement. Correctness, not patent unreasonableness, was the standard that applied to all other questions that might arise in the context of an arbitration. In the precedent case, then, giving meaning and content to such common or general law concepts as "vesting" and "accrued contractual rights" related to pension entitlements attracted no deference.[41]

It is important to note that the extent of judicial scrutiny of the meaning attributed to those terms is not based on their classification as jurisdiction or jurisdiction-conferring. At least in the absence of a strong privative clause, the approach concedes little or no scope for deference on matters *within* the tribunal's jurisdiction when those matters are not within the adjudicator's expected area of competence or expertise.

What has become clearer, however, is that a deferential approach is not confined to situations in which some degree of privative protection exists in the relevant legislation. Even where there is no privative protection and, indeed, even where access to the courts is not by way of general judicial review but by an explicit right of appeal created in the statutory authority's empowering or constitutive statute or some other applicable statute, the courts may accord deference to certain aspects of a tribunal's exercise of its authority.

This is not a completely new idea. Authority can be found from the 1940s onward in cases where the courts, exercising both appellate and review authority over economic regulatory bodies and professional disciplinary tribunals, accorded deference to those tribunals on matters that were seen as within their peculiar competence — for example, a professional disciplinary tribunal's elaboration of the contents of professional misconduct.[42] Sometimes this deference manifested itself in a classification of the issue as one of fact as opposed to one of law.[43] However, on other occasions, the court explicitly "limited" the scope of appellate capacity on the basis of a reasonableness standard or one that recognized the superior capacities of the first instance tribunal and the scope of the discretion that it had under the relevant statute.[44]

---

41 *Dayco (Canada) Ltd.* v. *CAW-Canada*, [1993] 2 S.C.R. 230. See also *United Brotherhood of Carpenters and Joiners of America, Local 579* v. *Bradco Construction Ltd.*, above, note 35.

42 See, for example, *Shulman* v. *College of Physicians & Surgeons (Ontario)* (1980), 111 D.L.R. (3d) 689 (Ont. Div. Ct.)

43 See, for example, *British Columbia (Minister of Social Services and Housing)* v. *Appeal Tribunal* (1992), 92 D.L.R. (4th) 326 (B.C.S.C.).

44 *Canadian Pacific Railway* v. *Québec (A.G.)*, [1965] S.C.R. 602.

The modern manifestations of this approach trace their origins to the judgment of Gonthier J. in *Bell Canada* v. *Canada (C.R.T.C.)*.[45] In an analysis of the scope of a statutory right of appeal to the courts on questions of law and jurisdiction from decisions of the CRTC, Gonthier J. stated that, while the patent unreasonableness standard did not apply in the face of such a right of appeal, the appellate court was required to recognize "the principle of specialization of duties" and pay some deference to the agency's determination of questions that came within that range. Subsequently, in *Pezim* v. *British Columbia (Superintendent of Brokers)*,[46] the Court applied this thinking in according deference to certain decisions of the British Columbia Securities Commission even though there was a statutory right of appeal on questions of law to the courts and even though the issues in question were classified as questions of law. After evaluating the expertise of securities commissions, Iacobucci J., for the Court, accorded deference to the Commission's determination of what constituted a "material change" in the affairs of a regulated company as well as the Commission's assessment of whether such a change had been reported "as soon as practicable." While these issues were considered questions of law, they also had a component that was peculiarly within the domain of what securities commissions are set up to do. Their meaning was also circumscribed by the Commission's role in protecting the public interest and developing standards to those with reference considerations. Basically, the courts should hesitate to intervene in the Commission's judgments on such matters and, in particular, should not review by reference to a correctness standard.

The final flowering of this approach is now to be found in the decision of the Court referred to above in which the Court differentiated between review on the basis of "unreasonableness" and review on the basis of "patent unreasonableness": *Canada (Director of Investigation and Research, (Competition Act)* v. *Southam Inc.*[47] , Iacobucci J. engaged in that differentiation in order to identify which that standard of review that should apply in the context of a statutory right of appeal on a question of mixed law and fact from the Competition Tribunal to the Federal Court. After an application to the questions under appeal of the "pragmatic and functional" analysis spelt out in *Bibeault*, Iacobucci J., concluded:

---

45   [1989] 1 S.C.R. 1722.
46   [1994] 2 S.C.R. 557.
47   *Southam*, above note 40.

[W]hat is dictated is a standard more deferential than correctness but less deferential than "not patently unreasonable." Several considerations counsel deference: the fact that the dispute is over a question of mixed law and fact; the fact that the purpose of the *Competition Act* is broadly economic, and so is better served by the exercise of economic judgment; and the fact that the application of principles of competition law falls squarely within the area of the Tribunal's expertise.[48]

After balancing those considerations against the presence of "an unfettered statutory right of appeal," Iacobucci J. held that the standard of review should fall somewhere on a "spectrum" that has correctness at one end and patent unreasonableness at the other. This point he described as review on the basis of unreasonableness or a decision which,

in the main, is not supported by any reasons that can stand up to a somewhat probing examination. Accordingly, a court reviewing a conclusion on the reasonableness standard must look to see whether there are any reasons that support it. The defect, if there is one, could presumably be in the evidentiary foundation itself or the logical process by which conclusions are sought to be drawn from it. An example of the former kind of defect would be an assumption that had no basis in the evidence, or that was contrary to the overwhelming weight of the evidence. An example of the latter kind of defect would be a contradiction in the premises or an invalid inference.[49]

Thereafter, he proceeded to draw the distinction between "unreasonableness" and "patent unreasonableness" outlined earlier.

6) Attributing Deference to Expertise

In understanding fully what the Supreme Court has done in this case, it is important to appreciate that this is not the standard that applies to all questions decided by securities commissions and the Competition Tribunal. The "pragmatic and functional" approach demands attention not only to the nature of the tribunal under appeal but also to the nature of the issue that is subject to that appeal. Only where there is some match between tribunal expertise and issue will this "reasonableness" form of deference be justified. In relation to all other matters of law and mixed fact and law, correctness scrutiny will be the order of the day. Nor should it be assumed that all tribunals will have an area of

---

48 *Ibid.* at p.775.
49 *Ibid.* at 776–77.

expertise calling for some degree of deference from the court, even in the presence of a statutory right of appeal.

The domain of human rights adjudication provides a graphic and controversial example of this latter observation. Across Canada, the decisions of human rights tribunals or boards of inquiry are generally subject to an appeal to the courts on questions of law or those decisions are not provided with any degree of privative protection.[50] At first blush, it might be thought that such tribunals would be entitled in some aspects of their functioning to the kind of deference that is acknowledged in *Pezim* and *Southam*. However, that is not the position. In a now quite lengthy series of judgments, the Supreme Court of Canada has emphasized that the only claim to deference that such tribunals have relates to matters of fact. Stressing that they are *ad hoc*, as opposed to permanently established, bodies, and referring to the courts' own considerable expertise in discrimination issues through exposure to them in the context of equality jurisprudence under section 15 of the *Charter*, the Supreme Court has simply refused to accord any deference to tribunal determination of issues of law arising out of human rights codes.[51] Indeed, this line of authority is referred to expressly in *Pezim* to distinguish between such tribunals and their tasks and the securities commissions and theirs. Moreover, in one of the more recent authorities, Iacobucci J. also cautioned that the patent unreasonableness standard of judicial scrutiny that applies to such tribunals' findings of fact should not extend to reaching inferences to be drawn from such facts; there, the policy reasons for deference are "significantly attenuated."[52]

Nor are human rights tribunals isolated on this question. Aside from various decision makers to which provincial superior courts and Courts of Appeal have not been prepared to concede little, if any, deference,[53] the Supreme Court of Canada in *Pushpanathan* v. *Canada (Minister of Citizenship and Immigration)*[54] refused to concede any degree of deference to a determination of the Immigration and Refugee Board. In so doing, the Court did rely on the nature of the particular question

---

50   However, the New Brunswick Act does contain a "finality" clause, a factor that led to a rather less intrusive review in *Ross* v. *New Brunswick School District, No. 15*, [1996] 1 S.C.R. 825.

51   *Zurich Insurance Co.* v. *Ontario (Human Rights Commission)*, [1992] 2 S.C.R. 321; *Canada (A.G.)* v. *Mossop*, [1993] 1 S.C.R. 554; *University of British Columbia* v. *Berg*, [1993] 2 S.C.R. 353; and *Gould* v. *Yukon Order of Pioneers*, [1996] 1 S.C.R. 571.

52   *Gould* v. *Yukon Order of Pioneers*, *ibid.* at 585 (Iacobucci J.).

53   See, for example, *Wedekind* v. *Ontario (Ministry of Community and Social Services)* (1994), 21 O.R. (3d) 289 (C.A.).

54   [1998] 1 S.C.R. 982 [*Pushpanathan*].

under consideration, the interpretation of the scope of terms in an international treaty, but also based its conclusions on other factors. The judgment of Bastarache J. cited the weakness of the relevant privative clause, the statutory qualifications of members of the board, and the human rights dimensions of the issue the Board had to determine. The Court also pointed out that any appeal from a first instance review decision by the Federal Court, Trial Division, depended on that judge's certifying an issue as one of "serious, general importance" as part of a leave to appeal process.

While it is unclear whether the Court in this instance was intending to lay down a general principle of correctness review in all such matters, what the judgment does suggest is that the Court is being much more careful in its willingness to concede expertise automatically to tribunals. It is taking considerable care to calibrate any claims for respect to expertise to the precise decision-making context. Now, it remains to be seen how far this marks the beginning of an era of decreasing deference to tribunals with lay membership, at least when they are engaged in determining issues of law.

However, Bastarache J., in delivering the judgment of the Supreme Court of Canada did seem to suggest at one point that there might have to be a re-evaluation of the Court's traditional posture of correctness review of human rights tribunals' findings of law.[55] Subsequently, Evans J. of the Federal Court, Trial Division, referred to this passage in *Public Service Alliance of Canada* v. *Canada (Treasury Board)*,[56] in justification of "being educated" by, if not deferring to, a human rights tribunal's reasons for its particular interpretation of an open-ended pay equity provision in the *Canadian Human Rights Act*.

7) Review of Factual Determinations

Even in an appeal situation, there will be occasions when the standard of review of factual determinations will be the more stringent one of patent unreasonableness. Thus, in the instance of the Competition Tribunal, the right of appeal is conditioned in the case of questions of fact on leave being given by the Federal Court of Appeal. Within such a statutory wording, it is possible to envisage the Federal Court declining to interfere with factual findings unless the evidence did not support them or the findings are patently unreasonable.

---

55   *Ibid.* at p.1017.
56   [2000] 1 F.C. 146 (T.D.).

Indeed, outside the domain of statutory appeals covering issues of fact, it needs to be emphasized that, even where there was no privative clause, the courts confined their review of factual determinations within jurisdiction to a complete absence of or "no evidence." To the extent that, because of the *O.S.S.T.F.* judgment, the Court has accepted a parallel between this species of review and review for "patently unreasonable" findings of fact, it is to be anticipated that, even absent a privative clause, judicial review of such determinations will continue to be constrained.

8) Authority to Deal Provisionally with Jurisdiction-Conferring Issues

In most situations where a tribunal or other statutory authority encounters a jurisdiction-conferring issue, the courts have had no difficulty in conceding to the tribunal the entitlement to proceed and make a preliminary or tentative determination of that issue. Even though it is one that affects or goes to the statutory body's jurisdiction, the body itself is entitled to consider it. In some cases, the reviewing court may even decline to become involved until the statutory authority has looked into the question, come up with tentative conclusions, and so created a record on which the court can then base its own review of the matter.[57]

However, as noted earlier in the chapter, this second order species of jurisdiction to consider jurisdictional issues or challenges is not always present. Traditionally, the courts seemed to have no difficulty with ceding to tribunals the entitlement to make tentative determinations of questions involving the *Constitution Act, 1867*.[58] Today, however, the position regarding issues arising under the *Canadian Charter of Rights and Freedoms* is somewhat different.

At first impression, it might be thought that the provisions of section 52(1) of the *Constitution Act, 1982* provided justification for all manner of statutory authorities making preliminary or tentative rulings on any *Charter* questions relevant to the exercise of their mandates. Section 52(1) declares the Constitution of Canada "the supreme law of Canada" and specifies that any law inconsistent with it is, to the extent of the inconsistency, "of no force and effect." This might be seen as a direction to all officials to heed the *Charter* and not to rely upon or enforce any

---

57   See, for example, *Northern Telecom Ltd.* v. *Communication Workers of Canada*, [1980] 1 S.C.R. 115 and *Northern Telecom Ltd.* v. *Communication Workers of Canada (No. 2)*, [1983] 1 S.C.R. 733.

58   See, for example, *Northern Telecom Canada Ltd.* v. *Communication Workers of Canada Ltd.*, *ibid.*

laws that conflict with it.[59] However, the Supreme Court has held that section 52 is not an independent source of jurisdiction for dealing with *Charter* issues.[60] Even here, the primary test is one of legislative intention based on a pragmatic and functional analysis. Does the empowering legislation either expressly or by implication authorize this tribunal to consider *Charter* questions that arise in any proceedings before it?

I return to consider this issue in detail in chapter 15 on the adjectival powers of statutory authorities.

D. CONCLUSIONS

In recent years, there have been a number of suggestions that the term "jurisdiction" be struck from the vocabulary of judicial review of administrative action. Advocates of this position point to its unfortunate history in this domain, the lack of clarity even today regarding what "jurisdiction" actually means, and the fact that it seems to mean different things in different contexts and, in some of which, it assumes a complexion far removed from any realistic sense of what are its limits.

Insofar as the principal points of contention in most substantive judicial review proceedings are, first, identification of the appropriate standard of review to be applied, and, second, according to that standard, discerning whether the statutory decision maker has erred, the terminology of jurisdiction does not fit all that easily. In most of these instances, in applying the pragmatic and functional analysis, the reviewing court is not really focusing on issues related to the scope of power and authority but rather on the respective qualifications of court and tribunal concerning the issue in question. The relevant statutory provisions are also read primarily for the purpose of discovering any indications as to how those responsibilities have been parcelled out. The term "jurisdiction," if it intrudes at all, does so largely as a rhetorical justification of what is being done: the *Constitution Act, 1867* enshrines judicial review for jurisdictional error, and among the wrongs that count for these purposes are patently unreasonable decisions. These, so it is said, cause a statutory decision maker to "lose" or "exceed" jurisdiction. However, there is seldom any sense that review on this basis stems from any *a priori* identification of a natural or

---

59   For a ringing endorsement of this position, see the dissenting judgment of McLachlin J. in *Cooper v. Canada (Canadian Human Rights Commission)*, [1996] 3 S.C.R. 854.

60   The most recent Supreme Court manifestation of this is *Cooper, ibid.*

immutable concept of what jurisdiction means. This too is just as pragmatic and functional as everything else in this domain.

Even conceding how malleable the term has proved to be in the hands of the courts, there is nothing necessarily problematic about its continued use. As long as judges realize the real values behind the term "jurisdiction," its effective reach and limits, as well as the policy basis behind the symbol, this code word can continue to serve a useful purpose in the evolution of the law and the Constitution in this area.

At a more fundamental level, however there is a narrower sense in which statutory decision makers and others involved in the administrative process use "jurisdiction"; a sense in which the word is more suited to colloquial use, and a sense which would be difficult, perhaps impossible, to remove from the rubric of administrative law. In the domain of questions that, on a pragmatic and functional analysis a statutory authority must answer correctly, there are many that are about jurisdiction in this more fundamental sense of the term. Do I have authority an inquire as to the *Charter* validity of this statutory provision? Am I a "court of competent jurisdiction" for the purposes of awarding *Charter* remedies? Have I the power to cite someone for contempt? Does the division of powers under the Constitution prevent me from dealing with this particular person or issue? Can I hear this particular matter or has the legislature assigned it exclusively to another statutory authority? All of these are questions that fit easily within the concept of "jurisdiction." Their inclusion within the term requires no instrumental justification; they represent bedrock, *a priori*, even if in practice relatively infrequent, examples. As such, they form an integral part of the whole framework of a system of judicial review.

FURTHER READINGS

ALLARS, M., "On Deference to Tribunals, With Deference to Dworkin" (1994), 20 Queen's L.J. 163

CHAPLIN, A.M., "Who is Best Suited to Decide? The Recent Trend in Standards of Review" (1994), 26 Ottawa L.R. 321

DYZENHAUS, D., "The Politics of Deference: Judicial Review and Democracy," in M. Taggart, ed., *The Province of Administrative Law* (Oxford: Hart Publishing, 1997) 278

LA FOREST, G.V. "The Courts and Administrative Tribunals: Standards of Judicial Review of Administrative Action," in *Administrative Law: Principles, Practice and Pluralism*, [1992] Special Lectures of the Law Society of Upper Canada 1

L'HEUREUX-DUBÉ, C., "The 'Ebb' and 'Flow' of Administrative Law on the 'General Question of Law,' in M. Taggart, ed., *The Province of Administrative Law* (Oxford: Hart Publishing, 1997) 308

HARVISON YOUNG, A., "Human Rights Tribunals and the Supreme Court of Canada: Reformulating Deference" (1993), 13 Admin. L.R. (2d) 206

HOLLOWAY, I., " 'A Sacred Right': Judicial Review of Administrative Action as a Cultural Phenomenon" (1993), 22 Man. L.J. 28

MACLAUCHLAN, H.W., "Reconciling Curial Deference with a Functional Approach in Substantive and Procedural Judicial Review" (1993), 7 Canadian Journal of Administrative Law & Practice 1

MCLACHLIN, B., "The Roles of Administrative Tribunals and Courts in Maintaining the Rule of Law" (1999), 12 Canadian Journal of Administrative Law & Practice 171

MULLAN, D., "Recent Developments in Administrative Law: The Apparent Triumph of Deference" (1999), 12 Canadian Journal of Administrative Law & Practice 191

MULLAN, D.J., "Deference Deferred: The Immigration and Refugee Board" (1999), 7 Reid's Administrative Law 97

CHAPTER 4

JURISDICTIONAL WRANGLING

In a number of instances, the principal reason for creating an administrative regime was to establish a jurisdiction that would supplant that of the regular courts or pre-empt the regular courts' entering a particular field. Among the most notable examples are those of workers' compensation, human rights commissions and their adjudicative arms, and the whole field of labour relations.

As we have already seen, over the years there have been many constitutional challenges to the creation of these regimes, constitutional challenges brought under sections 96 through 100 of the *Constitution Act, 1867* and relying on the guaranteed core of jurisdiction of the county, district, and superior courts. Beyond this, other litigation has involved the interpretation of the legislation creating administrative tribunals. What precisely is the scope of the jurisdiction conferred on the tribunal? Is that jurisdiction exclusive or does the tribunal share it with the regular courts or other administrative tribunals or agencies? If it is shared, which jurisdiction takes priority both in the hearing of matters and in the rare case where there are conflicting orders or directions emanating from different sources?

Human rights is one area where these issues have arisen quite frequently and a consideration of the most significant authorities in this domain will indicate the more precise nature of these disputes as well as judicial approaches towards their resolution.

This history begins with the 1981 judgment of the Supreme Court of Canada in *Seneca College of Applied Arts & Technology* v. *Bhadauria*.[1] There, the Supreme Court of Canada held that, in the face of the Ontario's enactment of a human rights code, there was no longer room for judicial recognition of a new common law tort of discrimination. The objectives and structure of the *Code* indicated that those who were victims of discrimination should take their complaints to the human rights commission. Unfortunately, if they were rebuffed there (as Bhadauria had been), the common law courts did not offer an alternative avenue of recourse.

Since then, it has become clear that the matter is not as straightforward as one reading of that case might suggest. In particular, the human rights commissions and their adjudicative arms do not have a monopoly on allegations of discriminatory conduct. This includes the specific grounds of discrimination expressly provided for in the Codes themselves. *Canada Trust Co.* v. *Ontario (Ontario Human Rights Commission)* was one of the first cases to confirm this.[2] There, the Court of Appeal held that the section 96 courts continued to possess jurisdiction over issues of discrimination that were raised as part of a cause of action already in existence at the time of the enactment of the *Code*. In this instance that existing jurisdiction was the section 96 courts' continuing equitable authority over charitable trusts. This included the adjudication of disputes as to whether the terms of such a trust were contrary to public policy by reason of their discriminatory objectives and impact. This led the Court of Appeal to rule not only that it had jurisdiction over the matter in issue, but that it should not defer to the mechanisms established by the Code. Similar assertions of continuing jurisdiction over issues of discrimination followed, in the context of wrongful dismissal actions.[3] And now there are serious questions still unresolved about whether the *Bhadauria* rule applies: to preclude the evolution of the constitutional tort of violating a person's section 15 equality rights as opposed to the common law tort of discrimination[4]

---

1   [1981] 2 S.C.R. 181 [*Bhadauria*].
2   (1990), 74 O.R. (2d) 481 (C.A.)
3   See, for example, *Lehman* v. *Davis* (1993), 16 O.R. (3d) 338 (G.D.).
4   See *Perera* v. *Canada*, [1997] F.C.J. No. 199 (T.D.) (Q.L.), aff'd in part and rev'd in part [1998] 3 F.C. 381 (C.A.).

Bearing upon this issue is the important Supreme Court of Canada judgment in *Weber* v. *Ontario Hydro*.[5] Here, the Court was dealing with a cause of action in tort (including an allegation of a violation of *Charter* rights) based on events that occurred in the course of an employment relationship covered by a collective agreement. As the dispute arose under the collective agreement, the Court held that the exclusive jurisdiction provisions of the labour relations statute and the terms of that collective agreement (including the right of grievance arbitrators to award monetary relief) combined to preclude any common law cause of action in tort. This included a cause of action based on *Charter* violations, a conclusion based in significant measure on the Court's determination that the grievance arbitrator was competent to address *Charter* questions and award financial relief where appropriate.

Could the same reasoning hold in the rather different statutory context of human rights codes? To date, it remains a moot point whether the *Weber* principles preclude the possibility of a cause of action for violation of section 15 rights in discrimination cases otherwise within the ambit of the codes. It also suggests yet another jurisdictional question that has subsequently come to the courts' attention. In situations where a collective agreement explicitly or implicitly incorporates the same protections against discrimination provinces for in the human rights codes, what are the jurisdictional consequences? More particularly, does *Weber* apply to preclude human rights commissions as well as the regular courts from taking such a complaint leaving exclusive jurisdiction to grievance arbitration under the collective agreement? Or, is it the other way around, with the complaint mechanisms in the codes superseding the collective agreement? Or, is this an area of shared jurisdiction? If so, on what basis should decisions regarding the exercise of that jurisdiction be made?

This very issue came before the Saskatchewan courts in *Saskatchewan Human Rights Commission* v. *Cadillac Fairview Corporation Ltd.*[6] Two employees in a unionized workplace had filed complaints of sexual harassment and discrimination against their employer with the province's human rights commission. On the appointment of a board of inquiry to adjudicate the complaint, the employer applied for an order to prohibit the hearing from proceeding. Callillac Fairview argued that the matter should have proceeded under the grievance provisions of

---

5   [1995] 2 S.C.R. 929 (and also *New Brunswick* v. *O'Leary*, [1995] 2 S.C.R. 967). See also the foundation judgment of the Court in *St. Anne Nackawic Pulp & Paper Co. Ltd.* v. *Canadian Paper Workers Union, Local 219*, [1986] 1 S.C.R. 704.
6   (1999), 173 D.L.R. (4th) 609 (Sask. C.A.), rev'g (1998), 162 Sask. R. 290 (Q.B.).

the collective agreement. At first instance, the application succeeded; the motions court judge applied *Weber*. Then on appeal, Vancise J.A., delivering the judgment of the Saskatchewan Court of Appeal, held that *Weber* was not governing. The Court considered the proper characterization of the dispute as one involving an alleged human rights violation. It also noted the superior character of human rights legislation and the nature of the mechanisms selected by the legislature for the resolution of such complaints. It concluded that the matter was properly before the board of inquiry. In terms of the labour relations legislation, despite the explicit incorporation of the human rights code standards into that agreement, the court also held that it was not in its essence a dispute arising out of the collective agreement.

Indeed, this judgment was part of a trilogy of decisions. In each, the court determined that the collective agreement did not pre-empt the jurisdiction of the statutory regime. The other two cases involved complaints about unsafe working conditions under occupational health and safety legislation[7] and claims under labour standards legislation based on the notice of layoff requirements of that statute.[8] In each, the Court characterized the nature of the dispute as one involving a claim under the specialized regime as opposed to one that arose out of the collective agreement.

What is interesting, however, is that the Court does not go so far as to assert that the claims could not have been brought under the collective agreement had the employees so wished. That obviously leaves open the possibility of shared jurisdiction, and if the jurisdiction is in fact shared, it raises the further problem of what would happen if the specialized jurisdiction statutory body — here, the human rights commission — wished to defer to the jurisdiction established by the collective agreement because of considerations such as workload. Would this be an appropriate exercise of discretion? Or could the person who has chosen that route rather than that of the collective agreement force the specialized regime to take the case? The reverse situation could also happen: a labour arbitrator might wish to defer to the specialized regime.

Subsequently, however, in another Saskatchewan case involving these issues,[9] the Supreme Court of Canada sustained the ruling of an

---

7   *Parr* v. *Prince Albert District Health Board* (1999), 173 D.L.R. (4th) 588 (Sask. C.A.).

8   *Dominion Bridge Inc.* v. *Routledge* (1999), 173 D.L.R. (4th) 624 (Sask. C.A.).

9   *Regina Police Assn. Inc.* v. *Regina (City) Board of Police Commissioners*, [2000] 1 S.C.R. 360. In so doing, the Court reversed the Saskatchewan Court of Appeal ((1998), 163 D.L.R. (4th) 145) and approved of the analysis of Vancise J.A., who dissented.

arbitrator that she did not have jurisdiction to deal with a grievance relating to the resignation of a police officer in the context of disciplinary charges. She held that the matters in issue came within the police discipline jurisdiction assigned to a special regime under the province's *Police Act*. In this instance, the Court applied *Weber* to a situation involving two administrative regimes rather than an administrative regime and the courts. It also held that the relevant inquiry was to determine which of the two regimes governed by reference to the essential character of the dispute and the indicators in the legislative scheme. In this particular case, there was no suggestion of the possibility that each regime might have jurisdiction over the dispute. The assumption throughout was that it had to be one or the other. At the same time, there is no assertion that shared jurisdiction over a dispute is impossible. Whether that can ever be the case must await further elaboration.[10] Indeed, the frequency with which such problems arise today suggests the efficacy of a legislative solution to this problem. Otherwise, a wide range of permutations and combinations may have to be litigated case by case. That would certainly not be in the best interests of affected constituencies.

One domain where there has been an attempt to deal with this matter legislatively is under the federal *Public Service Staff Relations Act*.[11] Section 91(1)(b) of that Act provides that employees may exercise the rights of grievance provided for under the Act, save where there is an "administrative procedure for redress . . . provided in or under an Act of Parliament." In *Mohammed v. Canada (Treasury Board)*,[12] the Federal Court of Appeal, sustaining earlier authority, determined that the exclusion covered complaints of discrimination within the scope of the *Canadian Human Rights Act*[13] even though there were non-discrimination clauses in the collective agreement. In so doing, the Court seemed to also accept that the Canadian Human Rights Commission could itself remit the matter by exercising its discretionary authority under section 41 of its Act to require the exhaustion of other modes of

---

10   It might be argued, I suppose, that the Court's approach in focusing on the "essential" character of the dispute amounts to an implicit assertion that all disputes have an essence that will indicate which of the two competing regimes will have jurisdiction.

11   R.S.C. 1985, c.P-35.

12   (1999), 181 D.L.R. (4th) 590 (F.C.A.).

13   Indeed, in one of the three cases that constituted this proceeding, the Court of Appeal held that recourse to the Commission was required even for a complaint of discrimination over which the Commission might have had no jurisdiction.

redress. Presumably, the tag-team routine would then end and the grievance process would be triggered, as there would be no further avenue of redress open to the grievor. Given complexities of this means of dealing with the issue there must, of course, be some doubt as to whether this is the best form of legislative solution.

This problem is not confined to situations concerning the threshold question as to the competence of one regime rather than another to deal with a matter. Sometimes, these questions also arise in the context of different bodies issuing conflicting orders. In those cases, the issue becomes which of the two inconsistent directions should the target of these orders obey. This matter came before the Supreme Court of Canada in *British Columbia Telephone Company* v. *Shaw Cable Systems (B.C.) Ltd.*[14] A labour arbitrator had ordered the telephone company to allow its unionized employees to attach cable television wires to its telephone poles, while the CRTC had ordered that the cable operators be permitted to do their own installations. According to the Supreme Court of Canada, pragmatic and functional considerations dictated which decision would prevail. In an analysis similar to that deployed by the Saskatchewan Court of Appeal in the trilogy of cases just discussed, the Court determined that this was more a matter involving the regulation of cable television than one of labour relations. The CRTC order therefore prevailed.

Of course, there are any number of situations where there is simply no possibility in law of shared jurisdiction. Either the matter belongs to one decision maker or to another; it cannot vest in both. In the previous section, we saw that, at least on occasion, where there are competing adjudicative claims to authority over a particular matter, the issue of which claim prevails may be a jurisdiction-conferring one on which the standard of judicial review will be that of correctness. This will almost invariably be the case in situations where the competing claims depend on constitutional allocation of authority. This is exemplified by cases involving a dispute as to whether an employer comes within the category of enterprise subject under the *Constitution Act, 1867* to federal legislative jurisdiction in general, and to the authority of the federal labour relations regime in particular.

Sometimes, however, primary responsibility for resolving the issue of mutually exclusive jurisdiction rests not with the courts in the context of judicial review but with a statutory body. As illustrated by the

---

14 [1995] 2 S.C.R. 739.

judgment of the Supreme Court of Canada in *Pasiechnyk* v. *Saskatchewan (Workers' Compensation Board)*,[15] that can happen even where the competing claimants are the section 96 courts and an administrative tribunal. There, the Court held that the Board had primary responsibility for determining a question of how far its jurisdiction precluded common law actions in the regular courts. Because of that, the Court held that the Board's determination of such questions was entitled to a high degree of deference, the patent unreasonableness standard of judicial review. The same may also be the case where both contending decision makers are administrative tribunals.

FURTHER READINGS

BROWN, R., & B. ETHERINGTON, "*Weber* v. *Ontario Hydro*: A Denial of Access to Justice for the Organized Employee" (1996), 4 Canadian Labour and Employment Law Journal 183

GRECKOL, S., "The Jurisdiction of Labour Arbitrators: The Debate Continues" in *Justice to Order — Adjustment to Changing Demands and Co-ordination Issues in the Justice System in Canada* (Montréal: Éditions Thémis, 1999) at 81

MULLAN, D., "Tribunals and Courts — The Contemporary Terrain: Lessons from Human Rights Regimes" (1999), 24 Queen's L.J. 643

NOMAN, K., "Through a Glass Darkly: Concurrent Jurisdictions in Workplace Human Rights Justice Systems" (1997), 7 Canadian Labour and Employment Law Journal 273

SWINTON, K., & K. SWAN, "The Interaction of Human Rights Legislation and Labour Law" in K. Swan and K. Swinton (eds.), *Studies in Labour Law* (Toronto: Butterworths, 1983)

VANCISE, W., "BUTTON, Button — Who Gets the Button?: Which Statutory Forum Has Jurisdiction," unpublished paper, The Annual Canadian Bar Association Administrative and Labour Law C.L.E. Update, "Staying Ahead of the Game," Ottawa, 19–20 November 1999

WITELSON, T., "Retort: Revisiting *Bhadauria* and the Supreme Court's Rejection of the Tort of Discrimination" (1999), 10 National Journal of Constitutional Law 99

---

15 [1997] 2 S.C.R. 890.

CHAPTER 5

ERROR OF LAW
AND ERROR OF
FACT REVIEW

A. INTRODUCTION

Before the recent emergence of the unifying or umbrella pragmatic and functional approach to judicial review of administrative action, error of law and error of fact review were treated as separate categories. While the precise parameters of these species of review have been the subject of prolonged judicial and academic debate, their general characteristics can be described in fairly short order.

In the domain of jurisdiction-conferring provisions, a statutory authority was technically subject to review on a correctness basis for all mistakes of both law and fact. Occasionally there were instances of judicial unwillingness to interfere with the factual findings of tribunals even on issues of "jurisdictional fact." That aside, the scope for judicial intervention was quite limited.

Where there was no privative clause, the courts traditionally would review on a correctness basis other errors of law, provided two conditions were met: that the tribunal was acting judicially or *quasi*-judicially and the error in question appeared on the face of the record. This kind of review was called variously "review for intrajurisdictional error of law" or "review for errors of law within jurisdiction." There were, however, doubts and confusion as to its availability as a ground of judicial review. How material to the outcome did the question of law have to be? What constituted the record for these purposes? With the advent of the procedural fairness doctrine and the lowering of the threshold for making procedural fairness arguments, and the increased availability of *certiorari*-type relief for these purposes, had the threshold for error of law review also become correspondingly lower? Was it now theoretically available for bodies that did not act judicially in the traditional sense? And, if that were the case, how low had the threshold dropped and what constituted the record in this new world of error of law review?

As for error of fact, for most of the twentieth century, the courts eschewed any capacity to review the decisions of tribunals for factual error on matters within jurisdiction. However, there was a complex and confusing body of case law to the effect that a complete absence of evidence to support a tribunal's finding constituted a reviewable error. That was never repudiated though there continued to be much dispute about the badges of this "no evidence" ground of judicial review. In particular, what constituted a sufficient absence of evidence? Did there have be to be at least some evidence supporting a tribunal's findings on all relevant issues? There was also the question of whether such review could survive the presence of a standard privative clause. Was it merely an intra-jurisdictional error of law or did it lead to a loss of jurisdiction?

Ultimately, the Supreme Court of Canada brought some clarity to this domain in *Skogman* v. *R.*[1] There, Estey J. categorized "no evidence" as a species of jurisdictional defect which meant that review was available on this basis in the face of standard privative clauses. He also held that there had to be some evidence on all points essential to making the relevant determination though was prepared to accept that the merest "scintilla"[2] of evidence would suffice.

Because a debate about the appropriate scope of review for error of law and error of fact had been ongoing for many years and showed no sign of abating or becoming marginalized, two of the major remedial reform exercises of the late 1960s and early 1970s reached into this substantive domain and attempted to bring some clarity and closure to this debate. In both cases, the legislation extended what up until then had been the generally accepted common law scope of this form of review. These were in the *Federal Court Act* of 1970[3] and the Ontario

---

1   [1984] 2 S.C.R. 93.

2   *Ibid.* at 108.

3   S.C. 1970–71–72, s. 1 (and also R.S.C. 1970, s. 10 (2nd Supp.). Now R.S.C. 1985, C-7 (as amended by S.C. 1980, s. 8).

Judicial Review Procedure Act[4] and *Statutory Powers Procedure Act (SPPA)* of 1971.[5]

The *Federal Court Act* provides that judicial review for error of law is available whether or not it appears on the face of the record.[6] Review for error of fact is redefined in terms of a tribunal that has "based its decision or order on an erroneous finding of fact that it made in a perverse or capricious manner or without regard for the material before it."[7]

The Ontario legislature dealt with these grounds of review in a somewhat different manner. Judicial review for error of law on the face of the record is available for all "statutory powers of decision,"[8] Under the definition in the *Judicial Review Procedure Act*,[9] this term is considerably wider than the reach of the former qualifying terminology — a tribunal obliged to act judicially. The *Statutory Powers Procedure Act* also contains a definition of what constitutes the record for those decision makers obliged to act judicially under the traditional law. Section 20 defines the record expansively and in a way that clarifies many of the doubts in the case law regarding what comprised the record at common law for judicial review purposes:

(a) any application, complaint, reference or other document, if any, by which the proceeding was commenced;

(b) the notice of any hearing;

(c) any interlocutory orders made by the tribunal;

(d) all documentary evidence filed with the tribunal, subject to any limitation expressly imposed by any other Act on the extent to or the purposes for which any such documents may be used in evidence in any proceeding;

(e) the transcript, if any, of the oral evidence given at the hearing; and

(f) the decision of the tribunal and the reasons therefor, where reasons have been given.

---

4   S.O. 1971, s. 48. Now R.S.O. 1990, s. J.1.
5   S.O. 1971, s. 49. Now R.S.O. 1990, s. S.22 (as amended by S.O. 1994, s. 27 and S.O. 1997, c.23).
6   S. 18.1(4)(c).
7   S. 18.1(4)(d).
8   S. 2(2).
9   S. 2(1).

Particularly in its reference to the evidence, transcript, and reasons, this provision almost certainly expanded the common law concept of what constituted the record.[10] Moreover, in the case of reasons, the section in the *SPPA* requiring tribunals coming within that Act to provide reasons on request[11] further increased the potential impact of this new definition of the record.

As for review on the basis of an absence of evidence, the Ontario *Judicial Review Procedure Act* provided its own formulation though not, it seems, in such a way as to preclude the continued existence of the common law no evidence rule. This formula applies where a body exercising a statutory power of decision is required by statute or law to base its findings "exclusively on evidence admissible before it" and on facts of which it may take official notice. In such cases, "if there is no such evidence and there are no such facts to support findings of fact made by the tribunal" the court may set the decision aside.[12]

In later remedial reform exercises, these precedents were followed in the same or modified form.[13] However, notwithstanding their expansionary tendencies, it is very difficult to see these statutory formulations having in any substantial manner increased the incidence of error of law and error of fact review. In fact, in the domain of error of fact review, the Courts have interpreted the relevant provisions in both the *Federal Court Act* and the Ontario *Judicial Review Procedure Act* as allowing for review in virtually the same terms as the accepted common law "no evidence" ground of judicial review.[14]

---

10   Thus, in jurisdictions where no statutory definition of the record in either primary legislation or rules of court exists, there are still debates over whether these items, and particularly the evidence, are part of the record: see, for example, *St. Elizabeth's Hospital* v. *Saskatchewan (Labour Relations Board)*, [1996] 7 W.W.R. 248 (Sask. Q.B.), which held that the record of the tribunal's proceedings did not include the transcript of the evidence.

11   S.17(1).

12   S. 2(3).

13   It is worth noting that while s. 3 of the British Columbia *Judicial Review Procedure Act*, R.S.B.C. 1996, c.241, replicated the Ontario provision on review for error of law, it did not contain an equivalent error of fact section.

14   *Judicial Review Procedure Act*: see *Re Keeprite Workers' Independent Union and Keeprite Products Ltd.* (1980), 114 D.L.R. (3d) 162 (Ont. C.A.), still the only sustained consideration of the reach of the section and its interrelationship with the common law. *Federal Court Act*: In *Rohm & Haas Canada Ltd.* v. *Canada (Anti-Dumping Tribunal)* (1978), 22 N.R. 175 (C.A.), the Court of Appeal expressed the view that the section would capture instances of failure to genuinely consider and weigh all the evidence and making a decision wilfully contrary to the evidence.

As already suggested, another counterinfluence on these various provisions has been the growth in the reach of judicial deference to the administrative process. Two aspects of this evolution, in particular, have diminished conventional judicial review for error of law on the face of the record and judicial review for no evidence, perhaps to the point of extinction.

First, when the Supreme Court of Canada accepted that patently unreasonable findings of fact[15] as well as patently unreasonable findings of law within jurisdiction were subject to judicial review, it seemed highly likely that this would replace the old terminology of or approach to review of intra-jurisdictional findings of fact, that of "no evidence." Second, the Supreme Court's willingness to move away from correctness to patent unreasonableness review or unreasonableness review, even in the absence of a standard privative clause and even in the context of a statutory right of appeal, has diminished significantly the role for error of law on the face of the record review. It has also reduced the number of occasions in any context when courts will review determinations of law on a correctness basis.[16]

Indeed, the only situations in which the "old" error of law on the face of the record review may continue to have relevance is where correctness review remains the standard and where it may be necessary still to prove any such error from the record of the proceedings. In such instances, supplementary affidavit evidence still may not be admissible,[17] and the courts may still have to confront issues of what constitutes the record at common law. For example, in what circumstances, if any, will it include the evidence and the reasons for the decision? Of course, given the amount of statutory reform in many provinces and federally, the number of jurisdictions in which these problems will arise is limited, though Nova Scotia

---

15   Definitively in *Lester (W.W.) (1978) Ltd.* v. *United Association of Journeymen etc. of the Plumbing and Pipefitting Industry, Local 740,* [1990] 3 S.C.R. 644.

16   Specifically, regarding the error of law and error of fact provisions of the *Federal Court Act,* Gonthier J., delivering the judgment of the majority of the Supreme of Court of Canada in *National Corn Growers Association* v. *Canada (Import Tribunal),* [1990] 2 S.C.R. 1324 at 1369–70, acknowledged explicitly that these statutory statements of the grounds of judicial review were themselves subject to judicial determination on a pragmatic and functional basis of how intensive judicial review should be in a particular instance.

and Saskatchewan provide at least two examples where litigation over these issues persists.[18]

What may also remain relevant concerns in limited situations of review and, more commonly, in the context of appeals restricted to questions of law or questions of law and jurisdiction, are, first, the differentiation of questions of law from questions of fact, and, second, whether the basis for the court's evaluation of whether there has been an error of law is affected in any way by the terms and context of the statute from which the application for judicial review or statutory appeal arises.

The first concern manifested itself in the early jurisprudence dealing with the nature of "no evidence" review with courts often accepting that for a statutory decision maker to reach a decision without any supporting evidence was to transcend the domain of factual error and in effect to commit an error of law.

Indeed, as already noted, at least from *Skogman* onwards, the Supreme Court accepted that such an error amounted to even more than an intra-jurisdictional error of law. It resulted in a loss of jurisdiction. The legacy of this link between errors of law and errors of fact persists today: courts scrutinizing statutory decision making for errors of law are willing to accept that it is a species of error of law to come to a conclusion based on the facts as found that no reasonable person

---

17   In situations where patent unreasonableness is the standard of judicial review, affidavit evidence is available to prove the error, and the applicant is not constrained by the record of the proceedings giving rise to the application. This is because the courts classify a patently unreasonable finding of fact or law as causing a loss or an excess of jurisdiction. It remains unclear whether the same analysis would be applied to situations where the standard of review is that of reasonableness. Does making an unreasonable finding of fact or law result in a loss of jurisdiction, opening up the possibility of affidavit evidence being used in support of an application of judicial review? Or, will the applicant be confined to the record in this intermediate category between correctness and patent unreasonableness? Indeed, the Supreme Court has yet to come to terms with the more fundamental question of whether a reasonableness standard of judicial review is ever appropriate regarding questions of fact. If the Court does move in this direction, it will mean that, in those situations, the courts will be far more interventionist on factual issues than previously under the generally applicable common law "no evidence" standard.

18   See, for example, *Waverley (Village) v. Nova Scotia (Minister of Municipal Affairs)* (1994), 129 N.S.R. 298 (C.A.), aff'g (1993), 126 N.S.R. (2d) 147 (T.D.) and *Bailey v. Saskatchewan Registered Nurses' Association* (1997), 153 Sask. R. 217 (Q.B.), var'd (1997), 154 Sask. R. 201 (Q.B.).

instructed in the law could ever have reached.[19] In other words, often the law/fact integration process is treated as a matter of law, not of fact. This is especially the case where there is an explicit right of appeal on mixed questions of law and fact. Examples are also common in review and particularly appeal restricted to questions of law.

As for the second consideration identified above, the terms of the relevant statute, in situations where the provision in issue was in broad or open-ended rather than circumscribed language, courts would commonly revert to the principles of review for abuse of discretion. Thus, in appeals or review from the exercise of a discretionary power, the court intervened only in the case of errors of principle.[20] These could include acting for improper purposes, failing to take account of relevant factors, taking account of irrelevant factors, asking the wrong question, or in the face of so-called *Wednesbury* unreasonableness.[21] And, of course, the broader the discretion, the fewer were the opportunities for this form of intervention.

Indeed, the contours of this area of review and appeal have now been modifying significantly. This is just one of the consequences of the Supreme Court's recognition in *Baker* v. *Canada* (*Minister of Citizenship and Immigration*)[22] of a spectrum of decision-making powers, ranging from the narrowest, most technical issues of law at one extreme to the broadest, most unconstrained political discretions at the other. To this the Court also brought its sense that, in the instance of most broadly based discretionary powers, the standard of review or appellate scrutiny is likely to be unreasonableness, if not patent unreasonableness.

B. ONUS AND STANDARD OF PROOF

The rules governing the onus and standard of proof in statutory decision making merit individual treatment from two perspectives. First, there is the question of the extent to which the courts should review

---

19 See, for example, *Re McCann*, [1970] 2 O.R. 117 (C.A.).

20 See, for example, *Carvery* v. *Halifax (City)* (1993), 105 D.L.R. (4th) 353 (N.S.C.A.).

21 Based on the judgment of Lord Greene M.R. in *Associated Provincial Picture Houses Ltd.* v. *Wednesbury Corporation*, [1948] 1 K.B. 223 (C.A.) at 229 and 234: "something so absurd that no sensible person could ever dream that it lay within the powers of the authority" or "a conclusion so unreasonable that no reasonable authority could ever have come to it."

22 [1999] 2 S.C.R. 817.

tribunal determination of these issues. Second is the issue of whether there are any general or overarching principles that apply to determining where the onus should lie and what degree of evidential burden should apply to statutory authorities in their decision making.

Quite clearly, an error with respect to the onus or standard of proof is an error of law. Absent other considerations, it will result in judicial review. More difficult questions arise in situations where the decision making in question is protected by a privative clause or there are other reasons for judicial deference to at least some aspects of the particular decision-making process. Here, the law is quite uncertain. On occasion, by classifying these as matters bearing on procedural fairness, the courts have reviewed issues of onus and standard of proof by reference to a correctness standard.[23] In particularly egregious circumstances or where there is a wrongful reversal of the onus of proof, the error may also be reviewable under the rubric of "no evidence."[24] On other occasions, the courts have treated errors of this kind as jurisdictional in their own right.[25] However, in yet other instances the courts have refused to intervene because the decision maker's rulings on issues of this kind were not patently unreasonable.[26]

On the substantive principles applicable, there is little reason to believe that the law on onus of proof differs as between proceedings in the regular courts and those before administrative tribunals. In both, it is always necessary to take account of the particular statutory language and context. As for the standard of proof, the burden, even in matters that may involve conduct that is also criminal (as in the case of professional discipline), is no more than proof on a balance of probabilities.[27] However, within the balance of probabilities there is an accepted range with the burden increasing in contexts such as serious professional misconduct charges to require "clear and convincing evidence of guilt."[28]

---

23 See, for example, *Bradley Air Services Ltd. (First Air) v. Landry* (1995), 90 F.T.R. 264, aff'd. (1996), 200 N.R. 305 (F.C.A.).

24 See, for example, *Ramoutar v. Canada (Minister of Employment and Immigration)*, [1993] 3 F.C. 370 (C.A.) [*Ramoutar*].

25 See, for example, *Hicks v. Langley Memorial Hospital* (1992), 16 Admin. L.R. (2d) 38 (B.C.S.C.)

26 See, for example, *Bouchard v. Manitoba (Workers' Compensation Board)* (1997), 48 Admin. L.R. (2d) 161 (Man. C.A.).

27 See, for example, above note 24.

28 See, for example, *Bernstein v. College of Physicians and Surgeons (Ontario)* (1977), 76 D.L.R. (3d) 38 (Ont. Div. Ct.).

FURTHER READINGS

EVANS, J.M., "Remedies in Administrative Law," [1981] Law Society of
Upper Canada Special Lectures (*Remedies*) 427

CHAPTER 6

ABUSE OF DISCRETION

A. INTRODUCTION

The courts will sometimes justify interference in the exercise of a power or function otherwise within the jurisdiction or authority of a statutory body by classifying it as involving a "discretion." Then they invoke one or more grounds of review for so-called abuse of discretion. Those grounds include bad faith, acting for an improper purpose or motive, taking account of irrelevant factors, failing to take account of relevant factors, undue fettering of discretion, and acting under the dictation of someone without authority. On occasion, the courts have also set aside an exercise of discretion as so unreasonable that no reasonable authority could ever have acted in that way.

The most riveting example of Supreme Court of Canada intervention for abuse of discretion remains the Court's 1958 decision in *Roncarelli* v. *Duplessis*.[1] This was a cause of action in damages against the then premier of Québec, Maurice Duplessis. It involved events in 1946, at the height of his government's concerted attacks on the civil liberties of Jehovah's Witnesses. Roncarelli was an adherent who had posted

---

1   [1959] S.C.R. 121 [*Roncarelli*].

bail for numerous Witnesses charged with a variety of offences, especially distributing pamphlets contrary to municipal by-laws. He also held a restaurant liquor licence. Acting under orders from the premier and after a spectacular lunchtime raid by the police, the general manager of the liquor commission revoked Roncarelli's licence and declared that he would never secure another. After many years, the case reached the Supreme Court of Canada where, by a majority, the Court held that Roncarelli was entitled to damages under the *Québec Civil Code* for abuse of power. Among the wrongs cited in this intimidatory excess of state power were Duplessis's arrogation to himself of a power that the statute had conferred on the general manager of the liquor commission; dictating what action the general manager, the official charged with responsibility under the relevant legislation, was to take; using power for an improper purpose or on the basis of irrelevant considerations; and seeking to punish Roncarelli for exercising a civil right all citizens possessed, that of posting bail. In so holding, the Court found the Premier had been motivated by a desire to interfere with the religious freedoms of Jehovah's Witnesses. Rand J., delivered the most memorable of the majority judgments of the Court:

> In public regulation of this sort there is no such thing as absolute and untrammelled "discretion," that is that action can be taken on any ground or for any reason that can be suggested to the mind of the administrator; no legislative Act can, without express language, be taken to contemplate an unlimited arbitrary power exercisable for any purpose, however capricious or irrelevant regardless of the nature or purpose of the statute. Fraud and corruption in the Commission may not be mentioned in such statutes but they are always implied as exceptions. "Discretion" necessarily implies good faith in discharging public duty; there is always a perspective within which a statute is intended to operate; and any clear departure from its limits or objects is just as objectionable as fraud or corruption.[2]

Rand J. then accumulated the wrongs that had been committed in this instance as bad faith in the exercise of public power, a classification that was necessary both to attach liability in damages under the *Quebec Civil Code* and to avoid the impact of prescriptive provisions in the relevant legislation:

---

2   *Ibid.* at 140.

"Good faith" in this context, applicable both to the respondent and the General Manager, means carrying out the statute according to its intent and for its purpose; it means good faith in acting with a rational appreciation of that intent and purpose and not with an improper intent and for an alien purpose; it does not mean for the purpose of punishing a person for exercising an unchallengeable right; it does not mean arbitrarily and illegally attempting to divest a citizen of an incident of his civil status.[3]

Roncarelli v. *Duplessis* remains a seminal case in Canadian law. Not only did it establish parameters within which a seemingly open and unfettered statutory discretion must be exercised but it also defined the circumstances under which civil liability as well as normal administrative law remedies can attach to abuses of power. Moreover, while the action for damages in that case was intimately connected to the provisions of the relevant legislation and then Article 1053 of the *Québec Civil Code*, subsequent jurisprudence has confirmed that the same rules govern the availability of damages for abuse of power at common law.[4]

Indeed, the only doubts that exist as to the authority of the statements made by Rand J. are in the domain of "improper purposes" review and the extent to which it can be invoked in the political domain. More specifically, how does this form of review apply to decision making by the Cabinet or, technically, by the governor or lieutenant governor in council? These doubts stem primarily from the unusually ambiguous judgment of Dickson J., as he then was, in *Thorne's Hardware Ltd.* v. *The Queen*.[5]

This involved a challenge to an order in council extending the limits of Saint John Harbour to include the appellant's riparian property so that ships docking there would have to pay harbour dues. The appellant contended that the sole purpose of the order in council was to increase the revenues of the National Harbours Board and that this was an improper purpose amounting to bad faith justifying the quashing of the order in council.

---

3   *Ibid.* at 143.
4   See, for example, *Gershman v. Manitoba Vegetable Producers' Marketing Board* (1976), 69 D.L.R. (3d) 114 (Man. C.A.).
5   [1983] 1 S.C.R. 106 [*Thorne's Hardware*].

In delivering the judgment of the Court, Dickson J. stated that there were limits on discretions conferred on the governor in council. In egregious cases, the courts could review orders that exceeded those limits. However, when it came to the specific argument of an improper purpose, he stated that it was not for the Court to weigh the evidence adduced by the appellant in an attempt to demonstrate such an error: "It is neither our duty nor our right to investigate the motives which impelled the federal Cabinet to pass the Order in Council." However, notwithstanding that statement, he proceeded to canvass the evidence to show that, in any event, it did not support the appellant's contention.

A number of interpretations can be advanced to explain the statement quoted above. At its extreme, it may establish an exception to the *Roncarelli* principles when allegations of improper motives or purposes are made against the Cabinet. Alternatively, it might be seen as a proposition dependent on the particular statutory configuration and the specific improper purposes allegation; given the scope of the power and the wrongful purpose alleged, there is no room for court inquiry. A further explanation draws some support from another section of Dickson J.'s judgment. When the courts are dealing with a multi-member body that does not provide reasons for its decisions and exercises very broad discretion, it is highly unlikely that there will be convincing evidence of an improper purpose. Unlike the situation in *Roncarelli* v. *Duplessis*, where the premier took the stand and was brutally frank about his motives, that kind of evidence is unlikely to be available in the case of Cabinet decision making. Thus, Dickson J. stated:

> I agree with the Federal Court of Appeal that the government's reasons for expanding the harbour are in the end unknown. Governments do not provide reasons for their decisions; governments may be moved by any number of political, economic, social or partisan considerations.[6]

As we shall see below, the Supreme Court of Canada has reiterated this particular point much more recently in the context of a wrongful purposes challenge to the actions of a municipal council in setting up a municipal inquiry, *Consortium Developments (Clearwater) Ltd.* v. *Sarnia (City)*.[7]

---

6   *Ibid.* at 112–13.
7   [1998] 3 S.C.R. 3 [Consortium Developments].

Thorne's Hardware also has to be read in the light of subsequent jurisprudence. Thus, albeit in a *Charter* context, the Court, in considering a challenge to an exercise of Cabinet power in *Operation Dismantle* v. *The Queen*,[8] held that the exercise of prerogative power[9] by Cabinet was subject to judicial review and also that there was no such thing as an American "political questions doctrine" in Canadian law.[10]

Then, subsequently, in *Shell Canada Products Ltd.* v. *Vancouver (City)*,[11] the Court reviewed the decision of another multi-member body, the council of the City of Vancouver, on the basis of improper purposes. On the facts, the purpose for which Council passed the impugned by-law was clear — to discourage Shell Canada from continuing to trade with South Africa. Despite the fact that a multi-member body was involved, the question for the majority of the Court was simply one of determining whether that purpose was a permissible reason for the municipality to enact a by-law "blacklisting" Shell.

It is also of some significance that the minority raised the question of whether it was permissible to review the actions of municipalities for improper motivation, though ultimately it did not resolve that issue. In raising it, McLachlin J. referred to *Thorne's Hardware* as establishing "that as a general rule the motives of governments enacting subordinate legislation should not be inquired into." By implication, the major-

---

8   [1985] 1 S.C.R. 441.

9   Note, however, the re-emergence in *Black* v. *Canada (Prime Minister)* (2000), 47 O.R. (3d) 532 (S.C.J.), of the argument that there are at least some forms of prerogative power that are unreviewable save as to the scope of their application. There, LeSage C.J.S.C. struck out Conrad Black's statement of claim alleging an abuse of discretion by the prime minister in forestalling Black's ambitions to become a member of the U.K. House of Lords. The conduct in question was classified as the exercise of the prime minister's prerogative powers in granting honours and conducting foreign relations. LeSage C.J.S.C. used the concept of "justiciability" from *Operation Dismantle* and, referring to *Thorne's Hardware* as well as to English authority on the unreviewability of certain species of surviving prerogative powers, he held that Black's statement of claim did not disclose a reasonable cause of action, at least on these matters.

10 The Court did not, however, set aside the exercise of power by holding that the applicants could never have laid a sufficient evidential basis for the claim they were making: that allowing U.S. testing over Canada of missiles carrying nuclear warheads would constitute a threat to their section 7 *Charter* right to "life, liberty and security of the person" because it would increase the risk of a nuclear war. In this sense, the dispute was not "justiciable." In itself, this constitutes another restriction on the review of discretionary decision making at least where the challenge is based on the impermissible effects of the exercise of the discretion.

11 [1994] 1 S.C.R. 231 [*Shell Canada*].

ity must be presumed to have rejected that proposition in the instance of municipalities or at least where the municipality purported to state its purposes in recitals to the impugned resolution. Indeed, even McLachlin J.'s statement might be read as indicating that, in the case of Cabinet, the rule is general but not universal or without exceptions. Ultimately, then, it is not to be supposed that the outcome in *Roncarelli* would or should have been any different had the legislation conferred the power to cancel licences on Cabinet to be exercised by order in council. The fact that Cabinet decided collectively to take the action for the very same reasons that motivated Duplessis makes no difference. Rather, the major problem in most such cases will remain that of proving the improper motivation.

B. THE NATURE OF DISCRETIONARY POWER AND LINKS WITH JURISDICTION

Archetypically, the use of the term "may" or "may in its discretion" in the language of the empowering section signifies the presence of a discretionary power. It connotes choice over a course of action as opposed to a duty to take action or to make a particular decision based on closely worded legislative language or even existing common law principles. Historically, such powers tended to be associated with those exercising executive or administrative functions. Indeed many theorists even regarded discretionary power as the antithesis of judicial power. Moreover, in the discourse of judicial review, an abuse or excess of discretion was usually described as producing an *ultra vires* decision as opposed to a jurisdictional error, the term used most often in review of judicial and *quasi*-judicial bodies.

However, two things are abundantly clear. Discretion is not necessarily antithetical to the functioning of even the most "judicial" of bodies, the regular courts. They possess all sorts of discretionary powers. Think of sentencing and the discretionary nature of equitable relief. Second, in the domain of agencies and tribunals, authority is conferred frequently in discretionary terms: "On being satisfied that the following conditions have been met, the tribunal *may* grant a licence to an applicant." As a consequence, abuse of discretion is a ground of judicial review that transcends the character of the decision maker and is available on a general basis. Hence, the real concerns are the nature of the link between review for abuse of discretion and review for jurisdictional error and whether the intensity of judicial review for abuse of discretion has any connection with the nature of the decision maker and the terms in which discretion is conferred.

Until very recently, these matters remained unresolved in Canadian administrative law. To the extent that they surfaced in particular cases, the discussion of the theoretical dimensions of the concerns was quite unsatisfactory. Reference can again be usefully made to *Canadian Union of Public Employees, Local 963 v. New Brunswick Liquor Corporation*.[12] As noted in chapter 3, part of the reason that Dickson J. adopted a deferential posture towards the Public Service Staff Relations Board was that the question in issue, the meaning of the relevant statutory provision, was one susceptible of a number of meanings. By according scope to the board's choice among those meanings to the extent of patent unreasonableness, the Court conferred autonomy on the designated decision maker to attribute meaning to certain statutory terms. In effect, the tribunal had a discretion as to the meaning of a statutory term. To the extent that this is accepted, any notion of a clear-cut distinction between issues of law and matters of discretion becomes lost.

What also becomes apparent (and Dickson J.'s judgment confirms this) is that the moment a court starts according a tribunal, (or any decision maker, for that matter) room to manoeuvre in attributing a meaning to statutory terms, it becomes necessary to ask whether that flexibility is controlled by any limitations other than that of reasonableness or patent unreasonableness. Do normal limits on the exercise of discretionary power (as reflected in the various categories of abuse of discretion) come into play in the case of a tribunal's attribution of meaning to statutory terms not explicitly couched in discretionary language?

The answer that Dickson J. apparently provided to this question in *New Brunswick Liquor* is an affirmative one. He drew on his own earlier judgment in *Service Employees' International Union, Local 333 v. Nipawin Union Hospital*,[13] where he had quoted approvingly from Lord Reid's judgment in *Anisminic v. Foreign Compensation Commission*.[14] He included within the scope of his definition of jurisdictional error such abuse of discretion grounds as "basing the decision on extraneous matters" and "failing to take relevant factors into account."[15] As already noted in chapter 3, when such terminology is applied to the review of a tribunal's interpretation of a relevant statutory provision, it can potentially undercut a general judicial philosophy of deference to tribunal decision making.

---

12 [1979] 2 S.C.R. 227.
13 [1975] 1 S.C.R. 382 [*Nipawin*].
14 [1969] 2 A.C. 147 (H.L. Eng.).
15 *Nipawin*, above note 13 at 389.

Indeed, to the extent that the explicit conferral of discretion in itself indicates the legislative reposing of trust in a particular statutory authority, the same argument could apply just as strongly, if not more so, in such instances. This was part of the thrust of McLachlin J.'s dissenting judgment in *Shell Canada Ltd.* referred to earlier. She was responding to an application to review for an improper motivation a municipality's exercise of a power to pass resolutions for the "good rule and government of the city" as part of a more general power to "promote the health, welfare, safety and good government of the municipality," McLachlin J. invoked *New Brunswick Liquor* in advocating a deferential approach to the review of decisions of municipalities. She suggested that there was little justification for holding municipal councillors to a higher standard of review than was the case with non-elected statutory boards and agencies.

That did not attract the support of the majority, which went along with the traditionally narrow interpretation of the scope of the powers of municipalities. The majority also treated the question of whether the purpose or motivation for which a resolution had been passed as a straight question of law. The Court attributed no discretion or judgment on the municipality's part as to what were the proper parameters of its resolution passing or by-law making capacities.

Of course, legislative language might also be decisive in this area. In *Sheehan v. Criminal Injuries Compensation Board*,[16] the Ontario Court of Appeal applied "patent unreasonableness" analysis to the Compensation Board's exercise of a discretionary power to grant compensation to victims of crime. In this exercise, the Board was directed to "have regard to all such circumstances as *it considers relevant* [emphasis added]." The Court of Appeal held that it could review the Board for taking into account irrelevant considerations only where the Board had made "relevant a consideration which is patently irrelevant." The subjective empowering language indicated the need for a posture of deference.

Now, as a consequence of *Baker v. Canada (Minister of Citizenship and Immigration)*,[17] it is clear that, even though the Supreme Court did not refer to *Sheehan*, the approach adopted by the Ontario Court of Appeal provides the basis for a more general reconciliation of the domains of review for jurisdictional error and review for abuse of discretion. More particularly, by extending the "pragmatic and

---

16   (1975), 52 D.L.R. (3d) 728 (Ont. C.A.).
17   [1999] 2 S.C.R. 817, [*Baker*].

functional" approach typical of review for jurisdictional error to review for abuse of discretion and by holding that review for abuse of discretion may range from incorrectness through unreasonableness to patent unreasonableness scrutiny, the Court has provided an overarching or unifying theory for review of the substantive decisions of all manner of statutory and prerogative decision makers. This is a most welcome development.

Baker involved a ministerial decision under the *Immigration Act*.[18] The minister refused to exercise a statutory discretion on humanitarian and compassionate grounds to allow a person subject to a deportation order to remain in Canada in order to seek permission to apply for permanent residence here. Among the many questions this litigation raised was that of the grounds on which the courts could review the exercise of this broad discretionary power by immigration officials acting on behalf of the minister.

L'Heureux-Dubé J. begins consideration of this dilemma by accepting the point illustrated earlier by reference to *New Brunswick Liquor*: there is no bright line distinction between the determination of questions of law and the exercise of discretionary decision-making powers. The resolution of questions of law will involve almost invariably elements of judicial discretion, and the exercise of discretion is just as invariably constrained in some measure by legal principles. As in many other aspects of administrative law, there is a range or a spectrum characterized at one end by extremely broad, unstructured discretion, the only non-constitutional limits on which are those that might be discerned from the overall purpose of the Act. At the other end of this spectrum, there are provisions that depend upon the application of legal terms sharply defined either in the statute itself or by clear common law principle.[19] She also observes the phenomenon, already noted, of tribunals that have broad discretionary powers. As an example, she cites the considerable discretion conferred on many tribunals in the award of remedies and the incorporation of deferential standards of review in the judicial scrutiny of the exercises of such statutory discretions.[20]

---

18   R.S.C. 1985, c. I-2, section 114(2) and section 2(1) of the *Immigration Regulations*, S.O.R./78-172, as amended by S.O.R./93–44.

19   *Baker*, above note 17 at paras. 54–55.

20   *Ibid.*, at para. 55.

Proceeding from this premise, L'Heureux-Dubé J. then accommodates all review of discretion within the mainstream of Canadian judicial review. However, this does not mean that the Court thereby diminishes the significance of legislative conferral of broad discretionary power. It simply incorporates it as a factor within the pragmatic and functional approach to determining the appropriate scope of judicial scrutiny of the exercise of public authority:

> Incorporating judicial review of decisions that involve considerable discretion into the pragmatic and functional analysis for errors of law should not be seen as reducing the level of deference given to decisions of a highly discretionary nature. In fact, deferential standards of review may give substantial leeway to the discretionary decision-maker in determining the "proper purpose" or "relevant considerations" involved in making a given determination. The pragmatic and functional approach can take into account the fact that the more discretion that is left to a decision-maker, the more reluctant courts should be to interfere with the manner in which decision-makers have made choices among various options.[21]

This point is given further content when she suggests that much will depend on whether the discretionary power is more polycentric in nature, having broad policy implications as opposed to one directed at an individual and having a significant impact on that person's rights, privileges, and interests.[22]

However, L'Heureux-Dubé J. then goes on to deal with the nature of judicial control that may be necessary even in relation to the broadest of discretions:

> [T]hough discretionary decisions will generally be given considerable respect, that discretion must be exercised in accordance with the boundaries imposed in the statute, the principles of the rule of law, the principles of administrative law, the fundamental values of Canadian society, and the principles of the *Charter*.[23]

There is a further consequence of incorporating review for abuse of discretion within the pragmatic and functional approach. Courts faced with review of statutory or prerogative decision making that would previously have been classified as discretionary must how ask which of the three standards of scrutiny currently deployed by the Supreme

---

21   *Ibid.* at para. 56.
22   *Ibid.* at para. 55.
23   *Ibid.* at para. 56.

Court of Canada will apply: (in)correctness, unreasonableness,[24] or patent unreasonableness. Moreover, in the extract just quoted, the Court provides some guidance as to the impact that this will have on traditional abuse of discretion grounds of review, such as taking account of irrelevant factors and failure to take account of relevant factors. The intensity of judicial review on those grounds will be determined by which of the three general standards of scrutiny applies in the individual case. On as yet unspecified occasions, the inquiry will be a correctness one. At the other extreme, when, for example, the court is confronted by a broad, policy-making power of polycentric dimensions, the court will approach its review task by asking whether, for instance, it was patently unreasonable for the decision maker to have failed to take a particular factor into account.

In this regard, the Court's deployment of the theory on the facts of *Baker* is also informative. In determining the standard of review, L'Heureux-Dubé J. noted the facial breadth of the discretion and the fact-sensitive quality of the determination as to whether to exercise it, the nature of the decision maker (formally, a minister of the Crown), and the expertise to be expected of those called upon to exercise the discretion on the minister's behalf. All of these considerations pointed in the direction of a deferential, not a correctness, standard of review. Nonetheless, and not surprisingly, the Court did not stretch this entitlement to deference beyond unreasonableness review. In this, it was influenced by the absence of a privative clause, the statutory contemplation of judicial review, and the fact that this aspect of the appeal was the core of the certified question on which the appeal was founded.[25] Even more significantly, it relied on the fact that, far from being a polycentric decision, it "relates directly to the rights and interests of an individual in relation to government, rather than balancing the interests of various constituencies or mediating between them."[26]

As a consequence, the Court went on to consider the determination of whether to exercise the discretion favorably based on a standard of "reasonableness *simpliciter*,"[27] whether the "humanitarian and

---

24 Sometimes, the Latin word "*simpliciter*" is added, as in the foundation judgment of *Canada (Director of Investigation and Research) v. Southam*, [1997] 1 S.C.R. 748 and once in *Baker*, above note 17, at para. 62. However, the only significance of the use of that word seems to be to distinguish from that which is just unreasonableness, *simpliciter* — patent unreasonableness.

25 *Ibid.*

26 *Ibid.* at para. 60.

27 *Ibid.* at para. 62.

compassionate" decision in this case crossed the boundary and was reviewable. In so doing, the Court does acknowledge the rather blurred nature of the difference between correctness review, and unreasonableness review when the allegation is a failure to take account or sufficient account of a factor implicitly relevant in the exercise of the discretion in question — in this instance, primarily[28] the best interests of Baker's children.

At one level, one can certainly use the language of unreasonableness to describe the basis for the Court's intervention. Having regard to the purposes of the Act and the relevant provision, the terms of the International Convention on the Rights of the Child, and the ministerial guidelines on exercising this discretion, the decision makers were unreasonable in attaching so little significance to the best interests of Baker's children. However, it is equally plausible to describe the conclusion of the Court as one which treated the failure of the immigration officers to make their decision "in a manner which was alive, attentive, or sensitive to the interests of Baker's children,"[29] as simply resulting from an incorrect appreciation of the legal nature and extent of the discretion conferred on the minister. In short, on many occasions, there may be little practical difference between reasonableness and correctness review of the exercise of broad discretions for failing to take account of relevant and taking account of irrelevant factors. Rather, the only difference will be the language in which the argument is dressed.

Another way of looking at this matter in terms of reasonableness might be to say that, having regard to best interests of Baker's children, this was an unreasonable outcome. However, the Court clearly did not go so far as to brand the outcome a necessarily unreasonable result. It did not reverse the decision; instead, it remitted the matter for reconsideration in accordance with proper principles. Only on exceptionally rare occasions will the Court exercise the statutory discretion itself and remit the matter for decision in a particular way. One is where there is only one option available to the discretion holder that is not patently unreasonable. The other is where the only reason identified for not exercising the discretion in a particular way was an improper one.

---

28 The Court also held that the officers had paid insufficient attention to other factors such as the hardship occasioned to Baker herself by a return to Jamaica after such a long period in Canada and her separation from her four Canadian children as well as needed medical care: *Baker*, above note 17, at para. 73.

29 *Ibid.* at para. 75.

These issues of the precise meaning of the judgment aside, will there ever be any situations where a statutorily or prerogative-conferred discretion will be subject explicitly to correctness review? The creation of a statutory right of appeal or reconsideration in sufficiently clear terms would seem to provide an example. Indeed, it is possible to conceive of legislative language that would permit the review to take place not simply on the record in order to determine by reference to normal appellate standards whether the decision-maker exercised that discretion correctly, but on the basis of a total or *de novo* "rehearing" of the matters in issue. Correctness review will also presumably be indicated in cases where the exercise of a discretion is conditioned explicitly on the tribunal taking into account certain legislatively specified considerations or factors. There, the courts will as a matter of fact determine whether they were taken into account. So too will this be the case where the authority is directed not to take certain factors into account.

As well, there is a more general issue as to which of the various grounds of review for abuse of discretion are swept up within the "new" theory. On one side of the fence, it is clear that challenges based on bad faith or acting under dictation will not be affected. On the other, taking account of irrelevant factors and failing to take account of relevant factors obviously come within its ambit. Acting for a wrongful purpose is more of a problem. As noted previously, the majority of the Court in *Shell Canada*, in the context of a challenge to a municipal resolution, seemed to accept that issues of motive and purpose were to be determined on a correctness basis. Moreover, in an extract cited earlier, L'Heureux-Dubé J. indicated that, even in relation to the broadest of discretions, the courts were responsible for ensuring that the decision maker adhered to the "boundaries imposed in the statute." This would seem to embrace judicial policing of the decision maker's faithfulness to the underlying purposes of the legislation. However, later, there is a much more explicit reference to wrongful purposes review that clearly states the opposite: "In fact, deferential standards of review may give substantial leeway to the discretionary decision-maker in determining the 'proper purposes' or 'relevant considerations' involved in making a determination."[30] Obviously, an internal tension exists here as well as a conflict with prior authority. Indeed, it is a matter of some concern whether the legislative delegation of discretionary power should ever go as far as requiring that the courts defer to determinations by the

---

30   *Ibid.* at para. 56.

beneficiary of that power as to the purposes for which the power may be exercised. Nonetheless, there is an argument that, in some situations, the comparative expertise and character of the discretionary decision maker will extend to judgments affecting the overall purposes of the legislation.

In municipal decision making, it is also worth noting that, in the aftermath of *Baker*, the Supreme Court has now accepted the position that McLachlin J. advocated in *Shell*: that the scope of review of municipal decision-making powers should be evaluated on a "pragmatic and functional" basis. This was established in *Nanaimo (City)* v. *Rascal Trucking Ltd.*,[31] a case that concerned a municipal determination that a pile of earth was a "building, structure or erection of any kind." In consequence of this, the municipality declared it a nuisance and ordered its removal. In sustaining the municipality's actions, the Court accepted that, on the statutory interpretation of whether the pile of earth was "an erection" in terms of the relevant section, the municipality had to be correct. Then, on the further issues of whether, as an erection, it constituted a nuisance that should be removed, the Court held that the municipality was entitled to deference and its decision was to be set aside only if "patently unreasonable." Thus, municipalities have been brought within the mainstream of judicial review theory. Left for another day is the issue of whether the approach of the majority in *Shell* will continue to prevail in cases where the specific basis for attack is that the municipality acted for a wrongful purpose. This was not an issue in *Rascal Trucking*.

Baker also leaves open a number of other questions. Among them is whether the case forecloses in Canada the ground of judicial review known as *Wednesbury* unreasonableness. I will return to that issue below. However, there also have to be some concerns from the general grounds of review listed above as to what L'Heureux-Dubé J. meant by and what influence the term "fundamental values of Canadian society" will have on review in this domain. Is this any more than a reformulation of the traditional "contrary to public policy" ground of judicial intervention which has played a significant role in the evolution of human rights law in Canada in judgments such as *Re Drummond Wren*[32] and *Canada Trust* v. *Ontario Human Rights Commission* demonstrate application of this principle.[33] Does the judgment have rather different pretensions or is it largely rhetorical? Indeed, even if L'Heureux-

31   [2000] 1 S.C.R. 342
32   [1945] O.R. 778 (H.C.).
33   (1990), 74 O.R. (2d) 481 (C.A.).

Dubé J.'s decision is viewed as merely reiterating the role of public policy principles in shaping the common law, it raises serious questions as to whether, in the pluralistic world of the new millennium, there is or should be much, if any room for this concept to play a role as a limiting principle. The one exception here is the obvious case of values entrenched in the *Charter* and other *Constitution Acts*. However a comprehensive, entrenched bill of rights, one would expect that there would be few opportunities for appeals to fundamental or accepted moral values outside the express terms and penumbra of that bill of rights.

Roncarelli v. *Duplessis* may provide some insight into this area. When, in the *pre*-Charter era civil liberties and freedom were at stake. The courts were often much more alert in their scrutiny of the exercise of discretionary power. In such a context, they sometimes saw themselves as the neutral guarantors of the underlying values of Canadian society our constitutional arrangements against statutory bodies with no particular insights in such matters and likely to be influenced unduly by more parochial or narrow concerns. This dimension also emerges in another of Rand J.'s famous judgments, *Smith and Rhuland* v. *The Queen*.[34] There, a majority of the Supreme Court quashed in the name of democratic, participatory values a decision of the Nova Scotia Labour Relations Board to withhold certification as a bargaining agent from a trade union. The secretary-treasurer of that union was a member of the Communist Party. The Communist Party had not been proscribed in Canadian law. Absent clear proof of an intention on the union's part to work against the intent and spirit of the labour relations legislation, it was contrary to the democratic values underlying Canada's constitutional arrangements to deny certification on the basis of the political beliefs of an influential officer of that union applying for certification.

Today, these specific concerns are by and large the stuff of the *Charter*, the *Canadian Bill of Rights*, and various provincial bills of rights. Nonetheless, this judicial approach, based in part on the implied bill of rights theory, may have modern equivalents and create room for concrete application based not only on the statements of L'Heureux-Dubé J. in *Baker* but also on the identification of the underlying principles of the Canadian Constitution in *Reference re Secession of Québec*.[35] I will return to this theme below.

---

34 [1953] 2 S.C.R. 95.
35 [1998] 2 S.C.R. 217 [*Secession of Québec*].

C. SPECIFIC GROUNDS

The cases discussed to this point have exemplified a number of the important grounds of review for abuse of discretion: acting under dictation, failing to take account of relevant factors, taking account of irrelevant factors, and acting for improper purposes or motives. These last two are the most common bases for review in this domain.

1) Failing to Take Account of Relevant Factors

Baker notwithstanding, failing to take account of relevant considerations or factors is not a common ground of judicial review. However, *Dalton v. Criminal Injuries Compensation Board* provided an example.[36] It involved the Ontario Criminal Injuries Compensation legislation amended in the wake of *Sheehan*, which directed the Board to "have regard to all relevant circumstances." In quashing the Board's decision to deny the compensation, the Court held that the Board had failed to take into account the severity of the injuries the claimant had suffered. A man with whom she had been drinking had pushed her from a van after when she rebuffed his sexual advances. The Board also failed to consider the possibility that the claim should have been reduced rather than denied outright because of what it believed to be the claimant's contributory conduct. In some senses, of course, this was a review of the tribunal's assessment and weighing of the evidence and also its reasoning processes. However, when the legislative direction to take account of all relevant factors is worded in objective, not subjective, language (as previously), the case for this form of intervention is that much stronger.

2) Fettering of Discretion

More common, particularly in recent years, have been cases where the allegation is that the decision maker failed to genuinely exercise its discretionary powers in an individual case; but rather made its decision on the basis of a pre-existing policy. In general, the courts have had no problem with agencies and tribunals adopting policies by which their work will be guided. From time to time, the courts have even suggested that this activity is a good practice even where not specifically sanctioned by legislation.[37] Nonetheless, this tolerance does not permit an

---

36   (1982), 36 O.R. (3d) 394 (Ont. Div. Ct.)
37   See, for example, the judgment of Laskin C.J. in *Capital Cities Communications Inc. v. Canada (Canadian Radio-Television and Telecommunications Commission)*, [1978] 2 S.C.R. 141.

agency to establish formal rules to govern in particular cases. That requires a specifically legislated, rule-making power. Thus, in *Ainsley Financial Corporation* v. *Ontario Securities Commission*,[38] the Ontario Court of Appeal declared a formal policy of the Commission on "penny stock" dealers *ultra vires* because of the way in which it was formulated. The OSC had instituted a binding set of rules, breach of which would attract sanctions, rather than informal guidelines to assist in its regulatory and policing functions. In the absence of a specific statutory power to promulgate such rules, the policy statement was therefore invalid.

Even absent such an illegitimate attempt to create what was in effect legislation, the courts demand that more informal policies and guidelines (whether publicized or simply used internally) must not become invariable rules applied automatically in every case. Individual matters are entitled to individual attention, and the discretion of the statutory authority should not be so fettered that it prevents the possibility of individualized consideration of particular cases. In *Brown* v. *Alberta*,[39] the Alberta Court of Queen's Bench set aside the suspension of a driver's licence as the product of the automatic application of a minimum period of suspension policy with no consideration given to whether it was appropriate to apply that policy in the particular case.[40]

In the case of elected bodies, questions arise as to the extent to which these principles apply when the members have been elected on the basis of a commitment to exercise a discretion in a particular way. The old New Zealand case of *Isitt* v. *Quill* provide good example.[41] The case involved the election of a slate of members to a local licensing commission who had campaigned on the basis of prohibition. Acting on this election promise, the commission automatically began refusing renewals on existing licences as they expired. In a decision of the New Zealand Court of Appeal in which some judges based their reasoning on bias and others on abuse of discretion, the Court held that the denial of a renewal in these circumstances could not stand. As the relevant legislation included no local preference option in the voting process, the adoption of a policy (albeit one sanctioned by the electorate) under which there would eventually be no licences in the district flouted the statute and the relevance of demand as a factor in determining the need for licences. As will be seen in chapter 14, similar

---

38   (1995), 21 O.R. (3d) 105 (C.A.).

39   (1991), 82 D.L.R. (4th) 96 (Alta. Q.B.)

40   I will return to this issue in greater detail in the chapter on the adjectival powers of statutory authorities.

41   (1893), 11 N.Z.L.R. 224 (C.A.).

considerations have been decisive in the municipal councillor cases decided in Canada under the rubric of bias. There a "totally closed mind" test has emerged as the touchstone for intervention.[42]

3) Discrimination

Discrimination in the exercise of discretionary power occasionally surfaces as a basis for judicial review. As a discrete ground for judicial intervention, it emerged originally in cases involving municipalities and their by-laws.[43] However, in *Forget v. Québec (A.G.)* the Supreme Court of Canada has now clearly accepted that it can be invoked on a broader canvas than that and, notably, in the case of regulations promulgated by provincial governments.[44] Whether it applies generally to statutory discretions still remains uncertain, particularly as the Supreme Court endorsed the principle in the following terms: "[T]he power to regulate does not include the power to discriminate."[45] Does the term "regulate" refer to all manner of discretionary or regulatory powers or does it take its meaning from the particular form of regulation in issue in that case — the making of subordinate legislation in the form of regulations?

There are also doubts as to the scope of review on the basis of discrimination. Discrimination was not deployed in *Forget* in the sense in which it forms the basis of human rights legislation and the various provisions of the *Canadian Bill of Rights* and the *Canadian Charter of Rights and Freedoms*.[46] That does not mean that violation of the standards of those enactments in the exercise of statutory discretions will not lead to judicial review; subject to the exclusivity of the jurisdiction of human rights commissions, they clearly will. This matter is explored in greater detail in the section that follows on the impact of the *Charter* on review for abuse of discretion.

However, even allowing that "discrimination" is potentially a broader category of review than is contemplated in its human rights and equality senses, it is nonetheless a remarkably elusive concept in

---

42 *Old St. Boniface Residents' Assn. Inc. v. Winnipeg (City)*, [1990] 3 S.C.R. 1170; *Save Richmond Farmland Society v. Richmond (Township)*, [1990] 3 S.C.R. 1213.
43 See, for example, *City of Montréal v. Arcade Amusements Inc.*, [1985] 1 S.C.R. 368 [*Arcade Amusements*]: "The rule that the power to make by-laws does not include that of enacting discriminatory provisions unless the enacting legislation provides the contrary has been observed from time immemorial in British and Canadian public law" (Beetz J. at 404).
44 [1988] 2 S.C.R. 90. (The argument was rejected on the facts.)
45 *Ibid.* at 105.
46 *Shell Canada*, above note 11, McLachlin J., (albeit dissenting.)

the domain of administrative law. Frequently, it amounts to just another way of characterizing a wrongful purpose review. This is exemplified by Supreme Court jurisprudence in the domain of review of municipal by-laws and resolutions.

In 1994, speaking for the majority of the Court, Sopinka J. held as an alternative basis for review that the municipal resolutions excluding Shell Canada[47] from doing business with the City of Vancouver were discriminatory. They created an impermissible distinction between oil companies which did business in South Africa and those which did not. At root, however, this part of the judgment amounts to merely a restatement of the main reason for the majority's decision — namely, that it was improper for the City to refuse to deal with Shell because it was trading in South Africa. It was beyond the purposes of a municipality to attempt to influence the extraterritorial conduct of private entrepreneurs. Thereafter, the Court declined to deal with the other species of discrimination alleged in the case: that in continuing to trade with another oil company that had dealings with South Africa, the City was discriminating in an unlawful manner against Shell. Such an allegation much more clearly involves discrimination as a free-standing ground of judicial review.

Nonetheless, earlier jurisprudence does suggest that discrimination is an independent ground of judicial review. In *Montréal (City)* v. *Arcade Amusements Inc.*,[48] Beetz J., delivering the judgment of the majority of the Supreme Court, found a by-law prohibiting those under the age of eighteen from using amusement arcades to be unlawfully discriminatory. In so doing, he seemed to distance himself from the City's contention that discrimination *per se* was not a ground for striking down a by-law.

The City had relied upon a statement by Lord Russell C.J., in the leading nineteenth-century English judgment of *Kruse* v. *Johnson*,[49] in which he had linked the concept of discrimination with the unreasonableness ground of judicial review. By-laws, he stated, could be struck down on the basis of unreasonableness if they

> were found to be partial and unequal in their operation as between different classes; if they were manifestly unjust; if they disclosed bad faith; if they involved such oppressive or gratuitous interference with

---

47   *Ibid.*
48   *Arcade Amusements*, above note 43.
49   [1898] 2 Q.B. 91.

the rights of those subject to them such as would find no justification in the minds of reasonable men.[50]

While conceding that any one of these grounds or any of them in combination could give rise to invalidity, Beetz J. also, reinforced the existence of a free-standing or "neutral" principle against discrimination. Under this principle, absent explicit statutory authorization, discriminatory by-laws could be condemned by the courts even if "the distinction on which they are based is perfectly rational or reasonable in the narrow or political sense, and was conceived and imposed in good faith, without favouritism or malice."[51] This, according to Beetz J., was a "principle of fundamental freedom".[52]

The Court cannot have intended by this decision to condemn all forms of differentiations among classes of person brought about by subordinate legislation or other exercises of discretion. Where, then, are the lines to be drawn? Obviously, age discrimination, shortly thereafter to achieve constitutional protection with the coming into force of section 15 of the *Charter*, is one domain where explicit authority seems to be required. Such civil liberties concerns also intrude, though somewhat more implicitly, in the earlier case of *R. v. Bell*.[53] In that instance, the Court struck down a by-law restricting the use of dwelling units to occupation by single families and defining a family in terms of persons related by consanguinity, marriage, or adoption. For now, however, it remains unclear how far these principles apply in relation to interests other than those that have achieved the status of rights and freedoms in the *Charter*.

Perhaps the nearest the Court has come recently to recognizing discrimination as a free-standing basis for intervention in domains not reached by the *Charter* is *R. v. Sharma*.[54] At stake was a municipal by-law that required permits to operate a street vending operation unless that operation was run by the owners of an abutting business. The Supreme Court reiterated its general theme that, in order to discriminate, a municipality must be able to point to statutory authority. Delivering the judgment of the Court, Iacobucci J. also quoted from *Arcade Amusements* to emphasize that it was not a matter of whether the categorization exercise was reasonable or not. It depended on whether authority

---

50   *Ibid.* at 99–100.
51   *Arcade Amusements*, above note 43 at 406.
52   *Ibid.* at 413.
53   [1979] 2 S.C.R. 212.
54   [1993] 1 S.C.R. 650.

could be found for it in the language of the empowering statute. In this instance, the language of the provisions relied upon could not be read as authorizing such distinctions in terms of the need for a permit.

In fact, there is a certain air of unreality in such an ostensibly neutral or value-free analysis of the relevant statutory scheme. Regulation necessarily involves choice and categorization, and the determination of which choices and categories should be sustained and which should not depend ultimately on a sense of the purpose of the statutory grant of power relied upon and a judicial assessment of the claims of more transcendent values as opposed to the categories and classes created in the regulatory exercise itself. In short, purposive analysis, explicit or implicit, is necessary. The only real choice may be in terms of onus of proof or presumption: are all discriminations not explicitly authorized presumptively good or presumptively bad?

As for the question that Sopinka J. left open in *Shell Canada* — whether discriminations within a class are justified — Iacobucci J. stated in *Sharma* that claims of discrimination could be made with respect to by-laws discriminating among members of a class and also with respect to discriminations between or among different classes. While this distinction is not without its own problems, this would seem to indicate that the Court will not tolerate distinctions among members of the same class or, to put it another way, in situations where there are no relevant distinctions to justify treating the relevant persons as members of different classes. Such an approach would presumably have placed a heavy onus on Vancouver to justify a boycott of Shell while it continued to deal with other oil companies trading with South Africa, even if a total boycott of all companies dealing with South Africa was justified.

Once one moves away from the context of by-laws and regulations, asserting discrimination as a general principle becomes more difficult. As recently as 1993, the Court issued a strong statement that inconsistency of treatment is not a general ground of judicial review.[55] Moreover, in the specific domain of prosecutorial discretion, the Court has rejected attempts to control such discretion in the name of even-handed treatment.[56] This means, that there continue to be considerable doubts about the availability under any guise of a general principle of review for discriminatory treatment within classes of persons with the same legally relevant characteristics.

---

55   *Domtar Inc. v. Québec (Commission d'appel en matière de lesions professionnelles)*, [1993] 2 S.C.R. 756.
56   *R. v. Smythe*, [1971] S.C.R. 680.

4) Unreasonableness

Aside from the specific categories already canvassed, at least until *Baker*, there has also been a general residual ground of review for abuse of discretion. This is the so-called *Wednesbury* standard of unreasonableness. It is derived from the judgment of Lord Greene, M.R., in *Associated Provincial Picture Houses* v. *Wednesbury Corporation.*[57] In that case, Lord Greene proclaimed that an exercise of discretionary power could also be reviewed if it produced a result that was so unreasonable that no reasonable authority could ever have reached it. As with patent unreasonableness in the domain of review for jurisdictional error, this was a rare ground of judicial review. The terms in which Lord Greene described it, in fact, were calculated to make it so, particularly when he equated it with review for bad faith.

A limited number of examples can be found in the Canadian jurisprudence. In *Re Stora Kopparbergs Bergslags Aktiebolag and Nova Scotia Woodlot Owners' Association,*[58] the Appeal Division of the Nova Scotia Supreme Court set aside the registration of an association as bargaining agent for woodlot owners. The association supplied only 6.8% of the pulpwood supplied to the mills in the province. To certify such an association amounted to unreasonableness in the *Wednesbury* sense. Of course, today, given that the decision was that of a tribunal, it is likely that a court would justify any judicial intervention in such a situation on the basis of *New Brunswick Liquor* and the jurisdictional error language of patent unreasonableness.

Much more recently, in 1995, *Wednesbury Corporation* was invoked in a case involving a challenge to a municipal by-law. At stake was a municipality's creation of a "local service area" for the purposes of making and financing improvements in telephone services. Within that designated area, the municipality authorized a property value tax to enable it to recover the cost of the enhanced facility. In so acting, the municipality defined the area in a geographically irregular manner, so that it could capture a CN Railway line. This meant that most of the cost of providing the enhanced service would be imposed on CN, the largest single landowner in the area, and this despite the fact that CN had no intentions of using the service to be provided. At first instance, in *Canadian National Railway Co.* v. *Fraser-Fort George (Regional District),*[59] the Court held that this amounted to reviewable unreasonable-

---

57   [1948] 1 K.B. 223 at 299 [*Wednesbury Corporation*].
58   (1975), 61 D.L.R. (3d) 97 (N.S.S.C. A.D.).
59   (1995), 29 Admin. L.R. (2d) 97 (B.C.S.C.), aff'd (1996), 140 D.L.R. (4th) 23 (B.C.C.A.).

ness of the kind outlined by Lord Greene, and the British Columbia Court of Appeal refused to interfere with the first instance judge's finding. In affirming the decision below, the Court of Appeal emphasized that the boundaries of the local service area were "eccentric and gerrymandered" and were so for one obvious reason. However, it is also worth noting that the Court of Appeal talked in terms of "patent unreasonableness" rather than the language of Lord Greene, stressing once again the increasing fungibility of review for abuse of discretion and review for jurisdictional error.[60]

Indeed, as a consequence of *Baker*, there may now be some question as to whether the specific *Wednesbury* unreasonableness test has disappeared entirely from the rubric of Canadian judicial review or, perhaps more accurately, has been subsumed by or parcelled out to the two categories of review that have a reasonableness focus. After citing[61] *Wednesbury Corporation*,[62] L'Heureux-Dubé J. makes no further specific reference to the terms of its test in formulating her conception of the appropriate principles of review. This may mean that it is safe to conclude that that test is no longer an independent or free-standing ground of review under Canadian law. On the other hand, Lord Diplock's subsequent parsing of the *Wednesbury* unreasonableness standard has considerable merit as a definition of at least one species of patent unreasonableness:

> It applies to a decision which is so outrageous in its defiance of logic or of accepted moral standards that no sensible person who had applied his mind to the question could have arrived at it.[63]

D. DISCRETIONARY POWERS AND THE *CHARTER*

In addition to the various common law grounds for reviewing the exercise of statutory powers or discretions, the *Canadian Charter of Rights and Freedoms* also acts as a limitation on the scope of discretion and the manner of its exercise. There are a number of ways in which the *Charter* may intrude.

---

60   It is also worth noting that reasonableness review of municipal by-laws has not always depended on meeting the strict the *Wednesbury Corporation* or *New Brunswick Liquor* conceptions of unreasonableness.

61   *Baker*, above note 17 at para. 53.

62   *Wednesbury*, above note 57.

63   *Council of Civil Service Unions* v. *Minister for the Civil Service*, [1985] A.C. 374 (H.L. Eng.) at 410.

At the level of actual decision making, the *Charter* can act as a brake on apparently broad discretions. Thus, in *Slaight Communications* v. *Davidson*,[64] the Supreme Court was confronted by a challenge to an order made by an adjudicator appointed under the *Canada Labour Code*. The applicant claimed that that order infringed its freedom of expression under section 2(b) of the *Charter*. The order in question required a company to provide a dismissed employee with a letter of reference with defined content and to confine any responses to requests for information about that person's employment status to providing that letter of reference.

The Court held initially that the adjudicator's order constituted "state" or governmental action. Hence it came within the reach of the *Charter* as delineated in section 52(1) of the *Constitution Act, 1982*. It then accepted that both of the orders violated the applicant's freedom of expression but proceeded to hold that they were saved by section 1 as "demonstrably justifiable in a free and democratic society." In so doing, Dickson C.J.C. (for the majority) contrasted the orders made here with those made by a labour board in *National Bank of Canada* v. *Retail Clerks' International Union*.[65] There, orders requiring the bank to write a letter expressing contrition for its unfair labour practices and support for the objectives of the *Canada Labour Code* were quashed as "patently unreasonable." The Court did so by reference to common law judicial review standards with Beetz J. suggesting in a concurring judgment that the orders were also contrary to section 2(b) of the *Charter*. The seeming implication of Dickson C.J.C.'s comparison is that the orders in that case would not have passed muster by reference to section 1.

Aside from the fact that the Court had no hesitation in holding that an order emerging from a statutory form of adjudication could constitute "state action," the judgment in *Slaight Communications* is also of general significance at two other levels. First, section 1 justifications for *Charter* violations can only be applied on the basis of "reasonable limitations *imposed by law* [emphasis added]." Therefore the Court must by implication be taken to have also found that the adjudicator's orders were "law." Secondly, in terms of methodology, Dickson C.J.C. — in contrast to Lamer J. in dissent — proposed that the initial question in such cases should probably be whether the orders under challenge violated the *Charter*. The issue was not whether they were patently unreasonable by reference to common law standards of judicial

---

64   [1989] 1 S.C.R. 1038.
65   [1984] 1 S.C.R. 269.

review. He went on to suggest that if an order, which on its face violated the *Charter*, was found nevertheless to be justifiable by reference to section 1, it would be highly unusual for that order then to be struck down as patently unreasonable on the common law test. In general, review by reference to a patent unreasonableness standard should not impose on a statutory authority obligations of justification more onerous than those required under section 1 of the *Charter*. Subsequently, in *Ross* v. *New Brunswick School District, No. 15*,[66] La Forest J. speaking for the Court, confirmed the approach which Dickson C.J.C. had advanced with some hesitation in *Slaight Communications*.

Had the applicant been successful in *Slaight Communications*, the result would have been a striking down of the orders as invalid or beyond the jurisdiction or capacity conferred by the legislation, as in the *National Bank case*. However, the scrutiny of the exercise of discretion by reference to *Charter* standards and a finding of insufficient attention to the *Charter's* dictates need not necessarily make a particular decision or order invalid. The rights and freedoms enshrined in the *Charter* may constitute factors that have to be taken into account in the exercise of a discretion, and a finding of failure to take them into account could produce not simply a quashing of a decision but also a remission back to the decision maker to perform the task once again, this time in the context of the *Charter* and a correct appreciation of its meaning and demands.

A good illustration of this often subtle difference is provided by the judgment of the Ontario Court of Appeal in *Eaton* v. *Brant County Board of Education*.[67] At issue here was the decision of a second level appeal tribunal that upheld a school board committee's decision that a disabled child could no longer be accommodated in a regular classroom setting and should be reassigned to a special class. Central to a challenge to this decision based on section 15 of the *Charter* was section 8 of the Ontario *Education Act*. This conferred on the Minister of Education a power to make appropriate special education programs

---

66   [1996] 1 S.C.R. 825.

67   (1995), 123 D.L.R. (4th) 43 (Ont. C.A.). This judgment was reversed by the Supreme Court of Canada: [1997] 1 S.C.R. 241. However, the primary basis for the reversal was on procedural grounds (inadequate notice had been given of the raising of a constitutional question). Also, while the Court indicated that it disagreed with the Court of Appeal's finding that the decision of the authorities violated *Charter* rights, it did so without calling into question the Court's ruling on what should be the appropriate disposition in the event that the *Charter* challenge was sustained. See, however, the separate judgment of Lamer C.J.C., concurred in by Gonthier J.

available for all exceptional children in Ontario. According to the Court of Appeal, on its face, this section and the regulations made pursuant to it violated the section 15 rights of disabled children; they contained no limitation on the capacity of the relevant decision makers to assign pupils to special classes by reference to their section 15 rights, not to be discriminated against on the basis of disability.[68] The appropriate disposition, however, was neither to strike down the provision nor to direct that the specific decision be reversed. Instead, the Court held that the section must be read to include a strong presumption that disabled children are to be educated in regular classrooms, with the matter remitted to a differently constituted tribunal for reconsideration according to the provisions of the statute interpreted or modified to include this presumption. Potentially left dangling is the interesting question of whether, on any subsequent review, the courts should be at all deferential to a tribunal that has now applied the correct methodology or whether the application of that methodology to the facts must be subjected to correctness scrutiny as is the case in other situations of judicial review of *Charter* determinations.[69]

In *Eaton*, the Court of Appeal[70] held by reference to principles laid down by the Supreme Court of Canada that engrafting such a restriction on the discretion conferred by section 8 was appropriate, as it "achieves *Charter* compliance while minimizing interference with the legitimate legislative objectives of the Act." At times, such a salvage operation may not be possible. A discretionary regime that fails to address explicitly *Charter* rights and freedoms or which on its face leaves too much room for derogation from those rights and freedoms may not survive. There may be either too much legislative engrafting to be done or an insufficient basis for performing that task by reference to the standard of the overall, legitimate objectives of the legislation.

---

68 In their separate judgment, Lamer C.J.C. and Gonthier J. expressed the view that the proper step to take in such a case is not even to call the validity of the relevant provision into question but simply to read it down or interpret it as not justifying exercises of power that violate the *Charter*. That seems standard, though not universal, fare. However, it does not call into question whether the proper disposition in some cases may be to remit the matter to be dealt with by reference to the *Charter* rights of the affected person.

69 See, for example, *Cuddy Chicks Ltd. v. Ontario (Labour Relations Board)*, [1991] 2 S.C.R. 5.

70 *Schachter v. Canada*, [1992] 2 S.C.R. 679.

Two prominent judgments illustrate this point graphically. In *R. v. Morgentaler*,[71] the therapeutic abortion committee provisions of the *Criminal Code* were found to violate section 7 of the *Charter*. In part, this was because they provided too little guidance on the procedures to be followed and the standards the committees were to apply in deciding whether to allow an abortion to take place. In short, the legislation left too much room for exercises of discretion in violation of a pregnant woman's rights to "life, liberty and security of the person." The British Columbia Court of Appeal reached the same kind of conclusion in *Wilson v. Medical Services Commission of British Columbia*.[72] The regulatory scheme under which new doctors and doctors coming from out of province[73] were to be assigned practitioner numbers was one that offended the principles of fundamental justice:

> It is based on the application of vague and uncertain criteria, which combined with areas of uncontrolled discretion, leaves substantial scope for arbitrary conduct.[74]

The Court then went on to reject the argument that the deficiencies of the scheme from a procedural fairness or natural justice perspective could be rectified by the application or engrafting of common law norms. The scheme was described as "so procedurally flawed that it cannot stand."[75]

This concern with precision also manifests itself in those situations where the courts have struck down legislation that creates regulatory offences that are too vague and overly broad. Such prohibitions must provide sufficient guidance to enable legal discourse about whether they have been infringed.[76]

In contrast, the Supreme Court has, on other occasions, resisted the notion that the mere existence of broad statutory discretion in domains where *Charter* rights and freedoms may be implicated directly or indirectly is not necessarily a basis for striking down such provisions. They can readily be interpreted subject to the constraints of the *Charter*, and judicial review is available to police those situations where

---

71   [1988] 1 S.C.R. 30.

72   (1988), 53 D.L.R. (4th) 171 (B.C.C.A.) [*Wilson*].

73   Controversially, the Court held that such a scheme was an infringement of the traditional "liberty" of the medical profession, thereby engaging section 7 of the *Charter*.

74   *Wilson*, above note 72 at 196.

75   *Ibid.* at 197.

76   See, for example, *R. v. Nova Scotia Pharmaceutical Society*, [1992] 2 S.C.R. 606 and *R. v. Morales*, [1992] 3 S.C.R. 711, where the Court held in the context of a provision governing pre-trial detention that "in the public interest" was too vague but that "public safety" was not.

there has been no or insufficient attention to the relevant *Charter* protections. A good example is provided by the Supreme Court's judgment in *R. v. Jones*.[77] This involved an unsuccessful challenge to an unstructured statutory discretion conferred on a ministerial official as to whether or not parents would be permitted to educate their children at home. The applicant alleged that leaving this to such a broad discretion interfered with the religious freedom of parents to choose home schooling as a matter of right. Referring to the need for such discretions in modern government, La Forest J. rejected the challenge to the validity of the statutory regime and the discretion that it created.

Where the line is actually to be drawn between overly broad discretionary power and permissible undefined discretion, nonetheless, remains a highly speculative exercise. However, it may be the case that where the statutory discretion trades directly or principally in *Charter* rights and freedoms, as in *Morgentaler*, the courts will be much more demanding of the legislature that confers that discretion and require that the provision be structured or confined with due regard to the *Charter* rights and freedoms that are at stake. In contrast, where, as in *Jones*, the discretion is one that does not directly, necessarily, or in most of its applications involve *Charter* rights and freedoms, there will be much more toleration for broad, unstructured discretion and more attention paid to individual exercises of the particular discretion. Indeed, there is warrant for this argument in La Forest J.'s subsequent judgment for the Court in *Eldridge v. British Columbia (Attorney General)*.[78]

At stake in *Eldridge* was the failure of the healthcare services authorities in British Columbia to make sign language interpreters available to the deaf when they needed medical services. The Court held that this policy or denial of benefits violated the section 15 rights of the deaf. However, the consequence of this was not the invalidity of the provisions under which the legislature had conferred discretion on hospitals and the province's Medical Services Commission regarding the services that would be provided and paid for. Rather, the proper disposition was to declare the particular exercise of discretion invalid. La Forest J. stated:

> Some grants of discretion will necessarily infringe *Charter* rights notwithstanding that they do not expressly authorize that result. . . . In such cases, it will generally be the statute, and not its application, that attracts *Charter* scrutiny. . . . In the present case, however, the discretion accorded to the Medical Services Commission to determine

---

77 [1986] 2 S.C.R. 284.
78 [1997] 3 S.C.R. 624 [*Eldridge*].

whether a service qualifies as a benefit does not necessarily or typically threaten the equality rights set out in section 15(1) of the *Charter*.[79]

E. OTHER CONSTITUTIONAL CONSTRAINTS

As already noted in the section on constitutional norms, before the advent of the *Canadian Charter of Rights and Freedoms*, there was much speculation about the role that the so-called "implied bill of rights" had to play in Canadian constitutional and administrative law. As reflected in *Roncarelli* v. *Duplessis*, there were occasions on which the Supreme Court restricted the exercise of otherwise broad statutory discretions by reference to underlying constitutional values, such as freedom of religion and speech, as well as such civil liberties as that of standing bail for those in custody after being charged with committing an offence.

Most of the rights and freedoms that were argued to make up the implied bill of rights found their way, first, at the federal level into the *Canadian Bill of Rights*, and, then for the whole country, into the *Canadian Charter of Rights and Freedoms*. There produced a sense that the implied bill of rights had been rendered redundant as a device for challenging legislation and calling into question particular exercises of discretion under otherwise valid legislation. However, it has now become apparent that the deployment of unwritten, underlying constitutional norms as a way of at least questioning particular exercises of discretion or executive actions may still be viable in certain circumstances.

In the context of *Baker* v. *Canada (Minister of Citizenship and Immigration)*, we have already noted the tantalizing statement by L'Heureux-Dubé J., on behalf of the Court, that not only must discretion be exercised within the boundaries of the power-conferring statute but also in accordance with "the principles of the rule of law, the principles of administrative law, *the fundamental values of Canadian society*, and the principles of the *Charter* [emphasis added]."[80] At this point, it remains a matter of conjecture whether the use of the emphasized words was merely a rhetorical device or was intended to have a bite. In that this statement finds its antecedent or pedigree in the fundamental organizing principles of the Canadian Constitution, identified by the Court in *Reference re Secession of Québec*,[81] there are already indicati-

---

79   *Ibid.* at 651.
80   *Baker*, above note 17 at para. 56.
81   *Secession of Québec*, above note 35.

ions that we may be on the verge of a new era of controlling executive discretion by reference to implied constitutional principles.

Here, the prime exhibit is *Lalonde* v. *Ontario (Commission de Restructuration des Services de Santé)*,[82] one of a number of cases that challenged to the activities of the Ontario Health Services Restructuring Commission. Here, the commission ordered the Hôpital Montfort in Ottawa, a hospital unique in the province by reason of its francophone character, to change significantly the nature of its functions and modes of operation. According to the Divisional Court, the Commission had not acted in accordance with the law in its restructuring order:

> In the circumstances of this case, by failing to take into account the importance of francophone institutions (including hospitals), as opposed to bilingual institutions, for the preservation of the language and culture of Franco-Ontarians, as not being "within the purview of the [Commission]," the Commission failed to comply with one of the fundamental organizing principles underlying the Constitution, namely that of the "protection of minorities."[83]

In particular, the Divisional Court saw warrant for its approach[84] in the Supreme Court's statements in the *Secession Reference* that the four organizing principles — federalism, democracy, constitutionalism and the rule of law, and the protection of minorities — were not simply "descriptive" of explicit rights. They actually had a substantive content of their own, "which constitute[s] substantive limitations upon government action."[85]

Of course, it remains to be seen whether this judgment holds up on appeal or is taken up by other courts. There must also be some question as to the number of situations to which this approach will be appropriate, particularly given the extent of the explicitly articulated rights and freedoms now found in the *Canadian Charter of Rights and Freedoms*, not to mention other "superior" forms of primary legislation such as the *Canadian Bill of Rights*, provincial bills of rights, and human rights codes. Nonetheless, the judgment does call upon those exercising discretion to be attentive to whether a decision in a particular matter has ramifications beyond the normal parameters of decision making under that statutory regime. Indeed, far more pervasive than the underlying principles of the Canadian Constitution and the "fundamental

---

82 (1999) 181 D.L.R. (4th) 263 (Ont. Div. Ct.).
83 *Ibid.* at para. 101.
84 *Ibid.* at para. 41.
85 *Secession of Québec*, above note 81 at 248–49.

values of Canadian society" may be the very factor to which the officials did not give any weight in *Baker*: the terms of Canada's international commitments, particularly in domains affecting civil liberties and human rights. To the extent that decision makers must take account treaties that Canada has ratified but not implemented legislatively, there may well be a whole range of overarching considerations that henceforth careful counsel will urge on statutory authorities and that they will be obliged to treat as relevant, albeit with varying levels of intensity.[86]

F. EVIDENTIAL AND OTHER ADJECTIVAL QUESTIONS

As already foreshadowed in the discussion of *Thorne's Hardware*,[87] there may be difficulties in securing evidence of the grounds on which broad discretionary powers were actually exercised. These difficulties are compounded in the case of collective decision making, such as that by Cabinet or multi-member tribunals. Indeed, on more recent Supreme Court of Canada authority seems to confirm the approach taken in *Thorne's Hardware* in the even broader context of decision making by municipalities.

In *Consortium Developments (Clearwater) Ltd.* v. *Sarnia (City)*,[88] the Supreme Court was confronted with an attempt to summon municipal councillors and officials to testify in proceedings challenging the setting up of a municipal inquiry. The applicant based its arguments on the premise that the relevant council had acted with improper motives or for wrongful purposes. Binnie J. delivered the judgment of the Court, affirming the striking out of the summonses. With reference to *Thorne's Hardware*, he expressed the view that the "motives of a legislative body composed of numerous persons are 'unknowable' except by what it enacts."[89] While then acknowledging that extrinsic evidence would be admissible on occasion to demonstrate "colourability" of purpose, he made the further point that, even if the municipal councillors had illegitimate expectations as to the scope of the judicial inquiry they were voting to create, "that wishful thinking" could not in effect turn it into an illegal surrogate for a police investigation. The judge

---

86   *Quaere* the extent to which this makes any call on those exercising powers under provincial legislation.

87   *Thorne's Hardware*, above note 5.

88   *Consortion Developments*, above note 7.

89   *Thorne's Hardware*, at 36.

conducting the inquiry was still constrained by the statutory and other constitutional limitations on his jurisdiction.

To the extent that this seems to undermine the possibility of bad faith or improper motivations as a free-standing ground for challenging the exercise of discretionary powers, it raises other serious problems. More generally, it further underscores the great practical difficulties confronting those making such allegations, difficulties that for judicial and *quasi*-judicial bodies are compounded further by the immunity accorded to members of such tribunals in their deliberative processes.

In some contexts, these problems may diminish because the statutory decision maker can be compelled to provide reasons for its decisions.[90] Of course, even with the moral force of oaths of office, formally meeting such a requirement may not always reveal the truth or the whole truth. Beyond that, in the leading House of Lords decision of *Padfield v. Minister of Agriculture, Fisheries & Food*,[91] the Court was willing to infer an abuse of discretion on the basis that the evidence presented by the applicant for review. The evidence made out a strong enough case to suggest that there could have been no good reason for the decision in question. Absent a response from the minister, that was sufficient to justify the grant of relief. There is now clear Canadian support for this proposition.[92]

Another difficulty can arise when the decision maker has made a decision for various reasons some defensible and others that on their own would amount to an abuse of discretion. Clearly, if there is a dominant purpose and it is an improper one, the courts will review.[93] Beyond that, however, the authorities are not consistent and there is no clear Supreme Court of Canada authority. However, given that the discretion is one conferred on the statutory authority and not the court, the better view may be that, as long as the decision was clearly influenced or affected by an improper purpose, the reviewing court should not speculate on whether the presence of "good" reasons or purposes would have led to the same result on their own.[94] Rather, the matter

---

90   Under principles now also established by *Baker*, above note 17.

91   [1968] A.C. 997 (H.L. Eng.).

92   See, for example, *Alkali Lake Indian Band v. Westcoast Transmission Co.* (1984), 7 Admin. L.R. 64 (B.C.C.A.).

93   *Warne v. Nova Scotia* (1969), 1 N.S.R. (2d) 150 (T.D.).

94   See, for example, *DiNardo v. Ontario (Liquor Licence Board)* (1974), 5 O.R. (2d) 124 (H.C).

should be remitted to the decision maker for reconsideration. In the context of a "Cabinet appeal," on the other hand, the Federal Court of Appeal, relying on a statement in *Thorne's Hardware*,[95] made the following statement:

> Even if one were to assume that the Governor in Council acted with a dual purpose in mind (one falling within his mandate, . . . and the other falling outside his mandate, . . .), I doubt that this could advance the respondents' case.[96]

Whether this amounts to a general principle or one confined to exercises of power by Cabinet in the context of broadly based Cabinet appeal provisions or regulation-making powers remains for the present a matter of speculation.

G. LEGAL CONSEQUENCES OF AN ABUSE OF DISCRETION

In general, the courts reject any attempt to direct a statutory authority to exercise its discretion in a particular way. Normally, a successful application for review for abuse of discretion results in a quashing or setting aside of the decision. If requested, the matter may be remitted to the statutory authority, with a direction that it re-exercise its discretion, this time in accordance with the law. However, on rare occasions — as exemplified by *Padfield* v. *Minister of Agriculture, Fisheries and Food*[97] if there are only two choices available, and if it would be unreasonable in the *Wednesbury* sense or, now presumably, depending on the context, incorrect, unreasonable, or patently unreasonable in the *Baker* sense to persist in the choice already made, the remission back to the decision maker may in effect direct the making of the "right" choice. Indeed, in such cases, where the applicant is seek nothing but is rather the subject of an order, remission back is probably redundant and a quashing of the decision will suffice.

---

95 *Thorne's Hardware*, above note 5 at 117.
96 *National Anti-Poverty Organization* v. *Canada (A.G.)* (1990), 60 D.L.R. (4th) 712 (C.A.) at 731.
97 [1968] A.C. 997 (H.L. Eng.).

FURTHER READINGS

BRUN H., & DENIS LEMIEUX, "Politisation du pouvoir judiciaire ed judiciaristion du pouvoir politique: la séparation traditionnelle des pouvoirs à-t-elle véçu?" (1977), 18 C. de D. 265

CHRISTIE, I.M., "The Nature of the Lawyer's Role in the Administrative Process," [1970] Law Society of Upper Canada Special Lectures 1

MULLAN, D.J., "Judicial Deference to Executive Decision-Making: Evolving Concepts of Responsibility" (1993), 19 Queen's L.J. 137

ROSS, J.M., "Applying the *Charter* to Discretionary Authority" (1991), 29 Alta. L.R. 382

CHAPTER 7

DELEGATED
LEGISLATION

A. INTRODUCTION

Delegated legislation, whether promulgated by central government in the form of regulations, by municipalities as by-laws, or, increasingly, as rules and policies issued by tribunals and agencies, is both a major source of law and instrument of governance in Canada. Indeed, it has long surpassed primary legislation as the quantitatively greater version of enacted law. As the scope for its promulgation continues to increase, often under almost completely unstructured grants of discretion, it brings increasingly into question the role of Parliament and the legislatures as the constitutionally most significant players in the development and refinement of our positive laws. Indeed, this debate is given particularly sharp focus in a jurisdiction such as present-day Ontario with the appearance in primary legislation of the often theoretically discredited "King Henry VIII clause." Such a provision authorizes subordinate legislation that conflicts with or overrides the terms of primary legislation.[1]

---

1   There are now more than ten such clauses in various forms in Ontario legislation. The following provision (s. 349(2)) from the *Fewer School Boards Act*, S.O. 1997, c. 3 is an example: "[I]n the event of a conflict between a regulation made under this Part and provision of this Act or of any other Act or regulation, the regulation made under this Part prevails."

Of course, delegated legislation in its various formats is an inevitable outgrowth, or by-product of a parliamentary system such as ours and the justifications for the phenomenon are notorious: Parliament does not have enough time to still be responsible for the consideration and passage of all legislated law in a complex democracy. The primary legislators should devote their attention to the matters of principle involved in and the detail of only the most far-reaching forms of legislation, leaving subordinate legislation to put the flesh on Acts. There is also a sense in which primary legislation becomes far less accessible in a practical sense if everything is crammed into it. Manageable statute books require physical limits. Subordinate legislation provides a forum for the working out of and often making rapid changes to matters of detail, the precise contours of which cannot be appreciated fully at the time that the primary legislation is enacted. If Parliament had to work out these issues of detail, there would often be lengthy delays in the enactment of legislation which, as a matter of principle, was needed quickly in the public interest.

To these relatively "benign" explanations for the proliferation of subordinate legislation has to be added what is really the single most significant reason for the extensive delegations of power so common in modern statutes: the continuing diminution in the real, or effective, power of Parliament and the legislatures in an era of extremely strong executive government. In many instances, the primary dictate in parliamentary conferral of extremely broad discretions, including the power to promulgate subordinate legislation, is a clear wish on the part of executives with effective voting control over the legislative branch to take more and more matters of general public significance out of the hands of Parliament and to arrogate it to themselves or agencies acting under their dictation, control, or strong influence. What was once generally justified only in time of war or other emergencies has become increasingly common: the enactment of legislation with very little opportunity for parliamentary debate and with both the principles and the detail left initially for the executive to work out and also subject to change at the executive's whim. In a way, we seem to be moving closer to a regime where legislatures have really ceased to be legislators in any traditional sense of that term. Now they provide the formal majority that the executive needs to get on with the business of both legislating and governing outside the parliamentary chamber. On occasion, through question period, they may also randomly bring mismanagement to the attention of the Canadian and provincial "publics." However, these matters aside, Parliament's and the legislatures' positive tasks are now remarkably few.

The focus for some, then, becomes that of providing antidotes to the erosions of parliamentary power in general and the proliferation of unchecked subordinate legislation in particular. In the case of subordinate legislation, these antidotes take three principal forms. The first has been the attachment, through legislation about subordinate legislation, of various forms of scrutiny and review, either in advance of its coming into effect, in the form of laying and approval requirements, or in subsequent scrutiny by subordinate legislation committees.

B. LEGISLATIVE SCRUTINY

This kind of legislation is not common in Canada. The federal *Statutory Instruments Act* does contain a weak form of provision for examination by the Clerk of the Privy Council in consultation with the Deputy Minister of Justice of regulations to check their validity, form, and content.[2] There are also two other checking requirements at the federal level. Section 3 of the *Canadian Bill of Rights* requires the Minister of Justice to scrutinize all proposed federal statutes and regulations for conformity with the provisions of that statute. While there is no similar provision in the *Charter*, since 1985, by virtue of section 4.1 of the *Department of Justice Act*, the Minister of Justice is similarly obligated to check bills and proposed regulations against the rights and freedoms enshrined in the *Charter*.[3]

The federal *Statutory Instruments Act* also provides,[4] as, does Saskatchewan's *Regulations Act*, for example,[5] that subordinate legislation "shall stand permanently referred to" any committee established for the purpose of "reviewing and scrutinizing statutory instruments." Ontario goes further by requiring the setting up of a standing committee on regulations. The Act makes it clear, however, that, in scrutinizing any regulations, the committee shall confine itself to questions of form and not consider the wisdom or merits of any policy behind any regulation.[6] Saskatchewan also creates a process for legislative disapproval of regulations.[7]

---

2   R.S.C. 1985, c. S-22, s. 3. However, a failure to engage in this process does not invalidate a regulation.
3   R.S.C. 1985, c. J-2 (as amended by S.C. 1985, c. 26, s. 106).
4   S. 19.
5   S.S., c. R-16.1, s. 16.
6   *Regulations Act*, R.S.O. 1990, c. R.21, s. 12.
7   S. 17.

Suffice it to say that the success of such checking devices depends in very large measure on the commitment of the executive to making them work. Do those responsible for the various tasks have the resources necessary to enable them to function effectively? To what extent do legislative committees set up to perform these tasks function along party or partisan lines? How little room is left for well-developed criticism of executive excesses? How often does this legislature sit? Is this work that continues out of parliamentary session?

For a comparatively brief period, there was reason to believe that the federal Standing Joint Senate/Commons Committee for Scrutiny of Regulations had both the resources and the level of independence to give it considerable credibility. It seemed equipped to evaluate the validity of federal subordinate legislation and provide pointed criticism of the substance of some subordinate legislation and the breadth of the legislative discretion under which it had been promulgated. However, evidence suggests that ultimately the pull of bi- or tripartisanship became too much and the committee surrendered its effectiveness. Indeed, if recent media exposure is any guide, there is little reason to believe that there is a parliamentary subordinate legislation committee anywhere in the country with a high enough profile role to draw the public's attention to excesses in and misuses of the promulgation of regulations and other forms of statutory instruments.

C. PUBLIC CONSULTATION

In the last few years, however, there has been a much greater tendency to move towards the kind of surrogate for legislative scrutiny and debate that American federal and state *Administrative Procedure Acts* provide: that so-called notice and comment procedure, which requires advance public notice of proposed regulations and the opportunity for the public to comment on those proposals. At least two high-profile legislative committees (one federally in 1968[8] and one in Ontario in 1983[9]) saw no need for a general notice and comment obligation, and Québec is still the only province to have such generally applicable legislation.[10] Yet there has been considerable expansion in the use of

---

8   The *Third Report of the Special Committee on Statutory Instruments* ("the MacGuigan Committee Report").

9   A report from the Standing Committee on Regulations and Private Bills. However, in a second report in 1988, (the "Fleet Committee Report"), the Committee did come around to accepting the utility of a general statute.

10 *Regulations Act*, S.Q. 1986, c. 22, ss. 8–14.

notice and comment procedures. First, it has now been incorporated legislatively into a number of specific high-profile regulatory regimes, such as the Ontario Securities Commission as a result of 1994 amendments to the Ontario *Securities Act*.[11] Second, in the federal domain, such provisions have become common in individual pieces of legislation[12] and, informally, as a result of initiatives taken in the mid-1980s. Annually, agencies of the federal government under the Federal Regulatory Plan[13] publish advance notice of planned regulatory initiatives and, subject to certain exceptions, provide a subsequent opportunity for the public to comment on draft regulations, which are annexed to the announcement of those initiatives.

How effective these mechanisms have been in providing effective surrogate accountability mechanisms awaits detailed study. There are many questions that need to be asked: To what extent do the exceptions under the various legislative and informal provisions operate to actually defeat effective participation? How accessible are such regimes to anyone other than well-funded lobby groups? Through their exercise of these procedural entitlements, these lobby groups may bring about or contribute to the regulatory capture of the relevant department or agency in a manner contrary to the public interest. Moreover, as suggested by some of the United States' experience with *Administrative Procedure Act* notice and comment, there is always the possibility that the process, whether by deliberate manipulation by participants or not, may produce regulatory paralysis, once again in a way inimical to the broader public interest. Despite this, on their face, such procedures are broadly democratic as they are open to use by all and, unlike legislative scrutiny committees, are not subject to quite the same kind of manipulation or appropriation by the government of the day.

---

11   Section 143.2 of the *Securities Act*, R.S.O. 1990, c. S. 5 (as inserted by S.O. 1994, c. 33, s. 8 and as amended by S.O. 1997, c. 19, s. 23).

12   See, for example, *Broadcasting Act*, S.C. 1991, c. 11, section 10(3), which requires that the CRTC provide a reasonable opportunity to make representations when exercising its regulation making powers.

13   Under this system, all government departments and agencies have to publish an annual federal regulatory plan outlining proposed regulatory initiatives. Thereafter, any proposed regulations coming out of that plan also have to be published in Part I of *The Canada Gazette*, along with a regulatory impact analysis statement. Those affected and the public generally then have an opportunity to make written comments.

D. JUDICIAL REVIEW

The third mechanism is that of judicial review. As with all forms of statutory authority, those responsible for promulgating subordinate legislation must act within the limits of the jurisdiction that has been conferred on them by the primary legislation-making authority, usually Parliament or the various provincial and territorial legislatures. Where those limits are not observed, judicial review remains available to those affected by these exercises of statutory power. In at least some cases, this includes individuals and groups acting in the public interest. Policing of the exercise of subordinate legislation-making powers tends to be random rather than regular and/or organized and is limited in its scope. It is not, therefore, a way to ensure ongoing, comprehensive substantive checks on the executive's exercise of such legislative powers. Nonetheless, it does fit in with the general theme of this book and is an important aspect of the overall system of judicial review of administrative action. As such, it warrants special or individual attention. Moreover, like judicial review in other contexts, its very random nature may help keep the drafters and promulgators of subordinate legislation honest.

Where statutory instruments legislation and other enactments prescribe certain steps for the effective enactment of subordinate legislation, those provisions will sometimes be treated as mandatory, leading to a finding of invalidity if they are not followed.[14] Such a challenge may arise directly, as in the case of an action for declaratory relief. Or, it may arise collaterally, as in a defence to proceedings based on a violation of the subordinate legislation in question. Unless a procedure such as notice and comment is prescribed by statute, there is no basis in general for asserting common law procedural fairness obligations in the context of subordinate legislation. As we shall see in the section on the threshold for applying of the rules of procedural fairness, such legislative powers are exempt from the obligation to provide any kind of process to those affected or potentially affected by such legislation. The only exception recognized by the Supreme Court of Canada in *Homex Realty and Development Corp. Ltd* v. *Village of Wyoming*[15] is in instances where the subordinate legislation is situation-specific and has the effect of solving an *inter partes* dispute, such as a dispute between the munic-

---

14   For a recent discussion of the principles governing determination of invalidity as automatic or dependent on proof of actual prejudice, see *Immeubles Port Louis Ltée c. Lafontaine (Village)*, [1991] 1 S.C.R. 326.

15   [1980] 2 S.C.R. 1011.

ipality and the person affected. In that instance, the municipality had attempted to finesse by a by-law withdrawing a development permit an ongoing controversy as to whether a property developer or the municipality was or should have been legally responsible for the costs of servicing a subdivision.

Obviously, as in the case of primary legislation, those with subordinate legislation-making powers are also constrained by the Constitution including the *Canadian Charter of Rights and Freedoms*. In fact, there has been at least one judicial suggestion that there may be constitutional problems with the use of King Henry VIII clauses to promulgate subordinate legislation that conflicts with the provisions of primary legislation, whether it be the empowering Act itself or some other primary legislation.[16] At some juncture, the passing on of authority to make subordinate legislation may constitute an impermissible subdelegation of the legislative authority of Parliament and the legislatures. Open-ended authority to promulgate subordinate legislation that contradicts primary legislation may represent the point at which those limits are engaged.

The authority to promulgate subordinate legislation also requires an express grant of power. There is no such thing as an implicit right to make subordinate legislation having the force of law, and while the Canadian courts have long sustained, even encouraged, the issuance of informal policies and guidelines by various agencies of government, they do not concede to them the status of law. Moreover, particularly in the domain of substance (as opposed to procedure), as we have already seen, any agency that follows such guidelines slavishly or attributes to them the force of law exposes the relevant decision to review for abuse of discretion in general, and a wrongful fettering of discretion in particular.

Nonetheless, guidelines, while not strictly law, can achieve legal significance. On occasion, the courts are willing to make use of the guidelines issued by statutory authorities as at least evidence of the content of the legal obligations owed by those or even other bodies. In the procedural domain, *Bezaire* v. *Windsor Roman Catholic Separate School Board*[17] provides an excellent example. There, the ministerial procedural policy on school closings and the Board's own procedural guidelines were treated as strong evidence of what procedural fairness required in the context of a decision to close a number of schools. In the

---

16   *Ontario Public School Boards' Association v. Ontario (Attorney General)* (1997), 151 D.L.R. (4th) 346 (Ont. G.D.) at p.362-65, though see *Re Gray* (1918), 57 S.C.R. 150.

17   (1992), 9 O.R. (3d) 737 (Div. Ct.).

domain of substantive requirements, *Baker* v. *Canada (Minister of Citizenship and Immigration)*[18] again provides a useful example. The Supreme Court relied upon the ministerial guidelines on the exercise of the humanitarian and compassionate discretion under the *Immigration Act* as an indication of the factors that the minister should have taken into account in dispensing with the normal requirements of the Act:

> The guidelines are a useful indicator of what constitutes a reasonable interpretation of the power conferred by the section, and the fact that this decision was contrary to their directives is of great help in assessing whether the decision was an unreasonable exercise of the H & C power.[19]

Subordinate legislation be it a regulation or by-law, is also subject to judicial review if *ultra vires*. The subordinate legislator cannot deal with subject matter that is beyond the express terms of the relevent empowering provision. As well as having to observe substantive limits imposed by the relevant regulation or by-law-making power, those with authority to promulgate such subordinate legislation must also act in good faith and, in theory, not for any improper purpose. Moreover, as with other statutory authorities, they must not exercise their power on the basis of irrelevant considerations or without taking account of relevant considerations. The rules against improper subdelegation also constrain those with subordinate legislation-making powers.

This is not to say that the courts set aside subordinate legislation regularly. Rather, and particularly in the case of regulations promulgated by the Governor General or the Lieutenant Governor in Council, judicial intervention is very restrained. There are a number of reasons for this. The power to pass such legislation is often expressed in broad subject matter terms as well as subjectively by the use of such language as "in her or his opinion" or "as he or she deems necessary." The courts have always interpreted both of these as indicators of the need for considerable deference to the judgment of the subordinate legislation-making authority. The court will intervene only if the regulation is one that on no reasonable view of the empowering language could come within the scope of the regulation-making authority's power.[20] In so doing, the courts have also taken an expansive view of what is reasonably incidental to the explicit conferral of power. In addition, the fact

---

18   [1999] 2 S.C.R. 817.
19   *Ibid.* at para. 72.
20   See, for example, *Canada (Canadian Wheat Board)* v. *Manitoba Pool Elevators*, [1952] A.C. 427 (P.C. Can.)

that the formal decision maker is in effect the Cabinet, a multi-member body, has a stifling effect on the availability of judicial review. This stems partly from the fact that the courts tend to be very reticent to interfere with what they often regard as a political judgment on the part of the apex of the executive branch of government. Also, as far as wrongful purpose allegations are concerned, the courts are singularly unwilling to countenance the making of such arguments against multi-member bodies because there is much room for differing reasons among the members of the group for supporting the promulgation of the legislation in question. When one adds to this the position adopted by some courts that the insinuation of bad motive or purposes does not necessarily trump otherwise permissible motives or purposes, it is very difficult to make out a case for invalidity on this basis.

The most graphic illustration of the courts' reluctance to become involved in a substantive *ultra vires* assessment of subordinate legislation remains *Thorne's Hardware Ltd.* v. *The Queen*,[21] which was discussed in chapter 6, on abuse of discretion. Orders in council made by the Governor General in Council "in matters of public convenience and general policy are final and not reviewable in legal proceedings." One slight concession exists: in an "egregious" case, review might be possible on "jurisdictional and other policy grounds."[22]

Nonetheless, there are certain grounds of judicial review of subordinate legislation that are more formal in their nature and that do not involve either an evaluation of the substance or content of the impugned regulation or by-law or an examination of the motives of those responsible for its promulgation. The courts have traditionally tended to be more comfortable with these bases for challenge. Included in this category are regulations and by-laws that conflict with express provisions in primary legislation, be it the empowering or some other Act; using a power to regulate an activity in order to prohibit it absolutely; and subdelegating a power to pass regulations to another authority directly, without structuring or confining or, more generally, attempting to legislate.

Canada (A.G.) v. *Brent*[23] illustrates this latter category well and it is on authority that the Supreme Court it has applied on subsequent occasions to the same effect.[24] There, the Governor in Council had power under the then immigration legislation to make regulations lim-

---

21   [1983] 1 S.C.R. 106.
22   *Ibid.* at 111.
23   [1956] S.C.R. 318 [*Brent*].
24   See *Brant Dairy Co.* v. *Ontario (Milk Commission)* (1972), [1973] S.C.R. 131; *Air Canada* v. *Dorval (City)*, [1985] 1 S.C.R. 861.

iting or prohibiting the admission into Canada of persons by reference to a list of categories. The Cabinet exercised this power simply by delegating to an official the discretion to deny someone admission into Canada by reference to the same categories and in the same language as the regulation-empowering section. Kerwin C.J., delivered the judgment of a unanimous Court:

> Parliament had in contemplation the enactment of such regulations relevant to the named subject matters, or some of them, as in His Excellency-in-Council's own opinion were advisable and not a wide divergence of rules and opinions; everchanging according to the individual notions of Immigration Officers and Special Inquiry Officers. There is no power in the Governor General-in-Council to delegate his authority to such officers.[25]

Historically, though seemingly less so today, the courts also were reluctant to read general grants of subordinate legislation-making powers as authorizing the imposition of certain categories of obligation or the restriction of certain kinds of interests. More particularly, express authority, rather than implied, was required for subordinate legislation that interfered with property rights (including common law rights to trade), restricted "civil liberties," imposed taxes, created offences, operated retroactively, and, more generally, created discriminations among classes of persons. As well, there was, and probably still is, a strong operating presumption that subordinate legislation that establishes procedures for adjudicative bodies must conform with the principles of natural justice or procedural fairness.

Indeed, these presumptions operate with greater influence on municipalities and their by-laws, where the Canadian courts have frequently exhibited a tendency to look for explicit grants of power and to read general grants of power narrowly. As opposed to regulations and other forms of subordinate legislation made by the central government, by-laws have also always been subject to challenge at common law on the basis of uncertainty[26] and plain unreasonableness. In the case of

---

25 *Brent*, above note 23 at 321.
26 Subordinate legislation of all kinds is, however, subject to the constraints imposed by the *Charter* and, in particular, the "void for vagueness" basis for challenge where section 7 rights to "life, liberty or security of the person" are affected by subordinate legislation. In such instances, the "principles of fundamental justice" require a sufficient level of certainty: *R. v. Nova Scotia Pharmaceutical Society*, [1992] 2 S.C.R. 606 and *R. v. Morales* [1992] 3 S.C.R. 711 (previously noted in Chapter 6).

unreasonableness, the test normally applied is still the famous statement of Lord Russell C.J. in *Kruse* v. *Johnson*[27]: "such oppressive interference with the rights of those subject to them as could find no justification in the minds of reasonable men." The Supreme Court of Canada used this statement in *R.* v. *Bell*[28] as justification of the striking down of a by-law which restricted the occupation of dwelling units to single families, with "family" defined in the by-law as persons related by consanguinity, marriage, or adoption. However, in the case of unreasonableness, most provinces have long had legislation preventing challenges on this basis to by-laws made in good faith.[29]

As we saw in the previous chapter, on abuse of discretion, unlawful discrimination has also proved a fruitful though very problematic basis for attacks on the validity of subordinate legislation, and of by-laws in particular. It is inevitable that legislation, whether primary or subordinate, will treat some persons differently from others. Yet, in the absence of explicit authority there are some kinds of choices that have been foreclosed to those promulgating subordinate legislation. Obviously, discrimination in the senses condemned by section 15 of the *Charter* and anti-discrimination codes gives rise to invalidity. However, even beyond this, the Supreme Court has condemned other species of discrimination perpetrated by those responsible for subordinate legislation and particularly by-laws.

At the end of the day, though, what the authorities demonstrate is that there can be no realistic principle of non-discrimination in the passage of a by-law divorced from an evaluation of the worth of the interests affected by the discrimination. While reasonableness may not be the touchstone of invalidity in this domain, what really is at stake is whether the Court accepts that there are public policy reasons for not engaging in the particular form of discrimination absent specific legislative authority for such actions.

FURTHER READINGS

HOLLAND, D., & J.M. MCGOWAN, *Delegated Legislation in Canada* (Toronto: Carswell, 1989)

---

27   [1898] 2 Q.B. 91 at 99–100.
28   [1979] 2 S.C.R. 212.
29   See, for example, *Vancouver City Charter*, S.B.C. 1953, c. 55, s. 148.

PART THREE

PROCEDURAL FAIRNESS

CHAPTER 8

THE REACH OF PROCEDURAL FAIRNESS RIGHTS

A. JUSTIFYING ADMINISTRATIVE PROCESS VALUES

One of the principal concerns of administrative law has always been the procedural fairness claims of those affected by governmental decision making of various kinds. This is reflected in the extent to the courts, by reference to constitutional[1] and common law standards as well as the provisions of statutory regimes, hold those decision makers to account for failures to accord procedural decencies. The design of appropriate processes or procedures also looms large as an important aspect of the development of most administrative structures. Either at the legislative drafting stage or subsequently by way of subordinate legislation (or internal, non-statutory codes) of those responsible craft rules of procedure for particular forms of decision making. Indeed, even absent such general rules, decision makers required to act in a particular matter may have to spend time working out an appropriate procedural framework for exercising their jurisdiction.

From some perspectives, this emphasis on process may seem misguided. After all, the fullest or fairest procedures may not guarantee the

---

1   Most notably, section 7 of the *Canadian Charter of Rights and Freedoms* and also, in the federal domain, the provisions of sections 1(a) and 2(e) of the *Canadian Bill of Rights*.

best or most appropriate substantive outcomes. There is always a danger that too much emphasis on procedures will be at the expense of other values that are important in the delivery of various government programs, especially in times of budgetary constraint. Adherence to procedural norms and values may delay the taking of important decisions in a manner prejudicial to the public interest and even the affected parties. Engaging in hearings costs money to both decision maker and participants. The delays inherent in some hearings may render the ultimate substantive outcome less valuable or more costly (such as public hearings into the location of a garbage disposal facility). Indeed, in the hands of the unscrupulous, the provision of participatory opportunities may present a means for the manipulation of the process to their advantage, resulting in the frustration of legislative objectives and the defeat of the public interest.

Nevertheless, the claims that have led to the incorporation of procedural norms into the administrative process are recognized as having considerable force. As in civil litigation and the criminal trial, there is a sense that hearing all the evidence and listening to all of the various perspectives on a question will produce better and fairer outcomes. For these purposes, there is also a generally held belief that some processes work better than others. Thus, where outcomes depend largely on factual issues and where credibility of witnesses may be vital, there is an assumption that oral or in-person hearings, including access to cross-examination rights, are superior to hearings confined to written evidence, such as affidavits or written depositions.

Another assumption looms large in the justifications of hearings as a prelude to the taking of decisions. Those parties affected, even if they do not ultimately prevail, will be far more likely to accept the outcome than they would be were the matter to be decided in secret by a faceless or nameless bureaucrat. The sense of having been able to participate in the decision-making process and confront the actual decision maker is a powerful antidote to disappointment over an adverse outcome. Indeed, this conception of the palliative value of procedures extends beyond the domain of resolving relatively confined disputes between particular individuals or between particular individuals and the state. Even when the terrain is that of broader public interest, policy-based decision making (again, think of choosing the location for a garbage disposal facility) as opposed to determinating narrow questions of law or questions of fact of the "Who did what to whom?" variety, many people regard participatory entitlements as having an important civic component. Particularly in an era when parliamentary processes may seem too remote from the ordinary citizen and increasingly irrelevant to the reality of political power, the provision of hearing opportunities in relation to such decision making can heighten a sense of belonging, of being part of public life, of having a voice. In this sense, some kinds of hearings represent a surrogate for parliamentary processes and a form of direct participation in the democratic state.

Making decisions by way of hearings to which the members of the general public have access, even if they are not directly affected by the outcome, also serves as an important accountability mechanism in certain situations. The continuing vibrancy of open courtrooms reinforces this principle. When forced to take decisions within the framework of an open[2] hearing process, decision makers tend to be more careful and reflective in the ways they act and in the conclusions they ultimately reach. Their conduct is also that much more subject to public scrutiny and criticism. Indeed, to the extent that there are formal levels of accountability for substantive outcomes and probity of conduct (such as by way of a statutory right of appeal on the substance to the courts or as reflected in a misconduct complaints regime), those processes themselves may work better when functioning against the background of a prior hearing.

Many of the various assumptions on which the range of claims to participatory entitlement exist have never been subjected to rigorous empirical testing. While this may depend largely on the values of a traditional and dominant legal culture, the persistence of such assumptions cannot be denied nor can their penetration of the broader public psyche. As noted already, they now form an explicit part of our constitutional framework. The "principles of fundamental justice," interpreted by the Canadian courts as embodying primarily values of process, are a key element in one of the most significant provisions of the 1982 *Canadian Charter of Rights and Freedoms*. While, section 7's protections are subject to both legislative override under section 33(1) and to demonstrably justifiable derogations in terms of section 1, nonetheless, they have come to represent an important value in both the design and evaluation of certain kinds of administrative processes. They represent the Canadian equivalent of the "due process" protections of the Fifth and Fourteenth Amendments to the United States Constitution, amendments which at certain times in the constitutional history of that jurisdiction have played a vital role in enhancing the quality of both criminal and administrative justice.

---

2   This can take the form of either an oral hearing that the public may attend or a written hearing where all the relevant material is available to the public at large.

B. SOURCES OF PROCESS CLAIMS

1) Constitutional and *Quasi*-Constitutional

a) Procedural Fairness as a Transcendent Constitutional Value

As we have seen already, in a constitutional regime where the fundamental value is that of the sovereignty of the legislature or Parliament,
there would appear to be little basis for arguing that there are transcendent procedural values that prevail even in the face of explicit legislative
exclusion. Moreover, even for those judges who accept the existence of
an implied bill of rights acting as a constraint on Parliament and the
provincial legislative assemblies, this has never been acknowledged
explicitly as involving any procedural norms. In the cases in which it
was recognized, its content was substantive. On the other hand, one of
Canada's most famous administrative lawyers, Professor John Willis,
gave an account of Canadian procedural fairness law in 1939 that supported the inclusion of procedural entitlements within the reach of any
such implied bill of rights theory.[3] He concluded that, in most instances,
when the courts imposed procedural fairness requirements on an otherwise silent statute or in excess of that which the statute required explicitly, that exercise was actually far more one based upon underlying
constitutional values than an exercise in statutory interpretation.

Far more recently, L'Heureux-Dubé J. rendering the judgment of
the majority of the Supreme Court of Canada in *Board of Education of
the Indian Head School Division No. 19 of Saskatchewan* v. *Knight*,[4] spoke
in terms of a "general right to procedural fairness, autonomous of the
operation of any statute."[5] Later in that same judgment, however, she
considered whether the plaintiff's procedural entitlements had been
excluded either by the legislation or by contract. This is a strong indication that she did not accept the possibility of an argument that procedural fairness claims could withstand specific legislative exclusion.[6]

---

3   John Willis, "Administrative Law in Canada" (1939), 53 Harvard Law Review 251.
4   [1990] 1 S.C.R. 653 [*Knight*].
5   *Ibid.* at 668.
6   In his judgment in *Kioa* v. *West* (1985), 159 C.L.R. 550, at 610–11, Brennan J. of the
     High Court of Australia dismissed out of hand the possibility of transcendent
     procedural norms under the Australian Constitution: "There is no freestanding
     common law right to be accorded natural justice by the repository of a statutory
     power. There is no right to be accorded natural justice which exists independently of
     statute. . . . The supremacy of Parliament, a doctrine deeply imbedded in our
     constitutional law and congruent with our democratic traditions, requires the courts
     to declare the validity or invalidity of executive action taken in purported exercise of
     a statutory power in accordance with criteria express or implied by statute."

Nonetheless, particularly given the recent resurgence in Supreme Court recognition of underlying constitutional values,[7] there may, even now, still be a slight possibility that, by reference to process values recognized as part of the United Kingdom's unwritten constitution in 1867, the Preamble to the Canadian *Constitution Act* of that year could become the source of guarantees of procedural protections, guarantees that can withstand legislative abrogation.

b) *The Canadian Charter of Rights and Freedoms*

As noted already, however, the clearest source of constitutional protection for procedural claims in Canada is found in section 7 of the 1982 *Canadian Charter of Rights and Freedoms*. It enshrines a right to "the principles of fundamental justice" in the face of the deprivation or threatened deprivation of "life, liberty and security of the person." The *Charter* contains other process values, too, most notably, in section 11. However, as we shall see when the *Charter's* provisions are discussed in detail, the Supreme Court of Canada has confined the protections of section 11, by and large, to the processes of the criminal law. Moreover, the guarantees that section 7 of the *Charter* provides (and section 11, for that matter) are not absolute. Sections 7 and 11 are among the provisions of the *Charter* subject to the legislative override created by section 33(1) — the notwithstanding clause. After some initial doubts, it now seems accepted that the government can justify a derogation from the principles of fundamental justice by reference to section 1. There are demonstrably justifiable reasons in a free and democratic society for not providing the benefit of the "principles of fundamental justice" when "life, liberty and security of the person" are at stake.

c) **The** *Canadian Bill of Rights* **and Various Provincial Bills of Rights**

Section 2 of the *Charter* provides that its guarantee of rights and freedoms is without prejudice to "the existence of any other rights and freedoms that exist in Canada." Among the rights and freedoms that existed in Canada in 1982 were those contained in the 1960 *Canadian Bill of Rights*, sometimes even now referred to as the "Diefenbaker *Bill of Rights*" after its ostensible progenitor. The *Canadian Bill of Rights* is an ordinary Act of the federal Parliament. Its principal provision, section 2(e), states that the rights and freedoms that the *Bill of Rights* recognizes apply against even subsequent legislation unless that legislation is

---

7   Most notably in *Reference re Secession of Québec*, [1998] 2 S.C.R. 217 and *Reference re Remuneration of Judges of Provincial Court of Prince Edward Island*, [1997] 3 S.C.R. 3.

"expressly declared" in the relevant Act to "operate notwithstanding" the provisions of the Bill.

The courts have implicitly attributed to this provision the legitimacy associated with a "manner and form" requirement; they have not attributed to it the illegitimacy of an attempt by Parliament to bind its successors on matters of substance. Because of this, the *Bill of Rights* in its area of operation, the federal arena, has assumed the status of a somewhat higher order of legislation or, as it is sometimes described, *quasi*-constitutional legislation. As with the *Charter*, it provides a basis on which both primary legislation and actual decisions may be invalidated for not complying with its norms.[8]

The principal provisions of the *Canadian Bill of Rights* affecting procedural claims within the administrative process are sections 1(a) and 2(e). Section 1(a) provides a "due process" guarantee when "life, liberty, security of the person and *enjoyment of property* [emphasis added]" are at stake; section 2(e) ensures, "the right to a fair hearing in accordance with the principles of fundamental justice" whenever a person's "rights and obligations" are being determined. These provisions will be examined in more detail shortly and their reach will be compared to that of section 7 of the *Charter*. Suffice it to say, for present purposes, that the differences between the two instruments may mean that the *Bill of Rights* provides a useful source of constitutionally protected procedural rights in the federal domain in at least some administrative decision making not covered by the *Charter*.

At the provincial level, there exist at least two examples of legislation such as the *Canadian Bill of Rights*, Acts of provincial legislatures containing general procedural obligations and which are expressed to prevail over subsequent legislation in the absence of express declarations to the contrary. Thus, Quebec has a *Charter of Human Rights and Freedoms*[9] that provides the procedural guarantee of a "full and equal, public and fair hearing" whenever a judicial or *quasi*-judicial body is determining "rights and obligations."[10] By section 52, derogations from that right require express legislative provision to that effect. Similarly, in Ontario, section 32 of its *Statutory Powers Procedure Act*[11] specifies the need for an express legislative provision to override the very

---

8   See, in particular, the judgment of Beetz J. in *Singh* v. *Canada (Minister of Employment & Immigration)*, [1985] 1 S.C.R. 177 and *MacBain* v. *Canadian Human Rights Commission* (1985), 22 D.L.R. (4th) 119 (C.A.).

9   R.S.Q. 1977, c.C–12.

10   See ss. 23 and 56.

11   R.S.O. 1990, c. S. 22 (as amended by S.O. 1994, c. 27 and S.O. 1997, c. 23).

detailed procedural obligations that that Act imposes on a range of statutory authorities operating in that province.

C. GENERAL PROCEDURAL CODES

As just noted, the province of Ontario has a "general" procedural code applicable to certain broad categories of decision maker. In other words, it represents a general set of procedural norms that the legislators wanted to apply across significant segment of the administrative process. The precedents for such procedural codes can be found in the United States *Administrative Procedure Act* of 1946 and its counterparts in all the states of the Union. However, with the exception of the provinces of Alberta, then Ontario, and, now much more recently, Québec, such generalization exercises have not attracted legislative support in Canada though, in the federal domain, in the early to mid-1990s, Justice Canada explored the introduction of such a code.

The Alberta *Administrative Procedures Act*,[12] which is far less detailed than its Ontario equivalent, depends for its application on designation by way of an order promulgated by the Lieutenant Governor in Council or, as has happened on some occasions, specific incorporation into primary legislation. As for the Ontario *Act*, it is predicated on whether the decision maker in issue comes within the ambit of a formula or definition contained in the *Act* itself:

> a proceeding by a tribunal in the exercise of a statutory power of decision conferred by or under an Act of Legislature, where the tribunal is required by or under the Act or *otherwise by law* [emphasis added] to hold or to afford to the parties to the proceeding an opportunity for a hearing before making a decision.[13]

As with the limitation on the procedural provisions of the *Québec Charter of Human Rights and Freedoms*, the courts have interpreted the term "otherwise by law" as restricting the *Act*'s application to those bodies or tribunals that, under traditional common law, are expected to act in a judicial or *quasi*-judicial manner. In other words, it does not embrace all decision making that has an impact on individual or group interests. Absent express legislative specification, it applies only to those decision-making functions that bear some connection to the kind of roles

---

12   R.S.A. 1980, c. A. 2.
13   S. 3(1).

that the regular courts normally play — determining discrete disputes between limited parties by reference to relatively clear standards of evidence and law.

In 1996, after a lengthy gestation period, Québec built upon the generally expressed obligation of procedural fairness contained in its *Charter of Human Rights and Freedoms* by enacting an *Administrative Justice Act*.[14] This *Act* came into force on September 1, 1997, and applies to government departments and other statutory authorities over which the government exerts significant control through the appointment of members and also auxiliary personnel.[15] Whenever such authorities make an individual decision on the basis of standards or norms prescribed by law, they owe a general duty to act fairly. The *Act* then provides for other procedural protections, the operation of most of which is governed by other conditions and limitations.

D. SPECIFIC STATUTORY REGIMES

Quantitatively, by far the most important sources of procedural obligations are primary and subordinate legislation specifying requirements for either specific decision makers or groups of decision makers. Obviously, the relevant empowering legislation and the regulations, by-laws, or orders made under it represent the first point of inquiry whenever a question as to procedural entitlements arises. On many occasions, the inquiry will start and end there. However, some qualifications do have to be made to the proposition that, if the legislature or appropriate subordinate legislation-making authority has dealt explicitly with procedures, that is the end of the matter.

First, whether one is dealing with primary or subordinate legislation, questions can arise as to whether the provisions of the relevant legislation constitute a complete code. Has the manner in which the legislation been formulated excluded the possibility that the procedures laid down could be supplemented by reference to common law principles? If legislative attention to procedural issues seems to be otherwise comprehensive and no provision is made for representation by counsel at hearings, does this mean that no such supplementary claim

---

14   S.Q. 1996, c. 54.

15   A majority of the members must be appointed by either the Minister or the Lieutenant Governor in Council, and the personnel must be appointed by and remunerated under the *Public Service Act*.

can be made? Indeed, in this context, it is interesting to note that even as extensive a procedural code as that provided by the Ontario *Statutory Powers Procedure Act*, until recent amendments, contained a heading proclaiming it a "minimum code" of procedures for those bodies to which it applied.

Second and, perhaps conversely, questions can arise as to whether invalidity follows automatically from a statutory authority's failure to observe the procedural rules laid down. The courts treat certain procedural provisions as "mandatory" and which must be adhered to strictly possibly subject to informed waiver. Then there are procedures described as "directory" only and which, absent proof of prejudice to a party, will not result in invalidity. These may include, for example, minor deviations from prescribed forms and some time limit provisions.

With both primary and subordinate legislation, it is also important to keep in mind that, in some cases, the procedures adopted will be subject to scrutiny by reference to constitutional standards or norms of the species already identified. For procedures adopted through subordinate legislation, there is a further possibility for challenging apparently inadequate protections. The subordinate legislation — be it a regulation made by the lieutenant governor in council or rules made by the agency itself — may be alleged to be invalid as not falling within the scope of the subordinate legislation-making authority that the empowering primary legislation conferred. The courts sometimes adopt the posture that, in conferring authority to make rules of procedure, Parliament or the legislature did not intend the subordinate legislator to devise rules contrary to normal or common law procedural standards.[16]

It should also be realized that sometimes the procedural rules to which tribunals adhere do not have the status of subordinate legislation in that they are not based on a formal exercise of regulation-making power. However, even without status as subordinate legislation in the technical sense of that term, procedures may have legal force to the extent that they arise out of the legitimate exercise of some other form of statutory authority, such as a power to issue guidelines and directives.[17]

Beyond this are procedures that do not derive from any formal authority in the relevant primary legislation. Instead they represent

---

16 See, for example, *Joplin v. Vancouver (City) Chief Constable* (1982), 144 D.L.R. (3d) 285 (B.C.S.C.), aff'd. (1985), 20 D.L.R. (4th) 314 (B.C.C.A.).

17 See, for example, *Bezaire v. Windsor Roman Catholic Separate School Board* (1992), 9 O.R. (3d) 737 (Div. Ct.), in which procedural guidelines issued by a minister under statutory authority were held to give rise to enforceable procedural rights [*Bezaire*].

internal, informal rules, often developed over time and through experience. Conventional wisdom would have it that, absent an argument of implicit statutory authorization, general management, or residual authority contained in the statute, these informal procedures are not "law"; they do not create any legally enforceable entitlement to their observance. However, even if this view continues to prevail, there are at least two ways that an affected person might use such rules in a complaint that a statutory authority did not adhere to those procedures. First, to the extent that the common law rules of procedural fairness vary considerably from situation to situation, the fact that an agency *itself* has chosen a particular way of proceeding as reflected in its internal rules may provide good or strong evidence of what the common law should require of that agency. Second, as we will see below, in recent years, the Canadian courts have accepted that procedural entitlements may arise by way of "legitimate expectation." Individuals may develop these legally enforceable expectations on the basis of their knowledge of and reliance on such informal rules and on assurance by the decision-maker that they will be followed either generally or in a particular case.

E. THE COMMON LAW

1) The Threshold

For centuries, the common law courts have engrafted hearing requirements onto statutes that have made no specific provision for procedural protections. In an important nineteenth century English case, *Cooper v. Board of Works for Wandsworth District*,[18] Byles J. described this process as one whereby "the justice of the common law will supply the omission of the legislature."

There are at least three possible justifications for this posture. The first two are based on theories of statutory interpretation. Under one, the legislature has been forgetful; if it had directed its mind to the matter, it would have included a provision for a hearing. Under the second, the legislature has not been forgetful. Rather, it has recognized the force of the common law to the effect that hearings will be required in certain situations where the legislation is silent. Armed with this knowledge and still remaining silent, the legislature has implicitly but advertently provided for a hearing. The third theory is that espoused by L'Heureux-Dubé J. in *Knight* and already referred to: procedural fairness is a tran-

---

18 (1863), 143 E.R. 414 (C.P.) at 420.

scendent norm that applies to a broad range of governmental decision making. Although it can be trumped by legislative exclusion, it is up to the legislature to actually to do that and do it explicitly. Of the three theories, this last is probably the most realistic in that it does not depend on any artificial construct of legislative intention.

As explained in *Cooper*, the strongest claims for a hearing in the face of legislative silence traditionally arose in cases in which the claimant's property or physical person was being affected by a decision. It "has been repeatedly recognised, that no man is to be deprived of his property without his having an opportunity of being heard."[19] Thus, in *Cooper* itself, where the plaintiff's claim was sustained, the decision or order under attack led to the demolition of a partially completed building. Moreover, in the precedents referred to by the Court, it becomes clear that, at least in some contexts, property rights or interests were conceived of broadly. Thus, more than a century earlier in 1723, in *Dr. Bentley's Case*, the governing council of Cambridge University and the College of which Dr. Bentley was Master revoked his university degrees and status. He argued that they could not do so without adhering to the rules of natural justice. The court upheld his claim and, in so doing treated his degrees and status as a form of property.[20]

In what is reflective of modern law in this domain, *Cooper* also emphasized that it was not simply the nature of the interest at stake that determines whether or not a hearing should be granted. The impact of the decision on that interest and the sanction to be imposed are also relevant. For these purposes, Erle C.J. noted that the power in issue was one that could be exercised in relation to a building under construction as well as to a fully completed building. Beyond this, however, the Court was concerned with the usefulness and the costs of the hearing. At one level, this involved a very crude cost benefit analysis: would the cost and inconvenience of a hearing outweigh the benefits it could achieve particularly in light of the interests at stake? More precisely, there is a focus on what would go on at a hearing to make it worthwhile; what could perhaps lead to a better, fairer, or more informed decision. Implicit in *Cooper* is the assumption that hearings are well suited to determining matters of disputed fact. Did Cooper infringe the statute by not sending the notice that that Act required of anyone about to engage in construction? However, it seems that *Cooper* was not a case where that failure was being contested. Nonetheless, even though the inquiry

---

19   *Ibid.* at 417 (Erle C.J.).
20   (1723), 1 Str. 557; 93 E.R. 698 (K.B.)

was then reduced to what, if any, sanction should be imposed, the Court saw potential value in allowing the plaintiff the opportunity to make what in today's criminal law arena we would describe as a plea in mitigation — to try to convince the Board why it should not exercise its discretionary power with respect to sanction in the most extreme fashion.

In line with the theory that what the courts are doing in this kind of case is statutory interpretation, the Court also searched the statute for any legislative indications to support its conclusion that a hearing was required. Here, the Court focused on the fact that there was a statutory right of appeal from the district board to a metropolitan board. At one level, this was seen as an indication that those affected by the actions of a municipal board were entitled to a hearing at some point. Moreover, in a situation where the demolition of a building could take place before the hearing of any appeal and perhaps where the metropolitan board had no authority to rectify the situation by awarding damages or ordering reconstruction of the building, the Court could give effect to the legislative intention to provide a hearing only by holding that the board could not act under the relevant provision unless a hearing was held first. More generally, the Court also read into the existence of an appeal right the assumption that appeals are normally conducted on the basis of a first instance decision-making process in which the affected parties have had an opportunity to participate.

It is interesting to contrast the principal judgment in *Cooper* with subsequent evolutions in English (and Canadian) law. Erle C.J. eschewed any notion that the function in question had to be a judicial one before a court was justified in engrafting a hearing requirement onto an otherwise silent statute. Before long, however, this did become one of the essential tests for making an argument for a procedural entitlement. The function in question had to be a judicial or, at the very least, a *quasi*-judicial one.

This requirement proved a telling blow for many superficially just claims. The whole situation was worsened that much more by the fact that the courts never provided a consistent, clear sense of what constituted a judicial or *quasi*-judicial function as opposed to the kind of function that was generally treated as its antithesis: a purely administrative or, sometimes, "ministerial" one. In many later cases, the pragmatic functionalism of *Cooper* was ignored and replaced by the ritual incantation of a highly problematic formula. This is not the place for a detailed examination of the possible meanings of the terms judicial and *quasi*-judicial. With the exceptions of the operation of the procedural protections of the *Quebec Charter of Human Rights and Freedoms* and the Ontario *Statutory Powers Procedure Act*, and possibly also the application of the doctrine of issue estoppel to the decisions of tribunals, this classification exercise has disappeared from our law. Suffice it to say that for at least half a century, it acted as a severe brake on the evolution and expansion of procedural fairness claims within the modern administrative state, a state in which a much broader range of interests than traditional property rights has since come to be recognized *by legislation* as an integral concern of public law.

Fortunately, modern Canadian procedural fairness law has returned to the functionalist base that characterized *Cooper*. The two key modern Supreme Court of Canada authorities are the 1978 judgment in *Nicholson* v. *Haldimand-Norfolk Regional Board of Commissioners of Police*[21] and *Knight*, which has already been referred to several times. These judgments are important at two levels. First, they provide important clarifications of and changes to the theory of procedural fairness law. Each also concerns a domain where procedural fairness claims have had a very significant impact in recent years: that of statutory office holders and various forms of employment under a statutorily provided for or sanctioned contract.

At the level of theory, *Nicholson*'s contribution is in its acceptance that procedural entitlements should no longer depend absolutely on the function, in issue being classified as judicial or *quasi*-judicial. Relying upon English authority, Laskin C.J.C., for a majority of the Court, held that the distinction between judicial functions and merely or purely administrative ones should no longer determine procedural claims. While the traditional rules of procedure — generally described as the rules of natural justice — might be reserved for judicial or *quasi*-judicial functions, this was without prejudice to the possibility that some lesser category of procedural entitlement, described by the English courts as a "duty to act fairly," could apply to the exercise of purely administrative functions.

In *Nicholson*, that theory was deployed as part of a statutory interpretation exercise to reach the conclusion that Nicholson, a probationary police officer, was entitled to an opportunity ("whether orally or in writing as the Board might determine"[22]) to respond to criticisms of his performance before he was dismissed. The relevant regulation provided that chiefs of police and other police officers and constables were entitled to a "hearing" and an appeal against dismissal. However, it also stated this did not affect the authority of the Board over those with less than eighteen months of service (probationers). According to Laskin C.J.C., the Ontario Court of Appeal had erred in reading that provision as having the effect of denying *any* procedural entitlements to proba-

---

21 [1979] 1 S.C.R. 311.
22 *Ibid.* at 328.

tionary constables. On the contrary, he wrote, the only exclusionary effect that such a regulation had was to deny to probationers the full procedural or hearing protections accorded to permanent police officers. It left room for the imposition of some lesser form of procedures in the dismissal of a probationary constable such as Nicholson — hence the Court's statement that whether the hearing was an oral or written one was a matter for the Board to decide, not the Court.

Nicholson did not, however, answer all questions about the reach of the new procedural fairness doctrine. For present purposes, the most important of those questions were the following two: did the case create two levels of requirement — natural justice applicable to judicial and *quasi*-judicial functions and procedural fairness applicable to purely administrative functions? Did the judgment afford at least some level of procedural entitlement to those affected by *any* exercise of statutory or prerogative power, or was there still a domain where procedural rights could not be asserted? In other words, while the threshold had been lowered dramatically, did a threshold still exist?

The answers to these questions were not that long in coming. In an important concurring judgment in *Martineau* v. *Matsqui Inmate Disciplinary Board*,[23] Dickson J., (as he then was) stated that, in general, the courts should not treat natural justice and procedural fairness as two different standards dependent for their respective application on whether the function in issue was judicial or *quasi*-judicial, on the one hand, or administrative, on the other. It was better, where possible, to conceive of procedural entitlements as operating on a spectrum or a sliding scale, not one artificially punctuated by such a bright line distinction.

In a judgment concurred in Laskin C.J.C., Dickson J. did, however, acknowledge that the need to classify a function might be compelled by the incorporation of such a standard of differentiation into a statutory regime. However, today, the examples of such incorporation are few. As noted already, they do exist in the legislative formulae establishing the reach of the procedural protections afforded by the *Québec Charter of Human Rights and Freedoms* and the Ontario *Statutory Powers Procedure Act*. Also, in circumstances such as provided by *Nicholson* itself, where the Court is confronted by a statutory provision implicitly stipulating a full, oral, adversarial or true natural justice hearing for certain categories of rights and interests, it may still be necessary to talk explicitly of a lesser guarantee of procedural "fairness" for other categories of interest existing under that statute.

---

23   [1980] 1 S.C.R. 602.

Conversely, there may be occasions on which it is necessary to use the classification of functions and the old terminology to make the point that it was not part of the intention or effect of *Nicholson* to lower or lessen the procedural obligations of those classified as exercising judicial or *quasi*-judicial functions. In *Prassad* v. *Canada (Minister of Employment and Immigration)*,[24] the Court refers to the entitlement of administrative tribunals to "control their own procedures subject to the proviso that they comply with the rules of fairness and, where they exercise judicial or quasi-judicial functions, the rules of natural justice."

In a judgment rendered slightly before *Martineau*, Dickson J. also provided a list of non-exclusive factors or considerations that should be used in determining whether a function was judicial or *quasi*-judicial in those limited situations where that distinction mattered. The court should:

a) consider the language and the general context of the empowering legislation were to be considered;
b) inquire whether the decision or order "directly or indirectly affect[s] the rights and obligations" of the applicant for relief;
c) also consider as relevant whether the "adversary process" was involved; and, finally,
d) ask whether the issue at stake was one that necessitated the application of "substantive rules to many individual cases" — as opposed to one involving a determination by reference to "social and economic policy in a broad sense."

Positive answers to the last three questions would strongly indicate a judicial or quasi-judicial function.[25]

As for the question of whether there were now no limits to the reach of procedural fairness obligations, the Supreme Court responded that the threshold had indeed been only lowered, not eliminated.[26] This prevented the application of procedural fairness obligations to the Governor in Council in hearing an appeal from a CRTC decision on a Bell Canada rate application. Estey J. in delivering the judgment of the Court, described, perhaps far too expansively or imprecisely, such a Cabinet appeal as involving "legislative action in its purest form."[27] Moreover, he held, relying once again on English

---

24 [1989] 1 S.C.R. 560 at 568–69.
25 *Minister of National Revenue* v. *Coopers & Lybrand*, [1979] 1 S.C.R. 495 at 504.
26 *Attorney General of Canada* v. *Inuit Tapirisat of Canada*, [1980] 2 S.C.R. 735.
27 *Ibid.* at 754.

authority,[28] that legislative actions were excluded from the ambit of even the "new" duty to act fairly. This idea of the exclusion of "legislative functions" from the ambit of the procedural fairness doctrine was also reiterated in an oft-quoted statement of Le Dain J. in another Supreme Court of Canada judgment, though not one where the outcome turned on the distinction:

> [A] duty of procedural fairness [lies] in every public authority making an administrative decision *which is not of a legislative nature* and which affects the rights, privileges and interests of an individual [emphasis added].[29]

Dickson J. provided a somewhat different formulation on at least two occasions:

> A purely ministerial decision, on broad grounds of public policy, will typically afford the individual little or *no* procedural protection [emphasis added].[30]

Even more recently, in *Knight v. Indian Head School Division No. 19*, where once again nothing really hinged on the definition, L'Heureux-Dubé J. stated:

> [N]ot all administrative bodies are under a duty to act fairly. Over the years, legislatures have transferred to administrative bodies some of the duties they have traditionally performed. Decisions of a legislative and general nature can be distinguished in this respect from acts of a more administrative and specific nature, which do not entail such a duty. . . . The finality of a decision will also be a factor to consider. A decision of a preliminary nature will not in general trigger the duty to act fairly, whereas a decision of a more final nature may have such an effect.[31]

What can be deduced from these various statements and their application in other judgments? First, it seems clear that the Canadian courts will not see any obligation of procedural fairness arising in the context of legislative action. For these purposes, legislative action obviously

---

28 *Bates v. Lord Hailsham of St. Marylebone*, [1972] 1 W.L.R. 1373 (Ch.), a case concerning denial of procedural fairness claims to a group of lawyers directly affected by the promulgation of subordinate legislation that abolished the tariff of fees applicable to solicitors' work.

29 *Cardinal v. Director of Kent Institution*, [1985] 2 S.C.R. 643 [*Cardinal*].

30 In *Martineau v. Matsqui Inmate Disciplinary Board*, above note 23 at 628 and in *Homex Realty & Development Co. Ltd. v. Village of Wyoming*, [1980] 2 S.C.R. 1011 at 1051.

31 *Knight*, above, note 4 at 670.

involves the making of both primary and subordinate[32] legislation, save perhaps subordinate legislation directed at a specific individual and that has the effect of resolving an ongoing dispute.[33] In some senses, the main significance of this exclusion may be that it eliminates in the short term any possible contention that common law procedural fairness could mandate an equivalent of the United States *Administrative Procedure Act's* "notice and comment" procedure as a prelude to the successful promulgation of subordinate legislation.

Beyond this, "legislative action," as conceived by both Estey and L'Heureux-Dubé JJ., extends to those tasks formerly performed by the legislature itself, a concept for which some enlightenment is provided by both the nature of the problem before the Governor in Council in *Inuit Tapirisat*, a rate balancing exercise of polycentric dimensions, and L'Heureux-Dubé J.'s description of the excluded functions as those of a "legislative and general nature." Taken together, these terms suggest that procedural fairness claims will not be readily generated in relation to broad, policy-based decision-making affecting a range of constituencies. Indeed, this concern is also the essential thrust of Dickson J.'s statements that the rules of procedural fairness will have little or no application in the domain of ministerial decisions taken by reference to broad policy considerations. Moreover, such a formulation also leaves open the possibility that there will be no claim to procedural protections in at least some contexts in which individual interests in real property are at stake notwithstanding the fact that this was the interest that the courts historically valued above virtually all others in this domain.[34]

However, the courts still have a difficult time drawing the line between policy making that is too broad in its purposes and reach to attract procedural fairness obligations and that which has a sufficiently narrow or individualized focus to justify procedural claims. Thus, in *Bezaire* v. *Windsor Roman Catholic Separate School Board,*[35] the Divisional Court, held that there should have been a consultation process

---

32 See, for example, *Re Groupe des éleveurs de volailles de l'Est de l'Ontario and Canadian Chicken Marketing Agency* (1984), 14 D.L.R. (4th) 151 (F.C.T.D.).

33 As in *Homex Realty and Development Co. Ltd. v. Village of Wyoming*, [1980] 2 S.C.R. 1011, where a by-law was passed deeming a subdivision plan not to be a registered plan of subdivision, this being the culmination of a dispute between the municipality and the developer over responsibility for the cost of servicing the lots in the planned subdivision.

34 See, for example, the post-*Nicholson* judgment of the Manitoba Court of Appeal in *Favor* v. *Winnipeg (City)* (1988), 47 D.L.R. (4th) 693 (Man. C.A.), applying the pre-*Nicholson* judgment of *Calgary Power v. Copithorne*, [1959] S.C.R. 24.

35 *Bezaire*, above note 17.

before the board closed nine schools within its jurisdiction. The Court distinguished decisions to close schools from those of reallocating classes of students within existing schools. This enabled the Court to avoid an earlier Ontario Court of Appeal judgment which held that a reallocation policy did not attract procedural fairness obligations.[36] It is, however, highly questionable whether school closing decisions are any more limited in their policy dimensions than the reassignment of classes of student and, at least from the point of view of those most directly affected, the pupils and their parents, the dislocative impact of both decisions is pretty much the same — the disruption caused by having to switch schools outside of the normal pattern of educational progression and, in many cases, the greater travel involved in reaching the new school.

The difficulties inherent in this new standard or threshold for the common law imposition of procedural fairness obligations also emerge dramatically from the diametrically opposed positions of a Federal Court, Trial Division judge and the Federal Court of Appeal in *Canadian Association of Regulated Importers* v. *Canada (Attorney General)*.[37] The minister had changed the allocation of import quotas for hatching eggs and chickens and the "historic" importers had claimed that, because of the economic impact of that change, they should have been given notice and an opportunity to respond before the change was put into effect. Recognizing that economic impact and the relatively small number of "historic" importers (meaning that the costs of providing a participatory opportunity would not be unduly high) Reed J., in the Trial Division, held that there was a procedural entitlement. She also stated that it was not appropriate to describe such an exercise of power as legislative. The mere fact that it involved policy was not determinative, and the importers did not need to establish a common law "right" to import in order to succeed. On appeal, this decision was reversed. Linden J.A., for the Court, held that, regardless of the numbers affected and the identity of the official responsible, changing quota policy was a legislative or policy decision excluded from the reach of procedural fairness obligations by reference to the tests established in *Inuit Tapiri-sat* and *Martineau*. He also noted that, in a number of other instances but not here, Parliament had stipulated participatory opportunities in the exercise of policy-making functions.

---

36   *Vanderkloet v. Leeds & Grenville (County Board of Education)* (1985), 20 D.L.R. (4th) 738 (C.A.).

37   [1993] 3 F.C. 199 (T.D.), rev'd [1994] 2 F.C. 247 (C.A.).

What seems to emerge from these contrasting judgments is a great deal of judicial uncertainty over the outer reaches of procedural fairness obligations. Clarification by the Supreme Court of Canada is needed. In the meantime, the paradigmatic situation for the implication of procedural fairness obligations, *Nicholson* notwithstanding, remains one where, in Le Dain J.'s terms, "the rights, privileges and interests of an individual" or a relatively discrete group of individuals are being affected on the basis of provisions approaching objective standards and criteria. To all of this, L'Heureux-Dubé J. would add a presumption against judicial implication of any procedural fairness obligations in situations of non-final decision making, an issue to which I return below.

All of this is not meant to suggest that *Nicholson* has not had an impact; it obviously has. It has expanded the situations in which individuals affected directly and personally by decision-making can claim procedural fairness. At this point, it is instructive to return to the specific domain at issue in both *Nicholson* and *Knight*, statutory forms of employment, a matter that was explored as part of the growing interaction between private and public law principles in chapter 1.

In the classic 1963 judgment of the House of Lords in *Ridge* v. *Baldwin*,[38] the Court held that the Chief Constable of Brighton was entitled as a public officer holder to the benefit of the principles of natural justice before he was dismissed from his position. Lord Reid, in one of the leading judgments, stated that, in order to apply the rules of natural justice, it was necessary to distinguish among three categories of employment: those who held a statutory office from which they could be dismissed only for cause, those who held a statutory office but only at the pleasure of the appointing authority, and those whose status was under an ordinary employment contract. Only the first category was entitled to the benefit of the rules of natural justice.

In *Nicholson*, Laskin C.J.C. acknowledged this situation. However, even though there was no mention in the relevant statute and regulation that probationary police officers could be dismissed only for cause, he was prepared to read that into the statute. This interpretation virtually elevated Nicholson to the same status as Chief Constable Ridge. In effect it lowered the test or standards for establishing the existence of a statutory office from which there can be dismissal only for cause.

Indeed, this can be seen as part of a sustained effort by a majority of the Supreme Court of Canada to accord a wider range of persons employed under statute the status of a public office holder. Dickson J.,

---

38 (1963), [1964] A.C. 40 (H.L. Eng.).

in a judgment rendered between *Nicholson* and *Knight* empasized this tendency, in sustaining the procedural claims of a university professor-who had been suspended: "A high standard of justice is required when the right to continue in one's profession or employment is at stake."[39]

Also noteworthy is that Laskin C.J.C. clearly intimated in *Nicholson* that, had it been necessary, he would almost certainly have re-evaluated Lord Reid's exclusion of offices held at pleasure from the benefits of procedural fairness claims. It was to this point that L'Heureux-Dubé J. and a majority of the Supreme Court of Canada returned in *Knight*. Knight's position as superintendent of a school board was one held at pleasure; nonetheless, he was entitled to a degree of procedural fairness. Even though the "pleasure" of the board was a sufficient basis for dismissing him and even though there was no need for legal cause, Knight was entitled to the opportunity to try to persuade the board to change its mind. More generally, the Court saw such broad discretionary powers as involving implications for the public interest. Requiring a hearing would impose better controls on and ensure greater public accountability for their exercise.

A further extension of the reach of the obligations of procedural fairness in statutory employment also emerges from *Knight*. In holding that Knight's status had a "sufficient statutory flavour" to take it out of the "pure master and servant" category,[40] L'Heureux-Dubé J. referred to Lord Reid's third category, those who were subject to the common law of employment. In so doing, she used language that narrowed the range of situations in which employees of statutory bodies could be denied procedural fairness.

Knight did not, however, eliminate that third category. Obviously, it will still be necessary in some cases to determine whether a person is an office holder or a mere employee albeit one employed by a statutory body and authorized by statute. While the case law on this point is not satisfactory, it does identify criteria for determining whether such a person is an office holder: the specific creation of the position in the relevant statutory regime and the specification in that regime of the incidents of the position — the powers and responsibilities of the person appointed.[41]

---

39 *Kane v. Board of Governors of the University of British Columbia*, [1980] 1 S.C.R. 1105 at 1113.
40 *Knight*, above note 4 at 672.
41 For these purposes, compare *Semchuk v. Board of Education of Regina School Division No.4 of Saskatchewan* (1986), 26 Admin. L.R. 88 (Sask. Q.B.), aff'd (1987), 37 D.L.R. (4th) 738 (Sask. C.A.) (graphic artist employed by school board was a mere employee) and *Hill v. University College of Cape Breton* (1991), 81 D.L.R. (4th) 300 (N.S.S.C. T.D.) (president of the University held to be an office holder).

As a comparison between *Knight* and *Nicholson* also reveals, the delineation between an office holder at pleasure and someone who can be dismissed only for cause may be equally problematic. Why is Knight, the director of education, in the first category while Nicholson, the probationary police constable, is in the second? Now that procedural fairness applies to both situations, the categories may not be all that legally significant as far as procedural entitlements are concerned, unless there is generally a difference in the level of procedures to which each is entitled. However, at least at the substantive level, the difference may be highly significant in that the grounds for removing an office holder at pleasure remain open-ended, while "cause" acts as an important constraint on the prerogatives of those responsible for office holders.[42] There is also a question as to whether there should be any claim to a hearing at all when an office holder at pleasure is being removed not (as in *Knight*) for any reasons specific to the performance of that person's responsibilities but for other non-personal reasons. Perhaps the position held has simply been eliminated[43] or the holder was a political appointee and now a new political party is in power.

Wells v. *Newfoundland*[44] may well have settled the first of these two examples. There, the Supreme Court of Canada held that the government owed Wells no duty of procedural fairness in a process whereby the board of which he was a member was abolished and he was not appointed to the successor agency. This was so notwithstanding the fact that he could otherwise be removed only for cause. The second example remains an open matter.

More than statutory employees have benefited from this broader conception of the categories of individuals who can claim procedural

---

42   Thus, in *Dewar* v. *Ontario* (1996), 30 O.R. (3d) 334 (Div. Ct.), aff'd. (1998), 37 O.R. (3d) 170 (C.A.), and *Murphy* v. *Ontario (Attorney General)* (1996), 28 O.R. (3d) 220 (G.D.), the ability of the incoming Ontario Conservative government to dismiss NDP appointees to the Ottawa Police Services Board and the board of Ontario Hydro respectively was defeated by the Courts' classification of each position as an office from which there could be dismissal only for cause.

43   This may also be an argument in the case of offices from which there can be dismissal only for cause. For these purposes, compare *Lund* v. *Estevan (City) Police Commissioners* (1993), 18 Admin. L.R. (2d) 245 (Sask. Q.B.), and *Vaydik* v. *Northwest Territories (Minister of Personnel)* (1991), 48 Admin. L.R. 95 (N.W.T.S.C.).

44   [1999] 3 S.C.R. 199. *Wells* is, however, a problematic judgment in another sense. The judgment seems premised at several points on the notion that the whole idea of tribunal members as "office holders" is outmoded and should be abandoned. It is not at all clear what the precise ramifications of this would be for the issues currently under discussion. This aspect of the judgment has already been discussed in chapter 1.

fairness. Under the previous law, in which the classification of functions played such a vital role, part of the conventional definition of a judicial function was one which involved a final determination of an individual's rights. After *Nicholson* the language of the test for procedural unfairness changed from "determines" to "affects," and embraced "interests and privileges" as well as "rights."[45] This greatly expanded the range of situations in which claims could be made. No longer was it necessary to identify the claimant as the holder of a pre-existing legal right rather than the possessor of a mere privilege or someone who was applying for but did not yet have a right.

Correctional law (penitentiary discipline and parole) provided a striking example. Previously, a sentence to time in custody was treated as involving a surrender of rights. Now, those subject to the correctional process achieved recognition as beneficiaries of procedural fairness. While the exigencies of the situation might sometimes demand action first and a hearing subsequently,[46] nonetheless, procedural obligations were attached to disciplinary decisions in a correctional law context which affected the amount of time served,[47] the location where a prisoner was detained,[48] and the continuation of parole and other forms of less secure custody.[49]

As well, those benefitting from various forms of social assistance, previously characterized as a "mere privilege," became entitled to procedural protections when their continued access to that assistance was threatened. For example, in a judgment delivered very shortly after *Nicholson*, the Ontario Court of Appeal in *Re Webb and Ontario Housing Corporation*[50] accepted that Webb, who occupied government-subsidized housing, deserved procedural fairness before the corporation's board of directors passed a resolution to make application to the court to terminate her tenancy.

---

45 See, for example, *Ibid.*
46 See, for example, *Ibid.*
47 See, for example, *Bull v. Prison for Women Disciplinary Tribunal* (1986), 25 Admin. L.R. 229 (F.C.T.D.).
48 See, for example, *Williams v. Canada (Regional Transfer Board, Prairie Region)* (1993), 15 Admin. L.R. (2d) 83 (F.C.A.).
49 See, for example, *Latham v. Canada (Solicitor General)* (1984), 5 Admin. L.R. 70 (F.C. T.D.).
50 (1978), 93 D.L.R. (3d) 187 (Ont. C.A.).

In *Webb* and elsewhere,[51] however, there continued to be a sense that those applying for licences and various other forms of government "largesse"[52] were not entitled to any degree of procedural fairness. In delivering the judgment of the Court in *Webb*, MacKinnon A.C.J.O. suggested that procedural entitlements were restricted to those who had been allocated government subsidized housing; no procedural fairness requirements attached to the allocation decision itself.

It is easy to appreciate the court's concerns with the costs of imposing hearing requirements on allocative decisions such as this, particularly when the number of applications is large and the available "places" few. Nonetheless, what needs to be recognized is that such decision making follows a process. Generally, applications are made in writing with supporting material, all that material is evaluated, and a decision is made according to established criteria. In most instances, good public administration demands that form of process. It is in that context that statements about the procedural fairness demands of applicants have to be evaluated and read as really saying that applicants have no claim to anything beyond the standard application procedure that the decision maker designed often for the purposes of administering effectively a high-volume jurisdiction.

Indeed, later jurisprudence makes it clear that it is impossible to generalize about access to procedural fairness demands for mere applicants. The nature of the interest at stake and the legislative framework within which the decision is taken may prompt the courts to recognize an applicant's demands for procedural fairness. For example, in *Hutfield* v. *Board of Fort Saskatchewan General Hospital District No. 98*,[53] legislative indicia (an "investigation" requirement) coalesed with the individual interest at stake (hospital privileges for an established physician), and a concern for the public interest (the range of services available to that doctor's patients) produce an entitlement to procedural fairness. The relevant committee of the board that was considering the doctor's application should have afforded him partcipatory opportunities.

---

51   See, for example, the English judgment of *McInnes* v. *Onslow-Fane*, [1978] 1 W.L.R. 1520 (Ch.), which held that an applicant for a boxing manager's licence was not entitled to procedural fairness. The regulatory body did not have to reveal to him what troubled it about his application, nor did it have to give him an opportunity to respond to that point.

52   As with "mere privilege," a loaded term in itself.

53   (1986), 24 Admin. L.R. 250 (Alta. Q.B.), aff'd (1988), 31 Admin. L.R. 311 (Alta. C.A.).

Perhaps even in high-volume jurisdictions, there may well be a claim for a hearing by a person whose application is being evaluated on the basis of information of which they are not aware, such as undisclosed allegations or suspicions of misconduct.[54] Some support for this position can be found in the judgment of the Federal Court of Appeal in *Lazarov* v. *Secretary of State of Canada*.[55] The Court placed an obligation of disclosure on the minister when he was of a mind to deny a citizenship application on the basis of information that had not come out at an earlier hearing before the Citizenship Court.

Much more recently, the Supreme Court recognized, without any detailed discussion, that the minister owed procedural fairness obligations to an over stayer who applied for permission to be allowed, on humanitarian and compassionate grounds, to apply for permanent residence in Canada without leaving the country. In *Baker* v. *Canada (Minister of Citizenship and Immigration)*,[56] the Court apparently approved the concession of the parties that Baker clearly had limited procedural entitlements notwithstanding the breadth of the discretion conferred on the minister. In terms of Le Dain J.'s formulation in *Cardinal*, the decision was one that affected her "rights, privileges and interests." This left as the only real issue whether those entitlements were more than minimal. It may, however, be of significance that, in deciding that the requirements were more than merely minimal, the Supreme Court emphasized the individual focus of the relevant inquiry and the absence of significant polycentric dimensions. Whether this implies that in the case of some kinds of polycentric decision-making affecting interests, there will be no, as opposed to minimal, procedural entitlements may, therefore, still remain an open question.

Indeed, even in individualized decision making, it is still necessary to take account of *Idziak* v. *Canada (Minister of Justice)*.[57] Cory J. described the minister's decision on whether to actually surrender an alleged fugitive from justice to a foreign power after a warrant of committal had been issued as "being at the extreme legislative end of *continuum* of administrative decision-making."[58] By this, he presumably

---

54   For example, where an application for admission to medical school may be evaluated on the basis of undisclosed allegations of sexual harassment in an undergraduate setting as well as the standard package of information generated by the applicant.

55   [1973] F.C. 927 (C.A.).

56   [1999] 2 S.C.R. 817 [*Baker*].

57   [1992] 3 S.C.R. 631.

58   *Ibid.* at 659.

meant that the Minister's decision was one that depended far more on unreviewable political considerations having to do with Canada's relationships with other powers than the particular circumstances of the affected individual. Because of this, the applicant's claims to further procedures after a full extradition hearing which had led to the warrant of committal were minimal at most, particularly given the normal assumption that, save in exceptional cases, surrender will follow pretty much automatically from the making of a such an order.

2) The Content

One point should be clear from the evolution of the legal threshold for any kind of procedural fairness: with the more expansive reach of modern common law imposing at least some common law procedural fairness obligations has come a much more diverse, context-sensitive approach to what constitutes sufficient procedural fairness protections. Indeed, as is apparent from the foundation judgment of *Nicholson*, the closer a decision-making function is to the legislative end of the spectrum, the fewer the procedural fairness obligations of the decision maker. Purely administrative decisions may now be caught in the web of procedural fairness law. What is sufficient to meet those requirements will, in the terminology of many of the judgments in this area, be minimal. What the courts needed to develop was a carefully calibrated series of factors or considerations that would assist in the assessment of how concentrated or full the procedural fairness obligations of particular decision makers would be.

It is clear that in the development of procedural fairness jurisprudence, the courts went a considerable way to identify the indicators of the extent of procedural fairness obligations. Aside from the obvious inquiries as to what is the best way to get at the information and arguments that are relevant to the exercise of the particular statutory or prerogative power, the courts have also recognized here, as in the determination of the prior threshold issue, that certain interests require greater procedural protections than others.

In *Nicholson*, the Court accepted that probationary police constables were entitled to certain procedural protections, but was not prepared to attribute to someone with that limited status more then minimal procedural entitlements. Laskin C.J.C. stated that whether the board thereafter heard Nicholson in writing or orally was a matter for its discretion. In contrast, Julius Kane, the tenured university professor, whether justifiably or not, was thought to possess a status that demanded a high level of procedural protection when it was under threat. In *Idziak* just discussed, the allegedly political character of the minister's decision coupled with the legislation's provision of a full hearing at an earlier point prevented a person subject to extradition from asserting other than minimal procedural fairness entitlements at the stage where the minister was deciding whether or not to surrender him to a foreign power. In contrast, Baker, the over stayer, was treated as having a significant interest in resisting enforced removal from Canada. While not going as far as entitling her to the full panoply of procedural rights normally characteristic of the regular courts in the exercise of their criminal and civil jurisdictions, this interest was certainly sufficient to justify a claim for more than simply the minimal procedures afforded by earlier Federal Court jurisprudence.

It was not, however, until L'Heureux-Dubé J.'s judgment in *Baker* that the Supreme Court really attempted to lay out authoritatively a methodology for dealing with the content question. Here, at long last, by reference to a range of factors or considerations that need to be taken into account, the Court provided some detailed guidance for lower courts confronting issues of this kind. Moreover, while there is nothing too surprising or novel in that list of factors or considerations, there is reason to believe that not only its endorsement but also the way in which it was applied to the facts in *Baker* will be useful in subsequent jurisprudence.

Not surprisingly, the first three factors parrot those specified in *Knight* and elsewhere as relevant to determine whether or not there are any procedural fairness obligations: the nature of the decision to be made; the precise statutory context in the sense of both the purpose of the relevant statute and the particular terms and context in which the relevant power exists; and the significance of the decision to those affected. With an eye to the facts of this case, L'Heureux-Dubé J. does, however, provide two useful points of detail. In terms of the statutory context, the absence of any right of appeal and the inability of those affected to seek any form of reconsideration are identified as factors pointing in the direction of a hearing. She also, by reference to English authority, alludes to the fact that the nature of the interest affected may have a decisive effect in that it will elevate the extent of procedural claims in situations where the other indicators may not be strong. Presumably, this foreshadows the discussion to follow in the judgment on whether the procedural claims of an over stayer are anything other than minimal, given the broad discretion conferred not on a tribunal but a minister of the Crown.

In addition, two further factors are provided in what is then described as a non-exclusive list. The first is the legitimate expectations of the person seeking the decision. Here too, there is no great surprise. Given the Supreme Court's earlier endorsement of this doctrine as a generator of procedural claims, it has clearly become part of the framework of Canadian procedural fairness law. What, however, is interesting is that it makes clear what was not clear in the foundation Supreme Court judgments. As well as generating procedural fairness claims where none could otherwise be advanced,[59] the doctrine also can serve as an enhancer of claims in situations where some procedural fairness is already an entitlement. Second, the Court recognizes, that tribunal or decision-maker choices of procedures are worthy of respect where either the statute confers an explicit discretion as to the content of procedures on the decision-maker or that decision-maker has expertise in such matters. This is very significant because it amounts to long overdue acceptance that the courts do not always have a monopoly on what constitute appropriate procedures in all contexts. In some situations at least, they should be deferential to agency and tribunal choice in such matters.

On the facts of the particular case, the Court concluded that the requirements of procedural fairness were more than minimal. While the minister had a broad discretion, while there were reasons to respect ministerial choice of the process to be used in dealing with such matters, and while there were no factors generating a legitimate expectation claim, the decision was one that "in practice has exceptional importance to the lives of those with an interest in the result — the claimant and his or her own family members."[60]

It is however significant that the Court rejected most of the details of the applicant's procedural fairness claims: an oral interview with the decision maker, notice to her children and the other parent of the interview, and the right of all to be assisted by counsel and to make submissions at the interview. The Court's response was that a paper hearing as conducted in the present case would suffice — one in which the applicant could submit an application with supporting documentation. Nonetheless, the significance of the applicant's interest did lead to the upholding of two other procedural claims. She was entitled to reasons,

---

59   In the foundation Canadian judgment of *Old St. Boniface Residents' Association Inc. v. Winnipeg (City)*, [1990] 3 S.C.R. 1170 at 1204, Sopinka J. gave the impression that the doctrine's operation was confined to producing procedural entitlements where none at all existed previously: "It affords a party affected by the decision of a public official an opportunity to make representations in circumstances in which there would otherwise be no such opportunity."

60   *Baker*, above note 56 at para. 31.

and the decision maker, by reference to a quite strict standard, had by the terms of his decision created a reasonable apprehension of bias.

Baker has obviously not provided a clear basis for answering all questions as to the detail of procedures to be followed in particular cases. However, it does provide a rational framework for dealing with such claims, particularly when coupled with the pragmatic aspects of the detail of the existing common law surrounding particular procedural claims. I will develop this detail below.

3) Substantive Fairness and Natural Justice

The very term "natural justice" is at least colloquially redolent of morality and substantive entitlements. In the English common law development of the grounds of review, there are examples of what might be characterized as review on the basis of substantive unfairness, as well as a more generalized sense that there is not really a sharp divide between procedure and substance. This is reflected most commonly in the cases where the English courts have reviewed decisions on the basis of inconsistency,[61] lack of proportionality,[62] and irrationality.[63]

In contrast, Canadian law has steadfastly refused to attribute any substantive content to the concepts of fairness and natural justice. Two situations in particular exemplify this judicial posture. First, the Supreme Court, as we will see in detail in the next section, has rejected any substantive content in the doctrine of legitimate expectation. On all three occasions on which it has confronted this doctrine, the Court has reiterated that it is purely procedural[64] in spite of some movement in English and Australian law in the direction of imbuing it with limited substantive content. Similarly, the Supreme Court has rejected out of hand claims that a decision may be tainted simply on the basis that it is inconsistent with previous rulings of the particular tribunal or agency.[65] Only where there is operational inconsistency in the sense of

---

61   *H.T.V. Ltd.* v. *Price Commission*, [1976] I.C.R. 170 (C.A.)

62   *R.* v. *Barnsley Metropolitan Borough Council, ex parte Hook*, [1976] 3 All E.R. 452 (C.A).

63   In *R.* v. *Minister for Civil Service, ex parte Council of Civil Service Unions*, [1985] A.C. 374 (H.L. Eng.), Lord Diplock purported to reduce the grounds of judicial review of administrative action to three core grounds: illegality, irrationality, and procedural impropriety.

64   *Old St. Boniface Residents' Association Inc.* v. *Winnipeg (City)*, [1990] 3 S.C.R. 1170; *Reference re Canada Assistance Plan*, [1991] 2 S.C.R. 525; *Baker*, above note 56.

65   *Domtar Inc.* v. *Québec (Commission d'appel en matière des lésions professionnelles)*, [1993] 2 S.C.R. 756.

the same person or body being confronted with conflicting or irreconcilable rulings on the same matter is this a basis for judicial review in
Canadian administrative law.[66] As well as these two explicit rejections,
there is a total lack of authority in Canadian law on proportionality as a
ground of review.

To this point, the same is largely true of the reach of the "principles
of fundamental justice" as enshrined in section 7 of the *Canadian Charter of Rights and Freedoms*. As opposed to the equivalent provision in
the *Canadian Bill of Rights*, section 2(e), the entitlement to fundamental justice is not expressed in terms of the "right to a fair hearing." This
has led the Supreme Court to accept that "fundamental justice" does
have a substantive component. However, the impact of this has for the
most part been confined to the criminal and *quasi*-criminal contexts.
There, it has been accepted that conceptions of fundamental justice
preclude the existence of absolute liability offences.[67] Criminal laws
can also be struck down on the basis that they are overly broad or
vague.[68] There is obvious room for the invocation of this ground of
review in the domain of administrative law which affects "life, liberty
and security of the person." Thus, as we have seen already, there have
been limited examples of laws being struck down or read down
because of the breadth of the discretion they have conferred on an
administrative official or authority with the ability to affect the protected rights.[69] However, this remains a largely undeveloped domain.

FURTHER READINGS

MACDONALD, R.A., "Procedural Due Process in Canadian
   Constitutional Law, Natural Justice and Fundamental Justice"
   (1987), 39 U. Florida L.R. 217

MULLAN, D.J., "Fairness: The New Natural Justice?" (1975), 25 U.T.L.J.
   251

MULLAN, D.J., "Natural Justice and Fairness — Substantive as Well as
   Procedural Standards for Review of Administrative Decision-
   Making?" (1982), 27 McGill L.J. 250

---

66 *British Columbia Telephone Co. v. Shaw Cable Systems (B.C.) Ltd.*, [1995] 2 S.C.R. 739.
67 *Reference re Section 94(2) of Motor Vehicle Act (British Columbia)*, [1985] 2 S.C.R. 486.
68 R. v. *Nova Scotia Pharmaceutical Society*, [1992] 2 S.C.R. 606.
69 See, for example, R. v. *Morgentaler*, [1988] 1 S.C.R. 30; *Wilson v. British Columbia
   (Medical Services Commission)*, [1989] 2 W.W.R. 1 (B.C.C.A.).

TUCKER, E., "The Political Economy of Administrative Process: A Preliminary Inquiry" (1987), 25 Osgoode Hall L.J. 555

WILLIS, J., "Administrative Law in Canada" (1939), 53 Harvard L.R. 251

CHAPTER 9

LEGITIMATE EXPECTATION

A. INTRODUCTION

When the courts are deciding whether the common law requires those exercising statutory or prerogative power to observe the principles of procedural fairness, usually they focus on the general nature of the power being exercised rather than the specific situation of the affected person.[1]

On occasion, however, the Canadian courts have justified their imposition of procedural fairness requirements on the basis of the particular circumstances of the individual case. Thus, in *T.E. Quinn Truck Lines Ltd.* v. *Ontario (Minister of Transportation and Communications)*,[2] Laskin C.J.C. held that, because a of delay in dealing with a report containing a recommendation, the minister had to give the applicant for a trucking licence a further opportunity to make representations. This opportunity would not have been available had the minister dealt with the relevant report promptly.

In other British Commonwealth jurisdictions, this individualized imposition of procedural fairness obligations has been most dramatic in the evolution of the doctrine of legitimate expectation. In certain instances, individuals affected by the exercise of a statutory or preroga-

---

1   For a clear example of this methodology, see *Durayappah* v. *Fernando*, [1967] 2 A.C. 337 (P.C. Cey.).

2   [1981] 2 S.C.R. 657.

tive power can, as a result of particular circumstances, expect that they will be given a hearing or consulted before it is in fact exercised.

A very early manifestation of this doctrine is Lord Denning M.R.'s concurring judgment in *R. v. Liverpool Corporation, ex parte Liverpool Taxi Fleet Operators' Association.*[3] Here, municipal officials had given an undertaking to a trade association that the City of Liverpool would not increase the number of available taxi licences without first consulting the Association. At least judged by the standards of the day, such a policy decision would not, independently of the circumstances of the particular case, have generated a claim by the trade association to participatory entitlement. However, Lord Denning was prepared to hold that the City officials' undertaking generated a legitimate expectation of consultation to which the court should give legal recognition.

Since the doctrine focuses on the reasonable and actual assumptions that persons have in dealing with government, its root is one found in the need to protect reasonable expectations. However, it also has as its focus the maintenance of credibility in the functioning of government. Standards of decent public administration and the reputation of government at a macro level depend at least in some measure on the extent to which governments deal with people consistently and with equal respect. Indeed, as will be discussed below, considerations such as this have led some courts and commentators to suggest that the doctrine should not be confined to situations where the applicant for relief has both known of and relied on an assurance or practice. Others have also argued that one of the chief benefits of recognizing an expansive doctrine of legitimate expectation is that it enhances democratic values. As David Wright has suggested, there may, however, be dangers in pushing this conception of the role of the doctrine too far. Although the doctrine is to protect the participatory expectations derived from consistent patterns of prior consultation, it may well cement the position of already powerful persons and groups at the expense of broadening the participatory base in government decision making. Universal access, notice and comment requirements, while not without the same kind of dangers, may be a more profitable way of pursuing the expansion of democratic participation.[4]

---

3   [1972] 2 Q.B. 299 (C.A.).

4   "Rethinking the Doctrine of Legitimate Expectations in Canadian Law" (1997), 35 O.H.L.J. 139.

B. LEGITIMATE EXPECTATION IN THE SUPREME COURT

Since *Liverpool Taxi Fleet Operators' Association*, the doctrine of legitimate expectation has gone on to provide a significant basis for procedural fairness arguments not only in England but also, for example, in Australian and New Zealand law. It is also a recognized doctrine in European Community law. However, to this point, though examples of its successful invocation exist and it has achieved explicit endorsement from the Supreme Court of Canada, its penetration of Canadian common law has been limited.

The principal reason for the limited application of the legitimate expectation doctrine in Canada law may well be the circumstances in and terms on which the Supreme Court of Canada has accorded it recognition as part of Canadian law. Indeed, in none of the three judgments in which the Court recognized the doctrine was the procedural claim successful. In itself, this has undoubtedly contributed to a restrained definition of the scope of the doctrine.

In the first case, *Old St. Boniface Residents' Association Inc.* v. *Winnipeg (City)*,[5] the Court referred to it as a purely procedural doctrine whereby claims for participatory opportunities could be made in circumstances where such opportunities were not normally required of the decision maker. This arose where "based on the conduct of the public official, a party has been led to believe that his or her rights would not be affected without consultation."[6] However, the Court decided there was no basis for the application of the doctrine given all of the other participatory opportunities available to the public interest body.

Except for outright rejection of any substantive, as opposed to procedural dimensions to the doctrine, there was nothing necessarily restrictive about the terms in which the Court described the doctrine in that case. However, in the next decision, *Reference re Canada Assistance Plan*,[7] Sopinka J. (again delivering the judgment of the Court) introduced some new elements in his refining of the general theory. These have cast considerable doubts on the use of the doctrine in Canadian law. Once again, the factual context was not one that lent itself easily to the application of the doctrine. Various provincial governments were trying to assert that the federal government was obliged by virtue of the

---

5   [1990] 3 S.C.R. 1170 [*Old St. Boniface*].
6   *Ibid.* at 1204.
7   [1991] 2 S.C.R. 525.

doctrine to consult them before introducing legislation in Parliament. This legislation would have had the effect of reducing the federal government's transfer payment obligations to those provinces under the *Canada Assistance Plan*. The Court rejected this argument primarily on the basis that the doctrine had no application to the legislative process. While it is easy to understand the Court's reluctance to impose legally enforceable consultation obligations here — obligations that would potentially inhibit governments' freedom to decide on a legislative agenda in the public interest — the problem emerges from the terms in which the Court described the limitations of the doctrine.

After again emphasizing that the doctrine was procedural only and had no substantive component by which the exercise of discretion could be limited or restrained, Sopinka J. also stated that the doctrine had no application to "purely legislative functions."[8] If he had stopped there, the extent of the exclusion of legislative functions would have taken its colour from the facts of the case: the parliamentary legislative process and perhaps the formulation and promulgation of subordinate legislation.[9] However, Sopinka J. then went on to define what constituted a legislative function by explicit reference to Dickson J.'s definition of "legislative function" in *Martineau v. Matsqui Institution Disciplinary Board*.[10] As already seen, that definition includes "a purely ministerial decision, on broad grounds of public policy."[11]

The major difficulty with the adoption of this definition of the excluded category is that it undercuts most of the ambit of the application of the doctrine of legitimate expectation. To say in one breath that "legitimate expectation" generates procedural claims where none would otherwise exist, and then to exclude those categories of decision that are outside the reach of normal procedural fairness obligations under Canadian law (legislative and broadly based policy decisions) is the ultimate in giving with one hand and taking away with the other. Under this interpretation, all that would be left for the doctrine would be situations where some level of procedural fairness would be required by reason of statute or common law and where an expectation of more procedures was generated by the assurances or other conduct of a public official.

---

8   *Ibid.* at 558.
9   This arising from the specific reference to *Bates v. Lord Hailsham*, [1972] 3 All E.R. 1019 (Ch.).
10   [1980] 1 S.C.R. 602.
11   *Ibid.* at 628.

This would be highly problematic, and perhaps room exists for a creative lower court to finesse this aspect of the Sopinka judgment. After all, in other parts of his judgment in *Canada Assistance Plan*, he refers with approval to English authority in the area and, at English law, policy making exercises have attracted the operation of the doctrine.[12] This might therefore generate a basis for reading the Dickson definition of legislative function as narrowly as possible or for interpreting *Canada Assistance Plan* restrictively and in fact confining its precedential impact to the actual factual situation in issue there or situations with clear parallels.[13]

In the more recent judgment of the Court in *Baker v. Canada (Minister of Citizenship and Immigration)*,[14] L'Heureux-Dubé J, although recognizing that the doctrine is an established part of Canadian law, does nothing to clarify this particular point. As well, she resisted holding that the terms of an international convention to which Canada was a party but which had not yet been implemented in Canada, could generate a legitimate expectation that greater than normal participatory rights would be available where the terms of the treaty were relevant to the exercise of a discretion. While acknowledging that legitimate expectations of procedures as opposed to substantive rights could arise not only from the promises or regular practice of a tribunal, but also from reasonable assumptions about particular results, she held that the articles of the treaty and their wording did not create such an expectation in this instance: "This Convention is not, in my view, the equivalent of a government representation about how. . . applications will be decided, nor does it suggest that any rights beyond the participatory rights discussed below will be accorded."[15] Tantalizingly, the judgment on this point concludes by stating that this is not meant to necessarily preclude the making of such an argument from the terms and content of other treaties.

---

12   As acknowledged by the House of Lords itself in *Council of Civil Service Unions v. Minister for the Civil Service*, [1985] A.C. 374 (H.L. Eng.), though its application was rejected in that case on the basis of a more specific "national security" justification.

13   As in *Hamilton-Wentworth (Regional Municipality) v. Ontario (Ministry of Transportation)* (1991), 49 Admin. L.R. 169 (Ont. Div. Ct.), involving the decision of a new government not to continue with the appropriation of funds for any further stages of a long term highway project.

14   [1999] 2 S.C.R. 817.

15   *Ibid.* at para. 29.

However, notwithstanding this last sentence concession of a possibility, the judgment of the Court in this case should probably also be read for what it does not state explicitly. In making the legitimate expectation argument in this case, Baker was relying on a judgment of the High Court of Australia in *Minister of State for Immigration and Ethnic Affairs* v. *Teoh*.[16] There, the High Court had accepted that a legitimate expectation of procedures had arisen out of the terms of the very treaty that was in issue in *Baker*.[17] Moreover, for these purposes, it mattered not whether the affected person had even known of the existence of the treaty, let alone relied on it in any way. In other words, the test for the application of the doctrine was an objective one and it was not at root reliance-based.

Unlike the judgment of the Federal Court of Appeal where *Teoh* was discussed and rejected,[18] the Supreme Court judgment contains no reference to it so it is impossible to know whether the Supreme Court's disagreement with it extends beyond the status of the treaty itself as a generator of legitimate expectations. Nonetheless, on this point, *Baker* again exemplifies the commitment of the Court to a narrow rather than an expansive version of the doctrine. It also leaves in a continuing state of uncertainty the question of whether it is only those who know of and rely on a representation, practice, or other state of affairs who can invoke the doctrine of legitimate expectation in Canada.

C. LEGITIMATE EXPECTATION IN THE LOWER COURTS

Not surprisingly, lower Canadian courts have had difficulty coping with the doctrine, its reach and, in particular, the threshold outlined in Sopinka J.'s judgment for the Supreme Court in *Canada Assistance Plan*. Thus, for example, in *Sunshine Coast Parents for French* v. *Sunshine Coast (School District No. 46)*,[19] a judge of the British Columbia Supreme Court apparently excluded from the operation of the doctrine a decision

---

16   (1995), 183 C.L.R. 273.
17   On January 5, 1997, the Australian Attorney General and Minster of Justice made an executive statement ostensibly reversing the effect of this judgment by stating that people should have no such expectations in the case of such unimplemented treaties. The statement also promised legislation to the same effect: see (1997), 8 Public Law Review 120.
18   [1997] 2 F.C. 127 (C.A.) at paras. 34–39.
19   (1990), 44 Admin. L.R. 252 (B.C.S.C.)

to close a French immersion program in the school district on the basis that such action was legislative. However, the Newfoundland Court of Appeal distinguished this decision in *Furey* v. *Roman Catholic School Board of Conception Bay Centre*[20] and held that the closing of a school, as opposed to a whole program, did attract the application of the doctrine. Of course, by describing the decision in question as administrative (and not legislative), the Court actually opened up the decision to procedural fairness obligations on a normal common law basis without the need to rely on the legitimate expectation doctrine.[21]

Indeed, these two cases exemplify other concerns with the application of the doctrine. In *Sunshine Coast Parents for French*, as an additional reason, the Court also held that only those who were aware of a past practice of consultation could use the legitimate expectation argument. Then, in *Furey*, the Court reversed the first-instance judge's application of the doctrine on the basis of affidavit evidence to the effect that the applicants did not believe that the Board would follow its past practice of consultation with parents in this instance. As already noted, these grounds for denying reliance on the doctrine raise questions as to the extent to which knowledge and actual detrimental reliance are components of the doctrine. Should it be possible for individual applicants to simply point to the past conduct or assurance of the public official and plead that that conduct or assurance of itself generates a claim that procedures should be followed irrespective of the fact that it only came to the attention of those affected after the event? Or, should it be only the legitimate expectations at the time of those now before the court, legitimate expectations that generated action or inaction on their part?

Lower courts have also dismissed attempts to rely on the doctrine on the basis that there has not been sufficient practice to generate a legitimate expectation. Typical in this respect is *Attaran* v. *University of British Columbia*,[22] in which students were challenging the decision of the University to increase fees without following the terms of a consultation policy. As that policy was quite new and had been adhered to only once previously, there was no basis for asserting a legitimate expectation that it would be followed before increasing tuition. Among

---

20   (1993), 104 D.L.R. (4th) 455 (Nfl'd. C.A.).
21   See, for example, *Bezaire* v. *Windsor Roman Catholic Separate School Board* (1992), 9 O.R. (3d) 737 (Div. Ct.). Indeed, this has now been acknowledged by the Newfoundland Court of Appeal: *Elliott* v. *Burin Peninsula School District No. 7* (1998), 161 D.L.R. (4th) 112 (Nfl'd. C.A.).
22   (1998), 4 Admin. L.R. (3d) 44 (B.C.S.C.).

other reasons, the court also noted that, while some members of the student association's executive may have known of the existence of the consultation policy, it was highly unlikely and certainly not established on the evidence that "the vast number of students at the University even knew about [it] at relevant times."[23]

Other limitations on the reach of the doctrine have stemmed from a literal reading of the initial statement as to the scope of the principle by Sopinka J. in *Old St. Boniface Residents' Association*. There he referred to a belief by a party "that her or his *rights* would not be affected without consultation [emphasis added]."[24] This was picked up by the British Columbia Court of Appeal in *Pharmaceutical Manufacturers' Association of Canada* v. *British Columbia (A.G.)*,[25] a case involving an attempt by the Association to argue on general procedural fairness grounds and legitimate expectation that the government should have consulted it before initiating changes to the province's drug payment program, changes that it alleged would have serious adverse economic impact on its members. As well as analyzing the function under consideration as "executive" in nature, the court held that the decision did not affect the Association's "rights." As a consequence, irrespective whether there was a sufficient pattern of prior consultation, the initial threshold for the invocation of the doctrine had not been reached.[26]

Finally, the courts have taken a broad view of what constitutes a "substantive" as opposed to a procedural claim. Promises such as to allow voting, to seek consent, or to permit other forms of participation in the actual taking of a decision have uncontroversially been treated as substantive.[27] Somewhat more marginal was the ruling of the Federal Court, Trial Division, in the litigation over the Krever Commission Inquiry into Canada's blood system that an assurance as to the scope of the inquiry was a substantive, not a procedural matter.[28]

Given all of these potential limitations, it should therefore be no surprise that, while the cases in which the doctrine has been argued are numerous, the situations in which that argument has been successful in Canada are almost certainly fewer than ten. Moreover, when the

---

23   *Ibid.* at 58.
24   *Old St. Boniface*, above note 5 at 1204.
25   (1997), 149 D.L.R. (4th) 613 (B.C.C.A.)
26   *Ibid.*, at 638.
27   See, for example, *Valhalla Wilderness Society* v. *British Columbia (Ministry of Forests)* (1997), 25 C.E.L.R. (N.S.) 197 (B.C.S.C.).
28   *Canada (A.G.)* v. *Canada (Commissioner of the Inquiry on the Blood System)* (1996), 37 Admin. L.R. (2d) 260 (F.C.T.D.).

courts have recognized a legitimate expectation argument, it has generally been in the most clearly archetypical of circumstances. This is exemplified by one of the earliest of the cases in which the doctrine was invoked: *Gaw v. Canada (Commissioner of Corrections).*[29] There, Gaw was dissuaded from pursuing litigation challenging the validity of an inquiry into his employment status by an assurance that he would be given a higher level of procedures than normal should the matter ever proceed to a more formal dismissal hearing. That assurance was held to be binding when the commissioner subsequently attempted to recant.

There, at least, the doctrine was applied. On the other hand, it also is the case that there are some times other ways in which the facts on which legitimate expectation arguments can be marshalled to produce an outcome favourable to the applicant. *Baker* provides an excellent example of this. While the Court held that the applicant had no legitimate expectation of enhanced procedures on the basis of the terms of the relevant treaty, the Court, in effect, went one step further than this when it held that, as a matter of substance, the minister had acted unreasonably and was thereby subject to review when departmental officials failed to attribute sufficient weight to the terms of that treaty. As a consequence, the outcome was the same as that in *Teoh* albeit for different reasons.

Similarly, the evolving doctrine of estoppel against public bodies[30] might enable judicial effectuation of expectations created by assurances and conduct that a particular decision would be taken by reference to an existing policy. This kind of case (which is neither purely substance nor purely procedure) has attracted the application of the reach of the legitimate expectation doctrine in some English cases.[31] Indeed, it now has the unequivocal support of the Québec Court of Appeal in a case presently under appeal to the Supreme Court of Canada: *Centre Hospitalier Mont-Sinaï c. Quebec (Ministère de la Santé et des Services Sociaux).*[32] There, the Court upheld the granting of a mandatory order against the minister directing the issuance of a licence to the hospital on terms that had been promised and that had led the hospital

---

29   (1986), 19 Admin. L.R. 137 (F.C.T.D.).

30   See, for example, *Aurchem Exploration Ltd. v. Canada* (1992), 7 Admin. L.R. (2d) 168 (F.C.T.D.), where a mining recorder was estopped from treating non-compliance with formal statutory requirements for the making of an application on the basis of a consistent pattern of accepting applications which deviated.

31   See, for example, *R. v. Secretary of State for the Home Department, ex parte Ruddock,* [1987] 2 All E.R. 518 (wiretapping policy).

32   (1998), 9 Admin. L.R. (3d) 161 (Qué. C.A.), leave to appeal granted on November 10, 1999: [1998] C.S.C.R. No. 595 (Q.L.).

to change the focus of its operations, engage in fund-raising, and relocate. Although acknowledging that the applicant hospital could not achieve its ends by relying on the doctrine of legitimate expectation, the court held that the relevant Supreme Court of Canada authorities did not preclude the use of the doctrine of promissory or equitable estoppel in cases such as this to achieve substantive ends.[33] Should that judgment be sustained on appeal, the Supreme Court, as in *Baker*, will have again marginalized legitimate expectation as a Canadian public law doctrine while at the same time created a powerful alternative to the use of legitimate expectation as a means to substantive ends.

For the moment, however, the practical impact of the actual doctrine of legitimate expectation in Canadian law has been very limited and, notwithstanding three Supreme Court of Canada examinations of its reach, even within its restricted area of operation, there are still major areas of confusion as to its scope in Canadian administrative law. Further clarification and elaboration are obviously needed.

FURTHER READINGS

CRAIG, P. "Legitimate Expectation: A Conceptual Analysis" (1992), 108 L.Q.R. 79

DYZENHAUS, D., "Developments in Administrative Law: The 1991–92 Term" (1993), 4 Supreme Court L.R. 177 at 189–95

MACPHERSON, P., "The Legitimate Expectation Doctrine and Its Application to Administrative Policy" (1995–96), 9 Canadian Journal of Administrative Law and Practice 141

MULLAN, D.J., "Legitimate Expectation in Canadian Public Law," *Contemporary Law, 1998* (Cowansville, Que.: Éditions Yvon Blais 1999) at 519

WRIGHT, D., "Rethinking the Doctrine of Legitimate Expectations in Canadian Law" (1997), 35 O.H.L.J. 139

---

33   This ruling and its likely impact, if sustained by the Supreme Court of Canada, is discussed in greater detail in the section on estoppel in public law in Chapter 15.

PROCEDURAL PROTECTIONS UNDER THE *CHARTER* AND THE VARIOUS BILLS OF RIGHTS

A. INTRODUCTION

To this point, our consideration of implied procedural protections has focused on the common law of procedural fairness and natural justice, theories developed by the common law courts that impose procedures on decision makers when the relevant legislation is silent and leaves room for this kind of judicial supplementation. On many occasions, this exercise proceeds as one in which the courts see themselves as engaged simply in an exercise in statutory interpretation. However, there is at least a degree of artifice about that and, as we have seen, some writers such as Willis treat these common law principles as more in the nature of unwritten constitutional guarantees that only cede to the clearest forms of statutory exclusion. In that respect, they have some kinship with the "implied bill of rights" theory that we canvassed in the section on constitutional norms.

Now we turn our attention to the various constitutional and near-constitutional sources of procedural protections and, most notably, the *Canadian Charter of Rights and Freedoms*, the *Canadian Bill of Rights*, and the *Québec Charter Human Rights and Freedoms*.

B. THE *CANADIAN CHARTER OF RIGHTS AND FREEDOMS*

As foreshadowed earlier, the *Canadian Charter of Rights and Freedoms* is a potential source of significant procedural protections. More particularly, section 7's guarantee of the protection of "the principles of fundamental justice" whenever the "right to life, liberty and security of the person" is in jeopardy provides a basis on which not only decisions but also legislation, both primary and subordinate, may be struck down for procedural inadequacy. Indeed, when the rights protected by section 7 are at stake, the principles of fundamental justice open up two possibilities: the recognition of procedural entitlements in situations previously not coming under the umbrella of common law procedural fairness, or an enhancement of the procedures previously or otherwise secured by the common law.

However, section 7 has not played all that key a role in the evolution of procedural fairness principles since it came into force in 1982. The reasons for this are not difficult to find.

First, as outlined already, for the *Charter* to have any application, the power in issue must either be one that is being exercised by a government decision maker, or itself be an inherently governmental function, or involve the implementation of a specific governmental policy or program. This requirement not only has precluded the application of the *Charter* to a range of statutory authorities, but also has continued to leave the status of others in a considerable degree of uncertainty.[1]

Second, even if a body is governmental or the authority that it is exercising it is inherently governmental or implementing a specific governmental program, it must at least have the potential to deprive someone of her or his right to life, liberty, and security of the person. Even after nearly two decades of the *Charter*, what counts for these purposes remains a somewhat problematic exercise. More importantly, the judgment of the Supreme Court of Canada in *Blencoe* v. *British Columbia (Human Rights Commission)*[2] has narrowed dramatically the opportunities for contending that administrative processes engage that right.

Third, after some initial misgivings on this question, the Supreme Court determined that it was not inconsistent with the very concept of fundamental justice to apply section 1 of the *Charter* to section 7 violations. In other words, it is possible for the state to establish that a process

---

1   For the discussion of this point, see chapter 2, on the *Canadian Charter of Rights and Freedoms*.

2   [2000] S.C.J. No. 43 (QL) (October 5, 2000)

that is contrary to the principles of fundamental justice is, nonetheless, demonstrably justifiable as a reasonable limit in a free and democratic society. The Court has also approved an approach to the interpretation of section 7 which is context-sensitive and under which, within section 7 itself, there is balancing between the demands of fairness and those of efficiency.

Fourth, in the foundation case of *Singh* v. *Canada (Minister of Employment and Immigration)*,[3] Wilson J. (speaking for herself and those members of the Court who decided this case by reference to section 7 of the *Charter*) made it clear that the Court should only deal with such *Charter* arguments if compelled by the situation before it to do so. Thus, in cases where the claim is one involving the engrafting of a procedural fairness requirement onto an otherwise silent statute, a court should first ask whether the common law of procedural fairness would allow this and move to any *Charter* argument only if it would not.

Moreover, beyond section 7, the other provisions of the *Charter* have done little or nothing to enhance procedural entitlements. The promise of section 11 in the administrative domain was rapidly reduced by the Supreme Court of Canada when the Court determined that its procedural content was limited in the administrative arena to situations of decision making having "true penal consequences."[4] Altough this does not exclude totally section 11's operation in what might be considered administrative law,[5] it certainly curtails that possibility very dramatically. As well, no headway has ever been made in trying to assert that the uneven distribution of procedural entitlements comes within the ambit of section 15's equality protection. With the confining of section 15's operation to the specifically designated and analogous categories of disadvantaged persons has come a threshold that is rarely going to be met in the domain of procedures. Only if someone is the victim of lesser procedural protections than the norm because that person comes within one of the protected categories will there ever be any possibility of a section 15 procedural inequality claim.

1) "Life, Liberty and Security of the Person"

a) General

The *Charter* had been in effect just over two years when the first administrative process, section 7 case reached it in 1984. This was

---

3   [1985] 1 S.C.R. 177 at pp. 188–89 [*Singh*].
4   *R. v. Wigglesworth*, [1987] 2 S.C.R. 541 at 559 [*Wigglesworth*].
5   As, for example, in *Wigglesworth* itself, involving internal discipline within the RCMP where there was the possibility of a prison term in the case of major service offences.

Singh v. *Canada (Minister of Employment and Immigration)*.[6] *Singh* involved procedural claims by a number of disappointed applicants for convention refugee status. The then Immigration Appeal Board had denied them the entitlement to appeal a negative decision by the Minister acting on the advice of the Refugee Status Advisory Committee. The claim was that the exercise of this statutory gatekeeping role by the Board had infringed their right to an oral or in-person hearing by a person or body with authority to determine their status.

Among the bases on which the applicants were making that claim was an assertion that the decision was one that deprived them of the right to life, liberty, and security of the person. Obviously, this gave the Supreme Court a great deal of difficulty for, after the oral hearing of the appeal had been concluded, the Court asked the parties to develop arguments on an alternative basis, that of whether the decision in issue was one that came within the ambit of section 2(e) of the *Canadian Bill of Rights*. Moreover, when the decision of the six-person Court was ultimately rendered, three of the judges upheld the applicants' claim by reference to section 2(e) and three by reference to section 7 of the *Charter*. Thus, even in this foundational judgment, there was no clear majority on whether the determination of convention refugee status involved a "life, liberty, and security of the person" interest.

The judgment of Wilson J., speaking for the three judges who did decide the case on this basis, reveals some of the problems that not only they but also the other judges obviously had with the application of section 7 to the plight of convention refugee claimants. By definition in the relevant treaty and legislation, a convention refugee was someone who has a genuine and well-founded fear of persecution in the event that he or she is returned to the country from which he or she came. In order to reach a life, liberty, and security of the person impact, it, therefore, became necessary to accept that the implication of the Canadian government in a potential threat to "life, liberty and security of the person" in another country was sufficient and that the determination of whether or not someone came within that category demanded the application of the principles of fundamental justice. In other words, the convention refugee determination process was all about whether or not someone's life, liberty, and security of the person were in jeopardy and, while many people making such claims did not come within this category, the task of deciding whether they attracted section 7 protections. To deny fair process was to be indifferent to and unnecessarily risk jeopardizing

---

6   *Singh*, above note 3.

the life, liberty, and security of the person rights of some claimants and that was sufficient to bring the determination process within the reach of the constitutionally protected entitlement.

Though it is now generally accepted that convention refugee claimants do have section 7 *Charter* rights, technically, there has never been Supreme Court of Canada majority support in favour of that proposition. There also remain considerable doubts as to the precise reach of section 7 in immigration settings. One of the principles of Wilson J.'s judgment in *Singh* has been accepted in that threats to life, liberty, and security of the person at the hands of a foreign power have qualified in the extradition setting. On the other hand, the status as section 7 claimants of resident non-citizens subject to deportation for the commission of serious crimes was put in serious question in *Chiarelli* v. *Canada (Minister of Justice)*.[7] Subsequently, the Court expressly declined to rule on the question of whether non-Canadians seeking admission to Canada at a port of entry had any section 7 rights.[8] Then, much more recently, the Court did not take the opportunity to clarify these issues when, in *Baker* v. *Canada (Minister of Citizenship and Immigration)*,[9] it declined to rule on whether an over stayer was entitled to claim the protection of section 7. What is at stake in each of these scenarios is, first, whether, as Wilson J. was prepared to accept in *Singh*, all persons physically present in Canada are entitled to the protection of section 7 and, second, even if they are entitled to make section 7 claims, whether their removal from this country would in and of itself constitute a threat to their life, liberty and security of the person.

More generally, what this second issue opens up is the whole troubled question of just how far section 7 and, in particular, liberty and security of the person reach. While the Supreme Court clearly accepted that they did not protect purely economic interests (including the right to work) or property rights, there still remained many areas of operation of the administrative state potentially covered by section 7. In its judgments, the Court also revealed the polarity that exists in terms of the overall purposes or reach of section 7. In one camp were those who see "liberty and security of the person" as involving aspects of personal integrity, dignity, and autonomy, as well as physical and mental well-being. Such a conception of liberty and security of the person has the potential to extend section 7 to a broad range of state activities as well as to impose on the state positive obligations such as the provision of at

---

7   [1992] 1 S.C.R. 711.
8   *Dehghani* v. *Canada (Minister of Employment and Immigration)*, [1993] 1 S.C.R. 1053.
9   [1999] 2 S.C.R. 817.

least subsistence level welfare assistance. This stretches the reach of section 7 well beyond the conception of restraint in the commonly accepted domain of its operation — active state deprivation of or inter-ference with life, liberty and security of the person interests in the domain of criminal law and other custodial settings.

In contrast, there is a much narrower conception of section 7, the principal adherent of which was Lamer C.J.C. Section 7 is implicated in the administrative process only to the extent of decision making that comes within the traditional realm of the courts' concern, "as guardian of the administration of justice system," to protect individuals from direct state interference with their physical liberty and security of the person:

> If liberty or security of the person under section 7 of the *Charter* were defined in terms of attributes such as dignity, self worth and emo-tional well-being, it seems that liberty would be all inclusive. In such a state of affairs there would be serious reason to question the inde-pendent existence in the *Charter* of other rights and freedoms such as freedom of religion and conscience or freedom of expression. [This] is the realm of general public policy dealing with broader social, political and all issues which are much better resolved in the political and legislative forum and not in the courts.
>
> . . .
>
> Put shortly, I am of the view that s.7 is implicated when the State, by resorting to the justice system, restricts an individual's physical liberty in any circumstances. Section 7 is also implicated when the State restricts individuals' security of the person by interfering with, or removing from them control over their physical or mental integ-rity. Finally, section 7 is implicated when the State, either directly or through its agents, restricts certain privileges or liberties by using the threat of punishment in cases of non-compliance.[10]

There statements, taken from his judgment in the *Prostitution Refer-ence,* stand in very stark contrast to some of the other conceptions of section 7, as, for example, identified by Wilson J. as early as *Singh*, and reiterated by her and Dickson C.J.C. in *R. v. Morgentaler*. La Forest J. refined these statements in the context of "liberty" claims in *B. (R.) v. Children's Aid Society of Metropolitan Toronto*,[11] and then re-enforced them in his concurring judgment in *Godbout v. Longueuil (City)*,[12] in which he was prepared to strike down as contrary to section 7 a munic-

---

10   *Reference re ss. 193 and 195(1)(c) of the Criminal Code*, [1990] 1 S.C.R. 1123 at 1177.
11   [1995] 1 S.C.R. 315 at 368.
12   [1997] 3 S.C.R. 844 [*Godbout*].

ipal law requiring employees of the city to reside within the city boundaries: "On the other hand, liberty does not mean mere freedom from physical restraint. In a free and democratic society, the individual must be left room for personal autonomy to live his or her own life and the make decisions that are of fundamental personal importance."[13]

In *New Brunswick (Minister of Health and Community Services)* v. *G. (J.) [J.G.]*,[14] however, there has been some narrowing of the apparent gap between these two camps at least in the domain of what comes within the reach of "security of the person." There, Lamer C.J.C. accepted that, at least in some contexts, "security of the person" embraced the physical and psychological integrity of the individual in domains beyond the criminal law. This case involved a claim by a mother for state-assisted legal aid in resisting an application by the province to renew a custody order over her children. According to Lamer C.J.C., this constituted "a serious interference with the psychological integrity of the parent,"[15] similar to that experienced by those exposed to the processes of the criminal law. Moreover, as opposed to situations when someone's child was sentenced to a term of imprisonment, the interference in this case was in a context in which the state was invoking a process which inquired into the "parent's fitness or parental status," one in which it was "usurping the parental role or prying into the intimacies of the relationship."[16] This was sufficient to trigger the application of section 7 and require that the process by which the determination was made comported with the requirement of fundamental justice.

At the very least, this suggested that a majority of the Court was prepared to accept a broader conception of those aspects of the administrative process that are reached by section 7. Moreover, while the majority of the judges declined to rule on whether the mother's right to liberty as well as security of the person was also at stake, three of the judges, concurring in the result, were prepared to go this far. The decision to remove children from the custody of their parents deprived the parents of "the right to make decisions on behalf of their children and guide their upbringing."[17] This was part of the right to liberty as protected by section 7.

In the domain of administrative law, the dilemmas presented by the often contrasting visions of the reach of section 7 are well illus-

---

13   *Ibid.* at para. 63, quoting Dickson C.J.C. in *R. v. Big M Drug Mart Ltd.*, [1985] 1 S.C.R. 295 at 368.

14   [1999] 3 S.C.R. 46 [*New Brunswick*].

15   *Ibid.* at para. 61.

16   *Ibid.* at para. 64.

17   *Ibid.* at para. 118 (*per* L'Heureux-Dubé J., Gonthier and McLachlin JJ. concurring).

trated by three contexts in which the application of section 7 has been highly controversial, one where the reference point has been "liberty" and the other two "security of the person."

b) Carrying on a Profession or Occupations

In *Wilson v. British Columbia (Medical Services Commission)*,[18] the British Columbia Court of Appeal was confronted with a legislative regime that restricted the opportunities for newly qualified doctors and those coming to British Columbia from out of province to secure registration that would enable them to bill the province's healthcare system for services rendered to patients. While recognizing that section 7 did not protect purely economic rights or the right to work as such, the court was of the view that the regulatory scheme interfered with the liberty interests of the affected doctors. The scheme operated to deny "the opportunity to pursue freely the practice of [a] profession" and this opportunity was a component of liberty that could only be removed in accordance with the principles of fundamental justice.

The bulk of subsequent authority, mainly in the professional disciplinary field, appears contrary to the position adopted in *Wilson*. Indeed, Lamer J. (as he then was) referred to it with apparent disapproval in the *Prostitution Reference* and may have in fact refused to follow it in his cryptic endorsement of the Prince Edward Island Court of Appeal judgment in *Walker v. Prince Edward Island*.[19] However, the theory on which it was at least in part based surfaced in La Forest J.'s concurring judgment in *Godbout*: "[C]hoosing where to live is a fundamentally personal endeavour, implicating the very essence of what each individual values in the ordering of his or her private affairs."[20] In large measure, this echoes those parts of the British Columbia Court of Appeal's judgment in *Wilson* where it found that the geographical restrictions aspect of the medical practitioner number scheme were an interference with the liberty of doctors to choose where to practise and live and went beyond a mere "right to work" interest.

c) Human Rights and Other Accusatory Processes

The second illustrative domain is the complaints process under anti-discrimination statutes. Does section 7 of the *Charter* provide any protection to those responding to complaints of discrimination brought under *Human Rights Acts* or *Codes*? Prior to *Blencoe v. British Columbia*

---

18   (1989), 53 D.L.R. (4th) 171 (B.C.C.A.).

19   [1995] 2 S.C.R. 407.

20   *Godbout*, above note 12 at 894.

(Human Rights Commission),[21] various appellate courts had differed dramatically on this question which was so critical not only to the domain of the investigation and adjudication of discrimination complaints but also to many other aspects of the administrative process which required individuals to respond to an allegation or a complaint. Now, the Supreme Court of Canada has provided an answer which, though not complete, has marginalized the prospects for section 7 having a significant impact in those domains.

There were various ways in which the Court could have determined that the British Columbia Human Rights Commission was subject to section 7 of the *Charter*. Depending on the meaning and content that the Court attributed to the right to "life, liberty and security of the person", section 7 could have applied because (*inter alia*):

(a) coercive proceedings which involve the possibility of any form of liability attract the protection of section 7 on the theory that these forms of state control and regulation of necessity affect the liberty and/or the security of the person of those affected.

(b) allegations of discrimination have a particular impact on the target of those allegations such that human rights proceedings generally raise liberty and/or security of the person concerns whenever a human rights commission acts on such allegations.

(c) allegations of discrimination which involve conduct which might also be criminal trigger the application of section 7 by virtue of the similarity between the stigma and anxiety that those accused of criminal offences can suffer, stigma and anxiety which affects the target's liberty and/or security of the person.[22]

(d) serious allegations of discrimination which are not resolved by a human rights commission within a reasonable period of time generate claims that the right to liberty and/or security of the person has been jeopardized.[23]

In addition, it is also feasible to describe a similar range of possibilities from the perspective of complainants starting with the proposition that whenever the state recognizes a category of harm as requiring legal protection, the state is *ipso facto* acknowledging a "life, liberty and

---

21 Above note 2.
22 In broad terms, this was the position of Prowse J.A. in the British Columbia Court of Appeal in *Blencoe*. See (1988), 160 D.L.R. (4th) 303 (B.C.C.A.).
23 Roughly, this was the basis for McEachern C.J.B.C.'s judgment in *Blencoe*.

security of the person" interest on the part of complainants which entitles them to the benefit of the principles of fundamental justice in the way in which their claims are processed and adjudicated.

On the respondent's side of this equation, the Court had no sympathy with arguments for the application of the *Charter* based on the first three possibilities or variations on them, nor did the Court admit of much room for claims based on the final formulation though here the matter was left somewhat open or unresolved. For these purposes, Bastarache J. engaged in a preliminary examination of the content of both "liberty" and "security of the person".

After emphasising that, where possible, the courts should treat liberty and security of the person as distinct rather than as a compendious right, Bastarache J. then defined "liberty" in such a way as to make it clear that it can be at stake outside of the domains where tribunals (such as the National Parole Board) are implicated directly in the physical restraint of individuals. Thus, he accepts that liberty is also engaged in the case of "state compulsions or prohibitions" which "affect important and fundamental life choices"[24].

What does this mean for tribunals? Well, as the case law demonstrates, situations where tribunals can demand that individuals testify or produce documents will be covered with the effect that, in such cases, fundamental justice will necessitate that such requirements be sufficiently respectful of the fact that such demands impinge on individual liberty. In addition, the substantive jurisdiction of certain tribunals involves decision-making about important and fundamental life choices as in the instance of *R. v. Morgentaler*[25] and the role of therapeutic abortion committees in the control that they exercised over a woman's choice to bear a foetus to term or have an abortion. The Court also lends its approval to the concurring judgment of La Forest J. in *Godbout v. Longueuil (City)*.[26] However, as had been the case with La Forest J. in *Godbout*, Bastarache J. was not about to allow the concept of fundamental lifestyle choice to become a vehicle by which the right to liberty would be engaged whenever the state placed restrictions or limitations on "any and all decisions that individuals might make in conducting their affairs."[27]

It encompasses only those matters that properly can be characterized as fundamentally or inherently personal such that, by their very

---

24   Above note 2
25   Above note 11
26   Above nove 12
27   Above note 2 at para. 51.

nature, they implicate basic choices going to the core of what it means to enjoy individual dignity and independence. This was a narrow field which he then suggested did not involve conceptions of economic liberty and security. Even more particularly, liberty was not automatically involved in a situation where the state mandated an inquiry into whether an individual had been responsible for discrimination. That did not prevent the person under inquiry from making any "fundamental personal choices." Putting it more generally, save to the extent that accusatory regimes with potential sanctions may involve testimonial compulsion and an obligation to produce documents, liberty is not engaged merely by reason of the fact that the state or an organ of the state is determining whether someone has failed to meet a prescribed standard of conduct.

It is, however, worthy of observation that in all of this there is no mention of *Wilson* v. *Medical Services Commission of British Columbia*.[28] Did the practitioner number scheme under attack in that case involve a "fundamental personal choice" analogous to choosing where one lives (as in *Godbout*) or was it more in the nature of a regulatory response to a problem which did not strike at "the core of what it means to enjoy individual dignity and independence"? The answer to that question probably must await another day.

The Court did, however, take much more seriously the argument that the process in which Blencoe was implicated affected his "security of the person." However, here too, the Court was adamant that simple subjection to processes in which the state was inquiring whether someone had failed to meet legislated standards was not enough to trigger the right to security of the person. Not all psychological stress induced by involvement in such processes counted, only that which was sufficiently serious. The actions of the state must have had "a serious and profound effect"[29] or impact in a domain involving "an individual interest of fundamental importance."[30] For these purposes, dignity, protection from stigma, and the preservation of one's reputation were not free-standing constitutional rights but underlying values which informed decisions as to whether there was sufficient interference with psychological integrity.

In terms of the impact of subjection to administrative processes, this led the Court to conclude that security of the person did not embrace:

---

28   Above note 18.
29   Above note 2 at para. 81.
30   *Ibid.* at para. 82.

. . . the ordinary stresses and anxieties that a person of reasonable sensibility would suffer as a result of government action.[31]

Bastarache J. then emphasises again in this context that, as with liberty, the right to security of the person is implicated only where delay in administrative processes interferes with the making of "profoundly intimate and personal choices."[32] Generally, that is not the case with "the type of stress, anxiety and stigma that result from administrative or civil proceedings."[33] Even assuming that there was a sufficient causal link between state action (or inaction) and the harm alleged, "personal hardship" of the kind undoubtedly suffered by the applicant in this case was simply not enough. The state had "not interfered with the respondent and his family's ability to make essential life choices."[34]

All of this suggests very strongly that involuntary subjection to regulatory proceedings will seldom in and of itself involve a sufficient threat to generate a "security of the person" claim. Indeed, the only instance really provided by the Court was *New Brunswick (Minister of Health and Community Services* v. *G. [J.].*[35] There, as opposed to the situation in *Blencoe*, direct state interference with the child/parent relationship did affect individual autonomy in a sufficiently serious way, and, in particular, involved the usurpation of the parental role and with it the right to make highly personal choices as to how to raise one's children.

Indeed, the only point at which the Court might have left much room for the assertion of section 7 rights in other situations of involuntary subjection to regulatory proceedings is in its discussion of why there is no analogy to be drawn between the criminal law and discrimination law regimes on the score of stigma. After reiterating that freedom from stigma is not a stand alone constitutional right, Bastarache J. distinguishes the criminal setting from that in issue in *Blencoe* emphasising the different objects and purposes of human rights legislation as reflected in the powers of Commissions — mediation and conciliation of complaints where possible, education and correction of attitudes and practices rather than punishment, closed rather than open processes within the Commission, less opprobrium attached to findings of

---

31   *Ibid.* at para. 81.
32   *Ibid.* at para. 83.
33   *Ibid.*
34   *Ibid.* at para. 86.
35   Above note 14.

responsibility than to criminal guilt with compensation being the remedial response, not punishment.

While there is a certain amount of overstatement in all of this, what it could be implying is that in relation to other regulatory enforcement regimes where a stronger analogy can be drawn with the processes of criminal law, the section 7 argument might work. Once again, professional discipline suggests itself immediately as a possible example. However, any such hopes appear dashed when, in the last paragraph of this section of the judgment, Bastarache J. states:

> If the purpose of the impugned proceedings is to provide a vehicle or act as an arbiter for redressing private rights, some amount of stress and stigma attached to the proceedings must be accepted. This will also be the case when dealing with the regulation of a business, profession, or other activity. A civil suit involving fraud, defamation or the tort of sexual battery will also be "stigmatizing."[36]

Once again, this indicates very strongly that section 7's security of the person protection will seldom, if ever be implicated in regulatory enforcement proceedings at least on the basis of the impact of such proceedings on one's psychological well-being and reputation in the community. Whether on the basis of the nature of the proceedings themselves or a combination of the nature of the proceedings and delay in their prosecution, claims of personal distress, familial fraying, and stigmatization in the broader community, will simply not suffice to engage the constitutional protection.

However, Bastarache J. does take particular care to state that the holding in *Blencoe* does not preclude entirely the possibility of section 7 being invoked in relation to human rights proceedings. Those reservations are expressed as follows:

> It is only in exceptional cases where the state interferes in profoundly intimate and personal choices of an individual that state-caused delay in human rights proceedings could trigger the section 7 security of the person interest.[37]

Nonetheless, given the nature of the allegations against Blencoe and the extent to which they had an impact on his career and life, it will obviously take very extreme circumstances in a human rights setting to trigger the application of section 7 through the "security of the person" route.

---

36 Above note 2 at para. 96.
37 *Ibid.* at para. 83. See also para. 98.

Of course, it may be that the reservation was expressed more out of consideration for the plight of complainants than for that of respondents; for situations in which the allegations of discrimination, if founded, involve continuing interference with "profoundly intimate and personal choices" such as instances of ongoing systemic workplace discrimination. It may also be possible to bring within this rubric instances where the process involves interim orders by the tribunal such as suspension from the practise of a profession pending the determination of professional disciplinary charges.

However, even in these two instances, it seems clear that mere involvement in the process will not be enough to trigger section 7's application. It is only when by reason of delay attributable to the functioning of the process which causes or exacerbates the relevant harm that those affected will be able to make the claim. In two senses that may represent a very narrow window of opportunity for the operation of section 7.

First, as is clear from the majority's subsequent discussion of delay as a ground for administrative law relief,[38] it will take a truly exceptional case even where "security of the person" is implicated for a court to rule that the delay has resulted in a failure of fundamental justice — at least in situations where the claim is based on abuse of process concerns as opposed to delay as a cause of prejudice to a person's ability to make her or his case.

Second, given that delay amounting to an abuse of process has now been recognized as a common law ground of procedural unfairness and also given that such allegations will seldom, if ever, involve statutorily authorized delay but rather delay caused by the dilatory nature of the internal functioning of the process, there will in most instances be no need to have recourse to the protections of the *Charter*. As the Court has reminded us time and time again, it is not appropriate to deal with cases on constitutional grounds where the common law provides a sufficient basis for the assertion of the relevant argument. This might, therefore, mean that the only case where an applicant needs the *Charter* is the rare situation where the common law would not normally intervene and it is necessary to establish that a

---

38   This aspect of the judgment is discussed in Chapter 13 under the heading "Timing of the Hearing — Delay".

Charter right is at issue to circumvent the reticence of the common law in providing relief.[39]

What then is the overall impact of *Blencoe* on the ability of those affected to make section 7 claims in relation to the functioning of administrative processes? First, the judgment in no way affects the accepted application of section 7 to proceedings having custodial implications. Second, the judgment makes it clear that section 7 will also operate to provide protections to the way in which some of the adjectival aspects of regulatory proceedings function such as compulsory testimony and production requirements. Third, liberty and security of the person will produce broadly-based fundamental justice protections in situations where the process involves restrictions on or compulsion with respect to choices on matters of fundamentally intimate and personal nature, though, here too there is nothing new in the case. The earlier judgments of the Court itself in *Morgentaler* and *G. (J.)* are produced as the prime examples in the administrative process setting of such cases. Fourth, mere subjection to regulatory enforcement proceedings will seldom, if ever otherwise generate a claim to section 7 protection. Finally, to the extent that the combination of the nature of the process and exceptional delay may on occasion coalesce to produce a claim even where the nature of the process itself would not, in almost all cases, this will also involve a situation where the reviewing court will not need to go to the *Charter* to provide relief. The common law protections against abuse of process or delay which prejudices the presentation of one's case will almost invariably suffice.

d) The Necessities of Life

In *Singh*,[40] Wilson J., in discussing the scope of "security of the person," made reference to a Law Reform Commission Working Paper, *Medical Treatment and Criminal Law* in which it had been suggested that "security of the person" could involve "not only protection of one's physical integrity, but the provision of necessaries for support."[41] It is in this conception of security of the person that rests the principal

---

39   In fact, in this respect, the argument could be made that the minority judgement did Blencoe a disservice in deciding the case by reference solely to common law principles. For the minority, the delay in question justified an order for the immediate hearing of the case rather than a permanent stay of the proceedings. There is nothing necessarily incorrect in this save that, if Blencoe could indeed point to interference with a *Charter* right, the argument for a permanent stay over a mere mandatory order might assume considerably more strength.

40   *Singh*, above note 3 at 206–7.

41   Working Paper No. 26 at 6.

basis for the advocacy of section 7 as reaching both the cutting off of various forms of welfare entitlement, but also as imposing a positive obligation to provide or to continue to provide that form of support.

To this point, however, there is little judicial support for the proposition that section 7 involves any positive obligations on the part of the state at least in the domain of assuring to citizens the wherewithal to lead at least a subsistence existence. Moreover, while the Supreme Court in G.(J.) was willing to accept that, in certain circumstances, the state was obliged to fund indigent persons whose life, liberty, and security of the person were at stake, it is significant that that ruling came in a context where the threat to rights was at the hands of those responsible for the operation of the justice system. Without such a state-funded applicant, the affected mother would not be deprived of the benefit of the principles of fundamental justice in a hearing to determine whether her child should remain in the custody of the province of New Brunswick. There is simply no suggestion in the judgment that there are positive duties on the state to support the maintenance of life, liberty, and security of the person outside of ensuring the proper functioning of hearing processes which have the potential for the deprivation of such rights.

2) "The Principles of Fundamental Justice": Immutable or Context Sensitive?

In *Singh*, Wilson J. was prepared to concede that it was possible that the principles of fundamental justice would not require an oral hearing every time life, liberty, and security of the person were in jeopardy. However, in that instance, because the applications raised serious issues of credibility, an oral hearing did constitute a requisite component.

This laid the foundations for what was almost an inevitable conclusion: as with the rules of natural justice and procedural fairness at common law, the procedural dimensions of fundamental justice vary with the particular context. Indeed, the wider the scope attributed to the reach of life, liberty, and security of the person, the greater the variety one would expect to find in the level of procedures demanded under the section.

In the Supreme Court of Canada jurisprudence that has followed *Singh*, it has become clear that Wilson J.'s initial instincts were correct. The requirements of fundamental justice are indeed context-sensitive. Two statements from La Forest J. exemplify the Court's continuing philosophy in this domain. In *R. v. Jones*,[42] he affirmed the need for a balance between "fairness and efficiency" and continued:

---

42 [1986] 2 S.C.R. 284 at 304.

The provinces must be given room to make choices regarding the type of administrative structure that will suit their needs unless the use of such structure is in itself so manifestly unfair, having regard to the decisions that it is called upon to make, as to violate the principles of fundamental justice.

This call for a considerable measure of respect for or deference towards legislative choice was given a slightly different twist the following year in *R. v. Lyons*: "It is also clear that the principles of fundamental justice are not immutable; rather they vary according to the context in which they are invoked. Thus, certain procedural protections might be constitutionally mandated in one context but not in another."[43]

Subsequently, Sopinka J. expressed the same idea in the following way:

> If the myriad of statutory tribunals that have traditionally been obliged to accord nothing more than procedural fairness were obliged to comply with the full gamut of the principles of fundamental justice, the administrative landscape of this country would undergo a fundamental change.[44]

In terms of judicial methodology, what this means is that, by and large, judicial assessment of section 7 claims has taken on the characteristics of the analysis that the courts conduct when dealing with common law procedural fairness claims. The same kinds of considerations or factors become relevant to determining the content of procedural obligations though obviously, at the nature of the interest at stake stage of that analysis, considerable weight should be given to the fact that a *Charter*-protected right is at stake.

A useful illustration of the extent to which context may diminish the content of the principles of fundamental justice even when *Charter* rights are at stake is provided by the processing of extradition application. In two cases where the claim was made that the minister was obliged to provide greater procedures before surrendering a person to a foreign power, the Court rejected out of hand the notion that the minister had to engage in some sort of adversarial process. In *Kindler v. Canada (Minister of Justice)*,[45] McLachlin J. referred to the procedural protections that had already been accorded at the extradition hearing prior to the issue of the warrant of committal that triggered the minister's discretion as to whether to actually extradite. A year later, in

---

43   [1987] 2 S.C.R. 309 at 361.
44   *Mooring v. Canada (National Parole Board)*, [1996] 1 S.C.R. 75 at 97–98.
45   [1991] 2 S.C.R. 779 at 856–57.

Idziak v. *Canada (Minister of Justice)*, the Court, through Cory J., while accepting that the minister was subject to a duty of procedural fairness, limited the content of that duty by reference to the proposition that the process in which the minister was engaged was "at the extreme legislative end of the continuum of administrative decision-making."[46] La Forest J. elaborated in a concurring judgment:

> [I]n considering the issue of surrender, the Minister was engaged in making a policy decision rather in the nature of an act of clemency. In making a decision of this kind, the Minister is entitled to consider the views of her officials who are versed in the matter. I see no reason why she should be compelled to reveal these views. She was dealing with a policy matter wholly within her discretion. . . .[47]

This characterization of the process not only led the Court to reject the enhanced process claims of the applicant but also to dismiss the further argument that the minister, having initially determined to proceed against the applicant by way of an extradition hearing, was thereafter disqualified by reference to principles against biased decision making from taking any further role. Given the nature of the process, the duality of the minister's role was not contrary to the principles of fundamental justice.

Of course, all problems do not disappear immediately with the use in section 7 jurisprudence of a similar balancing of interests framework to that deployed in common law procedural fairness review. Serious questions remain as to how much weight should be attributed to the fact that a *Charter*-protected right is in issue and how that greater weight is actually applied in the particular case. Even more important, there is the question of whether the fact that a *Charter* right is at stake will mean the advent of procedural fairness demands in the terrain where common law claims cannot presently be asserted: legislative action that under current common law seemingly includes a wide range of broad policy-making functions. Not only do the statements in *Idziak* foreshadow that debate but it is also interesting to note that Sopinka J., in his judgment in *Re Canada Assistance Plan* in which he holds that the doctrine of legitimate expectation cannot in Canada be invoked in the context of legislative action, expressly reserves on whether the position would be different were *Charter* rights in issue.

---

46   [1992] 3 S.C.R. 631 at 659.

47   *Ibid.* at 637.

3) Section 7 Rights and Section 1

In *Singh*, Wilson J. appeared to accept that section 1 could serve as a limitation on the rights enshrined in section 7. However, she was not prepared to entertain the arguments advanced by the minister in that case that the cost implications of recognizing the applicants' procedural fairness claims were exorbitant and provided justification for derogation from the panoply of procedural entitlements that the applicants were seeking. Aside from expressing concern with the evidence presented in support of this contention, Wilson J. stated that she had considerable doubts as to whether that "type of utilitarian consideration . . . can constitute a justification for a limitation on the rights set out in the *Charter*."[48]

Subsequently, in *Reference re Section 94(2) of the B.C. Motor Vehicle Act*,[49] in a separate judgment, Wilson J. went even further and expressed the view that a law that violated section 7 of the *Charter* and its guarantee of the principles of fundamental justice could never be justified by reference to section 1. However, in this, she was at odds with the rest of the Court and, as it transpired, statements in subsequent Supreme Court of Canada judgments. Thus, also in the *B.C. Motor Vehicle Act Reference*, Lamer J. (as he then was) accepted that there could be exceptional circumstances in which section 1 could be used in justification of derogations from section 7: "natural disasters, the outbreak of war, epidemics and the like."[50] Moreover, despite the fact that Wilson J. reiterated her position on section 1 and section 7 in subsequent cases, when it came to *Morgentaler*, she did a section 1 analysis of the therapeutic abortion provisions of the *Criminal Code* after holding that they violated section 7.

Despite regular court assessments of section 7 violations by reference to section 1, it is, however, difficult to find examples of a section 1 justification actually succeeding. However, in *Gallant v. Canada (Deputy Commissioner, Correctional Service)*,[51] one of the two majority judges in the Federal Court of Appeal, Pratte J.A., was prepared, in a penitentiary inmate transfer case, to hold that section 1 provided a justification for compromising normal procedural fairness entitlements to access to relevant contrary information. In contrast, the other majority judge, Marceau J.A., held that concerns about protecting confidential sources of information could be accommodated within the process of

---

48   *Singh*, above note 3 at 218.
49   [1985] 2 S.C.R. 486.
50   *Ibid.* at 518.
51   (1989), 36 Admin. L.R. 261 (F.C.A.).

teasing out what the principles of fundamental justice demanded in the particular case.

In fact, Marceau J.A.'s approach to the issue is quite in accord with section 7 jurisprudence emanating from the Supreme Court itself. Balancing of state interests against individual rights is an exercise that is now conducted regularly in the context of section 7 itself leaving no work for section 1 to do. *Chiarelli* provides an excellent example. There, *Chiarelli*'s claims to full procedures were balanced against and lost out to the state's "considerable interest in effectively conducting national security and criminal intelligence investigations and protecting police sources." Indeed, this kind of analysis has been obviously influenced at least in part by the kind of utilitarian considerations condemned by Wilson J. in *Singh*.

However, there is a good argument, particularly if utilitarian (including cost justifications) are going to be used to diminish or even eliminate what otherwise would be the normal fundamental justice procedural protections afforded to affected individuals, that it is for the state to justify such a conclusion. For those purposes, the appropriate location for state justification is section 1 and not internal balancing within section 7. Under section 1, the burden of justification rests with the state and it removes the possibility of the applicant having to establish as part of her or his case that there are no state interest impediments to the kind of procedures he or she wants to assert as part of the principles of fundamental justice.

This approach now seems to have garnered considerable support from the Supreme Court's judgment in *New Brunswick (Minister of Health and Community Services)* v. *G. (J.)* [*J.G.*].[52] In assessing whether section 7 required state provision of counsel to an indigent mother resisting the continuation of an order for provincial custody of her children, the Court's contextual analysis focused on the situation of the mother — the seriousness of the consequences to her, the complexity of the issues raised by the particular case, and her capacity to deal with those issues without legal representation. It was only in the consideration of section 1 and whether there were any constraints on the upholding of the mother's section 7 rights that the Court took into account state justifications such as the cost of a program that would guarantee state-funded counsel to persons in the position of the mother. Indeed, while it was clear, contrary to Wilson J.'s apparent position in *Singh*, that the Court was prepared to entertain cost of

---

52   *New Brunswick*, above note 14.

implementation justifications; nonetheless, the Court was also of the view that that argument was not sufficiently convincing in this context.

4) Section 11 and Other Potential Charter Sources of Procedural Protections

Section 7 is not the only potential source in the *Charter* of procedural protections for those embroiled in the administrative process. Section 8 protects against "unreasonable search or seizure" and, while the Supreme Court has been rather more generous to the state in the context of administrative as opposed to criminal proceedings,[53] it does act as a brake on this important adjectival power that accompanies many regulatory enforcement regimes.[54] Beyond that, section 13 bars the use of a person's testimony for the purpose of incriminating that person in other proceedings save in the cases of perjury or contradictory evidence. Section 14 creates the right to an interpreter in any situation where a party or a witness cannot either understand or speak the language in which the proceedings are being conducted. Both these provisions obviously have ramifications for the administrative process or, at least, that part of it involving formal hearings.

Section 11(d) also contains a right to "a fair and public hearing by an independent and impartial tribunal." However, as opposed to sections 7, 8, 13, and 14, section 11 is textually limited by its heading to "proceedings in criminal and penal matters," while the language just quoted from subsection (d) is prefaced by a reference to the presumption of innocence and expressed in the context of findings of guilt. Not surprisingly, the Supreme Court of Canada gave effect to this obvious limitation on the reach of section 11(d) when it confined its operation to the domain of proceedings that are criminal in their nature or by virtue of their truly penal consequences."[55]

This interpretation of section 11 has had the impact of excluding from its direct reach all but a very few situations normally regarded as coming within the ambit of administrative law.[56] RCMP major service

---

53 See *R. v. McKinlay Transport Ltd.*, [1990] 1 S.C.R. 627.
54 As established in the foundation case of *Hunter v. Southam*, [1984] 2 S.C.R. 145.
55 *Wigglesworth*, above, note 4.
56 There does, however, remain the tantalizing possibilities suggested by *Alex Couture Inc. v. Canada (A.G.)* (1991), 83 D.L.R. (4th) 577 (Qué. C.A.) that secton 11(d) can be relied upon if a tribunal has to power to punish or cite for contempt.

offences for which there is the possibility of imprisonment for up to a year[57] as well as court martial within the armed forces[58] activate the provision but not the regular internal discipline regimes of other police forces.[59] Indeed, the Supreme Court has gone so far as to exclude penitentiary discipline that can lead to loss of remission and solitary confinement. Despite the nature of the sanction, the Court emphasized that, in such cases, the penalty was imposed for the purposes of maintaining internal discipline within the penitentiary, not in order to redress a wrong done to society.[60]

However, the limited scope for the invocation of section 11(d) has not meant that the elimination of the argument that administrative decision makers which affect *Charter* rights have to be "independent and impartial" and hold "fair and open hearings." In most, if not all instances, these will be one of the components of the "principles of fundamental justice" whenever section 7 rights are in jeopardy.

C.   *THE CANADIAN BILL OF RIGHTS*

Ironically, it was only with the advent of the *Canadian Charter of Rights and Freedoms* that the *Canadian Bill of Rights* began to play any significant role in procedural fairness jurisprudence. Up until that point, its operation had been constrained by narrow interpretation of its relevant terms. Thus, the assertion in section 1(a) of an entitlement to the benefit of "due process of law" whenever a person was being deprived of the right to life, liberty, and security of the person or the enjoyment of property was constrained on occasion by the restrictive interpretation of "due process" to mean "in accordance with the terms of the relevant statute." Similarly, courts held that section 2(e)'s guarantee of the principles of fundamental justice for the determination of a person's "rights and obligations" had no application save where strict rights were being definitively removed in an administrative process. The granting or taking away of mere privileges did not trigger the operation of the section, nor did non-final decision making.

---

57   *Ibid.*
58   *R. v. Généreux*, [1992] 1 S.C.R. 259.
59   See, for example, *Burnham v. Metropolitan Toronto Police*, [1987] 2 S.C.R. 572.
60   *R. v. Shubley*, [1990] 1 S.C.R. 3.

Since the *Charter*, however, the Courts have breathed some life into the procedural protections enshrined in the *Bill of Rights* and especially into section 2(e). Two cases in particular were critical in this recasting of that section and the ambit of its application. For the three judges who decided *Singh* on the basis of section 2(e) of the *Canadian Bill of Rights* rather than section 7 of the *Charter*, the term "determination of his rights and obligations" was expanded to embrace not just terminations of existing rights and obligations but also the process of establishing whether someone was in law and in fact the holder of a right. Thus, given that convention refugees were in general entitled as a matter of legal right to remain in Canada, the process by which it was determined whether a person had that status had to conform to the "principles of fundamental justice." The same kind of approach characterized the judgment of the Federal Court of Appeal in *MacBain* v. *Lederman*,[61] in which it was held that section 2(e) of the *Bill of Rights* applied to the complaints process under the *Canadian Human Rights Act*. When the commission and the human rights tribunal were dealing with a complaint of discrimination, they were "determining" whether the respondent had breached her or his legal "obligation" not to engage in discriminatory conduct. This was sufficient to trigger the application of section 2(e).

Somewhat surprisingly, these two decisions did not spawn a whole lot of similar applications in the domain where the *Bill of Rights* applies — the federal arena. Notwithstanding the fact that, on many occasions, the path to sections 1(a) and 2(e) seems a whole lot clearer than that to the operation of section 7, the precedents are remarkably few. In the domain of section 2(e), there has also been at least one restrictive judgment: *National Anti-Poverty Organization* v. *Canada (A.G.)*.[62] There, the applicant had tried to invoke section 2(e) in the context of a CRTC decision making process that had ramifications for the rates that subscribers paid for telephone services supplied by Bell Canada.

At first instance, the Federal Court, Trial Division had determined that this also involved the "determination of right and obligations" and more specifically the extent of subscribers' financial obligations to Bell Canada should they wish to keep or connect to Bell Canada's service. However, on appeal, this argument was rejected on the apparent basis that the decision of the CRTC affected all of Bell Canada's subscribers whether they had participated in the regulatory proceedings or not.

---

61   [1985] 1 F. C. 856 (C.A.).
62   (1989), 60 D.L.R. (4th) 712 (F.C.A.).

"[N]o 'rights' or 'obligations' unique" to the applicants had been determined by the decision.[63] The message from this seems to be that section 2(e) has no or restricted application in situations where an administrative agency is making determinations that are broadly based in their impact; rather, the decision must be one that has individual focus. This, of course, raises the issue of whether the situation would have been different had the CRTC ordered Bell Canada to do something for its subscribers and Bell Canada had been the applicant for judicial review. Such a differentiation, while problematic in theory, seems suggested by the terms in which the Court's judgment is framed.[64]

The judgment also suggests that what may really be at stake here is the alternative argument advanced by Bell Canada and the intervenors, that section 2(e) (like the rules of procedural fairness) has no application to legislative or broadly based policy-making roles. It is difficult, however, to justify such an extrapolation from the language of section 2(e) though it may be a possible inference if the proper approach to take to the *Canadian Bill of Rights* in general and section 2(e) in particular is one that sees it as protecting individual as opposed to group rights. Nonetheless, even accepting such an approach, there will frequently be serious questions as to when a matter involves group, collective, or public rights and obligations as opposed to a coalition of separate individual or personal rights and obligations.

It is also worthy of note that the guarantee of the principles of fundamental justice in section 1(a) of the *Bill of Rights* extends beyond "life, liberty and security of the person" to deprivations of "the enjoyment of property." Somewhat surprisingly, this provision has generated very little attention even in the aftermath of the resurrection of the *Bill of Rights*. However, even though it is restricted in its application to "individuals," interpreted by the courts as excluding corporations, within that limited compass, there would seem to be considerable room for its exploitation by imaginative counsel.[65]

---

63   *Ibid.* at 727.

64   Assuming, of course, section 2(e) can be invoked by corporations, a matter that is still uncertain.

65   As exemplified by *Authorson v. Canada (Attorney General)*, [2000] O.J. No. 3768 (S.C.J.) (Q.L.) (October 11, 2000) in which the plaintiffs successfully invoked "the enjoyment of property" in a case involving a legislative attempt to prevent disabled veterans recovering arrears of pensions and interest from the federal Crown.

In further contrast to the *Charter*, the *Canadian Bill of Rights* has no equivalent to section 1. In other words, the state is limited to the use of the explicit override provision if it wishes to avoid the application of the *Bill of Rights*; it cannot argue that, for example, a violation of section 2(e) should be sustained because it is demonstrably justifiable in a free and democratic society. This potentially means that at least, on occasion, the *Bill of Rights* may provide a much more certain guarantee of procedural fairness before federal decision makers than is the case with the *Charter* and section 7 specifically. However, writers such as Hogg[66] have urged that this should not be overplayed and that the courts will still be inclined to engage in section 1–style balancing in teasing out the meaning and content of sections such as section 1(a) and 2(e). Suffice it to say, however, that to this point there has been no explicit judicial consideration of this point.

Also of significance is the fact that the *Canadian Bill of Rights* potentially reaches all exercises of federal statutory power. Unlike the *Charter of Rights and Freedoms*, its application is not limited to governmental bodies or to those performing essentially governmental functions. While it is unlikely that the courts would go as far as applying the provisions of the *Bill of Rights* to all bodies that owe their existence to federal statutes, such as corporations incorporated under the provisions of the *Canada Business Corporations Act*, what is far more likely is that, as opposed to the situation with the *Charter*, the application of the *Bill of Rights* will parallel the scope of the other principles of judicial review — it will reach those who are "public" as opposed to the more restricted category of government or governmental function.

D. *THE QUÉBEC CHARTER OF HUMAN RIGHTS AND FREEDOMS*

Three other jurisdictions in Canada have a Bill of Rights — Alberta,[67] Saskatchewan,[68] and Québec. Of these, the most significant at least in the procedural domain is the *Québec Charter of Human Rights and Freedoms*.[69]

---

66 Particularly in Peter W. Hogg, "A Comparison of the *Charter of Rights* with the *Canadian Bill of Rights*" in G.A. Beaudoin and E. Ratushny (eds.), *The Canadian Charter of Rights and Freedoms*, 2nd ed. (Toronto: Carswell, 1989), chapter 1.
67 *Alberta Bill of Rights*, R.S.A. 1990, c. A-16.
68 *Saskatchewan Human Rights Code*, S.S. 1979, c. S-24.1, Part VI.
69 R.S.Q. 1977, C-12 (re-enacted S.Q. 1982, c. 61, s. 16).

The *Québec Charter* is superior legislation to the extent that like the *Canadian Bill of Rights*, it is expressed to prevail against all other legislation (both prior and subsequent) save to the extent that that other legislation includes an express declaration to the contrary.[70] Section 23 then provides for a "full and equal, public and fair hearing by an independent and impartial tribunal" in situations where a person's "rights and obligations are being determined" and also in cases where a tribunal is determining the merits of a charge against someone.

As is obvious, some of the language mirrors that contained in the procedural protection provisions of the *Canadian Bill of Rights* and some of which was also repeated subsequently in the *Canadian Charter of Rights and Freedoms*. In particular, the references to an "impartial and independent tribunal" and the frequent litigation in Québec of what this means precisely has led to a situation where the Canadian law on this concept is much influenced by cases coming out of Québec.[71]

However, it is also important to realize that the Act defines "tribunal" and confines it to bodies acting judicially or *quasi*-judicially.[72] As a consequence, as noted already, section 23 of the Québec *Charter* remains one of the few pockets of administrative law where it is still necessary to make reference to the principles that applied prior to *Nicholson* in the determination of whether a public authority's powers were sufficiently judicial to attract the protection of the common law rules of natural justice. Indeed, in *2747–3174 Québec Inc.* v. *Québec (Régie des permis d'alcool)*,[73] quite a lot of time is devoted to a consideration of whether the province's liquor licensing authority came within the reach of sections 23 and 56 as a body that acted judicially or *quasi*-judicially. While it was indeed held to be such a body, the Québec Court of Appeal has also held that the proceedings of an academic appeal committee at Université de Montréal did not merit that classification.[74] What this clearly indicates is that, within this much more limited realm, there still remains much potential for problematic kinds of line-drawing that characterized the pre-*Nicholson* law on the threshold for the application of the rules of natural justice.

---

70   S. 52.
71   See, in particular, *2747-3174 Québec Inc.* v. *Québec (Régie des permis d'alcool)*, [1996] 3 S.C.R. 919.
72   S. 56.
73   Above note 53.
74   *Melanson* c. *Université de Montréal*, [1996] A.Q. No. 3239 (Q.L.).

FURTHER READINGS

EVANS, J.M., "The Principles of Fundamental Justice: The Constitution and the Common Law" (1991), 29 Osgoode Hall L.J. 51

GARANT, P., "Fundamental Rights, Fundamental Justice (Section 7)" in G.A. Beaudoin & E. Mendes *The Canadian Charter of Rights and Freedoms*, 3d ed. (Scarborough, Carswell, 1996) at chapter 9

CHAPTER 11

STATUTORY
PROCEDURAL CODES

A. INTRODUCTION

As is clear from the evolution of the common law of procedural fairness, process obligations differ quite dramatically across the whole range of statutory decision makers. Similarly, there are considerable variations in the content of the hearing obligations imposed on decision makers by their empowering statute. However, despite the obvious context-sensitive nature of such requirements, three Canadian jurisdictions have more general statutes that delineate certain common procedural standards for the range of decision makers which are within their ambit. They are the Alberta *Administrative Procedures Act*,[1] the Ontario *Statutory Powers Procedure Act (SPPA)*,[2] and the Québec *Administrative Justice Act*.[3]

B. ONTARIO

The most ambitious of these remains the Ontario *SPPA*, enacted first in 1971 and substantially amended in 1994. It contains not only a list of procedural obligations for decision makers coming within its ambit but

---

1   R.S.A. 1980, c. A.2.
2   R.S.O. 1990, c. S.22 (as amended by S.O. 1994, c. 27 and S.O. 1997, c. 23).
3   S.Q. 1996, c. 54.

also, since 1994, allows for additional procedures to be adopted by way of rules, an authority that is now conferred directly on the tribunals themselves.[4]

As opposed to the Alberta *Act*, where its application to particular tribunals is largely dependent on lieutenant governor in council designation,[5] the *SPPA* contains a formula that determines the *Act's* general application as well as some specific exclusions.

For the *SPPA* to apply requires the exercise of a "statutory power of decision." This is defined in section 1 as a power existing "by or under"[6] a statute to decide or prescribe

(a) the legal rights, powers, privileges, immunities, duties or liabilities of any person or party, or

(b) the eligibility of any person or party to receive or to the continuation of, a benefit or licence, whether the person is legally entitled thereto or not; . . .

The formula then makes the *Act* applicable whenever such a decision maker's empowering statute obliges it to hold a hearing or where a hearing "is required . . . otherwise by law."[7] The term "otherwise by law" clearly covers situations where the common law would require a hearing and probably now also includes decision makers that are subject to the dictates of "fundamental justice" as required by section 7 of the *Charter* when "life, liberty, and security of the person" are in jeopardy.

As for the application of the *SPPA* in situations where the common law would require a hearing, there is a crucial issue. In 1971, when the *SPPA* was first enacted, the common law required hearings of only those decision makers that were judicial or *quasi*-judicial in character. In the wake of the procedural fairness evolution brought about in 1978 by *Nicholson v. Haldimand-Norfolk Regional Board of Commissioners of Police*,[8] a question arose as to whether this judgment had expanded the reach of the *SPPA* to all statutory decision-makers which were now required to extend the benefits of procedural fairness to those affected by their decisions or actions.

---

4   S. 25.1(1).

5   S. 2.

6   The use of the word "under" catches powers conferred by subordinate legislation as well as authority existing directly by virtue of primary legislation.

7   S. 3(1).

8   [1979] 1 S.C.R. 311.

The answer to that question was not long in coming. In Re *Webb* and *Ontario Housing Corporation*,[9] decided that very same year, the Ontario Court of Appeal held that the *Act*'s ambit did not extend to all decision makers subject to the common law obligation of procedural fairness. In effect, the context in which the legislation was enacted in 1971 continued to dictate that the *Act* still apply only to those bodies which are judicial or *quasi*-judicial in nature. Thus, despite the fact that a benefit was being withdrawn, the right to occupy Ontario government subsidized housing, the *SPPA* was not triggered. The removal of such benefits did not attract the full panoply of natural justice protections, only more limited procedural fairness obligations.

In fact, this conclusion in a way was obvious from the fact that *Nicholson* itself was an Ontario case in which there was no suggestion that the probationary police constable was entitled to the benefits of the *SPPA* once it was held that procedural fairness was required. To the contrary, Laskin C.J.C. took pains to emphasize the flexible nature of the procedural demands that the judgment placed on the police commissioners.

As a consequence, whenever an issue arises as to whether a decision-maker "is required . . . otherwise by law" to give a hearing, the court must still ask whether that decision maker is a judicial or a *quasi*-judicial one; this remains a precondition of the application of the *SPPA*.

In section 3(2), there are also a number of specific exclusions. The *Act* does not apply to the Legislative Assembly or its committees nor to the ordinary courts. Arbitrators are also excluded as are inquests and public inquiries under the *Public Inquiries Act*. More generally, the *Act* does not apply to investigatory bodies that report in a way that does not legally bind or limit the person to whom the report is made.[10] As well, the subsection excludes the exercise of statutory powers to make regulations, rules, and by-laws.

Of course, this does not mean that these bodies have no procedural fairness obligations. Their own empowering statutes will, in most instances, impose a set of procedures. Moreover, as in the case of investigative bodies that merely report or make non-binding recommendations, the common law can still operate to impose procedural fairness requirements.[11]

---

9   (1978), 93 D.L.R. (3d) 187 (Ont. C.A.).

10 To a degree this provision is redundant since the definition section of the *Act*, section 1, makes it clear that a "statutory power of decision" covers only actions that decide or prescribe; it does not reach non-final decision-making.

11 See, example, *Abel* v. *Director (Penetanguishene Mental Health Centre)* (1979), 97 D.L.R. (3d) 305 (Ont. Div. Ct.), aff'd (1981), 119 D.L.R. (3d) 101 (Ont. C.A.).

In a practical sense, however, the most significant of the exclusions from the operation of the *SPPA* are those to be found in the empowering statutes of particular decision makers, exclusions which range from the whole *Act* to a single provision. Contemporaneously with the enactment of the *SPPA* in 1971, the Ontario Legislative Assembly also passed the *Civil Rights Statute Law Amendment Act, 1971*.[12] This amended numerous other statutes in order to custom fit the application of the *SPPA* to a whole host of decision makers. Moreover, this practice of tailoring the application of the *Act* continued apace under the current government's extensive legislative reform package. It therefore remains vital to consult the contents of the particular empowering statute in determining whether a decision maker is subject to any or all of the provisions of the *SPPA*. On the other hand, to the extent that the *SPPA* (or any of its specific provisions) is not expressly excluded or overridden in the relevant empowering legislation, it prevails in the event of conflict with that empowering legislation as well as against regulations, rules, or by-laws made under that legislation.[13]

Conversely, the *Act* is not an exclusive code. This was made abundantly clear in the heading to Part II of the 1971 *Act*, the Part in which the detailed procedural provisions were found. It was described as "a Minimum Code" of procedures. While that heading disappeared with the 1994 amendments, there is no reason to believe that this took place in order to make the Code exclusive and to prevent the assertion on a common law basis of other procedural obligations. To take one example, the *SPPA* does not mandate pre-hearing discovery; it simply provides that tribunals may provide for such discovery in their rules made under section 25.1(1) of the *Act*. The common law, however, does on occasion impose pre-hearing discovery obligations on tribunals.[14] In cases where a tribunal is subject to the *SPPA* but has not passed discovery rules, it should still be possible to assert an entitlement to discovery solely by reference to the common law procedural fairness principles.

In its original 1971 format, the *SPPA* was predicated on the traditional paradigm of an oral or in-person hearing proceeding along adversarial lines. In terms of the common law, there were probably no more than four or five provisions of particular interest. Section 8 required "reasonable notice of any allegations" before any hearing in which a party's "good character, propriety of conduct or competence

---

12   S.O. 1971, c. 50.

13   S. 32.

14   See, for example, *Ontario (Human Rights Commission)* v. *Ontario (Board of Inquiry into Northwestern General Hospital)* (1993), 115 D.L.R. (4th) 279 (Ont. Div. Ct.).

was in issue." Section 9 made all hearings open to the public save where material involving public security might be disclosed or where a privacy or other interest in "intimate financial or personal matters or other matters" outweighed the more general public interest that all such proceedings be open ones. Under section 16, tribunals were empowered to take notice of any facts that may be judicially noticed and also of "any generally recognized scientific or technical facts, information or opinions within its scientific or specialized knowledge." While these provisions all reflected what was probably the then current common law position, they at least provided some measure of certainty even if not total clarity. In contrast, however, section 17 was clearly in advance of the then common law. It mandated the provision of written reasons for a final decision or order whenever requested by a party.[15]

As well as delineating procedural obligations, the SPPA also had an impact on the conduct of judicial review and statutory appeals. Aside from the obvious benefits of a provision mandating the giving of reasons on request, the evidential aspects of judicial review and statutory appeals were also affected by section 20. This requires the compilation of a record of any hearing. Among the material to be included in that record are any documentary evidence (unless subject to a statutory exclusion or limitation), the transcript (if any) of any oral testimony, and, not surprisingly, the written reasons (if any). Section 25(1) also stated that, in the absence of any specific provision in the relevant statute, the taking of an appeal from a decision acted as a stay in the matter unless otherwise ordered by the court or other body to which the appeal was taken. However, an application for judicial review was expressly excluded from the ambit of this provision.[16]

By 1994, serious tears had begun to appear in the fabric of the Act. Certain matters that should have been apparent in 1971 had not been dealt with, such as specific authority for the making of interim decisions and orders,[17] the consequences of a presiding decision maker becoming disabled from continuing before the proceeding had concluded,[18] and the correction of typographical, calculation, or other similar errors.[19] There was also an emerging consensus that tribunals should have cer-

---

15   Baker v. Canada (Minister of Citizenship and Immigration), [1999] 2 S.C.R. 817 now establishes, of course, that there are circumstances where the common law of procedural fairness will require the giving of reasons.

16   S. 25(2).

17   Now, see s. 16.1.

18   Now, see ss. 4.3 and 4.4.

19   Now, see s. 21.1.

tain powers that would not generally have been conceded to them in 1971, such as those of re-opening and reviewing a decision or order already made[20] and of making their own procedural rules.[21]

Most significantly, there had also been a growing level of sophistication and variety in the kinds of processes utilized by administrative tribunals. The traditional paradigm of an oral or in-person hearing was no longer considered appropriate for all contexts coming within the potential reach of the *SPPA* and modern communications technology had also made other forms of "hearing" that much more efficient and accessible than had been the case in 1971. As well, pre-hearing processes had come to have that much greater significance in both the regular courts and also in some administrative tribunals.

In response to these modernization imperatives, a number of other new provisions were added to the *Act* though, in virtually every instance, the "new" procedures were not made mandatory. Rather, they would apply only when the particular matter was dealt with in the tribunal's own rules made under section 25.1. Thus, a tribunal may now proceed in writing[22] or electronically,[23] subject to certain restrictions and provided that those possibilities are opened up by the tribunal's rules of procedure. The same is true of the new and detailed provisions respecting pre-hearing conferences[24] and pre-hearing disclosure.[25] However, since 1994, many administrative tribunals have taken the opportunity now afforded to them to make their own rules of procedure and, in many instances, the relevant provisions have been triggered by provisions in those rules.

C. ALBERTA

The Alberta *Administrative Procedures Act* predates the *SPPA* by five years.[26] As already noted, whether it applies and the extent of its application depends generally on designation by the lieutenant governor in

---

20 Now, see s. 21.2.
21 Now, see s. 25.1.
22 S. 5.1.
23 S. 5.2.
24 S. 5.3.
25 S. 5.4.
26 S.A. 1966, c. 1.

council. Presently, there are approximately ten such designations.[27] However, a limited number of other tribunals function in accordance with its dictates by virtue of specific provisions in their empowering legislation.[28] Also, the procedural protections that it enshrines are expressed in terms of the exercise of a "statutory power."[29] That term is defined so as to exclude legislative powers, including the making of regulations. As with the Ontario legislation, it also seems restricted to actual decisions or orders and does not reach investigative and recommendatory functions.

It is much less detailed than the Ontario *Act* and, in some respects, does not go as far as the *SPPA*. Thus, for example, the right of a party to make representations does not necessarily entail a right to make oral representations or representation by counsel. If the authority considers that representations can be made adequately in writing, it can so limit the entitlements of a party.[30] In contrast, the provision with respect to reasons is more fulsome than its Ontario counterpart. Whenever a statutory power is exercised so as to affect adversely a person's "rights,"[31] reasons must be provided along with the findings of fact on which the authority based its decision.

There is no provision in the *Act* dealing explicitly with conflict between its provisions and those of any other statute. However, the *Act* is expressed to be without prejudice to the procedures designated under any other Act.[32] This at least ensures the protection of provisions in other legislation according greater procedural entitlements than are provided for in the *APA*.

---

27   For example, it applies in its entirety to the Public Utilities Board and to specified exercises of power by the Alberta Planning Board.
28   See, for example, Boards of Inquiry under the *Individual Rights Protection Act*, R.S.A. 1980, c. I-2, s. 29(2).
29   S. 1(c).
30   S. 6.
31   A term that is not defined in the Act.
32   S. 8.

D. QUÉBEC

In 1996, after a long gestation period,[33] the Québec National Assembly passed the *Administrative Justice Act*.[34] This legislation came into force on 1 September 1997. It applies to the organs of central government and other bodies where a majority of members is appointed by the government and their staff are appointed and remunerated in terms of the relevant public service legislation.[35] Within this category, the Act creates general duties of procedural fairness whenever individual decisions affecting citizens are being taken on the basis of norms or standards prescribed by law.[36]

For the most part, the obligation of such tribunals are stated at a greater level of generality than under the *SPPA*. Moreover, the *Act* does not have the same focus on oral or in-person hearings as either the Alberta and Ontario *Acts*. Rather, there is much more emphasis on providing clear information on the relevant issues and access to the relevant documentation, as well as the opportunity for those affected to add to or supplement the record or material in the possession of the decision maker.[37]

The Québec *Act* is also unique in making special provision for emergency or urgent action without adhering in advance to the *Act*'s procedural obligations though there is provision for a review or reopening in such cases.[38] The reasons provision also accords with the general access to information philosophy of the rest of the *Act*. Attached to the obligation to provide reasons is the supplementary requirement that the affected person be told of the opportunities available to challenge the decision other than by way of judicial review and the time limits for exercising any such recourse.[39] Finally, the *Act* is also unique in providing a statement of principles that should govern tribunals in the dispensing of administrative justice. This statement requires adherence to administrative norms or standards and other applicable rules of law; the utilization of simple, flexible, and informal rules; respect for affected constituencies as indicated by prevailing eth-

---

33   The origins of the legislation can be found in the 1987 Ouellette Report (*Rapport du Groupe de travail sur les tribunaux administratifs*).
34   S.Q. 1996, c. 54.
35   S. 3.
36   S. 2.
37   See ss. 5 to 7.
38   S. 5.
39   S. 8.

ical standards and norms; and good faith in the exercise of the statutory mandate.[40]

This *Act* also operates in tandem with the *Québec Charter of Human
Rights and Freedoms*.[41] As with the *SPPA*, this statute applies notwithstanding provisions to the contrary in either existing or subsequent
legislation.[42] Among its many guarantees is an entitlement to a "full
and equal, public[43] and fair hearing by an independent and impartial
tribunal" whenever rights and obligations or the merits of any charges
are being determined.[44] However, as with the *SPPA*, the reach of the
protection is confined to bodies exercising judicial or *quasi*-judicial
powers. This is a consequence of the definition of the term "tribunal"
so as to include authorities exercising *quasi*-judicial powers.[45]

E. ASSESSING THE CASE FOR STATUTORY PROCEDURAL CODES

As indicated by the fact that statutory procedural codes for administrative agencies have found legislative favour with only three Canadian jurisdictions, there is obviously some disagreement as to their
utility. The most immediate dilemma in the drafting of such a code is
to strike a balance between the general and the particular — to write
the statute in sufficiently specific language as to advance the broad
strictures of the common law but not to write it in so detailed and specific terms as to hamstring tribunals and impose on them unnecessary
procedural obligations.

Indeed, as exemplified by all three Canadian statutes, one way to
respond to these concerns is to realize that it will be impossible to draft
a statute that can apply to all forms of statutory decision making.
Choices in the range of the statute's application will have to be made
either, in the Alberta way, by leaving its application to executive designation or, in the Ontario and Québec manner, by use of a formula,
which brings within the range of the statute principally individualized
decision making of a final character affecting significant interests of cit-

---

40 S. 4.
41 R.S.Q. 1977, c. C-12.
42 S. 52.
43 The hearing may proceed *in camera* if demanded in the interests of morality or
    public order.
44 S. 23.
45 S. 56.

izens. However, as the sheer quantity of specific legislative exemptions from either all or portions of the Ontario *Act* may illustrate, even the most careful honing of the *Act*'s zone of application may amount to insufficient fine tuning.

On the other hand, statutes such as the *SPPA* do have the merit of both providing legislative drafters with a checklist and forcing specific attention to be paid to what items on that list should or should not be applicable to a new or revised "statutory power of decision" with an individual rights or interest focus. The penalty for not addressing that question deliberately is, of course, the overriding effect of the *SPPA*'s requirements.

This focusing of legislative inquiry can also have other salutary effects such as requiring specific justifications of deviations from the general provincial standard though how much emphasis can be placed on this consideration given the extent of recent deviations in Ontario from the norm is highly questionable. Similarly, questions can be raised about the impact or utility of provisions such as the Québec *Act*'s statement of administrative standards. At best, however, they do represent a reference point by which the performance of a tribunal can be evaluated, not just by affected constituencies but also in the context of judicial and other forms of review of individual exercises of power, as well as at the political level and in the public domain generally. Such powerful statements, when backed up by a general political and administrative process commitment to those values, might well have a difficult to quantify but overall advantageous impact on the functioning of the system of administrative justice.

This notion of commitment to the delivery of administrative justice also raises the controversial issue of one of the most obvious gaps in all three Acts: the absence of any provisions about independence and the appointment and performance of members of tribunals. In Ontario, this issue was forced onto the agenda of the Agency Reform Commission on Ontario's Regulatory and Adjudicative Agencies ("the Guzzo Commission") and, in its April 1998 Report,[46] the Commission laid down several principles that should govern appointments to administrative tribunals and agencies and the maintenance of their independence. However, there was no suggestion that these principles should be enshrined in the *SPPA*. Rather, they should inform government policies.

Of course, as will be discussed in detail later, where "life, liberty and security of the person" are at stake, section 7 of the *Charter* and the principles of fundamental justice will require an independent decision

---

46   *Everyday Justice* (Toronto: Queen's Printer for Ontario, 1998) at 15–16.

maker. The same is true of tribunals coming within the reach of the procedural protections in the *Québec Charter of Human Rights and Freedoms* and decision makers subject to section 2(e) of the *Canadian Bill of Rights*. Nonetheless, particularly given the strength of the arguments for adjudicative independence for many administrative tribunals and the ease with which that independence can be compromised under current arrangements, there is a serious case to be made for the inclusion within any general procedural code of provisions dealing with both the appointment and tenure of office of members of administrative tribunals and agencies.

Another element of the *SPPA*, introduced by the 1994 amendments, is the shifting of responsibility for the crafting of appropriate procedures from the legislature and executive branch (through the making of regulations) to the tribunals and agencies themselves. The rule-making authority conferred by section 25.1 allows for the development of certain aspects of procedures that are context-specific to particular tribunals. As well, it places the responsibility for the crafting of such rules in the hands of those who best appreciate the operational imperatives of the legislative mandate they have been charged with implementing.

It is, however, unfortunate that, for what were probably budgetary considerations, the 1994 amendments finally disbanded the moribund Statutory Powers Procedure Rules Committee. Under the 1971 *Act*, this Committee ostensibly had responsibility for superintending the procedural rules of all administrative tribunals and agencies across the province, whether subject to the specific procedural provisions of the *SPPA* or not. Such checks are important in ensuring that tribunal or agency self-interest does not impede the development of procedures that are responsive to constituency needs and the even-handed dispensing of administrative justice. It will therefore be instructive to observe how well the Québec Administrative Review Council, created by the *Administrative Justice Act*, functions in the fulfilment of its role of overseeing the operations of the administrative process in that province. It is also disappointing that consideration was not given to mandatory notice and comment rule-making as a possible substitute for the existence of such a superintending role.

In the absence of procedural rule-making "hearings" or an official monitoring body, it appears as though the maintenance of appropriate standards in Ontario is effectively in the hands of such voluntary organizations of tribunal members as the Conference of Ontario Boards and Agencies and the Society of Ontario Adjudicators and Regulators. There is also some evidence that, notwithstanding the room afforded by section 25.1 for the crafting of tribunal specific procedures, most are adopting a standard set of rules that is doing the rounds. What this says about the interests of flexibility and context-sensitive procedural rules is at this point an open question.

The Guzzo Report also raises other issues about the dispensing of administrative justice in the province which are of direct concern to the present state of the *SPPA*. In particular, the Report addresses the reality that, for many affected parties, a long, complex oral or in-person hearing hinders rather than aids the effective access to and delivery of administrative justice.[47] Many will simply not have the time or the resources to exercise their participatory entitlements to the extent provided and may be prejudiced by this. Also, to quote the hoary old maxim: justice delayed may be justice denied.

These considerations tie not only into the 1994 amendments and their provision for written hearings, but also to the possibilities for the greater use of ADR in the resolution of matters coming within the ambit of the *Act*. They also point to what is perhaps an immediate need for all three provincial statutes to address the issue of ADR directly if they are to remain relevant to the effective delivery of administrative justice in their respective jurisdictions. It may also demand (at least in the case of Ontario) that the option of written and other modes of dispute settlement not be left for too much longer as simply a matter of choice for tribunals under their rule-making capacities conferred by section 25.1. In this respect, the Québec *Act*, with its greater emphasis on the need for written hearings and its expression of a philosophy of "simple, flexible and informal rules" may well show the way.

---

47 Above, at 9–12. Indeed, a reading of this portion of the report reveals some ambivalence on the part of the Commission with the value of a statute such as the *SPPA*. At 11, it questions the utility of the "one size fits all" model but then goes on to assert: "Some changes are also needed to the *SPPA* to give all agencies the full range of powers needed to resolve problems as quickly as possible."

Interestingly, the Commission, at 12, also recommends "a process to review any proposed amendments or new legislation governing individual agencies. This will ensure that statutes governing agencies in individual ministries stay consistent with the reforms recommended in this report." Is this a re-evaluation of the need for a body such as the Statutory Powers Procedure Rules Committee?

FURTHER READINGS

ALLARS, M., "A General Tribunal Procedure Statute for New South Wales" (1993), 4 Public Law Review 19

MACDONALD, R.A., "Reflections on the Report of the Quebec Working Group on Administrative Tribunals (Ouellette Commission Report)" (1988), 1 Canadian Journal of Administrative Law and Practice 337

CHAPTER 12

CONSEQUENCES OF A DENIAL OF PROCEDURAL RIGHTS

A. IMPACT OF JUDICIAL REVIEW AND APPEAL RIGHTS

For a long time, there was considerable uncertainty in Canadian administrative law as to the consequences of a finding that there had been procedural unfairness. In particular, there was a question as to whether it was appropriate for the reviewing court to then proceed to ask whether the denial of procedural fairness had affected the substantive outcome of the matter under consideration. This dilemma was apparently resolved by the judgment of Le Dain J. for the Supreme Court of Canada in *Cardinal* v. *Director of Kent Institution*.[1] There, in responding to an argument that the same kind of penitentiary discipline would have been imposed on the applicant for relief even if there had been a hearing, he stated:

> [T]he denial of a right to a fair hearing must always render a decision invalid, whether or not it may appear to a reviewing court that the hearing would likely have resulted in a different decision. The right to a fair hearing must be regarded as an independent, unqualified right which finds its essential justification in the sense of procedural justice which any person affected by an administrative decision is entitled to have. It is not for the court to deny that right and sense of

---

1   [1985] 2 S.C.R. 643.

justice on the basis of speculation as to what the result might have been had there been a hearing.[2]

Indeed, in most instances, for the reviewing court to even speculate as to the outcome would be to compound the denial of procedural fairness. In a judicial review application that has as its focus the denial of procedural fairness, not the merits of the matter under consideration, the reviewing court is in an even worse position than the original decision maker as to the merits of the case. The court not only lacks the benefit of whatever might be produced by the participation of the applicant for relief, but it also comes to know of the material on which the decision maker acted only indirectly. In many instances, this occurs quite randomly, particularly when the record before the court does not include the evidence and where the primary focal points of the court's inquiry are the various affidavits of the parties and the submissions of counsel. Moreover, for the court to actually try to assess the merits more fully for these purposes would have the effect of extending significantly the scope and expense of this kind of case and, even more important, would amount to judicial usurpation of the task confided to the statutory decision maker — making a decision on the basis of a procedure that provided a fair opportunity for all parties to make their respective cases.[3]

It is therefore not surprising that the only subsequent occasion on which the Court has actually shown any retrenchment from this position, *Mobil Oil Canada Ltd.* v. *Canada-Newfoundland Offshore Petroleum Board*,[4] was one in which the application for judicial review involved two issues: an alleged denial of procedural fairness and an assertion that, as a matter of law, the party alleging procedural unfairness would have failed in its application in any event. In that context in which the question of law had been fully canvassed and resolved in favour of the respondent, the Court held that it would be inappropriate to remit the matter for rehearing when the outcome was legally inevitable. Indeed, it is dubious whether the Supreme Court would have denied relief here had the separate question of law not been determined already in the courts below.

Indeed, in another appeal from Newfoundland, *Newfoundland Telephone Co.* v. *Newfoundland (Board of Commissioners of Public Utilities)*,[5]

---

2   *Ibid.* at 661.

3   See also the majority judgment of La Forest J. in *Friends of the Oldman River Society* v. *Canada (Minister of Transport)*, [1992] 1 S.C.R. 3 at 80: "Prerogative relief should only be refused on the ground of futility in those few instances where the issuance of a prerogative writ would be effectively nugatory. For example, a case where the order could not possibly be implemented, such as an order in the nature of prohibition to a tribunal if nothing is left for it to do that can be prohibited."

4   [1994] 1 S.C.R. 202.

5   [1992] 1 S.C.R. 623.

the Court held that the principles of *Cardinal* applied to a successful bias challenge as well. The harm done by a reasonable apprehension of bias "cannot be cured by the tribunal's subsequent decision." "Procedural fairness is an essential aspect of any hearing before a tribunal. The damage caused by apprehension of bias cannot be remedied. The hearing, and any subsequent order resulting from it, is void."[6]

This sense that decisions tainted by a denial of procedural fairness are void, not just voidable, carries over into other domains. Thus, breaches of the rules of natural justice have always been treated as nullifying or voiding the decision so as to render inapplicable privative clauses preventing review of "decisions." Nullities are not decisions within the ambit of the clause's protection.[7] Nonetheless, this concept should not be pushed too far. In Chapter 1, I have already noted that breach of the rules of procedural fairness in the dismissal of the holder of a public office does not always result in relief in the form of reinstatement to that office. Also, as we shall see later, other discretionary considerations, such as undue delay in asserting one's rights or other forms of misconduct,[8] can result in the denial of relief even where there is an established denial of procedural fairness. Rather more strangely, when it comes to the issue of whether a decision maker is entitled to defend its decision against an application for judicial review, the Supreme Court has refused to treat an alleged denial of procedural fairness as crossing the threshold for those purposes. This is not a jurisdictional question on which the decision maker has standing to justify itself.[9]

However, there is one other area where the voidness of decisions tainted by procedural unfairness does have a significant impact: the operation of the principles of *res judicata* and finality. If a tribunal comes to accept that it has made a decision without according procedural fairness, it need not await a judicial quashing of that decision. Even where such a tribunal does not possess express or implied powers to generally reopen or reconsider a matter, it is justified in ignoring its decision and reopening the matter to correct the earlier procedural unfairness.[10]

One might have thought that the nullity of a decision tainted by breach of the rules of procedural fairness would, however, in general have pre-

---

6   *Ibid.* at 645.

7   *Toronto Newspaper Guild* v. *Globe Printing Co.*, [1953] 2 S.C.R. 18.

8   See, for example, *Homex Realty & Development Co.* v. *Wyoming (Village)*, [1980] 2 S.C.R. 1011.

9   *Canada (Labour Relations Board)* v. *Transair Ltd.*, [1977] 1 S.C.R. 722.

10 This principle was applied by the Supreme Court of Canada in *Chandler* v. *Association of Architects (Alberta)*, [1989] 2 S.C.R. 848, though it was not itself a case in which the decision was a nullity by reason of procedural unfairness.

vented any appeal from such a decision and, beyond that, the cure of any procedural deficiencies at the appeal level. However, for the purposes of statutory appeals, the Canadian courts have not used the device they sometimes deploy to avoid the impact of privative clauses: "decisions" are generally treated as coming within the scope of a statutory right of appeal even where they are otherwise "nullities." Thus, in most instances, breach of the rules of procedural fairness is a ground of appeal.

B. CURE OF DEFECTS ON APPEAL

Somewhat more complex and different issues are raised by the question of whether a statutory appeal body can itself cure the procedural defects of a first instance process. However, in its split decision in *Harelkin* v. *University of Regina*,[11] the Supreme Court of Canada accepted not only that this was theoretically possible, but also that that possibility actually existed on the facts of that case. Albeit that the decision requiring Harelkin to withdraw from the University on academic grounds was tainted by a denial of procedural fairness at lower levels, he had an appeal to the Senate. In the context of that appeal, the Senate of the University had the capacity to determine the issue afresh, in accordance with the rules of procedural fairness, and without attributing any weight to the decision under appeal. This led the Supreme Court to the conclusion that Harelkin should have taken his case to the Senate first rather than seeking judicial review.

Of course, not all appeal bodies will have the capacity necessary to engage in a process that will accord the person appealing the previously denied benefit of the rules of procedural fairness. However, the actual outcome in cases such as *Harelkin* is unaffected provided the appeal body can entertain the appeal on the grounds of procedural unfairness and, without itself curing the defect, nonetheless remit it back to the first instance body for rehearing. Indeed, in many instances even where the appeal body has curative capacities, if that first instance body is not otherwise tainted (such as by way of a reasonable apprehension of bias), that may be the appropriate step to take. The applicant in that way is provided with a procedurally fair hearing where it should have taken place initially — at first instance, not on appeal. Nonetheless, on other occasions, countervailing considerations of administrative convenience may indicate that the appeal body should exercise its curative capacities rather than have the matter go back to the initial stage once again.

As already indicated, however, when an appeal body purports to remedy or cure a lower level denial of procedural fairness, it is subject

---

11   [1979] 2 S.C.R. 561.

to certain obligations, one of which is not to repeat the procedural sins of the first instance tribunal and the other of which is to recognize that the tainted first instance decision can carry no substantive weight. A salutary example is provided by *Khan v. University of Ottawa*,[12] a decision of the Ontario Court of Appeal. Here, the University argued that any procedural deficiencies at the lower levels in hearing an appeal from a failing grade had been cured on appeal by the University's Senate. In delivering the majority judgment, Laskin J.A., while acknowledging the weight of *Harelkin*, continued:

> In the case before us the Senate Committee did not completely reconsider Ms. Khan's appeal or give her a hearing *de novo*. She was confronted with the adverse findings of the Examinations Committee, which were before the Senate Committee. The Senate Committee simply considered how the Examinations Committee reached its decision and whether it agreed with that decision. By importing a procedurally flawed finding into its own deliberations the Senate Committee's findings became tainted.[13]

In other words, even assuming the Senate had the capacity to cure the procedural defects at first instance, it did not embark upon its task in the manner required for the effectuation of such a cure. Laskin J.A. then went on to illustrate that the Senate had further compounded the procedural defects below by conducting a hearing in which those procedural defects were repeated. Among other flaws, in a case where the credibility of the student was crucial, the Senate, as was the case with the Examinations Committee, had refused an in-person or oral hearing.

This state of affairs can be contrasted with the situation in *McNamara v. Ontario Racing Commission*.[14] In this instance, whatever procedural failures had been committed when race track judges suspended McNamara's owner's licence were cured on appeal to the Ontario Racing Commission. In delivering the judgment of the Ontario Court of Appeal, Abella J.A. emphasized that, on the appeal, McNamara received "the benefit of every procedural safeguard."[15] She also noted that it was irrelevant that the proceeding was technically called an appeal: "What matters is what actually took place. And what took place was a hearing *de novo*, a fresh consideration of the events of September 12, 1997."[16]

---

12   (1997), 2 Admin.L.R. (3d) 298 (Ont. C.A.).
13   *Ibid.* at 312.
14   (1998), 9 Admin. L.R. (3d) 49 (Ont. C.A.).
15   *Ibid.* at 58.
16   *Ibid.*

CHAPTER 13

AUDI ALTERAM PARTEM (HEAR THE OTHER SIDE)

A. INTRODUCTION

The rules of procedural fairness or natural justice are divided into two separate categories. The first category comprises the various elements of the requirement that the decision maker provide adequate opportunities for those affected to present their case and respond to the evidence and arguments being advanced by other participants or in the knowledge or possession of the decision maker. The Latin term for this is *"audi alteram partem,"* though its admonition to hear or listen to the other side is somewhat underinclusive in terms of the obligations that this branch of the rules of procedural fairness comprehends. The second limb of the rules covers the requirement that decision makers be independent and unbiased. Here too, there is an underinclusive Latin term: *"nemo judex in sua propria causa debet esse"* — no one should be a judge in her or his own cause.

In this chapter, I will be reviewing the extent to which the first of these categories of procedural fairness is re-enforced by constitutional and other forms of statutory requirement and, in many instances, by the common law.

B. NOTICE

It is one of the fundamentals of procedural fairness that those affected by decisions coming within its ambit should in general receive notice of the process about to be undertaken in a sufficient degree of detail and in a timely enough fashion to enable the effectuation of their participatory entitlements. However, what this involves is a very context-sensitive inquiry. Moreover, as will be seen a little later in this chapter, there are also rare emergency situations in which notice comes and hearing opportunities are provided after a preliminary or interim decision or action has been taken.

As in many other situations involving the content of procedural entitlements, the requirements of notice will be more rigorous the nearer the nature of the decision-making process in question comes to approximating the paradigmatic kind of case arising in ordinary criminal or civil litigation. Thus, to take the example of professional discipline with career threatening ramifications, it will often be the case (whether by way of statute,[1] subordinate legislation, informal procedural rules or policies, or, failing all those, the common law) that the kind of process engaged in will be very similar in many aspects, including notice and other pre-hearing processes, to the model of a criminal prosecution. Disciplinary charges will be laid in the form of a document that specifies the nature of the professional misconduct alleged with reference to the particular provisions of the professional conduct regime that are being relied upon as well as setting out the potential consequences of any adverse finding.[2] That document or associated correspondence will also contain full details of the process that will follow along with a statement of the "accused's" various entitlements throughout that process. This material will be served personally on the subject of the proceedings if at all possible and, nowadays, this will often be followed by a discovery process akin to that followed in civil

---

1   For an example of a statutory codification of many aspects of what follows, see the Ontario *Statutory Powers Procedure Act*, R.S.O. 1990, c. S. 22 (as amended by S.O. 1994, c. 27, S.O. 1997, c. 23), s. 13, and S.O. 1999, c. 12, Scher B, s. 16. Indeed, this provision applied to all proceedings coming within the ambit of that statute save where expressly modified by particular empowering legislation.

2   See, however, *R. v. Ontario Racing Commission, ex parte Taylor* (1970), 15 D.L.R. (3d) 430 (Ont. C.A.) at 433, where the Court excused somewhat scanty notification of what was at stake at a hearing by the Commission on the basis that Taylor, as a horse trainer with "knowledge and experience in the racing business" should have realised that the hearing would involve his actions and possibly have consequences for his licence.

and criminal proceedings and, of which, there will be more in a later section of this chapter.

In stark contrast, where there is about to be a public hearing into a matter which affects either the public at large or a significant section of the public (such as a hearing on the location of a nuclear facility), the procedures in advance of the hearing may be somewhat less formal in the sense that not everyone will be served personally though those whose land will be particularly affected (such as "neighbours") may have to be. Rather, for most people, notice will come in the form of public advertisement in a newspaper or other communications medium (**see below**). Also, the manner in which the nature of the hearing is presented in that notice will also be quite different from the form of notice in a professional disciplinary proceeding. Most commonly, the proposed action or subject of the inquiry will be described in fairly general terms with a description of how those potentially affected can acquire further and more detailed information. There will then be information as to kind of participation that will or may be allowed as well as directions as to how those participatory entitlements can be exercised.

Ontario

ONTARIO ENERGY BOARD

ONTARIO HYDRO NETWORKS COMPANY

TRANSMISSION 2000 — COST ALLOCATION AND RATE DESIGN NOTICE OF APPLICATION

An application dated October 1, 1999 ("the Application") has been filed by Ontario Hydro Networks Company Inc. ("OHNC") with the Ontario Energy Board ("the Board") under sections 78 and 129 of the Ontario Energy Board Act, S.O. 1998, c. 15, and pursuant to the direction of the Board in the Transitional Rate Order for Transmission Rates dated April 1, 1999 (RP-1998-0001). Any customer of Ontario Hydro Networks Company Inc. may be affected by the Board's decisions regarding the Application.

Particulars of The Application

ONHC has applied for an order or orders approving a cost allocation and rate design proposal for transmission of electricity. The rates and other charges for which approval is requested would be effective upon the declaration of open access by the Government of Ontario in the year 2000. The rates which are proposed in the Application are designed to recover the revenue requirement approved by the Board for the year 2000 in the Transitional Rate Order issued April 1, 1999 (RP-1998-0001). The Board has designed file number RP-1999-0044 to the Application.

The Evidence
The Application will be supported by written and oral evidence. The written evidence for the application has been pre-filed and may be amended before the review of that evidence is completed. Conferences involving OHNC, Board Staff and other intervenors may be held to clarify the prefiled evidence and attempt to identify and resolve issues. Any agreement reached on issues will be submitted for its consideration.

How to See the Applicant's Pre-filed Evidence
Material supporting the Application will be available for public inspection at the Board's offices, and at the offices of Ontario Hydro Networks Company Inc. in Toronto. Copies of the complete pre-filed evidence supporting the notified of the time and place of the hearing, and of your presentation. If you wish to comment in the French language at the hearing, your letter must state this.

IMPORTANT
IF YOU DO NOT FILE A LETTER OF INTERVENTION OR A LETTER OF COMMENT OR INDICATE TO THE BOARD SECRETARY THAT YOU WISH TO COMMENT AT THE HEARING, THE BOARD MAY PROCEED IN YOUR ABSENCE AND YOU WILL NOT BE ENTITLED TO ANY FURTHER NOTICE OF THESE PROCEEDINGS.

Procedural Orders
The Board may issue Procedural Orders as to how the Application will proceed and copies will be sent to all intervenors. A copy of the Board's Rules of Practice and Procedure is available from the Board Secretary and on the Board's website at www.oeb.gov.on.ca

Ce document est disponible en français.

Addresses
Ontario Energy Board
P.O. Box 2319
2300 Yonge Street,
26th Floor
Toronto, Ontario
M4P 1E4
Attn: Mr. Paul B. Pudge
       Board Secretary
       1-888-632-6273

How to Intervene

If you wish to intervene (i.e. actively participate) in any part of the proceeding relating to the Application, you must file a written notice of intervention within 14 days after the publication of this Notice. Your notice of intervention must be delivered or mailed to the Board's Secretary and to OHNC at the addresses below.

The notice of intervention must state:

• which part of the application you are interested in;
• the issues you intend to address during the proceeding; and
• whether you intend to seek an award of costs.

If you wish to participate in the proceeding using the French language, your letter must state this. All intervenors granted party status by the Board will receive notice of the time and place of any pre-hearing conferences and of the hearing. The Board Secretary will distribute a list of intervenors to all parties and to OHNC.

How to Observe

If you wish to monitor (i.e. not actively participate in) the proceeding related to the Application, you must file a written notice requesting observer status within 14 days after the publication of this notice. Your notice requesting observer status must be delivered or mailed to the Board Secretary at the address below.

How to Comment

If you wish to comment on the Application without becoming an intervenor, you may write a letter of comment to the Board stating your views and any relevant information. All letters of comment will be provided to OHNC and will become part of the public record in the proceeding. Alternatively, you may write to the Board Secretary to state that you prefer to make your comments orally at the hearing, in which case you will be

Ontario Hydro Networks Company Inc.
5th Floor
250 Yonge Street
Toronto, Ontario
M5B 2L7

All documents related to the Application should be directed to the following address.

If sent by mail or delivered:

Ontario Hydro Networks Company Inc.
5th Floor
250 Yonge Street,
Toronto, Ontario
M5B 2L7
Attn: Mr. David Curtis
       Manager, Transmission Regulation
       (416) 506-2712 (Voice)
       (416) 506-5031 (Fax)
       david.curtis@ohsc.com

DATED at Toronto October 8, 1999

Ontario Energy Board

Paul B. Pudge
Board Secretary

Nonetheless, even in this second category, there is at the very least
an obligation on the tribunal to make wise choices as to the medium or
media through which the affected portions of the public are to be notified and to provide information that is both ample enough to alert the
public as to what is at stake and which, at the very least, is not misleading. Two examples will assist in the illumination of these points.

Re Central Ontario Coalition and Ontario Hydro[3] concerned the adequacy of an announcement of a hearing into the siting of transmission
lines to be held by a joint panel of the Ontario Municipal and Environmental Assessment Boards. The hearing and its subject matter had
been publicized widely by a combination of personal service and newspaper advertising. However, a problem arose when the joint board
decided to reject the primary proposal and approve an alternative
route. While the proceedings had been announced in newspapers in
the area covered by the alternative proposal, those advertisements
described the area potentially affected as "Southwestern Ontario," a
description that was clearly very general and, also in relation to the
area ultimately affected, even misleading. Given the potential consequences of the joint board's approval (including the possibility of

---

3   (1984), 10 D.L.R. (4th) 341 (Ont. Div. Ct.)

expropriation of private property), Reid J. had no hesitation in holding that the notice was inadequate in the circumstances.

Nisga'a Tribal Council v. *Environmental Appeal Board*[4] provides a similar example. The Nisga'a lived in a remote valley where there was no local newspaper. They were concerned about the prospect of the spraying of pesticides in the valley and had made it clear to the environmental authorities that they wished to be informed of the issuance of any permit to spray in that area. In this communication, they also suggested how they should be informed — by direct service on the Tribal Council and by posting at public access areas to their various communities. When such a permit was in fact issued, the administrator left it to the applicant how to fulfil the obligation spelled out in the relevant regulations to publish its details "in one or more newspapers with local distribution." The applicant responded by placing an announcement in a newspaper serving a community 150 miles from where the Nisga'a lived and failed to advertise it in the newspaper of the community which was nearest to the valley, some 55 miles distant. The Court held that this was insufficient compliance with the spirit of the regulations and the demands of natural justice. Indeed, the implication is that, in this instance, given the remoteness of the valley, newspaper advertising of any kind was inadequate and there was an obligation on the administrator to ensure notification in the manner requested by the Tribal Council.

In many, if not all instances, notice will have to be given again if during the course of a hearing new issues arise particularly when additional persons stand to be affected by the decision. Indeed, in such cases, the tribunal must be responsive to requests for adjournments or delay made by those already attending the hearing or participating in the process. Clearly, if they are taken by surprise by the expansion or change in direction of the hearing, their ability to participate effectively is compromised seriously unless they are given ample time to prepare to deal with the new issues and dimensions of the hearing.

C. DISCOVERY

One of the bedrock principles of natural justice or procedural fairness is that affected individuals have timely notice of what is at stake in sufficient detail to enable them to participate effectively in the decision-making process. This principle is not only the basis of the common law

---

4   (1988), 32 Admin. L.R. 319 (B.C.S.C.)

jurisprudence in this domain but it also is manifest in statutory provisions such as section 8 of the Ontario *Statutory Powers Procedure Act.*[5] It provides:

> 8. Where the good character, propriety of conduct or competence of a party is an issue in a proceeding, the party is entitled to be furnished prior to the hearing with reasonable information of any allegations with respect thereto.

In recent years, however, demands have surfaced for more than just "reasonable information." In certain contexts, parties have been seeking full discovery rights or access to *all* relevant material in the hands of the decision maker and other parties. Much of the impetus for these demands came with the judgment of the Supreme Court of Canada in *R. v. Stinchcombe*,[6] in which the Court prescribed extensive discovery rights in the criminal trial process. Indeed, there have been at least some positive responses to such demands.

For example, in 1993, in *Ontario (Human Rights Commission) v. Ontario (Board of Inquiry into Northwestern General Hospital)*,[7] the Human Rights Commission was unsuccessful in its challenge to a discovery order made by a board of inquiry into an allegation of discrimination prosecuted by the Commission following a formal investigation of a complaint. This order obliged the Commission to provide discovery of

> all statements made by the Complainants to the Commission and its investigators at the investigation stage, whether reduced to writing or copied by mechanical means [as well as] the statement and identity of any witness interviewed by the Commission or its agents who the Commission does not propose to call and whose statements might reasonably aid the Respondents in answering the Commission's case.

In justification of its denial of judicial review of the order, the Divisional Court emphasized the serious ramifications of a finding of discrimination and, in this context, expressed the view that justice would be served better "when there is complete information available to the respondents."[8] In this, the Court's points of reference were not only *Stinchcombe* but also the fact that, well before *Stinchcombe*, full discovery had been a feature of civil litigation.

---

5   R.S.O. 1990, c. S. 22 (as amended by S.O. 1994, c. 27 and S.O. 1997, c. 23).
6   [1991] 3 S.C.R. 326.
7   (1993), 115 D.L.R. (4th) 279 (Ont. Div. Ct.) at 284 (quoting the judgment of Sopinka J. in *Stinchcombe*).
8   *Ibid.*

Despite this promising beginning, there has not yet been universal acceptance of discovery as a component of procedural fairness across a broad spectrum of administrative processes. In this respect, the *Northwestern General Hospital Board* case stands in stark contrast to the judgment of the Federal Court of Appeal in *CIBA-Geigy Ltd.* v. *Canada (Patented Medicine Prices Review Board).*[9] The latter involved a hearing into whether a drug was being sold at an excessive price and the target of that hearing was seeking pre-hearing disclosure of all relevant documents in the Board's possession, including the report that led to the scheduling of the hearing and all material relating to the conduct of the investigation leading to that report.

The Board itself had refused discovery on the basis that to provide the documentation requested could undermine the Board's need to have "candid, complete and objective advice from its staff." In sustaining that ruling, the Federal Court, Trial Division not only relied upon the fact that these were not criminal proceedings but also expressed concern about the impact of such discovery rights on the efficient dispatch of its business; to provide access to all this material would have the tendency of increasing the length of proceedings.[10] This judgment was affirmed by the Federal Court of Appeal which also emphasized that the proceedings were not criminal ones nor, in distinguishing *Northwestern General Hospital*, were they proceedings that "affect human rights in a way akin to criminal proceedings." The domain of economic regulation was a different one.

On its face, the differentiation made between allegations of discrimination and allegations of charging excessive prices for medicine is by no means totally convincing. How much more damaging is it to be accused of discrimination than it is to be accused of price gouging? How much more deserving of protection are the investigative staffs of the Patented Medicine Prices Review Board than the staff of the Ontario Human Rights Commission? Moreover, to the extent that the Court in *Northwestern General Hospital* relied on the analogy of board of inquiry proceedings to the *civil litigation* process, it is not really appropriate to see it as a judgment that depended in large measure on the *criminal process* precedent of *Stinchcombe*.

---

9   (1994), 170 N.R. 360 (F.C.A.) [*CIBA-Geigy*].

10   (1994), 77 F.T.R. 197 at 209 [*CIBA-Geigy*].

In other jurisprudence, discovery rights have been held to exist in the context of a convention refugee claim hearing[11] as well as professional discipline,[12] but not in the instance of a commission having a broad mandate to order the closure, amalgamation, or restructuring of hospitals in the province of Ontario.[13] That does suggest that there may at least be something to be made of the differentiation also suggested in *CIBA-Geigy* between tribunals engaged in economic and other forms of policy-oriented regulation, and those adjudicating on matters involving the application of more precise norms to individual situations. The only problem with *CIBA-Geigy* would then be the classification of what was at stake in that case as being more in the nature of economic regulation than the assigning of individual responsibility. In any event, the precise parameters of entitlements to discovery in the administrative process are still far from being established.

As in other aspects of procedural fairness, demands for discovery become attenuated to the extent that the person or body from which a discovery order is being sought is engaged in investigation as opposed to final decision-making. This has two aspects. First, those called upon to testify before a commission of inquiry have no entitlement to pre-testimonial discovery of all relevant material in the possession of the commission.[14] Indeed, as illustrated by *Masters v. Ontario*[15] and *Chiarelli v. Canada (Minister of Justice)*,[16] discussed elsewhere, there are some situations where investigative authorities are not obliged to reveal all the information they have secured either before or at any other stage of the hearing. Secondly, to the extent that an investigation has not yet led to the setting up of a hearing, there will generally be no entitlement to discovery. Thus, in *Northwestern General Hospital*, it was not the conclusion of the investigation that triggered discovery rights but the setting up of a board of inquiry as a result of that investigation.[17]

---

11 *Nrecaj v. Canada (Minister of Employment and Immigration)* (1993), 14 Admin. L.R. (2d) 161 (F.C.T.D.), though see *Siad v. Secretary of State*, [1997] 1 F.C. 608 (C.A.) [*Nrecaj*].

12 See, for example, *Bailey v. Registered Nurses' Assn (Saskatchewan)* (1996), 39 Admin. L.R. (2d) 159 (Sask. Q.B.).

13 *Pembroke Civic Hospital v. Ontario (Health Services Restructuring Commission)* (1997), 36 O.R. (3d) 41 (Div. Ct.).

14 *Labbé v. Canada (Commission of Inquiry into the Deployment of Canadian Troops to Somalia)* (1997), 146 D.L.R. (4th) 180 (F.C.T.D.)

15 (1994), 18 O.R. (3d) 551 (Div. Ct.).

16 [1992] 1 S.C.R. 711.

17 See, for example, *British Columbia (Securities Commission) v. Stallwood* (1995), 7 B.C.L.R. (3d) 339 (S.C.).

Where rights to discovery exist, it may also be necessary to specifically assert them. Thus, in *Siad* v. *Canada (Secretary of State)*,[18] the failure of the immigration authorities to disclose all relevant material prior to a convention refugee hearing did not amount to a breach of their duty when counsel did not request that material until the hearing had commenced. Indeed, this foreshadowed a similar 1998 modification by the Supreme Court of Canada of the principles of discovery in criminal cases.[19]

There is also another dimension to the availability of discovery in the administrative process that does not necessarily surface in the context of the civil and criminal litigation processes given the inherent and statutory jurisdiction of the regular courts. That issue is the extent to which administrative tribunals have the capacity or authority to make discovery orders. Of course, when, as in *CIBA-Geigy*, the relevant material is in the possession of the actual decision maker in advance of the hearing, there is no problem. The decision maker will generally be free to provide pre-hearing access to that material. However, this is not necessarily the case where the material is not in the hands of the decision maker but rather is being held by one of the parties, as in *Northwestern General Hospital*. The requested material was in the possession of the Commission which was the party that had the carriage of the case against the hospital before the board of inquiry.

Administrative tribunals and agencies do not have any inherent powers; only those that are conferred on them by statute either expressly or by necessary implication.[20] Thus, they will require express authority to make an order for discovery, it being unlikely that such authority will arise by necessary implication for the mere fact of an entitlement to conduct hearings. In *Northwestern General Hospital*, the Divisional Court purported to find that express authority in section 8 or 12 (or the combined effect of both) of the *Statutory Powers Procedure Act*.[21] This is highly dubious. Section 8 with its reference to "reasonable information" is a doubtful source, while the relevant portion of section 12 deals with the production of evidence at the hearing itself. In *Canadian Pacific Airlines Ltd.* v. *Canadian Air Line Pilots Association*, the Supreme

---

18   *Nrecaj*, above note 11.

19   *R.* v. *Dixon*, [1998] 1 S.C.R. 244.

20   *Canadian Pacific Airlines Ltd.* v. *Canadian Air Line Pilots Association*, [1993] 3 S.C.R. 724, [*Canadian Pacific Airlines*].

21   A further alternative identified in *Coopers & Lybrand Ltd.* v. *Wacyk* (1996), 94 O.A.C. 292 (Div. Ct.) is section 23(1) which provides that a "tribunal may make such orders or give such directions in proceedings before it as it considers proper to prevent an abuse of its processes."

Court indicated that such provisions meant what they said and could not be applied to compel access to material at a pre-hearing stage.[22]

However, what section 12 does suggest is that there is more than one way of skinning a cat. Even in the absence of a specific power to order pre-hearing discovery, a tribunal with the authority to order the production of evidence at a hearing has the ability to suggest voluntary pre-hearing discovery under the threat of such an order at the hearing itself coupled with an adjournment[23] to enable the other parties to evaluate that evidence and consider their response. On occasion at least, that should prove sufficient. In addition, for Ontario purposes, the *Statutory Powers Procedure Act* has now been amended to clothe decision makers coming within its ambit with the authority to order pre-hearing discovery provided they have passed rules to that effect.[24]

As is the case in the civil and criminal litigation processes, access to discovery in administrative proceedings is also subject to the restrictions imposed by various forms of evidential privilege. Thus, in penitentiary disciplinary proceedings, any claim to discovery would be subject to the constraints imposed by informer's or solicitor/client privilege.

Claims of privilege were in fact made and rejected by both the board of inquiry and the Divisional Court in *Northwestern General Hospital*. Whatever litigation privilege existed as between the lawyers to the Commission and their clients did not extend to the investigative stage under the *Ontario Human Rights Code*. Similarly rejected was a claim for a class privilege for communications between complainants and officers of the Commission. Whether such a class privilege might exist in terms of the relationship between a tribunal and its staff remains an open question. In *CIBA-Geigy*, it was certainly suggested that this was indeed a relationship of confidentiality that was worthy of protection. There is also the possibility that, even before a hearing, some of these communications might achieve the protection of deliberative secrecy.[25] Also, in the context of a legislated discovery regime, a claim of public interest privilege was sustained in *Canada (Director of Investigation & Research, Competition Act)* v. *D. & B. Companies of Canada Ltd.*[26] This was with respect to both staff reports and the complaint

---

22 *Canadian Pacific Airlines*, above note 20 at 735 *ff.*
23 See *Bailey v. Registered Nurses' Assn (Saskatchewan)* (1996), 137 D.L.R. (4th) 224 (Sask. Q.B.), where the Court held that providing full discovery during the hearing itself was not adequate.
24 See section 5.4 (as inserted by S.O. 1994, c. 27).
25 See *Tremblay v. Québec (Commission des affaires sociales)*, [1992] 1 S.C.R. 952.
26 *CIBA-Geigy*, above note 9.

received by the Director along with the submissions and material provided by the complainant.

One final aspect of *CIBA-Geigy* also merits emphasis. To the extent that the provision of discovery or the making of a discovery order is a matter within the discretion of an administrative tribunal or agency, it is possible that any ruling about discovery will be subject to judicial review not on a correctness but on a patent unreasonableness standard. This possibility is clearly foreshadowed in the judgment of McKeown J. at first instance in which the board's refusal of disclosure is described as a decision that was entitled to "curial deference unless fairness or natural justice requires otherwise."[27] Subsequently, deference to the tribunal's sustaining of a public interest claim also featured in the Federal Court of Appeal's judgment in *Canada (Director of Investigation & Research, Competition Act)* v. *D. & B. Companies of Canada Ltd.*[28] Indeed, such an approach is now rendered that much more likely since the Supreme Court in *Baker* v. *Canada (Minister of Citizenship and Immigration)*[29] proclaimed the need for judicial deference to tribunal procedural choices particularly where the tribunal is given a broad discretion over such procedural matters in its empowering statute or possesses the kind of expertise or experience that should lead a reviewing court to respect its judgment in such matters.

D. THE NATURE OF HEARINGS

For a common lawyer, the term "hearing" conjures up visions of the kind of process typified by the proceedings in a regular court of law: a trial-type adversarial hearing in which the proof and arguments are presented orally or in person and where testimony is subject to testing by way of cross-examination. And, in fact, many administrative processes adhere very closely to this traditional model of adjudication. This is particularly so where the matters being canvassed within the administrative process approximate closely the kinds of issue or subject matter dealt with in either the criminal or civil courts, with professional disciplinary proceedings often providing a typical example. However, the range of processes that can satisfy the common law requirements of a hearing is far more extensive than that and, more

---

27   *CIBA-Geigy*, note 10 at 208.
28   (1994), 176 N.R. 62 (F.C.A.).
29   [1999] 2 S.C.R. 817 [*Baker*].

and more, particularly in this electronic age, the concept of what can count as a sufficient hearing is expanding dramatically. It has therefore become increasingly important to be able to identify the conditions that necessitate the typical or conventional in-person, truly adversarial hearing, and those that indicate the adequacy of some other form of process such as one conducted entirely in writing.

Over twenty years ago, in Re *Webb* and *Ontario Housing Corporation*,[30] MacKinnon A.C.J.O., delivering the judgment of the Ontario Court of Appeal, expressed the opinion that those applying for access to government-assisted housing could not expect any degree of procedural fairness. As opposed to those from whom the Corporation was removing this benefit, mere applicants had no expectation of a hearing. However, when one thinks about how bureaucratic structures work typically or are assumed to work, as well as the possible range of what may count as hearing, this statement is highly problematic. If when Ms. Webb had made her application for subsidized housing, the responsible officer at the Ontario Housing Corporation had simply torn up her application knowing full well what it was, most people would surely accept that she had not been treated in a procedurally fair manner. Why? Because we conceive of fair process in such a situation as one involving the administration of an application form in which relevant questions are asked, the evaluation of the answers and other material provided, and the allocation of the scarce resource on the basis of who best fits the criteria on which the competition for the benefit has been established. Only in the comparatively rare situation of benefits allocated by lottery or on a first-come, first-served basis would we approve of any other way of determining the question of access. In fact, even in the case of a lottery or first-come, first-served allocations, there will generally need to be some consideration of whether those filing applications are eligible to compete in the competition.

What this example is meant to convey is that, on some occasions, the right to a hearing may mean no more than the opportunity to submit a written application and to have one's eligibility actually considered and determined by reference to the criteria on which the questions asked in the application form are based. Nonetheless, minimal though the participatory rights may be in such a case, they are still in a very real sense a "hearing."

This evolving sense of what may constitute an adequate form of hearing finds expression in the 1994 amendments to Ontario's *Statutory*

---

30   (1978), 93 D.L.R. (3d) 187 (Ont. C.A.) at 195.

Powers Procedure Act.[31] The original 1971 legislation, which applied to statutory bodies performing judicial or *quasi*-judicial functions, was based on the traditional model of a trial-type, in-person hearing with a few nods in the direction of more flexible processes such as discretion over whether or not to always allow cross-examination. In the 1994 version, albeit that the *Act's* coverage has not expanded, what is now admitted is the possibility not just of paper or written hearings[32] but also electronic hearings.[33] In other words, even within traditional hearing domains, flexibility has become the order of the day.

The same is also true of the common law. Indeed, with the expansion of the reach of procedural fairness obligations into the realm of administrative functions in *Nicholson v. Haldimand-Norfolk Regional Board of Commissioners of Police*,[34] the judicial recognition of a range of hearing processes that could satisfy common law procedural requirements depending on the context became inevitable. Thus, in *Nicholson* itself, Laskin C.J.C., delivering the judgment of the Court, was perfectly content to leave to the Board the kind of procedure that it would follow in dealing with Nicholson in the wake of the Court's quashing of the original termination decision.

Subsequently, in *Singh v. Canada (Minister of Employment and Immigration)*,[35] the leading judgment on the procedural entitlements of those claiming convention refugee status, Wilson J. was prepared to concede that, even where section 7 *Charter* rights were in peril, it might not always be necessary to hold an oral or in-person hearing. On unspecified occasions, a written hearing could suffice. However, on the particular facts, Wilson J. did apply conventional analysis to a situation where the credibility of claimants was perceived as a crucial consideration. As a consequence, the determination of *Charter* rights in this particular context did demand an oral or in-person process in front of an actual decision maker in order to satisfy the demands of the "principles of fundamental justice."

Wilson J.'s sense that an oral hearing might not always be a necessary component of the "principles of fundamental justice" was, in fact, confirmed by the Court in *Kindler v. Canada (Minister of Justice)*.[36] Here, the Court held that, despite the fact that extradition could affect

---

31   R.S.O. 1990, c. S. 22 (as amended by S.O. 1994, c. 27 and S.O. 1997, c. 23).
32   S. 5.1.
33   S. 5.2.
34   [1979] 1 S.C.R. 311.
35   [1985] 1 S.C.R. 177.
36   [1991] 2 S.C.R. 779

the applicant's section 7 right to "life, liberty and security of the person," nonetheless, the minister was not obliged to afford him an oral or in-person hearing prior to making the formal order surrendering him to the custody of the requesting foreign power. The procedural obligations of fundamental justice at the "legislative" end of the extradition process had been met by the provision of an opportunity to make submissions in writing.

In *Knight* as well,[37] the Court exhibited a flexible approach to what could constitute a form of hearing sufficient to meet the requirements of procedural fairness. In a judgment that has considerable relevance for various forms of ADR as sufficient to fulfil hearing obligations, the Court held that Knight, through the negotiations conducted by his lawyer over the renewal of his contract, had adequate notice of what was troubling the school board and sufficient opportunity to meet those concerns. When negotiations thereafter broke off because he was not willing to accept the board's offer of a limited renewal and he was dismissed, Knight could not complain that the Board had taken away his position without a "hearing."

Very recently, the Court has revisited the issue of written versus oral hearings in an immigration setting. This was in the case of *Baker v. Canada (Minister of Citizenship and Immigration)*,[38] in which Baker, an over-stayer, had applied to the minister for permission on humanitarian and compassionate grounds to make an application for permanent residence in Canada without leaving the country. Among the grounds on which she challenged the rejection of her application was the failure of the immigration officials exercising the ministerial discretion to afford her any kind of in-person hearing. Rather, she had been forced to make her case for discretionary consideration on a paper basis and had thereafter been given no further opportunity to meet the immigration officials' concerns with her application.

In delivering the judgment of the Supreme Court of Canada, L'Heureux-Dubé J. proceeded, first, to analyze the nature of Baker's claim to an in-person hearing by reference to the standard criteria by which courts determine not only the existence of an entitlement to any degree of procedural fairness but also the content or dimensions of any procedural fairness obligations. Her conclusion in this part of the judgment, rejecting earlier Federal Court of Appeal authority, was that Baker's procedural entitlements clearly went beyond the "minimal." Nonetheless,

---

37 [1990] 1 S.C.R. 653.
38 *Baker*, above note 29.

even then, "meaningful participation can occur in different ways in different situations."[39] Thereafter, she concluded that, at least on these facts, the officials were not obliged to provide more than an opportunity to make the case for humanitarian and compassionate consideration through the documentation supplied along with the formal application. In other words, Baker's entitlement went no further than the kind of process suggested above for applicants for government-assisted housing — knowledge of the relevant criteria and the chance to provide written evidence and submissions in support of the contention that she was deserving within the parameters of those relevant criteria.

Nevertheless, the Court was careful not to overstate its satisfaction with a limited form of written hearing. Its conclusion is expressed explicitly in terms of the facts of this case. Also, part of the context referred to by the Court in justification of this conclusion is the fact that Baker was represented by a lawyer, and it further appears as though there were no crucial issues of credibility and limited areas of factual dispute or confusion. By implication, therefore, the Court may be saying that, in other situations, the applicant would at least be entitled to an interview. Among the more obvious situations are those of an unrepresented applicant whose first language is not English or French or who is barely literate or even illiterate. The claim for an interview or at least the opportunity to be confronted with the concerns of the immigration officers would also seem to be magnified in situations where the immigration officers are intending to rely upon information unfavourable to the applicant which they have obtained from other sources. Indeed, even in situations where the demands of procedural fairness may be minimal, such as applying for subsidized housing or admission to law school, fairness would seem to demand that applicants be provided with an opportunity to respond to information secured otherwise by the decision makers that suggested, for example, that the application be denied because the candidate was a thief.

As in the domain of civil and criminal processes, the standard assumption of the courts is that the demand for an in-person confrontation in administrative proceedings has its greatest pull in situations where credibility is an issue. Only by seeing the witnesses and allowing their stories or versions of events to be tested by cross-examination will the chances of the "truth" emerging be maximized. A vivid example of this approach is provided by *Khan* v. *University of Ottawa*.[40] This case

---

39   *Ibid.* at para. 33.
40   (1997), 2 Admin. L.R. (3d) 298 (Ont. C.A.).

involved an appeal from a failing grade on a law faculty examination. In contention was whether or not the candidate had submitted a booklet at the end of the examination that subsequently had gone missing. In delivering the judgment of a majority of the Ontario Court of Appeal, Laskin J.A. held that, as the credibility of the candidate's story was of central importance to the determination of the appeal and because the committee's denial of her appeal was based on its disbelief of her story, Ms. Khan should have had an in-person hearing and an opportunity to make representations orally.

This approach, of course, reflects continued acceptance of the empirical validity of the proposition that the best way for adjudicators to determine whether someone is telling the truth is by observing that person's demeanour in giving testimony and responding to cross-examination, as well as his or her ability to maintain a consistent story throughout the time on the witness stand. To the extent that the assumptions behind this posture are relatively untested and to the extent that meeting the test may depend upon reactions and overall performance that are culturally specific, there must now be some doubts as to whether this testing is anywhere near as reliable as is often claimed. Nonetheless, to the extent that it remains the operating basis within the criminal and civil litigation processes, it is not likely to come under sustained attack in an administrative law setting and will continue to present the strongest justification for an oral hearing. On the other hand, there are some indications that in the training of members of certain tribunals, greater attention is being paid to issues that have culturally sensitive aspects to them such as ways of "testifying" and reaction to the experience of confrontation in an adjudicative setting. Moreover, as suggested above, in a country of ever-increasing cultural diversity, oral or in-person hearings will frequently be an imperative in situations of unrepresented parties who cannot communicate in writing in either English or French.

The right to an in-person hearing also does not necessarily mean that the whole hearing has to be conducted orally and in the presence of the person affected. Thus, in the sensitive area of sexual harassment, the Ontario Divisional Court in *Masters* v. *Ontario*,[41] sustained the fairness of an investigative/recommendatory process in which the alleged victims and perpetrators were interviewed separately. Provided that the substance of what the accusers were alleging was conveyed adequately to the target of the investigation, there was no procedural unfairness. This kind

---

41   (1994), 18 O.R. (3d) 551 (Div. Ct.).

of procedure, which of course has necessary ramifications for the further right to cross-examine witnesses, was also sustained by the Federal Court of Appeal in *Shah* v. *Canada (Minister of Employment and Immigration)*.[42] This involved the procedure to be followed by immigration officials in dealing with humanitarian and compassionate applications, the terrain of *Baker*. There, the Court held that it was permissible to interview a claimant and his spouse separately, and, while there is now reason in the wake of *Baker* to doubt the Court's holding that there was no obligation to put the contents of the spousal interview to the claimant, the interviewing process itself would probably still pass muster.

E. TIMING OF HEARING

1) Emergencies

As already discussed in the section on notice, the normal requirement is that those affected have sufficient advance notice of the hearing to enable them to prepare properly and attend or otherwise take part effectively in whatever process is being used. In some situations, this will also involve an adequate opportunity to instruct a lawyer or agent and have that lawyer provide representation at the hearing. Indeed, where these rights have been compromised without any fault on the part of the person affected, the decision maker may be under an obligation to grant an adjournment or delay of the process to enable effective participation.

On rare occasions, however, a decision maker may be justified in postponing a hearing until after the event. In certain emergency situations or where legislative objectives might be compromised by a hearing in advance of taking action, a statutory authority may act first and then evaluate the decision taken in the light of a subsequent hearing.

The Supreme Court of Canada has affirmed this possibility on at least two occasions and the facts of these two cases provide ample illustrations of the exceptional circumstances where a hearing after the event at which the initial decision is reconsidered will suffice. In *R.* v. *Randolph*,[43] the Court held that there was no obligation of procedural fairness prior to the making of an interim order withdrawing mail service from an individual suspected of using the mail for criminal purposes. In justification of this conclusion, Cartwright C.J.C. stated:

---

42   (1994), 170 N.R. 238 (F.C.A.).
43   [1966] S.C.R. 260.

The main object of section 7 is to enable the Postmaster General to take prompt action to prevent the use of the mails for the purpose of defrauding the public or other criminal activity. That purpose might well be defeated if he could take action only after notice and a hearing.[44]

Subsequently, in *Cardinal* v. *Director of Kent Institution*,[45] Le Dain J. held that the placing of inmates in segregation without a prior hearing in the context of an emergency situation was justified as long as there was a subsequent hearing at which the initial decision was reviewed. In that instance, a number of inmates had been placed in segregation on their arrival at a new penitentiary to which they had been transferred after they had been charged criminally with holding a guard hostage at knife point.

The litigation in *Cardinal* pre-dated the *Charter*. However, subsequent authority in the Federal Court supports the proposition that the need for urgent action in the public interest may trump normal procedural rights under both the *Charter* and the *Canadian Bill of Rights* and justify the taking of action without a prior hearing. This was in *Bertram S. Miller Ltd.* v. *R.*,[46] where trees being imported to Canada were seized and destroyed under provisions in the *Plant Quarantine Act* when they were found to be infested with larvae. The authorities did not wait to give the owners a hearing. Of course, in such a case, a hearing after the event, save on possible issues of compensation, will be of no use.

In fact, in *Randolph*, section 2(e) of the *Canadian Bill of Rights* was advanced in support of the argument for procedural fairness but this argument was rejected on the basis that section 2(e) applied only in the instance of final determinations, not interim suspensions.

2) Delay

In contrast to situations where the administrative process moves too quickly there is an increasing incidence of cases in which relief is sought on the basis that it has taken too long to bring a matter on for a hearing. Resource constraints have meant that many tribunals are having trouble in managing their case load and, on occasion, this will result in situations where to proceed after a considerable lapse of time would amount to a breach of the rules of natural justice or procedural fairness.

The most common basis on which an argument of undue delay arises is where the proceeding involves the determination of allegations

---

44   *Ibid.* at 266.
45   [1985] 2 S.C.R. 643.
46   [1986] 3 F.C. 291 (C.A.).

of wrongdoing against an individual such as professional discipline or discrimination under human rights legislation. In that context, it will generally be argued, as in the true criminal arena, that the delay in convening the hearing has prejudiced the mounting of an effective defence. Important testimony may no longer be accessible because key witnesses have died or are otherwise no longer available. Even where all the relevant witnesses can be assembled, the passage of time can lead to the dimming of memories. However, general assertions of these phenomena are not enough. Prejudice will not be presumed. It is for the person affected to provide concrete evidence of the likely impact of unacceptable delay on the presentation of her or his case.[47]

Albeit that they were developed in the context of a human rights case in which it was held that the affected person's right to "life, liberty and security of the person" as protected by section 7 of the *Charter* was at stake,[48] the following criteria provide a useful non-exclusive checklist on which the courts analyze undue delay arguments:

> (1) whether the delay complained of was *prima facie* unreasonable, having regard to the time requirements inherent in such a remedial proceeding, (2) the reason or responsibility for the delay, having regard to the conduct of the complainants (at whose instance the proceedings were initiated), the conduct of the Commission (who by the provisions of the *Code* has carriage of the proceedings) including the inadequacy of or limitations to its institutional resources and the conduct of the alleged discriminator, including whether he failed to object or waive any time period, and (3) the prejudice or impairment caused to the alleged discriminator by the delay.[49]

In that case, a consideration of these criteria and the supporting affidavit evidence as to difficulties with locating witnesses and their fading memories led the Saskatchewan Court of Appeal with some reservations to uphold the first instance judge's ruling of prejudicial delay for which the applicant for relief was not responsible.[50] That delay was one

---

47   *Blencoe* v. *British Columbia (Human Rights Commission)* [2000] S.C.J. no. 43 (QL).

48   Now in the wake of *Blencoe*, above note 47, a highly unlikely scenario in either human rights or professional disciplinary proceedings.

49   *Kodellas* v. *Saskatchewan (Human Rights Commission)* (1989), 60 D.L.R. (4th) 143 (Sask. C.A.) at 158–59. As Bayda C.J.S. admitted freely, the criteria are based on those developed by the Supreme Court of Canada in the leading *Charter*, criminal law case of *R.* v. *Rahey*, [1987] 1 S.C.R. 588.

50   *Ibid.* at 161.

of three years and eleven months from the time of the filing of the complaints and over four years since the alleged events occurred.

Of these criteria, the only controversial or problematic one has to be that of institutional resources. In the case itself, it is suggested that had the commission been able to demonstrate that its failure to proceed more quickly had been the result of a lack of institutional resources, the result might have been different. However, it is questionable whether the person affected by the delay should bear the brunt of such a lack of resources. Indeed, at most, perhaps this is a factor or consideration which in a close case should be seen as explaining the delay from the commission's perspective in response to an allegation that the commission could have avoided the delay had it been of a mind to do so.

As far as prejudice is concerned, questions also arose as to whether this concept included other kinds of disadvantage not related to the presentation of the case. While most of the case law has rested almost exclusively on impairment to the mounting of a response, there were instances in which other considerations intruded. One example was *Misra v. College of Physicians and Surgeons (Saskatchewan),*[51] where the court took into account the extent to which a doctor's practice of medicine and other aspects of his life had been affected by a delay in the processing of professional discipline proceedings as well as the conduct of the professional body in the way in which the matter proceeded. In so doing, the court included within its concept of natural justice abuse of process as an independent value and described its ability to intervene in cases of undue delay in terms of both "unfairness and prejudice."

Now, as a result of *Blencoe v. British Columbia (Human Rights Commission),*[52] it is clear that delay which results in other forms of prejudice and amounts to an abuse of process can give rise to relief in an administrative law (as well as a criminal process) setting even where the applicant's section 7 *Charter* rights are not in issue. However, at least in situations where the relief sought is a stay of further proceedings, as opposed to an order for an expedited hearing,[53] the onus on the

---

51 [1988] 5 W.W.R. 333 (Sask. C.A.) at 347. See also *Stefani v. College of Dental Surgeons (British Columbia)* (1996) 44 Admin L.R. (2d) 122 (B.C.J.C.); *Brown v. Association of Professional Engineers and Geoscientists of British Columbia* [1994] B.C.J. No. 2037 (S.C.) (Q.L.); and *Ratzl aff v. British Columbia (Medical Services Commission)* (1996), 17 B.C.L.R. (3d) 336 (C.A.).

52 Above note 47.

53 This is the relief that the minority would have awarded in *Blencoe*. To the extent, that the majority judgement is generally predicated on the fact that the applicant was seeking a stay, it may well be that the obstacles will be fewer in situations where the relief sought is not a stay but an expedited hearing.

applicant will be an exceptionally heavy one. According to Bastarache J., delivering the judgment of the majority of the Supreme Court:

> Where inordinate delay has directly caused significant psychological harm to a person, or attached a stigma to a person's reputation, such that the human rights system would be brought into disrepute, such prejudice may be sufficient to constitute an abuse of process. . . . It must however be emphasised that few lengthy delays will meet this threshold.[54]

For these purposes, the reviewing court has to weigh competing public interests: the importance of a fair process against the harm that results when enforcement proceedings are stayed.

Among the factors relevant in this balancing exercise and the determination of whether a delay has been inordinate are "the nature of the case and its complexity, the facts and the issues, the purpose and nature of the proceedings, whether the respondent contributed to the delay or waived the delay, and other circumstances of the case."[55] In this regard, the Court elaborated on the extent to which different considerations intruded in the case of proceedings under typical human rights legislation than in the case of criminal prosecutions. In particular, it emphasised the gatekeeping role played by the commission. That function was there to ensure for the protection of respondents that only claims which had some basis advanced to the hearing stage. It also required not only investigation but also participatory opportunities and the exploration of the possibility of settlement through mediation. As such, it was a process that would frequently involve much more time than the taking of the decision to lay a criminal charge. In other words, there is no automatic transposition of the criminal process precedents and the point at which delay becomes inordinate in that setting to administrative processes. Because of the nature of the administrative process in issue, the courts may have to tolerate far more lengthy processing periods.

The way in which the Court applied these principles to the facts of the particular case is also instructive. First, it noted that the commission handled this matter in the same way as it handled other complaints. In so doing, it discounted the argument that the commission should have proceeded more expeditiously than normal because of the high profile of the respondent; he had not asked for any priority. Second, the Court looked at data on the time other human rights commis-

---

54   *Ibid.* at para. 115.
55   *Ibid.* at para. 122.

sions took to process complaints as well as the length of delay that had given rise to successful abuse of process claims in previous case law. On this score, it reached the conclusion that twenty-four months from the filing of the complaints to the setting up of a tribunal was not out of line with the time it would have taken to deal with such a matter in other jurisdictions and settings. Third, the Court took account of the extent of the delay for which the Commission had no explanation: five months. This was not in itself sufficient to tip the balance in the respondent's favour. In sum, even conceding that the time taken in processing the claim had resulted in prejudice (in the form of anxiety, stigma, affront to dignity, and loss of reputation) to the respondent and his family, it was not of such a magnitude as to have offended "the public's sense of decency and fairness."[56]

In attempting to generalize from this judgment to other contexts in which claims of abuse of process by reason of delay might arise, it is also important to take into account that complaints of direct discrimination made against individuals under human rights legislation are among the most serious and reputation threatening matters dealt with by way of an administrative process. If, out of an understandable concern that alleged victims of discrimination not be deprived of the opportunity to establish their case, the Supreme Court is willing to tolerate considerable delays in a context such as that, then, in other settings, it is almost certainly going to be as, if not more difficult to establish prejudice of the magnitude required.

When allegations of undue delay are made, the courts are often willing to determine those allegations by way of an application to prohibit or enjoin the commencement of the hearing. However, there is also the possibility that, as a matter of discretion, the court will rule that the tribunal should itself be allowed the opportunity to assess whether the delay will be prejudicial to the conduct of the affected person's defence.[57] Indeed, there will be occasions on which that judgment can only be made in the wake of the actual hearing when all the evidence has been heard. In contrast, as in a case such as *Blencoe*, where the allegation is one based not on evidentiary concerns but on abuse of process, there may be no reason for the court to provide the tribunal with an opportunity to deal with that issue.

---

56 *Ibid.* at para 132..
57 See, for example, *Ontario College of Art v. Ontario (Ontario Human Rights Commission)* (1992), 99 D.L.R. (4th) 738 (Ont. Div. Ct.).

F. OPEN OR CLOSED HEARINGS

1) Introduction

At common law, it was generally a matter of discretion for a tribunal or agency whether to hold its hearings in public or behind closed doors. Indeed, as James Sprague has noted in an extensive survey of the case law and the policy issues underlying that case law,[58] it will frequently be difficult to identify any natural justice or procedural fairness considerations relevant to either the exercise of that discretion or the existence of any overriding entitlement of those affected to have the proceedings open to the public. In many instances, the effective presentation of one's case and countering the case presented by the other side will not be enhanced in any way by the opening of the proceedings to the public. Indeed, in some instances, being subject to the "glare of the public spotlight" might very well cause some to be less effective in the way in which they argue their cause or provide evidence. This may be particularly the case where sensitive personal information is at stake.

Nonetheless, there may be situations where to close a hearing does constitute a potential threat to the effectiveness of participatory rights. Of necessity, where the matter is one in which the public at large or a significant segment thereof is entitled to participate, generally, open hearings would seem to be a necessary corollary of the legislative recognition of the public interest. There is also a sense in relation to at least some hearings that openness, particularly when attended by publicity through media reporting, may lead to the emergence of other witnesses and relevant evidence, thereby contributing to a decision based on more complete information. Some would also maintain that forcing parties and witnesses "to tell their stories" in public will at least, on occasion, have a healthy tendency to ensure truth-telling and serve as a guard against perjury. Finally, public hearings serve in an indirect way to assist those who subsequently make allegations of breaches of the rules of natural justice. Especially when the ground of review is a reasonable apprehension of bias by reason of the way in which an adjudicator behaved at the hearing, the making out of that case will, in many instances, be easier when members of the public attending the hearing are available to provide corroborative testimony. This avoids the reduction of the resolution of such matters to what will often be the conflicting testimony as to what actually happened from the party alleging

---

58 James L.H. Sprague, "Open Sesame!: Public Access to Agency Proceedings" (1999), 13 Canadian Journal of Administrative Law and Practice.

bias, on the one hand, and from the party or parties adverse in interest and the impugned adjudicator, on the other.

More commonly, however, debate as to whether or not a hearing should be open to the public is one centred on more general conceptions of open government and the ability of the populace to learn either first- or second-hand through the media about the activities of what is in and of itself an important feature of governance and one which also (as in the case of commissions of inquiry) has frequently as its principal objective the regulation or supervision of other aspects of government or matters of broad public concern. In other words, requirements of openness are more commonly thought of as promoting accountability through visibility. In the hands of the press and other media, this then translates into an issue involving freedom of expression and in particular, "freedom of the press and other media of communication." In most instances, only by allowing the media to be present and to report on the conduct of a hearing will the public come to know in any numbers as to the functioning of the administrative process itself and the areas of public interest regulated by that process. Seen in this light, it is therefore not surprising that the most prominent recent case law in this whole area involves media challenges on the basis of section 2(b) of the *Charter* to both statutory and tribunal-ordered prohibitions or limitations on access to and reporting of the functioning of various aspects of the administrative process.

2) Statutory Provisions

Some statutes creating statutory authority to make decisions following a hearing will make it clear that the hearing in question will normally have to be open to the public. Thus, section 29 of the *Immigration Act* provides that all hearings must be open to the public unless the adjudicator is satisfied that to hold an open hearing would imperil the life, liberty, and security of any person.[59] On other occasions, as mentioned already, the requirement of an open hearing will arise by inference from the terms of the statute and the nature of the questions in issue.

Vancouver (City) v. *British Columbia (Assessment Appeal Board)*[60] exemplifies the kind of case in which the court was prepared to draw this inference in rejecting a ruling by the Assessment Appeal Board which would have closed part of a hearing to the public. Among the

---

59   S.C. 1992, c. 49.
60   (1996), 39 Admin. L.R. (2d) 129 (B.C.C.A.).

factors to which the Court of Appeal referred in holding that the board had to open its hearings to the public, notwithstanding the silence of the legislation, were: the ramifications of the property assessment process for a large portion of the province's population as well as the possibility that assessment on other properties could be reopened in the event that the particular proceedings demonstrated or suggested that they had been undervalued for rating purposes.

However, Sprague may be on strong ground when he suggests that Laskin J.A. (as he then was) went too far when, in R. v. *Tarnopolsky, ex parte Bell*,[61] he suggested in passing that there was a presumption in favour of open hearings at common law in the case of silent statutes. While Laskin J.A.'s position is against the weight of Canadian authority in the context of tribunals, it does, however, reflect the position at common law with respect to the regular courts and may still have a strong claim to recognition at least in the case of tribunals such as human rights boards of inquiry that act in a manner that approximates proceedings in regular courts and that deal with disputes of a kind that resemble closely those dealt with by regular courts of law. In the particular case of human rights tribunals, there is also the further consideration that part of the statutory objectives is the education of the public in the evils of discrimination. Open hearings could contribute to the achievement of that objective.

More particularly, in the province of Ontario, however, the *Statutory Powers Procedure Act* (which applies to *Human Rights Code* Boards of Inquiry) mandates that, in general, hearings subject to that *Act* be open to the public.[62] The only exceptions are where this provision is expressly overridden in the relevant empowering legislation or where the tribunal is of the opinion that

(a) matters involving public security may be disclosed; or

(b) intimate financial or personal matters may be disclosed at the hearing of such a nature, having regard to the circumstances, that the desirability of avoiding disclosure thereof in the interests of any person affected or in the public interest outweighs the desirability of adhering to the principle that hearings be open to the public.

---

61   (1969), 11 D.L.R. (2d) 658 (Ont. C.A.). However, it does have the support of Hugessen J.A. in *Armadale Communications Ltd.* v. *Canada (Minister of Employment and Immigration)*, [1991] 3 F.C. 242 (C.A.).

62   S. 9.

However, judicial interpretation of this provision has accepted that sub-section (b) is not triggered simply because of the stigma and public embarrassment occasioned by a person having to submit to an inquiry as to whether he or she has been "guilty" of some form of misconduct.[63]

Interestingly, there is no equivalent provision in the Alberta *Administrative Procedures Act*. Moreover, in response to an attempt by a lawyer to force the Law Society to hear disciplinary charges against him in public despite a provision that they be heard *in camera*, a judge of the Alberta Court of Queen's Bench held,[64] after a survey of common law authorities,[65] that an open hearing was not a requirement of "due process of law" as guaranteed by section 1(a) of the *Alberta Bill of Rights*.[66] As the common law of natural justice did not require an open hearing, it was not a component of due process so as to override the provisions of the relevant legislation.

The 1994 amendments to the Ontario *Statutory Powers Procedure Act* also highlight another problematic aspect of the "open hearings" debate.[67] Up until this point, the *Act* was predicated on the holding of an oral hearing. The amendments introduced the possibility of written and electronic hearings. In those situations, what constitutes an open hearing? The simple answer would seem to be immediate or, at the very least, speedy access by the public to all documents and electronic data filed by the parties and generated by the tribunal or agency. However, without an open web site on which all such material is located, there are some obvious logistical problems in ensuring that not only is the material readily available to interested members of the public but also that they are alerted promptly to the fact that new data have been filed.[68]

Clearly, these considerations gave the drafters of the legislation difficulties. Thus, in the case of written hearings, as provided for under the *Act*, the public are entitled to only "reasonable" access. Moreover, in the case of electronic hearings, there is no requirement of any form of

---

63 *Pilzmaker v. Law Society of Upper Canada* (1989), 70 O.R. (3d) 126 (Div. Ct.); *Ottawa Police Force v. Lalande* (1986), 57 O.R. (3d) 509 (Dist. Ct.).

64 *Midgley v. Law Society of Alberta* (1980), 109 D.L.R. (2d) 241 (Alta. Q.B.) [*Midgley*].

65 In particular, the judgment of the Alberta Court of Appeal in *Re Penner and Board of Trustees of Edmonton School District No. 7* (1974), 46 D.L.R. (2d) 222 (Alta. C.A.) and *Re Millward and Public Service Commission* (1974), 49 D.L.R. (2d) 295 (F.C.T.D.).

66 R.S.A. 1980, c. A-16.

67 S.O. 1994, c. 27.

68 Of course, as Sprague points out forcefully (above, note 56 at 5–7), there can be serious logistical difficulties on occasion in providing facilities at a hearing which will enable it to be effectively open to all those who want to attend.

public access. The implications of this are somewhat startling. By moving to a hearing by way of teleconference or videoconference, a tribunal will be able to remove effectively the normal public right of access to the hearing. The potential for frustrating the *Act*'s basic policy is obvious and it seems equally obvious that either the basic policy should be rethought or the *Act* should be amended to provide for some surrogate form of public access in the case of hearings by way of teleconference or videoconference. Of course, with the growing sophistication of the information highway and the increasing use of the Internet, many of the logistical difficulties (not to mention cost) of providing timely public access to other than oral hearings may well diminish considerably and, as suggested above, it will become quite feasible to ensure openness by the use of publicly accessible web sites through which all relevant data must be filed.

3) The Impact of the *Charter*

The issue of open hearings has arisen quite frequently under the *Charter*. However, the focal point for the assertion of a *Charter*-based claim to an open process has not been the principles of fundamental justice as guaranteed in certain limited contexts by section 7.[69] Rather, as noted above, the challenges have been based primarily on section 2(b) and its guarantee of "freedom of expression, including of freedom of the press and other media of communication." Moreover, not surprisingly, the major protagonists in this litigation have been media interests.

Essentially, the courts have held, in a way that perhaps lends some support to Laskin J.A.'s perception of the common law expressed in *Bell*, that section 2(b) can create an entitlement to access in situations involving administrative tribunals that function like regular courts. In other words, while the section's reach has no explicit limits, it has not been treated to this point as amounting to a constitutionally protected guarantee of access or freedom of information to all governmental operations. It has, however, been held to invalidate legislation which created a presumption against an open process in the case of adjudica-

---

69   This does not mean, of course, that s. 7 has no role to play. However, not only would it require establishing that the administrative proceedings in question involved a threat to "life, liberty and security of the person" but also that, in at least the specific context, the "principles of fundamental justice" involved an open hearing. For the latter to occur would require the court to have a rather different perspective on the issue than that of the Alberta Court of Queen's Bench in *Midgley*, above note 64.

tors operating under the predecessor to the *Immigration Act* provision identified above. This was in *Pacific Press Ltd.* v. *Canada (Minister of Employment and Immigration)*,[70] where MacGuigan J.A. found the task in which adjudicators were involved was sufficiently judicial to justify the hearing being treated as court proceedings for the purposes of the protection of section 2(b). The court then went on to rule that the objectives of a closed process were over-inclusive (the protection of those who were the subject of a hearing as well as their family) and that the section could not be justified under section 1. Among the factors taken into account were the failure of the section to contemplate the possibility of intermediate steps such as a publication ban, the fact that much of the information provided at such hearings was otherwise accessible in public documents, the imposition of an over-rigorous standard on those seeking an opening of the hearing,[71] and the application of the *Act* to a wide range of immigration proceedings and not just those involving convention refugees.

What, of course, is interesting in all of this is that the court is not condemning outright the use of closed hearings but rather is urging that there at least be far more careful legislative calibration of the circumstances under which they can take place. In this respect, the legislative response of a reversal of the onus may have been an overreaction to the court's concerns.[72]

4) Alternatives

As just noted, the *Pacific Press* case identifies at least one alternative to a totally closed hearing: a publication ban on some or all of the proceedings. This is a compromise that may be relevant not only for the purposes of section 2(b) of the *Charter* but also, in a purely common law setting, when issues of natural justice or tribunal abuse of discretion over the control of its processes are raised. Similarly, there may be justification for partial closures where certain kinds of testimony are

---

70   (1991), 127 N.R. 325 (F.C.A.).

71   The relevant provision, s. 69(2) of the *Immigration Act*, R.S.C. 1985, c. I-2, required that the person seeking an opening of the hearing satisfy the adjudicator that to do so would not "impede" the conduct of the hearing and that the hearing could be conducted openly without affecting adversely those whose interests the provision was aimed protecting.

72   Sprague, above note 58, also questions whether the judgment in *Pacific Press*, in its generous treatment of the s. 2(b) claims, is totally in accord with the approach of the Supreme Court of Canada in the later judgment in *Dagenais* v. *Canadian Broadcasting Corporation*, [1994] 3 S.C.R. 835.

being given and, in some instances, this may be either legally necessary (as in the case of information having national security dimensions or criminal intelligence-gathering techniques) or justified even to the extent of excluding one of the parties. These issues are dealt with in greater detail later. Any obligation to hold open hearings is also without prejudice to the normal entitlement of tribunals to exclude those who have still to testify.

G. REPRESENTATION

The right to representation in administrative proceedings is the established norm in Canadian administrative law. This is so both statutorily and at common law. Thus, section 10 of the Ontario *Statutory Powers Procedure Act* and section 23 of the *Québec Charter of Human Rights and Freedoms* provide that parties to proceedings covered by those Acts are entitled to be represented by counsel or an agent. At common law, where serious interests are at stake, such as employment or liberty in a correctional setting, the courts have commonly recognized an entitlement to representation. More generally, the more complex the legal and factual issues and the less likely it is that a person will be able to represent her or his interests effectively, the greater will be the obligation on the decision maker to allow for representation. Indeed, in most instances, this will mean legal representation. In other words, the courts will not sustain attempts to preclude the use of lawyers as opposed to other forms of representative. As well, the courts have, on occasion, recognized that witnesses, as well as parties, are entitled to legal representation. There is also sometimes an obligation to inform those affected that they are entitled to representation by counsel.

However, it is also clear that the right to representation is not an absolute requirement in all administrative proceedings. In contrast to the Ontario and Québec statutory provisions, section 6 of the Alberta *Administrative Procedures Act* explicitly provides that those statutory authorities that are subject to the *Act* do not necessarily have to allow representation by counsel, though the section expressly reserves situations where that right is recognized in other legislation. Even the Supreme Court of Canada in *Dehghani* v. *Canada (Minister of Employment and Immigration)*,[73] has recognized exceptions to the right to representation in the case of the secondary examination by an immigration

---

73   [1993] 1 S.C.R. 1053.

officer of those seeking admission to Canada at a port of entry. Even assuming that this process affects the section 7, "life, liberty and security of the person" rights of those affected, the Court held that the imposition of a right to counsel on this interview process would add a further unnecessary complication. More generally, the entitlement to counsel lessens in the context of investigative and inquiry as opposed to true adjudicative processes, part of the thinking obviously being that there will be later opportunities for representation should the inquiry or investigation open up the possibility of further proceedings.[74] Also, the relatively minor nature of the matters at stake and the nature of the context in which a decision is being made may dictate that there is no need to recognize a right to representation by counsel. Thus, in a correctional setting, not all decisions involving penitentiary inmates will generate an entitlement to a hearing.[75] There has also been judicial acceptance of university rules precluding legal representation in student disciplinary settings at least where the potential sanction is not as severe as expulsion or suspension.[76]

It is also important to recognize that the right to the assistance of a lawyer or an agent does not trigger a single, undifferentiated form of representation. On occasion, the representation may be confined to providing advice at a hearing but not extend as far as cross-examining witnesses or making submissions.[77] However, in general, it will involve the right to have one's representative present throughout the proceedings. Indeed, in some instances, considerations of confidentiality may dictate that only the representative and not the person affected be present or have access to certain information and then on the basis of an undertaking to keep that information confidential even from the client. Two situations in which the courts have accepted this uneasy compromise have been the instance of commercially sensitive information[78] and mental health inquiries[79] where there is a fear that the revelation to

---

74   Indeed, in delivering the judgment of the Court, Iacobucci J. makes express reference to the later opportunity for an oral hearing before the applicant's status was determined finally: *ibid.* at 1078.

75   In the context of penitentiary discipline, see the distinctions made in *Howard* v. *Stony Mountain Institution* (1985), 19 D.L.R. (4th) 502 (F.C.A.).

76   *Morgan* v. *Acadia University (Board of Governors)* (1985), 16 Admin. L.R. 61 (N.S.S.C.T.D.).

77   See, example, *Egglestone* v. *Ontario (Advisory Review Board)* (1983), 150 D.L.R. (3d) 86 (Ont. Div. Ct.) [*Egglestone*].

78   See *Magnasonic Canada* v. *Anti-Dumping Tribunal*, [1972] F.C. 1239 (C.A.).

79   *Egglestone*, above note 77.

the person affected of certain kinds of medical information may imperil that person's prospects for recovery or the safety of those providing that information.

The right to representation by counsel does not necessarily involve the right to representation by a particular counsel. This principle has its highest profile in situations where the counsel of choice is unavailable on the date set for the hearing of the proceeding. While conflicts in scheduling are unavoidable and where some accommodation of counsel and their clients by administrative tribunals may be necessary, the courts have recognized that there is no universal entitlement to an adjournment in such cases in order to permit the attendance of retained counsel. This is particularly the case in situations where there is any hint that the demand for an adjournment on these grounds is in any way part of a strategy of delay.

While, as noted already, the Supreme Court of Canada has gone as far as holding that representation by counsel is not always a necessary component of the principles of fundamental justice when section 7 *Charter* rights are at stake, there is conversely no doubt that, in general, where *Charter* rights and freedoms are at stake, the intensity of claims to representation by counsel heighten considerably. This is exemplified by the jurisprudence involving those embroiled in the correctional system and the extent to which rights to counsel in that domain increased with the advent of the *Charter*.[80]

More recently, the Court has gone even further and held that, in certain instances, section 7 may demand that the state actually provide counsel in situations where the protected rights are at stake. *New Brunswick (Minister of Health and Community Services) v. G. (J.) [J.G.]*[81] involved a denial as a matter of legal aid policy of counsel to a woman who was opposing the extension of the custody of her three children by the province. In resisting the assertion of the right to state-funded counsel, the province relied (*inter alia*) on the earlier judgment of the

---

80   See, example, *Howard v. Stony Mountain Institution* (1985), 19 D.L.R. (4th) 502 (F.C.A.) for an elaboration of the circumstances under which there is a right to counsel in penitentiary disciplinary proceedings. Indeed, in the New Brunswick Court of Appeal in *New Brunswick (Minister of Health and Community Services) v. G. (J.) [J.G.]* (1997), 145 D.L.R.(4th) 349 (N.B.C.A.), Bastarache J.A. read the judgments in *Howard* as going as far as establishing an entitlement to state-funded counsel in those circumstances where the right was triggered. This is a dubious reading of *Howard*. However, as a consequence of the Supreme Court's judgment in *G. (J.), infra*, it may now, in fact, have a claim to be the law in at least some situations of penitentiary discipline.

81   [1999] 3 S.C.R. 46 [*New Brunswick*].

Court in *R. v. Prosper*,[82] in which the Court had refused to interpret section 10(b)'s guarantee of the right of a detained or arrested person "to retain and instruct counsel" as involving any claim to state-funded or provided counsel. However, the Court rejected this contention. *Prosper* did not necessarily involve the further proposition that there could never be a claim to state-funded counsel in situations where section 7 rights were at stake and that representation by counsel was necessary to ensure a fair hearing.

This distinguishing of *Prosper* opened the door for the Court considering the claim in this case. Having identified that the interests of the mother involved her right to security of the person and possibly also a liberty interest, the Court then proceeded to hold that, at least in certain circumstances where section 7 rights were at stake, the state was obligated to provide counsel. For these purposes, the Court identified three factors or considerations: "the seriousness of the interests at stake, the complexity of the proceedings, and the capacities of the appellant."[83] These factors look remarkably similar to those that are relevant to the threshold determination of whether there is any entitlement to representation by counsel, let alone state-financed counsel. However, it is manifest that the Court predicated all its discussion of this issue on the fact that the affected parent was indigent. This would, therefore, seem to be a "jurisdictional" threshold to any claim of this kind. The Court also made it clear that not every child custody proceeding would produce such an entitlement. The three factors would not always point to that as a necessity. What, however, does seem to follow is that the judgment opens up the possibility of such a claim being made in all section 7 cases where there is otherwise a right to representation and the person affected is indigent.

H. CONFIDENTIALITY

1) Introduction

If the principles of natural justice or procedural fairness have an essence, it must surely be that the parties affected by a potential decision or action must have sufficient knowledge of what is at stake to enable them to marshal evidence and arguments in support of their position and to counter what is being alleged in opposition to their

---

82 [1994] 3 S.C.R. 236.
83 *New Brunswick*, above note 81 at para. 75.

interests. Effective participation demands that those affected are aware of the issues and at least the nature of the contrary evidence. Without that, they can but speculate and such speculation may be sadly astray, not to mention a serious hindrance to the efficient conduct of the hearing process. While considerations of efficiency may sometimes lead to the conclusion that the parties' entitlement does not extend to a hearing at which all evidence is given in person subject to testing on cross-examination and that written summaries of the matters in issue will suffice, the minimum that is required is that those affected be at least provided with the "gist" of what is at stake both in terms of the issues and the evidence.

Indeed, Lord Denning once went so far as to suggest that, if the decision maker could not reveal at least the "gist" of the contrary evidence, that material could not be used.[84] This was in response to a situation in which it was claimed that considerations of confidentiality prevented the disclosure of relevant material to a party who was the subject of an inquiry. Whether Canadian courts would react in exactly the same way in the face of a confidentiality claim remains an open question.

In this section, I will first illustrate the basic principle that procedural fairness generally dictates that those affected have access to all relevant information before considering the contexts in which the Canadian courts are prepared to give complete or qualified recognition to confidentiality claims.

2) The Basic Principle

Cases involving an unadorned consideration of issues or evidence not made known to the affected person do not occur all that often. In general, the context in which these issues arise is one in which a claim is being made on various grounds of an entitlement to act in this manner for reasons of confidentiality. However, the Supreme Court of Canada judgment in *Kane* v. *University of British Columbia*[85] does provide an excellent illustration of the strength of the principle that natural justice or procedural fairness demands that the contrary arguments and evidence be revealed to those affected by a proposed decision in order to vindicate effectively participatory rights.

In *Kane*, the applicant was a professor who had been suspended from his duties at the university on the ground that he had been making

---

84 *In re Pergamon Press Ltd.*, [1971] Ch. 388 (C.A.) at 400.
85 [1980] 1 S.C.R. 1105 [*Kane*].

improper use of computer facilities. He appealed this decision to the board of governors of the university. In the course of considering Kane's appeal, the board of governors met with the president of the university over dinner. It was the president who had suspended Kane and it appeared from the affidavit evidence filed in support of Kane's application for judicial review that the president had supplied the board with further information during the course of the meal. Despite the fact that the president was a member of the board of governors, the Supreme Court held that the provision of such information behind the back of Kane was contrary to the rules of procedural fairness. Indeed, even to create a reasonable apprehension that such conduct had occurred would have been sufficient in the circumstances. While Dickson J. emphasized, in the course of delivering the judgment of the Court, that a high standard of procedural fairness is always required when someone's career or job is in jeopardy, the principle is one that has general application at least in situations where the focus of the hearing is the conduct or status of an individual or discrete group of individuals.

It does, however, deserve to be emphasized that the duty to reveal all relevant information may not be of quite the same order in situations where the context is a broad, policy-making one and the allegations of breach of the principles of procedural fairness are coming from individuals or public interest groups who have been given standing to participate in hearings on the proposed policy. Thus, in *Pembroke Civic Hospital v. Ontario (Health Services Restructuring Commission)*,[86] the Ontario Divisional Court rejected an argument for complete access to all relevant information made by those participating in the process by which the commission was determining how Pembroke's existing hospitals were to be restructured. In particular, the applicant hospital alleged that it had been refused access to "lists and copies of all the submissions made by others" and, as a result, it was not aware of the case it had to meet. In rejecting this argument, Campbell J., delivering the judgment of the court, made the following observation:

> The Commission is a policy making and implementation body, not an adversarial forum. As a policy making body, the Commission is entitled to listen to anyone who may have helpful information or opinions. Having listened to and considered submissions, it is under no obligation to follow the adversarial procedure of discovery and disclosure of all the information and materials submitted to it or considered by it.[87]

---

86   (1997), 36 O.R. (3d) 41 (Div. Ct.).
87   *Ibid.* at 47.

He then went on to state that the terminology of "a case to meet" had far less application to "a complex polycentric decision-making task" such as involved in the restructuring of the province's healthcare delivery system.[88] In so doing, he also stressed that the hospital could have been under no illusion as to what was potentially at stake, in reasonably specific terms, in the case of Pembroke's hospitals.

3) The Disputed Territory

The justification advanced most commonly for not revealing information as part of an administrative process is that of confidentiality. Behind these frequently advanced claims are a variety of concerns: to allow a business rival access to commercially valuable information will confer a competitive advantage; to provide the affected person with information that has a negative impact on her or his interests will be to invite reprisals against the providers of that information; giving some people knowledge about themselves may be harmful to their physical and mental health; public exposure of certain information may cause unnecessary embarrassment to those it concerns; law suits might result from the public dissemination of certain information if it proves to be untrue and defamatory; relationships of trust and confidence are cultivated better and greater frankness is ensured when the parties to those relationships have an assurance that their communications will be privileged; the state has an interest in preserving the secrecy of various species of information affecting the national interest or public security.

From time to time, tribunals and courts have had to deal with all these various claims and many others. Frequently, the resolution of the competing claims of confidentiality, on the one hand, and the need to have access to participate effectively, on the other, is not an easy task. On occasion, this leads tribunals and courts to explore compromise solutions.

One domain where access to information claims eventually triumphed was that of medical reports in disputed workers' compensation claims. Fears of reprisals from disappointed claimants, the spectre of possible lawsuits, and a general sense that such reports would be far less frank and helpful if open to claimants, led the medical profession to be skeptical about opening such reports to scrutiny in the context of appeals from negative decisions. However, in a strong judgment in

---

88   *Ibid.*

1981, the British Columbia Court of Appeal rejected these arguments in *Re Napoli and Workers' Compensation Board*.[89]

Here, while the board was prepared to provide Napoli with summaries of the evidence against his claim to workers' compensation, it denied him access to the actual medical reports on which the summaries were based. Faced with summaries that alleged without attribution that Napoli was feigning injury or was a malingerer, the court held, that without access to the actual reports and the authors of those reports, he would not be able to counter effectively the damaging evidence against him. In so doing, Nemetz C.J.B.C., delivering the judgment of the Court of Appeal, rejected expressly arguments to the effect that, if doctors knew that their reports were available to claimants, they would "sanitize" them in order to prevent reprisals from claimants and avoid potential legal liability and, in so doing, would render their reports practically useless for the task at hand. Nemetz C.J.B.C. was much more convinced by the usual contrary argument to the effect that the knowledge that the reports would be available to claimants would encourage physicians to "prepare them with greater care and diligence."[90] Moreover, in any event, the entitlement to procedural fairness required that "the reports be revealed in order that the claimant can effectively answer the case against him."[91]

While the issues that were at stake in Napoli's claim were essentially those of fact involving allegations that his own conduct undercut his claim for workers' compensation, the judgment precipitated a change in policy across the country on access to medical and other personal files in the workers' compensation process. In other words, the impact of the judgment extended to access to reports that were confined to purely medical diagnosis.

It is, however, clear that *Napoli* did not establish a general principle of universal access by subjects to medical reports in administrative proceedings where those reports were relevant to the determination of the matters at stake. Thus, the Ontario Divisional Court, in *Re Egglestone and Mousseau and Advisory Review Board*,[92] would not countenance the revelation of institutional reports to a person detained in a psychiatric facility and whose status was being reviewed to determine whether he should be released. Obviously, despite the fact that the case involved the

---

89 (1981), 126 D.L.R. (3d) 179 (B.C.C.A.).
90 *Ibid.* at 186.
91 *Ibid.*
92 (1983), 150 D.L.R. (3d) 86 (Ont. Div. Ct.).

applicant's right to liberty in terms of section 7 of the *Charter*,[93] the court's concerns were with potential repercussions at the hands of the patient for the authors of the relevant reports and also the patient's own health — to reveal certain kinds of information might hinder recovery. However, in a compromise that has also been used in other settings, the court did allow counsel of the patient access to the file on the basis that he or she not reveal that information to the client, a process which the court conditioned on the consent of the affected person.

Not surprisingly, one of the areas where concerns about release of information to those affected has surfaced quite frequently is where there are attempts to secure the release of information which has been gathered by police or security forces and which is now being used in situations that have the potential for a serious impact on someone's status as, for example, in the instances of those applying for Canadian citizenship and various forms of security clearance and non-Canadian residents subject to deportation proceedings.

In *Lazarov* v. *Secretary of State of Canada*,[94] after Lazarov had convinced a citizenship court judge that he qualified for Canadian citizenship, the minister exercised a residual discretion to deny him that status on the basis of confidential information provided by the RCMP and not revealed to Lazarov. Setting aside this decision, the Federal Court of Appeal held that, even if the confidential report or its contents did not have to be revealed, at the very least the minister should have revealed the "pertinent allegations which if undenied or unresolved would lead to the rejection of his application."[95] Moreover, this had to be to "an extent sufficient to enable him to respond to them."[96]

However, in similar contexts, the Supreme Court seems to have been somewhat less generous in its willingness to require the provision of the "gist" of such significant security or intelligence information. In *Prata* v. *Canada (Minister of Manpower and Immigration)*,[97] a deportation proceeding, the Federal Court of Appeal rejected a claim for access to criminal intelligence reports on the basis that to reveal these would run the serious risk of the sources for such reports drying up in a manner that would defeat the broader public interest. Indeed, the Supreme Court

---

93   In this very early *Charter* case, the majority asserted in one brief paragraph that if the court's prescriptions as to revelation of the relevant reports were observed that would amount to compliance with the "principles of fundamental justice."

94   [1973] F.C. 927 (C.A.).

95   *Ibid.* at 940.

96   *Ibid.* at 941.

97   [1976] 1 S.C.R. 376, aff'g. [1972] F.C. 1404 (C.A.).

of Canada went so far as to hold that Prata did not have any right to a hearing on the issuance of a certificate from two ministers of the Crown curtailing his normal right to contest a deportation order before the then Immigration Appeal Board. In the context of these rulings, both Courts also rejected an argument that this was a situation in which Prata had an entitlement to the principles of fundamental justice by reference to section 2(e) of the *Canadian Bill of Rights*.

Much more recently, in *Chiarelli* v. *Canada (Minister of Justice)*,[98] another deportation case involving someone convicted of a serious offence and suspected of involvement in organized crime, the Court ruled, that, even assuming that the deportation of a non-resident Canadian affected that person's section 7 *Charter* rights, the principles of fundamental justice did not demand that Chiarelli have access to the full details of information on his activities provided to the Security Intelligence Review Committee. In so doing, the Court referred to the state's "considerable interest in effectively conducting national security and criminal intelligence investigations and in protecting police sources."[99] It is, however, also significant that, in terms of *Lazarov*, Sopinka J., delivering the judgment of the majority of the Supreme Court, did conclude that the summaries provided to Chiarelli of this *in camera* evidence had given him "sufficient information to know the substance of the allegations against him, and to be able to respond."[100]

Not surprisingly, a related domain where the threat of reprisals has had its greatest impact on access to information for the purposes of administrative proceedings is that of correctional law and, more particularly, prison discipline and parole suspension and revocation. On many occasions, the demands for protection in such cases are also based on the need to prevent the dissemination of evidence as to police and penitentiary authority information-gathering techniques.

Gallant v. *Trono, Deputy Commissioner, Correctional Service Canada*[101] is an illustrative though inconclusive authority. The context was a decision to transfer an inmate from one penitentiary to another. The basis for this allegation was that, while incarcerated, he had been involved in the supply of drugs and extortion. While the authorities provided some details, they declined to reveal the names of six informants or to provide further details that might reveal their identities. To do so would be to expose them to the possibility of reprisals. By a

---

98   [1992] 1 S.C.R. 711.
99   *Ibid.* at 744.
100 *Ibid.* at 746.
101 (1989), 36 Admin. L.R. 261 (F.C.A.).

majority of two to one, the Federal Court of Appeal sustained the transfer decision. However, the majority judges differed in their approach to the procedural unfairness arguments, arguments that were made under the umbrella of section 7 of the *Charter* and its demand for adherence to the principles of fundamental justice.

According to Pratte J.A., the failure to provide greater detail and the names of the informants had had a seriously adverse impact on Gallant's ability to contest the proposed transfer. Because of this, the proceedings had not been in accordance with the principles of procedural fairness or fundamental justice. However, he went on to hold that such a compromise of Gallant's entitlements was demonstrably justifiable by reference to section 1 of the *Charter*. In contrast, Marceau J.A. did not see procedural fairness or fundamental justice as requiring complete revelation of all the details. Having regard to the nature of decision (the transfer of an inmate from one institution to another for administrative and good order reasons), the procedural demands were not as exacting as they might be in other contexts even accepting that the transfer decision deprived Gallant of the "right to life, liberty and security of the person." In particular, as guilt was not really the issue but whether there were sufficient grounds for concern to justify a transfer, procedural fairness and, in particular, a "meaningful" participation in the process were achieved with the provision of the level of detail that had been given. They did not demand anything fuller and, in particular, the identity of the informants or further information by which they might possibly be identified.

In many ways, however, Desjardins J.A.'s dissent is even more revealing than the majority judgments. Like Pratte J.A., she accepted that, on the basis of the information provided, Gallant "probably did not have enough information to defend himself."[102] However, at least in the context of a penitentiary transfer decision, she did not seem prepared to go as far as Lord Denning and hold that, if the authorities felt that they could not reveal the relevant information to Gallant, they could not use it. Rather, she apparently accepted that, in some contexts, informers were entitled to protection but that the information they provided could nonetheless be used. What, however, was problematic in this instance was the failure of the authorities to provide to Gallant or the court a sufficient foundation in justification of this significant compromise of normal procedural fairness entitlements.

---

102   *Ibid.* at 280.

Drawing on an earlier judgment of Reed J. of the Federal Court, Trial Division,[103] Desjardins J.A. suggested that this justification should come in two forms: sealed affidavits explaining the exact nature of the evidence and identifying how specifically the authorities anticipated its revelation would compromise the safety of informants and the security of penitentiary information-gathering techniques, as well as independent, objective evidence that indicated that the authorities had taken steps to verify the reliability of the informants and the information they had provided. Without that kind of material, she was not prepared to countenance the use of the information in a way that was contrary to the normal dictates of procedural fairness.

Subsequently, in *Gough v. Canada (National Parole Board)*,[104] another correctional law case with rather more serious consequences, parole revocation on the verge of the former inmate securing his "unconditional liberty," the Federal Court indicated that it would not readily countenance the use of unrevealed information at a post-suspension hearing to determine whether suspension should become revocation. In this context, Reed J., in a judgment that in effect was confirmed by the Federal Court of Appeal,[105] indicated grave concerns with the justifications advanced for not revealing the details of the relevant incidents or the names of the alleged victims. In so far as those justifications were ones based on the potential danger to informants and the undermining of the operation of the parole system, they amounted to mere assertions not supported by a sufficient factual underpinning. Moreover, the authorities had refused the opportunity for an *in camera* hearing at which they would have the opportunity to lay the factual foundations for the beliefs expressed in the relevant affidavits.[106] Given that, without further detail, the applicant would not have sufficient information as to the "gist" of what was at stake "to enable him to respond intelligently"[107] in a matter affecting his section 7 rights, the decision revoking his parole could not stand.

It is also significant that Reed J. at one point in *Gough* defined the issue in terms of whether or not the Parole Board "is required to either release the information to the applicant (when disclosure will necessar-

---

103 *Cadieux v. Director of Mountain Institution*, [1985] 1 F.C. 378 (T.D.) at 402.
104 (1990), 45 Admin. L.R. 304 (F.C.T.D.) [*Gough*].
105 (1991), 47 Admin. L.R. 226 (F.C.A.).
106 Reed J. envisaged that counsel for Gough would be present at such a hearing provided that an undertaking was given not to reveal the information proffered to the client.
107 *Gough*, above note 104 at 314.

ily reveal the source of that information) or forego reliance on that information in making a decision on the applicant's parole."[108] While she never says so explicitly and the matter is not without ambiguity,[109] it may therefore be a reasonable implication from her quashing of the original revocation decision and remission of the matter to a differently constituted panel of the Parole Board that the authorities have to either provide the relevant information or not rely upon it in making their case before the Board. At least in this context, Lord Denning's position that if the gist cannot be revealed, the information may not be relied upon may have achieved acceptance.

Whether this is the position generally under Canadian law remains, however, a matter of speculation. The courts have not fully come to terms with the difficult question of whether information can be relied upon if it identifies a source who would thereafter be in jeopardy. Indeed, there is still uncertainty as to the extent to which information can be used without revealing the source of that information at least in situations where the ability of the affected person to counter that information effectively may be seriously compromised without knowledge of who has supplied it.

One of the non-*Charter* domains where this has surfaced often but without definitive resolution by the courts[110] is in the context of faculty members seeking preferment (appointment, renewal, tenure, promotion) in a college or university setting. Can the college or university rely upon references and other forms of assessment that are not revealed to the faculty member? If there is an obligation to reveal that material to the faculty member, may the college or university expunge the name of the person supplying that information? Does it matter for these purposes whether the person supplying the information is an external referee, a colleague, or a student? Does the nature of the information matter? For example, is there a difference between a student asserting that the candidate is a poor teacher and an allegation that the faculty member has engaged in inappropriate conduct? Is it relevant that the faculty member might be described in the old terminology as a privilege seeker rather than as a rights holder? Are decisions about appointment, renewal, ten-

---

108   *Ibid.* at 320.

109   Giving the authorities an opportunity to lay a fuller factual foundation for their position on non-disclosure can be seen as inconsistent with a "reveal or not use" posture.

110   These are, however, issues that are very much central in the negotiation of collective agreements in tertiary educational settings and, in those collective agreements, they are dealt with in varying ways and with varying levels of specificity.

ure, and promotion all of the same order of significance for these purposes? What about participation in salary increases?

These questions point out what can be at stake in determining whether ensuring the rights of individuals to participate in a decision-making process can ever be suspended in a significant fashion by reference to overriding public interest considerations. In particular, is the perception that the truth will only emerge in certain contexts if those supplying information are given protection from exposure to the person who is the subject of that information correct? To the extent that relying upon secret information goes against the very essence of what a participatory opportunity is all about, there is a case for arguing that such compromises of procedural fairness can never be tolerated. Information which is not subject to testing should never be relied upon. The danger that it will be unreliable is simply too great, even though it may mean that, in certain circumstances, the "truth" will never come out.

However, experience does tell us that, in some regulated contexts, reprisals are a real possibility and, human nature being what it is, most of us are also, to a greater or lesser extent, unwilling or reluctant to face those whom we "accuse." It is simply too uncomfortable and disruptive at all sorts of levels. Whether the public interest dictates formal acknowledgment and accommodation of these realities, particularly the second, is, of course, another question. Nonetheless, what Reed J. and Desjardins J.A. have pointed to in their judgments in this domain is the possibility of a reasonably satisfactory compromise at least in some domains. In limited circumstances, the relevant authorities will be entitled to rely upon secret information without revealing its detail to affected persons provided, in the event of challenge, that they can convince the court that they have subjected the information in questions to alternative and reliable verification techniques.

4) Commercially Sensitive Information

Many regulatory settings require businesses to reveal to regulators a range of commercial information that could be of very considerable value both to existing competitors and those with the ability to enter the particular field of commercial endeavour. Aside from the obvious instance of such things as secret formulae, recipes, programs, and other inventions that serve to give a particular business a competitive edge, businesses also will frequently have a considerable competitive interest in keeping financial information, the terms on which they are prepared to do business, and information as to the way in which they have structured their business out of the hands of competitors and potential competitors.

In our current form of capitalist economy, all of these generally are recognized as being legitimate interests that, in most situations, will have to be accommodated within the statutory framework of regulation and the practices of the regulator. In some situations, this leads to rather secretive regulation with the protection of the public interest, in general, and a competitive market, in particular, being entrusted to the wisdom and expertise of the regulator. However, this is not universally the case and it is now very common for both the public generally and even competitive interests to be accorded a role in the ongoing regulation of business as reflected in rights of participation at regulatory hearings of various kinds.

When this happens, the legislature and, failing that, the regulator and, in a reserve capacity, the courts will have to find a reasonable accommodation between the expectation on the part of the public and competitors of effective participation in the regulatory process and the need of the regulated business for protection of its various "commercial secrets." As in other areas, that compromise may be in the form of providing the "gist" but not the detail of the relevant information to competitors and public interest participants. Here too, regulators and courts have found a role for the device of giving access to the relevant information to counsel for the competitors and public interest groups on the giving of an undertaking that it not be revealed to the client. On yet other occasions, the regulator or the courts will require that those participating make out a very clear case that their participation will effectively be negated if they do not have access to particular information. As well, in extreme cases, the regulator may be forced to determine that it alone should have access to the relevant information because there is simply no way of sharing it with other participants without damaging the competitive position of the regulated business in a way that conflicts with or undercuts the whole purpose of the statutory regulatory regime.

In fact, the Canadian jurisprudence in this domain is not particularly rich.[111] In part, that may well be a consequence of carefully tailored statutes, regulations, internal rules, or regulatory practices that participants have come to accept as the necessary "rules of the game" in particular areas. In an era where the Canadian courts are also beginning to accord some deference to the expertise of at least certain tribu-

---

111   For some of the few examples, see *Magnasonic,* above, note 76; *Sarco Canada Ltd.*
      v. *Canada (Anti-dumping Tribunal),* [1979] 1 F.C. 247; *Scott* v. *Nova Scotia (Rent
      Review Commission)* (1977), 81 D.L.R. (3d) 530 (C.A.); *Ogilvie Mills Ltd.* v. *Canada
      (National Transportation Agency)* (1992), 140 N.R. 278 (F.C.A.); and *McCain Foods
      Ltd.* v. *Canada (National Transportation Agency),* [1993] 1 F.C. 583 (C.A.).

nals in the crafting of appropriate procedures, it is not to be expected that there will be any great surge in judicial setting aside of such compromises in the handling of access to information particularly in situations where those compromises have been the product of a rule-making process. Indeed, given the highly context-sensitive nature of problems about information in the world of business, this is an area crying out for settlement by way of constituency-based rulemaking with the courts playing a very reserved and deferential role once that process has concluded.

5) Crown or Executive Privilege

Confidentiality claims may also arise in other guises or formats. Thus, for example, the invocation of various evidential privileges, such as lawyer/client privilege or adjudicative privilege may prevent or limit the efforts of those participating in administrative proceedings or subsequent judicial review to obtain full information on all relevant matters. Of particular interest in this domain is executive or Crown privilege which provides the executive in certain circumstances with a mantle of secrecy and which may have an impact on the conduct of administrative proceedings.

At common law, since the judgment of the Supreme Court of Canada in *Carey* v. *Ontario*,[112] it has been clear that the courts have ultimate reserve authority over any claim to executive privilege even in the instance of security claims. In practice, this means that, if a decision maker invokes executive privilege as a basis for not revealing information relevant to the taking of a particular decision, or a witness or potential source of information in an administrative proceeding declines to reveal relevant information on the basis of executive privilege, the matter may be tested in the courts. In that context, the court may accept the claim on the basis of the affidavits filed by the government. However, the potential exists for the court to call for the relevant information so that it might be inspected and the merits of the claim to privilege assessed.

Federally, the situation is rather different in that the whole issue of Crown or executive privilege is not determined by reference to common law principles but in terms of a statutory regime contained in sections 37 to 39 of the *Canada Evidence Act*.[113] Under that regime, in the instance of "a confidence of the Queen's Privy Council for Canada," an

---

112   [1986] 2 S.C.R. 637.
113   R.S.C. 1985, c. C-5.

objection to disclosure lodged by either a minister of the Crown or the Clerk of the Privy Council is conclusive. In such a case, disclosure "shall be refused without examination or hearing of the information" by either the court or relevant statutory decision maker. Indeed, the way in which the section is couched seems to suggest that the court or decision maker cannot even inquire whether the information is genuinely such a confidence as defined in the *Act*. It is the certificate that it is such a document that creates the immunity. It is also significant that "a confidence of the Queen's Privy Council for Canada" is defined to include not only the deliberations of and documents presented to the Privy Council, Cabinet, and Privy Council and Cabinet committees but also

(d) a record used for or reflecting communications or discussions between Ministers of the Crown on matters relating to the making of government decisions or the formulation of government policy;

(e) a record the purpose of which is to brief Ministers of the Crown in relation to matters that are brought before, or are proposed to be brought before, Council or that are the subject of communications or discussions referred to in paragraph (d); and

(f) draft legislation.

To this point the courts have resisted all attempts to challenge the constitutional validity of this extremely broad provision that may be without parallel in the common law world.[114]

In terms of its impact on the functioning of administrative processes, this provision can obviously be used to justify non-disclosure of certain kinds of information relevant to decisions taken by the authorities coming within the ambit of the provision. It also allows the government considerable latitude in preventing courts, tribunals, and other decision makers and those affected by their decisions from seeking access to such information even when it is highly relevant to adjudicative and other decision making tasks in which they are involved. In

---

114   See *Canadian Association of Regulated Importers* v. *Canada (Attorney General)* (1991), 87 D.L.R. (4th) 730 (F.C.A.); *Canada (Attorney General)* v. *Central Cartage (No. 1)*, [1990] 2 F.C. 641 (C.A.); *Singh* v. *Canada (Attorney General)*, [1999] 4 F.C. 583 (T.D.), aff'd. [2000] 3 F.C. 185 (C.A.). It was, however, conceded in *Singh* that a bad faith or malicious abuse of the power conferred by s. 39 was reviewable and could not be constitutionally immunized from review. Within that realm is included Cabinet use of s. 39 to prevent unconstitutional conduct coming to light. However, it was for the person asserting such an allegation to provide the court with a sufficient factual basis for lifting the veil created by s. 39. See also *Babcock* v. *Canada (Attorney General)*, [2000] B.C.J. No. 1127 (QL) (June 6, 2000) holding that the Crown had waived its right to rely on section 39.

such cases, the decision makers and affected constituencies are at the mercy of the government in the sense of having to hope that the government will not abuse its authority to issue a certificate but rather save such exercises of power for cases where there is genuine state interest in the security of the relevant information.

6) Additional Dimensions

As we have seen already in the section on discovery, one area where the courts have sometimes strived to protect what they regard as a relationship of confidentiality is with respect to reports prepared by staff to regulatory agencies for the purposes of assisting that agency or a particular panel in the determination of a matter that is before them. Questions do, however, arise as to the extent to which the fostering of a frank relationship between tribunal members and assistants can be at the expense of the parties' right to have access to all relevant material and to be confronted with all relevant opinions. In fact, this is really part of the broader issue of consultations between those charged with taking the decision and others. I will, therefore, return to it below in the section on consulting with others. As well, before that, I will deal with the issue of the extent to which the expansion of the scope of judicial notice in proceedings before administrative tribunals and regulatory agencies requires, at least in some contexts, the decision maker to reveal the facts of which he or she is proposing to take notice so that the parties will have an opportunity to contest them.

I. RULES OF EVIDENCE

Both the Alberta *Administrative Procedures Act*[115] and the Ontario *Statutory Powers Procedure Act*[116] provide that decision makers covered by these Acts are not constrained by the rules of evidence applicable to courts exercising civil or criminal jurisdiction nor does evidence have to be given under oath. Parallels also exist in other jurisdictions in statutes conferring decision making powers on individual tribunals and agencies. Thus, for example, section 16(c) of the *Canada Labour Code*[117] provides that the Canada Industrial Relations Board has power "to receive and accept such evidence and information on oath, affidavit

---

115 R.S.A. 1980, c. A-2, section 9.
116 R.S.O. 1990, c. S.22 (as amended by S.O. 1994, c. 27 and S.O. 1997, c. 23), s. 15.
117 R.S.C. 1985, c. L-2 (as amended by S.C. 1998, c. 26, s. 5).

or otherwise as the Board in its discretion sees fit, whether admissible in a court of law or not."

These various provisions do not however alter the common law; rather, they reflect the common law position: in general, the normal rules of evidence do not apply to administrative tribunals and agencies. Thus, in a variety of contexts,[118] Canadian courts have cited with approval the classic statement of Lord Loreburn L.C. in *Board of Education* v. *Rice*: "They can obtain information in any way they think best, always giving a fair opportunity to those who are parties in the controversy for correcting or contradicting any relevant statement prejudicial to their view."[119] Obviously, the opening clause of this sentence concedes considerable discretion to the decision-maker in determining how information will be obtained. On the other hand, such a discretion, whether existing at common law or by reason of specific statutory provision, does not provide an excuse for compromising the general principles of procedural fairness.

A good illustration is provided by the 1955 judgment of the Supreme Court of Canada in *Mehr* v. *Law Society of Upper Canada*.[120] At issue there was the solicitation and use by the Society's Discipline Committee of a joint declaration made by persons outside Canada who were not available for cross-examination. This declaration contradicted sworn oral testimony that had been given by the lawyer who was the subject of the disciplinary proceedings and ultimately disbarred. In the circumstances, the Court held that the "reception of such evidence was . . . wrongful and fatal to the validity of the proceedings."[121] Indeed, the Court went on to express reservations as to the position adopted in the Court of Appeal that the committee was not obliged to adhere to court rules of evidence. This suggests that, where a professional career is at stake, the common law might well require adherence to or at least close approximation to the ordinary rules of evidence.

However, since then, the ordinary rules of evidence have become that much more relaxed with respect to the use of hearsay in general, including statements made outside the course of the hearing by persons not only disabled from testifying directly or unwilling to do so. As a consequence, it now seems highly unlikely that, even in professional disciplinary proceedings, the courts would refuse to countenance the

---

118   See, example, *British Columbia (Labour Relations Board)* v. *Traders Services Ltd.*, [1958] S.C.R. 672.

119   [1911] A.C. 179 (H.L. Eng.) at 182.

120   [1955] S.C.R. 344 [*Mehr*].

121   *Ibid.* at 349.

use of hearsay evidence or written depositions by administrative tribunals. Indeed, in the context of the professional disciplinary proceedings involving Dr. Khan, the physician whose criminal trial provided the context for the redefinition of the hearsay rule in criminal proceedings,[122] the Ontario Court of Appeal explicitly sustained the use of hearsay evidence.[123]

Nevertheless, where, in matters of this kind, hearsay evidence or various forms of deposition are used, there will generally be an obligation on the part of the tribunal relying on such material to treat such materials with caution and be acute to the need for other indicators of their reliability. Moreover, the lesson from *Rice* still holds: the person affected must still be accorded an ample opportunity to counter the evidence from such sources. While this does not necessarily involve always making the source of such evidence available for cross-examination, there may well be circumstances where that or a close surrogate will be a requirement.[124] Moreover, to the extent that *Mehr* involved a tribunal securing a written contradiction of sworn testimony by the subject of the disciplinary proceedings without making the authors of the declaration available for cross-examination, it is almost certainly still good law on its facts.

In fact, a useful contrast is provided by the judgment of the Alberta Court of Appeal in *Re County of Strathcona No. 20 and Maclab Enterprises*.[125] This involved a hearing by the Provincial Planning Board in which a decision to admit a report by an expert on pollution in the relevant area was under challenge. Although the author of that report was not available for cross-examination, the court accepted that, in the circumstances, the opportunity afforded and in fact taken to provide written responses to the content of that report was enough to meet the requirements of natural justice or procedural fairness. In terms of *Rice*, this represented a sufficient opportunity to "correct or contradict" any "statement prejudicial to their view." What this clearly illustrates is that standards in this domain will vary depending both on the nature of the evidence in question and the subject matter of the hearing, with the courts far more inclined to look closely at the justifications for the use of such material and hearsay evidence in situations involving

---

122   *R. v. Khan*, [1990] 2 S.C.R. 531.

123   *Khan v. Ontario College of Physicians and Surgeons* (1992), 94 D.L.R. (4th) 193 (Ont. C.A.).

124   *Bond v. New Brunswick (Management Board)* (1992), 95 D.L.R. (4th) 733 (N.B.C.A.).

125   (1971), 20 D.L.R. (3d) 200; leave to appeal refused [1971] S.C.R. xii.

allegations of the "who did what to whom?" variety in the context of proceedings having career-threatening possibilities.

Indeed, the closer the character of the proceedings is to the kind of matter typically dealt with by a court of criminal or civil jurisdiction, the more likely it is that other aspects of the law governing the leading of evidence will apply to an administrative tribunal. Two examples will suffice. In professional disciplinary proceedings, it is generally impermissible to introduce new allegations and evidence after the "prosecution" has closed its case.[126] Likewise, usually, it is procedurally unfair to take evidence and submissions on penalty before the determination of "guilt" or responsibility.[127]

As well as leading to a breach of the rules of natural justice or procedural fairness, the wrongful admission or use of evidence can also, on occasion, give rise to another ground of judicial review: a complete lack of evidence to support the findings made by the tribunal. This will occur in a situation where, without the challenged evidence, there is no basis in fact for the decision maker's finding on a key issue or issues.[128]

A refusal to allow evidence to be led or otherwise entered can also create a breach of the rules of natural justice or procedural fairness, or, indeed, other forms of reviewable error. Thus, for example, if a tribunal wrongly determines that evidence is protected by some form of statutory or common law privilege, there will be judicial review of the exclusion of that evidence. Similarly, even where tribunals are given broad powers to control their proceedings and exclude evidence that it is unreliable, repetitious, or irrelevant, an exercise of that power that defeats the right of party to advance its case may give rise to a breach of the rules of natural justice. Indeed, in this sense, a refusal to consider hearsay evidence may in some instances constitute a breach of the rules of natural justice or procedural fairness.

A modern but problematic example of review based on the exclusion of evidence is provided by *Syndicat des employés professionnels de l'Université du Québec à Trois Rivières* c. *Université du Québec à Trois Rivières*.[129] The context was a grievance brought by two researchers who had been dismissed "because of a lack of funds" to support the

---

126 Discussed in *Hryciuk* v. *Ontario (Lieutenant Governor)* (1994), 26 Admin. L.R. (2d) 271 (Ont. Div. Ct.).

127 *Hirt* v. *College of Physicians and Surgeons (British Columbia)* (1986), 63 B.C.L.R. 185 (S.C.), aff'd. (1986), 10 B.C.L.R. (2d) 314 (C.A.).

128 *Robertson* v. *Scott* (1973), 35 D.L.R. (3d) 451 (B.C.S.C.), rev'd. on other grounds (1974), 42 D.L.R. (3d) 143 (B.C.C.A.).

129 [1993] 1 S.C.R. 471 [*Syndicat*].

research that they had been conducting. In the course of the hearing, the grievance arbitrator had refused to admit evidence to the effect that the lack of funds had resulted from the conduct of the researchers. Acting under a broad discretion over the admission of evidence, the arbitrator had determined that this represented an attempt by the university to insinuate a fresh justification for the dismissal of the two employees. However, the Supreme Court of Canada rejected this characterization of the purpose and effect of the impugned evidence. Rather, the Court ruled that the exclusion of the evidence went to an issue that was central to the grievance, the competence of the researchers. As such, the refusal of the arbitrator to admit that evidence had led to a breach of the rules of natural justice.

In reaching this conclusion, the Court emphasized that judicial review was not available for every wrongful refusal to admit evidence. Particularly in situations such as this where there was not only a wide discretion in the decision maker as to the admission of the evidence but also a privative clause protecting the arbitrator's definition of the scope of the arbitration from judicial review, it was only errors that led to a breach of the rules of natural justice that would justify a setting aside of the decision under attack. However, in this context, given that a lack of funds could, as accepted by the arbitrator, be a ground for dismissal only if the employees were to blame for that state of affairs, the arbitrator's failure to admit evidence on that very issue had led to a breach of the rules of natural justice.

While there is nothing controversial in the general proposition that evidential errors which have that consequence should be set aside, what the case does illustrate, however, is that there may on occasion be a very blurred line separating a ruling on the admissibility of evidence from a ruling on the proper scope of a hearing. According to the arbitrator in this instance, when the university justified its actions on the basis of a "lack of funds" without any specific reference to the conduct of the employees, that defined the scope of the grievance. It was incumbent on the university to establish that there was in fact a lack of funds and that, in terms of the collective agreement, this was a freestanding basis for dismissal. Thereafter, it was too late to introduce a new ground based on the conduct of the employees as the basis for the lack of funds. This looks very much like a determination as to the proper legal scope of the arbitration. However, in categorizing the refusal to admit that kind of evidence as a breach of the rules of natural justice, the Court in effect is holding that implicit in the university's communication of the basis for dismissal is a statement to the effect that the employees were responsible for that state of affairs.

Only when viewed in this light can the intervention begin to be justified and, of course, even then, it almost certainly involves second-guessing the grievance arbitrator's reading of the university's initial justification for its actions.

Given that the Court in recent years has generally been ill-disposed towards arguments that attempt to finesse the policy of deference to the substantive decisions and rulings of expert tribunals, this judgment can be seen as somewhat of an anomaly. In particular, it should probably not be read as giving encouragement to those who seek to disguise substantive merits review in a procedural fairness, evidential error cloak. Indeed, as already noted, the majority, over the dissent on this issue of L'Heureux-Dubé J., took particular care to emphasize that mere error on an evidential exclusion question was not sufficient to justify judicial review; it had to have unfairness consequences. This does not suggest a Court overly anxious to open this up as a basis for review. However, even when read in this limited way, it does illustrate the perils for the procedural and substantive prerogatives of tribunals and agencies in the too ready acceptance of this species of argument.[130]

Linked also with issues about the admissibility and use of evidence are questions as to its sufficiency, where the onus or burden of proof lies, and what is the appropriate standard of proof. While these issues are sometimes treated as giving rise to procedural fairness concerns, they are more generally conceived of as part of the law governing the review of determinations of law and fact. Accordingly, they have been dealt with in chapter 5.

J. OFFICIAL NOTICE

As already discussed, there are many tribunals that are obliged to follow a basically judicial or adversarial hearing process, one of the key elements of which is the obligation to make a decision on the basis of the evidence adduced at the hearing. Thus, such a tribunal will offend the rules of natural justice or procedural fairness if it or any of its members engages in an independent search for further evidence or data.[131]

---

130   For another example of the problem, see *Timpauer v. Air Canada* (1986), 18 Admin. L.R. 192 (F.C.A.).

131   See, example, *Sivaguru v. Canada (Minister of Employment and Immigration)* (1992), 16 Imm. R. (2d) 85 (F.C.A.), where an adjudicator secured evidence for the purposes of laying a trap for an applicant, thereby exposing himself to disqualification on the basis of a reasonable apprehension of bias.

However, as in the world of the regular courts, there is an important qualification to this general principle. Just as judges in regular courts have the capacity to take judicial notice of certain notorious facts, so too may adjudicative tribunals take what is commonly called "official notice" of certain kinds of facts.

Not only is this a common law principle but it is also provided for explicitly in the Ontario *Statutory Powers Procedure Act*.[132] Indeed, the terms of the relevant provision of that *Act* are useful in illustrating the proposition that the scope for official notice may in some instances be somewhat broader than the rather narrow confines of traditional judicial notice. Section 16 provides that decision makers coming within the ambit of the *Act* as well as taking notice of facts that may be judicially noticed are also entitled to

(b) take notice of any generally recognized scientific or technical facts, information or opinions within its scientific or specialized knowledge.

Given the reasons behind the creation of many administrative regimes — the timely resolution of issues or disputes by those with expertise in the particular field — this is a perfectly understandable provision that gives concrete recognition to such a policy. However, there may well be many occasions where simply to take notice of the kind of material specified in this subclause will be detrimental to the effective participation of those affected.

This is illustrated well by one of the few cases in which the parameters of this provision have been explored though by no means in a definitive manner: *Township of Innisfil* v. *Township of Vespra*.[133] This case involved an application by a municipality to annex three other neighbouring townships. Among the issues that were pertinent to this application was the question of whether industry would be attracted to such an expanded city. In determining such matters, the Ontario Municipal Board used what was called "a vacancy factor." How much vacant land would it take to induce an industry to relocate expressed in terms of a multiplier of the area of land it was occupying at its present location? In this instance, the part of the board's decision dealing with this issue referred to evidence that had been given in a previous case involving another application by the same municipality. This evidence was based on the recollection of a member of the panel who had sat on the previous application and was not put to the parties.

132   R.S.O. 1990, c. S. 22 (as amended by S.O. 1994, c. 27 and S.O. 1997, c. 23).
133   [1981] 2 S.C.R.145, rev'g (1978), 95 D.L.R. (3d) 298 (Ont. C.A.), aff'g (1978), 7 O.M.B.R. 233 (Div. Ct.).

In the Divisional Court, varying stances were taken on the use of this evidence. One judge was of the view that this was not a "generally recognized scientific or technical fact." As such, it did not come within the section and could not be relied upon unless entered formally in evidence. Another judge felt that the use of such information was quite proper. However, it was a requirement of natural justice that the parties be informed of the tribunal's intention to take it into account and be given an opportunity to respond to it with their own evidence and arguments. On appeal, the majority of the Court of Appeal agreed that, where a tribunal is of a mind to rely on a precedent or evidence given in an earlier proceeding, it should inform the parties. However, the court was also of the view that there was independent evidence on the record supporting the board's finding on this issue and that the reference to the previous proceeding was merely an illustrative example. On this issue, the Supreme Court of Canada supported the Court of Appeal.

What emerges from this decision are concerns as to what precisely qualifies as appropriate terrain for the operation of the doctrine of official notice whether under the common law or a statutory formulation such as Ontario's. More particularly, what are hallmarks of "generally recognized scientific facts, information or opinions"? Moreover, what also becomes clear from the discussion of the issue by the various judges is that it may be necessary to think in terms of not just two but three categories of evidence in this domain: material that must be entered and proved in the regular manner; facts, information, and opinions of which the tribunal may take notice without alerting the parties; and facts, information, or opinions that do not have to be entered in the regular way but that the tribunal is under an obligation to reveal and to provide an opportunity for the parties to contest before they are taken into account.

Indeed, the more specialized the area of regulation and the more likely it is that those appearing before the tribunal will not have had knowledge of or even access to the information in question, the more convincing is the case for the third category to be the norm and the second category the exception. In this regard, it is informative to consider the terms of the special official notice regime created in the *Immigration Act*[134] for proceedings before the Refugee Division of the Immigration and Refugee Board. While the Board is entitled to the benefit of the judicial notice rule and also to take account of "any other

---

134   R.S.C. 1985, c. I-2, ss. 68(4),(5).

generally recognized facts and any information or opinion that is within its specialized knowledge,"[135] the relevant section goes on to provide that, save in the case of judicial notice, "the Board shall notify the Minister, if present at the proceedings, and the person who is the subject of the proceedings of its intention and afford them a reasonable opportunity to make representations with respect thereto." It is quite likely that this is also a requirement both at common law and, implicitly, under section 16 of the Ontario *Statutory Powers Procedure Act*.

K. CROSS-EXAMINATION

As we have seen already, one of the reasons commonly advanced for arguments in support of a requirement that witnesses testify in person and that hearsay evidence be admitted with caution is the need to facilitate one of the key features of the traditional common law system of fact ascertainment: the testing of evidence through cross-examination. However, as we have also seen, in the context of many administrative proceedings and particularly those where the credibility of witnesses is not a vital concern, the courts have been prepared to accept alternative methods of providing testimony and the availability of surrogates for cross-examination.[136]

Nonetheless, cross-examination remains one of the key features of many administrative proceedings. Indeed, on the limited occasions on which the issue of cross-examination in administrative proceedings has been before the Supreme Court of Canada, the Court has endorsed the existence of the entitlement in the strongest terms. Thus, in *Township of Innisfil* v. *Township of Vespra*,[137] a case we have already encountered in the domain of official notice, Estey J. waxed lyrical about the importance of cross-examination in the context of municipal annexation proceedings:

> It is within the context of a statutory process that it must be noted that cross-examination is a vital element of the adversarial system applied and followed in our legal system, including, in many instances, before administrative tribunals since the earliest times.

---

135   To the extent that the term "generally recognized" qualifies only "facts" and not information and opinion, this provision is probably broader in scope than s. 16 of the Ontario *Act* and desirably so.

136   See *Re County of Strathcona No. 20 and MacLab Enterprises* (1971), 20 D.L.R. (3d) 200 (Alta. S.C. A.D.)

137   [1981] 2 S.C.R. 145.

Indeed, the right to cross-examination and the right to meet the case being made against the litigant, civil or criminal, is the procedural substructure upon which the common law itself has been built. That is not to say that because our Court system has been founded upon these techniques and procedures that administrative tribunals must apply the same techniques. Indeed, there are many tribunals in the modern community that do not follow the traditional adversarial road. On the other hand, where the rights of the citizen are involved and the statute affords him the right to a full hearing, including a hearing of his demonstration of his rights, one would expect to find the clearest statutory curtailment of the citizen's right to meet the case against him by cross-examination.[138]

This echoed the comments of Gale J. some thirty years earlier in *Toronto Newspaper Guild and Globe Printing*.[139] There, he described cross-examination as "a cardinal privilege which [the company] enjoys under our jurisprudence."[140] In that instance, the context was a Labour Relations Board denial to an employer of the right to cross-examine employees whom it suspected had quit the applicant union after an application for certification had been filed.

The right to cross-examine is also provided for in both the Ontario and Alberta procedural codes though in somewhat different terms. Section 10.1(a) of the Ontario *Statutory Powers Procedure Act*,[141] which was applicable to the proceeding in issue in *Township of Innisfil*, assumes an automatic entitlement to cross-examine witnesses at oral or electronic proceedings covered by that *Act* to the extent that the exercise of that right is "reasonably required for a full and fair disclosure of all matters relevant to the issues in the proceeding." Under section 5 of the Alberta *Administrative Procedures Act*,[142] the entitlement to cross-examine is expressed in somewhat more qualified terms. The affected party must convince the tribunal that a "fair opportunity" to "contradict or explain" facts or allegations made against her or him requires that the persons making those statements be available for cross-examination.

While it is questionable whether these different modes of expressing the entitlement will produce all that much difference in practice,

---

138   *Ibid.* at 166–67.
139   [1951] 3 D.L.R. 162 (Ont. H.C.), aff'd [1952] 2 D.L.R. 302 (Ont. C.A.), aff'd [1953] 2 S.C.R. 18.
140   *Ibid.* at 181.
141   R.S.O. 1990, c. S.22 (as amended by S.O. 1994, c. 27 and S.O. 1997, c. 23).
142   R.S.A. 1990, c. A-2.

what is interesting about both provisions and some of the older common law authorities is the extent to which they go further than is the case today even in proceedings in the regular criminal or civil courts. This is particularly so given the relaxation of the traditional restrictions on the use of hearsay evidence,[143] and has been further underscored by the judgment of the Supreme Court of Canada in the sexual assault case of *R. v. F. (W.J.) [W.J.F.]*,[144] in which the Court allowed the use of the record of previous statements by the alleged child victim of sexual assault in a situation where the child would no longer testify. In so doing, the Court liberalized the circumstances under which considerations of necessity would justify the use of such evidence.

Such a ruling has obvious ramifications for the right of the accused to test the evidence against her or him and presumably must have consequences for at least those increasingly large pockets of the administrative process where issues of sexual misconduct are in issue. Assuming that the obligations to allow cross-examination in the administrative process are somewhat less onerous in any event, will the courts be disposed to accept these kinds of reasons for not making the victims of sexual misconduct available for cross-examination?

In a number of instances involving accusations of sexual harassment, the courts have sustained tribunal decisions not to make the complainants of sexual harassment available for cross-examination.[145] However, the jurisprudence is not consistent and, on other occasions, the unavailability of the alleged victim for cross-examination has proved fatal to the validity of the proceedings. Thus, in *Re B. and Catholic Children's Aid Society of Metropolitan Toronto*,[146] the Ontario Divisional Court set aside the entry of the appellant's name on a child-abuse register. The victim of the alleged abuse was not made available for cross-examination and, given that the only evidence against the appellant was hearsay and that no reasons were provided for the alleged victim not testifying other than she had changed her story, the proceedings had been tainted by a denial of natural justice. What, however, both this case and the criminal law jurisprudence do suggest is that, on occasion, an administrative tribunal will be justified in relying

---

143 *R. v. Khan*, [1990] 2 S.C.R. 531.

144 (1999), 178 D.L.R. (4th) 53 (S.C.C.).

145 See, for example, *Masters v. Ontario* (1994), 18 O.R. (3d) 551 (Div. Ct.); *Semchuk v. Regina School Division No.4 (Saskatchewan Board of Education)* (1986), 26 Admin. L.R. 88 (Sask. Q.B.), aff'd (1987), 37 D.L.R. (4th) 738 (Sask. C.A.); *Y.B. v. R.W.* (1985), 16 Admin. L.R. 99 (Ont. Div. Ct.)

146 (1987), 38 D.L.R. (4th) 106 (Ont. Div. Ct.).

on records of prior statements by principal witnesses as well as other forms of hearsay as to their version of events despite their unavailability for cross-examination. This will be particularly so if there are sufficient reasons for either believing that the giving of testimony and exposure to cross-examination will endanger the health of that person or where that person is otherwise not available for cross-examination. However, in such circumstances, the tribunal may have to be particularly vigilant in assessing the reliability of the hearsay evidence and the strength of the corroborative or surrogate testimony. In particular, extreme care should be taken in basing the final decision simply on the basis of hearsay testimony.

Rights to cross-examination have also traditionally been attenuated or even non-existent in the case of certain kinds of inquisitorial or investigative function,[147] a domain which in Ontario is explicitly excluded from the operation of the *Statutory Powers Procedure Act*.[148] Indeed, this principle has recently been extended to justify the correctional authorities not making the authors of clinical reports available for cross-examination in proceedings to determine whether an inmate should be released from an indeterminate sentence. In justifying the Parole Board's ruling, the Federal Court of Appeal categorized the process as an inquisitorial one which did not necessitate cross-examination even where the clinical reports in question conflicted with the reports of the inmate's own experts.[149]

L. THE RIGHT TO PRESENT PROOFS AND ARGUMENTS

The question of whether the rules of evidence apply to proceedings before administrative tribunals and agencies is one aspect of the broader issue of the extent to the which the rules of natural justice guarantee the entitlement of parties to present proofs and arguments in support of their position. Thus, as illustrated by *Syndicat des employés professionnels de l'Université du Québec à Trois Rivières c. Université du Québec à Trios Rivières*,[150] a wrongful refusal to admit

---

147   *Irvine v. Canada (Restrictive Trade Practices Commission)*, [1987] 1 S.C.R. 181; *Masters v. Ontario* (1994), 18 O.R. (3d) 551 (Div. Ct.).
148   By the definition of "statutory power of decision" in section 1(1).
149   *MacInnis v. Canada (A.G.)* (1996), 41 Admin. L.R. (2d) 22 (F.C.A.), leave to appeal to the S.C.C. denied (1997), 46 C.R.R. (2d) 375 (note).
150   *Syndicat*, above note 129.

evidence may involve a denial of the right to participate fully and effectively in the hearing.

Administrative tribunals and agencies have control over the conduct of their proceedings and this includes the ability to place limits on the right of parties to adduce evidence and to make submissions in support of their position. Without such authority, decision makers would be in the thrall of anyone anxious to disrupt the timely operation of the administrative process. Nonetheless, the exercise of these powers is conditioned by a number of considerations.[151] Generally, it will depend on an appropriate judgment by a tribunal that further evidence or submissions should not be permitted on the basis of inadmissibility, irrelevance, or repetition. An erroneous assessment on any of these bases can lead to a reviewable denial of procedural fairness.

Far more controversial, however, is the extent of the entitlement of tribunals to limit participatory rights simply by reference to considerations of efficiency and the need for the expeditious carrying out of the statutory mandate. Indeed, even in the common situation where the relevant legislation provides that a tribunal is to proceed expeditiously, courts have been reluctant to allow this a basis for denying the right to call witnesses who may add something of relevance to the matter under consideration.[152] There is also precedent condemning a policy of confining hearings to a set length at least when it can be established that rigid adherence to the policy in the particular case would potentially affect the normal natural justice entitlements of a participant.[153] On the other hand, in the context of public hearings on broadly based policy issues, the courts do concede considerable latitude to those conducting the hearings to limit participatory rights, including the confining of some public interest advocates to written submissions.[154] Indeed, in the context of the Commission of Inquiry into the Deployment of Canadian Forces to Somalia, this was held to include a limit on the number

---

151 S. 23(1) and (2) of the Ontario *Statutory Powers Procedure Act* expressly confer on decision makers coming within its ambit not only the general right to control abuse of their processes but also the discretion "to reasonably limit further examination or cross-examination of a witness where it is satisfied that the examination or cross-examination has been sufficient to disclose fully and fairly all matters relevant to the issues in the proceeding."

152 See, for example, *Timpauer v. Air Canada* (1986), 18 Admin. L.R. 192 (F.C.A.).

153 *Mackey v. Saskatchewan (Medical Care Commission)* (1988), 32 Admin. L.R. 279 (Sask. Q.B.).

154 *Doctors Hospital v. Ontario (Health Services Restructuring Commission)* (1997), 103 O.A.C. 183 (Div. Ct.).

of witnesses that could be called by persons facing the possibility of criticism in the final report of the commission.[155]

In some instances, the right to present proofs and arguments will also encompass a right to lead evidence in reply, to reopen one's case, and to present further evidence or submissions. Thus, in a situation where a tribunal changes its mind and treats an issue as relevant which it initially treated as irrelevant, there will normally be an obligation to allow those who have already completed their evidence and arguments a further participatory right to deal with the newly emerging concerns.[156] Indeed, in situations where tribunals possess a continuing jurisdiction over the matter under consideration, the obligation to receive and consider further evidence will extend beyond the apparent conclusion of the formal hearing.[157]

M. THE RIGHT TO A HEARING BEFORE AND A DECISION BY THE DESIGNATED DECISION MAKER: LIMITS ON THE DELEGATION OF ADJUDICATIVE RESPONSIBILITIES

There has always been a presumption that judicial power cannot be delegated. Thus, if a statute confers an adjudicative power on a particular tribunal in specific terms, the designated tribunal must exercise that power itself and cannot delegate the decision-making task to another. In the domain of natural justice and procedural fairness, there is also a doctrine to the effect that he or she who hears must decide. The practical effect of this doctrine generally is to exclude from a decision-making role those who have not heard or considered all the evidence and arguments. These two principles coalesce to produce a still strong set of rules mandating that, in most instances, the decision-makers not only assume full responsibility for the outcome of any hearing but also participate in all aspects of the decision-making process.

---

155 *Addy v. Canada (Commission of Inquiry into the Deployment of Canadian Forces to Somalia)* (1997), 149 D.L.R. (4th) 118 (F.C.T.D.).

156 *I.A.M. Lodge 2309 v. Canada (Canada Labour Relations Board)* (1988), 33 Admin. L.R. 227 (F.C.A.).

157 *Vairavanathan v. Canada (Minister of Citizenship and Immigration)* (1996), 43 Admin. L.R. (2d) 121 (F.C.T.D.).

Under the paradigm situation of an oral hearing having serious consequences for individual rights or interests in which issues of credibility are raised, this means that the member or members of the tribunal should not only sit at the hearing but also be present and attentive throughout and thereafter reach their own independent decision on the basis of the evidence adduced and arguments presented by the parties.[158] However, that paradigm does not by any means exhaust the variety of decision making undertaken by statutory or prerogative authorities. Moreover, even where there is a close fit, there are important nuances that have to be taken into account.

As far as delegation is concerned, where responsibilities are assigned in general terms to a corporate entity that performs many other functions, delegation of adjudicative responsibilities to a committee or smaller unit within that entity will generally not give rise to problems. Thus, in situations where the senate or board of governors of a university is given responsibility for the discipline of the students of the university, there is likely no problem with the senate adopting a disciplinary code and delegating responsibility for adjudications on whether a student has breached that code to a discipline committee consisting of members of the university. Even though ultimate responsibility for expulsion of a student may still rest with the senate or board of governors, the nature of the way in which the power has been conferred and practical considerations suggest strongly that there is no reason to assume that the legislature wanted hearings on such matters to be conducted by all the members of the senate or board of governors.[159]

Particularly in situations where credibility is not an issue, the courts have also long recognized that there are many occasions on which the gathering and even distillation of evidence can be delegated by the ultimate decision maker. Moreover, such gathering of evidence may follow a variety of paths depending on the context. On occasion, the delegate will be charged with proactively gathering material in the form of documentary evidence and interviews. In other instances, the delegate will act in a much more structured way in the sense of conducting an oral hearing on behalf of the decision maker and either producing a transcript of the evidence for consideration by the actual

---

158   See, for example, *Ramm v. Public Accountants Council (Ontario)*, [1957] O.R. 217 (C.A.).

159   See, for example, *Morgan v. Acadia University* (1985), 15 Admin. L.R. 61 (N.S.S.C. T.D.), though *cf. King v. Institute of Chartered Accountants (Nova Scotia)* (1993), 99 D.L.R. (4th) 425 (N.S.S.C. T.D.).

decision maker or even going so far as summarizing and distilling that evidence with recommendations for the benefit of the decision maker. Four examples will provide a flavour of what may be acceptable.

As early as 1915, in *Local Government Board* v. *Arlidge*,[160] the House of Lords confronted a process under which the board was charged with considering appeals from orders of local authorities, *inter alia* closing private dwelling houses. As required by the relevant legislation, the board appointed an inspector to hold a public inquiry and to report back. The board, which was located within a government department and included the relevant Minister, was given power to determine its own procedure, and the question arose as to whether it was appropriate for it to decide the appeal simply on the basis of the material contained in the inspector's report or whether it had to hold a separate oral hearing. In delivering the judgment of the Court sustaining the Board's actions, Viscount Haldane L.C. made the following observations:

> [The Minister] is responsible not only for what he himself does but for all that is done in his department. The volume of work entrusted to him is very great and he cannot do the great bulk of it himself. He is expected to obtain the bulk of his materials vicariously through his officials and he has discharged his duty if he sees that they obtain these materials for him properly. To try to extend his duty beyond this and to insist that he and the other members of the Board should do everything personally would be to impair his efficiency.[161]

Obviously, the House of Lords was influenced in this case by the general principle that ministers of the Crown are, in most instances, entitled to act through responsible officials in their department. However, it is significant that the Court was not deterred from the application of this principle by the fact that an important property interest was at stake or that the issues involved were ones typical of an adjudicative setting.

A far more recent example of this is provided by *Baker* v. *Canada (Minister of Citizenship and Immigration)*.[162] In this case, the Supreme Court had no difficulty with a regime in which a senior official within the relevant government structure exercising a discretion formally reposed in the minister made a decision on the basis of evidence gathered and a recommendation made by a more junior official. However, to the extent that the senior official apparently just adopted the report

---

160   [1915] A.C. 120 (H.L. Eng.).
161   *Ibid.* at 133.
162   [1999] 2 S.C.R. 817.

of the junior official, the Court did attribute the faults and bias apparent in that report to the senior official.

That the ability of those charged with regulatory responsibilities to delegate the gathering and sifting of evidence is not confined to powers exercised by ministers of the Crown is underscored by the advice of the Judicial Committee of the Privy Council on an appeal from the New Zealand Court of Appeal. In *Jeffs* v. *New Zealand Dairy Production and Marketing Board*,[163] the Privy Council was confronted by a situation in which the board appointed a committee consisting of some of its members to hold a hearing and report back with recommendations on a matter involving zoning of districts for the purposes of marketing milk and cream. Here, once again, the allegation was that this constituted an improper delegation of the board's adjudicative responsibilities and that, in any event, the whole board should have considered "all the evidence, notes and submissions" and not relied on the report of the committee in making its final decision.

Viscount Dilhorne, in providing the advice of the Judicial Committee, was quite prepared to accept that, in matters of this kind, at least where credibility of witnesses was not involved, it was appropriate for the board "to hear and receive evidence and submissions from interested parties for the purpose of informing the board of the evidence and submissions."[164] Indeed, he went so far as to concede that in some instances "an accurate summary of the evidence and the submissions would suffice." However, in this instance, the board's ultimate decision was tainted because the "committee's report did not state what the evidence was and the board reached its decision without consideration of and in ignorance of the evidence."[165]

Much more recently, in *Armstrong* v. *Canada (Commissioner of the Royal Canadian Mounted Police)*,[166] in a context having career-ending consequences, Rothstein J. then of the Federal Court, Trial Division in effect applied the principles accepted in *Jeffs* and concluded that the requirements for consideration of the matter by the actual decision maker had been met. Armstrong was a member of the RCMP. The force's Discharge and Demotion Board had determined that she should be dismissed for "unsuitability." She appealed this decision to the Commissioner and, as part of that process, an independent External Review Committee had rec-

---

163 [1967] 1 A.C. 551 (P.C. N.Z.).
164 *Ibid.* at 568.
165 *Ibid.* at 569.
166 [1994] 2 F.C. 356 (T.D.). See also *Masters* v. *Ontario* (1994), 18 O.R. (3d) 551 (Div. Ct.).

ommended that her appeal be allowed. However, the Commissioner ultimately rejected Armstrong's appeal acting on the basis of a report prepared by a subordinate in which, along with summarizing the evidence and identifying possible courses of action, the subordinate had called into question the committee's conclusions. In giving reasons for so doing, he incorporated the first sixteen pages of the delegate's report.

In sustaining the process adopted by the Commissioner and, in particular, his sole reliance on a report prepared by a delegate, Rothstein J. emphasized that the appeal was on the record and did not involve an oral rehearing of the matter. He also noted that, given his other responsibilities and the enormity of the task of reviewing all of the evidence, the Commissioner could not be expected to act in such matters without the benefit of assistance from subordinates. What was also clear in this instance was that the report from the delegate did summarize the relevant evidence and, despite his wholesale incorporation of the factual and other components of that report into his decision, the balance of the Commissioner's determination made it clear that he had made up his own mind on the basis of the material put before him by the delegate.

In the next section, I consider in greater detail the extent to which all manner of statutory and prerogative authorities are entitled to rely on staff and other sources in preparing for, during and in the aftermath of their hearings. In general, however, this jurisprudence underscores the principles enunciated in these cases: the responsibility of the decision maker will in many instances be satisfied by the making of an independent decision on the basis of an adequate knowledge of the matters in issue as developed by the parties to the proceedings. For these purposes, adequate knowledge may be acquired through reports on the evidence and submissions prepared by delegates or subordinates.

Nonetheless, it is important to note that not only in *Jeffs* but also in *Armstrong*, the courts were clear that the situation will almost certainly be different when the disposition turns on issues of credibility. There and also in other situations where the legislative scheme actually indicates the right to an oral or in-person hearing before the actual decision maker, the delegation of evidence collection let alone summary will not be permissible. Indeed, in such cases, the paradigm of constant and attentive attendance during the hearing will be necessary. Thus, in strong *obiter dicta*, in *Mehr* v. *Law Society of Upper Canada*,[167] Cartwright J. expressed the view that invalidity would follow from the fact that the composition of the Law Society's discipline committee had changed three times in the course of the hearing with nothing to sug-

---

167   *Mehr*, above note 120.

gest that all the various participants had not taken part in the final decision. Indeed, it has also been suggested that, in situations of multi-member boards, the obligation to act collectively extends beyond the actual hearing to the decision-making stage:

> [A]t some point in time, the panel must reach a decision collectively and each member must "participate" individually in that collective decision in agreeing with it or dissenting from it. There must be a meeting of the minds, each member being informed at least in a general way of the point of view of each of his colleagues.[168]

N. THE RIGHT TO HAVE A MATTER DECIDED ON THE BASIS OF THE EVIDENCE AND ARGUMENTS PRESENTED AT THE HEARING

1) Official Notice and Independent Evidence Gathering

Courts operating in the common law tradition are expected to resolve disputes on the basis of the issues as framed by the parties[169] and the evidence presented by the parties. Save to the extent provided by the doctrine of judicial notice, judges are not entitled to take into account evidence within their personal knowledge nor can they act as roving commissioners seeking to supplement from other sources apparent gaps in the evidence presented or in an endeavour to resolve inconsistencies in that evidence.

By and large, these same principles govern the functioning of adjudicative tribunals.[170] Certainly, the scope for official notice may be

---

168 *IBM Canada Ltd.* v. *Deputy Minister of National Revenue, Customs and Excise*, [1992] 1 F.C. 663 (C.A.) at 673–75 (*per* Décary J.A.).

169 Or, at least, where the court conceives of another way of viewing the issues surrounding the dispute, to put that to the parties for the purposes of argument: for example, *Singh* v. *Canada (Minister of Employment and Immigration)*, above, note 35, where the Court asked the parties to provide submissions on the possible applicability to the case of section 2(e) of the *Canadian Bill of Rights*. However, for an instance of where the Court did not live by this principle, see *Homex Realty & Development Co.* v. *Wyoming (Village)*, [1980] 2 S.C.R. 1011, where over the dissent of Dickson J. (as he then was), the Court denied judicial review of a decision taken in breach of the rules of natural justice because of the developer's misconduct despite the fact that this argument had not been raised by the village and without giving the parties an opportunity to make submissions on it.

170 For these purposes, it is necessary to draw a distinction between investigatory bodies and also agencies charged with a broad policy development mandate and those adjudicating individual claims or *inter partes* disputes. The former will in general have much greater leeway in all these respects.

somewhat more expansive in the case of many tribunals. Nonetheless, within this extended version of the judicial notice doctrine, the decision maker generally will be expected to confront the parties with the material of which it proposes to take official notice and to provide an opportunity for them to deal with it. Moreover, unless expressly authorized by statute, those tribunals are also expected to confine themselves to the evidence presented by the parties. Seeking evidential aid from other sources is proscribed by the common law.

Indeed, as well compromising the entitlement of the parties to a reasonable opportunity to deal with the contrary evidence,[171] such conduct can also bring into serious question the impartiality of the tribunal. This is well illustrated by *Sivaguru* v. *Canada (Minister of Employment and Immigration)*.[172] There, a member of a panel adjudicating a convention refugee claim became convinced that the claimant was not telling the truth. He therefore went in search of other evidence with a view to laying a trap for the claimant. To do this and to spring the trap (even though it worked at least in part) gave rise to a reasonable apprehension of bias. Along the same lines, in *Kane* v. *University of British Columbia*,[173] as we have seen in another context, the Supreme Court quashed a decision in a university disciplinary context on the basis that for the president of the university to be present at the deliberations of the hearing panel created a reasonable apprehension of procedural unfairness. Even without proof that new material had been provided to the panel by the president, the mere sequestering of the president with the decision makers was sufficient without more to raise legitimately in Kane's mind that that kind of inappropriate conduct had taken place.

2) Consulting With or Seeking the Advice of Others

The rigour of these rules would tend to suggest that there is very little room at least for the members of adjudicative tribunals to engage in consultations with others either before, during, or after a hearing. Whether it be their staff, lawyers, colleagues, or complete outsiders, such contacts must perforce be limited, if not totally proscribed. However, it is clear from the jurisprudence that this overstates the legal position.

---

171   See, for example, *Budge* v. *Alberta (Workers' Compensation Board)* (1985), 42 Alta. L.R. (2d) 26 (C.A.) (breach of the rules of natural justice for board to conduct a further investigation after hearing of claim for workers' compensation).

172   [1990] 2 F.C. 374 (C.A.).

173   *Kane*, above note 85.

While the case law on the subject is surprisingly far from comprehensive, many tribunals clearly can utilize their staff in preparing for a hearing. In the case of those engaged in broad regulatory tasks, the use of staff can extend as far as the gathering of evidence and the compilation of reports on matters that will be pertinent at the hearing.[174] The same holds true for certain adjudicative tribunals at least in situations where there is a combined investigative and adjudicative role or where effective representation of the public interest rests at least in some measure with the decision maker itself.[175] However, unless the material compiled by staff is of a purely background variety, not really relevant, or otherwise available to the parties, there is clearly an obligation on the decision maker to give timely notice of at least the essential gist of such material, if not the totality of it to the parties.[176] There will also be some adjudicative tribunals, particularly those involved in disciplinary hearings or the resolution of certain kinds of *inter partes* disputes where such a proactive role is not appropriate and where complete responsibility for the gathering and presentation of the evidence rests with the parties and the parties alone.[177] This will also be indicated in situations where, under the relevant statutory regime, there is a clear separation of investigative and adjudicative aspects of the process.[178]

Staff (including lawyers) may also be deployed in both the pre-hearing, actual hearing, and post-hearing phases in summarizing and commenting on the evidence and issues raised by the parties and even in the drafting of part of the reasons for decision. Here too, however, the insinuation of new evidence and issues raises problems. Indeed, it may well be that, once the actual hearing has begun, there are serious limitations in any kind of case on the introduction of other evidence by a tribunal's staff or anyone else, for that matter, other than by way of formal proof through whatever kind of hearing process the tribunal is employing. Moreover, at the point at which the hearing concludes, there is no room at all for the gathering of further evidence except under an authority to reopen a concluded hearing. As for the raising of

---

174 See, for example, *Trans Québec & Maritimes Pipeline Inc.* v. *Canada (National Energy Board)* (1984), 8 Admin. L.R. 177 (F.C.A.)

175 *CIBA-Geigy Ltd.* v. *Canada (Patented Medicine Prices Review Board)*, [1994] 3 F.C. 425 (C.A.).

176 *Toshiba Corporation* v. *Canada (Anti-dumping Tribunal)* (1984), 8 Admin. L.R. 173 (F.C.A.).

177 As in the separation between human rights commissions that investigate complaints and the tribunals and boards of inquiry that adjudicate them.

178 For a discussion of the problems of overlapping roles, see *2747-3174 Québec Inc.* v. *Québec (Régie des permis d'alcool)*, [1996] 3 S.C.R. 919.

new issues or a recasting of the issues as framed by the parties, at all stages, these come within the permissible ambit of staff and, indeed, colleague activity. However, in such cases irrespective of when it happens, the new or recast issues and arguments should be revealed to the parties to enable them to respond or comment.

The leading authorities in this domain are two judgments of the Supreme Court of Canada, *I.W.A., Local 2-69* v. *Consolidated-Bathurst Packaging Ltd.*[179] and *Québec (Commission des affaires sociales)* v. *Tremblay.*[180] In both, the Court was concerned with the particular problem of the relatively common practice of post-hearing consultations between the members of the panel of the tribunal that actually heard the matter and other non-sitting members of that tribunal as well as lawyers and staff to the tribunal. However, in terms of some of the matters dealt with by the Court, it is clear that the principles enunciated are not confined to the particular facts of the case but are pertinent to a broad range of use of staff and consultations irrespective of the point at which they occur.

Gonthier J. delivered the judgment of the Court in each of these cases. In *Consolidated-Bathurst*, as well as condemning the presentation of any new evidence to the panel in the absence of the parties, he also held that, in general, there should not even be any discussion of the facts between those who had heard the evidence and those who had not. As for policy or legal issues arising out of the evidence submitted and the arguments made by the parties, Gonthier J. held that such discussions were justified particularly in situations where the issues involved had an impact beyond the immediate interests of the parties. Indeed, such practices were praised as ways of

> seek[ing] to avoid inadvertent contradictory results and [of achieving] the highest degree of coherence possible under these circumstances.[181]

However, he also made it clear

> that the parties must be informed of any new ground on which they have not made any representations. In such a case, the parties must be given a reasonable opportunity to respond and the calling of a supplementary hearing may be appropriate.[182]

Certainly, as far as the introduction of new grounds are concerned, these remarks seem apposite irrespective of the context. Similarly, the admonition with respect to the introduction of new evidence has broader

---

179   [1990] 1 S.C.R. 282 [*I.W.A., Local 2-69*].
180   [1992] 1 S.C.R. 952 [*Tremblay*].
181   *I.W.A., Local 2-69*, note 177 at 328.
182   *Ibid.* at 338.

ramifications. However, on the matter of discussion of the evidence, the Court itself is not totally unequivocal even in the context of discussions with colleagues who have not heard the evidence. Where staff have been present at the giving of the relevant testimony or where the evidence is written rather than given orally, the constraint on discussion may not have quite the same force.

As well as concerns with the entitlement of the parties to have the opportunity to both know and respond to the relevant evidence and arguments taken into account by the tribunal, these two cases also raise problems of adjudicative independence. The person charged with taking the decision must actually decide the matter and not delegate that task to someone else or act under dictation from someone not assigned the responsibility for making a decision.

In articulating a policy in *Consolidated-Bathurst* generally favouring such consultations, Gonthier J. conceded that it was unrealistic to think that the discussions might not have an "influence" on the members of the particular panel and could contribute to a change of mind on a vital issue thereby altering the eventual outcome. After all, if that is not a possibility, there seems little purpose in having such meetings. What must, however, be avoided are processes "which may effectively compel or induce panel members to decide against their own conscience and opinions."[183]

Given that the identification of whether such illegitimate compulsion or inducing has taken place is, like the existence of actual bias, beyond the realm of truly objective inquiry, the Court concentrated in both this case and *Tremblay* on the actual conditions under which such consultations took place. In *Consolidated-Bathurst*, the processes passed scrutiny. They did not do so in *Tremblay*. What were the differences?

In *Consolidated-Bathurst*, the practice was a long-standing one. It required a request from a member of the hearing panel and could not be imposed. It also was tailored so as not to have as its focus the forging of a consensus. Rather, the emphasis was on free and open discussion. Minutes were not kept, there were no votes, attendance was not compulsory, nor was a record of attendance taken. In contrast, in *Tremblay*, the consultative process could be initiated by both the members of the panel and the president of the commission. As well, the objective was to arrive at a consensus, votes were generally taken as well as attendance, and minutes were kept. This led the Court to conclude that the process "may exert undue pressure on decision-makers."[184]

---

183   *Ibid.*at 333.
184   *Tremblay*, above note 180 at 975.

Whether the conclusion of the Supreme Court is an appropriate one is not at all clear. For example, the keeping of a formal record of what took place can be seen as a safeguard of independence rather than a factor indicating illegitimate pressure. In some circumstances, having knowledge of who was present can assist in assessing the pressures created by the process. Moreover, creating incentives for all members of the tribunal to attend such important meetings seems desirable if the objective is the development of a collective position on what are important issues of principle. Indeed, this last consideration leads inexorably to the fundamental question: In a statutory regime where tribunals function in panels because of case load, why is something stronger than mere influence such a bad thing? After all, to the extent that the Supreme Court of Canada has asserted that inconsistency is in and of itself not a basis for judicial review,[185] and has left the resolution of jurisprudential conflicts to tribunals themselves, the case for an effective central harmonization process becomes that much stronger and the claims for the adjudicative independence of "rogue" members or panels of multimember tribunals that much weaker.

Aside from these pragmatic considerations, there is also a question as to whether the criteria embraced by the Supreme Court for determining whether there has been compulsion as opposed to mere influence are all that reliable as indicators. The focus of the inquiry in any judicial review application is on the formal rules governing the way in which such consultations will take place. However, as illustrated graphically by other aspects of the judgment in *Tremblay*, the really significant factor is not the formal rules or lack thereof for whole tribunal consideration of major issues but the actual internal dynamic of the particular tribunal and, especially, the role and influence of the chair or president. Thus, even conceding the impossibility of determining whether a tribunal member has been compelled as opposed to merely influenced, it is questionable how reliable an indicator are the actual rules governing consultation processes. They may tell little, if nothing about the internal dynamics of a tribunal's operations. Indeed, in many instances, the most important consideration may well be the chair's suasion in the reappointment process.[186]

---

185   *Domtar Inc.* v. *Québec (Commission d'appel en matière des lésions professionnelles)*, [1993] 2 S.C.R. 756.

186   See David J. Mullan, "Common and Divergent Elements of Practices of the Various Tribunals: An Overview of Present and Possible Developments" in *Administrative Law: Principles, Practice and Pluralism* (Special Lectures of the Law Society of Upper Canada) (Toronto: Carswell, 1992) at 469–74.

Once again, while the judicial review focus has been on post-hearing consultations, the principles established by the Supreme Court of Canada also have relevance to earlier stages in the adjudicative process. Dominance by either the chair, a cabal of tribunal members, or even an individual member, lawyer to the tribunal, or anyone else will violate the independence of judgment required of those exercising adjudicative roles.

3) The Use of Lawyers

This is particularly well illustrated by a series of cases involving the proper role of lawyers to tribunals. In this jurisprudence, it is made clear that, while tribunals may seek assistance from a lawyer during the course of the hearing, responsibility for running the hearing and making procedural and other interlocutory rulings remains that of the tribunal members. Thus, for a lawyer to the tribunal to take over the hearing and act as though he or she were the tribunal chair is not only to usurp the functions of the tribunal members but also, in many instances, to give rise to a reasonable apprehension of bias.[187] Similarly, in disciplinary and related proceedings, for counsel to the tribunal to act as though he or she were prosecuting counsel will create the potential for bias allegations.[188] Indeed, in such matters, there may also need to be a formal separation between the prosecutorial branch of the professional body and those charged with advising and assisting disciplinary committees.[189]

As indicated by *Consolidated-Bathurst* and *Tremblay*, lawyers to tribunals are also restricted in the role they can play in the wake of the hearing. Preferably, the tribunal members should themselves take responsibility for the drafting of their decisions and seek advice and guidance from counsel on the basis of a draft. However, this may be a counsel of perfection and the courts have been willing to tolerate the writing of an initial draft by counsel provided that there is sufficient evidence of instructions as to the contents of the key portions of the decision from the tribunal members and adequate opportunity thereafter to review and revise the decision to ensure it accords with the

---

187 See *Matthews v. Ontario (Physiotherapy Board)* (1990), 44 Admin. L.R. 147 (Ont. Div. Ct.).

188 See *Adair v. Ontario (Health Disciplines Board)* (1993), 15 O.R. (3d) 705 (Div. Ct.)

189 See *Mitchell v. Institute of Chartered Accountants (Manitoba)*, [1994] 3 W.W.R. 704 (Man. Q.B.); *2747-3174 Québec Inc. v. Québec (Régie des permis d'alcool)*, above note 178.

actual positions of the members of the tribunal. In all of this, the key concern remains one of whether the tribunal members actually make the decision. If the court has reason to believe that the real decision maker is the lawyer to the commission or someone else, the decision will be set aside.[190]

4) Proving Infringments

In many respects, observance of the strictures on internal consultation is also dependent on voluntary compliance on the part of tribunals. The protections afforded to tribunal decision making in the name of deliberative secrecy[191] require those alleging infringement of the principles and rules to make out a case from independently generated evidence that the constraints have been violated. Absent a dissident member of the tribunal or the proverbial unattributed brown paper envelope, this may be impossible. Suspicions do not count and fishing expeditions are not allowed.

Ellis-Don Ltd. v. *Ontario Labour Relations Board*,[192] currently on appeal to the Supreme Court of Canada, provides graphic evidence of this. Here, as a result of a full board discussion and the asserted adoption of a different legal test than it had applied in its draft reasons, a panel of the board changed its decision in a case involving the abandonment of bargaining rights. Besides accepting the board's explanation of the nature of the change and that it had not resulted from interference with the fact-finding process, the Court of Appeal, affirming the Divisional Court, reiterated that, in such matters, there was a presumption of regularity and it was for the applicant to prove otherwise. Moreover, no adverse inferences should be drawn from the fact that the board declined to disclose the content of its internal delibera-

---

190   I return to this issue and an evaluation of the jurisprudence in the next section on the Provision of Reasons.

191   As outlined in *Tremblay*, above note 180.

192   (1998), 38 O.R. (3d) 737 (C.A.), aff'g. (1995), 89 O.A.C. 45 (Div. Ct.). See also in the context of an international commercial arbitration: *Noble China Inc.* v. *Lee* (1998), 42 O.R. (3d) 69 (G.D.). However, cf. *Glengarry Memorial Hospital* v. *Ontario (Pay Equity Hearings Tribunal)* (1993), 99 D.L.R. (4th) 682 (Ont. Div. Ct), varied in part (1993), 99 D.L.R. (4th) 706 (Ont. Div. Ct.), reversed on other grounds (1995), 124 D.L.R. (4th) 82 (Ont. C.A.), where, (pp.704–5), O'Leary J. made an order for the examination of a dissenting member of a tribunal who had made statements giving the impression that the principles of natural justice had been compromised seriously by the actions of the other members of the panel.

tions nor was there any entitlement in the applicant to examine the members of the board as to those deliberations.[193]

However, *Tremblay* does make it clear that the principles of deliberative secrecy are not as protective or absolute in the case of adjudicative tribunals as they are in a regular court setting. In appropriate circumstances, tribunal members and their staff can be questioned as to the process that was used in reaching a conclusion in a particular case. This will include attempts to ascertain whether the tribunal breached any of the principles of procedural fairness before, during, or after the hearing and, in particular, failed to observe the strictures on post-hearing consultation laid down by the Supreme Court in the two principal authorities. Provided the questioning does not probe the actual reasoning processes of the adjudicator, it will be legitimate.

Moreover, in *Payne* v. *Ontario Human Rights Commission*,[194] the Ontario Court of Appeal specified a comparatively liberal standard for whether there could be pre-trial or application examination of tribunal members and staff under the relevant rule of the Ontario Rules of Civil Procedure (Rule 39.03). Where the examination could raise deliberative secrecy concerns, the test was whether the applicant for relief has presented "some basis for a clearly articulated and objectively reasonable concern that a relevant legal right may have been infringed".[195] Nevertheless, in that instance, the justification (as in so many of these cases) was an affidavit from a disenchanted former member of the commission detailing how the commission had allegedly determined whether to refer a complaint to a board of inquiry in the wake of an investigator's report.

Provisions conferring testimonial immunity or even prohibiting the giving of testimony may also impede the efforts of applicants to secure information on whether a tribunal or its members have violated the relevant procedural fairness principles. Such a provision featured in earlier interlocutory proceedings in *Ellis-Don* in which the board was applying to quash subpoenas issued against the chair, vice-chair, and registrar of the board requiring them to submit to pre-application examination as to the procedures that the board had adopted in dealing with the matter in issue. The relevant section prohibited members of the board and the registrar, save with the consent of the chair, from giving testimony "in any civil suit...respecting information obtained in

---

193   This particular ruling was the product of an earlier interlocutory proceeding: (1994), 16 O.R. (3d) 698 (Div. Ct.), leave to appeal refused by the Ontario Court of Appeal on June 13, 1994 and by the Supreme Court of Canada on January 12, 1995.

194   (2000), 2 C.C.E.L. (3d) 171 (Ont. C.A.).

195   *Ibid.* at para. 177.

the discharge of their duties or while acting within the scope of their employment". The Divisional Court held that this was sufficient to prevent examination in the present circumstances.[196] There could be no exception for allegations of breach of the rules of natural justice, though the Court did concede that an allegation of misconduct such as tampering with witnesses might be different. In such a case, the member would not be acting within the realm of the statute and her or his duties.

Subsequently, in *Payne*, the Court of Appeal distinguished this holding on the basis that the relevant provision in the *Human Rights Code* applied only up to the end of the investigative part of the commission's processes. It did not "protect" the commission's determination of what to do on the basis of the investigation. Even more fundamentally, O'Leary J., at the interlocutory stage in *Glengarry Memorial Hospital* v. *Ontario (Pay Equity Hearings Tribunal)*,[197] held that such provisions were unconstitutional to the extent that they could place an insuperable impediment in the way of an applicant establishing a breach of the rules of procedural fairness. To the extent that sections 96 to 100 of the *Constitution Act, 1867* guaranteed judicial review for jurisdictional error and that procedural unfairness was a species of jurisdictional error, the legislature could not remove that entitlement either directly through a privative clause or indirectly through a testimonial immunity or prohibition. It remains to be seen whether that position will commend itself to a higher court should the occasion arise.

O. THE PROVISION OF REASONS

1) Introduction

When a public authority takes a decision after an oral or even a written hearing, it is likely that most people whose rights or interests are affected by that decision would expect the decision maker to provide reasons. However, the traditional common law position was that statutory authorities were not obliged to provide reasons for their decisions either as a substantive requirement or as a component of the rules of natural justice or procedural fairness. The most common defence of this position was the argument by way of analogy to the situation in the regular courts. If the courts themselves did not have to give reasons

---

196   (1004), 110 D.L.R. (4th) 731 (Ont. Div. Ct.).

197   Above note 192.

in justification of their judgments, there was simply no basis for the imposition of such a requirement on other adjudicative fora let alone those charged with the exercise of broad statutory discretions.

However, just as there was always a certain amount of unease with a rule that exempted the regular courts from giving reasons, so too were there serious reservations about a similar blanket exemption for tribunals. The kinds of issues that many tribunals decide are just as important to those affected as much of what is dealt with by regular courts. Indeed, to the extent that political patronage intruded in the selection of members of certain tribunals and that there were doubts about the capacities of some tribunal members to decide what could be complex legal issues, some made the case that there was a far greater need to subject tribunals to a reasons requirement than in the case of the regular courts. It was an important accountability mechanism.

2) Evolution

This kind of thinking was very much reflected in the drafting of both the Alberta *Administrative Procedures Act*[198] and the Ontario *Statutory Powers Procedure Act*,[199] both of which contain a reasons requirement. Under section 7 of the Alberta *Act*, authorities coming within the reach of that *Act*, when making decisions "adversely affecting the rights of a party," are obliged to render a written decision. That decision must contain both the findings of fact on which the authority based its decision and the reasons for that decision. The Ontario requirements are somewhat different. The obligation to provide written reasons set out in section 17 is triggered only by a request from a party and there is no further attempt to specify their required content. However, in contrast to the Alberta *Act*, the Ontario provision is not restricted (at least on its face) to decisions which affect "rights"; rather, it applies, absent express legislative exclusion, to all statutory authorities coming within the ambit of that *Act*.

Much later, section 8 of the 1996 Québec *Administrative Justice Act*[200] imposed a reasons requirement when a decision maker coming within the *Act* made a decision that was unfavourable to an individual. As well, in those jurisdictions without any kind of procedural code, there are often reasons requirements attached to the exercise of particular statutory powers.

---

198   R.S.A. 1980, c. A-2.
199   R.S.O. 1990, c. S.22 (as amended by S.O. 1994, c. 27 and S.O. 1997, c. 23).
200   S.Q. 1996, c. 54.

In contrast, the courts exercising their common law jurisdiction remained generally unsympathetic to arguments for judicially imposed reasons requirements. Indeed, this sentiment was one that gained considerable re-enforcement from an important judgment of the High Court of Australia in 1986, *Osmond v. Public Service Board of New South Wales*.[201] This case involved the refusal of a tribunal to give reasons for a decision denying an appeal from a losing candidate for promotion to a senior position in the civil service. Reversing a strong New South Wales Court of Appeal,[202] the High Court held that, at that point in the evolution of the principles of administrative law, any imposition of a reasons requirement on statutory authorities had to come from the legislature, not the courts in the exercise of their common law powers.

Nonetheless, there were some indicators in Canada that at least some judges in some contexts had a different mind set. Thus, four years earlier than *Osmond*, the Nova Scotia Supreme Court, Appeal Division had held that the provision of reasons would be necessary in certain situations to effectuate a statutory right of appeal.[203] Without the benefit of reasons from the statutory authority under appeal, the making of arguments for reversal would, in many instances, require guess work or speculation on the part of the appellant as to the basis for the decision. That was simply not satisfactory in the face of a legislative provision of a right of appeal.

Both in Nova Scotia and elsewhere, judicial support for this argument grew. Indeed, subsequently, in *Future Inns Canada Ltd.* v. *Nova Scotia (Labour Relations Board)*, that same court took this position to what seemed to many to be its logical conclusion and held that, as judicial review for jurisdictional error was a constitutionally guaranteed right, reasons would at least on occasion be required in order to protect that constitutional entitlement.[204] In this, the court was picking up on an earlier judgment of Grenier J. of the Québec Superior Court.[205]

In sharp contrast and contemporaneously, in *Williams* v. *Canada (Minister of Citizenship and Immigration)*,[206] the Federal Court of Appeal

---

201   (1986), 159 C.L.R. 656.

202   [1984] 3 N.S.W.L.R. 447 (with the principal judgment delivered by Kirby J., now a judge on the High Court of Australia).

203   *RDR Construction Co. Ltd.* v. *Nova Scotia (Rent Review Commission)* (1982), 139 D.L.R. (3d) 168 (N.S.S.C. A.D.).

204   (1997), 160 N.S.R. (2d) 241 (C.A.).

205   *Société des services Ozanam Inc.* v. *Québec (Commission municipale du Québec)*, [1994] R.J.Q. 364 (Qué. S.C.)

206   [1997] 2 F.C. 646 (C.A.).

continued to deny any common law basis for the imposition of a reasons requirement on statutory bodies. In so doing, the court explained its position in terms of the theory of deference. Supreme Court-ordained deference to administrative tribunals required respect for the judgment of statutory authorities that reasons were not necessary in particular circumstances. Nonetheless, the court did accept that, at least in some circumstances, judges would be justified in drawing the inference from an absence of reasons that there had been a reviewable abuse of discretion. This reflected the English position at least from the time of *Padfield* v. *Minister of Agriculture, Fisheries and Food.*[207] It spoke to the rare situation where an applicant for judicial review could adduce sufficient evidence in support of a substantive position that would justify the reviewing court in assuming, in the absence of reasons or rebuttal material from the decision maker or other party, that there could be no legally good basis for the decision that had been made.

The Supreme Court of Canada forewent the opportunity to resolve the growing confusion in this area when it denied leave to appeal in both *Future Inns*[208] and *Williams.*[209] However, it did show its hand in *C.U.P.E., Local 301* v. *Montréal.*[210] In dealing with an argument that the absence of a transcript constituted a basis for judicial review of a labour tribunal's ruling, the Court accepted that, at least in some instances, an applicant's constitutionally protected entitlement to judicial review for jurisdictional error could be compromised by the failure of a tribunal to make a transcript of its proceedings. Nevertheless, given the grounds on which this particular application was advanced and the ability of the applicant to make out its case adequately by the use of other available sources, there had been no adverse impact on the constitutionally protected right in this instance.

This echoed the position of the Nova Scotia Court of Appeal in *Future Inns* and certainly foreshadowed the Supreme Court's application of that same theory to the absence of reasons as well as the lack of a transcript. In addition, it was also becoming clear that other comparable jurisdictions were changing their position on the whole issue of reasons. English case law had started to accept that there was a right to reasons at least in certain categories of case and particularly where an

---

207 [1968] A.C. 997 (H.L. Eng.).
208 (1997), 164 N.S.R. (2d) 240 (note) (S.C.C.).
209 (1997), 150 D.L.R. (4th) viii (note) (S.C.C.).
210 [1997] 1 S.C.R. 793.

interest highly regarded by the law was at stake.[211] Indeed, there were some indicators that this might also apply in certain situations in the case of the regular courts. Even more dramatically, the post-apartheid South African Constitution mandates reasons in situations where administrative action affects individual rights.[212]

3)   *Baker* v. *Canada (Minister of Citizenship and Immigration)*

All of this set the scene for *Baker* v. *Canada (Minister of Citizenship and Immigration),*[213] in which, for the first time, the Supreme Court of Canada accepted that a failure to give reasons could taint a decision. As we have seen already in the chapter on abuse of discretion, this involved an exercise of discretionary power by the minister to deny an over stayer subject to deportation the opportunity on "humanitarian and compassionate grounds" to make an application for permanent residence without leaving Canada. Notwithstanding Federal Court authority denying the existence of any obligation to give reasons in such cases, the Court, in a judgment delivered by L'Heureux-Dubé J., held that, in the particular circumstances, the provision of reasons was a component of the duty of procedural fairness.

In so doing, the Court identified a number of values that are advanced by the crafting of reasons. The discipline imposed by the task can contribute to more careful reasoning processes thereby promoting better decision making. Public justification of decisions may inspire greater public and constituency confidence in the integrity of a decision-making process. Echoing, though not referring to either *Future Inns* or *C.U.P.E., Local 301*, the Court also accepted that the provision of reasons was important in the facilitation of any rights of appeal, reconsideration, or judicial review.

In response to the standard contrary arguments that to impose a reasons requirement would impede efficient administration, creating delays and imposing extra cost burdens, and also lead to a lack of candour in the sense of formulaic, boilerplate sets of reasons having as their principal aim the avoidance of judicial review or reversal on

---

211   R. v. *Secretary of State for the Home Department, ex parte Doody,* [1994] A.C. 531 (H.L. Eng.); R. v. *Civil Service Appeal Board, ex parte Cunningham,* [1991] I.C.R. 816 (C.A.).

212   *The Constitution of the Republic of South Africa,* Chapter 2: Bill of Rights, section 33(2): "Everyone whose rights have been adversely affected by administrative action has the right to be given written reasons."

213   [1999] 2 S.C.R. 817.

appeal, L'Heureux-Dubé J. countered that at least the first of these concerns could be met in large measure by judicial flexibility as to the form of the reasons that would be acceptable. Thus, in the particular case, the Court held that the obligation had been met by the notes of the front line immigration officer in which he or she outlined the basis for a recommendation that Baker's application be denied. In other words, the reasons did not have to be crafted by the senior immigration officer who exercised the statutory discretion on behalf of the minister. In cases where that officer added nothing to the reasons identified by the front line officer, the courts would be justified in attributing those reasons to the actual decision maker. It is also of some significance that at no point did the Court suggest that reasons always had to be given in writing. Moreover, to the extent that the Court found the reasons provided to be legally impeachable, the Court made it clear by necessary inference that there was a distinction between the obligation to provide reasons and the exposure of the content of the reasons to judicial review. Just because the reasons given revealed reviewable substantive error did not mean that there had been a breach of the duty to provide reasons.

However, what was even more important was that the Court made it clear that it was not imposing a duty to give reasons on all statutory and prerogative authorities. As in many aspects of judicial review law, whether the requirement existed in any particular case required a context-sensitive inquiry. Relevant to this inquiry were the nature of the interest at stake, whether there was a statutory right of appeal, and unspecified "other circumstances." In this particular instance, it was the first factor that was decisive: "It would be unfair for a person subject to a decision such as this one which is so critical to their future not to be told why the result was reached."[214]

The particular significance of this is the Court's attachment of a high value to the interest of Baker in remaining in Canada notwithstanding that the vindication of that interest depended upon the exercise of a facially open-ended discretion formally conferred on a minister of the Crown, and that the extent of procedural entitlements owed in this kind of case was considerably short of the typical trial-type, adversarial hearing. Indeed, the Court reached this position without ever responding to Baker's argument that the decision affected her *Charter* rights.

It now remains to be seen what other interests attract this kind of treatment and whether an entitlement to reasons will be automatic if *Charter* rights are in fact at stake. There is also the question of the

---

214 *Ibid.* at para. 43.

extent to which the exercise is one that will involve the balancing of the interest at stake against the nature and the breadth of the discretion accorded to the decision maker. In this respect, it is significant that, in other portions of this extremely important judgment, the Court emphasized the individualized quality of the decision under challenge in this case. This, in the Court's mind, differentiated it from other discretionary decision making involving broad policy determinations with polycentric characteristics. This indeed suggests that it is not simply a case of identifying relevant interests and that there may not even be an automatic entitlement to reasons when *Charter* rights are in issue — at least when those rights are being affected in the context of a broad policy-making exercise.

As well as the elucidation of the nature of the interests which will attract a reasons requirement, there are questions as to what, if any, limitations there are on rights of appeal, to reconsideration, and judicial review as generators of an entitlement to reasons, and what constitute "other circumstances" spawning such a right. There is also the issue of whether, even if the interest at stake is one that would normally generate an entitlement to reasons, an absence of reasons will inevitably produce invalidity or whether, if the basis for the impugned decision is otherwise discernible, there is no justification for intervention at least on this ground. This leads to the still further question of whether a failure to provide contemporaneous reasons can be overcome by appropriate affidavits in response to the application for judicial review. In other words, is this a free-standing or automatic basis for judicial review?

In sum, while the principle has been established clearly, there is still a lot of detail to be filled in. On the other hand, the Supreme Court was probably well advised to eschew spelling out a code in the context of this particular case. Flexibility in such matters was a principle that appealed to the Court and the judgment certainly leaves room for manoeuvre and refinement in other contexts.

In attempting to predict how far *Baker* will extend, it is, however, important to be sensitive to the policy and theoretical bases on which the Supreme Court found its support of a reasons requirement. While L'Heureux-Dubé J. classifies the requirement of reasons as a component of the rules of procedural fairness, thereby echoing the standard categorization, the justifications provided for supporting the providing of reasons are not all procedural fairness arguments or, perhaps more accurately, conventional procedural fairness justifications.

To accept a reasons requirement because it effectuates judicial review, reconsideration, or appellate entitlements, is to focus not on the procedural fairness of the process by which the decision under review was reached but on the procedural fairness of what is to come. In that sense, the reasons requirement is more in the nature of a notice requirement of what is at stake so that the parties will have an appropriate focus in the conduct of the review, reconsideration, or appeal. Similarly, requiring reasons as a way of improving substantive decision making speaks at least in part to a point beyond the actual hearing and imposes a form of deliberative discipline which is in some ways divorced from the normal objectives of procedural fairness obligations — the provision of an adequate opportunity to present proofs and arguments in support of one's position. On the other hand, to the extent that the spectre of having to write reasons may force decision makers to be attentive at the actual hearing, the requirement does focus on what has to be one of the primary objectives of all procedural fairness rules — that the parties be heard in the sense that their proofs and arguments are listened to.

In the notion that reasons will promote trust and confidence in tribunal processes and integrity, there are also obvious links with the rationale behind the reasonable apprehension of bias rule. Those participating in such processes are entitled to an appearance of the even-handed dispensing of administrative justice. However, the more general transparency and public confidence arguments for reasons as well as the value of a reasons requirement in the building up of a body of tribunal jurisprudence are rather more difficult to classify as components of procedural fairness. Rather, their ambitions are much more substantive in nature and serve to emphasize that, at the margins, procedural and substantive considerations tend to blur. Indeed, this slippage into reasons as a substantive or adjectival rather than a procedural requirement is even more obvious if one treats the failure to provide reasons as a basis for drawing adverse inferences against a decision maker absent the submission of surrogate material supporting the position reached.

Of course, it must be said that there is nothing at all wrong with combining procedural, adjectival, and substantive ambitions in the development of and justification of a particular rule or ground for judicial intervention or review. On the other hand, the realization that requiring reasons can involve all of these ambitions may well be important in making and understanding the context-sensitive arguments that the judgment of the Court in *Baker* clearly demands. Indeed, as will be discussed below, there is a sense in which this is true not simply in determining whether there is an obligation to provide reasons but also in discerning the appropriate remedial response when any such duty has not been met.

4) Content of Reasons

As noted already, the Supreme Court in *Baker*, while setting the decision aside as unreasonable, nonetheless, was satisfied that the form and content of the reasons provided by the front line immigration officer satisfied the formal requirements of the obligation to give reasons. Albeit in note form, they provided a clear indication of the facts and considerations on which the officer was recommending to her or his superior that the application be rejected. In so doing, the Court emphasized that there was no universal or standard template for the meeting of the obligation. Indeed, it is in this domain that notions of deference do have a role to play. As stated over twenty-five years ago by Dickson J. in *S.E.I.U., Local 333* v. *Nipawin District Staff Nurses' Association*,[215] it is not for the courts to meticulously parse the decisions of administrative tribunals in the search for error:

> The reasons for decision of the Board do not state the number of persons employed by the S.R.N.A. and the Board did not expressly find that the S.R.N.A. was an employer or employer's agent but I do not regard that as fatal to the Board's jurisdiction. A tribunal is not required to make an explicit written finding on each constituent element, however, subordinate leading to its final decision.

In the context of a legal obligation to give reasons, what this statement supports clearly is the giving of leeway to tribunals in the way in which they choose to craft their reasons and, in particular, recognizing that the constituencies in which many tribunals operate will be sensitized to the formulae and shorthand used in the reasons provided. Not every "i" need be dotted nor every "t" crossed.[216]

Nonetheless, if one takes the reasons provided albeit in rough and ready fashion by the immigration officer, what is clear is that, had it been applicable, they would have met the demands spelled out in the Alberta *Administrative Procedure Act*'s prescription of what the provision of reasons should entail: the key findings of fact and an explanation of how those findings coalesced to produce the final result. In this instance, the "explanation" was the listing of factors that the decision maker took into account and those that were discounted. Where the decision making function is one that depends more heavily on the

---

215   [1975] 1 S.C.R. 382 at 391.
216   See, for example, *Islands Protection Society* v. *British Columbia (Environmental Appeal Board)* (1988), 34 Admin. L.R. 1 (B.C.S.C.), to the effect that the Board did not have to make explicit findings on each issue.

interpretation of statutory provisions or precedents, one would expect the explanation provided to reveal how the decision maker reasoned with the legislative language and the relevant precedents. Whether anything less than that should ever suffice is questionable.

This dilemma is well illustrated in the domain of factual findings. On occasion, Canadian courts have been prepared to excuse a tribunal from the obligation of making specific factual findings on the basis that it is clear from the transcript of the proceedings that the tribunal has adopted a particular version of the facts in reaching its decision.[217] On other occasions, courts have held, particularly where credibility is an issue, that the decision maker must not only make an explicit finding on credibility but also provide a reasoned basis for that finding.[218] It is not enough to assert that "having seen the witnesses and heard their testimony, I prefer X's version of events to Y's." While the latter approach seems in most instances to place excessive demands on statutory decision makers, nevertheless, context is everything and there may well be occasions where a failure to address the question of credibility fully and clearly will amount to a failure to meet either the common law or statutory obligation.

5) Authorship

In general, the statutorily designated decision maker is legally responsible for the writing of the decision. The principles against delegation and dictating that the person who hears must herself or himself decide both support this rule.[219] However, as *Baker* itself makes clear, there are exceptions. In a situation where the statute formally reposed the discretionary power in the Minister, the normal principles against delegation of the decision-making function did not apply and the Court was prepared to sustain the formal making of the decision by one departmental official on the basis of reasons provided by another in what was seemingly a recommendation.

Authorship issues have arisen most commonly in the context of tribunals that rely on lawyers and other experts for assistance. What are the legal limits on such assistance and, in particular, do they extend as

---

217 See, for example, *Khaliq-Kareemi v. Nova Scotia (Health Services and Insurance Commision)* (1989), 89 N.S.R. (2d) 388 (N.S.S.C. A.D.).

218 See, for example, *Mehta v. Mackay* (1990), 47 Admin. L.R. 254 (N.S.S.C. A.D.).

219 See, for example, *Sawyer v. Ontario Racing Commission* (1979), 26 O.R. (2d) 673 (Div. Ct.), where a decision was quashed because the lawyer prosecuting the case before the commission wrote the reasons finding Sawyer "guilty."

far as allowing the lawyer to write the decision for signature by the tribunal members?

A series of Ontario cases involving the discipline of lawyers and other professionals[220] suggested that the role of counsel assisting the disciplinary committee in the actual writing of the decision was confined to "journalistic and editorial" assistance.[221] According to *dicta* in one judgment:

> It is highly desirable that a tribunal draft its own reasons and I deplore the practice of the committee in not drafting its own findings and the reasons for its findings. It is a responsibility of the office.[222]

Nonetheless, in that case, the fact that the clerk to the committee had "drafted" the decision was not fatal. This was because there was affidavit evidence to the effect that the clerk had drafted the decision under instructions from the chair; the chair had reviewed the draft with the clerk on two separate occasions; and the chair and the other committee members made further changes to it before its release.

Subsequently, in a medical discipline case,[223] a similar process was followed (though this time after the preparation of an initial draft by a committee member), Doherty J.A., of the Ontario Court of Appeal, emphasized that "the judicial paradigm of reason writing cannot be imposed on all boards and tribunals."[224] Nor should the influence of others be excluded in all contexts. Rather, the extent of permissible assistance depended, as is so often the case, on a range of considerations — the nature of the proceedings, the issues raised, the composition of the committee, the terms of the governing legislation, the available support structures, and the committee's workload.

Thus, to make just one comparison, what may not be acceptable in a professional disciplinary context where the decision makers are themselves lawyers may very well be perfectly permissible in the context of the Immigration and Refugee Board which is composed of hundreds of members and sits all across the country. Achieving some degree of consistency in decision making, maintaining quality control, and ensuring

---

220 See, for example, *Bernstein v. Ontario (College of Physicians and Surgeons)* (1977), 15 O.R. (2d) 447 (Div. Ct.); *Emerson v. Law Society of Upper Canada* (1983), 44 O.R. (2d) 729 (Ont. H.C.); *Spring v. Law Society of Upper Canada* (1988), 30 Admin. L.R. 151 (Ont. Div. Ct.).

221 Craig J., in *Spring, ibid.* at 158.

222 Labrosse J., *ibid.* at 155.

223 *Khan v. Ontario (College of Physicians and Surgeons)* (1992), 9 O.R. (3d) 641 (C.A.).

224 *Ibid.* at 673.

conformity with a corporate style of decision making all coalesce to suggest the legitimacy of assistance in the writing of reasons by the members of this high-volume board, members who frequently will have had no prior legal training. Thus, the availability of templates for decisions in particular kinds of case and the use of counsel for the vetting of draft decisions may not be a problem. Indeed, in *Bovbel* v. *Canada (Minister of Employment and Immigration)*,[225] the Federal Court of Appeal approved the board's Reasons Review Policy, a policy that called for mandatory scrutiny of decisions by the legal staff.

What remains important, however, is that the designated decision maker actually make the decision. This principle has been endorsed strongly by the Supreme Court of Canada in the two leading authorities on post-hearing consultations between members of the panel hearing a particular case and tribunal staff and other members.[226] Where that line is crossed is also exemplified by *Adair* v. *Ontario (Health Disciplines Board)*.[227] There, the Ontario Divisional Court quashed a decision in which the language used was that of the lawyer to the board and where the ground on which the case was decided was one that had been promoted by that lawyer during the course of the hearing. In penning the decision, the lawyer had in effect also illegitimately made it.

6) Impact of a Failure to Provide Reasons

Because the Court concluded in *Baker* that the reasons provided met the formal requirements, there was no explicit consideration of the consequences of a failure to meet that obligation. However, in a situation such as *Baker* where the applicant for judicial review is in the position of seeking something from the state, there are at least three possible remedial responses, precedents for two of which can be found in existing Canadian case law. One possibility is for the court to quash the decision and remit it for reconsideration. Another is the making of an order directing the provision of reasons without quashing the original decision. A more extreme step, for which there is no precedent, would be to grant or direct the granting of the "benefit" the applicant is seeking.

As between the first two, there is much to be said for not choosing either as the general rule but rather to allow the reviewing court discretion as to which step is more appropriate in the circumstances. Thus, if

---

225 [1994] 2 F.C. 563 (C.A.).
226 *I.W.A., Local 2-69* v. *Consolidated-Bathurst Packaging Ltd.*, *supra*, note 177; Québec (Commission des affaires sociales) c. Tremblay, above note 180.
227 *Adair*, above note 188.

the court is of the view that the failure to provide reasons is indicative of a lack of deliberation, the former may be more appropriate. Indeed, in such cases, the most appropriate disposition may be a remission back to a different decision maker. On the other hand, if the applicant's primary concern is the development of a sufficient basis to enable the effectuation of judicial review, statutory appeal, or reconsideration rights, that purpose may be served sufficiently by an order directing the provision of reasons. As for the third possibility, it should probably remain a reserve possibility.

Where the decision is one that affects an existing right or interest, the same possibilities still exist. However, it may be that, in such cases, the first alternative should be the presumptive remedial response unless all the applicant seeks is an order mandating reasons. Some have also suggested that, in this context, a straight quashing of the decision with no possibility of reconsideration would constitute an appropriate remedial response particularly in the face of a complete failure to meet a mandatory statutory requirement to provide reasons.

While there is some English *dicta* to the effect that a failure to meet an obligation to provide reasons is not necessarily a ground for review but will depend on the reviewing court's assessment of whether there is any real purpose to be served by remitting the matter for reconsideration or the provision of reasons,[228] there are few situations in which such an approach would seem justifiable. Certainly, to the extent that such a response involves an assessment by the reviewing court of the substantive outcome, it bespeaks inappropriate judicial involvement in the merits of tribunal decision making. However, if the only purpose that the applicant has in seeking reasons is the effectuation of judicial review, appellate, or reconsideration rights, there is the possibility, illustrated by *C.U.P.E., Local 301*, of a court determining that those rights have not been prejudiced by the absence of reasons. The grounds on which the applicant is seeking judicial review may not require reasons in order to be asserted effectively; the case can be made as forcefully in other ways.

---

228   *Save Britain's Heritage v. Number 1 Poultry Ltd.*, [1991] 1 W.L.R. 153 (H.L. Eng.) at 167 (Lord Bridge).

FURTHER READINGS

ADELL, B., "Arbitral Discretion in the Admission of Evidence: What Limits Should There Be?" (1999–2000), 1 & 2 Labour Arbitration Yearbook 1.

BLUE, I., "Common Evidentiary Issues before Administrative Tribunals and Suggested Approaches" (1993), 14 Advocates' Quarterly 385

CASEY, J.T., "Discovery in Administrative Proceedings: Does *Stinchcombe* Apply?" (1997), 5 Reid's Administrative Law 121

CRAIG, P., "The Common Law, Reasons and Administrative Justice" (1994), 53 C.L.J. 282

ELLIS R., & P. ATERMAN, "Deliberative Secrecy and Adjudicative Independence: The *Glengarry* Precipice" (1994), 7 Canadian Journal of Administrative Law and Practice 171

Gorsky, M.R., "Effective Advocacy and the Continuing Significance of the Rules of Evidence before Administrative Tribunals" (1988), 2 Canadian Journal of Administrative Law and Practice 47

HAWKINS, R.E., "Behind Closed Doors I" (1995–96), 9 Canadian Journal of Administrative Law and Practice 267 and "Behind Closed Doors II" (1996-97), 10 Canadian Journal of Administrative Law and Practice 39

HAWKINS, R.E., "Reputational Review III: Delay, Disrepute and Human Rights Commissions" (2000), 25 Queen's L.J. 599

HOULE, F., "The Use of Official Notice in a Refugee Determination Process" (1993), 34 C. de D. 573

KUSHNER,H., "The Right to Reasons in Administrative Law" (1976), 24 Alta. L.R. 305

LEMIEUX D., & E. CLOCCHIATTI "Official Notice and Specialized Knowledge" (1990), 46 Admin. L.R. 126

MACDONALD R.A. & D. LAMETTI, "Reasons for Decision in Administrative Law" (1990), 3 Canadian Journal of Administrative Law and Practice 123

MORRIS, M.H., "Administrative Decision-Makers and the Duty to Give Reasons: An Emerging Debate" (1997), 11 Canadian Journal of Administrative Law and Practice 155

MULLAN, D.J., "The Role of Lawyers to Professional Disciplinary Bodies" (December 1994) The Advocates' Society Journal 10

MUNRO, K.M., "Howe Troublesome: Do Natural Justice or Fairness Require Full Disclosure?" (1995), 4 Reid's Administrative Law 97

RATUSHNY, E., "Rules of Evidence and Procedural Problems before Administrative Tribunals" (1988), 2 Canadian Journal of Administrative Law and Practice 157

RANKIN M., & LEAH GREATHEAD, "Advising the Board: The Scope of Counsel's Role in Advising Administrative Tribunals" (1993), 7 Canadian Journal of Administrative Law and Practice 29

SPRAGUE, J.L.H., "Evidence before Administrative Agencies: Let's Forget the 'Rules' and Just Concentrate on What We're Doing" (1995), 8 Canadian Journal of Administrative Law and Practice 263

SPRAGUE, J.L.H., "Open Sesame!: Public Access to Agency Proceedings" (1999), 13 Canadian Journal of Administrative Law and Practice 1

SPRAGUE, J.L.H., "A Summary of the Application of the *Stinchcombe* Disclosure Principles to Administrative Agencies" (1996), 2 Administrative Agency Practice 41

STEELE, G., "Tribunal Counsel" (1997), 11 Canadian Journal of Administrative Law and Practice 57

TAGGART, M., Should Canadian Judges be Legally Required to Give Reasoned Decisions in Civil Cases?" (1983), 33 U.T.L.J. 1

CHAPTER 14

BIAS AND LACK OF
INDEPENDENCE

A. INTRODUCTION

The second limb of the traditional natural justice rules requires that decisions not be tainted by bias. The Latin phrase used to express this concern was *nemo judex in sua causa debet esse* or "no one should be a judge in her or his own cause." The clearest manifestation of this principle (applicable to both regular courts and administrative tribunals) is in situations where an adjudicator has a direct stake in the outcome of the proceedings in the manner of a litigant. A typical example is where an adjudicator is a shareholder in a company which is party to the proceedings before the court or tribunal.[1]

However, beyond this kind of clear case, there is a huge variety of situations that give rise to allegations of bias in its original sense. Moreover, the concern of the courts has been with not only demonstrable financial interests of the kind just indicated but also attitudes and relationships to both the parties and the relevant issues such as would create in a reasonable observer serious qualms or misgivings as to whether the decision maker will approach and determine the matters in issue in a sufficiently dispassionate or disinterested way.

---

1   As in the classic judicial bias case, *Dimes v. Proprietors of the Grand Junction Canal* (1852), 10 E.R. 301 (H.L. Eng.), where the Lord Chancellor held shares in a company that was a party to litigation coming before him.

In their reflection of these principles, the courts have also indicated frequently that they are more concerned with the appearance of bias than with the actual existence of bias. Two justifications are generally advanced for this posture. First, the courts recognize the difficulty of determining in any satisfactory manner whether a person is actually biased in the sense of being unable to put any potentially illegitimate interests out of her or his conscious or subconscious mind. Second, the aphorism that it is as equally important that justice be seen to be done as that justice actually be done has been adopted specifically as a governing policy in this domain. The reputation of the justice system for integrity and impartiality is diminished in a way that is contrary to the public interest if the participants and the public generally have grounds for believing that an adjudicator may be subject to illegitimate influences or predispositions.

B. EXPANDING THE REACH OF THE BIAS PRINCIPLES

Until the procedural fairness evolution, in an administrative law setting, those affected could advance allegations of bias only in the case of decision makers who were acting in judicial or quasi-judicial capacities. If the decision maker did not pass this threshold, the attack would have to be framed in terms of such abuse of discretion grounds of judicial review as bad faith, taking into account irrelevant factors, or acting for an improper purpose. However, in the wake of *Nicholson v. Haldimand-Norfolk Regional Board of Commissioners of Police*,[2] the Canadian courts decided that the bar for bias allegations had now been lowered or liberalized to embrace administrative as well as judicial functions.[3]

However, just as with the expansion in the reach of the *audi alteram partem* rule, the broader terrain now subject to allegations of potentially biased decision making is one in which the expected standards vary depending on the nature of the decision-making process. Thus, for example, the Supreme Court of Canada accepted that it would not hold municipal councillors engaged in adjudicative func-

---

2   [1979] 1 S.C.R. 311.
3   For an early example, see *Energy Probe v. Canada (Atomic Energy Control Board)* (1984), 8 D.L.R. (4th) 735 (F.C.T.D.), aff'd (1984), 15 D.L.R. (4th) 48 (F.C.A.) [*Energy Probe*].

tions in the performance of their duties to the same strict rules about lack of prior involvement with the parties or the issues[4] as apply, for example, in professional disciplinary matters. Similarly, the Federal Court of Appeal has ruled on at least two occasions that those acting in an investigatory capacity (such as a commissioner under general inquiries legislation) will not be assessed on the more rigorous basis that pertains to those exercising truly adjudicative functions.[5]

Moreover, just as claims for participatory entitlements have been rejected in the domain of "legislative" decision making, it is also to be anticipated that even the less rigorous standards applicable to municipal councillors will not affect those involved in the "legislative" process. Once again, however, that does not mean that legal standards of proper conduct will be inapplicable to those engaged in such decision making. Conflict of interest standards (whether policed by the regular courts or by the legislative bodies themselves and often legislated) will act as a brake on certain types of association with parties and issues in the legislative process.

C. BIAS AND MULTIMEMBER TRIBUNALS

As elaborated already, in common with the *audi alteram partem* limb of the rules of procedural fairness or natural justice, bias provides an automatic basis for judicial review.[6] The right to be dealt with by an unbiased adjudicator is an "independent and unqualified right" and cannot be remedied by the actual decision of the tribunal and any sense that the outcome was the correct one in any event.[7] One apparent consequence of this is that generally the courts have treated the bias of any one member of a multimember tribunal to be disqualifying of the

---

4   *Old St. Boniface Residents Association* v. *Winnipeg (City)*, [1990] 3 S.C.R. 1170; *Save Richmond Farmland Society* v. *Richmond (Township)*, [1990] 3 S.C.R. 1213.

5   *Beno* v. *Canada (Commissioner & Chairperson, Commission of Inquiry into the Deployment of Canadian Forces to Somalia)*, [1997] 2 F.C. 527 (C.A.); *Zündel* v. *Canada (Minister of Citizenship and Immigration)* (1997), 154 D.L.R. (4th) 216 (F.C.A.)

6   However, as is also the case with breaches of the *audi alteram partem* rule, certain discretionary grounds for the denial of relief, such as delay and waiver, may affect the assertion of an allegation of bias. The scope for these defences will be addressed later in the chapter.

7   *Newfoundland Telephone Co.* v. *Newfoundland (Board of Commissioners of Public Utilities)*, [1992] 1 S.C.R. 623.

whole process. It is assumed that the disqualified member will have had an impact.[8]

Also, though there is yet to be a successful challenge on this basis, the courts have acknowledged that there are situations where all members of a tribunal may be disqualified from adjudicating particular matters by reason of "corporate taint." An example of where this argument came close to succeeding was in *E.A. Manning Ltd.* v. *Ontario Securities Commission.*[9] There, the whole Ontario Securities Commission barely survived disqualification from adjudicating in proceedings being taken against "penny stock" dealers. Since the commission as a whole had developed an *ultra vires* rule condemning the activities of these dealers who were now subject to disciplinary processes, there had been new appointees to the commission who were held not to have been tainted by either the rules in question or by the activities of the chair which had independently given cause for problems with his participation in the matter.

It is also worth noting that a finding of corporate taint may not lead necessarily to regulatory paralysis. The courts have acknowledged that there might be an overriding doctrine of necessity which will, in extreme instances, allow for adjudication by otherwise biased adjudicators.[10] In addition, in Ontario, section 16 of the *Public Officers Act*[11] provides for the appointment of *ad hoc* adjudicators where those charged with exercising a statutory power are "disqualified by interest." This provision was invoked successfully in *Service Employees International Union* v. *Johnson.*[12] There, in the context of an unfair labour practice application, the union raised issues as to whether a member of the government had intimidated the members of the Ontario Labour Relations Board by discussions he had had with the chair. These discussions had allegedly concerned the criteria by which Management Board of Cabinet would determine which vice-chairs of the board would have their appointments revoked. The chair had given all the vice-chairs information about this meeting and it was deter-

---

8   See, for example, *International Union of Mine, Mill & Smelter Workers* v. *U.S.W.A.* (1964), 48 W.W.R. 15 (B.C.C.A.).

9   (1994), 18 O.R. (3d) 97 (Div. Ct.), aff'd (1995), 23 O.R. (3d) 257 (C.A.) [*E.A. Manning*].

10 The issue is discussed in *E.A. Manning, ibid.* See also *Finch v. Association of Professional Engineers and Geoscientists (British Columbia)* (1996), 18 B.C.L.R. (3d) 361 (C.A.).

11 R.S.O. 1990, c.P.45.

12 (1997), 35 O.R. (3d) 345 (O.C. G.D.) [*Johnson*].

mined that this tainted the entire board from dealing with the particular unfair labour practice application. However, on the application of the union and given the refusal of the minister to appoint someone, the Court exercised the power conferred on judges of the General Division under section 16 to indicate that it would appoint a "disinterested person" to hear that application and would take submissions as to who that person should be.

D. THE TESTS

In the case of pecuniary bias,[13] the mere existence of an actual financial stake in the outcome of proceedings will be sufficient to disqualify a person from adjudicating. No further inquiry is thought to be necessary. For these purposes, the size of the financial or other proprietary stake is generally treated as irrelevant. However, some limits are placed on the extent to which this principle is applied. To have a stake in the outcome involves the existence of tangible, incontrovertible links.[14]

Thus, the Supreme Court has reiterated the need for the stake to be "direct" before it is automatically disqualifying. In *Pearlman* v. *Manitoba Law Society Disciplinary Committee*,[15] the Court therefore rejected a claim of disqualification of the professional disciplinary committee based on the assertion that the members had a financial interest in making an award of costs against a disciplined professional. The contention was that such an award would reduce the operating costs of the

---

13 The House of Lords has recently accepted that there are other situations in which there will be automatic disqualification: *R.* v. *Bow Street Metropolitan Stipendiary Magistrate, ex parte Pinochet Ugarte (No. 2)*, [1999] 2 W.L.R. 272 (H.L. Eng.). In that case, the House of Lords ruled that one of its members should not have sat on the appeal involving Spain's application to have former Chilean dictator, General Pinochet extradited to stand trial in that country. The fact that Lord Hoffmann was a director of a charity closely allied to one of the parties supporting the position of Spain in the proceedings, Amnesty International, was automatically disqualifying. There was no need to ask whether this also gave rise to a reasonable apprehension of bias. Public adherence to or promotion of particular causes can be just as problematic as an economic interest.

14 Note also the recognition in the English jurisprudence of a *de minimis* exception. See *Locabail (U.K.) Ltd.* v. *Bayfield Properties Ltd.* (1999), [2000] 1 All E.R. 65 (C.A.). How far this extends is, of course, an interesting question. However, it would presumably apply in situations where a member of a tribunal adjudicating a claim against a particular company was a member of widely dispersed pension or mutual fund which owned shares in that company.

15 [1991] 2 S.C.R. 869.

society in a way that would benefit the members of the committee in terms of their dues or fees. However, the Court held that the connection between the power to award costs and the financial advantage of the members of the committee was too remote and speculative as to constitute a direct financial benefit. Similarly, in an earlier decision, the Federal Court of Appeal rejected a pecuniary bias challenge to the participation of someone whose company might secure contracts as a result of the relicensing of a nuclear facility.[16] According to the majority of the judges, the interest of the member in question was "indirect and uncertain and too remote to constitute either direct pecuniary interest, or bias."[17]

This is not, however, meant to indicate that indirect or speculative financial interests cannot be relevant considerations in bias litigation. They are simply not the stuff of automatic disqualification for pecuniary bias. Rather, they can be either independently or in combination with other factors operative features of an argument for disqualification on the basis of a "reasonable apprehension of bias," the standard generally applied to other species of allegedly disqualifying bias.

Obviously, a test of disqualification for bias concerned with the existence of a reasonable apprehension is a reflection of the concern of the law for appropriate appearances identified earlier. In Canadian law, the details of this test are spelled out in the dissenting judgment of de Grandpré J. of the Supreme Court of Canada in *Committee for Justice and Liberty* v. *National Energy Board*.[18] For an apprehension to be reasonable, it must be one that would be

> held by reasonable and rightminded people, applying themselves to the question and obtaining therefrom the required information. In the words of the Court of Appeal, that test is "what would an informed person, viewing the matter realistically and practically — and having thought the matter through — conclude."

Despite the fact that this was contained in a dissenting judgment, it has nonetheless been applied subsequently by lower courts and endorsed by the Supreme Court of Canada itself.[19]

On its face, this test requires the court to put itself in the shoes of an artificial construct, the "reasonable and rightminded" person, and to attribute to that person a certain amount of knowledge about the rele-

16 *Energy Probe*, above note 3.
17 *Ibid.* at 54.
18 [1978] 1 S.C.R. 369 at 394–95.
19 In *Canadian Pacific Ltd.* v. *Matsqui Indian Band*, [1995] 1 S.C.R. 3.

vant process and the adjudicator under scrutiny. While "reasonable person" tests are the stuff of much of the common law, there is considerable uncertainty under this particular variant as to the amount of information the reasonable person should be deemed to possess. In other words, what makes up the "required knowledge" to which de Grandpré J. refers in his formulation?

Ostensibly, this test does not focus on the knowledge in fact possessed by the person whose apprehensions of bias have led to the bringing of the case. It does not have as its reference point a reasonable person knowing that which the applicant in fact knows or knew. On the other hand, it might be founded on the information that a person in the position of the applicant would have been able to ascertain by diligent inquiry. The sense here would be that challenges based on an apprehension of bias are serious matters and those mounting them are obliged to move beyond initial impressions and perhaps incomplete information and to seek some verification of their version of the facts before commencing litigation.

The Canadian bias jurisprudence has never really probed this question of the information base on which the courts should decide whether a reasonable apprehension of bias exists. However, the practical reality is that the parties to the litigation submit all the relevant evidence in their possession, generally by way of affidavit, and the court, on the basis of the knowledge that it acquires through the process, then makes a decision. Indeed, this reality has led the English courts to finesse the question of how much knowledge to attribute to the reasonable and rightminded bystander. The court is seen as personifying the reasonable person and the court reaches its conclusions on all of the material available to it at the hearing of the application for review.[20] This seems highly pragmatic even allowing for the fact that it opens up the possibility that what was a reasonable apprehension on the part of the applicant at the commencement of the case stands to be countered by evidence introduced during the review process itself by the respondent adjudicator.

There is, however, a more general question common to all reasonable person tests that surfaces when the court sees itself, as the English courts have done, as the personification of the "reasonable man" for these purposes. This difficulty is manifest in the very fact that the House of Lords in 1993 still defined this role in terms of the "reasonable man" and it is the problem of whether the court is justified, particularly in a domain where impressions are said to count, in abjuring any

---

20 R. v. *Gough (RB)* (1993), 155 N.R. 81 (H.L. (Eng.)) and as refined in *R. v. Inner West London Coroner, ex parte Dallaglio*, [1994] 4 All E.R. 139 (C.A.) at 151–52.

attempt to locate itself in the minds of those who are the constituents of a particular tribunal. Take the example of a coroner's inquest into the shooting of a black youth by a white police officer. If the coroner's participation is challenged on the basis of an apprehension of bias, should the court in any way attempt to see the facts as presented to it through the eyes of the victim's family and the community groups which have been accorded standing at the inquest? Or, should an ostensibly neutral, universal viewpoint, that of the "reasonable person" (as opposed to the "reasonable man") continue to prevail?

To the extent that deference to the integrity of administrative processes is an underlying policy of Canadian judicial review law, at the very least, there is a case to be made for attention to be paid to the apprehensions of those who are closest to the process under scrutiny: the parties to the proceedings and the general constituency of that tribunal or authority. However, that concern for one affected constituency must also be tempered by the fact there might be other persons affected by the proceedings whose interests are also entitled to regard in any consideration of whether the perceptions of the applicants for disqualification should prevail. As the coroner's inquest example clearly suggests, the court must also pay some regard to the extent to which acceding to the perceptions of the deceased's family and the community groups will create a sense of bias in the mind of the police officer whose conduct is subject to scrutiny.

The universality of the test proposed by de Grandpré J. in *Committee for Justice and Liberty* also has to be qualified in the light of the Supreme Court's clear acceptance of the notion that what constitutes an illegitimate bias is context-sensitive. In some instances, any recent prior involvement with parties particularly in relation to the matter now before the adjudicator will be disqualifying as will any expression of opinion whether prior to or during the hearing indicating an existing view as to the proper outcome of the proceedings. In other instances, the courts are willing to tolerate such conduct. In the value system of the "reasonable and rightminded" person, expectations of adjudicative neutrality vary depending on the nature of the process that is before the court.

Thus, in the world of municipal politics, councillors may have campaigned on issues or they may have assisted constituents in matters that then come before them in an adjudicative capacity as exemplified most commonly in planning and zoning applications.[21] Members of regulatory bodies may have been appointed because of their associa-

---

21 The leading Supreme Court of Canada judgments already referred to contain some of these elements: *Old St. Boniface Residents Association* and *Save Richmond Farmland Society*, above note 4. In each, the participation of the councillor was sustained.

tion with a particular sector of the regulated community or affected constituencies and may continue to see themselves as champions of the community from which they have been appointed and as vindicators of causes that they have espoused publicly from within that community.

Such was the case in *Newfoundland Telephone Co.* v. *Newfoundland (Board of Commissioners of Public Utilities)*.[22] A former municipal councillor and long-time consumer advocate was appointed to the board and promised to continue his support of consumer causes during his term of office. More specifically, he railed against the salaries being paid to the senior executive officers of Newfoundland Tel as well as their enhanced pension plan. These were matters under investigation by the board, an investigation that led to a hearing on whether the board should order rollbacks on those items. Notwithstanding the scheduling of the hearing, the member in question continued to make public pronouncements about his concerns with these items and this persisted even after the actual commencement of the hearing and a challenge by the company on the ground of bias to his participation in that hearing.[23]

In delivering the judgment of the Supreme Court of Canada, Cory J. found that members of regulatory boards of this kind were more akin to municipal councillors exercising adjudicative functions and, as such, they were not to be disqualified from participation merely because they held strong views that they expressed publicly on policy issues being investigated by the board. However, the Court did find that the member in question had crossed the line in the statements he made once the matter had been set down for hearing. At that stage, it was prudent for the public statements to stop and for the traditional test of a reasonable apprehension of bias to be applied. Moreover, in this instance, the public statements during that period had even crossed the threshold that the Court regarded as the appropriate one to apply to members of this kind of regulatory agency during the pre-hearing investigative period, a test which was the one applied previously in the municipal councillor cases. The strength of the statements indicated "he had a closed mind on the subject." To use the language of one of the municipal councillor cases, they proved that he was no longer "amenable to persuasion."[24]

---

22 [1992] 1 S.C.R. 623. [*Newfoundland Telephone*].
23 The Board declined to deal with challenge on the basis of lack of jurisdiction to rule on such matters.
24 Incidentally, in the final decision, the member in question was part of the majority that rolled back the enhanced pension plan and ordered reimbursement of consumers. However, he concurred in the decision not to make any order with respect to the salaries of the senior executive officers.

E. COMMON SITUATIONS IN WHICH A REASONABLE APPREHENSION OF BIAS MAY OCCUR

Whatever the uncertainties as to the meaning and application of the test for bias, there are many situations where disqualification is almost inevitably going to occur. Adjudicating in cases involving close friends, personal enemies, business associates, and rivals, not to mention family members, provide clear, though nowadays infrequent examples. Indeed, the rules of many tribunals contain codes identifying relationships of this kind that are either disqualifying or at the very least have to be declared. Behaviour during the course of the hearing may also be disqualifying. Adjudicators should not engage in intemperate questioning or cast gratuitous aspersions on the character or physical appearance of a participant or, for that matter, a participant's counsel or representative. Other indicators of prejudgment such as not paying attention may also attract sanction though cases such as this are also classifiable under the *audi alteram partem* limb of the rules of procedural fairness.

Prior active involvement in the actual matter before the tribunal will also generally be disqualifying. The prior involvement may take the form of an adjudicator having played other roles in the administrative process preceding the hearing. A recent example of this is provided by the decision of the Supreme Court of Canada in *2747-3174 Québec Inc. v. Québec (Régie des permis d'alcool)*.[25] Here, the Court held that the Régie's impartiality was compromised by the fact that the structure and operating procedures of the Régie left open the possibility that a Régie lawyer could be involved in every stage of the Régie's process in a particular matter from the initial investigation to the adjudication. In addition, the chair had the capacity to initiate an investigation, decide to hold a hearing, and then constitute the panel to conduct the hearing, a panel on which he or she could choose to sit. Even directors had the ability to make a decision that a hearing was necessary and then sit on that hearing. Given the potential for such overlapping and conflicting roles, the Court was of the view that the process would create in an informed person a reasonable apprehension of bias in a substantial number of cases. This was not only a breach of the common law requirements but also an infringement of section 23 of the *Québec*

---

25   [1996] 3 S.C.R. 919 [*Québec*].

Charter of Human Rights and Freedoms[26] and its requirement of an "impartial and independent" tribunal in such cases.

Disqualifying prior involvement may also arise from associations with the matter now before the tribunal in an earlier professional or other capacity. This second category of case is exemplified by *Committee for Justice and Liberty* itself, the precedent out of which the standard Canadian test for bias emerged. This litigation involved the disqualification of the chair of the National Energy Board from presiding over the hearing of an application for permission to build a pipeline. The basis for this disqualification was the chair's involvement before his appointment to the board in the development of the proposal that eventually led to the application now before the board. In his earlier capacity, he had both supported the project and had helped develop some of the terms on which the application came to be made.[27]

A striking contrast can, however, be seen between the Supreme Court's decision in *Committee for Justice and Liberty* and that of the Ontario Divisional Court in *Large v. Stratford (City)*.[28] At stake in the latter was whether a decision by a human rights adjudicator in a mandatory retirement case should be quashed when the adjudicator had, in his capacity as president of a national association of employees, made a speech after the release of his decision in which he advocated a regime of flexible rather than mandatory retirement. Aside from the fact that these statements were made in another context, the Divisional Court, in denying the application for judicial review, noted that they were not pertinent to the issue before the board of inquiry in that the parties had accepted for the purposes of the case that mandatory retirement was *prima facie* discriminatory and the only issue before the tribunal was whether it could be justified as a *bona fide* occupational requirement in this instance.

---

26 R.S.Q. 1977, c. C-12.

27 The way in which the matter came before the courts provides an interesting illustration of how bias challenges can be processed. Prior to the formal hearings commencing, concerns were raised by the lawyer for the applicant about the chair assigning himself as a member of the panel. This led the chair at the outset of the hearings to read out a statement detailing his prior involvements and asking if any of the parties and intervenors objected to his participation. While the vast majority of those involved had no objections, a few (but not the applicant) did and the chair then adjourned the hearing to enable the board to state a case to the Federal Court of Appeal on whether or not he was disqualified from participating. Before both the Federal Court of Appeal and the Supreme Court of Canada, three public interest groups appeared to argue that the chair was disqualified.

28 (1992), 9 O.R. (3d) 104 (Div. Ct.)

What this case also raises, however, and what it shares in common with the *Newfoundland Telephone* case discussed earlier is the issue of attitudinal bias, one which is presently giving the Canadian courts some difficulties. In delivering the judgment of the Divisional Court, Campbell J. noted:

> Human rights inquiry boards are drawn from those who have some experience and understanding of human rights issues. To exclude everyone who ever expressed a view on human rights issues would exclude those best qualified to adjudicate fairly and knowledgeably in a sensitive area of public policy.[29]

In the context of an agency engaged in economic regulation, Cory J., quoting Hudson Janisch, expressed similar sentiments in the *Newfoundland Telephone* case:

> He observed that Public Utilities Commissioners, unlike judges, do not have to apply abstract legal principles to resolve disputes. As a result, no useful purpose would be served by holding them to a standard of judicial neutrality. In fact to do so might undermine the legislature's goal of regulating utilities since it would encourage the appointment of those who have never been actively involved in the field. This would, Janisch wrote . . . result in the appointment of "the main line party faithful and bland civil servants." Certainly there appears to be great merit in appointing to boards representatives of interested sectors of society including those who are dedicated to forwarding the interest of consumers.[30]

What emerges from these statements is that, in general, far from being a reason for disqualification, prior experience with and the expression of views on issues arising in the regulated area is a strong reason for appointment. Indeed, even in the case of tribunals adjudicating disputes of an essentially binary nature, a record of advocacy for the principles on which the legislation has been based should not be disqualifying nor generally should membership in groups that support the cause of those likely to benefit from the legislation.[31] Further, to

---

29   *Ibid.* at 107.
30   *Newfoundland Telephone*, above note 22 at 639.
31   However, note in contrast *R. v. Bow Street Metropolitan Stipendiary Magistrate, ex parte Pinochet Ugarte (No. 2)*, above note 13, where the House of Lords held that Lord Hoffmann's continued association with a group having close links with a party taking a highly adversarial role in the proceedings was *automatically* disqualifying.

have been an active and vocal supporter of the expansive interpretation of human rights legislation and, indeed, of the parliamentary extension of its reach should not be a reason for disqualification from membership on the list of human rights adjudicators, albeit that the nature of that involvement and advocacy may dictate recusing oneself from cases involving specific issues on which a prior position has been taken. And, of course, what is true of tolerance for such involvements on the part of adjudicators involved in the resolution of binary disputes is more so in the instance of those involved in polycentric regulatory tasks where the range of interests is diverse and, as Cory J. (endorsing Janisch) points out, the policy components of the decision-making process generally far exceed in significance the resolution of narrow questions of statutory interpretation.

However, as *Newfoundland Telephone* demonstrates graphically, there are limits on the extent to which advocacy of and adherence to a particular cause can be carried even in such regulatory environments. This point is also illustrated by another human rights case from Ontario, a case which, while problematic in its outcome, does illustrate well the dimensions of the problem in marginal cases. In *Gale v. Miracle Food Mart*,[32] a human rights adjudicator was disqualified from participation in a case where systemic employment discrimination against women was being alleged. This was primarily on the basis that the adjudicator had been on the record at the time the hearing commenced as one of the complainants in another case before the commission in which allegations of systemic employment discrimination on the basis of sex were being made. As a consequence, the Court did not feel it necessary to take any position on the wider argument of the applicants, that being one that focused not only on the activist role that the adjudicator had played as an academic and in other capacities in the cause of combatting "sex discrimination" but also on the fact that she had allegedly taken a public position on the very kind of issue that was before her in this case.

Clearly, if one accepts the arguments of Campbell J. in *Large*, there is little or no basis for a challenge based on general activism in the area. On the other hand, for a decision-maker to have taken a prior public position on, for example, a disputed question of law now before her or him in an adjudicative capacity might be seen by some as raising

---

32 (1993), 109 D.L.R. (4th) 214 (Ont. Div. Ct.).

different considerations,[33] particularly when this is the first case in which the issue has been raised squarely.[34] Nonetheless, even if we think of this issue in terms of the supposedly paradigmatic neutral forum, the section 96 courts, having once taken a position as an advocate or an academic on a particular legal question has never been seen as requiring a judge to recuse herself or himself from participation in a case in which that question is raised.

The examples of *Large, Gale* and *Newfoundland Telephone* do, however, suggest other examples of potentially problematic situations. While advocacy of the ends and purposes of the legislation in question should not be a basis for disqualification, the appointment of members with a known record of hostility towards those aims and purposes may give rise to quite different considerations. Indeed, as exemplified by *Baker* v. *Canada (Minister of Citizenship and Immigration)*,[35] to render a decision in a matter that reflects a lack of sympathy with the legislative objectives and an impatience with the way in which the legislative scheme is being administered can also be disqualifying.

As we have seen in a number of other contexts, *Baker* involved an immigration officer charged with determining on behalf of the minister whether an over stayer now subject to a deportation order should be allowed on humanitarian and compassionate grounds to make an application for permanent residence without leaving the country. In recommending that the minister deny her application and, thereby, "play[ing] a significant role in the making of" the decision,[36] the immigration officer complained in his reasons about the administration of an immigration scheme that took so long to root out and deal with over stayers as well as attributing negative characteristics to the applicant that were at odds with the whole purpose of the *Act*'s creation of a

---

33   In one of the four cases before the English Court of Appeal, *Locabail (U.K.) Ltd.* v. *Bayfield Properties Ltd.*, above note 14, a part-time judge was held to be disqualified from a case where an insurance company had admitted liability and the sole issue was the determination of damages. In recent professional and academic writings, he had expressed strong criticism of insurance companies and their behaviour in resisting legitimate claims, including contesting liability on dubious grounds. Despite the fact that, in this instance, the insurance company had conceded liability, the Court of Appeal agreed with its assertion of a reasonable apprehension of bias.

34   The Divisional Court notes in *Gale* that there had at that point been no case under the *Ontario Human Rights Code* which had found systemic sexual discrimination in employment.

35   [1999] 2 S.C.R. 817.

36   *Ibid.* at para. 45.

"humanitarian and compassionate" exemption from deportation or at the very least were irrelevant to the resolution of the matter.

In delivering the judgment of the whole Court on this issue, L'Heureux-Dubé J. identified what for these purposes was the proper approach to take in the best spirit of the legislative regime:

> Because they necessarily relate to people of diverse backgrounds, from different cultures, races, and continents, immigration decisions demand sensitivity and understanding by those making them. They require a recognition of diversity, an understanding of others, and an openness to difference.[37]

In a rather different vein, there may also exist some basis for challenge where the government of the day chooses to staff a regulatory agency exclusively with those representing or supportive of the interests of one element of the various interests affected by the regulatory task — all consumer advocates or all with past associations with telephone company interests in the context of the legislative scheme in *Newfoundland Telephone*.

In the first instance, lack of sympathy with the statutory objectives should be disqualifying and governments should be denied the opportunity to frustrate the achievement of legislative goals through the appointments process as opposed to direct legislative repeal or amendment. Indeed, in the other instance, legislative goals are also in issue in that it might be argued that even if not explicitly, then at least implicitly, the legislation creating agencies engaged in economic regulation contemplates appointments that reflect some measure of balance in terms of the various affected interests and constituencies. For the moment, however, the outcome of any case raising either of these possibilities remains a matter for speculation.

F. LINKS WITH REVIEW FOR ABUSE OF DISCRETION

Before *Nicholson* opened up the possibility of challenging purely administrative decisionmaking on the basis of bias, as noted already, a surrogate basis for attack that was sometimes available was one of the various forms of abuse of discretion and, most commonly, bad faith, taking account of irrelevant factors or considerations, and failure to

---

37   *Ibid.* at para. 47.

take account of relevant factors or considerations. Indeed, even today, both types or species of judicial review will often be pleaded in the same application. Moreover, as exemplified by *Baker* v. *Canada (Minister of Citizenship and Immigration)*,[38] both can be successful. There, not only did the immigration officer's notes reveal a reasonable apprehension of bias (as outlined above) by reason of her or his approach to the task of dealing with Baker's application but also many of those same factors or considerations meant for the Supreme Court that there had been an unreasonable exercise of the ministerial discretion. More particularly, by being "completely dismissive of the interests of Ms. Baker's children," the immigration officer had failed to exercise the discretion "in a manner that is respectful of humanitarian and compassionate considerations" and, therefore, "was inconsistent with the values underlying the grant of discretion" and not capable of "stand[ing] up to the somewhat probing examination required by a standard of reasonableness."[39] In short, there had been actual bias on the part of the immigration officer which had led to substantive error.

Another link between review for abuse of discretion and review for bias exists in the domain of unlawful fettering of discretion. The Canadian courts have never had any difficulty in accepting that, at least in some contexts, while it is perfectly permissible for agencies and tribunals to indicate in advance how they will exercise their discretion in particular matters, these often informal policy instruments or statements should not be couched in immutable terms. The agency or tribunal must always show at least a reserve clause willingness to re-evaluate the policy or at least to consider the possibility of creating an exception or not applying it in the context of individual adjudications. Not to do so is to unduly fetter one's discretion and to deny the affected person the individual consideration of her or his case contemplated by the legislative conferral of a discretion to be exercised on a case by case basis. And, of course, to approach an individual case with too great a commitment to such a policy will also lead to allegations of a reasonable apprehension of bias. Thus, in *E.A.Manning*,[40] referred to already, the Ontario Court of Appeal was concerned with the ramifications of the Securities Commission involvement with illegal informal rule making. According to the Court, this policy or rule in effect condemned the activities of "penny stock" traders prior to the holding of a hearing against them under the Act. As a consequence, the parties were

---

38   *Ibid.*
39   *Ibid.* at para. 65.
40   *E.A. Manning,* above note 9.

justified in their claim of reasonable apprehension of bias against all those members of the commission who had participated in the formulation of the relevant illegal policy.

G. STATUTORY AUTHORIZATION

At times, in fact, the relevant legislation will make it clear that a state of affairs that would normally give rise to an allegation of bias is sanctioned legislatively either expressly or by necessary implication.

One of the most obvious examples of this is provided by tripartite models of adjudication (common in the case of arbitration of labour disputes) in which the parties to a bilateral dispute each select a member of the panel which will adjudicate. While there is considerable disagreement in the jurisprudence and among the commentators as to what limits, if any, exist on the capacity of the parties to choose any adjudicator they wish, what is clear is that, without legislative sanction, allowing one of the parties to a proceeding to choose or select an adjudicator would lead to a successful challenge.[41]

In terms of the jurisprudence on statutory authorization, the most commonly litigated question involves situations of overlapping roles; cases in which the adjudicator has been involved in earlier stages of the process in question such as receiving a complaint, determining whether an investigation is necessary, directing, or otherwise participating in that investigation, deciding whether charges should be laid and a hearing convened and then presiding at that hearing. In the context of the enforcement activities of Securities Commissions,[42] the courts have generally been prepared to sustain such a multiplicity of roles. This conclusion has been reached on the basis of the structure of the relevant legislation and the courts' perception of the environment in which securities commissions operate.

In *Brosseau* v. *Alberta (Securities Commission)*,[43] the Supreme Court relied particularly on the fact that all of the allegedly conflicting roles were by the legislation conferred on the commission without any indication that members of the commission engaged at one stage were thereafter disqualified automatically from participation in any later

---

41 See, for example, *MacBain* v. *Lederman*, [1985] 1 F.C. 856 (C.A.).
42 Starting with *Re W. D. Latimer & Co. and Bray* (1974), 6 O.R. (2d) 129 (C.A.), aff'g. (1973), 2 O.R. (2d) 391 (Div. Ct.).
43 [1989] 1 S.C.R. 301.

stage of that same or related process. In addition, the Court emphasized the practical reality that securities commissions will have repeated
dealings with certain companies and traders over the course of time
and also the role of the commission in regulating the securities industry and protecting the public interest. These considerations had the
effect of diminishing the claim that those affected by the enforcement
role of the commission had a right to precisely the same kind of process they would receive in a regular court.

However, the Court did emphasize in *Brosseau* that the defence of
statutory authorization was not a blanket authorization for the performance of multiple functions. Rather, the "mere fact" of involvement in
more than one stage was not sufficient in itself to give rise to disqualification. Subsequently, this particular point was taken up by the Ontario
Divisional Court and Court of Appeal in *E.A. Manning Ltd.* v. *Ontario
Securities Commission.*[44] There, the limits of what was permissible were
transgressed when the commission, in the context of what was later
found to be an *ultra vires* policy statement, in effect determined the guilt
of the companies the activities of which were the subject of the hearing.
Moreover, the reiteration of this position in a public statement by the new
chair of the commission also led to his disqualification from the hearing.

Statutory authorization will also fail as a defence when the applicant is able to challenge successfully the validity of the terms of the legislation by reference to norms such as those contained in section 7 of
the *Charter* and section 2(e) of the *Bill of Rights*. Thus, for example, in
MacBain v. *Lederman*,[45] the Federal Court of Appeal condemned by reference to section 2(e), a statutory scheme under which the Canadian
Human Rights Commission, having determined that there was a basis
for a hearing, then appointed the members of the tribunal to hear the
case and "prosecuted" the case before the tribunal.

H. LACK OF INDEPENDENCE

In recent years, lack of independence has surfaced as a separate ground
for challenging a perceived lack of integrity in decision-making processes. One of the reasons for this has been the use of the term "independent and impartial tribunal" in section 11(h) of the *Canadian*

---

44 *E.A. Manning*, above note 9.
45 Above note 41.

Charter of Rights and Freedoms,[46] language also found in section 2(f) of the earlier *Canadian Bill of Rights* as well as section 23 of the *Québec Charter of Human Rights and Freedoms*.[47] While, ultimately, the Supreme Court of Canada interpreted section 11(h) in a manner which meant that it has very little impact on the administrative process, the specific recognition of the dual standards of independence and impartiality has carried over to section 7 and the contents of the principles of fundamental justice. Moreover, the jurisprudence interpreting the meaning of "independent" in the context of section 11(h), while principally concerned with the criminal process, has obvious lessons for and found analogies in the administrative process. As a consequence, independence arguments also started to surface in the administrative law setting and not just in cases involving *Charter* or *Bill of Rights* challenges to legislative regimes. Additionally, the courts recognized lack of independence as a basis for challenging the actual practices of administrative tribunals as well as subordinate legislation and internal rules of process which created structures and environments in which adjudicative independence was at risk.

In adopting a test by which the independence of adjudicative bodies is evaluated, the Supreme Court has transposed into this arena the de Grandpré J. bias or impartiality test from *Committee for Justice and Liberty*. However, in the foundation case of *R. v. Valente*,[48] Le Dain J. made it clear that the focal point of the courts' inquiries about the state of the reasonable person's mind in such cases was directed at that person's perception of

---

46 Indeed, as *Reference re Remuneration of Judges of Prince Edward Island Provincial Court*, [1997] 3 S.C.R. 3, makes abundantly clear, the principle of independent adjudication has a much longer pedigree under Canada's constitutional arrangements than 1982, the date of the *Charter*. Sections 96 to 101 of the *Constitution Act, 1867* provide a constitutional guarantee of independence for superior court judges and, now after this judgment, the Preamble to the old *BNA Act* and its recognition of a "Constitution similar in principle to that of the Untied Kingdom" provides at least one basis on which similar protections may apply to provincial court judges. It now remains to be seen whether the Preamble will also be read as extending similar protections to administrative tribunals and particularly those adjudicating in domains once reserved to provincial court judges or sufficiently analogous to the jurisdiction of that and the superior court judiciary [*Remuneration of Judges*].

47 R.S.Q. 1977, c. C-12.

48 [1985] 2 S.C.R. 673.

whether the tribunal enjoys the essential objective conditions or guarantees of judicial independence, and not a perception of how it will in fact act, regardless of whether it enjoys such conditions or guarantees.[49]

As revealed in the litigation, the requirement of adjudicative independence has intersecting dimensions. A lack of independence may arise out of influences extraneous to the adjudicative process. However, it may also be a product of the internal structures and protocols of the adjudicative process itself. Most commonly, though not invariably, the first category is one that infects all of the members of the adjudicative body and is accurately characterized as a concern for institutional independence. On the other hand, the second category will generally involve concerns with the adjudicative independence of particular adjudicators.

In terms of insulating adjudicators from improper external threats to their independence and the government or executive branch in particular, the main preoccupations of the courts have been with security of tenure, financial security, and institutional independence with respect to administrative decisions pertaining to the fulfilment of the adjudicative mandate.[50] In the context of the Competition Tribunal and a challenge to its independence under section 11(h) of the *Charter*,[51] the Québec Court of Appeal[52] was content, on the first score, with periods of appointment that were either as a matter of legislation or actual practice in the five- to seven-year range with protection against dismissal save for cause. As for financial security, the focus was on the payment of lay members with the court rejecting the first instance judge's holding that there was too much potential for executive interference in the setting of that remuneration by the governor in council and in the appraisal system in place for salary increments. Finally, on the question of institutional independence in administrative matters, the court was not prepared to treat the absence of a requirement that the chair could be replaced only for misconduct as in itself compromising the independence of the tribunal. All three criteria did not have to be equally satisfied for a tribunal to be independent.

---

49   *Ibid.* at 689.

50   *Ibid.* at 694–714.

51   The Court justified its use of section 11(h), normally confined to criminal matters, on the basis of the tribunal's authority to deal with contempt.

52   In *Alex Couture Inc. v. Canada (Attorney General)* (1991), 83 D.L.R. (4th) 577 (Qué. C.A.).

What emerges from this case are a number of important elements in any assessment of the independence of administrative tribunals, considerations that were to be confirmed by subsequent Supreme Court of Canada authority. First, to reiterate, the three criteria do not represent immutable, fixed standards but rather constitute a list of matters to be taken into account. Second, and this is connected to the first point, standards will vary depending on statutory context and, clearly, those applicable to administrative tribunals will not be as demanding as those applicable to regular courts. Indeed, as among various administrative tribunals, there may be considerable deviations in expectations as to the indicators of independence. Third, as well as the legislation, the courts will look at actual practice. Thus, even where the legislation leaves open some possibility that independence may be compromised, there is room for arguing that actual practice in such matters as salary assessment and length of appointment will convince a court that there is no problem in reality.

In particular, the endorsement of this approach can be found in the Supreme Court of Canada's short judgment upholding that of the British Columbia Court of Appeal in *Katz* v. *Vancouver Stock Exchange*.[53] This case concerned the disciplinary procedures of the exchange and questions were raised about the absence of any form of formal tenure for those hearing disciplinary cases as well as the fact that peers on the committee did not receive remuneration and there were no express provisions covering the reimbursement of the external legal members of the panel. In its judgment, the British Columbia Court of Appeal had stressed the self-governing, peer discipline character of the exchange in holding that the standards of independence appropriate in such a context were not as exacting as those applicable to other adjudicative bodies. In particular, the court expressed the view that there was no problem in members being subject to discipline at the hands of fellow members who were giving their services on a gratuitous basis. Indeed, to the extent that the lawyer members charged on a fee-for-service basis and the lay members were not doing this as a career or job, concerns with the absence of the protection of financial security were not really relevant in this context. As for security of tenure of both the peer and legal members of the panel from which adjudicators were drawn for particular cases, the court went to the actual practice, practice which revealed that members continued to serve until resignation or death.

---

53   [1996] 3 S.C.R. 405, aff'g (1995), 128 D.L.R. (4th) 424 (B.C.C.A.).

In endorsing this judgment, the Supreme Court simply stated its concurrence with the Court of Appeal's posture that the actual practice of the administrative process was an important consideration. It also emphasized that the self-regulatory context differentiated this case from the situation in its earlier decision in *Canadian Pacific Ltd.* v. *Matsqui Indian Band.*[54] In that case, two of the judges forming the majority of the Court had based their decision on the lack of independence possessed by those charged under band by-laws with determining appeals from taxes imposed on those using land within Indian reserves. In that context, an absence of any security of tenure or provision guaranteeing financial remuneration plus the fact that the members of the appeal bodies could be members of the band which had initially imposed the tax were all seen by the two judges as fatal to the validity of the relevant by-laws.

A contrast can also be drawn between *Katz* and another judgment of the British Court of Appeal in a case presently before the Supreme Court of Canada: *Ocean Port Hotel Ltd.* v. *British Columbia (General Manager Liquor Control).*[55] Here, the court was concerned with members of the province's Liquor Appeal Board who, under the statute, served at the pleasure of the lieutenant governor in council and in reality were appointed on a part-time basis for a year[56] with no guarantee of ever hearing a case. Given the severity of the economic consequences of a licence suspension that could be imposed on licensees for infringement of the licensing laws,[57] Huddart J.A. (delivering the judgment of the unanimous court) held that the degree of independence possessed by members of the tribunal should approach that expected of a court at common law. Seen in those terms, the tenuous nature of the members' appointments was insufficient to satisfy the security of tenure aspects of the independence requirements. In so doing, Huddart J.A. applied the standards established by the Supreme Court of Canada in *2747-3174 Québec Inc.* v. *Québec (Régie des permis d'alcool).*[58]

---

54   [1995] 1 S.C.R. 3.

55   (1999), 174 D.L.R. (4th) 498 (B.C.C.A.).

56   According to the Court, (*idid.* at 508) this did not prevent the lieutenant governor in council removing a member without cause at any time. It did not change the "at pleasure" nature of the appointment. All it created was an entitlement to damages under the terms of the appointment. *Cf. Hewat* v. *Ontario* (1998), 156 D.L.R. (4th)193 (Ont. C.A.).

57   In so doing, Huddart J.A. noted (*ibid.* at 503–04) that, under the alternative enforcement mechanism provided for in the *Act,* a regulatory prosecution, the penalty was a fine that had nowhere near the financial consequences of any significant licence suspension, yet in such cases the licensee received a hearing before a regular court.

58   *Québec,* above note 25.

There, the challenge was based on section 23 of the *Québec Charter of Human Rights and Freedoms* and involved allegations of lack of independence on the part of the Régie des permis d'alcool, the Québec liquor licensing body. In its judgment, the Court confirmed the approach in *Couture* that, in general, administrative tribunals would pass the security of tenure test if their members were given a reasonably lengthy period of appointment (three years or more) and were removable only for cause during that period. Obviously, the level of security of tenure was much greater than that possessed by the members of the Liquor Appeal Board in *Ocean Port*. However, what *Ocean Port* raises clearly is the issue of the extent to which there may be constraints not only on at pleasure but also part-time appointments to tribunals of this kind. It also suggests that there might at least on some occasions be concerns about the failure of those responsible for assigning hearings to assign cases to duly appointed members for whatever reason.

Somewhat more seriously in *Régie*, questions were also raised about the third criterion, the administrative independence of the Régie and its chair and directors from the minister under whose umbrella the Régie operated. In the Québec Court of Appeal, this institutional relationship had been held to have compromised the independence of the Régie. However, this aspect of the judgment was reversed by the Supreme Court of Canada. In so doing, the Court emphasized that it was not unusual for administrative tribunals to be subject to the general supervision of ministers of the Crown. Moreover, notwithstanding the many encounter points between the minister and the Régie and the minister's other role as the official responsible for the police forces enforcing the liquor laws of the province, there were no facts on the record that indicated that this involved the minister in day to day regulation and scrutiny of the administrative functioning of the Régie. This was in the hands of the chair. The Court also noted the terms of the oath of office sworn by the directors of the Régie.

Internal as well as external influences can represent a threat to the independence of individual members of tribunals. Thus, the power possessed by the chair of a tribunal may have an independence-threatening impact on the adjudicative capacities of one or more members. Control or influence over reappointment, preferment, and salary may all produce inducements to conform to the chair's wishes. Illegitimate pressure can also arise from the collective weight of the other members of the tribunal and also, in some instances, through conduct of staff and particularly lawyers.

Traditionally, these possibilities have been dealt with by reference to principles such as those instructing that the person that hears a case must decide it or that the person charged statutorily with responsibility for making a decision should not act under dictation. However, at root here is a problem of lack of independence or decisional autonomy. Moreover, this has spawned in recent years a now significant body of jurisprudence where the concern of the courts has been with institutional structures (either legislated directly or evolving as a matter of practice) which contribute to a reduction in the autonomy of individual members of tribunals.

The most dramatic manifestation of this concern has come in situations where tribunals have put in place structures for dealing with problem cases coming before individual panels of particular tribunals. As we have seen already, part of the concern here is with the exclusion of the parties from discussions that have the potential to generate new arguments and evidence. However, they also can lead to unacceptable compromises of the independence of the members of the panel charged with actually deciding the case.

Thus, while the Supreme Court in *International Woodworkers of America, Local 2-69* v. *Consolidated-Bathurst Packaging Ltd.*[59] found no problem in general with meetings of the whole of a tribunal to discuss cases coming before individual panels that raised novel or controversial issues, nonetheless, the Court made it clear that the way in which such meetings were structured was very important. There were some forms of "consultative practices" that might indeed cross the boundary of what was permissible and "force or induce decision-makers to adopt positions with which they do not agree." For these purposes, structures that allowed for influence were alright but those that opened up the possibility of compulsion were open to challenge.

Subsequently, in *Tremblay* v. *Québec (Commission des affaires sociales)*,[60] the Supreme Court held that the limits laid down in *Consolidated-Bathurst* had indeed been exceeded. Albeit that the consultative process in issue had been put in place as the result of a request by the members of the Commission, the degree of formality that it involved as well as the powerful influence of the chair in the whole process led to its invalidity.

As opposed to the situation in *Consolidated-Bathurst*, the consultation process in *Tremblay* was one that could be set in motion not only by the members of the particular panel but also by the chair of the commission. This was provided for explicitly in the formal rules that

---

59   [1990] 1 S.C.R. 282.
60   [1992] 1 S.C.R. 952.

had been promulgated and re-enforced by a practice under which the decisions of particular panels required the imprimatur of the commission's lawyer or, in her or his absence as in the case under review, of the chair. Gonthier J. found this feature sufficient in itself to condemn the process adopted by the commission. In addition, he also cautioned against the use in such processes of some of the other features present in the commission internal directives, notably "[v]oting, the taking of attendance and the keeping of minutes." They can all lead as in this instance to "systemic pressure" to conform. To the extent that consistency was one of the objectives of such mechanisms, it had to yield to the greater value of the integrity and independence of individual members of the commission.

As the facts of *Tremblay* indicate, independence can be compromised internally not just by the chair and fellow members of the tribunal, but also by staff and particularly lawyers to the relevant agency. Aside from such obvious situations as using lawyers to one of the parties to assist in the writing of the decision,[61] the independence of adjudicators is also infringed when lawyers appointed to assist and advise or to act as counsel in effect take over the proceedings and act as though they are members of the tribunal hearing the case.[62] In like vein, it may also be necessary to ensure a separation within certain tribunals (such as the disciplinary arms of professional societies) between the lawyers responsible for enforcement and prosecution and those charged with providing advice and assistance to the disciplinary committee itself.[63] Moreover, as we have seen in the section on the provision of reasons, while using lawyers to assist in the writing of reasons for decision and for the purpose of vetting decisions are not in and of themselves grounds for challenge, there are limits that must be recognized. The assistance should not turn into effectively making the decision, and compulsory or mandatory vetting may be just as offensive to the courts as were the compulsory consultations in *Tremblay*, particularly if associated (as there) with restraints on independent release of the decision.

---

61 *Canadian Pacific v. Ontario Highway Transport Board*, unreported judgment of Ontario Divisional Court, October 3, 1979.

62 See, for example, *Venczel v. Association of Architects* (1990), 45 Admin. L.R. 288 (Ont. Div. Ct.).

63 See, for example, *Re Bernstein and College of Physicians and Surgeons of Ontario* (1977), 15 O.R. (2d) 447 (Div. Ct.). See also the discussion in *2747-3174 Québec Inc. v. Québec (Régie des permis d'alcool)*, above note 25.

Especially critical in recent litigation have been issues of the impact on independence of government proposals to change the composition of tribunals either by non-renewal of expiring appointments or even dismissal. The early case law in this domain rejected such challenges on the basis that those seeking renewal would realize that the government of the day would be looking at their performance in terms of their overall discharge of their duties in terms of the general philosophy and dictates of the empowering statute. It was simply inappropriate to presume that members of a tribunal might act in such a way as to favour government interests in particular cases in order to enhance their chances of reappointment.[64] More recently, confronted by the spectre of governments blatantly and unapologetically using their powers of appointment, reappointment, and dismissal to achieve political ends and political rebalancing, such arguments are now making some headway.

Service Employees International Union, Local 204 v. Johnson,[65] already dealt with in the section on corporate or institutional taint, provides a graphic example. The prospect that the members of the Ontario Labour Relations Board possibly had knowledge of the criteria by which the orders in council appointing them to the board would be revoked was sufficient to disqualify the whole board at least from the particular case in which this was being raised on an unfair labour relations complaint. Also, on a narrower point, McGillis J. of the Federal Court, Trial Division invalidated a provision in the *Canadian Human Rights Act* that put in the hands of the minister of justice the fate of a hearing by a tribunal member whose appointment was due to expire before the case was completed.[66] Given the relationship between the minister and the commission which had the carriage of the complaint before the tribunal,

---

64   See, for example, *Sethi* v. *Canada (Minister of Employment and Immigration)*, [1988] 2 F.C. 537 (C.A.).

65   *Johnson*, above note 12.

66   *Bell Canada* v. *Canadian Telephone Employees Association* (1998), 143 F.T.R. 241 (T.D.). An appeal from that judgment was adjourned *sine die* in some measure because the relevant legislative provisions had been amended. See (1999), 246 N.R. 368 (F.C.A.). However, subsequently, there was another successful challenge to the provisions of the Act: *Bell Canada* v. *Canadian Telephone Employees Association*, [2000] F.C.J. No. 1747 (T.D.) (Q.L.) (November 2, 2000). Under the amendments, the chair of the Canadian Human Rights Tribunal Panel now made the decision on whether a member whose term of office was about to expire could continue to hear a case. This too was held to be an illegitimate threat to the independence of panel members. As well, the Court held that the ability of the commission to issue guidelines that would be binding on panels determining pay equity cases was also a violation of the principles of fundamental justice (including the right to an independent adjudicator) guaranteed by section 2(e) of the *Canadian Bill of Rights*.

this represented far too great a potential threat to the independence of the process. The court also held that the statutory scheme was further tainted by the control that the commission at that time had over the levels of remuneration and the expenses of tribunal members.

As the examples detailed above demonstrate, lack of independence arguments can arise in a variety of ways. In some instances, the challenge will stem from a particular incident or perhaps a practice of the tribunal or agency. In such cases, aside from the setting aside of the decision or proceedings under attack, the only other response called for by the tribunal is to ensure that the incident is not repeated or that the institutional practices that gave rise to the successful attack are changed to bring them into conformity with the law's requirements of a sufficient degree of independence. On occasion, as in *Katz* and *Matsqui Indian Band*, the threat to independence is found in subordinate legislation — regulations, by-laws. In those situations, the remedial response will be a striking down of not just the relevant decision or proceedings but also the subordinate legislation.

Where, however, the lack of independence is imbedded in primary legislation, the courts' ability to act is contingent on whether or not there is a *Charter* right that is at stake or whether the matters in issue come within the ambit of other forms of superior legislation such as the *Canadian Bill of Rights* or the *Québec Charter of Human Rights and Freedoms*. Without such a basis for striking down the legislation itself, the court will be forced to conclude that, because the lack of independence is statutorily authorized, nothing can be done about it. However, since the judgment of Lamer C.J.C., in *Reference re Remuneration of Judges of Prince Edward Island Provincial Court*,[67] the possibility may have opened up that arguments for a guarantee of tribunal independence might also be advanced on the basis of the Preamble to the *Constitution Act, 1867*, at least when those tribunals are performing traditional adjudicative tasks. If the Preamble can be deployed to challenge compromises of independence in the case of non-section 96 judges, it is not much of a stretch to extend that to adjudication by tribunals.

I. ASSERTING A CLAIM OF BIAS OR LACK OF INDEPENDENCE

Frequently, though not invariably, the facts giving rise to possible disqualification on the basis of bias or a lack of independence will be

---

67 *Remuneration of Judges*, above note 46.

known to the relevant party prior to the hearing. On other occasions, they will become apparent during the course of the hearing.

In such instances, it is incumbent on the party affected to put the allegation and the facts on which that party is relying to the decision maker at the earliest possible moment. Not to do so is to risk a finding of waiver should the allegation not be raised until some later point. It also provides the decision maker with an opportunity to evaluate the allegations and to decide whether or not to voluntarily recuse herself or himself. Indeed, there is probably a duty on the decision maker to make that assessment.

Should the adjudicator refuse to disqualify herself or himself, more difficult questions arise. Having put the allegations on the record, has the affected party protected her or his position or might further steps need to be taken at this point to avoid a later allegation of waiver? One point is clear, that the party need not abandon the proceedings in the sense of refusing to take part. Indeed, not only does the law not require this but it is also very dangerous to take this step since it assumes that at some point a court will rule in that party's favour on the bias allegation. If that does not happen, the right to a hearing has effectively been abandoned.

On many occasions, the next step is to ask the adjudicator to adjourn the proceedings to enable the refusal to recuse to be tested by way of a judicial review application. However, it is by no means clear whether this is a step that must always or sometimes be taken. Similarly, if the adjudicator refuses to adjourn the proceedings on this basis, there is no clear law on whether at that point the party affected is at least sometimes, if not always, obliged to institute an application for judicial review and, in conjunction with that, to apply for a stay of proceedings or an interim injunction to prevent the matter proceeding until such time as a court can deal with the substance of the bias or lack of independence allegation.

One of the principal reasons for this uncertainty stems from the fact that, even where all of the facts are known or able to be ascertained in the context of an application for judicial review, the courts may, nonetheless, treat an application for relief in the nature of prohibition or an injunction on the basis of bias or a lack of independence as premature.[68] In so doing, the courts will rely on considerations such as the costs of fragmenting judicial review and the avoidance of potentially unwarranted interference with the functioning of the administrative process. All of this would seem to suggest that affected parties, having put their objections on the record, will in most cases be justified in not pursuing the challenge any further at that point. Rather, they should

---

68   See, for example, *Ontario College of Art v. Ontario (Ontario Human Rights Commission)* (1992), 99 D.L.R. 738 (Ont. Div. Ct.).

await the outcome of the hearing and find out whether, despite their concerns, they have been successful on the merits. If not, they can then apply for judicial review not only on the basis of the allegation of bias or lack of independence but also on any other grounds that have emerged during the course of the hearing.

However, it is not universally the case that the courts will refuse to intervene before or during the hearing process[69] and this always raises questions as to whether there might also be occasions on which the affected party takes a risk of waiver or loss of her or his claim if the pre-emptive action is not taken. These are not easy issues and they will be returned to in more detail and with reference to the jurisprudence in the section on discretionary reasons for the denial of relief and, in particular, the sometimes conflicting concepts of waiver and prematurity.

FURTHER READINGS

BRYDEN, P., & RON HATCH, "British Columbia Council of Administrative Tribunals Research and Policy Committee: Report on Independence, Accountability and Appointment Processes in British Columbia Tribunals" (1999), 12 Canadian Journal of Administrative Law and Practice 235

DES ROSIERS, N., "Toward an Administrative Model of Independence and Accountability for Administrative Tribunals" in *Justice to Order - Adjustment to Changing Demands and Co-ordination Issues in the Justice System in Canada* (Montréal: Editions Thémis, 1999) at 53

GINN, D., "Recent Developments in Impartiality and Independence" (1997), 11 Canadian Journal of Administrative Law and Practice 25

HAIGH, R., & J. SMITH, "Independence After *Matsqui*" (1998), 12 Canadian Journal of Administrative Law and Practice 101

RANKIN, M., "Perspectives on the Independence of Administrative Tribunals" (1993), 6 Canadian Journal of Administrative Law and Practice 91

RANKIN, T.M., "Case Comment: *Ocean Port Hotel Limited v. B.C. (General Manager, Liquor Control)*" (1999), 57 The Advocate 709

SHORES, W., and D. Jardine, "Institutional Bias — A Sharpened Sword for Attacking the Administrative Structure of Tribunals" (1997), 6 Reid's Administrative Law 197

---

69 As in *Committee for Justice and Liberty v. National Energy Board*, above note 18.

CHAPTER 15

THE ADJECTIVAL OR ANCILLARY POWERS OF ADMINISTRATIVE TRIBUNALS

A. INTRODUCTION

The Supreme Court of Canada has made it clear that, unlike the superior courts, administrative tribunals and agencies have no inherent powers.[1] As a consequence, there are considerable limitations on the exercise of ancillary or adjectival powers by statutory authorities. Unless the particular power is conferred directly by statute or arises by necessary implication from the nature and purposes of the statute in general and the decision-making regime in particular, it is unlikely that the courts will concede to the tribunal the authority that it is claiming.

Thus, in the chapter on the contents of procedural fairness, we saw how the courts have generally recognized that, without explicit statutory authority, administrative tribunals do not have the ability to order pre-trial discovery or, even for that matter, the compulsory production of materials at a hearing. Even though the availability of evidence would seem to be vital to the full determination of the issues at stake, tribunals do not have any inherent or necessarily incidental power to order its production either before or even during the conduct of a hearing. Moreover, to the extent that the absence of access to this information may compromise the procedural fairness entitlements of other affected per-

---

1   *Canadian Pacific AirLines Ltd.* v. *Canadian Air Line Pilots Association*, [1993] 3 S.C.R. 724.

sons, the most that can be done is for the tribunal to draw inferences from that against the party refusing access to the material evidence.

However, it is also clear that there are other kinds of power or authority that the courts are willing to concede to administrative tribunals and agencies almost automatically, such as the power to control or regulate proceedings over which they preside and the authority to issue policy statements and guidelines indicating how they are likely to exercise discretion in individual cases. Indeed, in such cases, there is seldom much pretence to the effect that what the courts are engaging in is an exercise in statutory interpretation. Rather, they are simply assuming that, in the absence of legislation expressly withdrawing that power, considerations of efficiency and expediency indicate that the tribunal or agency should have the particular power.

Seen in this light, it therefore becomes necessary to identify how the courts are going to approach particular assertions of ancillary or adjectival powers by administrative agencies and tribunals. On what occasions will the courts require that there be express statutory authority? On what occasions will they require at least some strong indications from the statutory context that this is the kind of power that the legislature has implicitly authorized the agency or tribunal to exercise? On what occasions, will they simply assume the existence of the power absent an express legislative exclusion?

As might be inferred from the example already provided of discovery and other forms of compulsory production of documents and other evidence, explicit authority[2] is most often going to be required in situations involving the use of the coercive power of the state against individuals and, particularly, where the recognition of such a power would involve privacy interests that have traditionally been a concern of the common law. Thus, *Entick* v. *Carrington's*[3] proscription against warrantless searches, now re-enforced by section 8 of the *Charter*, makes it impossible that a court would ever uphold a tribunal's claim to engage in any kind of search and seizure without express legislative authority. The same also holds for sanctions such as detention, seizure of goods, and the award of monetary remedies in the shape of either fines or damages. It is also true of the awarding of costs. The courts have traditionally been

---

2   As illustrated graphically by *Canadian Pacific Airlines Ltd., ibid.*, this manifests itself
     in two ways. If there is no statutory provision that could be interpreted as granting
     the power, that power does not exist, and, even if there is a possible statutory source
     of power, it will generally have to be quite explicit with any ambiguity interpreted
     against the existence of the authority asserted by the tribunal or agency.

3   (1765), 19 St. Tr. 1030; 95 E.R. 807 (K.B.).

unwilling to allow tribunals and agencies any authority to grant interim relief, though recent jurisprudence recognizes that, at least on occasion, tribunals can ask the superior courts to exercise their own inherent or statutory power to grant interim relief in aid of the administrative process. Also, in recent times, the Supreme Court of Canada has proved sympathetic to arguments for a liberal reading of broad discretions conferred on tribunals over the crafting of appropriate remedial orders.

The power to deal with contempt is one where explicit authority would usually be expected. However, for historic reasons, the designation of a tribunal as "a court of record" generally has been seen as carrying with it an automatic right to deal with contempt in the face of the tribunal.[4]

Once we move away from situations that have coercive elements, the courts will not generally be looking for express statutory authority and are more willing to accept that the tribunal or agency possesses the authority in question simply on the basis of functional and pragmatic considerations. However, as we will see, sometimes, even in this domain, lingering concerns about the overall competence and appropriateness of the administrative process will hinder the advancing of some claims to ancillary and adjectival power. In the minds of some judges, there are simply some tasks that should not be left to administrative tribunals and agencies and that are better left to be carried out by courts. The story of the first area that I will consider in detail, the right of tribunals and agencies to consider *Charter* questions, certainly has elements of that in it. Thereafter, I will deal with a number of other aspects of the adjectival powers of statutory authorities that have caused difficulties over the years and on which there is generally a rich body of illustrative jurisprudence: the delegation of powers; control over procedures and the making of procedural rulings; the making of representations and the giving of assurances; issuing of policy statements and guidelines; and reopening and reconsidering a matter that has already been dealt with.

B. JURISDICTION OF TRIBUNALS AND STATUTORY AUTHORITIES GENERALLY TO DEAL WITH *CHARTER* AND OTHER CONSTITUTIONAL ISSUES

Before the advent of the *Canadian Charter of Rights and Freedoms*, administrative tribunals and, more generally, statutory and prerogative

---

4   *Chrysler Canada Ltd.* v. *Canada (Competition Tribunal))*, [1992] 2 S.C.R. 394.

authorities, seldom encountered issues as to their competence to consider constitutional questions. Nonetheless, in the context of proceedings in which doubts were raised as to whether a matter was properly within federal or provincial jurisdiction, as we have seen, tribunals such as labour relations boards routinely entertained these questions and made rulings on them albeit subject to the judicial review jurisdiction of the courts.[5] Indeed, where such an issue surfaced, the courts expected the tribunal to at the very least develop an adequate factual record on which any subsequent judicial review proceedings could be adjudicated. Not to do so invited a remission of the matter back to the tribunal.[6] This continues to be accepted jurisprudence.[7]

However, with the *Charter* came a dramatic increase in other kinds of constitutional litigation. No longer were constitutional cases virtually restricted to division of powers issues. Rather, courts were being asked to strike down both legislation and administrative action on the basis that they infringed the rights and freedoms guaranteed by the various provisions of the *Charter*. Indeed, on occasion, litigants sought more than striking down; in the case of allegedly underinclusive statutes and orders, the courts were asked to extend the legislation's reach to accommodate the guarantees contained in the *Charter* and, in particular, section 15's right to equality. Similar demands also soon came to be made of administrative tribunals. Both quantitatively and qualitatively, this was a problem of a rather different order than the odd case in which a tribunal had to deal with a largely fact-centred inquiry into whether a matter was properly before it by reference to the division of powers principally contained in sections 91 and 92 of the *Constitution Act, 1867*.

Some of these new scenarios are not all that problematic and they serve to demonstrate that administrative tribunals and agencies do have jurisdiction to consider *Charter* issues albeit that the Supreme Court has not surprisingly ruled that, in dealing with any such question, they have no entitlement to deference from the courts on any subsequent judicial review application.[8] Thus, by and large, where a tribunal that makes decisions that have the potential to deprive a person of the right to life, liberty, and security of the person as guaranteed by section 7 of the *Charter*, there would seem to be no difficulty, at

---

5   See, example, *Northern Telecom Ltd.* v. *C.W.O.C. (No. 2)*, [1983] 1 S.C.R. 733.
6   *Northern Telecom Ltd.* v. *Communication Workers of Canada*, [1980] 1 S.C.R. 115.
7   *Douglas/Kwantlen Faculty Association* v. *Douglas College*, [1990] 3 S.C.R. 570, [*Douglas/Kwantlen Faculty Association*].
8   *Cuddy Chicks Ltd.* v. *Ontario (Labour Relations Board)*, [1991] 2 S.C.R. 5 [*Cuddy Chicks*].

least where the particular claims are not dealt with expressly by statute, with that tribunal responding to an argument that the "principles of fundamental justice" require a certain level of procedures.[9]

However, the matter takes on a rather different complexion where the challenge involved requires the tribunal or decision-maker to consider the validity of its empowering statute and, even more so, when the challenge is based on the contention that that statute is underinclusive in its protection of either substantive or procedural guarantees of rights and freedoms contained in the *Charter*. Since the coming into force of the *Charter*, there has been much debate, indeed fierce controversy on these issues. That controversy is epitomized by the split among the judges of the Supreme Court of Canada in that Court's most recent visiting of crucial aspects of this whole question: *Cooper* v. *Canada (Human Rights Commission)*.[10] This followed a trilogy of earlier Supreme Court judgments in which the issue had been explored with varying results.

1) Tribunals and Assertions of Legislative Invalidity and Underinclusiveness

a) The Trilogy

In the foundation judgment of the Supreme Court of Canada in *Douglas/Kwantlen Faculty Association* v. *Douglas College*,[11] the particular context was a grievance arbitration challenging the termination of employment and involving a section 15 challenge to the mandatory retirement policy in a collective agreement. La Forest J., delivering the judgment of the Court, found statutory authorization for the arbitrator considering the *Charter* issues[12] in a section of the relevant legislation that authorized the arbitrator to interpret and apply any Act intended to regulate employment. This was sufficient to round out the arbitrator's jurisdiction over the parties, the subject matter, and the remedy sought. Not only could the question be considered but also, if the *Charter* argument prevailed, the arbitrator had jurisdiction to allow the grievance against termination and order the reinstatement of the relevant employees.

---

9   See, however, *Re C.(J.)* (1992), 3 Admin. L.R. (2d) 233 (Ont. G.D.).

10   [1996] 3 S.C.R. 854 [*Cooper*].

11   [1990] 3 S.C.R. 570 [*Douglas/Kawantlen Faculty Association*].

12   Did the *Charter* even apply and, if it did, did the mandatory retirement provisions of the collective agreement violate s. 15 and, if they did, were they saved by s. 1?

Subsequently, the same kind of approach was deployed in *Cuddy Chicks Ltd.* v. *Ontario (Labour Relations Board).*[13] Here, the issue was whether, in the context of a certification application, the board could[14] consider the validity (again by reference to section 15) of a statutory exclusion from the benefits of collective bargaining of a certain category of employee. This time, the Court found the statutory justification in a provision authorizing the board "to determine all questions of law and fact that arise in any matter before it." If it determined that the statutory exclusion violated the *Charter*, the board could then grant the certification application, that which it was being asked to do by an applicant otherwise properly before it. This conclusion was re-enforced for the Court by "practical considerations":

> It is apparent that an expert tribunal of the calibre of the Board can bring specialized expertise to bear in a very functional and productive way in the determination of *Charter* issues which make demands on such expertise. In the present case, the experience of the Board is highly relevant to the *Charter* challenge to its enabling statute, particularly at the s.1 stage where policy concerns prevail. At the end of the day, the legal process will be better served where the Board makes an initial determination of the jurisdictional issue arising from the constitutional challenge.[15]

What these two cases left open, however, was the question of whether the presence of legislative provisions of the kind that were relied upon in each of them was an essential requirement for a finding of legislative authorization or whether the courts could imply legislative authorization from the character of the tribunal and the nature of the *Charter* issue even absent such legislative indicia. In fact, it is possible to read a positive answer to this question into the final of this initial trilogy of such to come before the Supreme Court. Despite the fact that, in *Tétrault-Gadoury* v. *Canada (Employment and Immigration Commissioner),*[16] the Court held that a board of referees under the *Unemployment Insurance Act* did not have authority to consider a *Charter* challenge to a limitation on entitlement to a benefit, the Court did not see the possibility of such authority being defeated necessarily or auto-

---

13 *Cuddy Chicks*, above note 8.
14 Indeed, the Ontario Court of Appeal, the **decision** of which was affirmed on appeal, went so far as to hold that the board *had* to rule on the *Charter* issue: (1989), 62 D.L.R. (4th) 125 (Ont. C.A.).
15 *Ibid.* at 132.
16 [1991] 2 S.C.R. 22. [*Tétrault-Gadoury*].

matically by the absence of provisions such as those found in the two earlier cases. On the facts, however, practical considerations in favour of the board having the capacity to consider such questions did not overcome the weight of the legislative indicators and, in particular, the fact that, on appeal from the board of referees, umpires were given authority to deal with all questions of law and fact that arose in any matter properly before them. Without that provision, the Court's conclusion could have been different, and La Forest J., again delivering the judgment of the Court, conceded as much.

b) *Cooper*

Cooper involved an attempt by two complainants under the *Canadian Human Rights Act* to challenge a provision in that *Act* that had the effect of disabling the Canadian Human Rights Commission from considering their complaint and determining whether it merited reference to a tribunal for adjudication. The section in question provided an answer to a challenge to age discrimination in employment. As long as the normal age of retirement from a particular position represented the industry norm, there was no discrimination proscribed by the *Act*.

In the case of these two complainants, the industry (airline pilots) norm was sixty and they were seeking to have that provision read out of the *Act*. However, rather than commencing an action in the courts for a declaration that the provision was *ultra vires* as violating the *Charter*, Cooper and Bell asked the Human Rights Commission to determine whether or not they had an arguable case that the provision violated the *Charter* and, if so, to refer the matter to a tribunal for determination. By a majority of five to two, the Court determined that neither the commission nor a tribunal had authority to determine this question.

One member of the majority, Lamer C.J. was of the opinion that statutory authorities had no jurisdiction to determine *Charter* issues irrespective of the context. Indeed, any attempt to clothe them with that jurisdiction would itself be unconstitutional as trenching upon both the guaranteed judicial role of the superior courts under sections 96 to 101 of the *Constitution Act, 1967* and the partial separation of powers between the legislative and executive branches of government implicit in that same *Constitution Act, 1867*; it was not the role of the executive (including, for these purposes, administrative tribunals and agencies) branch of government to pronounce on the legitimacy of the acts of the legislative branch. The only use that tribunals and other forms of statutory authority could make of the *Charter* was as a guide to the interpretation of statutory language.

The minority judgment of McLachlin J. (in which L'Heureux-Dubé J. concurred) is towards the other end of the spectrum on this issue. Starting from the position that all law and all law makers must conform to the *Charter*, McLachlin J. took the stance that all tribunals and commissions that had authority to determine questions of law of necessity had the jurisdiction to consider *Charter* issues that arose for consideration in the course of their functions. Only where the legislature had expressly withdrawn that capacity from them or expressly confined them to the determination of questions of fact alone would a tribunal or agency lack authority to consider the *Charter* including challenges to the constitutionality of a provision under which the tribunal or agency was acting.

Indeed, it is possible to take the logic of McLachlin J.'s position a step further and argue that section 52(1)'s proclamation that the *Charter* is the "supreme law of Canada" is directed at all with authority to apply and administer the law and not just tribunals and commissions. A further corollary of this would be that Parliament and the legislatures would lack the capacity to withdraw this imperative and that all exercising statutory and prerogative authority would be obliged to confront any *Charter* issues raised by those affected or, even perhaps, simply apparent in matters coming before them. To this point, there is no judicial opinion supporting this position.

McLachlin J. also justified the position that she adopted in *Cooper* not just on the basis of constitutional theory but also by reference to practical considerations. Many of those for whom the administrative justice system was designed would have great difficulty ever raising *Charter* issues were they obliged to do so in the context of an action or application for a declaration in the regular courts. Unless they were able to raise the matter for consideration by the administrative tribunal from which they were normally entitled to seek justice, there might be no effective way of ever having it dealt with.

Once again, the majority judgment in *Cooper* was delivered by La Forest J. and it adopted yet a third position on the issue of the capacity of tribunals and agencies to deal with *Charter* challenges to their empowering language. Building on or, perhaps more accurately, modifying the thrust of the trilogy, La Forest J. ruled that tribunals and agencies have no inherent jurisdiction to consider *Charter* challenges to the constitutionality of their enabling legislation. It was all a question of whether or not the legislature has explicitly or implicitly conferred that jurisdiction.

This reflected the earlier Supreme Court judgments. Indeed, as we have seen, in those cases, the Court had accepted that one of the indicators of the legislative conferral of this jurisdiction or capacity was a provision to the effect that the tribunal or agency had authority to deal with all or general questions of law[17] arising in matters coming before it, if truth be told a rather slim basis on which to make a judgment of legislative intent to confer such jurisdiction. La Forest J. then proceeded to deal with the question the "trilogy" had left uncertain: whether and, if so, under what other circumstances, a statutory authority would possess an implied grant of jurisdiction to deal with *Charter* challenges to its empowering legislation. As is now so true of much of Canadian judicial review law, he stated that, in many cases, this determination depended on "pragmatic and functional policy concerns" such as "the composition and structure of the tribunal, the procedure before the tribunal, the appeal route from the tribunal, and the expertise of the tribunal."[18] In the instance of the Canadian Human Rights Commission, all of the relevant indicators were negative. While the commission had explicit authority to perform certain tasks that depended in some instances on the evaluation of questions of law, there was no provision in the empowering legislation that conferred authority on it to deal with general questions of law. Functionally, it was not an adjudicative body. Rather, its role in this context was the reception, processing, and screening of complaints. At a practical level, it was not set up in a way that would enable it to deal with such challenges fully and appropriately in that it did not perform its functions in a truly adjudicative setting. Moreover, the undertaking of such inquiries could jeopardize seriously its ability to fulfill its mandate in "an accessible, efficient and timely manner." The issues at stake were also of a dimension on which the commission's members would not necessarily have any expertise. In short, the matters raised were best left for a court of law in the context of an action for a declaration of invalidity.

Seen simply in this light, *Cooper* clearly establishes that, absent explicit indicators in the legislation, bodies that perform administrative, investigatory, and filtering functions are seldom, if ever, likely to have the implied authority to determine challenges to the constitutional validity of their empowering statutes. Indeed, the thrust of this part of the judgment might also be somewhat more encompassing in that some of the factors detailed above and, in particular, those relating

---

17   As typified by section 106(1) of the Ontario *Labour Relations Act*, R.S.O. 1980, c.223, which was under consideration in *Cuddy Chicks*. It conferred on the board "exclusive jurisdiction" "to determine all questions of law or fact that arise in any matter before it. . . ."

18   *Cooper*, above note 10 at 888.

to resources and institutional setting, would also seem to suggest that those making administrative or discretionary decisions outside an adjudicative setting will not likely have authority to determine *Charter* challenges. Thus, for example, if a minister has a discretionary power to confer certain benefits and it is claimed that the legislative scheme infringes the guarantee of equality found in section 15, it is not likely that a court, mindful of *Cooper*, would find that the minister had authority to deal with that challenge in the exercise of her or his discretionary power under the relevant statute.

However, all of this would seem without too much relevance to the jurisdiction of adjudicative tribunals to deal with *Charter* issues. Of course, it followed in *Cooper* that, if the commission could not consider this particular challenge, neither could a Human Rights Tribunal under the *Act*. For a tribunal to become seized of this issue of necessity would involve the commission referring to it a matter which, on the face of the statute, was beyond the tribunal's jurisdiction. When the only potential way for that to be achieved, a tentative ruling by the commission that the statute was constitutionally underinclusive was proscribed by the Court, the case for tribunal jurisdiction fell by reason of that alone and not for more general functional and pragmatic considerations or because of other statutory indicators. Indeed, La Forest J. went on to acknowledge that, in matters properly before a tribunal, constitutional questions could be raised such as a *Charter* challenge to the remedial regime under which the tribunal operated or division of powers issues.

If the judgment had stopped there, it might have been concluded that the Court had merely qualified its judgments in the earlier trilogy. However, La Forest J. proceeded to make some further observations about the capacities of human rights tribunals that have caused subsequent courts and commentators to treat *Cooper* as having engaged in a significant retrenchment of the capacities of Canadian tribunals to deal with *Charter* challenges to the validity of their empowering legislation:

> I would add a practical note of caution with respect to a tribunal's jurisdiction to consider *Charter* arguments. First, as already noted, a tribunal does not have any special expertise except in the area of factual determinations in the human rights context. Second, any efficiencies that are *prima facie* gained by avoiding the court system will be lost when the inevitable judicial review proceeding is brought in the Federal Court. Third, the unfettered ability of a tribunal to accept any evidence it sees fit is well suited to a human rights complaint determination but is inappropriate when addressing the constitutionality of a legislative provision. Finally, and perhaps most decisively,

the added complexity, cost, and time that would be involved when a tribunal is to hear a constitutional question would erode to a large degree the primary goal sought in creating the tribunals, that is, the efficient and timely adjudication of human rights complaints.[19]

On this basis, he went on to rule that, although human rights tribunals[20] might have jurisdiction to consider "general" constitutional questions, they had no authority to "question the constitutional validity of a limiting provision of the Act."[21]

To the extent that all tribunals in varying degrees possess at least some of the characteristics identified in this extract from the judgment, this would suggest that there is now a very strong presumption (absent the magic formula) against any tribunal being competent to consider a *Charter* challenge based on the underinclusivity of empowering legislation. It, in effect, marginalizes *Cuddy Chicks*, where the Court sustained this kind of jurisdiction on the part of the Ontario Labour Relations Board and suggests that, absent the authority of the board to consider all questions of law and jurisdiction that arise in the course of its proceedings, the outcome would have been different. Indeed, even with respect to general constitutional questions, whatever they embrace, this extract at the very least hints that, without the formula, the authority of tribunals is by no means automatic.

c) Applying *Cooper*
Subsequently, there has only been limited lower court consideration of the impact of *Cooper*. However, some of that jurisprudence does exemplify the mixed messages emanating from the judgment. In *Nova Scotia (Workers' Compensation Board)* v. *O'Quinn*,[22] the Nova Scotia Court of Appeal held that *Cooper* prevented a human rights board of inquiry from ruling that a provision of the province's *Workers' Compensation Act* was invalid by reference to the *Charter*. This ruling that had opened the way for a finding by the board of inquiry that the Workers' Compensation Board had discriminated contrary to the provisions of the

---

19   *Ibid.* at 897.
20   See e.g. *Collins* v. *Abrams* (1999), 19 Admin. L.R. (3d) 269 (B.C.J.C.) upholding the right of a human rights tribunal to entertain a *Charter*-based bias challenge and the extent to which the *Act*'s anti-discrimination provision are qualified by freedom of expression as guaranteed by s. 2(b) of the *Charter*.
21   *Ibid.* at 898.
22   (1997), 143 D.L.R. (4th) 259 (N.S.C.A.) [*O'Quinn*].

Human Rights Act. The primary basis[23] for this conclusion was that *Cooper* had established that

> it would be more efficient, both for the parties and to the system in general, that a declaration of constitutional invalidity ought to be sought in a superior court rather than have the matter determined by a tribunal . . . [I]n such a setting the issue could be debated in the fullness it requires and proper expertise brought to bear in its resolution.[24]

In contrast, in *Northwest Territories (Workers' Compensation Board) v. Nolan*,[25] a challenge to an exclusion from coverage in workers' compensation legislation, the court upheld the right of the board to entertain such a challenge. In so doing, the Court emphasized that, while the Supreme Court in *Cooper* had seemed to take a rather restricted view of the practical advantages of tribunals dealing with such *Charter* questions, that had to be understood as influenced heavily by the role of the human rights commission and did not represent a change of position from the earlier "trilogy."

While it is, of course, feasible to distinguish these two judgments, what they obviously reveal is very differing views as to the impact of *Cooper* and this is also reflected in the academic commentary on the impact of the judgment. At some point, therefore, it will probably be necessary for the Supreme Court to revisit this problem yet again to straighten out the general confusion.

d) Where the Statutory Authority Has No Relevant *Charter* Jurisdiction

Indeed, the confusion does not end with this general issue of the appropriate starting point from which lower courts should evaluate assertions of tribunal competence to deal with *Charter* issues. In the wake of *Cooper*, there has also been a division of judicial opinion on the question of how such challenges should be mounted absent tribunal jurisdiction. In *Cooper* itself, the only feasible alternative was for the two airline pilots to apply to a superior court for a declaration of constitutional invalidity.

---

23   As a subsidiary, yet much more convincing, reason, the Court also held that express language would almost invariably be necessary to justify a tribunal entertaining a collateral constitutional challenge to the validity of a provision in another statutory regime.

24   *O'Quinn*, above note 20 at 272.

25   (1999), 45 C.C.E.L. (2d) 215. Subsequently, the Nova Scotia Court of Appeal reached the opposite conclusion in the case of its Workers Compensation Appeal Tribunal: *Martin v. Nova Scotia (Workers Compensation Board)*, [2000] N.S.J. No. 353 (QL) (November 8, 2000).

Indeed, this is the recourse identified by La Forest J. himself as the appropriate one in that instance, if not generally. However, there is another possibility. The refusal of jurisdiction could be challenged on a straight judicial review application in which the court would be asked to do what the tribunal or statutory authority could not have done in taking the decision under attack: rule on the constitutionality of an exclusion or otherwise suspect under-inclusive legislation.

There are problems with such a course of action in the sense not only that La Forest J.'s statements in *Cooper* as to the proper way of dealing with such matters implicitly excluded this as an alternative but also because judicial review applications and statutory appeals are conventionally directed to matters that the decision maker under review properly had or, at least, could and should have addressed in coming to her or his decision. Nonetheless, given the extent that the *Charter* has revolutionized Canadian law and given growing judicial recognition of flexibility in the world of remedies, there is much to be said for courts being open to this as an alternative.

However, such a possibility may have been precluded explicitly by the even earlier judgment of La Forest J. in the third case in the trilogy: *Tétrault-Gadoury* v. *Canada (Employment & Immigration Commission)*.[26] There, he held that, in the context of a judicial review application from the declining of authority to deal with a *Charter* challenge, the Federal Court of Appeal had jurisdiction to determine only the challenge to the board of referees' jurisdictional ruling; it had no authority to thereafter determine the constitutional question in the context of that application for judicial review. This flowed from the terms of section 28 of the *Federal Court Act*, which restricted the initial review court, the Federal Court of Appeal, "to overseeing and controlling the legality of decisions of administrative bodies and to referring matters back to those bodies for redetermination, with directions where appropriate."[27]

Nonetheless, there is a conflict among the post-*Cooper* judgments. In some cases, the apparent position of La Forest J. in both *Cooper* and *Tétrault-Gadoury* has simply been followed.[28] However, in others, the more expansive notion of the capabilities of a standard application for judicial review or a statutory right of appeal has been sustained. Thus,

---

26   *Tétrault-Gadoury*, above note 16.
27   *Ibid.* at 37.
28   See, for example, *Gwala* v. *Canada (Minister of Citizenship and Immigration)*, [1998] 4 F.C. 43 (T.D.); *Zündel* v. *Canada (A.G.)*, [1999] 4 F.C. 289 (T.D.) [*Zündel*].

the Manitoba Court of Appeal held in *R.* v. *Hoeppner*[29] that, when it was hearing an appeal on any question of law from a review board established under the mental health provisions of the *Criminal Code*, it had authority to deal with *Charter* issues pertaining to the detention of the appellant even if the board itself did not. In so doing, the court referred to another statement of La Forest J. in *Tétrault-Gadoury*, one to the effect that, while the board of referees could not consider the *Charter* challenge, the umpire on appeal from the board's decision could do so.

Rothstein J. then of the Federal Court, Trial Division in *Shubenacadie Indian Band* v. *Canada (Human Rights Commission)*, reached the same conclusion in the context of a judicial review application from a decision of a Canadian human rights tribunal.[30] Just because, as a consequence of *Cooper*, the tribunal itself could not deal with an attack on the constitutional validity of the reach of the *Canadian Human Rights Act* and other aspects of the challenge, this did not preclude the court from entertaining such an argument in the context of a judicial review application from the decision of the tribunal. The court could not ignore challenges which in effect undercut or nullified all or part of the tribunal's decision. In contrast, however, to *Tétrault-Gadoury*, this was a situation in which the applicants for judicial review were using constitutional arguments to limit the reach of the human rights regime, not to expand the ambit of the *Act*.[31]

This matter needs clarification and raises the following questions: can the courts in the context of either judicial review or a statutory appeal deal with *Charter* issues that were beyond the competence of the agency subject to scrutiny? Is there a difference between statutory appeal and judicial review for these purposes? Might the conclusion differ depending upon how the judicial review or statutory appeal regime is legislatively established or worded? Does it matter for these purposes whether the constitutional attack has as its aim the extension or contraction of the reach of the relevant legislation?

e) Where Jurisdiction Exists — Mandatory or Discretionary?

In rather stark contrast to the Supreme Court's parsimonious attribution to tribunals and statutory authorities generally of the capacity to

---

29 (1999), 134 Man. R. (2d) 163 (C.A.). On an application for leave to appeal to the Supreme Court of Canada, this case was remitted back to the Manitoba Court of Appeal with directions for reconsideration on matters having nothing to do with this issue: [1999] S.C.C.A. No. 237 (Q.L.).

30 [1998] 2 F.C. 198 (T.D.)

31 The same was the case in *Zündel*, above note 28, so at this level, these two judgments almost certainly conflict.

deal with *Charter* issues, the position of the Court appears to be that, in those cases where that capacity exists, it must be exercised. There is no discretion to decline jurisdiction or leave the matter for resolution. Thus, in the second case in the earlier trilogy, *Cuddy Chicks*, La Forest J. stated that the Ontario Labour Relations Board "not only has the authority but a duty to ascertain the constitutional validity" of the challenged provision.[32] This position was also presumably reflected in the actual disposition in the third of the trilogy, *Douglas/Kwantlen Faculty Association* v. *Douglas College*.[33] There, the Supreme Court remitted the actual resolution of the *Charter* issue to the arbitration board which had declined to deal with it.

Subsequent authority also supports this position. In *Falkiner* v. *Ontario (Minister of Community and Social Services)*,[34] the Ontario Divisional Court dismissed an application for judicial review of regulations partially on the basis that the *Charter* issue that they raised should be dealt with initially in the context of an appeal to the province's Social Assistance Review Board from a decision denying benefits on the basis of the impugned regulations. Not only might the appeal be allowed on other grounds but the board, having jurisdiction to consider the *Charter* issues, could set the scene for subsequent efficient and informed judicial consideration of those issues in the context of a judicial review application or statutory appeal by the development of a full record and the giving of a reasoned decision.

Some commentators have, however, questioned whether tribunals with authority or jurisdiction to consider *Charter* issues should always be under an obligation to do so. Thus, John Evans has suggested that tribunals be recognized as having a discretion to decline to do so when the benefits of a tribunal determination of that issue are outweighed by the advantages "of obtaining from a court an early authoritative ruling on the constitutional question."[35] Indeed, under such a regime, the court itself would continue to be able to play ping-pong by second-guessing the tribunal's assessment of the situation and remitting the matter back, though one would expect some degree of judicial deference to the tribunal's assessment of the impact on its resources of determining such an issue and, indeed, the tribunal's profession of a lack of expertise and capacity. However, given that such a regime con-

---

32 *Cuddy Chicks*, above note 8.

33 *Douglas/Kwantlen Faculty Association*, above note 11.

34 (1996), 140 D.L.R. (4th) 115 (Ont. Div. Ct.).

35 "Administrative Tribunals and *Charter* Challenges: Jurisdiction, Discretion and Relief" (1997), 10 C.J.A.L.P. 355 at 364.

flicts with the current position of the Supreme Court and given that the whole question is one of statutory interpretation, Evans suggests that the matter be resolved by statutory provision and, in the case of Ontario, by the inclusion of such a discretion in the *Statutory Powers Procedure Act*.

f) Tribunals as "Court[s] of Competent Jurisdiction"

Under section 24(1) of the *Charter*, anyone whose rights and freedoms have been violated may apply to a "court of competent jurisdiction" for "such remedy as the court considers appropriate and just in the circumstances." Moreover, in such proceedings, section 24(2) goes on to provide that the court shall, subject to certain conditions, exclude any evidence that was obtained in violation of any of the rights and freedoms guaranteed by the *Charter*.

Right from the outset, there have been questions raised as to the relationship between these provisions and the issue just canvassed, the authority of tribunals to consider issues as to the *Charter* validity of legislation. In the trilogy and *Cooper*, however, the Court has made it clear that it sees no necessary link between section 24 and jurisdiction over *Charter* issues. Thus, in *Cooper*, La Forest J. reiterated the standard line: "It should be emphasized that there is no need to determine if either the Commission or a tribunal under the Act is a court of competent jurisdiction under s. 24(1) of the *Charter*. That is not the inquiry before us."[36] However, a few lines later, a note of confusion is introduced when La Forest J., by reference to *Cuddy Chicks*, then asserts as a precondition to a tribunal having authority over *Charter* issues that it have "jurisdiction over the parties, the subject matter before it and the remedy sought by the parties."[37] Aside from drawing attention to the obvious, that those trying to have a tribunal to consider *Charter* issues will want consequences to flow from that, the use of the word "remedy" does indeed suggest a close, if not necessary link with section 24. Moreover, the very language used is that of the test to determine in other contexts whether a regular court has authority to respond to section 24 demands.[38]

Indeed, it may well now be time that the Court accepted that the two questions are, in many instances, inextricably linked. Initially, the caution of the Court was understandable. To the extent that there had been no authoritative conclusion to the issue of whether the word

36   *Douglas/Kwantlen Faculty Association*, note 7 at 888.
37   *Ibid.*
38   Starting with *R. v. Mills*, [1986] 1 S.C.R. 863.

"court" in the English version of section 24[39] extended beyond courts in the traditional or colloquial sense, the divorcing of the two issues could be understood as being the product of a desire not to pre-empt tribunals considering *Charter* validity questions should the reach of section 24 be confined to regular courts. Now that there is general acceptance that at least some tribunals may be "court[s] of competent jurisdiction" for section 24 purposes and that the classification of a body as a "court of competent jurisdiction" does not mean automatically the conferring of a general, at large remedial capacity, these concerns have been diminished to the point of disappearance. However, be that as it may, the Supreme Court has yet to acknowledge explicitly this reality.

In any event, what is clear is that, whether or not an administrative tribunal is a "court of competent jurisdiction," it does not have constitutional competence to issue a declaration of invalidity with respect to legislation; this is a role reserved to sections 96 and 101 courts.[40] Thus, in situations where a tribunal can rule on the constitutional validity of legislation, the options open, irrespective of section 24, are confined to those of ignoring totally the unconstitutional provision; treating the invalid part of the provision as severed and applying the balance; reading in language so as to rectify an under-inclusive provision; and reading down the provision so as not to apply it to the situation before the court. In deciding whether any or all of these steps are appropriate, the tribunal should obviously be guided by the same principles that the courts deploy when engaged in this kind of exercise.

In terms of section 24, there is now a growing body of jurisprudence on the circumstances in which a tribunal will be a "court of competent jurisdiction" for both the formal granting of remedies and the exclusion of evidence. Two Supreme Court of Canada judgments are sufficiently illustrative.

In *Mooring v. Canada (National Parole Board)*,[41] the Supreme Court determined that the National Parole Board was not "a court of competent jurisdiction" with respect to the exclusion of evidence at a parole revocation hearing on the basis that that evidence had been obtained in the violation of the parolee's *Charter* rights. The controls on the reception and use of such evidence were those of the common law of procedural fairness and the section 7 guarantees of the principles of fundamental justice, principles applicable in parole suspension and revocation hearings. In so ruling, the Court in fact engaged in a func-

---

39 The French version reads "tribunal."
40 This was clearly laid down in *Cuddy Chicks*, above note 8.
41 [1996] 1 S.C.R. 75.

tional analysis of the National Parole Board very akin to that which it applied to the Human Rights Commission in *Cooper*, thereby providing further evidence of the links between the two issues, the jurisdiction of tribunals to consider *Charter* challenges and their status under section 24. This functional analysis stressed, *inter alia*, the inquisitorial nature of the board's proceedings, the fact that it was not set up structurally in a way that facilitated the adjudication of such issues and the balancing of interests involved in their resolution, as well as the board's primary concern in risk assessment with the protection of society.

In somewhat stark contrast to this stands the earlier judgment of the Court in *Weber* v. *Ontario Hydro*.[42] Here, the Court decided that a board of arbitration under a collective agreement was "a court of competent jurisdiction" for the purposes of providing relief for violation by a government employer of an employee's *Charter* rights.[43] In terms of the standard criteria of jurisdiction over the subject matter, the parties, and the remedy that was being sought, the arbitration board qualified. The dispute arose out of the collective agreement, the relevant parties were within the jurisdiction of the arbitrator, and damages were an available remedy for violations of employee rights arising out of the collective agreement. Indeed, given the exclusivity of the arbitrator's jurisdiction over disputes arising out of the collective agreement, there was no other recourse available to the affected employee. The option of suing in the regular courts in tort, including the tort of violation of constitutional rights, was simply not available.

C. DELEGATION

In 1943, the Canadian Bar Review published an article by John Willis entitled "Delegatus Non Potest Delegare."[44] Although almost sixty years have passed, this article remains the seminal articulation of the law governing the subdelegation of statutory and discretionary powers. In particular, it remains accurate in its description of both the approach that the Courts take generally when such issues arise and

---

42   [1995] 2 S.C.R. 929.
43   In delivering the judgment of the Court, McLachlin J. made it clear that the word "court" in the English version of section 24 should not be interpreted narrowly. It was the powers that the body exercised, not its title that was decisive in this context. In so doing, she drew attention to the use of "tribunal" in the French version: *Ibid.* at 962.
44   (1943), 21 Can. Bar. Rev. 257.

most of the detail of the relevant law. Indeed, it has influenced the jurisprudence that has followed it.[45]

Literally translated, the Latin maxim of Willis's title involves the proposition that those to whom power is delegated cannot themselves further delegate that power. Translated to the world of statutory powers, if literally applied, it would mean that, absent express statutory permission,[46] those to whom Parliament, the legislatures, and indeed the makers of subordinate legislation have delegated power must exercise that power personally and cannot subdelegate its exercise to someone else. In fact, the maxim has never been applied by the Canadian courts in anything resembling that absolutist position. At most, Canadian courts have traded in the concept that while legislative and judicial powers cannot be delegated, there is no outright prohibition on the delegation of purely administrative powers.

However, as Willis demonstrates amply, even in the domain of legislative and judicial powers, at best, the *delegatus non potest delegare* maxim is a rule of construction or an operating presumption; it is by no means an absolute prohibition. Indeed, given the exigencies of modern government in all of its manifestations, the application of anything close to an absolute rule against subdelegation would be totally unrealistic and have the potential to lead to administrative chaos.

As we have already seen in the section on *Audi Alteram Partem*, the maxim has a strong pull in the domain of those who are charged with the exercise of truly adjudicative responsibilities. It reflects itself in more detailed rules that, at least in certain situations, those who perform such functions must themselves listen to or otherwise gather all the relevant evidence, be personally attentive to all the contending arguments, make up their own minds on the basis of that evidence and those arguments, and compose the decision. However, as modern jurisprudence demonstrates, even in those cases, the holders of the power are not only entitled to the benefit of ongoing expert assistance but may also seek advice from peers and consultants in the wake of the hearing. Moreover, outside the traditionally adjudicative settings, there are many situations in which common law obligations of procedural fairness will not be compromised

---

45   A quick search of the CJ database on QL reveals at least forty citations to the article with one of the most recent being by the Supreme Court of Canada in *Comeau's Sea Foods Ltd.* v. *Canada (Minister of Fisheries and Oceans)*, [1997] 1 S.C.R. 12.

46   A not uncommon situation. See, for example, s. 4.1 of the *Canada Oil and Gas Operations Act*, R.S.C. 1985, c. O-7 authorizing the National Energy Board to "delegate any of its powers" under certain sections of the *Act* "to any person."

by the person charged with the ultimate decision delegating evidence-gathering and sifting roles to administrative and other personnel.

In the section on subordinate legislation, we have also seen how the courts have been willing to countenance significant "subdelegation" of powers by regulation, statutorily authorized policy instruments, and municipal and other kinds of by-law. Subject to constraints on the straight passing on the very power that has been granted (as reflected in the need for some form of structuring and constraining) and the conferral of power on persons outside the administrative hierarchy or control of the original delegate, subordinate legislation delegating responsibilities will generally pass muster.

Indeed, in the case of powers that are conferred on ministers of the Crown, the maxim has very little role to play. In this domain, the operating presumption is in effect reversed and, absent express provision or other clear indicators, ministers are assumed to be able to act through responsible officials in their departments and in the agencies for which they are responsible.[47] Re-enforcing this common law provision are also provisions such as those in the federal and provincial and territorial *Interpretation Acts* specifically authorizing ministers of the Crown to be exercised by a deputy.[48]

Indeed, most commentators do not treat the situation of ministers of the Crown as even coming within the purview of the principles governing the subdelegation of statutory powers and discretions since the power is commonly exercised in the name of the minister. Nonetheless, some of the exceptions to the proposition that ministers can act through their responsible officials clearly do have reference back to the maxim particularly in those cases where exceptions are inferred simply

---

47   The leading authority remains the 1943 judgment of the English Court of Appeal in *Carltona Ltd.* v. *Commissioner of Works*, [1943] 2 All E.R. 560 (C.A.). There is also support for the operation of the *Carltona* principle with respect to the operations of the Crown representative in Council *Maraj* v. *Canada (Minister of Employment & Immigration)* (1993), 14 Admin. L.R. (2d) 169 (F.C. T.D.) and also the Federal Treasury Board *Mancuso Estate* v. *R.*, [1980] 1 F.C. 269 (T.D.), aff'd [1982] 1 F.C. 259 (C.A.) and Public Service Commission *Brooker* v. *Canada (Attorney General)*, [1973] 1 F. C. 327 (C.A.) as well as Deputy Ministers *Ahmad* v. *Canada (Public Service Commission Appeal Board)*, [1974] 2 F.C. 644 (C.A.).

48   See, for example, *Interpretation Act*, R.S.C. 1985, c. I-11, s. 24(2) [as amended by S.C. 1992, c. 1, s. 89(4)]. Indeed, *Interpretation Acts* make provision for the appointment of and exercise of powers by deputies of all manner of public officers or functionaries: *ibid.* s. 24(1). However, as with other provisions in interpretation legislation, such provisions give way in the face of express or implied provision to the contrary.

on the basis of the nature of the power conferred by statute. Thus, where a statute required the consent or *fiat* of the attorney general to the commencement of a prosecution, the Supreme Court of Canada sustained a judgment to the effect that this power was so important to the rights of the individual that it had to be exercised personally by the attorney general.[49]

Some of the jurisprudence involving exceptions to the proposition that the minister can always act through her or his responsible officials is also relevant to the general law in this area particularly in so far as it bears upon the relevance of statutory indicia and the nature of the interest at stake. Thus, in *Ramawad v. Canada (Minister of Manpower and Immigration)*,[50] the Supreme Court held that a power conferred on the minister to give relief from provisions in regulations prohibiting the issuance of work visas had to be exercised personally by the minister on the basis that it was clear from the way in which responsibilities had been assigned in other parts of the relevant regulations that this was a decision that the governor general in council had intended to be taken by the minister personally. Indeed, the use of the expression "the Minister himself" led to the same conclusion in *Québec (A.G.) c. Carrières Ste-Thérèse Ltée*[51] in the context of a power conferred on the minister under public health legislation to order, as a matter of urgency, the closing down of a hazardous plant.

To the extent that all these precedents requiring the personal exercise of power by the minister rely on judgments about legislative reposing of special trust in the person or body designated to exercise the relevant power, they have obvious ramifications in considering the meaning of legislative conferral of power on other administrative officials and statutory tribunals. Also relevant in determining whether a delegation of power is sustainable besides the nature of the interests at stake, the character of the person on whom the power is conferred, and the terms of the relevant statutory provisions, will be the nature and scope of the delegation as well as the character of the delegate. Delegations are far less likely to be sustained when there is a straight passing on the power in the same terms in which it was conferred initially. On the other hand, the courts will be disposed to accept a delegation of

---

49   *R. v. Horne & Pitfield Foods Ltd.*, [1985] 1 S.C.R. 364, aff'g. [1982] 5 W.W.R. 162 (Alta. C.A.). Though now see *R. v. Frisbee* (1989), 48 C.C.C. (3d) 386 (B.C.C.A.), to the effect that this case should not be seen as foreclosing the exercise of this power by the attorney general's designated deputy as generally authorized by the terms of the *Interpretation Act*.

50   [1978] 2 S.C.R. 375.

51   [1985] 1 S.C.R. 831.

authority if it involves only a part of the area over which the delegating person or body has power and in situations where the designated authority in delegating narrows the scope of the discretion conferred by statute in the sense of confining or structuring the ways in which it can be exercised by the delegate. There is also more of a tendency to uphold delegations to persons operating within the same institutional framework as the person on whom the power has been formally conferred. In contrast, where the power has been given to some private organization operating outside normal channels of responsibility, the courts will tend to look askance at the delegation.

A good example of where the Supreme Court of Canada rejected an unlawful subdelegation argument on the basis of some of these principles is to be found in *Forget* v. *Québec (A.G.)*.[52] Among the issues raised by this case was the assignment to a committee by the Office of the French Language of responsibility for setting French language examinations for professionals wishing to practise in Québec. Not only did the legislation contemplate the appointment of a committee to assist the office in its assigned statutory tasks but the office had also established criteria on which the examinations were to be based and the committee had to adhere to those standards in the performance of its task.

In contrast, in *Air Canada* v. *City of Dorval*,[53] the Court struck down a by-law authorizing the setting of taxes by annual resolution. To the extent that the relevant legislation contemplated the setting of tax rates by by-law, it was incompetent for the municipality to delegate that task to be performed annually in a different modality and in no way constrained by the terms of the delegating instrument. In such a case, it did not matter that the municipality had retained the power itself.

Finally, an excellent example of the improper surrender of regulatory responsibility is provided by *Re Niagara Wire Weaving*.[54] Here, the Ontario Court of Appeal struck down a ruling by the Ontario Securities Commission on an application by the company for exemption from certain statutory disclosure requirements. It was not permissible to engage in a subdelegation of that task by conferring the decision on whether there should be disclosure in any particular case on the shareholders of the applicant company even where the order required that there be 90 percent consent. The task of granting exemptions had been assigned to the commission and it could not effectively relinquish that statutory responsibility by giving it away to the shareholders.

---

52   [1988] 2 S.C.R. 90.
53   [1985] 1 S.C.R. 861.
54   [1972] 3 O.R. 129 (C.A.).

Indeed, it is important to recognize that, whatever connotations the colloquial sense of the term "delegation" might have, for these purposes, it does not involve acceptance of a permanent conferral of authority on someone else. The original delegate or decision maker is always entitled to resume the power in question though not in a retroactive manner. However, in the recent Supreme Court of Canada judgment in *Comeau's Sea Foods* v. *Canada (Minister of Fisheries and Oceans)*,[55] the Supreme Court held that the minister could withdraw a delegation of power to make a licensing decision before it had been exercised formally by the actual issuance of a licence in a particular case.

D. CONTROLLING PROCEDURES AND MAKING PROCEDURAL RULINGS

Administrative tribunals achieve control over the procedures that they follow in a number of ways. Their empowering legislation may confer on them specifically the authority to control their own procedures or to make procedural rulings either generally or in relation to particular matters. In some situations, as for example under section 25.1 of the Ontario *Statutory Powers Procedure Act*, the tribunal may be empowered to make rules having the force of subordinate legislation governing the procedures to be followed in matters coming before them. Even without explicit statutory authorization, the courts have always conceded to tribunals the ability to control their own processes and make procedural rulings as a power that is a necessary incident of the effective exercise of their jurisdiction and this may extend to making informal or internal rules by which they will be guided in all matters coming before them.

Thus, in delivering the judgment of the Supreme Court of Canada in *Kane* v. *Board of Governors of University of British Columbia*, Dickson J. stated that, in an appeal to the board of governors from a disciplinary suspension of a member, "the Board is free, within reason, to determine its own procedures."[56]

Subsequently, in discussing the question of jurisdiction to grant an adjournment, the Court, in *Prassad* v. *Canada (Minister of Employment and Immigration)*,[57] spoke generally of administrative tribunals:

---

55   [1997] 1 S.C.R. 12.
56   [1980] 1 S.C.R. 1105 at 1112.
57   [1989] 1 S.C.R. 560 at 568–69.

[T]hese tribunals are considered to be masters in their own house. In the absence of specific rules laid down by statute or regulation, they control their own procedures subject to the proviso that comply with the rules of fairness and, where they exercise judicial or quasi-judicial functions, the rules of natural justice. Adjournment of their proceedings is very much in their discretion.

Statements such as this would therefore seem to accord tribunals the capacities they need to both keep their proceedings under control and to determine (at least as a matter of first impression) what the principles of fairness demand in each case or even generally. Indeed, in *Bezaire* v. *Windsor Roman Catholic Separate School Board*,[58] the Ontario Divisional Court treated non-statutory procedural guidelines developed by the relevant minister and the board as either independently creating a right to have them observed[59] or as, at the very least, amounting to strong evidence of what procedural fairness demanded in the particular matter before the Court.

Somewhat more problematic, however, are situations in which the tribunal attempted to argue for some entitlement to judicial deference towards its rules or rulings. Some read the 1984 judgment of the Supreme Court of Canada in *Bibeault* v. *McCaffrey*[60] as providing support for the application of a patent unreasonableness standard to at least some categories of procedural ruling. There, the Court had held that the decision of the Québec Labour Court on whether to accord status to employees at a particular stage of proceedings could be set aside only if patently unreasonable. However, in a subsequent case,[61] the Court stated that this holding was restricted to statutory provisions which dealt explicitly with the subject matter of the ruling in issue; it did not make room for the according of deference to other procedural rulings made by a tribunal in the course of exercising its jurisdiction. As suggested by the extract from *Prassad*, cited above, the power to control one's own procedures was always subject to the constraint of the rules of natural justice and procedural fairness and these were matters on which tribunals had to be correct.

---

58 (1992), 9 O.R.(3d) 737 (Div. Ct.)
59 One way of justifying this would be on the basis of the doctrine of legitimate expectation. However, it was not mentioned specifically.
60 [1984] 1 S.C.R. 176.
61 *C.A.I.M.A.W., Local 14* v. *Paccar of Canada Ltd.*, [1989] 2 S.C.R. 983 at 1014–17 (*per* La Forest J.).

Much more recently, however, the Court has indicated that it is no longer willing to take such a restricted stand on the parcelling out of the entitlement to deference in procedural matters. In *Baker* v. *Canada (Minister of Citizenship and Immigration)*,[62] L'Heureux-Dubé J. stated:

> Fifth, the analysis of what procedures the duty of fairness requires should also take into account and respect the choices of procedure made by the agency itself, particularly when the statute leaves to the decision maker the ability to choose its own procedures, or when the agency has an expertise in determining what procedures are appropriate in the circumstances. . . . While this, of course, is not determinative, important weight must be given to the choice of procedures made by the agency itself and its institutional constraints.

This suggests that, at long last, the Court is willing to give up on its claim to superior expertise on all questions of natural justice and procedural fairness. How far and in what circumstances this new posture of deference will go remains uncertain. However, at the very least, one would now expect considerable degrees of deference to be accorded procedures that are the result of an open rule-making exercise or which have been forged through negotiations with all relevant affected constituencies, as in the New Zealand case of *Furnell* v. *Whangarei High Schools Board*.[63]

E. POLICIES AND GUIDELINES

It is accepted without question that statutory authorities charged with the exercise of discretionary powers have authority, even when not specifically authorized by statute, to issue policy statements on the subject matter of their discretion and to provide guidelines on how they are likely to exercise that discretion in particular cases.

The first explicit acknowledgment of this by the Supreme Court of Canada came in *Capital Cities Communications Inc.* v. *Canadian Radio-television and Telecommunications Commission*.[64] This involved a challenge to a CRTC decision in which the commission had relied upon a policy that it had developed earlier on the conditions under which cable companies would be allowed to delete commercial messages from pro-

---

62 [1999] 2 S.C.R. 817 at para. 27.
63 [1973] A.C. 660 (P.C. N.Z.).
64 [1978] 2 S.C.R. 141.

grams they were taking off the airwaves for transmission by cable. In delivering the judgment of the Court, Laskin C.J.C. held that, even though the Commission had authority to deal with such matters by way of regulation, it was still within its capacity to also issue non-statutory guidelines. While acknowledging that, if there were relevant regulations, they would of necessity prevail over the guidelines, nonetheless, in the absence of regulations, the setting of guidelines was a valuable exercise:

> [H]aving regard to the embracive objects committed to the Commission under s. 15 of the Act . . . it was eminently proper that it lay down guidelines from time to time as it did in respect of cable television. The guidelines on this matter were arrived at after extensive hearings at which interested parties were present and made submissions. An overall policy is demanded in the interests of prospective licensees and of the public under such a regulatory regime as is set up by the *Broadcasting Act*. Although one could mature as a result of a succession of applications, there is merit in having it known in advance.[65]

This position has been reiterated on a number of subsequent occasions, as, for example, by McIntyre J., in the context of a ministerial discretion in *Maple Lodge Farms Ltd.* v. *Canada*:

> There is nothing improper or unlawful for the Minister charged with the responsibility for the administration of the general scheme provided for in the Act and Regulations to formulate or state general requirements for the granting of import permits. It will be helpful to applicants for permits to know in general terms what the policy and practice of the Minister will be.[66]

What these extracts emphasize is not only that the issuance of informal policies and guidelines is permissible but also that they may be extremely helpful to affected constituencies. Knowing how the holder of a discretion is likely to exercise it in a particular instance may be of great assistance in the conduct and planning of one's affairs. Moreover, as is suggested especially by Laskin C.J.C., the development of such policies, particularly if affected constituencies are involved in that exercise, may lead to a better framework for the exercise of that discretion in individual cases than would emerge from a gradual accretion of practice or precedent over a lengthy period.

---

65 *Ibid.* at 170.
66 [1982] 2 S.C.R. 2 at 6–7 [*Maple Lodge Farms*].

Without this capacity, whether conferred by statute or not, carrying on the business of effective government in Canada would, in an age of such extensive discretion, be an impossible task. The structuring of discretion by both formal and informal methods is how government agencies operate and, without it, both agencies and those on whom they have an impact would be affected detrimentally. Just consider what would happen to the effective administration of the national income tax regime and the commercial life of the country if the Canada Customs and Revenue Agency was no longer able to issue interpretation bulletins or to provide advance rulings.

In reality, there will be many situations in which "informal" policies and guidelines will achieve the status of *de facto* law. Because of their longevity and the expectations built up around them they will be treated as though they were binding both by the agency responsible for promulgating them and the regulated community. Nonetheless, Canadian courts have never conceded them official status. Thus, in *Pezim* v. *British Columbia (Superintendent of Brokers)*,[67] Iacobucci J., speaking of the policies of the British Columbia Securities Commission, stated: "However, it is important to note that the Commission's policy-making role is limited. By that I mean that their policies cannot be elevated to the status of law; they are not to be treated as legal pronouncements absent legal authority mandating such treatment."[68]

The practical effect of this not only is that the policies can be altered just as informally as they were created but also that reliance on their existence cannot create any entitlements to their application on the basis of estoppel or legitimate expectation.[69] Indeed, as McIntyre J. makes clear in *Maple Lodge Farms*, even where still in existence, they are nonetheless not binding on the relevant authority; policies do not give rise to legally enforceable rights. To do this would be to "elevate ministerial directions to the level of law, and fetter the Minister in the exercise of his discretion."[70] In that instance, the consequence was that the appli-

---

67   [1994] 2 S.C.R. 557.

68   *Ibid.* at 596.

69   Recollect the normal principles that public authorities cannot be estopped from exercising their statutory powers and discretions and that the doctrine of legitimate expectation cannot be used to establish substantive entitlements: *Reference re Canada Assistance Plan*, [1991] 2 S.C.R. 525. Whether the Supreme Court will expand the domain of estoppel in public law awaits its judgment on the appeal in *Centre Hospitalier Mont-Sinaï c. Québec (Ministère de la Santé et des Services Sociaux)* (1998), 9 Admin. L.R. (3d) 161 (Qué. C.A.) [*Centre Hospitalier Mont-Sinaï*].

70   *Maple Lodge Farms*, above note 64 at 7.

cants would have had no entitlement to an order directing the minister to issue them a permit in terms of the policy even if that policy had been apparently unqualified and not contained the word "normally."

In bringing such policies within the ambit of review for abuse of discretion based on unlawful fettering, the Court is, however, creating a regime that can cut both ways. On the one hand, such policies and guidelines cannot confer legally enforceable entitlements, while on the other, the rule against fettering also prevents the agency from applying them automatically to particular situations. In *Capital Cities*, there was nothing wrong with the CRTC promulgating a commercial deletion policy, but it was also important that the commission held a hearing at which it dealt with the particular application and determined in good faith how the policy should be applied to the circumstances. Often, it will be a nice question as to whether this is a matter of substance or form, particularly when it seems accepted that there is nothing wrong with having a predisposition against exceptions and in favour of the existing policy.[71]

Earlier, in the chapter on abuse of discretion, we encountered an example of an exercise of discretion that came down on the wrong side of this particular fence: *Brown* v. *Alberta*.[72] Here, the Court struck down the automatic application of a policy specifying a minimum period of licence suspension for those guilty of particular driving offences. The evidence established that there had been no attention paid to the particular facts of the case.

It is, however, worth recollecting that, in *Newfoundland Telephone Co.* v. *Newfoundland (Board of Commissioners of Public Utilities)*,[73] the Supreme Court was prepared in an economic regulatory setting to accept that, at the pre-hearing stage, it was only in cases of conduct indicating a totally closed mind that individual members of the agency would be disqualified from participation in particular proceedings on the basis of bias. If that is the standard applicable to individual agency members, it would seem inconsistent with that not to cede to those who have laid down policies and guidelines some degree of commitment to those policies in the context of individual cases.

Important aspects of this difficult issue were raised in *Ainsley Financial Corporation* v. *Ontario Securities Commission*,[74] a case involving an Ontario Securities Commission policy statement on the activi-

---

71 See *British Oxygen Co.* v. *Board of Trade*, [1971] A.C. 610 (H.L. Eng.), cited in both *Capital Cities* and *Maple Lodge Farms*.
72 (1991), 82 D.L.R. (4th) 96 (Alta. Q.B.).
73 [1992] 1 S.C.R. 623.
74 (1995), 21 O.R. (3d) 104 (C.A.).

ties of securities dealers in the "penny stock" market. The policy statement in question was a detailed code of conduct which "read like a statute" and had a coercive tone in the sense of suggesting that enforcement or disciplinary action would be taken in the face of any failure to meet its precise terms. This led the Ontario Court of Appeal to hold that this policy "crossed the Rubicon between a non-mandatory guideline and a mandatory pronouncement having the same effect as a statutory instrument."[75] As a consequence, this kind of policy needed explicit statutory authorization. Without it, it was invalid and the plaintiff dealers were entitled to a declaration to that effect.

At one level, this suggests a significant limitation on the ability of tribunals and agencies to issue guidelines. They will be valid exercises of power only if general in their contents or, perhaps, if specific, acceptable only to the extent that they are hedged with language such as "usually" or "normally." However, it is also possible to read the judgment somewhat more narrowly than that, particularly if one takes into account the dual factors giving rise to the declaration of invalidity. In effect, the terms and tone of the policy amounted to a statement that certain practices were, of necessity, infringements of securities legislation in circumstances where that issue was more properly determined in the context of individual enforcement proceedings.

Indeed, to foreclose in all circumstances those charged with the exercise of broad discretion from the promulgation of detailed specifications would have a very limiting effect on the scope of policy statements and guidelines. In the delivery of broad-based government programs such informal structuring is vital. Even in the area of government regulation and standards, detailed statements of what the regulator regards as inappropriate activities can play a significant role in the effective performance of a legislative mandate and, as Laskin C.J. implied in *Capital Cities*, have strong claims to legitimacy when forged through a process of hearings or negotiation involving all relevant interests. It is therefore to be hoped that the judgment in *Ainsley* not be applied according to its broadest possible reading.

Even where the making of policies is authorized explicitly by statute, problems may arise. This is well exemplified by *Whelan v. Workplace Health, Safety and Compensation Commission*.[76] This involved a workers' compensation decision upholding the deduction of vacation pay from the injured worker's benefits despite the fact that the vacation

75   *Ibid.* at 109.
76   (1999), 181 Nfl'd. & P.E.I.R. 192 [*Whelan*].

pay had accrued before the occurrence of the relevant injury. Under the Act, as interpreted by the Court, there was a discretion as to whether to make a deduction for such benefits. However, acting under section 5(1) of the *Workplace Health, Safety and Compensation Act*,[77] the commission had established a policy to the effect that such payments should always be deducted and both the commission and its review division had simply applied that policy stating that there was no room for departing from it. In these circumstances, the dilemma for the Court was whether the statutory authority to issue policies having statutory force went so far as authorizing the commission to issue policies that constrained or fettered discretions that had been created by the Act. Despite the argument that, as with subordinate legislation, such policies cannot override the *Act* and, more particularly, be inconsistent with the creation of discretions in the primary legislation, the Court held that the policy-making function was a central feature of the *Act* and consonant with the broad responsibilities conferred on the board for the operation of the workers' compensation scheme. As such, "the legislature must have intended to grant the Commission authority under subsection 5(1) that would include the making of policies that would have the effect of fettering the exercise of its discretion under provisions such as section 81(1)."[78]

It is a nice question whether this is the correct approach to take to the extent of the policy-making role conferred on the commission particularly given that the policies and programs adopted under the relevant section were directed to be "consistent with this *Act* and regulations." Is it more consistent with the *Act* to allow the policy to stand on the basis that to do so respects the broad scope of the commission's assigned responsibilities or to reject it on the basis that making mandatory that which is otherwise optional runs counter to the whole reason for making certain considerations discretionary?[79] Putting it another way, does the conferral of the power to make policies necessarily involve the capacity to structure or confine discretions created by the *Act* in a manner that either eliminates or reduces their discretionary nature by making certain outcomes obligatory?

---

77   R.S.N. 1990, c. W-11.
78   *Whelan*, above note 74 at para. 39.
79   However, see also, interpreting the same policy making provision, *DGH Construction Ltd.* v. *Workers' Compensation Commission* (1997), 150 Nfl'd. & P.E.I.R 50 (Nfl'd. S.C. T.D.), referring to *Blackpool Corporation* v. *Locker*, [1948] 1 K.B. 349 (C.A.).

F. ESTOPPEL

To this point in Canadian public law, there has been very limited use of the doctrine of estoppel as a basis for preventing public authorities from going back on their assurances even where there has been detrimental reliance on those assurances. The principal reason for this has been generally unquestioning acceptance of the theory that statutory authorities cannot disable themselves from the future exercise of their jurisdiction or powers by the giving of assurances.

At one level, this reluctance is based on the purely formal consideration that nothing less than the actual exercise of statutory or prerogative powers can give rise to legal consequences. However, there is also a very clear sense that it is contrary to public policy to disable a statutory or prerogative authority from the full exercise of its powers by according legal effect to promises or assurances as to how those powers are going to be exercised in the future.[80] The recognition of a species of promissory estoppel in the domain of public law would place impediments in the way of decision making in the public interest as it exists at the time when a statutory power actually falls to be exercised. In many instances also, to give effect to such promises or assurances or reasonable expectations based on the conduct of statutory or prerogative authorities could actually lead either to a failure to fulfill a statutory or prerogative obligation or involve the taking of action or making of a decision for which there was no jurisdiction or authority. Moreover, even in the area of discretionary powers, the application of the doctrine of estoppel against a statutory authority runs into difficulties with the rule against unlawful fettering of discretion. It is impermissible to lay down a rigid policy by which a discretionary power is always going to be exercised. Indeed, as already discussed in both the chapter on abuse of discretion and the previous section, this doctrine can cut both ways in that, on occasion, the person affected will not want rigid adherence to a policy on the exercise of a discretion.

A typical example of the traditional position is provided by *Lidder v. Canada (Minister of Employment & Immigration)*.[81] This involved the processing of an application for the sponsorship of a young family member for immigration to Canada. Ultimately, the application was

---

80   See, for example, *Pacific National Investments Ltd. v. Victoria (City)*, [2000] S.C.J. No. 64 (QL) (December 14, 2000) holding that the City could not by contract better its legislative authority over the zoning of land.

81   (1992), 6 Admin. L.R. (2d) 62 (F.C.A.).

denied on the basis that the formal application had been made after the family member had reached the age beyond which applications could no longer made. Despite assurances to the sponsor prior to the application being filed that all was in order and the continued processing of the application after it should have become clear that the application was out of time, the Federal Court of Appeal refused to set aside the denial of the application. According to Desjardins J.A., "the doctrine of estoppel cannot interfere with the operation of the law."[82] As the age limit on filing the application was mandatory, the actions of the authorities could not give rise to an estoppel compelling them to ignore that time limit.

In denying the application of the doctrine of estoppel in *Lidder*, the Federal Court of Appeal relied upon *Granger* v. *Canada (Employment and Immigration Commission)*,[83] a case in which the Supreme Court of Canada had simply endorsed the judgment under appeal. In *Granger*, the Court had been confronted with a situation in which the commission had made representations as to the revenue consequences of taking a pension in a particular way. Granger then relied on these representations only to discover that they were inaccurate. He then tried to resist enforcement of the law as it was written on the basis of his detrimental reliance on the commission's representations. In delivering the judgment of the majority in the Federal Court of Appeal, Pratte J. asserted that "[a] judge is bound by the law. He cannot refuse to apply it, even on grounds of equity."[84]

This does not mean, however, that the doctrine of equitable estoppel has no application in public law. More than fifty years ago, Lord Denning provided a frequently referred to example in *Robertson* v. *Minister of Pensions*.[85] There, the authorities had made representations that caused Robertson not to gather further evidence in support of his application for a disability pension. Thereafter, they could not deny him a pension on the basis of inadequate supporting evidence particularly as that evidence was no longer available. This application of equitable estoppel to the adjectival aspects of public law also finds examples in Canada. Thus, in *Aurchem Exploration Ltd.* v. *Canada*,[86] Strayer J., of the Federal Court, Trial Division, held that a mining authority was estopped from denying an application on the basis that

---

82   *Ibid.* at 68.
83   [1989] 1 S.C.R. 141, aff'g. [1986] 3 F. C. 70 (C.A.).
84   *Ibid.* at para. 9.
85   [1949] 1 K.B. 227.
86   (1992), 7 Admin. L.R. (2d) 168 (F.C.T.D.).

the application was not in the proper form. Given its practice of accepting non-complying applications and the reliance on that practice in the particular case, it could not revert to a requirement of strict compliance without providing adequate notice. The difference between this case and *Lidder* and *Granger* lies, of course, in the fact that the statutory requirement in issue here was a formal one as opposed to a substantive limit on jurisdiction or authority. Sometimes, however, the line between these two categories is not necessarily a bright line one.

Indeed, even in the domain of revenue cases such as *Granger*, the courts have created another distinction. Where the liability in question is based on a discretionary provision in the relevant legislation, the possibility exists that the doctrine of estoppel will be applied to prevent recovery or greater recovery. Thus, the Québec Court of Appeal, in a case referred to with some skepticism in *Granger*, had refused to allow the provincial tax authorities to revisit a tax assessment on the basis that the interpretation of the relevant provision of the *Act* involved elements of discretion and that the original interpretation on which the taxpayer had relied was not unreasonable.[87]

Indeed, there is a strong argument that this kind of approach has the support of the Supreme Court of Canada from its treatment of a situation which has strong analogies. This was in *Kenora (Town) Hydro Electric Commission* v. *Vacationland Dairy Co-operative Ltd.*,[88] where the Court held that the commission could not collect arrears from a consumer. Distinguishing earlier authority holding that there was no defence to such a claim,[89] the Court held that, as opposed to the earlier case, the legislation in this instance neither created a positive obligation to collect accounts nor imposed sanctions on consumers for failing to pay. Given that the mistake in this instance had been negligent and that the consumer had been both unaware of it and had relied upon it in its pricing, there could be no recovery of the arrears.

Indeed, to the extent that there was actually a mistake of law made by the authorities in the *Kenora* case, this seems to create a rather large exception to the notion that public authorities cannot be estopped from applying the law. Moreover, as with the distinction between formal and substantive statutory requirements, there will also obviously be difficulties in drawing clear lines between statutory provisions that

---

87   *Sous-ministre du Revenu du Québec* c. *Transport Lessard (1976) Ltée*, [1985] R.D.F.Q. 191 (C.A.)

88   [1994] 1 S.C.R. 80.

89   *Maritime Electric Co.* v. *General Dairies Ltd.*, [1937] 1 D.L.R. 609.

involve some element of discretion in their interpretation from those that do not.

What these authorities do suggest very strongly, however, is that there should no longer be any problem with the application of the doctrine of equitable estoppel as a matter of principle to those powers that are obviously discretionary. In other words, the rules with respect to unlawful fettering of discretion may sometimes at least have to be subordinated to the interests of those who have relied upon promises as to how a discretion will be exercised in the future.

In fact, clarification by the Supreme Court of Canada of this vitally important issue may not be long in forthcoming as the Court has given leave to appeal from the judgment of the Québec Court of Appeal in *Centre Hospitalier Mont-Sinaï c. Québec (Ministère de la Santé et des Services Sociaux).*[90] Here, the Québec Court of Appeal compelled the minister to issue a licence to the hospital for a certain number of long-term and intermediate-term beds. It did so on the basis of assurances by those in authority that, if certain steps were taken including the relocation of the hospital, the permits would be issued. The hospital, relying on these assurances, engaged in fund-raising, altered its orientation, and moved its location. In these circumstances, the Court of Appeal held that the doctrine of estoppel applied and the minister was obliged to issue the licences or permits in the terms promised.

In delivering the judgment of the Court, Robert J.A. conceded that, under the law as presently conceived by the Supreme Court of Canada, the doctrine of legitimate expectation cannot be applied in Canada to achieve a substantive result. However, he also ruled that this jurisprudence did not necessarily preclude the operation of the doctrine of equitable estoppel to reach the same end. In so doing, he stressed the need for a clear representation by words or conduct by those in authority and also relied on the discretionary nature of the minister's authority over permits. However, he doubted whether proof of detrimental reliance should be a requirement in such cases though, in case it was, he was quite clear that it existed here. He also resisted arguments based on the sense that estoppel could not be used as a sword, only as a shield. In modern authority emanating from the Supreme Court of Canada in the private law domain, he found justification for the proposition that, in appropriate cases, estoppel could be deployed to create a cause of action sustaining positive entitlements.

---

90   *Centre Hospitalier Mont-Sinaï*, above note 69. For a British equivalent, see *Re Preston*, [1985] A.C. 835 (H.L. Eng.).

In reaching his conclusion on this point, Robert J.A. cited[91] the following extract from the leading Canadian article on estoppel in public law:

> A public authority cannot be estopped from exercising its powers. But once the authority has decided that a particular exercise of power is appropriate, it must act accordingly, at least where there has been reliance on that decision. A promise of future execution is binding precisely because it necessarily involves a decision that the promised action is an appropriate exercise of the power. To this point, nothing more is involved than the proposition that decisions made cannot be reconsidered even though they may not have been implemented by executive action.[92]

It remains to be seen whether and to what extent this expansive version of the possibilities for the operation of the doctrine of estoppel in public law will be endorsed by the Supreme Court of Canada. In particular, aside from the general questions of the use of estoppel in situations where a discretionary power is in issue and the technical requirements for the operation of the doctrine, there are some obvious problems about the relationship between estoppel and the fettering doctrine in such cases. Indeed, more generally, there is an issue raised as to whether there is or should be any basis for the holder of the power to invoke overriding public interest concerns in justification of a failure to live up to assurances as to how a discretion is going to be exercised. In the English authorities relying upon legitimate expectation to achieve these ends, there is clearly some concern that, at least on occasion, broader public interests may have to prevail.[93]

G. REOPENINGS AND RECONSIDERATIONS

Under many statutory regimes, tribunals and other decision makers have express authority to review, reopen, or reconsider a determination or decision. Indeed, section 21.2(1) of the Ontario *Statutory Powers Procedure Act*[94] contemplates the possibility of all decision makers coming within the scope of that *Act* being able to review decisions as

---

91   *Ibid.* at 198.

92   P. McDonald, "Contradictory Government Action: Estoppel of Statutory Authorities" (1979), 17 O.H.L.J. 160 at 180–81.

93   See, for example, *R. v. Secretary of State for the Home Department, ex parte Khan*, [1985] 1 All E.R. 40 (C.A.), cited by Robert J.A. at 180–81.

94   R.S.O. 1990, c.S.22 (as amended by S.O. 1994, c.27 and S.O. 1997, c.23).

long as they make procedural rules to that effect. Quite clearly, in such instances, the common law doctrine of *functus officio* applicable to proceedings in the regular courts has no relevance. However, for a long time, it was assumed that, without such express authority, adjudicative tribunals at least were bound by the rule. They could not reopen their final decisions save for very limited purposes such as correcting clerical errors, or where proper notice of the hearing had not been given or a party otherwise had been prevented from taking advantage of his or her right to a hearing.

All that seemingly changed with the judgment of the Supreme Court of Canada in *Chandler* v. *Association of Architects (Alberta)*.[95] There, Sopinka J., delivering the judgment of the Court, stated that there was certainly a general rule based on "a sound policy reason"[96] that a tribunal could not revisit a final decision simply because it had "changed its mind, made an error within jurisdiction or because there had been a change in circumstances."[97] However, he then went on to state that the application of the *functus officio* doctrine

> must be more flexible and less formalistic in respect to the decisions of administrative tribunals which are subject to appeal only on a point of law. Justice may require reopening of administrative proceedings in order to provide relief which would be otherwise available on appeal.[98]

Among those situations were ones where there were statutory indicia that a decision could be reopened in order to enable it to discharge its statutory function. In addition, where a tribunal has failed to deal with a matter that has been fairly raised in the proceedings before it, it should be allowed to complete its statutory task.

Chandler itself came within the latter category. At the conclusion of a practice review, the association's Practice Review Board had found a group of architects guilty of professional misconduct and imposed various sanctions. This conclusion was set aside by the Alberta Court of Appeal on the basis that the board had no direct jurisdiction over professional discipline. Its authority was as a statutory body concerned with improving the quality of professional practice. As such, its powers were confined to making reports to the council of the association with recommendations, though it did also have the ability to refer matters to

---

95 [1989] 2 S.C.R. 848.
96 *Ibid.* at 861.
97 *Ibid.*
98 *Ibid.* at 862.

the association's complaints review committee. Following this setting aside, the board gave notice that it intended to resume its proceedings for the purposes of preparing a report for council and possibly referring matters to the complaints review committee. It was alleged that this was impermissible by reference to the *functus officio* principle.

In rejecting this argument, a majority of the Supreme Court of Canada held that, notwithstanding the absence of any power of reopening, when a tribunal's decision is quashed because it has acted in excess of jurisdiction, it may, nonetheless, still resume its proceedings of its own initiative and complete its unfinished legitimate business — in this instance, the making of a report and considering whether or not there was any warrant for referring a matter to the complaints review committee.

In fact, there was nothing particularly novel about the actual holding in this instance. Previous authority had confirmed the right of tribunals to reopen a hearing in the face of judicial nullification of part of its proceedings. Indeed, a tribunal that realized that it had committed a nullifying error (such as the denial of procedural fairness) could also act on its own initiative to rehear such a matter without awaiting judicial reversal or quashing. The Court also made it clear that it was not endorsing, as a general matter, the existence of broader powers of reopening, review, or reconsideration such as the revisiting of a discretion over relief in the light of subsequent events or a preservation of continuing jurisdiction in situations where the statutory regime did not allow for such ongoing supervision of the parties and the relief granted.

It is therefore important to recognize that, while the Court's general statements indicated a lessening of the rigidity of the doctrine of *functus officio* in the context of statutory authorities, the particular facts of and other discussion in the *Chandler* case provide little in the way of concrete clues as to when this liberalization might have a bite. Indeed, it is only by its endorsement of the judgment of Martland and Laskin JJ. in the earlier case of *Grillas v. Canada (Minister of Manpower and Immigration)*[99] that the Court provides a different kind of example. There, in a dissenting judgment which on this point had the support of the majority, Martland and Laskin JJ. read a provision in the immigration legislation giving the then Immigration Appeal Board authority to suspend the operation of a deportation order on, *inter alia*, humanitarian and compassionate grounds, as conferring an ongoing jurisdiction on the board including the right to reopen a matter in the event of new evidence becoming available. To Sopinka J. this was the kind of situa-

---

99   [1972] S.C.R. 577.

tion that he had in mind when he conceded the relevance of legislative indicia that the *functus officio* rule would not apply in a tribunal setting.

Chandler has been cited on numerous occasions since it was decided in 1989 but, in fact, its greatest impact has been on the activities of other than formal adjudicative tribunals. Thus, there is a strong, though by no means consistent body, of jurisprudence recognizing the right of visa officers and immigration officers to revisit in the light of new evidence and circumstances decisions they have already made. Reed J., of the Federal Court, Trial Division, encapsulated her sense of the law in the following statement:

> As I read the jurisprudence, I think the need to find express or implied authority to reopen a decision in the relevant statute is directly related to the nature of the decision and the decision-making authority in question. Silence in a statute with respect to the reopening of a decision that has been made on an adjudicative basis on a formal hearing, and after proof of the relevant facts may indicate that no reopening is intended. Silence in a statute with respect to the reopening of a decision that is at the other end of the scale, a decision made by an official pursuant to a highly informal procedure, on whom no time limits are imposed, must be assessed in light of the statute as whole. Silence in such cases may not indicate that Parliament intended that no reconsideration of the decision by the relevant official be allowed. It may merely mean that discretion to do so, or to refuse to do so was left with the official.[100]

In like manner, the British Columbia Court of Appeal in *Zutter* v. *British Columbia (Council of Human Rights)*,[101] was disposed to find in the province's human rights legislation authority to reconsider a gatekeeping decision denying a person complaining of discrimination access to an adjudication of the allegation. Among the factors relevant to this ruling was the absence of any right of appeal from the council's decision. This was a reflection of the English origin of the rule or principle in the context of the regular courts — the creation of a right of appeal to a Court of Appeal under the *Judicature Acts* making previous entitlements to reconsideration redundant. Indeed, the court went so far as to hold that the council's denial of the applicant's request had led to a breach of the rules of natural justice. Also, the council's policy of never reopening such decisions was branded as an unlawful fettering of discretion.

---

100   *Nouranidoust* v. *Canada (Minister of Citizenship and Immigration)* [2000], 1 F.C. 123 (T.D.) at para. 24.
101   (1995), 122 D.L.R. (4th) 665 (B.C.C.A.).

Another clear example of the doctrine's different application in the domain of discretionary decision making by statutory authorities that do not function in a typically adjudicative environment is provided by the Supreme Court's judgment in *Comeau's Sea Foods Ltd.* v. *Canada (Minister of Fisheries and Oceans)*.[102] Here, the Court refused to find fault with the minister, on the basis of changed policy considerations, withdrawing authorization for the issuance of a fisheries licence before the licence itself had been formally issued.

What has also become clear is that the courts are now generally prepared to be somewhat more liberal in the scope they attribute to "exceptions" to the operation of *functus officio*. Thus, clerical errors have been expanded to encompass the recasting of incomplete and ambiguous decisions.[103] A similar example is provided by *Grier* v. *Metro International Trucks Ltd.*,[104] where an employment standards referee allowed an appeal on the basis of an agreed statement of facts that contained what may well have been a crucial factual error. Describing the referee's initial decision as a "nullity," MacPherson J., (as he then was) for the court, held that the referee had erred on a jurisdiction-defining question when he had held subsequently that the principles of *functus officio* applied and prevented a reopening of the matter for reconsideration in accordance with the true facts. The court therefore quashed both rulings and remitted the matter to the referee for reconsideration.

In *Grier*, MacPherson J. described the court's approach as an example of the flexibility endorsed by the Supreme Court of Canada in *Chandler*. What remains to be seen is how far this flexibility will go. However, what is clear to this point is that the courts that have applied *Chandler* do not appear to have placed much emphasis on the nature of the interest that is at stake in the relevant proceedings. Thus, *Grier* involved an *inter partes* dispute between employers and employees as did *Zutter*, while the immigration and visa cases involve both sides of the fence with the request for reopening sometimes coming from the person seeking the favourable exercise of discretion by the state and, on other occasions, from the state seeking to revisit a decision in favour of the person seeking a state benefit.

What also needs to be factored into any evaluation of the scope for reopenings is the extent to which the ability to reopen a decision will be

---

102 [1997] 1 S.C.R. 12.
103 *Severud* v. *Canada (Minister of Employment and Immigration Commission)*, [1991] 2 F.C. 318 (F.C.A.).
104 (1996), 28 O.R. (3d) 67 (Div. Ct.).

affected by detrimental reliance. In other words, there may well be situations where theoretically the right to reopen exists but the statutory authority might well be estopped from doing so because of actions that have been taken on the basis of the decision in question. This concern is reflected in section 21.2(2) of the Ontario *Statutory Powers Procedure Act* which requires any review of a decision to take place within a reasonable time. It is also reflected in those cases that attach a duty of procedural fairness to the question of whether or not a matter should be reopened.[105] However, as seen already, the whole question of the extent to which the principle of estoppel applies to the exercise of power by statutory authorities is a matter of considerable uncertainty and the balance of authority to this point is to the effect that estoppel cannot be pleaded where the reopening or reconsideration is based upon the jurisdictional infirmity or nullity of the original decision. On the other hand, as we have seen earlier, in *Centre Hospitalier Mont-Sinaï c. Québec (Ministère de la Santé et des Services Sociaux)*, the Québec Court of Appeal accepted that the doctrine of estoppel could apply in public law in the case of a lawful exercise of discretion.[106] Though involving actions by a minister of the Crown and not an adjudicative tribunal, if it is upheld by the Supreme Court of Canada, this judgment will obviously have ramifications for the operation of the *functus officio* doctrine.[107]

H. COMMISSIONS OF INQUIRY

1) Introduction

One of the most important instruments of public policy in Canada is the commission of inquiry. It comes in various guises and is deployed for a variety of tasks. At one end of the spectrum are inquiries that have as their sole task the factual determination of why a particular event or series of events occurred — to find out and explain to the public in general and affected constituencies in particular. More commonly, these fact-finding functions are also, as in the case of most coroner's inquests, set up with a view to coming up with recommendations to prevent or lessen the possibility for the recurrence of the events that are the subject of the inquiry. On occasion, part of the objective may also be to ascer-

---

105   See, for example, *Commercial Union Assurance v. Ontario (Human Rights Commission)* (1988), 30 Admin. L.R. 183 (Ont. C.A.).

106   *Centre Hospitalier Mont-Sinaï*, above note 69.

107   Leave was given on 10 Nov. 1999: see [1998] C.S.C.R. No. 595 (Q.L.).

tain whether there is any basis for legal proceedings of a criminal, regulatory, or civil variety. In recent times, the Inquiry into the Deployment of Canadian Troops to Somalia, the Inquiry into the Deaths Underground at the Westray Mine, the Arbour Commission of Inquiry into the Strip Searching of Female Inmates at the Kingston Penitentiary for Women, and the Krever Inquiry into the Working of the Canadian Blood Supply System all involved some or all of these objectives. Something had gone seriously wrong culminating in tragedy or serious violations of rights and it became necessary to find out what had actually happened and why, with a view to preventing similar occurrences and also assigning responsibility where that was appropriate or providing a basis on which appropriate proceedings could be taken.

In rather stark contrast to these "who did what to whom and why?" inquiries are those which are part of a far broader, forward-looking policy agenda. What are the likely directions of higher education in Canada in the first quarter of the new millennium and what can be done to accommodate those evolutions in a way that will redound for the benefit of all Canadians? A typical example of this form of commission is the Royal Commission on the Economic Union and Development Prospects for Canada or the "Macdonald Commission" as it was known after its chair, the Honourable Donald Macdonald.

Over the years, commissions of inquiry and particularly those of the "who did what to whom?" variety have raised a broad range of legal questions, many of which have been the subject of judicial review applications at various points — on the setting up of, during the life of, or at the conclusion of the relevant inquiry. Particularly in the context of inquiries set up by provincial governments, there have been issues of constitutional competence. Questions have also arisen as to whether or not the relevant legislation authorizes an inquiry on the terms specified by the government or other body setting it up. Thereafter, there may be allegations that the scope of the inquiry has exceeded the mandate allocated to it by the government or the relevant legislation. Most commonly, allegations will be made that an inquiry has trampled on the procedural rights of those whom it is investigating or summoned as witnesses. Or there may be allegations that, in the exercise of its powers of entry, search, and the compelling of testimony, the inquiry has infringed various common law, statutory, and constitutional protections, most commonly with respect to search and seizure and self-incrimination. Finally, challenges may be made based on the scope of the inquiry's recommendations and, in particular, impermissible or unfounded findings that are seen as amounting to findings of civil and/or criminal responsibility.

As a consequence of all these challenges, some stemming from the largely skeletal nature of Canada's various pieces of general and specific inquiries legislation, there has come to be a significant body of common or case law governing the conduct of commissions of inquiry in this country. While, at one level, these precedents are but more detailed applications of the generally accepted principles of constitutional and judicial review law, the institution of the commission of inquiry is now deployed so frequently in Canada and so fundamental to the process of government that they do deserve separate treatment in a work of this kind.

2) Constitutional Dimensions

Because many commissions of inquiry have their origins in the infliction of harm and perceptions of misconduct, there is often the possibility that what the commission is investigating may also involve action or inaction which is criminal or for which there could be civil liability. There is nothing necessarily wrong about that. Indeed, were the setting up of commissions of inquiry impermissible where the matters under investigation involved criminal conduct or potential civil liability, the use of this public policy instrument would be curtailed drastically.

However, what is clear, at least in the case of provincially established commissions of inquiry, is that they cannot trench upon the federal criminal law power in section 91(27) of the *Constitution Act, 1867.* Put more bluntly, they cannot be in pith and substance a surrogate for a police investigation and preliminary inquiry into a possible criminal offence. This proposition is well illustrated by *Starr* v. *Houlden.*[108] The commission of inquiry in this case was set up in order to investigate suspicions of political corruption on the part of a named individual and a corporation. While the commissioner was expressly prohibited from actually making any findings of criminal responsibility, the Supreme Court of Canada, nonetheless, held that the terms of reference had stepped over the line into the territory of the criminal law. In particular, because those terms of reference were in virtually the same language as the relevant criminal offence in the *Criminal Code,* were directed specifically at the conduct of the named persons, and did not contain any broader public purpose than simply finding out facts from which inferences of criminal responsibility would be drawn readily, the commission was *ultra vires* of the provincial government.

---

108   [1990] 1 S.C.R. 1366.

Whether there are any limitations on the constitutional capacity of the federal Parliament to authorize a commission of inquiry which amounts to a criminal investigation is somewhat more problematic as is the issue of whether the federal government or the provinces could create commissions of inquiry with the effect of determining issues of civil liability. In *Canada (A.G.)* v. *Canada (Commissioner of Inquiry into the Blood System)* ("the Krever Commission case"),[109] the judgment of the Supreme Court assumes that, had the notices to parties whom the commission might name in its final report actually been couched in terms of criminal and civil responsibility, they would have been *ultra vires*. However, the legal foundation for such a finding is never identified and there are at least three possibilities — that such a finding would be outside the commission's terms of reference; beyond the powers for which a commission could be established under the existing federal inquiries legislation; or unconstitutional.

For what reason might a finding of civil and criminal liability by a federal commission of inquiry be unconstitutional? First, to allow a federal commission of inquiry to go this far might infringe sections 96 to 101 of the *Constitution Act, 1867*, now apparently applicable to the federal Parliament as well as the provincial legislatures. Albeit that the commission could attach no sanctions to its findings, such a role may, nonetheless, involve an assumption of too many of the attributes of a section 96 court. Second, the use of commissions of inquiry for these purposes may infringe the principles behind the Preamble to the *Constitution Act, 1867*, the principles so recently deployed by Lamer C.J.C. in *Reference re Remuneration of Judges of Prince Edward Island Provincial Court*[110] to justify the need for an independent provincial court judicial system. Third, if the finding of civil and/or criminal liability (albeit without direct sanction) could be seen to involve the "life, liberty and security of the person" of those found responsible in such terms, then the process leading to these conclusions might well (principally because of its coercive and inquisitorial nature) be contrary to section 7 of the *Charter* and the "principles of fundamental justice," and not justifiable by reference to section 1. For the moment, however, these other possible constitutional constraints on the creation of commissions of inquiry must remain largely conjectural.

---

109   [1997] 3 S.C.R. 440.
110   [1997] 3 S.C.R. 3.

3) Inquiries Legislation

All of the provinces and the federal government have general legislation authorizing the creation of commissions of inquiry. While there are considerable variations in the details of the various statutes, there are basically two models. The first, exemplified by Ontario, provides for the setting up of an inquiry by the lieutenant governor in council in order to inquire into matters affecting the good government of the province, the conduct of any part of its public business, the administration of justice in the province, or that the lieutenant governor in council declares to be a matter of public concern.[111] In contrast, as exemplified by the federal *Inquiries Act*[112] and the British Columbia legislation,[113] some statutes allow for two separate categories of inquiry: a departmental investigation established by the relevant minister and more general inquiries set up by the governor general in council "into and concerning any matter connected with the good government of Canada or the conduct of any part of the business thereof."

Once established, a commission of inquiry still remains under the control of its creator to the extent that the terms and conditions of its mandate may be changed and its life extended or cut short. This principle was established in the context of the Somalia Inquiry when the Federal Court of Appeal sustained the legality of a modification of the terms establishing that commission of inquiry and, in particular, requiring it to report by a certain date. Despite protests that this was an impermissible interference with the operation of an independent body, the court in *Dixon v. Canada (Commission of Inquiry into the Deployment of Canadian Forces to Somalia)*[114] held that the creation of a commission of inquiry did not carry with it any guarantee of its continued existence until its original mandate expired; it remained within the discretion of the government to terminate its operations. The only potential consequences for such an action were political, not legal.

In addition to inquiries established under general inquiries legislation, there are, however, many other species of inquiry and investigation provided for under other specific legislation, and some of these forms of inquiry and investigation have a permanent or free-standing existence as exemplified by the coroner's inquest. In such cases, without legislative amendment, executive interference with the conduct

---

111   *Public Inquiries Act*, R.S.O. 1990, c. P. 41, s. 2.
112   R.S.C. 1985, c. I-11, Parts I and II.
113   *Inquiry Act*, R.S.B.C. 1996, c. 224.
114   (1997), 149 D.L.R. (4th) 269 (F.C.A.)

and completion of the inquiry or the investigation may indeed be illegal. Frequently, however, the legislation providing for such inquiries and investigations will incorporate some or all of the relevant provisions in the general inquiries legislation relating to the procedures to be followed and the powers of the board of inquiry or investigator. Outside of inquiries provided for expressly by legislation, governments will from time to time establish internal inquiries and investigations by reference to general powers of departmental or agency management or even the residual royal prerogative.[115]

4) Procedures

As mentioned already, general inquiries legislation is skeletal in many respects and particularly as to the procedures to be followed. Typically, the legislation places the conduct and procedures of the inquiry within the discretion of the commission itself and then goes on to deal with a limited number of procedural and adjectival matters such as standing to participate, openness, the rules of evidence, and the coercive powers of the commission. What also characterizes these more specific provisions is the breadth of the discretion they confer on the commission. Thus, under the Ontario *Act*, while it states that the proceedings of commissions of inquiry will be open to members of the public, the commission has a relatively broad discretion to close the inquiry.[116] In the case of evidence, flexibility is also the order of the day with the commission not bound by the strict rules of evidence but rather given a broad discretion to take evidence in any form provided it is reasonably relevant to the subject matter of the inquiry.[117]

In general, the existence of these broad procedural discretions has led the courts to accord a considerable degree of deference to the procedural rulings of commissions. Indeed, it is not just the language of the various provisions that creates this environment of deference. The courts also appeal to the overall nature and purposes of commissions of inquiry. Their primary aim is to generate findings and recommendations in the public interest. Even in "who did what to whom?" inquiries, the commission is not engaging in an adjudicative task even though it may ultimately make findings of responsibility and make recommendations. It does not impose penalties or civil liability. In such a context, the procedural claims of those who are implicated in the proceedings of

---

115   See, for example, *Masters v. Ontario* (1994), 18 O.R. (3d) 551 (Div. Ct.) [*Masters*].
116   *Above*, note 111, s. 4.
117   *Ibid.* s. 11.

a commission of inquiry are attenuated. Indeed, this reflects traditional common law which, at one time, denied procedural protections and the remedy of *certiorari* to those whose interests were affected by non-final or recommendatory bodies,[118] and, even today, treats the non-final nature of a decision as a highly relevant consideration in determining whether there should be any procedural protections at all[119] and, if so, the level of those protections.[120] Indeed, it is also reflective of a policy of limited procedural entitlements that the Ontario *Statutory Powers Procedure Act* excludes explicitly from its operation not only commissions of inquiry under the *Public Inquiries Act* but also all those charged with conducting an investigation and making a report with or without recommendations provided that the report is for information or advice and does not have legally binding consequences.[121]

Nonetheless, there is a growing recognition of the reality that commissions of inquiry can, in certain circumstances, have drastic consequences for the reputations and careers of those whom they target particularly in situations where the task of the inquiry is directed to wrongdoing and may lead to immediate and serious repercussions for those named as responsible. Typical in this regard are investigations and inquiries which are directed specifically at the investigation of misconduct by a single individual in the performance of a public office. However, even here, as exemplified by *Masters* v. *Ontario*,[122] the procedures can still be relatively informal and do not have to accord with those of a trial or even regular disciplinary hearings in a professional setting. In *Masters*, the Divisional Court rejected the argument that the target of an investigation into allegations of sexual misconduct had a right of direct access to the responses to his answers to the complaints. As long as those responses added nothing substantial to the record, there was no requirement that they be revealed to him even though the ultimate outcome could be a recommendation that he be dismissed from an important public position.

As far as inquiries under general inquiries legislation are concerned, the focal point for the courts' insistence on procedural protections is generally on either the standing provisions of such legislation or, more

---

118 See *Guay* v. *Lafleur*, [1965] S.C.R. 12.
119 See the judgment of L'Heureux-Dubé J. in *Indian Head School Division No. 19 (Saskatchewan Board of Education)* v. *Knight*, [1990] 1 S.C.R. 653.
120 *Irvine* v. *Canada (Restrictive Trade Practices Commission)*, [1987] 1 S.C.R. 181.
121 R.S.O. 1990, c. S.22 (as amended by S.O. 1994, c. 27 and S.O. 1997, c. 23, ss. 3(2)(f) and (g)).
122 *Masters*, above note 115.

particularly, the statutory requirement that prevents a commission of inquiry from making a finding of misconduct against anyone unless that person has been given reasonable notice of the nature of the alleged misconduct and a full opportunity to be heard at the inquiry in person or by counsel. In the domain of standing, that has produced judgments in which the courts have reviewed the determination of a commission as to whether someone had a sufficient interest in the inquiry to entitle them to participate.[123] As far as the right to respond is concerned, the most thorough recent examination of such provisions and their import is to be found in the various judgments of the Federal Court and the Supreme Court of Canada in the Krever Commission litigation.[124]

Aside from raising the issue of whether the commission could make findings of civil or criminal responsibility for the maladministration of Canada's blood supply and whether the required notices were couched inappropriately in such terms, the applicants for relief challenged the timing of the giving of the notices. They alleged that the notices had come far too late in the proceedings (the final day of the scheduled hearings) and had failed to give them a sufficient time in which to respond. In delivering the judgment of a unanimous Supreme Court of Canada, Cory J. emphasized the need to accord procedural fairness to those whose reputation might be stained by the commission's final report. This could be ensured by issuing the required notices in confidence to those likely to be named in the final report and providing as much detail as possible.

On the particular facts of this case, however, the Court did not believe that the commission had acted in a procedurally unfair manner save in relation to one of the many persons receiving notices. The fact that the notices had been delayed until the last day of the scheduled hearings was not necessarily fatal to their validity. Although it was desirable that the notices be given as early as possible, this was one of those kinds of inquiry where, because of its complexity, it was practically impossible for the notices to be issued before all of the material was before the commission. It was also significant that, save for one person, all those named were aware that they were among the targets of the inquiry and had, save for two persons, one of which took a calculated gamble, participated fully in the proceedings. What was ultimately important was whether those notices contained sufficient details

---

123   See, for example, *Parents of Baby Gosselin* v. *Grange* (1984), 8 Admin. L.R. 250 (Div. Ct.)

124   *Canada (A.G.)* v. *Canada (Commissioner of the Inquiry on the Blood System)*, [1996] 3 F.C. 259 (T.D.), aff'd. [1997] 2 F.C. 36 (C.A.), aff'd. [1997] 3 S.C.R. 440.

and were given in a timely enough fashion to enable a proper opportunity to respond. On the first score, the Court had no problems and, on the second, was prepared to accept the commission's judgment on an appropriate timetable for indicating whether there would be a response and, subsequently, for the making of that response.

It is also the case that the courts exhibit much greater flexibility in applying the principles against bias in the context of inquiries and investigations treating those involved in such tasks as subject to a test somewhere between the reasonable apprehension of bias associated with truly adjudicative functions and the "totally closed mind" test applied to those exercising broad-based policy-making or regulatory powers. Thus, in *Beno v. Canada (Commissioner & Chairperson, Commission of Inquiry into the Deployment of Canadian Forces to Somalia)*,[125] the Federal Court of Appeal set aside a Trial Division judgment prohibiting the chair of the commission from participating in any findings with respect to a member of the Canadian Forces who had been served with a notice. Despite the fact that, in an extrajudicial setting, the chair had made disparaging remarks about the evasiveness and untruthfulness of the testimony of this officer, that was not a basis on which to disqualify him given the rather different standards applicable to commissions of inquiry.[126]

FURTHER READINGS

ANISMAN, P., "Jurisdiction of Administrative Tribunals to Apply the *Canadian Charter of Rights and Freedoms*" in *Administrative Law: Principles, Practice and Pluralism*, [1992] Special Lectures of the Law Society of Upper Canada 89

ANISMAN, P., "Regulation Without Authority: The Ontario Securities Commission" (1994), 7 Canadian Journal of Administrative Law and Practice 195

BEAUDOIN, G.A., "Les tribunaux administratifs et la *Charte canadienne des droits et libertés*" (1998), 61 Sask. L.R. 277

BERZINS, C., "Policy Development By Labour Relations Boards in Canada: In There a Case for Rulemaking" (2000), 25 Queen's L.J. 479

---

125 [1997] 2 F. C. 527 (C.A.).
126 See also *Zündel v. Canada (Minister of Citizenship and Immigration)* (1997), 154 D.L.R. (4th) 216 (F.C.A.).

BILODEAU, J.-L., "L'affaire *Ainsley* et le contrôle politique de la régulation du marché des valeurs mobilières au moyen de normes de portée générale" (1997), 22 Queen's L.J. 297

BROWN. R., AND B. ETHERINGTON, "*Weber* v. *Ontario Hydro*: A Denial of Access to Justice for the Organized Employee" (1996), 4 Canadian Labour and Employment Law Journal 183

CRANE, M.C., "Administrative Tribunals, *Charter* Challenges, and the "Web of Institutional Relationships" (1998), 61 Sask. L.R. 495

D'OMBRAIN, N., "Public Inquiries in Canada" (1997), 40 Canadian Public Administration 86

EVANS, J.M., "Administrative Tribunals and *Charter* Challenges: Jurisdiction, Discretion and Relief" (1997), 10 Canadian Journal of Administrative Law and Practice 355

JANISCH, H.N., "The Choice of Decisionmaking Method: Adjudication, Policies and Rulemaking" in *Administrative Law: Principles, Practice and Pluralism*, [1992] Special Lectures of the Law Society of Upper Canada 259

JANISCH, H.N., "Further Developments with Respect to Rulemaking by Administrative Agencies" (1995), 9 Canadian Journal of Administrative Law and Practice 1

LORDON, P., "Administrative Tribunals and the Control of Their Processes" (1998), 11 Canadian Journal of Administrative Law and Practice 179

MCDONALD, P., "Contradictory Government Action: Estoppel of Statutory Authorities" (1979), 17 O.H.L.J. 160

MCMILLAN, J., "Tribunals and the *Charter*: The Search for Implied Jurisdiction — A Case Comment on *Cooper* v. *Canada (Human Rights Commission)*" (1998), 32 U.B.C.L.R. 365

MOLOT, H., "The *Carltona* Doctrine and the Recent Amendments to the *Interpretation Act*" (1994), 26 Ottawa L.R. 259

PROSS, A.P., INNIS CHRISTIE, AND JOHN A. YOGIS, eds., *Commissions of Inquiry* (Toronto: Carswell, 1990)

ROMAN, A.J., "Case Comment: *Cooper* v. *Canada (Human Rights Commission)*" (1997), 43 Admin. L.R. (2d) 243

SCHUCHER, K., "A Further Diminishing of the Role of Human Rights Tribunals: *Cooper* v. *Canadian Human Rights Commission, Bell* v. *Canadian Human Rights Commission*" (1997), C.L.E.L.J. 173

SCHWARTZ, B., "Public Inquiries" (1997), 40 Canadian Public Administration 72

TREBILCOCK M.J., & LISA AITKIN, "The Limits of the Full Court Press: Of Blood and Mergers" (1998), 48 U.T.L.J. 1

WILLIS, J., "Delegatus Non Potest Delegare" (1943), 21 Can. Bar. Rev. 257

PART FOUR

REMEDIES

CHAPTER 16

GENERAL

A. INTRODUCTION

At common law, judicial supervision of the administrative process developed through the evolution of a series of common law remedies known as the prerogative writs. Indeed, until quite recent times, the scope of judicial review of administrative action was frequently seen through the lenses of the modern-day equivalents of these historic forms of relief. However, the prerogative writs were not the only ways in which the lawfulness of administrative action could be tested. The validity of administrative decisions and orders could be put in issue in the context of proceedings taken to enforce those decisions and orders. Today known as collateral (as opposed to direct) attack, this enabled someone, for example, to resist prosecution for alleged breach of a by-law or regulation on the basis that the relevant subordinate legislation was invalid. In time, also, the equitable remedy of injunction as well as declaratory relief were called in aid of the prerogative writs frequently because of technical and often archaic limitations on the scope of those normal remedies. As in private law, equity came to the rescue when the common law forms of relief proved unequal to the task. Under limited circumstances, unlawful administrative action could also generate a cause of action in damages. Finally, and today this probably represents the highest incidence of proceedings questioning the validity of administrative action of various sorts, statutes conferring statutory authority would frequently create a specific right of appeal to the courts so that those affected would not have to rely on the common law and equitable remedies in order to secure redress for unlawful administrative action. They had a direct and explicit route to judicial intervention.

In Canada, the last thirty-five years of the twentieth century were characterized by a number of important legislative reforms to the remedial pattern of administrative law. Perhaps most significantly, remedial jurisdiction over federal statutory decision makers was in 1970 transferred almost, though not quite completely, from the provincial superior courts to the newly created Federal Court of Canada, a court that replaced the former Exchequer Court of Canada, which had had only very limited judicial review jurisdiction. Almost contemporaneously, Ontario was engaged in simplifying the remedies of judicial review and conferring most judicial review authority on a three-judge bench of the then Ontario High Court, the Divisional Court. These efforts at remedial simplification followed a less ambitious but nevertheless significant remedial reform in Québec and were themselves to be followed over the next three decades by remedial reform exercises of varying levels of intensity in virtually all of the provinces and territories.

From time to time, serious consideration has also been given to the question of whether there should be a separate system of administrative courts. Among the models considered have been the French Conseil d'état and the Commonwealth of Australia's Administrative Appeals Tribunal, which has appellate jurisdiction over the merits of decisions taken by an extensive range of departments and agencies of the federal government. So far, however, the province of Québec is the only jurisdiction to have taken up these proposals. As a result of two statutes enacted in 1996 and 1997 respectively and which came into force on 1 April 1998,[1] there is now an administrative appeal body, le Tribunal administratif du Québec, fashioned along the lines of the Australian model[2] and providing appellate recourse, generally by way of *de novo* merits review, from a broad spectrum of those exercising statutory powers in the province. It functions in four divisions[3] and, in those matters over which it has jurisdiction, stands between the origi-

---

1   *Loi sur la justice administrative*, S.Q. 1996, c. 54, Titre 2 and *Loi sur l'application de la Loi sur la justice administrative*, S.Q. 1997, c. 43.

2   Titre 3 of la *Loi sur la justice administative* also provides for un Conseil de la justice administrative justice, another parallel with the Australian system where there is an Administrative Review Council exercising similar supervisory functions.

3   La Section des affaires sociales, la Section des affaires immobilières, la Section du territoire et de l'environnement, and la Section des affaires économiques.

nal administrative process and traditional judicial review,[4] access to which is thereafter preserved but limited by a privative clause to questions of jurisdiction. This represents a bold experiment in the delivery of administrative justice and, if successful, will undoubtedly regenerate debate in at least some of the larger jurisdictions as to the desirability of moving in that direction.[5]

In this chapter, I will start by describing the nature and reach of the old prerogative writs, an exercise which is more than simply one of historical interest. Notwithstanding the breadth of remedial reform in Canada, in a number of the provinces, the latter-day successors of these writs along with the supplementary equitable jurisdiction still form the backbone of judicial review of administrative action. Thereafter, I will examine some of the statutory reform initiatives and assess the extent to which they have simplified the processes of judicial review by removing technical impediments to the application of appropriate substantive standards of judicial scrutiny. I will also devote specific attention to statutory appeals, collateral attack, and actions in damages and for other forms of monetary relief as alternative ways of securing relief for unlawful administrative action. As well, I will be looking separately at some of the important remedial issues that transcend most of the individual forms of relief — issues of standing to seek relief and the various discretionary grounds for the denial of relief such as prematurity, waiver, delay, and, particularly, the availability of a more suitable avenue for the vindication of the rights and interests being asserted. I will then conclude with a brief consideration of some of the extrajudicial modes of securing relief and, in particular, the office of the ombudsman.

B. THE PREROGATIVE REMEDIES

Streamlined versions of the old prerogative writs (along with declaratory and injunctive relief) still provide the foundations for judicial review of administrative action in Manitoba, Newfoundland, Nova

---

4   In the case of expropriation decisions, there is also a further right of appeal to la Cour du Québec, the Québec provincial court.

5   In what has to be a setback to this regime, the Superior Court has struck down several provisions of the *Loi sur la justice administrative* pertaining the members of the tribunal as not providing a sufficient guarantee of impartiality and independence as guaranteed by section 23 of the Québec *Charter of Human Rights and Freedoms*, R.S.Q. 1977, c. C-12: *Barreau de Montréal* v. *Québec (Procureur général)*, (1999), [2000] R.J.Q. 125 (S.C.).

Scotia, and, to a lesser extent, in Québec and Saskatchewan. As well, in those provinces that now have a simplified application for judicial review applicable to most, if not all, aspects of judicial review of administrative action, that application for judicial review was established legislatively by reference to the prerogative forms of relief. As a consequence, it remains important across Canada to have some knowledge of the nature of those various species of relief.

C. *HABEAS CORPUS*

Constitutionally, the most significant of the prerogative writs was that of *habeas corpus*. As with at least three others, the name of the writ is taken from the Latin terminology used in the writ itself to express the form of relief that the applicant is seeking. In this case, the instruction that went out to the government[6] official or agency from the court was "Let me have the body (alive)" of the person who is the subject of the application. More specifically, it called on those responsible for the detention of an individual to produce that person to the court so that the validity of the detention could be ascertained by the court. In cases where there was no justification for either the original or continued detention of the person before the court, the court would order her or his release. As a consequence, *habeas corpus* represented an extremely powerful instrument for the maintenance of the rule of law in an era where arbitrary arrest and imprisonment and illegal detentions were well-known weapons in the arsenal of those wanting to silence political rivals and eliminate any form of dissent.

As opposed to the Constitution of the United States, the *Constitution Act, 1867* contains no guarantee of the continued availability of *habeas corpus* to test the validity of any detention though it is conceivable that the courts could have read such a guarantee into the Constitution by reference to the preamble and the implied bill of rights theory. Today, however, that issue is largely redundant. Section 2(c)(iii) of the 1960 Diefenbaker *Canadian Bill of Rights* contains a guarantee of *habeas corpus* in the case of detentions by federal authorities and this has now been built into section 10(c) of the *Charter*. How-

---

6   In fact, historically, the remedy was not restricted to detentions by public officials as exemplified by the famous case of *Somerset v. Stewart* (1772), Lofft 1 (K.B.), in which Mansfield C.J. directed the writ to the captain of a ship in which a slave was being kept in irons pending his forced return to Jamaica.

ever, there are some lingering concerns as to the extent that this constitutional guarantee covering all forms of government and government agent detentions is subject to both section 1 justifications of derogations and the section 33 override.

In fact, today, *habeas corpus* does not figure all that often in the court lists. However, it remains a potentially efficacious remedy for testing the validity of the continued detention of those in the custody of the various federal and provincial correctional services as well as the police, immigration, and child welfare authorities, the military and RCMP, and mental health institutions. Indeed, in 1971, when the Federal Court took over the provincial superior courts' existing jurisdiction over judicial review of federal statutory authorities, one of the few domains reserved for the continued jurisdiction of the provincial superior courts in federal matters was that of *habeas corpus*. The thinking behind this was that judges should be available to consider an application for *habeas corpus* at any hour of the day or night and, with so few Federal Court judges centred mainly in Ottawa, the efficacy of this theory would be compromised seriously were this jurisdiction to be removed from the provincial superior courts.

The Supreme Court of Canada also gave a boost to the reach of *habeas corpus* in two important ways. First, it held that, in a correctional facility setting, it was available to test the validity of the transfer of an inmate from a less to a more secure form of custody under the so-called prison-within-a-prison argument.[7] The Supreme Court also held that the *Federal Court Act*'s conferral on the Federal Court of exclusive jurisdiction to grant relief in the nature of *certiorari* against federal statutory authorities did not compromise the ability of the provincial superior courts to grant *certiorari* in aid of *habeas corpus* with respect to such bodies. This was a separate form of relief not touched by the exclusionary provision in the *Federal Court Act*.[8] The impact of this was to preserve the authority of the provincial superior courts to scrutinize the validity of detentions by reference to material beyond the warrant authorizing the detention and, in effect, to go behind the warrant and investigate by reference to a wider form of record and affidavit evidence, any underlying infirmities in the continued detention of the subject matter of the application.

---

7   See the trilogy *R. v. Miller*, [1985] 2 S.C.R. 613 [*Miller*]; *Cardinal v. Kent Institution (Director)*, [1985] 2 S.C.R. 643; *Morin v. Canada (National Special Handling Unit Review Committee)*, [1985] 2 S.C.R. 662.

8   *Miller, ibid.*

All of this still remains the case though as will be seen below, the use of *habeas corpus* against federal statutory authorities has been diminished by a body of law that basically acknowledges the discretion of the provincial superior courts to decline to deal with such applications where there is an appropriate alternative form of relief available from the Federal Court. Indeed, more generally, the use of *habeas corpus* has diminished with the increase in the number of specialized statutory regimes for the review and testing of detentions of various kinds.

D. CERTIORARI

Both historically and today, the most common prerogative remedy has been that of *certiorari*. It called upon a statutory authority to produce the record of its proceedings so that the court could become "more certain" that the authority had not committed a reviewable error in reaching its decision. The consequence of a finding of such an error is the quashing of the relevant decision or order.

Over time, the efficacy of *certiorari* as a remedy increased dramatically as a result of two evolutions. First, the English courts recognized that it was not confined in its scope to jurisdictional or invalidating errors; it was available for the questioning of intrajurisdictional errors of law provided they appeared on the face of the record of the authority under review. Second, as far as allegations of jurisdictional or invalidating error were concerned, the courts were also prepared to accept that affidavit evidence could be adduced in support of such grounds of review; judicial scrutiny of the impugned decision was not restricted to what could be ascertained from the formal record. This second evolution was particularly instrumental in the growth of *certiorari* as a means of raising issues of procedural impropriety particularly as the courts were, at least for these purposes, prepared to treat a breach of the rules of natural justice as an invalidating error as opposed to one within jurisdiction and subject to the constraints of what could be established from the formal record. This remains the situation in Canada today save insofar as these principles have been modified in the context of some of the remedial reforms.

Regrettably, the history of the evolution of *certiorari* was not a totally expansionary one. As a result of restrictive judicial rulings as to its scope, it became rooted in the domain of decision makers who made final decisions affecting rights and who, in doing so, were obligated either by statute or the common law to act judicially or *quasi*-judicially. In other words, *certiorari* went from being the vehicle through which procedural among other rights could be vindicated to a remedy that was constrained in its general application to bodies which at common law were subject to the principles of natural justice. It did not expand, at least until quite recently, to provide relief on substantive grounds against all forms of statutory and prerogative authorities whether or not they were obliged to act judicially or comport themselves in accordance with the principles of natural justice. Moreover, when the courts began to take a restricted or at least inconsistent stand on what it meant in the language of the "leading" English precedent to have "legal authority to determine the rights of subjects" as well as a "superadded duty to act judicially,"[9] serious doubts were raised as to whether the courts were acting in the best interests of citizens in their attempts to secure justice against the state. Too often, the substantive consideration of a challenge was derailed by technical, remedial considerations having nothing to do with the merits of the applicant's case.

Indeed, while in time the action for declaratory relief became available with respect to decision makers not technically within the realm of *certiorari*, not only did this condemn the citizen to have to proceed by the more complicated and expensive proceeding by way of action as opposed to a by then relatively simple and straightforward application procedure, but also there was always the risk that the state respondent would raise the argument that declaratory relief was not available because the decision-making process in issue was indeed the territory of *certiorari*. Moreover, if this plea were successful, because of the incompatability of an action with an application, the aggrieved person would have to start her or his challenge all over again.

Such a state of affairs was clearly not in the public interest and, indeed, it provided much of the impetus for the series of remedial reforms starting in Canada in the late 1960s. Its impact was also diminished significantly in the aftermath of *Nicholson* v. *Haldimand-Norfolk Regional Board of Commissioners of Police*.[10] In subsequent cases, it was accepted that the lowering of the threshold for the making of procedural fairness arguments and the application of principles of procedural fairness to a significant range of purely administrative bodies had also lowered the threshold for the reach of the remedy of *certiorari* and its pre-decision equivalent, prohibition.[11] It was no longer necessary to

---

9   R. v. *Legislative Committee of the Church Assembly*, [1928] 1 K.B. 411, explaining *R. v. Electricity Commissioners, ex parte London Electricity Commissioners*, [1924] 1 K.B. 171 (C.A.), the infamous "gloss" by Lord Hewart C.J. on *dicta* by Atkin L.J. (as he then was).

10   [1979] 1 S.C.R. 311.

11   *Martineau* v. *Matsqui Inmate Disciplinary Board*, [1980] 1 S.C.R. 602.

apply the traditional formula for the availability of those forms of relief. Now, there is also limited authority for the proposition that *certiorari* as become a general all- purpose remedy available for checking reviewable error irrespective of the formal categorization of the function in issue.[12] While this proposition does not have explicit Supreme Court of Canada support, the combination of the clearly established lowering of the threshold and the impact of remedial reform in most jurisdictions has meant the virtual disappearance of judicial review litigation in which the central question is whether the applicant has selected correctly as between *certiorari* and some other form of relief and, most notably, a declaration.

E. PROHIBITION

Certiorari provides relief when a decision or order has already been made. Sometimes, of course, relief may be justified in advance of the taking of a decision or an order. For example, faced with the prospect of a lengthy hearing in front of a decision maker who may be disqualified by reason of a reasonable apprehension of bias, the parties may be keen to have the matter clarified rather than potentially wasting all the time and resources involved in proceeding with the hearing only to have the decision quashed after the event for bias. Indeed, not to take the point to court when it first arises may in such cases give rise to a discretionary defence of waiver to a subsequent *certiorari* application. Prohibition provides the facility whereby those affected can at least on occasion take pre-emptive strikes of this kind.

In the pre-*Nicholson* era, prohibition was also subject to all the same limitations applicable to *certiorari*, and just as the action for a declaration came to occupy some of the territory where *certiorari* would not go, so too did equity in the form of injunctions and interlocutory injunctions make up for some of the deficiencies of prohibition as a pre-decisional remedy. Prohibition also suffered from the disadvantage of no longer being available once the relevant decision had been taken or order made. Indeed, this was one of the reasons why, in its initial remedial reform in 1965, Québec combined *certiorari* and prohibition into a single remedy, that of evocation. In other jurisdictions where the prerogative remedies survive, the applicant is dependent on the willingness of the court to convert an application for relief in the nature of prohibition into an application for relief in the nature of *certiorari*.

---

12   *Minister of National Revenue v. Kruger Inc.*, [1984] 2 F.C. 535 (C.A.); *Alberta v. Beaver (County No. 9)* (1984), 7 Admin. L.R. 119 (Alta. C.A.).

F. MANDAMUS

Mandamus literally translated means "we order" or "we command" and that gives a very clear clue as to the purpose that it serves in the judicial review remedial firmament. It is available when a statutory authority has failed to respond to a request that it fulfill or perform a currently existing legal duty. Unlike *certiorari* and prohibition, *mandamus* was never constrained in its reach to bodies that act judicially or quasi-judicially. Thus, it was typically available to compel the performance of duties owed to an individual or specific individuals by officials of various kinds such as the issuance of a licence when the applicant had met all statutory preconditions. Indeed, the only such limitation is the unavailability of relief in the nature of *mandamus* against the Crown. This limitation was based in part on general conceptions of Crown or executive immunity and in part on the rather dubious notion that it was in some way unseemly or inappropriate for the "Royal" courts to direct mandatory decrees against the monarch. However, while at times the courts did extend this immunity to ministers of the Crown, the general tendency in the more modern authorities is to treat statutory duties imposed on members of the executive as not being owed on behalf of the Crown but as the statutorily designated instrumentality for giving effects to the dictates of the legislation.

Relief in the nature of *mandamus* is sometimes combined with an application for relief in the nature of *certiorari*. A typical example is provided by the situation where someone seeking a benefit has been denied that benefit in a manner that infringes the principles of procedural fairness. In such a situation, for the court merely to quash the invalid decision does not achieve the applicant's purposes. Accordingly, the court will generally respond positively to an application for a combination of *certiorari*-type relief and an order in the nature of *mandamus* compelling the statutory authority or a replacement to reconsider the matter this time in accordance with the obligations of procedural fairness.

G. QUO WARRANTO

Quo warranto is a virtually obsolescent prerogative remedy that calls on an administrative official to demonstrate "by what warrant or authority" he or she is purporting to act. In its original form, it presented a way of questioning whether or not an administrative official had been properly appointed to the position he or she purported to occupy or whether such an official still possessed the capacity and the qualifications to exercise that power. Typical examples of intervention were situations where the official lacked the designated statutory qualifications for the office in question or where her or his term of office had expired. However, to the extent that these questions were also ones that could be raised on an application for relief in the nature of both *certiorari* and prohibition and by way of an action for an injunction, the use of this form of relief diminished. However, it still does have a life in at least a couple of the provinces and notably Québec and New Brunswick where it is sometimes used as a way of challenging the authority of municipal councillors on the basis of a prohibited conflict of interest.[13]

H. EQUITABLE AND OTHER RELIEF

The supplementing of the prerogative forms of relief with the declaration and the injunction dates back to the nineteenth century. As already intimated, during the time when there were severe restrictions on the availability of *certiorari* and prohibition particularly, this ability to have recourse to equity was a very valuable accretion to the spectrum of judicial review remedies.

The use of such forms of relief did, however, involve what was often the disadvantage of having to proceed by way of the more cumbersome procedure of an action. On some occasions, though, this was an advantage rather than a disadvantage. Where complex factual issues were at stake, being able as a matter of course to rely on the usual evidential facilities of the trial process (examinations for discovery and *viva voce* evidence) rather than by way of the record and affidavit evidence, could be extremely useful. Access to interim relief was also a factor that on occasion influenced the choice of the equitable rather than the prerogative route. There was no such creature as an interim prohibition nor any generally recognized jurisdiction to give a stay of proceedings pending the disposition of an application for prohibition. In contrast, while the courts would not historically award an interim declaration, interim or interlocutory injunctions were a regular feature of the courts' exercise of their injunction jurisdiction. Also, in situations where the aggrieved party was wanting damages for the unlawful administrative action, it was only through the vehicles of an action for a declaration or an injunction that this objective could be achieved in conjunction with other judicial review remedies. Damages were not

---

13   See, for example, *R. v. Wheeler*, [1979] 2 S.C.R. 650.

available by way of application, only in an action, and hence could not be combined with an application for one of the prerogative forms of relief. While, in most jurisdictions, these rigid divisions have been removed either by way of legislative or rule of court reform, the considerations on which they were based continues to have relevance in limited contexts.

Injunctive relief did, however, suffer from the same restriction as that applicable to relief in the nature of *mandamus*; it was not available against the Crown. This principle has been eroding slowly over the past two decades but, even prior to that, it was and is a feature of crown proceedings legislation to include provisions confirming the normal rule but also providing that the court can award a declaration in such instances in lieu of an injunction.[14]

As well as serving the same objectives as prohibition, that of preventing a matter from proceeding to consideration or a final decision, the public law injunction was and is also available to prevent the execution of decisions already taken and orders already made on the basis that they are *ultra vires*. In this extended sense, the injunction, of course, plays a similar role to that of *certiorari*. The declaration is also used in situations involving an allegedly *ultra vires* decision or order by a statutory authority not amenable to *certiorari*. If the plaintiff or applicant makes out a case on the merits, the court will generally declare the decision or order *ultra vires*. While it is generally assumed that bare declarations of this kind are not necessarily binding,[15] it is highly unusual for such a decree to be ignored. In effect, therefore, it will be as if the court had actually quashed the relevant decision. As with the injunction, the declaration also has another dimension which takes it out of the domain of *certiorari* and prohibition and more into the territory of *mandamus*. On occasion, a declaration will be available as an original remedy to declare someone's rights under a statute. Although this is subject to the discretionary consideration that the use of a declaration for these purposes should not pre-empt statutorily specified mechanisms for the determination of the matters in issue, it does fill a very useful role in those instances where there is a dispute about an alleged statutory entitlement and no other way in which the claim can be legally established. This is particularly so in situations where the claim is one against the Crown, since, as in the case of the injunction,

---

14   See, for example, *Proceedings Against the Crown Act*, R.S.A. 1980, c. P-18, section 17(1).

15   Hence the availability of declarations in lieu of injunctions against the Crown.

the traditional common law position has been that relief in the nature of *mandamus* is not available against the Crown.

I. INTERIM RELIEF

1) Introduction

The same considerations that make the availability of interim relief so important in private law are present frequently in challenges to the validity of administrative action. If an order is executed or allowed to remain in effect or proceedings go ahead while the applicant awaits the final determination of an application for judicial review, there may be no utility to any remedy that ultimately the applicant obtains or the applicant will have suffered irreparable or irremediable harm in the meantime. As a consequence, interim relief plays an important though, as we will see, limited role in the context of judicial review of administrative action.

2) Forms of Interim Relief

There are various forms in which interim relief is available to suspend action or proceedings pending the hearing of an application for judicial review. Historically, the most common form of interim relief has been the interlocutory or interim injunction sought in the context of an action for a permanent injunction. Indeed, to the extent that the courts never recognized any form of interim relief in support of applications for relief in the nature of the prerogative writs, this represented another advantage that sometimes accrued in commencing an action for an injunction instead of an application for a prerogative remedy. In fact, it was also an advantage that the injunction possessed over the declaration since the courts traditionally would not grant either an interim declaration or an interlocutory injunction in support of an application for an injunction.

In today's remedial world, however, the courts recognize a much broader jurisdiction to issue interim relief in public law matters. An application for a stay of proceedings is now available under most rules of court in support of any other form of relief. The courts themselves have also become that much more flexible and have come to recognize the availability of interim injunctions to protect the integrity of forms of judicial review proceeding other than an action for a permanent injunction. Most significantly, however, interim relief is now provided for specifically in the statutes and rules of court reforming the remedies of judicial review of administrative action. Thus, to take just one example, section 18.2 of the *Federal Court Act*[16] provides:

> 18.2 On an application for judicial review, the Trial Division may make such interim orders as it considers appropriate pending the final disposition of the application.

Moreover, by virtue of section 28(2), that provision also applies to proceedings commenced in the Federal of Court of Appeal.

Given this jurisdictional scope for interim relief and given that the principles applied in determining the availability of interim relief in its various forms tend to be exactly the same, I will not dwell further on the general issue of authority save in one respect: the ability of the courts to give interim relief which is not an adjunct to other proceedings before the courts but simply in support of proceedings before a statutory authority. I will deal with this issue in a separate section.

3) The Test for Interim Relief in Public Law Litigation Generally

It is now accepted[17] that, with one important refinement, the general (though not necessarily universal) test for interim relief in public law matters is the same as that first developed by the House of Lords in *American Cyanamid Co.* v. *Ethicon Ltd.*[18] Under that test, the court inquires whether there is a "serious case to be tried" on the merits of the claim for final relief. If the answer to that question is in the affirmative, the court then moves to consider whether the applicant will suffer irreparable harm in the event that the interim relief is not granted and he or she were to prevail ultimately on the principal claim for relief. Should the answer to that question also be an affirmative, the court then assesses the balance of convenience as between the applicant for interim relief and the other party or parties to the proceedings. Included within the court's evaluation of the balance of convenience is the issue of irreparable harm to the respondent. Will the respondent suffer irreparable harm if the interim relief is granted and he or she is ultimately successful in defending the principal claim? Finally, in a situation where, as between the parties, the balance of convenience or

---

16 R.S.C. 1985, c. F-7 (as amended by S.C. 1990, c. 8).
17 *Manitoba (A.G.)* v. *Metropolitan Stores (MTS) Ltd.*, [1987] 1 S.C.R. 110, as refined in *RJR-MacDonald Ltd.* v. *Canada (A.G.)*, [1994] 1 S.C.R. 311 [*Metropolitan Stores*].
18 [1975] A.C. 396 (H.L. Eng.).

inconvenience favours neither side, the court is, at that point, justified in looking further at the merits of the principal claim.

In public law litigation, the one important refinement of this test is that, at the balance of convenience stage, the court must also take into account the public interest in the matters at stake. A good example of how this works is in fact provided by the foundational Supreme Court of Canada judgment in *Manitoba (A.G.)* v. *Metropolitan Stores (MTS) Ltd.*[19] This involved an employer attempt to secure a stay of an application before the provincial labour relations board for the compulsory imposition of a first collective agreement pending resolution of a *Charter* challenge to the validity of the relevant provisions in Manitoba's labour relations legislation. In restoring the first instance judgment denying the stay, the Court relied on the general proposition that courts should exercise caution in denying effect to any legislation passed in the public interest and also on the basis of the maxim that labour relations delayed is labour relations denied. This approach or presumption was said to be particularly appropriate in so-called "suspension" cases where the direct effect of a stay would be the temporary (at least) ineffectiveness in all contexts of the impugned legislative provisions. Moreover, while it would sometimes be less applicable in "exemption" cases where the direct target of the injunction was (as in this case) a single proceeding, the Court also recognized that to grant the application here would almost certainly lead to either the board in fact not exercising its powers in other cases or the making of similar applications in all other pending first contract applications.

4) Application of the Test in Purely Administrative Law Settings

How precisely these principles operate in an administrative law setting is not immediately clear. These uncertainties manifest themselves in several ways. For example, it has been held[20] that the first question in the *American Cyanamid* test is not always appropriate in judicial review proceedings at least where the success of the judicial review application depends on establishing that the impugned decision is patently unreasonable. Given the difficulty of passing that test on the actual judicial review application, it has been held that the court should demand more than just proof of a serious question to be tried on the

---

19   *Metropolitan Stores*, above note 17.

20   *Sobeys Inc.* v. *UFCW, Local 1000A* (1993), 12 O.R. (3d) 157 (Div. Ct.).

application for interim relief; rather, the former general test of whether or not there was a *prima facie* or strong *prima facie* case on the merits was the appropriate basis on which to commence any consideration of such an application.

It is, of course, questionable whether "patent unreasonableness" cases do in fact necessitate a reversion to the former standard first question. After all, as part of determining whether there is a serious issue to be tried, the motions court judge will presumably pay heed to or factor in the high standard that the relevant legal test prescribes for making out a case on the merits. Nonetheless, it does illustrate well the problems in knowing how far there can be a straight transfer of the principles from the constitutional and *Charter* cases to the purely administrative law arena.

What is also true of applications for interlocutory relief in purely administrative law cases is that they are much more likely to be exemption cases or ones having no immediate impact on other proceedings. A good example is provided by a bias challenge based on an allegation of personal animosity on the part of the adjudicator towards a person accused of professional misconduct. Granting interim relief pending the outcome of a judicial review application in such cases will not affect other proceedings. However, even here, there are other public interest considerations that may point against the granting of relief. The public interest in the speedy and efficient rooting out of professionals who engage in misconduct should not be frustrated readily by making interim relief staying proceedings too readily available to those who stand charged with such misconduct. (Indeed, this factor may become even more significant if the application for interim relief is aimed at a suspension from practice order made after a hearing.[21]) Are these also situations where the applicant should be required to make out more than simply "a serious issue to be tried"?

On the other hand, the professional seeking the interim relief is always going to point to the potential adverse consequences to participating in possibly tainted proceedings or living with a possibly invalid suspension or striking off the rolls — damage to reputation and the economic costs of a potentially wasted proceeding or, more importantly, being unable to practise. Indeed, the latter consideration may be particularly significant to the extent that, in matters of this kind, the courts do not require public authorities, as part of resisting the award

---

21 See, however, *Smoling v. Canada (Minister of Health and Welfare)* (1992), 8 Admin. L.R. (2d) 285 (F.C. T.D.).

of interim relief, to ever give an undertaking to pay the costs of a subsequently quashed proceeding or the harm suffered by the operation of an order. There may also be further questions raised in some cases as to whether or not professional disciplinary proceedings might prejudice the professional's defence in any parallel criminal proceedings and whether this is a factor the courts should take into account.[22]

When one couples to these considerations the high degree of fact sensitivity in such cases and the absence of a significant body of Court of Appeal jurisprudence, it is, therefore, no wonder that it is extremely difficult to generalize in the domain of pure administrative law cases of the exemption variety as to how the balance of public interest and the protection of the interests of the individual is going to be assessed by the courts in particular situations. Nonetheless, it should be recognized that there are sometimes ways of finessing the problem. One such way is suggested by the provision in Ontario's *Judicial Review Procedure Act* to the effect that, in cases of urgency, an application for judicial review may be brought on before a single judge.[23] More generally, the more quickly applications for judicial review can be heard, either the less need there will be on many occasions for interim relief or the less harmful to the public and other relevant interests will be the award of that relief. Flexibility in the managing of court lists and compelling parties to be ready for an early hearing of the principal application can solve a lot of problems.

5) Interlocutory Relief in Aid of the Administrative Process

Until quite recently, the conventional wisdom supported by respectable authority[24] was that a court could only grant interlocutory or interim injunctions in support of final relief already being sought or about to be sought in that court. However, Canadian courts began to re-evaluate that position in the wake of House of Lords' recognition[25] that interim relief was available even where the court did not have

---

22   See the apparently conflicting judgments of *Williams* v. *Nova Scotia (Superintendent of Insurance)* (1993), 125 N.S.R. (2d) 323 (S.C. T.D.) and *Canada (Minister of Employment and Immigration)* v. *Lundgren* (1992), 13 Admin.L.R. (2d) 305 (F.C.T.D.).

23   R.S.O. 1990, c. J.1, s. 6(2).

24   See, for example, *Lamont* v. *Air Canada* (1981), 126 D.L.R. (3d) 266 (Ont. H.C.).

25   *Channel Tunnel Group Ltd.* v. *Balfour Beatty Construction Ltd.*, [1993] 2 W.L.R. 262 (H.L. Eng.).

jurisdiction over the principal proceedings. This re-evaluation received the endorsement of the Supreme Court of Canada in 1996 in *B.M.W.E.* v. *Canadian Pacific Ltd.*[26]

This case involved an application by the union for an interlocutory injunction preventing the employer implementing amendments to a work schedule pending the outcome of an arbitration in which those changes were being grieved by the union. The *Canada Labour Code* under which the relevant collective agreement existed made no provision for any such relief[27] nor did the collective agreement itself. In accepting that the British Columbia Supreme Court had jurisdiction to entertain the application for interim relief, the Supreme Court in effect rejected the argument that the *Code* and the agreement represented an exclusive code. Rather, it accepted the existence of a residual jurisdiction to fill such gaps in the scheme otherwise governing the relationship between the parties to the collective agreement; to supplement where "no adequate alternative remedy exists" under that scheme. The basis for this jurisdiction was asserted to be, in general, the inherent jurisdiction of provincial superior courts and, more specifically, the provision in the British Columbia *Law and Equity Act*,[28] which conferred jurisdiction on the British Columbia Supreme Court to grant an injunction "in all cases in which it appears to the court to be just and convenient that the order should be made." In this context, the Supreme Court made it clear that it mattered not that there was no underlying cause of action already proceeding in the British Columbia superior court. That court could act to fill gaps in other remedial regimes.

Affirmation and indeed extension of this principle came with *Canada (Canadian Human Rights Commission)* v. *Canadian Liberty Net.*[29] This case involved an application by the Commission to the Federal Court, Trial Division, for an interim injunction preventing Liberty Net from operating a telephone message line until such time as a tribunal appointed under the *Canadian Human Rights Act* could determine whether the activities of Liberty Net violated the *Act*. Despite the fact that the Supreme Court of Canada could find no explicit or implied warrant in the terms of the *Canadian Human Rights Act* itself for the commission seeking such an injunction, it was prepared to ground the availability of such relief in the principles enunciated in *B.M.W.E.* and

---

26   [1996] 2 S.C.R. 495.
27   *cf.* section 16.1 of the Ontario *Statutory Powers Procedure Act*.
28   R.S.B.C. 1979, c. 224, s. 36.
29   [1998] 1 S.C.R. 626.

section 44 of the *Federal Court Act*,[30] a provision virtually identical to the provision on which jurisdiction was based in *B.M.W.E.*.

There are two salient features of this decision. First, as the Federal Court of Canada is a purely statutory court, unlike the provincial superior courts, it has no inherent jurisdiction. As a consequence, inherent jurisdiction alone could not have provided a basis for jurisdiction in this instance; it depended necessarily on the scope of section 44 or some other provision in the *Federal Court Act*.[31] Second, the injunction being sought was of a rather different nature than the one that was granted in *B.M.W.E.* In the earlier case, the injunction was of a conserving nature; the *status quo ante* was being preserved pending a determination of whether the change in working conditions was permissible. Here, an enforcement authority was asking for an injunction against conduct, the legality of which had still to be determined.

In fact, the Supreme Court was well aware of the intrusive nature of the injunction being sought. Nonetheless, it held that this was a matter that was irrelevant to the jurisdiction of the Federal Court to grant such relief in aid of the administrative process. Rather, the preemptive nature of this form of injunction was a discretionary consideration to be taken into account in determining whether an injunction should in fact be granted.[32] For these purposes, the Court did suggest, because "pure speech" as opposed to commercial speech was in issue, that one of the components of the normal test for the availability of interlocutory and interim injunctions would have to be modified. The commission would have to do more than show that there was a serious issue to be tried by the tribunal on the merits; rather, it had to demonstrate a much greater likelihood of success before the tribunal of its contention that the conduct of Canadian Liberty Net amounted to a violation of the *Canadian Human Rights Act*.

The importance of these two judgments lies in the fact that they enable re-enforcement of regulatory regimes in the regular courts even when the legislation creating those regulatory regimes makes no express provision for such remedies and interim injunctions in particu-

---

30   R.S.C. 1985, c. F-7.
31   However, the Supreme Court did make it clear that, despite the fact that a federal regime was in issue, a provincial superior court could also have granted relief in this instance.
32   Indeed, similarly, in *B.M.W.E.*, the Court held that arguments based on management rights and the principle in collective agreement and arbitration law of "obey now; grieve later" were matters that went not to jurisdiction but to the merits of the application for an interim injunction.

lar. Adoption of the principle that superior courts may provide such relief on a free-standing basis and without an underlying cause of action in that court opened that door. However, it is important to underline that whether the relief will actually be available in any situation still depends on an evaluation of the particular statutory regime in support of which the claim arises. Interim relief will not be available if, on an assessment of that statutory regime, a court concludes that the regime was indeed intended to be an exclusive code and preclude the availability of any other form of relief.

However, given the fact that the two Supreme Court cases arose in the contexts of collective agreement arbitration and human rights adjudication respectively, it seems unlikely that, without an express legislative prohibition in the relevant legislation, there will be all that many situations in which the courts will hold that this form of relief is unavailable as a matter of principle. After all, the regimes of collective agreement arbitration and human rights adjudication have generally been regarded as being as self-contained as any that exist under Canadian regulatory legislation. What, of course, may be far more likely is that courts will deny an application for an interim injunction on the basis of the standard tests governing the availability of such relief.

Thus, for example, a judgment such as that of the Ontario Divisional Court in *Stevenson* v. *Air Canada*[33] may still be good law. There, the court denied interlocutory relief preserving the employment status of airline pilots who had reached the retirement age specified in the collective agreement. They were seeking such relief pending the determination by the Canadian Human Rights Commission of a complaint against the mandatory retirement regime. The court denied relief primarily on the basis of a consideration of the balance of convenience as between the interests of the pilots in preserving the continuity of their employment and those of Air Canada and its reliance on a regime that had been adopted in the collective agreement. The court also had a perception that this was not a particularly strong case on the merits.

J. THE CONSEQUENCES OF A SUCCESSFUL APPLICATION FOR JUDICIAL REVIEW

When the court quashes a decision or makes a declaration that a decision or action is a nullity, the normal assumption is that the effect of this is to restore the situation to the point before the challenged decision or action

---

33   (1981), 132 D.L.R. (3d) 406 (Ont. Div. Ct.), rev'g 126 D.L.R. (3d) 242 (Ont. H.C.).

was taken. Thus, in the case of the wrongful removal of a licence, the licence is in effect restored unless, of course, it would have expired in the period between the wrongful removal and the successful application for judicial review. Indeed, if the reviewing court does not want the granting of judicial review to have that effect, it may have to make an order granting the application for judicial review on terms or subject to conditions.[34]

One domain where the issue of the effect of a quashing order or a declaration of nullity has caused particular problems is that of office holders who have been deprived of their office in breach of the rules of natural justice or otherwise unlawfully. As we have seen already in Chapter 1, in such cases, difficulties may arise not just because the successful applicant's term of office has since expired but, even more problematically, in situations where a successor has been appointed.[35] Thus, while the court might declare the applicant's dismissal to have been unlawful, there will be a reluctance to follow through with all of the logical consequences of branding a decision a nullity or *ultra vires* and, in particular, requiring the successor to vacate his or her office in favour of the "true" holder of that office. Indeed, even if reinstatement is possible theoretically because there has been no successor appointed, questions may still arise as to whether the court has any overriding discretion to deny that form of relief because, for example, of some of the same considerations that lead courts to deny specific performance of contracts under private employment law — a reluctance to force the continuation of a working relationship characterized by incompatibility.

It is therefore becoming increasingly important to identify precisely what are the parameters of financial relief at private or common law in such cases. The authorities seem clear that normally the person who has lost office is entitled to all of the emoluments of that office that would have been earned in the meantime whether reinstated or not. Indeed, at first instance, in *Hewat v. Ontario*[36] *and Dewar v. Ontario*,[37] the Ontario Divisional Court held that the wrongfully dismissed vice-chairs of the Labour Relations Board and members of the Ottawa-Carleton Police

---

34   See, for example, *Sparvier v. Cowessess Indian Band No. 73* (1993), 13 Admin. L.R. (2d) 266 (F.C.T.D.), the details of which are discussed in chapter 20, "Limits of Review — (iii) Remedies — Refusal on Discretionary Grounds."

35   See, for example, *Brown v. Waterloo Regional Board of Commissioners of Police* (1983), 150 D.L.R. (3d) 729 (Ont. C.A.), where a new chief of police was well ensconced by the time of the ultimate disposition of his predecessor's application for judicial review.

36   (1997), 32 O.R. (3d) 622 (Div. Ct.).

37   (1996), 30 O.R. (3d) 334 (Div. Ct.).

Services Board were entitled to those emoluments for any as yet unex-pired term of their office, despite the fact that they would not render any services that would normally be a condition of entitlement to pay-ment. Whether the Court of Appeal's leaving the consequences of its order to be sorted out between the parties indicates some unease with such a solution is, however, a matter of speculation.[38]

Aside, of course, from the concern about dismissed personnel not being entitled to pay for which they have not worked, there might be reason for hesitancy on the part of the courts because of a concern with whether common law principles of mitigation have any application in this domain. Interestingly, in subsequent proceedings in the famous case of *Nicholson*,[39] Nicholson was held entitled to his salary up until the point at which he should have submitted to a reconsideration of the allegations against him; however, the Court did make a deduction for moneys earned elsewhere in the meantime.[40] The same occurred in the Supreme Court of Canada judgment in *Emms* v. *R.*[41] Whether this is simply an accounting for actual mitigation rather than an acceptance that there was in fact a need to take mitigating opportunities is quite unclear. However, to the extent that there remains a tendency on the part of the courts to be more liberal in finding that someone is an office holder rather than a statutory employee to enable procedural unfair-ness arguments to be made,[42] it can be expected that, at the remedies end of the litigation, the courts may be more willing to apply ordinary contractual principles to those who seek judicial review and have no real prospect of reinstatement to their office. A failure to mitigate may be held against them, particularly in situations where the appointment to the office is not time limited.

This may be particularly so in cases where a person dismissed from a public office or position chooses not to seek reinstatement or a public law declaration of invalidity but rather simply relies on her or his con-tractual rights. In such instances, as exemplified by *Cohnstaedt* v. *Uni-versity of Regina*,[43] the normal principles of damages for wrongful

38 See (1998), 37 O.R. (3d) 161 (C.A.) and (1998), 37 O.R. (3d) 170 (C.A.), respectively.
39 *Nicholson* v. *Haldimand-Norfolk Regional Board of Commissioners of Police*, [1979] 1 S.C.R. 311.
40 (1980), 117 D.L.R. (3d) 604 (Ont. Div. Ct. and C.A.).
41 [1979] 2 S.C.R. 1148.
42 See, for example, *Board of Education of Indian Head School Division No.19 of Saskatchewan* v. *Knight*, [1990] 1 S.C.R. 653.
43 [1995] 3 S.C.R. 451, aff'g the dissenting judgment of Sherstobitoff J.A.: (1994), 113 D.L.R. (4th) 178 (Sask. C.A.).

dismissal will apply. More particularly in that instance in which the plaintiff was a tenured university professor, the damages amounted to the amount of salary and benefits until the age of retirement with a deduction to reflect the obligation to mitigate.

Subsequently, this position has been re-enforced by the judgment of the Court in *Wells* v. *Newfoundland.*[44] In terms of computing the damages to which Wells was entitled when his term of office came to an end because of the statutory abolition of the board on which he served, the Court held that the Newfoundland Court of Appeal had been correct in making deductions for mitigation and all the usual contingencies. In other words, Wells did not have any automatic claim to all the benefits that would have flowed to him between the date of his dismissal and his reaching the age of seventy, some fifteen years hence.

FURTHER READINGS

CHRISTIE I.M., AND D.J. MULLAN, "Canadian Academic Tenure and Employment: An Uncertain Future?" (1982), 7 Dalhousie L.J. 72

FLOOD, C., "*Hewat* v. *Ontario*" (1998), 6 C.L.E.L.J. 263

---

44   [1999] 3 S.C.R. 199.

CHAPTER 17

STATUTORY REFORM

A. *THE FEDERAL COURT ACT*

1) Introduction

Where the exercise of a federal statutory or prerogative power is in issue, the principal forum for judicial review is the Federal Court of Canada. This is a statutory court that was created in 1970[1] and became operational in 1971 by virtue of the powers conferred on the Parliament of Canada by section 101 of the *Constitution Act, 1867* to establish additional courts for the "better administration of the laws of Canada." It replaced the existing Exchequer Court, a court that possessed limited administrative law jurisdiction.

The creation of a Federal Court with virtually exclusive jurisdiction over judicial review of federal administrative action was justified by its promoters on two interconnected bases. First, it was thought that, by taking this jurisdiction away from the provincial superior courts and relocating it in a federal court, there would a greater assurance of the development of an appropriate level of judicial expertise with respect to the federal administrative process. Second, with ten superior courts across the country all having the potential to exercise judicial review jurisdiction over federal statutory authorities, there was

---

1   By virtue of the *Federal Court Act*, S.C. 1970–71-72, c. 1.

a growing concern about the likelihood of inconsistent decisions or rulings in an era when judicial review applications in the federal arena were becoming that much more common.

2) Reach of Jurisdiction

By virtue of the *Federal Court Act*,[2] review authority over a "federal board, commission or other tribunal" is vested primarily in the Federal Court with section 2(1) of the Act defining "federal board, commission or other tribunal" expansively as

> any body or person or persons having, exercising or purporting to exercise jurisdiction or powers conferred by or under an Act of Parliament or by or under an order made pursuant to the prerogative of the Crown, other than any such person or persons appointed under or in accordance with the laws of a province or under section 96 of the *Constitution Act, 1867*.

In other words, the term "federal board, commission or other tribunal" does not have its narrow colloquial sense but extends to all federal statutory authorities exercising powers under federal law whether that law be primary legislation, subordinate legislation, or orders made under a regime established by the royal prerogative. The only ostensible exceptions are the powers exercised under federal statute by superior court judges and situations where federal power is exercised by provincially appointed officials. However, the mere fact of incorporation under federal legislation (whether public or private) does not bring the entity in question within the Federal Court's review jurisdiction[3]; only to the extent that such bodies are given explicit jurisdiction to exercise authority over others will jurisdiction exist.[4]

While the impression created by the wording of the *Act* is that of a legislative attempt or intention to confine all challenges to federal statutory and prerogative authorities to the Federal Court, there are some very significant exceptions to that exclusivity regime.

The exclusivity of the court's review jurisdiction may be affected by the provisions of other statutes. While this has occurred infrequently,

2   R.S.C. 1985, c. F-7 (as amended by S.C. 1990, c. 8).
3   *Canada (A.G.) v. Lavell*, [1974] S.C.R. 1349 at 1379 (*per* Laskin J.).
4   *Rural Dignity of Canada v. Canada Post Corporation* (1992), 7 Admin. L.R. (2d) 242 (F.C.A.).

two examples in particular merit identification. First, arbitrators exercising jurisdiction under collective agreements entered into under the *Canada Labour Code* are deemed not to be a "federal board, commission or other tribunal," meaning that their decisions will be subject to review by the appropriate provincial superior court.[5] Second, under the North American Free Trade Agreement, binational panels are established a substitute for judicial review in the Federal Court of decisions of the Canadian International Trade Tribunal in matters involving Canada and its NAFTA partners, the United States and Mexico.[6]

The fact that the *Act* does not (save in the limited case of members of the Canadian forces serving out of the country) confer any *habeas corpus* jurisdiction on the Federal Court also means that jurisdiction over that historically significant prerogative remedy remains the preserve of the provincial superior courts in cases where detentions by federal statutory authorities are in question. Indeed, as seen above,the Supreme Court has held that, for the purposes of such proceedings, *certiorari* sought in aid of *habeas corpus* is not the same form of *certiorari* over federal statutory authorities which section 18 has removed from provincial superior court jurisdiction.[7]

More recently, in the context of deportation proceedings where the interests of the deportee's children are involved, attempts have been made to attack the deportation order collaterally in the provincial superior courts by invoking the *parens patriae* jurisdiction of those courts.[8] However, those efforts have been rebuffed by at least two provincial Courts of Appeal, the British Columbia Court of Appeal[9] and, more recently, the Ontario Court of Appeal.[10] However, these courts dealt with the issue in somewhat different terms. The British Columbia Court of Appeal held that the exclusivity provisions of the *Federal Court Act* meant that there was no basis for the invocation of the *parens patriae* jurisdiction of the

---

5   R.S.C. 1985, c. L-2, s. 58(3).

6   As implemented by the *Special Import Measures Act*, R.S.C. 1985 (as amended).

7   *R. v. Miller*, [1985] 2 S.C.R. 613.

8   In another context entirely, the Supreme Court suggested in *Canada (Canadian Human Rights Commission)* v. *Canadian Liberty Net*, [1998] 1 S.C.R. 626, that the provincial superior courts could also provide interlocutory relief in aid of federal administrative tribunals and statutory authorities.

9   *Torres-Samuels* v. *Canada (Minister of Citizenship and Immigration)* (1998), 166 D.L.R. (4th) 611 (B.C.C.A.).

10 *Francis (Litigation guardian of)* v. *Canada (Minister of Citizenship and Immigration)*, (1999), 179 D.L.R. (4th) 421 (Ont. C.A.). [*Francis*].

provincial superior courts as a way of challenging the deportation order.[11] In contrast, the Ontario Court of Appeal dealt with it as a matter of discretion by reference to *Baker* v. *Canada (Minister of Citizenship & Immigration).*[12] Since *Baker* established that the immigration authorities were obliged to take account of the best interests of the children of deportees in determining whether to allow deportees to remain in Canada on humanitarian and compassionate grounds, failure to do so gave rise to a basis for seeking a remedy under the *Federal Court Act.* Given the availability of an adequate basis for protecting the interests of children within the regime of relief available in the Federal Court, the Ontario courts should in general refrain from exercising their *parens patriae* jurisdiction in such cases. It remains to be seen which of these positions prevails ultimately.

More fundamentally, the Supreme Court has also held that, to the extent that the *Federal Court Act* confers jurisdiction on the court to deal with constitutional challenges to not only legislation but also decisions and orders made under federal legislation, that jurisdiction is shared with the provincial superior courts. By virtue of sections 96 to 100 of the *Constitution Act, 1867,* the traditional jurisdiction of the provincial superior courts to deal with issues of constitutional law is itself constitutionally sacrosanct.[13] This principle was established in division of powers cases and, after some conflict of authority, it now seems clear that it also applies to *Charter* challenges to federal legislation.[14] Doubts do however persist in the case of *Charter* challenges to decisions and orders made by federal statutory and prerogative authorities. In particular, there are questions as to whether the provincial superior courts possess jurisdiction where the basis for the *Charter* challenge is not the legislation on which the order under challenge is based[15] but

---

11 In doing so, the Court distinguished *R.* v. *Miller,* above note 7 and the provincial superior courts' continuing jurisdiction over *habeas corpus* in aid of *certiorari* with respect to detentions by federal authorities. It did, however, also refer to the first instance judgment in this case, where the matter had been dealt with as a matter of judicial discretion, not jurisdiction: (1998), 42 Imm. L.R. 290 (B.C.S.C.).

12 [1999] 2 S.C.R. 817 [*Baker*].

13 *Attorney General of Canada* v. *Law Society of British Columbia,* [1982] 2 S.C.R. 307 [a.k.a. *Jabour*]; *Paul L' Anglais Inc.* v. *Canada (Conseil canadien des relations de travail),* [1983] 1 S.C.R. 147.

14 *Reza* v. *Canada,* [1994] 2 S.C.R. 394 [*Reza*]. See also the judgment of Sopinka J. in *Kourtessis* v. *Minister of National Revenue,* [1993] 2 S.C.R. 53 at 113-14.

15 See, for example, *International Fund for Animal Welfare Inc.* v. *Canada* (1998), 157 D.L.R. (4th) 561 (Ont. Gen. Div.), where the Court asserts jurisdiction where the challenge to a decision is based on the invalidity of the legislation underlying that decision and, in so doing, distinguishes the cases where provincial superior courts declined jurisdiction where the challenge was to *Charter* violations by those making the impugned order.

violations of the *Charter* by the authority making that order. Here, the current weight of authority is to the effect that such cases are within the exclusive authority of the Federal Court.[16] Moreover, the residual jurisdiction of the provincial superior courts almost certainly does not extend as far as situations where federal subordinate legislation is being challenged not on *Constitution Act, 1867* or *Charter* grounds but rather on the basis that it is *ultra vires* the scope of the empowering statute.[17] To go that far would come perilously close to establishing the Federal Court had no exclusive jurisdiction in administrative law matters.[18]

It should also be noted that the mere fact that the provincial superior courts have this constitutionally guaranteed jurisdiction does not mean that they will necessarily exercise it. The Supreme Court has confirmed that, at least in some instances, the provincial superior courts may defer to the jurisdiction of the Federal Court.[19] I will return in the section on judicial discretion to an account of the types of case and the grounds on which this discretion to decline jurisdiction has been exercised.

Additionally, there may exist certain kinds of constitutional challenge where the provincial superior court will have to take jurisdiction because the Federal Court lacks the authority to deal with the issue at least in the context in which it is being raised. More specifically, there remain doubts as to whether the Federal Court has any jurisdiction to issue a bare declaration that federal legislation is unconstitutional.[20] However, this is without threat to the Federal Court's jurisdiction to deal with constitutional (including *Charter* challenges) in the context of an application for judicial review of a particular decision or order.[21]

Another pocket of provincial superior court or indeed provincially created court review of federal statutory authorities also exists in the domain of damages claims against the Crown in right of Canada. Since 1992, jurisdiction over this kind of claim has been shared between the Federal Court and the provincial superior courts or, depending on the amount at stake, the provincial courts. To the extent that such an action depends on establishing the invalidity or unlawfulness of an action or decision taken under federal statutory or prerogative author-

---

16   *Mousseau v. Canada (A.G.)* (1994), 107 D.L.R. (4th) 727 (N.S.C.A.), appl'd in *Nolan v. Canada (A.G.)* (1998), 155 D.L.R (4th) 728 (Ont. Div. Ct.)

17   *Saskatchewan Wheat Pool v. Canada (A.G.)* (1993), 17 Admin. L.R. (2d) 236 (Sask. C.A.).

18   This is issue is elaborated in greater detail later in this chapter.

19   *Reza*, above note 14. *Reza* was applied in *Francis*, above note 10.

20   See *Jabour*, above note 13 at 322–26 and the judgment of Foisy J.A. in *Pearson v. Canada (Canadian Radio-television Telecommunications Commission)* (1997), 48 Admin. L.R. (2d) 257 (Alta. C.A.) at 263–64.

21   *Native Women's Association of Canada v. Canada*, [1994] 3 S.C.R. 627.

ity, the provincial superior or created court engaged in hearing the case will be reviewing in territory normally reserved to the Federal Court. Indeed, the same will be true in the now very limited domain of collateral attack in situations where federal statutory authorities are using the provincial superior or created courts for the enforcement of orders made under federal statutes.

3) Allocation of Review Jurisdiction Between the Trial Division and the Court of Appeal

Within the *Federal Court Act*, the key sections are sections 18, 18.1, and 28. They not only establish the procedure for seeking judicial review but also allocate original jurisdiction in judicial review matters between the Court's Trial and Appeal Divisions. Under section 18, the Trial Division is given exclusive original jurisdiction to grant relief in the nature of the historic prerogative writs (with the exception of *habeas corpus*)[22] and their equitable supplements, the declaration and the injunction. Section 18(3) then goes on to provide that the various species of relief are available by way of an application for judicial review. Later, in section 28, there is a derogation from the seemingly exclusive jurisdiction conferred on the Trial Division by section 18. It provides that, in the case of fifteen listed tribunals, all applications for judicial review will be made in the first instance to the Federal Court of Appeal. The tribunals listed include many of the most prominent in the federal system of administrative justice.[23] However, that is not always the case. Significant omissions are the Immigration and Refugee Board

---

22   In s. 18(2), there is a specific conferral of jurisdiction to award relief in the nature of *habeas corpus*. However, it is restricted to members of the Canadian forces serving abroad.

23   The list is as follows: the Board of Arbitration established by the *Canadian Agricultural Products Act*; the Review Tribunal established under the same *Act*; the Canadian Radio-Television and Telecommunications Commission ("the CRTC"); the Pensions Appeal Board; the Canadian International Trade Tribunal ("the CITT"); the National Energy Board ("the NEB"); the Canada Industrial Relations Board ("the CIRB"); the Public Service Staff Relations Board ("the PSSRB"); the Copyright Board; the Canadian Transportation Agency ("the CTA"); the Tax Court of Canada; umpires appointed under the *Employment Insurance Act*; the Competition Tribunal; assessors appointed under the *Canada Deposit Insurance Act*; the Canadian Artists and Producers Professional Relations Tribunal.

and the Canadian Human Rights Tribunal.[24] All judicial review applications involving these two tribunals as well as the Canadian Human Rights Commission must be commenced by way of an application for judicial review in the Federal Court, Trial Division.

Two explanations are usually given for the allocation of original jurisdiction over the listed tribunals to the Federal Court of Appeal: first, it is more seemly that such important and often multimember bodies be reviewed at first instance by a three-judge Court of Appeal than by a single Trial Division and, second, their proceedings potentially will be subject to less delay under a regime in which there is only one further possible level of appeal, an appeal to the Supreme Court of Canada and then only with leave.

4) Forms of Relief

The key feature of section 18.1 (which applies to proceedings in both the Trial Division and the Court of Appeal[25]) is its statement in subsection 4 of the various grounds of judicial review. For the most part, these grounds are couched in the familiar language of the common law (jurisdiction, natural justice, procedural fairness, and so on). However, there are some variants. Error of law review is available irrespective of whether it appears on the face of the record.[26] There follows a statutory specification of error of fact review: "based its decision or order on an erroneous finding of fact that it made in a perverse or capricious manner or without regard to the material before it." Action or inaction on the basis of "fraud or perjured evidence" is then listed and, finally, there is a general catchall category: "acted in any other way that was contrary to law."

Given that the Supreme Court of Canada has made a number of its pronouncements as to varying standards of review over errors of law and fact in the context of cases coming up to it from judicial review

---

24 The explanations for the choices that were made are not on the surface all that ready to discern. However, there is certainly a sense abroad that those choices were not necessarily all principled ones. Rather, lobbying and politics played a role. However, in the case of the Immigration and Refugee Board, it was almost certainly excluded for reasons of more efficient judicial administration: to remove a high volume area of first instance judicial review jurisdiction from the Federal Court of Appeal (where it was located on the basis of the formerly applicable statutory formula) and relocate it in the Trial Division.

25 S. 28(2).

26 S. 18.1(4)(c).

proceedings under the *Federal Court Act*,[27] it is highly unlikely that at this stage an argument would be countenanced to the effect that the provisions of the *Act* mandate correctness review in all cases of alleged error of law. Rather, the essential thrust of the provision is to open up the *possibility* of error of law review in one of its three manifestations (incorrectness, unreasonableness, and patent unreasonableness) whether or not that alleged error is manifest from the decision maker's record. Similarly, there have been few indications that the Federal Court is willing to treat the statutory form of review of questions of fact as extending or significantly modifying the restricted opportunities that exist for such review at common law. More particularly, insofar as such review is available at common law only in the case of "patently unreasonable" determinations of fact, it is relatively easy to treat the language of the relevant provision as but one example of such an error.

While the current *Act* does not mention privative clauses and their impact on the judicial review capacities of the court, it is worthy of note that the original 1970 version of section 28 applied notwithstanding the provisions of any other Act. This meant that the Federal Court of Appeal could intervene on any of the grounds specified irrespective of the existence of privative clauses in at least prior legislation. That clause did not survive the 1990 amendments to the legislation and it must now be assumed that privative clauses as well as other provisions (such as leave requirements) in particular legislation may affect the scope of scrutiny of administrative action in both the Trial Division and the Court of Appeal.

The *Act* also contains provisions for interim relief[28] and the reference of matters of law, jurisdiction, practice, and procedure to the court by a "federal board, commission or other tribunal."[29] As well, the *Act* establishes the primacy of various statutory forms of appeal over judicial review. Thus, in section 18.5, it is provided that the judicial review jurisdiction of the court is precluded to the extent that there is a right of appeal not only to the court itself but also to the Supreme Court of Canada, the Court Martial Appeal Court, the Tax Court of Canada, the governor in council, and the Treasury Board. However, it is important to note that, if the appeal provided does not cover the whole range of the grounds of review established in section 18.1(4),

---

27   See, for example, *National Corn Growers Association* v. *Canada (Import Tribunal)*, [1990] 2 S.C.R. 1324; *Pushpanathan* v. *Canada (Minister of Citizenship and Immigration)*, [1998] 1 S.C.R. 982, amended [1998] 1 S.C.R. 1222; *Baker*, above note 12.

28   S. 18.2.

29   S 18.3.

the review jurisdiction of the court is unaffected as far as those particular grounds are concerned.

One deficiency in the remedial powers created under section 18.1 and the statutory form of judicial review application is the absence of any explicit authority to award damages in conjunction with relief under that section. This probably means that any attempt to secure damages in connection with the exercise of federal statutory power will have to be by way of action under section 17 of the *Act*. In this context, it remains doubtful whether there can be an amalgamation of section 17 and section 18.1 claims.

B. JUDICIAL REVIEW PROCEDURE ACTS

1) Introduction

The first significant remedial reform in Canada took place in Québec in 1965.[30] This was relatively modest and involved primarily the combination of relief in the nature of *certiorari* and prohibition into a single remedy, evocation. However, it was the Ontario *Judicial Review Procedure Act* of 1971[31] that was to provide the lead in comprehensive remedial reform over the next twenty-five years. It was followed by a virtually identical statute in British Columbia[32] and had influence in varying degrees on subsequent changes to the remedial schemes in the public law domain in Alberta, New Brunswick, Prince Edward Island, and Saskatchewan. Indeed, the model was also exported to New Zealand and, eventually, with the 1990 reforms to the *Federal Court Act*,[33] its success was reflected in the extension of the single application for judicial review from the Federal Court of Appeal to the Trial Division.

2) The 1971 *Ontario Judicial Review Procedure Act*

The basis of the Ontario *Act* was simple. It introduced a single application for judicial review that consolidated all the former public law remedies available in the province with the exception of *habeas corpus* and

---

30 See *Code of Civil Procedure*, R.S.Q. 1977, c. C.25, art. 846.
31 S.O. 1971, c. 48 (now R.S.O. 1990, c. J.1).
32 Now R.S.B.C. 1996, c. 241.
33 *Federal Court Act*, R.S.C. 1985, c. F-7 (as amended by S.C. 1990, c. 8), section 18.1.

quo warranto.[34] On the coming into force of the *Act*, a challenge to allegedly unlawful administrative action could be commenced by this application for judicial review, and the court could take jurisdiction provided the grounds on which the review application was based and the relief that was sought came within the range of what was previously available by way of relief in the nature of *certiorari*, prohibition, and *mandamus* as well as an action for a declaration or an injunction.[35]

One of the features of the *Act* was the room that it created for the use of a simplified application procedure not only in the old prerogative remedy territory but also in the case of declaratory and injunctive relief. Indeed, the *Act* made it clear that relief in the nature of *certiorari*, prohibition, and *mandamus* was no longer available outside of the *Act*; it had to be sought henceforth by way of an application for judicial review.[36]

In the case of declaratory and injunctive relief, the situation was somewhat different. In order to prevent the use of an application for judicial review in the private law domain, the reach of the *Act* in relation to declaratory and injunctive relief was restricted to exercises of "statutory power" as defined in the *Act*. The *Act* also left open the possibility of such relief being sought outside the *Act* even when exercises of a statutory power were involved. There were primarily two reasons for this. First, on occasion, even in public law matters, there are advantages to having issues resolved by way of trial or action rather than largely on the basis of affidavit evidence in the context of a simple application procedure. Second, the *Act* made no provision for the combination of a claim for damages or other forms of monetary relief with the new application for judicial review. Damages still had to be sought outside of the *Act* and, most commonly, by way of action. As a consequence, the continued availability of declaratory and injunctive relief outside the *Act* allowed for the combination in appropriate cases of those remedies in their public law guise with a claim for various monetary forms of relief. It is, however, noteworthy, that the choice of whether to seek declaratory or injunctive relief by way of action was not given over to the absolute control of the party seeking judicial review. Any other party could apply to the court for the matter to be converted into an application for judicial review.[37] Conversely, it also

---

34   In the case of *habeas corpus*, including *certiorari* in aid of *habeas corpus*, section 11(2) preserved the existing regimes for the seeking of such relief. In contrast, the *Act* was silent as to *quo warranto*.

35   S. 2(1).

36   S. 7.

37   S. 8.

remained within the capacity of the court to deny an application for judicial review on the basis that the matters in issue would be adjudicated more appropriately within the context of an action for declaratory and injunctive relief.[38]

As well as establishing a single application for judicial review occupying the field of most of the former remedies of judicial review, the *Act* also included other provisions that had as their objective the removal of formal or technical impediments to the court cutting to the merits of any application for judicial review and dealing appropriately with situations where there were grounds for intervention. Thus, if an application was launched for one of the old forms of relief, the court was directed to treat it as an application for judicial review.[39] Conversely, as long as the application set out in sufficient detail the grounds on which relief was being sought and the nature of that relief, it was no impediment to the court taking the case and granting a remedy that the applicant did not specify how this application came within the scope of the previous system of remedies.[40] Out of an abundance of caution probably, the *Act* also made it clear that in situations where previously the court was confined to issuing declaratory relief, it now possessed a discretion to make an order quashing or setting aside the decision.[41]

Other provisions of the *Act* also had as their objective the removal of obstacles to and technical limitations on the availability of judicial review. Thus, there was express provision for the granting of interim relief, a recourse not previously available in support of applications for relief in the nature of the prerogative writs.[42] The *Act* provided for relief against the operation of time limits in other statutes provided that this would not cause "substantial prejudice or hardship" to anyone affected

---

38   See, for example, *Seaway Trust Co. v. Ontario* (1983), 41 O.R. (2d) 532 (C.A.).
     While it might be read as standing for a broader exclusion of the operation of the
     Act, see *Falkiner v. Ontario (Minister of Community and Social Services)* (1996),
     44 Admin. L.R. (2d) 256 (Ont. Div. Ct.) holding that it was appropriate to bring
     proceedings for a declaration outside the *Act* when the purpose of those
     proceedings was to establish that subordinate legislation was invalid by reference
     to the *Charter*. See also *Re Service Employees International Union and Broadway
     Manor* (1984), 48 O.R. (2d) 225 (C.A.) at 233, to the effect that bare declarations
     of unconstitutionality are not available under the *Act*; there must be at least a
     matter pending which provides a focus for the application for judicial review in
     order to satisfy the requirement of a "statutory power."
39   S. 7.
40   S. 9(1).
41   S. 2(4).
42   S. 4.

by the delay.[43] Section 10 obliged the decision maker under attack on being served with an application for judicial review to file the record of the proceedings leading to the decision under review. For statutory authorities coming within the ambit of the *Statutory Powers Procedure Act*,[44] essentially tribunals acting in a judicial manner, the extent of that obligation was given clear definition by an expanded list of materials that constituted the record, including the reasons, if any.[45] That *Act* also mandated the decision maker to provide written reasons on request.[46]

In two respects, the *Judicial Review Procedure Act* also actually dealt with the substantive scope of judicial review and probably expanded it from its common law reach. Subject to the effect of privative clauses, judicial review for error of law on the face of the record was "extended" beyond its traditional common law ambit of bodies that acted judicially or *quasi*-judicially to the apparently broader category of all those who were engaged in the exercise of a "statutory power of decision."[47] This term was defined expansively in the *Act* to include all decision makers that decided or prescribed

(a) the legal rights, powers, privileges, immunities, duties or liabilities of any person or party, or

(b) the eligibility of any person or party to receive, or to the continuation of, a benefit or licence, whether that person is legally entitled thereto or not.[48]

Similarly, the *Act* dealt with review for an absence of evidence for bodies exercising a statutory power of decision and that were required by any statute or the common law to base their decisions "exclusively on evidence admissible before [them] or on facts of which [they] may take judicial notice."[49] However, the formulation of the criteria for this species of review was one that did not appear to go further than most conceptions of what up until that time had been permissible under common law "no evidence" review. Only where there was "no such evidence" or "no such facts to support findings of fact" was review available. Indeed, subsequent jurisprudence pretty much confirmed

---

43   S. 5.
44   Now R.S.O. 1990, c. S. 22 (as amended by S.O. 1994, c. 27 and S.O. 1997, c. 23).
45   *S.P.P.A.*, s. 20.
46   *S.P.P.A.*, s. 17(1).
47   *J.R.P.A.*, s. 2(2).
48   S. 1.
49   S. 2(3).

this assessment of the impact of this section.[50] It has also been the case that the "expanded" scope for review for error of law on the face of the record has had little or no impact on Ontario judicial review.

It is in fact unfair to characterize the *Act* as one that focused exclusively on improving the situation of those seeking judicial review or as one that had as its primary objective the more ready exposure of the province's administrative process to judicial scrutiny and ultimate review. Thus, the *Act* made it clear that the existing discretionary grounds for the denial of relief survived[51] and though, in its basic provision, the *Act* speaks in terms of an application for judicial review being available "despite any right of appeal,"[52] the Ontario courts have never interpreted this provision as removing the power of the reviewing court to hold that an applicant for judicial review should have exercised a right of appeal rather than seeking judicial review. The *Act* also explicitly preserves the effect of privative clauses and other forms of limitation, save prescription periods, on the availability of judicial review found in other legislation.[53] As well, the court has a discretion both to refuse judicial review and to validate a decision where the only ground made out for review is "a defect in form or a technical irregularity" provided, of course, "no substantial wrong or miscarriage of justice has occurred."[54]

The requirement that all applications for judicial review be served on the attorney general obviously was aimed at ensuring that, if the public interest needed representation in a particular case, the attorney general would have the notice necessary to enable this to happen.[55] Moreover, as discussed below, in the chapter on standing, there is at least some case law under the Ontario *Act* to the effect that section 9(2)'s statement to the effect that the decision maker may be a party to the proceedings creates a situation different from the ordinary common law position under which the decision maker under attack is very limited in the role that it may take in defending the decision under review.[56]

---

50   See *Re Keeprite Workers' Independent Union and Keeprite Products Ltd.* (1980), 114 D.L.R. (3d) 162 (Ont. C.A.).

51   S. 2(5).

52   S. 2(1).

53   S. 11(1).

54   S. 3.

55   S. 9(4).

56   See *Re Consolidated-Bathurst Packaging Ltd. and International Woodworkers of America, Local 2-69* (1985), 20 D.L.R. (4th) 84 (Ont. Div. Ct.), though *cf. Gale* v. *Miracle Food Mart* (1993), 12 Admin. L.R. (2d) 267 (Ont. Div. Ct.) at 278.

The *Act* also makes it clear that the primary location[57] for the hearing of applications for judicial review is the three-judge Divisional Court, provision for which was made in parallel legislation. In this, there seems to have been some sense that the issues raised by judicial review were of sufficient significance that they normally required the attention of three, rather than just one, superior court judge. It was also thought by some that the existence of a separate division within the then High Court was a sign of implicit legislative expectation that that division would be staffed regularly by judges with a particular interest and expertise in administrative law. Suffice it to say that, throughout the history of the *Act*, assignments to the Divisional Court have not always been based on that philosophy.

Probably the most reliable indicator of the success of any exercise in legislative reform is the extent to which it passes the test of time without the need for its parameters having to be established by resort to litigation. In contrast to the judicial review provisions of the *Federal Court Act* of 1970, Ontario's *Judicial Review Procedure Act*, after a couple of early misguided "hiccoughs" and subject to one significant exception, has necessitated neither amendment nor a significant body of litigation. In other words, it has been a success and, in particular, remedial technicalities seldom intrude in Ontario judicial review litigation so as to prevent the Divisional Court going immediately to the merits of an application for judicial review. As for the hiccoughs, they are largely of historical interest and will not be dealt with here. However, I will consider the one really problematic area with the *Act*'s reach after a brief description of the British Columbia parallel legislation. The same issues have arisen there but the thrust of the jurisprudence is somewhat different.

3) The British Columbia *Act*

British Columbia followed Ontario's lead in 1973.[58] In most respects, its *Judicial Review Procedure Act* was identical. However, there were some significant differences. The British Columbia reforms were not accompanied by the creation of a Divisional Court or the equivalent of Ontario's *Statutory Powers Procedure Act*. The former meant that in British Columbia first instance judicial review continued to be heard before a single Supreme Court judge. The latter led to the inclusion

---

57   S. 6(2) provides for a single superior judge hearing an application for judicial review under the Act where the case is "one of urgency and that the delay required for an application to the Divisional Court is likely to involve a failure of justice."

58   S.B.C. 1979, c. 209 (now R.S.B.C. 1996, c. 241).

within the *Act* of a definition of the "record" for the purposes of an application for judicial review.[59] This definition was the same as that in the Ontario *Statutory Powers Procedure Act*. However, the *Act* did not make the filing of the record mandatory; that depended on an exercise of judicial discretion and could involve a direction to file only a portion of the record. As a potential cost-saving measure, this has merit.[60]

While the British Columbia Act contains the same provision as the Ontario *Act* extending the ambit of error of law on the face of the record review, it does not have an equivalent error of fact provision. However, in four other ways, the British Columbia *Act* clarified matters left in a state of some uncertainty under the Ontario *Act*.

(a) First, there is no reference to *quo warranto* in the Ontario *Act*. The British Columbia *Act* abolishes informations in the nature of *quo warranto* and goes on to provide that judicial review under the *Act* is available to deal with challenges to the capacity of someone to act or continue to act in office.[61]

(b) Second, there is a broader definition of "statutory power" in the British Columbia *Act*, a provision that controls the availability of declaratory and injunctive relief under both the Ontario and British Columbia Acts. Under the British Columbia *Act*, a statutory power includes a power or right conferred by an enactment "to make an investigation or inquiry into a person's legal right, power, privilege, immunity, duty or liability."[62]

This filled an obvious gap in rounding out the reach of the application for judicial review in public law matters, a gap that has given rise to some difficulty under the Ontario *Act*.[63] It would, however, have also been useful had the reach of declaratory and injunctive relief in each statute been extended explicitly to exercises of prerogative as well as statutory powers.[64]

---

59   S. 1.

60   S. 17.

61   S. 18.

62   S. 1.

63   *Masters v. Ontario* (1994), 18 O.R. (3d) 551 (Div. Ct.), affirming the availability of relief in the nature of *certiorari* under the *Act* for the conduct of an investigation conducted under prerogative powers and leading to a report on the basis of which Masters was reassigned to another position. However, the court also made it clear that declaratory relief was not available under the *Act* given that the violations of Master's rights did not "relate to the exercise of a statutory power."

64   Indeed, this gap would probably have meant that the British Columbia Supreme Court would have decided *Masters*, above, differently on the issue of the availability of declaratory relief.

(c) Third, in what probably was a product of an abundance of caution, the *Act* explicitly provides for the court to refer a matter back to the decision maker with explicit directions as to how the decision maker is to reconsider the matter.[65]

(d) Finally, while the Ontario *Act* makes no reference to the Crown, section 19 of the British Columbia *Act* specifies that its version is subject to the provisions of the *Crown Proceedings Act*, thereby both implicitly making it clear that the *Act* applies to the Crown but continuing to immunize the Crown from injunctive relief.

It is also worth noting that the British Columbia courts have interpreted the provision entitling the decision maker under attack to be a party to the application for judicial review as not altering the restrictions that the common law has placed on the participatory rights of the decision maker.[66]

4) The Outer Reaches of the Two *Acts*

The most obvious purpose of these two largely parallel statutes was the simplification and amplification of the remedies for securing relief in public law matters and, in particular, in relation to the decision-making capacities of provincial statutory authorities.

In Ontario, some of the early judicial interpretations of the *Act* went against the spirit of this objective by reading the definition of "statutory power" as limiting not only the availability of declaratory and injunctive relief but also relief in the nature of *certiorari*, prohibition, and *mandamus*.[67] This created a problem particularly given that, in the Ontario *Act* as noted above, the term did not include investigative and inquisitorial functions. Moreover, it was an interpretation that was simply not warranted on the wording and structure of the relevant provision.

Subsequently, the Ontario courts repudiated this approach and no longer viewed relief in the nature of the former prerogative remedies as dependent on the presence of a "statutory power" as defined in the *Act*.[68] However, in some instances, courts went rather further in the

---

65   Ss. 5–6.

66   See, for example, *Quintette Coal Co. Ltd.* v. *British Columbia (Assessment Appeal Board)* (1984), 54 B.C.L.R. 359 (S.C.).

67   Indeed, in *Robertson* v. *Niagara South Board of Education* (1973), 41 D.L.R. (3d) 57 (Ont. Div. Ct.), the Divisional Court went as far as holding that the availability of judicial review under the Ontario *Act* was limited by the even more restricted terms of the definition of "statutory power of decision."

68   See, for example, *Bezaire* v. *Windsor Roman Catholic Separate School Board* (1992), 9 O.R. (3d) 737 (Div. Ct.).

opposite direction. The relevant provision speaks in terms of the availability by way of an application for judicial review of relief that could have been obtained previously by way of "application for an order in the nature of" one of the three named prerogative remedies. According to some judges, the use of the words "in the nature of" indicated that the legislature intended the reach of judicial review under the *Act* to extend beyond the traditional scope of judicial review of administrative action and to reach the activities of at least non-state or non-governmental bodies not previously amenable to the old prerogative remedies. This argument was based on the assertion that the kinds of remedies available to correct jurisdictional excesses and failures of procedural fairness committed by such bodies was sufficiently like the forms of relief and grounds of intervention offered by the prerogative remedies to be "in the nature of" them. As a consequence, there is Ontario case law supporting the availability of an application for judicial review against consensual arbitrators,[69] the internal membership decisions of trade unions,[70] as well as the United Church of Canada,[71] and a private school.[72]

In very marked contrast, the British Columbia courts rejected this approach holding that the regime established by the *Judicial Review Procedure Act* had the purpose to consolidate existing modes of public law relief without expansionary objectives. Moreover, there was a more credible explanation for the use of the term "in the nature of." The old prerogative writ procedures had long ago been simplified by the civil procedure rules in both jurisdictions. Orders in the nature of the old writs were substituted.[73]

In a way, of course, this issue is linked with broader questions as to the reach of public law principles and modes of relief and, in particular, whether certain "private" bodies should be treated as exercising public functions. It is also complicated by the fact that many of these

---

69 *Re Ontario Provincial Police Association and the Queen* (1974), 46 D.L.R. (3d) 518 (Ont. Div. Ct.).

70 *Re Rees and United Association of Journeymen & Apprentices of the Plumbing and Pipefitting Industry of the United States and Canada, Local 527* (1983), 150 D.L.R. (3d) 493 (Div. Ct.). However, *cf. Pestell v. Kitchener-Waterloo Real Estate Board Inc.* (1981), 34 O.R. (2d) 476 (Div. Ct.), holding that the *Act* did not apply to the disciplinary actions of a voluntary Real Estate Board.

71 *Lindenburger v. United Church of Canada* (1985), 17 C.C.E.L. 143 (Ont. Div. Ct.)

72 *D.(C.) (Litigation guardian of) v. Ridley College* (1996), 44 Admin. L.R. (2d) 108 (Ont. Gen. Div.).

73 *Mohr v. Vancouver, New Westminster and Fraser Valley District Council of Carpenters* (1988), 33 Admin. L.R. 154 (B.C.C.A.).

bodies do have a statutory basis at least to the extent that they owe their legal status to a statutory form of incorporation either under a general statute or, in the instance of the United Church of Canada, to a special Act of Parliament.[74]

Nonetheless, as a matter of statutory interpretation, the British Columbia position appears the more plausible at least in terms of the assumptions of the drafters at the time of the enactment of these two statutes. Of course, in an era of privatization, corporatization, and out-sourcing, it may be that the wider version of the *Act's* reach provides the path by which the *Act* may continue to be deployed to capture the con-tinuing public law aspects of activities formerly performed by govern-ment itself. However, if the example of the United Kingdom has any lessons in this domain,[75] there is a danger that the substantive issues raised by this at times dramatic reconfiguration of government will not be faced squarely but become disguised or distorted by technical legal debate as to the language and scope of the *Judicial Review Procedure Act.*

---

74   Indeed, this raises yet another issue as to the reach of the *Judicial Review Procedure Acts* of both jurisdictions. To what extent do they apply to the limited range of federal decision-making review of which may still take place in the provincial superior courts? Suffice it to say that to this point the general assumption of the Ontario courts has been that the *Act* does apply. Presumably, the basis for this is some sense of the capacity of provincial legislatures to enact statutes dealing with remedial consequences of unlawful administrative action even with respect to federal statutory authorities in much the same way as they have the capacity directly or indirectly to establish the rules of civil procedure for all disputes coming before the provincial superior courts irrespective of whether a federal body or matter is involved. See *Williams* v. *Kaplan* (1983), 3 Admin. L.R. 113 (Ont. Div. Ct.). I am not sure that it is quite as obvious as that. Indeed, there is British Columbia authority to the effect that applications for judicial review of the decisions of arbitrators dealing with grievances arising under collective agreements within the *Canada Labour Code,* over which the Federal Court's jurisdiction was explicitly excluded, must take place outside the *Judicial Review Procedure Act.* See, for example, *Seaspan International Ltd. (Victoria Division)* v. *Office & Technical Employees' Local Union No. 15* (1983), 1 Admin. L.R. 98 (B.C.S.C.).

75   There, issues as to the reach of substantive principles of public law have often taken place in the context of disputes as to zone of operation of Order 53, that being the Order governing the seeking of public law remedies. See *R.* v. *Panel on Take-overs and Mergers, ex parte Datafin plc,* [1987] Q.B. 815 (C.A.).

C. OTHER REMEDIAL REFORMS

Since the enactment of the *Judicial Review Procedure Acts* in Ontario and British Columbia and the earlier reforms in Québec, all of the other provinces (with the exception of Manitoba) have wrought significant changes to their scheme of public law remedies. However, they vary in their methodology. Only Prince Edward Island has enacted a *Judicial Review Act*[76] and there are doubts as to the extent that it excludes the parallel existence of the old forms of relief.[77] In the other jurisdictions, the reforms have been accomplished by changes in the rules of civil procedure. In the instances of Alberta,[78] Saskatchewan,[79] and New Brunswick,[80] these changes have involved the adoption of a single application for judicial review. However, in Nova Scotia[81] (followed by Newfoundland[82]), the old separate forms of relief have been preserved but most of the anomalies and complications resulting from the different ways of commencing proceedings for relief in the nature of the prerogative writs and those for declaratory and injunctive relief have been eliminated. Thus, for example, it is now possible to commence an application for declaratory and injunctive relief and to include within that application a prayer for relief in the nature of the prerogative writs.

As a consequence, across the country, remedial technicalities now play a far less significant role than was formerly the case. Only under the *Federal Court Act*, and even there to a lesser extent since the 1990 reforms, do remedial disputes regularly distract a court from reaching the merits of the decision under attack.

---

76 R.S.P.E.I. 1988, c. J.3.
77 See *Big John Holdings Ltd.* v. *Prince Edward Island (Island Regulatory & Appeals Commission)* (1993), 18 Admin. L.R. (2d) 307 (P.E.I.S.C. T.D.).
78 *Alberta Rules of Court*, Alta. Reg. 390/68, RR. 753.01-753.19 (all en. Alta. Reg. 457/87, s.3.
79 *Saskatchewan Queen's Bench Rules*, Rule 664(1).
80 *New Brunswick Rules of Court*, Rule 69.01. In fact, the foundation for this rule can be found in the *Judicature Act*, R.S.N.B. 1978, c. J-2, s. 36(1) [re-en. 1981, c. 36, s. 12], (2) [re- en. 1981, c. 36, s. 12; am. 1983, c. 43, s. 7(a), abolishing the prerogative writs and making reference to an application for judicial review to be provided for in the Rules of Court.
81 See *Nova Scotia Civil Procedure Rules*, Rules 5.01, 9.02, and 56.
82 *Rules of the Supreme Court, 1986.*

FURTHER READINGS

MEEHAN, E., & N. FERA, "Jurisdictional Changes in the Federal Court" (1993), 15 Advocates' Quarterly 257

MORRIS, M., & G. SINCLAIR, "The Exclusive Jurisdiction of the Federal Court of Canada over Federal Administrative Law?: Ongoing Jousting over Ousting" (1999), 12 Canadian Journal of Administrative Law and Practice 119

SGAYIAS, D, M. KINNEAR, D.J. REMIE & B.J. SAUNDERS, *Federal Court Practice 1998* (Scarborough: Carswell, 1998)

CHAPTER 18

STANDING

A. INTRODUCTION

In the vast majority of judicial review applications, no question of standing to bring the proceedings surfaces. The applicant is the sole or primary target of the decision or action under challenge. However, in two situations in particular, issues as to the status of the applicant may arise. The first is where the decision or action in question affects a broad cross-section of the public in largely undifferentiated ways and the second involves cases where the decision affects a range of interests in differentiated ways and someone other than the primary target or most affected person seeks judicial review.

B. STANDING: THE TRADITIONAL LAW

Under traditional concepts of standing developed somewhat haphazardly as an incident of various judicial review remedies, there were major difficulties in the path of anyone in either of these two categories seeking judicial review. Generally, though the courts did claim a rarely exercised jurisdiction to accord status to "strangers," the prerogative remedies of *certiorari* and prohibition were available only to those who were directly affected or aggrieved. Applicants for *mandamus* had to demonstrate the existence of an unfulfilled legal duty that was owed specifically to them. In actions for a declaration or an injunction, the plaintiff was obliged to show that either her or his rights were affected by the decision or, in matters involving public rights, that he or she was suffering harm or loss over and above that being suffered by other members of the public. The Canadian courts also frowned on representative-type proceedings particularly as a way of presenting an accumulation of interests to finesse the possible lack of standing on the part of individual members of the applicant or plaintiff group.[1]

In fact, the concept of a person or group bringing a judicial review application in the name of the public interest was quite alien to a system under which the accepted constitutional convention was that the attorney general was the appropriate spokesperson for or vindicator of the public interest in litigation. Only if the attorney general was prepared to allow an individual to commence proceedings in her or his "name" (relator proceedings) could issues as to standing be put to rest. Moreover, the decision of the attorney general on whether or not to lend such support was a prerogative power immune from any form of judicial review or oversight.

Indeed, this notion of the attorney general as the sole litigation guardian of the public interest had remarkable persistence in Canadian law notwithstanding the fact that this role was one that had to be exercised on occasion in relation to the decisions of the Cabinet of which the attorney general was a member or in relation to the decisions of ministerial colleagues or of departments or agencies for which ministerial colleagues were theoretically responsible both in Parliament or the legislature, and more generally.

However, there was a much more legitimate side to the courts' reluctance to recognize public interest standing. That came from a sense that to allow private individuals and groups through the courtroom doors as representatives of the broader public interest was to countenance the definition and appropriation of that public interest by self-appointed watchdogs whose perspective would in many instances itself be narrow or confined to matters involving a not necessarily enlightened self-interest.

Concerns about appropriation also play a role when the applicant for judicial review is not the primary target or person affected most detrimentally by the decision under attack. There is an important sense in which even certain species of public law wrong are the "property" of the person most directly harmed and no one else. If a person is dis-

---

1   *L'Association des propriétaires des Jardins Tâché v. Les entreprises Dasken Inc.*, [1974] S.C.R. 2.

missed from a public office contrary to the principles of procedural fairness, there seems good reason, save in exceptional circumstances, to reserve judicial review to that person and that person alone. The interest is particularly personal and the wrong is in large measure a wrong that is an affront to that person and no one else. If the primary victim is not of a mind to seek judicial review, that decision should perhaps be by and large respected.[2]

C. REPRESENTATIVE ACTIONS

In recent times, these traditional concerns and positions have been subject to three principal modifications. First, and probably least controversially, the courts have begun to recognize group or representative actions in the public law domain, though not necessarily as a way of allowing the frailty of individual claims to standing to be overcome by the weight of a numbers of similarly affected persons.

As far as representative groups of affected persons were concerned, the breakthrough judgment was *Conseil du Patronat du Québec* v. *Québec (A.G.).*[3] This was a *Charter* challenge in which the Supreme Court of Canada, by reference simply to the dissenting judgment of Chouinard J.A. in the Québec Court of Appeal, recognized the standing of the largest employers' organization in Québec to challenge the validity of anti-scab labour legislation. Even more recently, in another *Charter* case, *Vriend* v. *Alberta*,[4] the Court accorded standing to gay and lesbian groups to be parties to proceedings in which the provisions of the Alberta *Individual Rights Protection Act* were being challenged for not proscribing discrimination on the basis of sexual orientation.

D. PUBLIC INTEREST STANDING

Second, and more significantly, the Supreme Court in *Finlay* v. *Canada (Minister of Finance)*,[5] extended the reach of the more general concept of public interest standing from the constitutional to the administrative

---

2   Though see *Re Ratepayers of New Ross Consolidated School* (1979), 102 D.L.R. (3d) 486 (N.S.S.C. T.D.) for an example of where a group of parents was allowed to challenge the process by which a teacher dismissed without any discussion of the propriety of such a proceeding.

3   [1991] 3 S.C.R. 685, rev'g (1988), 16 Q.A.C. 11 (C.A.).

4   [1998] 1 S.C.R. 493 [*Vriend*].

5   [1986] 2 S.C.R. 607 [*Finlay*].

law arena. This case involved a challenge by Finlay, a welfare recipient to the alleged failure of the federal government to require the provincial authorities in Manitoba to observe the terms of the *Canada Assistance Plan* in the dispensing of welfare benefits to its residents. Finlay, who claimed that he had been affected detrimentally by this failure, after failing to persuade the welfare authorities that they were acting illegally, then tried to secure relief directly against the Manitoba government in the courts of that province. However, on failing there as well, he turned his attention to the federal government and sought both declaratory and injunctive relief, the first to establish that the Federal government was acting illegally in continuing to make transfer payments to the Province while it was in breach and the second to enjoin the continuation of those payments until Manitoba was willing to live up to the terms of the legislation and on which it was entitled to the money.

When his standing to seek this relief was put in issue, Finlay argued, first, that he came within the normal principles of standing to seek declaratory and injunctive relief. However, this argument was rejected by the Supreme Court of Canada. To have standing in his own right, the Court proclaimed that he must necessarily gain some advantage from the granting of the relief sought. Here, it did not follow from the grant of relief that such an advantage would necessarily accrue to Finlay. Faced with a judgment preventing the Federal government from making any further transfer payments until Manitoba came into line, the Province might just forego the transfer payments and go it alone. As a result, Finlay was going to succeed in arguing the merits only if the Court recognized him as having public interest standing to advance the case.

Since 1975 and the judgment of Laskin J. for a majority of the Court in *Thorson v. Canada (A.G.),*[6] the Supreme Court had recognized the existence of a discretion to allow groups or individuals to bring challenges to the constitutional (including, since 1982, *Charter*) validity of legislation. The purpose was stated to be that of ensuring that unconstitutional legislation as well as decisions and orders would not be immunized from judicial scrutiny. That could occur where the Attorney General was refusing to take action personally or to lend her or his name in relator proceedings to a person or group wanting to bring such an action. In such cases, there might be no person or group of persons sufficiently affected personally to enable a challenge to be brought under the normal rules of standing. Alternatively, there might

---

6   [1975] 1 S.C.R. 138. See also *Nova Scotia Board of Censors v. McNeil*, [1976] 2 S.C.R. 265 and *Minister of Justice v. Borowski*, [1981] 2 S.C.R. 575.

be persons peculiarly or especially affected but they too (like the attorney general) were not willing to launch a challenge or did not have the resources to do so. Indeed, this latter situation is well exemplified by *Nova Scotia Board of Censors* v. *McNeil*,[7] where those most directly or immediately affected by a regime of movie classification and censorship — the film theatres and the movie distributors — were not going to challenge the constitutional validity of the legislative scheme. In those circumstances, McNeil, a journalist and moviegoer, was accorded public interest standing to launch a challenge.

As the constitutional cases involving public interest standing proliferated, more and more questions were asked as to whether they extended to purely administrative law litigation. When the issue finally reached the Supreme Court of Canada in *Finlay*, Le Dain J., delivering the judgment of a unanimous Court determined that they did. In so doing, he adopted the reasoning in *Thorson* as also justifying the recognition of public interest standing in purely administrative law cases. If the attorney general did not act to take issue in the courts with potential illegality, the courts should have a discretion to recognize the standing of a public interest litigant to do so.

Le Dain J. then went on to identify how that discretion should be exercised to control the according of standing and, in so doing, held that Finlay himself had crossed the relevant thresholds in this case. The elements of this assessment are:

(a) whether or not there is a justiciable issue, reflecting "concern about the proper role of the courts and their constitutional relationship with the other branches of government."

(b) whether or not the challenge involves a serious issue raised by someone with a "genuine" interest in its determination, reflecting a "concern about the allocation of scarce judicial resources and the need to screen out the mere busybody."

(c) whether or not there is any other "reasonable and effective manner in which the issue may be brought before a court", reflecting the concern that the "courts should have the benefit of the contending points of view by those most directly affected by them."[8]

In these terms, Finlay qualified. Despite the fact that the case involved the relationship between the federal and provincial branches of government, the issue nonetheless turned on the interpretation of a

---

7   *Ibid.*
8   *Finlay*, above note 5 at 631.

statute, clearly a justiciable question. Finlay, as someone who came close to meeting the test for standing in his own right and as someone "in need" in terms of the statute, was clearly not a busybody. Finally, given the fact that it was clear that the attorney general would not have taken proceedings or given consent to a relator action if he had been asked and that there was no one else more affected in this matter than someone in Finlay's position, there was no other more effective way in which this important question could come before the court. In so ruling on this latter point, the Court made it clear that it would not require in every case that the public interest applicant or plaintiff have first sought the assistance of the relevant attorney general. Le Dain J. also went on to emphasize that the ruling applied to both the declaratory and injunctive relief, thereby indicating that the nature of the relief sought was not a factor in the exercise of the court's discretion.

In the jurisprudence that has followed *Finlay* on public interest standing, the most commonly addressed factor (not at all surprisingly) has been the third, whether there is any more reasonable and effective manner in which the issue could be placed before a court. This was particularly manifest in the Supreme Court's next incursion into the arena of standing, *Canadian Council of Churches* v. *Canada (Minister of Employment and Immigration)*,[9] a *Charter* challenge to a range of amendments to the *Immigration Act* brought by a prominent coalition of Christian churches with a long history of work and advocacy on behalf of immigrants to Canada. While having no difficulty with the first two factors, justiciability and seriousness of the issue, Cory J., delivering the judgment of the Supreme Court, held that the Canadian Council of Churches did not pass the third branch or element in the test. In so doing, he took notice of the fact that there were any number of cases already before the courts in which immigrants affected by the relevant amendments were in fact making *Charter* challenges to their validity. While the Council might be an appropriate intervenor in those proceedings, the fact that persons directly affected by the legislation were actually taking many of the same issues being raised by the Canadian Council of Churches meant there were "other reasonable methods of bringing the matter before the courts."

This seems an unduly mechanistic application of the *Finlay* test. First, it appears to have elevated the third branch of the test to a decisive role and to have defined it in a particularly narrow manner: if there are other more directly affected persons actually launching challenges,

---

9   [1992] 1 S.C.R. 326.

that is the end of the matter. However, as indicated by the very facts of this case, the mere fact that individuals are taking challenges does not mean that the courts are necessarily going to have the most sharply focused, legally skilled representation of the contending issues. Much will depend on the resources available to individuals embroiled in the system, particularly in comparison with the resources both legal and financial available to a body such as the Council.

Second, given that the Council in this case was attempting to place before the Federal Court a constitutional case that depended at least in part on an evaluation of the overall effect or impact of the amendments, it was in fact making a different kind of case from that which was being advanced by individual immigrants. Finally, and in any event, if one turns one's focus from the third to the second element of the test, there is a strong argument that scarce judicial resources will be conserved by allowing the matter to go forward in this global manner to be settled once and for all rather than having a situation in which the relevant provisions are picked off one or two at a time in the context of applications by individual litigants.[10]

Subsequently, though without any explicit acknowledgment that it was doing so, the Supreme Court in *Vriend*[11] seemed to step back from the rigidity of this position. In *Vriend*, Vriend and gay and lesbian groups were challenging the wholesale exclusion from the Alberta *Individual Rights Protection Act* of any protection against discrimination on the basis of sexual orientation. The precipitating cause was the refusal of the authorities to process a complaint by Vriend made when he was dismissed from his position as a teacher ostensibly on the basis of his sexual orientation. Despite the fact that the proceedings involved a challenge to all relevant provisions from which sexual orientation was excluded and not just the employment provision on which Vriend had relied, Cory J., writing the judgment of the Court on this issue, upheld the standing of both Vriend and the gay and lesbian groups:

> With respect to the third criterion, the only other way the issue could be brought before the Court with respect to the other sections would be to wait until someone is discriminated against on the ground of

---

10   There may, of course, be situations where the court's proper understanding of a problem will need a concrete fact situation as exemplified by the plight of a person who meets the normal requirements for standing. Considering the problem presented in the abstract by a public interest litigant may not be good enough. In this sense, the "best arguers" will sometimes be those who can put the case before the court on the basis of their own factual situation.

11   *Vriend*, above note 4.

sexual orientation in housing, goods, services, etc., and challenge the validity of the provision in each particular case. This would not only be wasteful of judicial resources, but also unfair because it would impose burdens of delay, cost and personal vulnerability to discrimination for the individuals involved in those eventual cases.[12]

The Court went on to note that the various challenged provisions were similar and did not depend on the establishing of further facts.

While this does not necessarily mean that *Canadian Council of Churches* must now be taken as having been decided incorrectly on its facts, at least, this approach is one that treats the third criterion in a somewhat more flexible manner and with more regard to the realities of litigation and overall resource considerations. It also suggests that judgments such as that of MacPherson J. (as he then was) in *Unishare Investments Ltd.* v. *The Queen*[13] were decided correctly. There, a corporation that sold flowers to vendors was given standing to challenge a by-law affecting the street vendors' operations. While the street vendors themselves were more directly affected, MacPherson J. allowed the corporation standing on the basis of its greater resources and the unlikelihood that an individual vendor would mount such a challenge. Indeed, it is also significant, that, at least in *Charter* cases, the Court has acknowledged an even broader discretion, that of ignoring the issue of whether a person or group meets the *Finlay* test for public interest standing in, for example, situations where a case has been argued fully on the merits.[14]

E. INTERVENOR STATUS

The final aspect of modern "standing" law that should be noted is the significant degree to which (particularly in constitutional cases but also in purely administrative law proceedings) the opportunity for intervention in litigation commenced by others has expanded. Certainly, the right to intervene is not automatic. The courts generally require that the intervenor bring a perspective to the case that would not otherwise be before the court. There is also a concern that the intervention not change the focus of the litigation and in effect appropriate its scope and conduct from the parties. Nonetheless, it does represent a significant avenue for not only public interest groups but also

---

12   *Ibid.* at 528.
13   (1994), 18 O.R. (3d) 603 (Gen. Div.).
14   *Canadian Egg Marketing Agency* v. *Richardson*, [1998] 3 S.C.R. 157.

for others whose interests are affected indirectly or collaterally particularly in the context of broad-based policy-making exercises.

F. STANDING IN THE FEDERAL COURT

Finlay v. *Canada (Minister of Finance)*,[15] the foundation authority on public interest standing in administrative law matters commenced in the Federal Court, Trial Division. At that time, judicial review proceedings in the Federal Court, Trial Division, were commenced by way of one of the traditional remedies for judicial review such as a declaration or injunction, as in *Finlay*, or an order in the nature of one of the prerogative writs. The relevant standing principles or rules therefore depended, as under the ordinary common law on the remedy being sought. In contrast, in matters coming within the Federal Court of Appeal's original judicial review jurisdiction, the form of proceeding was an application to review and set aside with standing accorded by section 28(2) of the *Federal Court Act*[16] to either the attorney general or "any party directly affected."

In the wake of *Finlay*, questions were raised immediately as to whether the recognition of public interest standing in that case could have any application in cases commenced in the Federal Court of Appeal. After all, the restriction of standing to a "party directly affected" looked much like a statutory codification by reference to the strict standard of some of the common law authorities on the issue of standing.[17] This problem was compounded by the 1990 amendments to the *Federal Court Act*[18] in which the simplified application to review and set aside was extended to proceedings commenced in the Federal Court, Trial Division, with standing in both divisions of the court now described in terms of "anyone directly affected."[19] This looked suspiciously like a legislative reversal of *Finlay* for the purposes of Federal Court proceedings.

---

15   *Finlay*, above note 5.

16   R.S.C. 1985, c.F-7.

17   Thus, for example, Le Dain J., in holding that Finlay did not have standing as of right or by reference to the traditional principles, described his interest as "indirect": above note 5 at 617–24.

18   S.C. 1990, c. 8.

19   See s. 18.1(1), applicable to proceedings commenced in the Federal Court of Appeal by section 28(2).

While this question cannot as yet be regarded as resolved authoritatively, the argument was rejected in at least one case, *Friends of the Island Inc. v. Canada (Minister of Works)*.[20] Reed J., delivering the judgment of the Federal Court, Trial Division, according standing to a public interest group to challenge the construction of the bridge between Prince Edward Island and the mainland, was not willing to attribute such an intention to Parliament.

> I think the wording in subsection 18.1(1) allows the court discretion to grant standing when it is convinced that the particular circumstances of the case and the interest which the applicant holds justify status being granted.[21]

For the moment, therefore, the principles of standing can be taken to be the same in matters within the jurisdiction of the Federal Court as in the provincial superior courts with the recognition of public interest standing coming within the discretion of the court.

G. STANDING OF THE TRIBUNAL OR AUTHORITY UNDER ATTACK

A very specific and perennial problem of standing concerns the status of the decision maker in any application for judicial review attacking its decisions and processes. Put starkly, the conventional wisdom has been that the decision maker should not be heard from in such proceedings save in defence or justification of its jurisdiction. Moreover, in this context, the term "jurisdiction" does not include allegations of breaches of the rules of natural justice or procedural unfairness. For these purposes, it matters not whether the context is an application for judicial review or a statutory appeal, or whether the statutory authority is there as either a formal respondent or other party to the proceedings or as an intervenor.[22] However, in recent years, not only have doubts been raised about the universality of the general principle but there has also been further elaboration of it by the Supreme Court of Canada.

---

20 [1993] 2 F. C. 229 (T.D.).
21 *Ibid.* at 283.
22 The standard authorities are *Northwestern Utilities Ltd. v. City of Edmonton*, [1979] 1 S.C.R. 684; *Central Broadcasting Co. Ltd. v. Canada Labour Relations Board*, [1977] 1 S.C.R. 112; and *Re Canada Labour Relations Board and Transair Ltd.*, [1977] 1 S.C.R. 722.

In *CAIMAW* v. *Paccar of Canada Ltd.*, La Forest J. reviewed the conventional position in the context of an argument that the Supreme Court itself had not been faithful to that position. The source of this argument was the judgment of the Supreme Court in *Bibeault* v. *McCaffrey*[23] in which the decision makers under attack had been heard in defence of their ruling that employees were not entitled to participatory rights at a particular stage of an investigation being conducted under the *Québec Labour Code*. At first blush, this looked like a situation in which the decision makers were defending themselves against an allegation of breach of the principles of procedural fairness. However, in that case, the Court had treated the question not so much as an issue of natural justice as the interpretation by the decision makers of a particular statutory provision in which the issue of participatory rights was dealt with. Review of such a determination was therefore subject to the standard of patent unreasonableness and this meant that the issue was in the nature of a jurisdictional challenge. Given that, the decision makers were entitled to be heard from.

This position was reaffirmed by La Forest J. in *Paccar*. The general prohibition on tribunals defending themselves against allegations of procedural impropriety still existed. However, in the limited category of situation where a procedural entitlement depended on the interpretation of a specific provision in the empowering legislation for which the appropriate standard of judicial review was that of patent unreasonableness, the decision maker had status. Indeed, La Forest J. used this as a springboard for asserting that tribunals were entitled to be heard in all contexts in which they were subject to attack on the basis of patent unreasonableness. Putting it another way, the defence of jurisdiction for these purposes now seemed to include patent unreasonableness within the category of jurisdictional error.

In admitting that the decision maker under attack could defend itself against an allegation of patent unreasonableness, La Forest J. drew a distinction between the methodology of such a defence and the impermissible defence of the correctness of a decision. The mode of argument approved by the Court was one in which counsel for the tribunal explained how it had proceeded and that it had taken into account all the arguments that had been made as well as the authorities that had been presented. All this was with a view to demonstrating that it had not acted in a patently unreasonable fashion. That, of course, is all very well but patent unreasonableness is not just a matter of meth-

---

23   [1984] 1 S.C.R. 176.

odology; it involves an assessment of whether the substantive choice made by the tribunal came within the range of rationally permissible options possible on a reading of the relevant legislation. To move from an explanation of methodology to that kind of argument must, as a practical matter, make distinguishing between correctness arguments and patent unreasonableness arguments difficult to sustain in both written facta and oral submissions.

Indeed, subsequent Federal Court of Appeal authority suggests that La Forest J. should not be read as providing *carte blanche* to the tribunal in defending itself against allegations of patent unreasonableness.[24] Only where the tribunal "may cast some light imperceptible to ordinary mortals" should such participation be allowed. This was not the case in determining whether the labour board had made a patently unreasonable determination on whether there had been a sale of a business in terms of the *Canada Labour Code*. In addition, the Federal Court ruled that the board could not be heard on a challenge to its determination that the company was a federal undertaking, a determination on which, as a matter of constitutional law, the board's jurisdiction depended. Such constitutional issues were not within the ambit of "jurisdiction" in terms of the traditional authorities. If there needed to be representation on such an issue aside from that provided by the parties, that was the responsibility of the attorney general, not the board.

Subsequently, however, in creating the new Canada Industrial Relations Board, Parliament specified:

> The Board has standing to appear in [judicial review proceedings] for
> the purpose of making submissions regarding the standard of review
> to be used with respect to decisions of the Board and the Board's
> jurisdiction, policies and procedures.[25]

This provision is almost certainly unique in Canadian legislation and, in effect, amounts to a legislative rebuke to the Federal Court for not observing the legal principles laid down by the Supreme Court. It still, however, leaves open the question of how the Federal Court will henceforth treat other tribunals trying to be heard on these issues.

It is also useful to compare the stance of the Federal Court to the apparent position in matters coming before the Ontario Divisional Court under that province's *Judicial Review Procedure Act*.[26] Under sec-

---

24   *Ferguson Bus Lines Ltd. v. ATU, Local 1374*, [1990] 2 F.C. 586 (C.A.).
25   *Canada Labour Code*, R.S.C. 1985, c. L-2, s. 22 (1.1), as inserted by S.C. 1998, c. 26, s. 9.
26   R.S.O. 1990, c. J.1.

tion 9(2) of that *Act*, it is provided that the person who is authorized to make the decision which is the subject of the application for judicial review "may be a party to the application." At first instance in *Re Consolidated-Bathurst Packaging Ltd. and International Woodworkers of America, Local 2-69*,[27] this was treated as providing the tribunal with a choice on whether to participate, a choice which, when exercised, entitled the tribunal to be heard on the natural justice issue raised by that case: the discussion by the whole board of a matter that had been heard by a particular panel of the board. Indeed, subsequently, the Ontario Labour Relations Board was heard on this question without further objection in both the Ontario Court of Appeal and the Supreme Court of Canada.

It may, however, be dangerous to place too much reliance on this decision. Subsequently, in *Gale* v. *Miracle Food Mart*,[28] the Ontario Divisional Court castigated as "wrong" the representation by counsel of an adjudicator against whom there was an allegation of bias. Also, in British Columbia, notwithstanding the entitlement of a decision maker to become a party to judicial review proceedings at its "option,"[29] the normal restrictive principles have been applied as evidenced by the fact that *Paccar* was a case that started as an application for judicial review under the British Columbia *Judicial Review Procedure Act*.[30]

Obviously, this is a domain fraught with uncertainty for any statutory authority evaluating whether or not it should attempt to defend itself in judicial review proceedings. Obviously also, there is a need for a fundamental rethinking of the whole issue. Going back to first principles, there are a number of interconnected reasons why courts have been reluctant to accord status or recognition to tribunals or other statutory bodies attempting to defend their decisions or actions in the context of judicial review or statutory appeal.

Principal among those justifications is the analogy drawn to the situation of the regular courts. Regular courts do not defend their decisions in resistance to appeals from their judgments or verdicts. They have had the opportunity to justify their position in reasons for judgment. It is also perceived to be inappropriate and as bringing into question their independence if they were to take an adversarial role in the

---

27   (1985), 20 D.L.R. (4th) 84 (Div. Ct.) [*Consolidated-Bathurst*].

28   (1993), 12 Admin. L.R. (2d) 267 (Ont. Div. Ct.) at 268.

29   *Judicial Review Procedure Act*, R.S.B.C. 1979, c. 209, s. 15.

30   See to the same effect *Dairy Producers Co-operative Ltd.* v. *Saskatchewan (Saskatchewan Human Rights Commission)* (1993), 109 D.L.R. (4th) 726 (Sask. Q.B.) (interpreting a statutory provision entitling the commission to be a party to any appeal from its decisions).

context of an appeal. At a more practical level, there will generally always be someone there to defend the decision of the court in the person of the losing party at first instance. Failing that, the possibility exists for intervention in support of the judgment under appeal by the appropriate attorney general or the appointment of an *amicus curiae*.

In many instances, some of these same conditions apply to the administrative process. However, on occasion, the analogy may not be appropriate. Where the decision under attack is not one involving a *lis inter partes* as, for example, in the case of the denial of an application for a licence, there may be no opposing party available to defend the tribunal's position and the attorney general may be unwilling or lack the resources to act as a surrogate. Indeed, even where the decision under attack is the culmination of a *lis* or contest, the winning party may also lack the resources to resist effectively an application for judicial review or a statutory appeal. Even where there is an unsuccessful party willing to appear in defence or in justification of the tribunal's decision, the matters raised by way of an application for judicial review may be matters that stem not from the merits of the decision under attack but from facts of which the respondent party would have at best incomplete knowledge such as assertions of inappropriate post-hearing consultation as in *Consolidated-Bathurst*, claims of legitimate expectation arising from previous conduct or statements,[31] and even allegations of bias by reason of various associations and involvements (as in *Gale*).[32] There, the only way the full facts and possible justifications will emerge will be by conceding a role to the tribunal. Finally, in a domain where courts acknowledge frequently the need for considerable deference to tribunals because of their expertise and experience, an argument arises that the courts' relative unfamiliarity with the substantive matters being dealt with by the tribunal may necessitate an opportunity for the tribunal to explain particularly in situations of alle-

---

31   See, for example, the judgment of Reed J. in *Canada (A.G.) v. Canada (Human Rights Tribunal)* (1994), 19 Admin. L.R. (2d) 69 (F.C.T.D.).

32   This is also a problem in the domain of regular courts. Where an allegation of bias is raised, the judge may have had no prior opportunity in her or his reasons for decision to address the issue and may also have facts in her or his possession that are relevant to the determination of the issue. Under the normal rules, where the appeal is by the Crown on the basis of an acquittal tainted by bias, the judge will be forced to rely on the accused/respondent to defend against that issue (see, for example, *R. v. S. (R.D.)*, [1997] 3 S.C.R. 484. That may or may not be satisfactory and, of course, the Attorney General is in an obvious conflict of interest in such a case with the only way out seemingly being the appointment of an *amicus curiae* to put the case resisting the allegation.

gations of patent unreasonableness. True respect or deference especially where the customary form of reasons provided by the tribunal do not contain essential background may require an opportunity for the tribunal to provide that background and relate it to the facts of the case. Indeed, this may be so even where there is a respondent actively participating in the proceedings.

In this regard, one of the interesting observations made by Osler J. in *Consolidated-Bathurst* was that

> the rule restricting the right of a tribunal to make submissions before the Court is a rule of the Court rather than a rule of law, and the extent of the participation to be permitted to the [tribunal] must depend on the circumstances of each case.[33]

Whether or not that does represent the current state of Canadian law in this area, Osler J.'s approach has much to commend it. The issue of tribunal participation would be far better conceived of in terms of judicial discretion than as a set of precise rules where tribunal participation depends on the grounds on which appeal or review is being pursued.

Under a discretionary approach, the principal question should probably be whether the participation of the tribunal is needed to enable a proper defence or justification of the decision under attack. If that decision will almost certainly be presented adequately by the losing party at first instance or by some other party or intervenor such as the attorney general, there may be no need for tribunal representation irrespective of the ground of judicial review or appeal. On the other hand, where no one is appearing to defend the tribunal's decision, where the matter in issue involves factors or considerations peculiarly within the decision maker's knowledge or expertise, or where the tribunal wishes to provide dimensions or explanations that are not necessarily going to be put by a party respondent, then there should clearly be room for that kind of representation to be allowed within the discretion of the reviewing or appellate court. Indeed, in at least some instances, a true commitment to deference and restraint in intervention would seem to necessitate it.

---

33   *Consolidated-Bathurst*, above note 27 at 102.

FURTHER READINGS

Bogart, W.A., "Understanding Standing, Chapter IV: *Minister of Finance of Canada* v. *Finlay*" (1988), 10 Supreme Court Law Review 377

Janisch, H.N., "Standing of the Decision Maker in Proceedings for Judicial Review" in I. R. Feltham, ed., *International Trade Dispute Settlement: Implications for Canadian Law* (Ottawa: The Centre for Trade Policy and Law, 1996) at 11

McIntyre, S., "Above and Beyond Equality Rights: *Canadian Council of Churches* v. *The Queen*" (1992), 12 Windsor Yearbook of Access to Justice 293

Roman, A.J., and M. Hemingway, "Standing to Intervene" (1987), 26 Admin. L.R. 49

Ross, J.M., "*Canadian Council of Churches* v. *The Queen*: Public Interest Standing Takes a Back Seat" (1992), 3 Constitutional Forum 100

CHAPTER 19

OTHER METHODS OF JUDICIAL SCRUTINY OF ADMINISTRATIVE ACTION

A. INTRODUCTION

As already noted in the Introduction to this Part, issues as to the validity or legality of administrative action can arise in proceedings other than applications for the various forms of relief or remedy by way of judicial review. Albeit that this mode of attack has been increasingly codified in statutory form, the origins of judicial review lie in the common law as supplemented by equity. Judicial review was not the product of a legislative determination that such a recourse should be available to the victims of unlawful administrative action. The same is true of one of the other two modes of judicial scrutiny of administrative action: collateral attack. This too represented the evolution of a common law principle that allowed citizens to question the validity of administrative action in various other proceedings in which such issues were relevant such as a defence to a charge based on a defective summons. In contrast, the first category dealt with in this chapter, rights of appeal against administrative action, is indeed one that is the product of legislative choice. Nonetheless, notwithstanding this contrast between the sources of judicial review and those of statutory appeals, increasingly, as will be seen in what follows, there is a correspondence between the principles governing the two modes of securing redress from the courts.

B. STATUTORY APPEALS

Quantitatively, administrative action is tested most commonly in the context of statutory appeal. Judicial review is the exception; appeal is the norm. Unlike judicial review, however, there is no such thing as a common law right of appeal. Appeals are purely creatures of statute. Unless there is a statutory foundation for an appeal, there is no right of appeal, and affected persons must look to other avenues of recourse such as an application for judicial review. Indeed, the Canadian courts have to this point accepted that, as opposed to judicial review, there is never a constitutionally guaranteed right of appeal even where *Charter* rights are in issue.[1] Moreover, rights of appeal are in no sense standardized. They come in all shapes and sizes and their scope is determined by the language of the statute creating them and a set of common law principles that has evolved over the years determining the legal contours of particular statutory appeal formulae.

It must also be kept in mind that the courts almost invariably will require the exhaustion of rights of appeal before being willing to entertain a judicial review application. Indeed, in many instances, the existence of a right of appeal will totally pre-empt the availability of any other form of remedy. It is therefore important to check the relevant statutes to ascertain whether there is any form of statutory appeal or review whenever a challenge to an administrative decision or action is being contemplated.

On occasion, there will be an internal right of appeal or review in the sense of an appeal to another body within the administrative structure of the original decision maker. As we have seen from the cases of *Harelkin v. University of Regina*[2] and *Khan v. University of Ottawa*,[3] appeals to the senate from student disciplinary decisions are common in the settings of colleges and universities. Internal appeals are also a feature of tribunals with high-volume jurisdictions such as workers' compensation boards.[4] As well, there are many examples where the form of appeal is a right to seek a reconsideration by the person or body who took the initial decision. This is particularly the case with

---

1   See, for example, *Chiarelli v. Canada (Minister of Justice)*, [1992] 1 S.C.R. 711.
2   [1979] 2 S.C.R. 561.
3   (1997), 148 D.L.R. (4th) 577 (Ont. C.A.)
4   See, for example, the appellate jurisdiction of the Ontario Workplace Safety and Insurance Appeals Tribunal: *Workplace Safety and Insurance Act*, S.O. 1997, c. 16, s. 123.

tribunals and agencies with ongoing regulatory responsibilities over a particular person or enterprise as in the instance of the regulation of public utilities.[5] At other times, the appeal will be to an umbrella or external administrative body. The most significant example of this is le Tribunal administratif du Québec, this country's nearest approximation to a general, all-purpose administrative appeals tribunal. More limited sectoral varieties are found in appellate authorities such as the Professions Tribunal in Québec, a body that serves as a general appeal tribunal in professional disciplinary and other regulatory matters,[6] or, the Ontario Municipal Board in the instance of appeals from a range of decisions made by municipalities across the province. Thereafter, there will sometimes be a further right of appeal to the courts while, on other occasions, the courts will be the first avenue of appeal.

Just as there is great variety in the form of appeal mechanisms, so too is there great variety in the scope of appeals. At one end of the spectrum are so-called *de novo* appeals in which the matter in issue is completely reheard, sometimes without any weight at all being attributed to the first instance decision. At the other end are decisions restricted to issues of law that are heard on the basis of the record compiled by the first instance decision maker. Not all appeals are as of right. They may depend on the aggrieved person obtaining leave from the decision maker or, more commonly, the appellate body. Thus, in the case of the Immigration and Refugee Board, leave to appeal must be obtained from the Federal Court, Trial Division, and any further appeal to the Federal Court of Appeal depends on the Trial Division judge who has heard the appeal certifying that the case involves a serious question of general importance.[7]

Despite the fact that, in many situations, particularly where there is a general or unadorned right of appeal, the role of the appeal authority will be to substitute its judgment on the merits for that of the body under appeal, restraint or deference also features in much of the relevant jurisprudence. Thus, where the appeal is on the basis of the record of the proceedings below, there may be reluctance to second-guess the

---

5   See, for example, *Utilities Commission Act*, R.S.B.C. 1996, c. 473, s. 99, which provides that: "The commission may reconsider, vary or rescind a decision, order, rule or regulation made by it, and may rehear an application before deciding it."

6   Its jurisdiction was not absorbed into le Tribunal administratif du Québec.

7   *Immigration Act*, R.S.C. 1985, c. I-2, ss. 82.1(1), 83(1).

tribunal appealed from on issues of evidence and particularly the credibility of witnesses.[8] Even before the emergence of deference as a dominating concept in the domain of judicial review, courts hearing appeals from certain tribunals, such as those engaged in economic regulation or professional discipline, were disinclined to intervene too readily, particularly in the case of determinations where expertise or professional judgment formed the basis for the decision below. Among the ways the courts facilitated this were to adopt a broad concept of what constituted issues of fact in appeals confined to questions of law[9] and, most effectively, to describe the decision appealed from as one involving the exercise of discretion. This restricted the scope of the appeal to a consideration of whether the first instance decision maker had committed an error in principle or fallen into one of the other grounds which the courts treated as an abuse of discretion in the context of judicial review.[10]

As we have already seen, this often unarticulated policy of judicial restraint has now been explicitly acknowledged with the bringing of statutory rights of appeal within the umbrella of deference-based judicial review. More particularly, by reference to the concept of "specialization of duties," the Supreme Court has accepted that there will often be occasions where correctness is not the appropriate standard of scrutiny to apply the decision under appeal but rather one of the other less intrusive standards of patent unreasonableness or, more commonly, unreasonableness *simpliciter*.[11]

As with the other aspects of the law governing appeals, the statute is crucial in determining what an appeal tribunal or court can do when it finds the grounds of appeal made out. However, in situations where the statute is silent, the normal assumption will be that the appellate authority can reverse the decision under appeal or, in some instances, remit the matter for reconsideration or rehearing. However, where the statute speaks explicitly to the powers of the appeal body, the statute is governing.

---

8   See, for example, *Laba v. Dental Association (Manitoba)* (1988), 54 Man.R. (2d) 17 (Q.B.).

9   See, for example, *British Columbia (Minister of Social Services and Housing)* v. *Appeal Tribunal* (1992), 92 D.L.R. (4th) 326 (B.C.S.C.).

10   *D.R. Fraser & Co.* v. *Minister of National Revenue*, [1949] A.C. 24 (P.C. Can.).

11   As discussed extensively in chapter 3 and culminating in *Canada (Director of Investigation and Research)* v. *Southam*, [1997] 1 S.C.R. 748.

C. COLLATERAL ATTACK

Unlawful administrative action is challenged most commonly by way of an application for judicial review or statutory appeal,[12] proceedings that have as their direct or immediate target the relevant decision or order. However, the validity of administrative action may also be raised collaterally in the course of proceedings which do not have as their express objective the quashing of, declaring as invalid, or reversing that administrative action.

One of the most famous judgments in the evolution of procedural fairness law presents a typical example. In *Cooper* v. *Wandsworth Board of Works*,[13] the plaintiff was suing the defendant for the tort of trespass. The action giving rise to the litigation was the demolition by order of the board of works of a structure that the plaintiff was in the course of building. As a defence to the plaintiff's claim for damages, the public authority relied on a demolition order that had been issued as a consequence of the alleged failure of the plaintiff to give the board the statutorily required notice of its intention to build. In responding to this defence, the plaintiff then put in issue the validity of the demolition order; the board had issued it without affording the plaintiff a fair hearing. In accepting this argument and allowing the plaintiff to succeed in his claim in tort, the court found the administrative action invalid in the context of proceedings not having as their immediate or formal focus the decision or order in question.

In contemporary Canadian law, the most common species of collateral attack involves situations where, in defence to charges or enforcement proceedings in the courts, the defendant or accused challenges the validity of the statutory provision or order on which the proceedings are based. Thus, in recent years, the Supreme Court of Canada has dealt with cases in which, by way of defence to a charge of violating a municipal by-law, the validity of that by-law has been put in issue.[14]

---

12   Some theorists classify statutory appeal as itself being a form of collateral attack: see Mark Aronson, "Criteria for Restricting Collateral Challenge" (1998), 4 Public Law Review 237 at 238. However, to the extent that a statutory appeal has as its direct target the relevant administrative action, there are problematic aspects to such a categorization. Of course, to the extent that statutory appeals are seen as collateral attack, what is clear in current Canadian law is that, in virtually every instance, this is a form of collateral attack that not only can but generally must be used instead of judicial review.

13   (1863), 143 E.R. 414 (C.P.).

14   *R.* v. *Sharma*, [1993] 1 S.C.R. 650; *R.* v. *Greenbaum*, [1993] 1 S.C.R. 674.

However, the extent to which collateral attack is available has not been without controversy. Historically, the theory on which collateral attack depended was the jurisdictional infirmity of the relevant statutory provision or order. If the statutory provision was *ultra vires* or the order had been made without jurisdiction, it was incapable of having legal force and, as such, could be called into question in the context of any proceedings in which the effectiveness of that statutory provision or order was at all relevant to the issues raised.

Even under this traditional conception of the reach of collateral attack, there was not an exact parallel between the scope of applications for judicial review and most statutory appeals (direct attack) and collateral attack. To the extent that, in certain circumstances, the courts accepted that non- or intra-jurisdictional errors of law on the face of the record could be reviewed on an application for judicial review, the courts recognized a basis for direct attack that had no parallel in the domain of collateral challenges. Collateral attack was not possible for anything less than jurisdictional infirmity. Orders based on an intra-jurisdictional error of law were not candidates for any such challenge. They were not nullities or void but merely voidable. They had to be challenged directly or not at all.

However, it also became clear that the traditional jurisdiction-based theory itself was too expansive in its recognition of the opportunities for collateral attack. The courts therefore rejected an absolute theory of nullity and other considerations came to dictate that, even where there was an allegation of jurisdictional infirmity in the statute or order being relied on by the government or administrative authority, collateral attack was not always available. Indeed, as a result of two 1998 judgments of the Supreme Court of Canada, the availability of collateral attack in the context of enforcement proceedings has been circumscribed in a very restrictive but appropriate manner.

R. v. *Consolidated Maybrun Mines Ltd.*[15] and *R.* v. *Al Klippert Ltd.*[16] both involved failures by companies to obey orders issued under statute by administrative officials. Under the applicable legislation in each case, there was a right of appeal to an administrative tribunal from the relevant orders and, thereafter, access to the regular courts by way of further appeal. However, rather than exercise those rights of appeal or seek judicial review, the respective companies chose simply to ignore the orders in question. Not surprisingly, this prompted regulatory

---

15   [1998] 1 S.C.R. 706 [*Consolidated Maybrun Mines*].
16   [1998] 1 S.C.R. 737 [*Al Klippert*].

offence charges being laid against the two companies. It was in the context of those charges that the companies for the first time challenged the validity of the orders on which the charges were based. In the case of *Consolidated Maybrun*, the company alleged that the relevant administrative official had acted in a patently unreasonable manner in determining that the statutory standards for the making of the relevant order were present. In *Al Klippert*, the company pleaded that it in fact had legal authority to engage in the mining operations that were the basis of the prohibition and cleanup orders made by the administrative official.

In each case, a unanimous Supreme Court of Canada held that the orders could not be attacked collaterally by way of defence to the regulatory enforcement proceedings and this notwithstanding the fact that, at least in *Al Klippert*, the ground of attack was based on an allegation of a complete lack of jurisdiction to make the order in issue; a case in which the jurisdiction *ab initio* of the administrative official might be said to have been in issue.

In large measure though not completely adopting the judgment of Laskin J.A. in the Ontario Court of Appeal in *Consolidated Maybrun*,[17] L'Heureux-Dubé J. held that the availability of collateral attack should in each of these cases depend on a consideration of five factors:

> (1) the wording of the statute under the authority of which the order was issued; (2) the purpose of the legislation; (3) the existence of a right of appeal; (4) the kind of collateral attack in the light of the expertise of raison d'être of the administrative appeal tribunal; and (5) the penalty on a conviction for failing to comply with the order.[18]

Focusing on these five factors would enable a court to make a judgment as to the "legislator's intention as to the appropriate forum"[19] for challenges to the orders now being attacked collaterally.

In each instance, this evaluation led the Court to the conclusion that the legislator's intention was that those concerned about the validity of such orders were normally obliged to utilize the particular form of statutory appeal or review provided by the empowering legislation. Not only had the legislature provided a statutory right of appeal, but also both the tribunal and the court on further appeal had the legal and institutional capacity to deal with the companies' challenges to the validity of the relevant administrative order. Indeed, it was in this con-

---

17 (1996), 28 O.R. (3d) 161 (C.A.).

18 *Al Klippert*, above note 16 at 746.

19 *Consolidated Mayburn Mines*, note 15 at 728.

text that L'Heureux-Dubé J. took issue[20] with the Ontario Court of Appeal to the extent that it seemed to suggest in *Consolidated Maybrun* that the outcome might have been different had the challenge been not on the basis of patent unreasonableness but on the basis of an absence of jurisdiction *ab initio*. Aside from the problems created by distinguishing among categories of jurisdictional infirmity, L'Heureux-Dubé J. reiterated that the real question was not the nature of the jurisdictional error but whether the appeal structure created by the *Act* was designed to deal with it.

The Supreme Court also emphasized in *Consolidated Maybrun* the pre-emptive or preventive nature of the orders being made for environmental protection purposes and the undesirability of allowing challenges to be delayed to the order enforcement stage. If the validity of such an order was to be attacked, it was in the public interest that it be done as early as possible and within the specific framework created by the legislation. As well, the penalties provided for at the enforcement stage did not include imprisonment and the fines were comparatively small. In fact, in this aspect of the Court's judgment, while not actually using the terminology, the Court is in fact relying upon arguments and considerations that the British courts have deployed in rejecting certain forms of collateral attack on the basis that they amount to an abuse of process.[21]

While the Supreme Court has indicated in this and other contexts that it does not look favourably on postponing challenges to the validity of administrative action until the enforcement stage, the possibility of such forms of collateral attack is not precluded entirely. For example, it would be surprising if the criteria adopted in *Consolidated Maybrun* and *Al Klippert* precluded the making of collateral attack in municipal by-law enforcement proceedings. In most instances, there is simply no reason to expect that persons prosecuted under the relevant by-law would have had an earlier reason or opportunity to challenge it directly. Rather, the prosecution will often be the defendant's first direct encounter with the relevant legislation. And, indeed, the Court in *Consolidated Maybrun* refers with obvious approval to the recent by-law jurisprudence on collateral attack.[22]

On the other hand, though the third factor among those to be considered speaks in terms of the existence of statutory rights of appeal, it seems fairly clear that a failure to seek judicial review would in most

---

20   At 729–31.
21   Starting with *O'Reilly v. Mackman*, [1983] 2 A.C. 237 (H.L. Eng.).
22   *Consolidated Maybrun Mines*, above note 15 at 721.

circumstances be treated as of the same character as a failure to exercise a statutory right of appeal. Indeed, earlier jurisprudence from the Court clearly indicates that this is the case. Thus, in *Canada (Human Rights Commission)* v. *Taylor*,[23] the Supreme Court held that it was too late for an allegation of bias to be raised against a human rights tribunal at the stage at which the respondent before that tribunal was being proceeded against for contempt for breach of the final order made by that tribunal. The issue should have been raised by way of a timely application for judicial review.

Indeed, subsequent authority seems to make it clear that even the actual launching of a challenge does not provide any justification for disobeying a tribunal's order. Absent a stay, the order should normally be obeyed in the meantime. In *Canada (Canadian Human Rights Commission)* v. *Canadian Liberty Net*,[24] the Federal Court of Appeal upheld a conviction for contempt even though, in parallel proceedings,[25] the order on which it was based was found to be beyond the jurisdiction of the Court that had made it on the application of the commission in aid of its processes. This position was sustained by the two judges in the Supreme Court of Canada who agreed with the position of the Federal Court of Appeal on the invalidity of the order.[26]

What is also significant about these other cases is that they involved rather more serious penal consequences than in either *Consolidated Maybrun* or *Al Klippert*, and although concerned with court rather than tribunal or agency orders must be regarded as having some weight on the question of the relevance of the nature of the penalty involved. Severe penalties for disobedience, the fifth factor, may not necessarily provide a justification for collateral attack. In sum, the key factor, or question, may really be the opportunities that exist for direct attack and the desirability of affected persons taking advantage of such opportunities rather than hiding in the weeds and waiting for enforcement proceedings to become a reality.

Indeed, the philosophy of the Supreme Court in the recent jurisprudence also suggests that foregoing an application for judicial review and subsequently seeking damages may not always be a wise tactic.

---

23 [1990] 3 S.C.R. 892.

24 [1996] 1 F.C. 787 (C.A.).

25 [1996] 1 F.C. 804 (C.A.).

26 *Canada (Canadian Human Rights Commission)* v. *Canadian Liberty Net*, [1998] 1 S.C.R. 626 (*per* McLachlin J., Major J. concurring). The other members of the Court did not have to deal with this issue because of their disagreement with the Federal Court of Appeal on the issue of the validity of the Court's order.

This position was espoused by at least one judge of the Federal Court of Appeal in *Comeau Sea Foods Ltd.* v. *Canada (Minister of Fisheries and Oceans)*[27]: decisions depriving a licensee of an occupational licence should be challenged by way of judicial review and not postponed to the context of an action in damages for bad faith or misfeasance in the exercise of a statutory power. This issue was not reached when the case went to the Supreme Court of Canada[28] but it does suggest that in today's world, Roncarelli would have had yet another defence raised against him by Duplessis in the famous case of *Roncarelli* v. *Duplessis*.[29] The actions of the manager of the Québec Liquor Commission and the premier of Québec could have been challenged immediately by way of an application for judicial review, assuming that such a recourse was otherwise available, to question the cancellation of Roncarelli's restaurant liquor licence. Failing to seek such direct relief, allowing the allegedly invalid action to have effect until such time as serious financial consequences ensued, and then suing for damages based on misfeasance in public office may be an inappropriate course of action in such a case, leaving open the possibility of dismissal of the tort or extra-contractuelle action.

In short, the modern philosophy of the Supreme Court towards collateral attack may reflect both a more general recognition of the problems that delay in attacking allegedly unlawful action can create for the administrative process as well as the relevance of principles of mitigation in both public and private law. As a consequence, the Court has moved a long way from the absolute theory of nullity on which the availability of collateral attack was based originally. In so doing, it has rejected hard and fast distinctions based on the nature of the alleged error and has instead located the consideration of such questions within the domain of statutory interpretation and the pragmatic and functional analysis that characterizes so much of the Court's view as to the appropriate scope of judicial scrutiny of administrative action. In such an environment, collateral attack will become an even more exceptional recourse than it has been historically.

---

27 (1995), 123 D.L.R. (4th) 180 (F.C.A.) (Stone J.A.). While not going quite so far, Linden J.A. was of the opinion that a failure to challenge the decision promptly by way of judicial review would be a matter affecting damages by reference to the principles of mitigation.

28 [1997] 1 S.C.R. 12.

29 [1959] S.C.R. 121.

FURTHER READINGS

ARONSON, M., "Criteria for Restricting Collateral Challenge" (1998), 4 Public Law Review 237

BILSON, B., "Lying in Wait for Justice: Collateral Attacks on Administrative and Regulatory Orders" (1999), 12 Canadian Journal of Administrative Law and Practice 289

BROWN, D.J.M., & J.M. EVANS, "Collateral Challenges to the Validity of Administrative Action" (1999), 4 Reid's Administrative Law 73

CHAPTER 20

LIMITS ON REVIEW

A. ISSUE ESTOPPEL

The doctrine of issue estoppel prevents the retrial of issues which have already been determined finally in judicial proceedings involving the same parties. Though the Supreme Court of Canada has yet to rule on the matter, it has become clear in recent years from a number of Court of Appeal judgments that it can apply not just to the determination of issues by regular courts but also to decision making by administrative tribunals and other forms of statutory authority. In other words, there are occasions on which the doctrine will operate to foreclose the reopening before either a regular court or even another administrative tribunal of an issue that has already been the subject of an adjudication by a statutory authority.[1] What remains highly controversial, however, are the precise circumstances under which it will be invoked in the case of the resolution of issues by decision makers other than the regular courts.

---

1   See, for example, aside from the judgments discussed below, *Raison* v. *Fenwick* (1981), 120 D.L.R. (4th) 622 (B.C.C.A.); *Rasanen* v. *Rosemount Instruments Ltd.* (1994), 112 D.L.R. (4th) 683 [*Rasanen*], leave to appeal to the Supreme Court of Canada refused (1994), 19 O.R. (3d) xvi; and, for an identification of Federal Court authority on the point, see *Canada (A.G.)* v. *Symtron Systems Inc.*, [1999] 2 F.C. 514 (C.A.) at note 21.

A striking illustration of the possible operation and reach of the doctrine as it affects administrative tribunals and other forms of statutory decision maker is provided by *Danyluk* v. *Ainsworth Technologies Inc.*[2] This case involved a determination by an employment standards officer under Ontario's employment standards legislation. The employment standards officer held that Danyluk, a dismissed employee was entitled to two weeks' termination pay but refused to award her a much higher sum for unpaid commissions and wages to which she claimed to be entitled. At that time, the Ontario *Act* expressly preserved an employee's common law rights and, relying on that, Danyluk commenced an action in the Ontario Court of Justice (General Division) for damages for wrongful dismissal and for unpaid wages and commissions. In so doing, she forewent the opportunity provided by the *Act* at that time to apply to the director of employment standards for the appointment of an adjudicator to conduct a hearing and review the decision of the employment standards officer. In response to the commencement of the action, the employer moved to have the claim for unpaid wages and commissions struck out on the basis of issue estoppel. The motions court judge agreed and this ruling was upheld by the Ontario Court of Appeal.

In dismissing the appeal, the Ontario Court of Appeal was not troubled by two of the three normal requirements for the operation of the doctrine of issue estoppel. The claim for unpaid wages and commissions was the same question that had been decided by the employment standards officer, and the parties to the two proceedings, the employments standards complaint and the civil litigation, were identical on this issue even if not on other aspects of the wrongful dismissal claim. More problematic was the third requirement, that of whether there had been a final, judicial determination of the relevant issue.

The *Act* provided both employers and employees with the right to seek review of a determination by an employment standards officer. Also, that officer was not compelled to reach a conclusion but could instead make a report to the director simply to the effect that there *may* have been a violation of the rights created by the *Act*, such a report opening up the appointment of a referee to make a final determination.[3] Nonetheless, the Court of Appeal held that, in this instance, there had been a final determination in the sense demanded by the principles governing the operation of the doctrine and the fact that

---

2   (1998), 167 D.L.R. (4th) 385 (Ont. C.A.) [*Danyluk*].
3   Indeed, the earlier Ontario Court of Appeal judgment in *Rasanen*, above note 1, had established that the doctrine applied to determinations by referees.

there was a right of appeal or possibility of review of the decision did not affect the finality of the employment standard's officers determinations in this case. It was final in the crucial sense that it was not open to that officer to rescind her or his decision.[4]

More problematic was the issue of whether the employment standards officer was sufficiently judicial for the doctrine to operate. The court acknowledged that not every determination of rights and interests by a statutory body would qualify as a judicial determination. However, the court went on to suggest that provided that the decision maker in question was one who, on the basis of the law prior to the judgment of the Supreme Court in *Nicholson v. Haldimand-Norfolk Regional Board of Commissioners of Police*,[5] would have been categorized as exercising a judicial function, that requirement for the operation of the doctrine was satisfied.

The effect of this is, of course, to re-insinuate into the law one of the most problematic distinctions ever encountered in Canadian judicial review law. It is, however, interesting that, relying on earlier Court of Appeal authority based on a slightly different version of the legislation,[6] the court was prepared to hold that the employment standards officer was indeed exercising a judicial function for these purposes. Despite the fact that the way in which the officer functioned under the *Act* was more in the nature of an inquisitorial than a traditionally adversarial process, the court in the precedent case had accepted that the crucial element was the ultimate adjudicative function performed by the officer — the establishment of rights and liabilities by applying the facts as found to the law as laid down in *Act*.

> [T]hese requirements could be met without the formalities of a full-scale hearing or other time-consuming procedures that could defeat the statute's purpose of giving the employee a speedy and effective remedy.[7]

---

4   In an era where, by statute and common law, tribunals are given greater latitude in the reopening of matters that they have heard, it would, in fact, not be surprising to see this concept of finality re-evaluated. After all, there may be no necessary contradiction between what the requirement of finality should involve for the purposes behind the principles of issue estoppel and the expanded capacity of some tribunals to reopen a matter they have already decided.

5   [1979] 1 S.C.R. 311.

6   *Re Downing and Graydon* (1978), 21 O.R. (2d) 292 (C.A.).

7   *Rasanen*, above note 1 at 307–8, cited in *Danyluk*, above note 2 at 402.

This represents a liberal conception of what constitutes a "judicial" function at least by reference to the state of the law at the time of *Nicholson* and also in light of the rather more formal hearing requirements applicable in the case of any subsequent internal review of the officer's decision. Nonetheless, there is also support for this approach in the judgment of the Supreme Court of Canada in *MacDonald Tobacco Inc.* v. *Canada (Employment and Immigration Commission)*,[8] rendered after *Nicholson* in 1981. There, on the basis of much the same principles though for quite different purposes, the Court had held that a commission officer making employment insurance decisions in a setting quite different from a fully adversarial one was acting judicially. This conclusion was in no way affected by the fact that there was an appeal from that officer to a board of referees that proceeded in a much more formal, judicialized way.

It is also of significance that the Court came to this conclusion despite the fact that it accepted that the employment standards officer had breached the rules of natural justice or procedural fairness in this particular instance. This was not a matter that was at all relevant to the operation of the doctrine of issue estoppel. Relying on standard authorities such as *Harelkin* v. *University of Regina*[9] and *Canadian Pacific Ltd.* v. *Matsqui Indian Band*,[10] the Court held that it need not have concern with whether the final judicial determination in this case had been preceded by adherence to the rules of procedural fairness. There was an appropriate and available appeal route for dealing with such allegations with the prospect of judicial review thereafter should the appeal on this ground be unsuccessful or should the adjudicator not cure the procedural deficiencies before the employment standards officer.

The Court also found further support for this proposition in the recent Supreme Court of Canada jurisprudence on collateral attack and, in particular, *R.* v. *Consolidated Maybrun Mines Ltd.*[11] Danyluk should have raised these issues directly on an application to the director for the appointment of an adjudicator, not collaterally by way of trying to resist the application of the doctrine of issue estoppel.

Both in terms of the operation of the doctrine of issue estoppel and the concomitant refusal to treat a breach of the rules of natural justice or procedural fairness as in any way relevant to the operation of that doctrine in this case, the Court of Appeal was determined to respect

---

8   [1981] 1 S.C.R. 401.
9   [1979] 2 S.C.R. 561.
10 [1995] 1 S.C.R. 3.
11 [1998] 1 S.C.R. 706.

the integrity of the relevant administrative process as well as giving effect to the more usual policy behind the issue estoppel doctrine — to protect the courts' own processes and the interests of other parties to disputes from the relitigation of issues that have already been dealt with once in another forum. Three additional considerations underscore the Court's commitment to the direction it took. First, under the then *Act*, the pursuit of remedies through the employments standards route was expressly stated to be without prejudice to the right of the affected individual to pursue common law remedies in the regular courts. According to the Court, that did not necessarily pre-empt the possibility of issue estoppel being raised in the context of a subsequent exercise of the preserved common law right. Second, on the face of the *Act*, the director had a discretion as to whether to respond positively to a request by an aggrieved employee for the appointment of an adjudicator to review the employment standard officer's decision. However, the Court doubted whether this provided a basis for denying a right of appeal when the employee had followed the statutory prerequisites laid down in the *Act*. Finally, despite concerns expressed by the appellant as to the status of employment standards officers as civil servants, the Court did not see this as calling into question their independence such as to disable them from the status of judicial functionary for the purposes of the application of the principles of issue estoppel.

As a consequence, though subject to the Supreme Court's judgment on the appeal from this decision,[12] *Danyluk* amounts to a particularly broad conception of the reach of the principles of issue estoppel in the domain of determinations by tribunals and other forms of statutory adjudicator. Nonetheless, it is one that is rooted very firmly in the policies of respect for the integrity of administrative processes so evident in such recent case law as *Matsqui Indian Band*, *Consolidated Maybrun*, and *Weber* v. *Ontario Hydro*.[13] Account should, however, be taken of other jurisprudence that is not quite so expansive in its treatment of issue estoppel arguments in the context of the administrative process.

Among a number of even more recent judgments, the Nova Scotia Court of Appeal has distinguished *Danyluk* and, in so doing, has shed light on other aspects of the principles of issue estoppel. This was in *Braithwaite* v. *Nova Scotia Public Service Long Term Disability Plan Trust Fund*.[14]

---

12   Leave to appeal was granted on 4 Nov. 1999: [1999] S.C.C.A. No.47 (Q.L.) and the decision of the Court is now under reserve.

13   [1995] 2 S.C.R. 929.

14   (1999), 176 N.S.R. (2d) 173 (C.A.).

Braithwaite had been on long-term disability. However, his coverage was discontinued when the carrier determined that he was no longer disabled. Braithwaite then exercised a right of appeal on medical grounds to a medical appeal board. That appeal was dismissed and rather than seeking judicial review of the board's decision, Braithwaite sued the plan civilly, claiming that he was disabled as defined in the plan, and therefore entitled to benefits. The plan then moved to strike out his statement of claim on the basis that the issue of his disability was *res judicata* as a consequence of the determination of the medical appeal board and that he was therefore estopped from "litigating it again."

In affirming the motion judge's dismissal of this application, Cromwell J.A. (delivering the judgment of the majority) accepted that there was at least some doubt as to whether the question of eligibility for benefits under the plan had necessarily been foreclosed by the determination of the medical appeal. Given this doubt as to the identity of the issues at stake in the two proceedings, he accepted that the matter should not be resolved definitively in the context of a motion to strike out. In so doing he also noted that, as opposed to *Danyluk*, there were no internal rights of appeal or other designated modes of recourse from a decision of the medical appeal board, simply judicial review. This led him to speculate on whether, given the discretionary nature of the court's authority to refuse to deal with cases on the basis of issue estoppel and *res judicata* as well as under the concept of limited access to judicial review, it might be simply better and fairer to allow the case to go forward as an action than holding that the plaintiff should have had recourse to judicial review.

In so doing, Cromwell J.A. also relied on yet another Ontario Court of Appeal authority,[15] judgment in which had been rendered after *Danyluk* but in which there had been no reference to *Danyluk: Minott* v. *O'Shanter Development Co.*[16] The principal basis for the conclusion of the Court of Appeal in *Minott* that the doctrine of issue estoppel or *res judicata* did not apply was its determination that the first instance judge had been correct in her holding that there was not a sufficient identity of issues. The fact that the board of referees had upheld the denial of employment insurance benefits on the basis that a dismissed employee had lost his job "by reason of his own misconduct" in terms of the relevant legislation was not the same issue as whether, under common law, he been dismissed for cause. In that sense, *Minott* is an

---

15   *Ibid.* at 189.
16   (1999), 42 O.R. (3d) 321 (C.A.).

even clearer example of the first requirement than *Braithwaite*; the need for an identity of issues.

Indeed, it has been applied subsequently on this point in yet another Ontario Court of Appeal incursion into this troubled area of the law: *Heynen* v. *Frito Lay Canada Ltd.*[17] This too involved a determination by an employment standards officer, and Goudge J.A., in delivering the judgment of the court, held that the issue determined by that officer was not the same issue that was before the first instance court in subsequent wrongful dismissal proceedings. The officer had denied a jailed employee termination pay on the basis of a provision in the legislation dealing with contracts that had been frustrated or become impossible to perform. In the civil litigation, the employer had not raised frustration as a defence. The issues were therefore not identical. In so holding, the court, quoting from the judgment of Morden A.C.J.O. in *Rasanen* v. *Rosemount Instruments Ltd.*,[18] expressed the view that it was necessary to take a "fastidious approach" to the requirement that there be an identity of issues.[19]

As well, the Court of Appeal in *Minott* ruled that one of the other three prerequisites for the application of the doctrine had not been satisfied. To the extent that the employer had not been a participating party in the unemployment insurance proceedings, the requirement as to identity of parties had not been met. For these purposes, the court did not treat the supply of information to an officer of the commission as amounting to a sufficient degree of participation as to make it a party. Indeed, even greater active participation would seemingly have not made a difference since the court was very wary of the dangers of creating incentives for employers to take a significant role in unemployment insurance proceedings, proceedings in which they did not have any direct financial stake in the outcome. This too distinguished the case from *Danyluk* in that, there, the employer had participated actively as a respondent in the investigation by the employment standards officer, though, perhaps more importantly, it was a party in the sense of having direct financial responsibility in the event of a finding of a breach of the *Act*.

However, the court then went on to make some pronouncements that at first blush seem quite at odds with the position adopted by a differently constituted Court of Appeal a mere five weeks earlier in *Danyluk*. First, while accepting that a board of referees under what was then the *Unemployment Insurance Act* was sufficiently judicial to qualify for the application of the issue estoppel doctrine, the court seemed clearly of the

---

17   (1999), 179 D.L.R. (4th) 317 (Ont. C.A.) [*Heynen*].
18   *Rasanen*, above note 1.
19   *Heynen*, above note 17 at para. 20.

view that that protection would be lost not only if the governing legislation infringed the principles of procedural fairness but also if there had been a failure to afford procedural fairness in the particular case. Second, and perhaps most significant, the court emphasized the discretionary nature of the deployment of the doctrine of issue estoppel particularly in the case of findings by administrative tribunals and other forms of statutory authority. This was so even where the three requirements were met.

In the particular context of unemployment insurance disputes, Laskin J.A., delivering the judgment of the court, cited five considerations. If issue estoppel principles apply to a regime that is meant to provide quick, inexpensive, and summary justice, it could have the contrary effect of making it important for all such cases to be argued as though the dispute was before a regular court. Employees embroiled in this system are generally in a very vulnerable state, having just lost their jobs and, as a consequence, not necessarily well located to make their claim to optimum effect. The financial stakes are also not as likely to be as high as in a subsequent wrongful dismissal action. Moreover, even conceding that the board does comply with the rules of procedural fairness, there are significant procedural differences between its processes and the fuller protections of a civil action. Finally, there is a considerable difference between the nature of the expertise of a board of referees and that of a judge adjudicating on a wrongful dismissal suit. As a consequence, Laskin J.A., stated that, had the court not rejected the application of the doctrine on the basis of the three-stage test, it would have done so as an exercise of judicial discretion.

Given that some or all of these considerations can also be applied in the case of employment standards adjudications and particularly at the employment standards officer level, there are very obviously tensions between the two judgments. Indeed, more generally, the court in *Minott* is clearly very cautious in the approach that it takes to the invocation of the doctrine of issue estoppel in the case of administrative tribunals as reflected by the assertion of such a broad discretion. In contrast, in *Danyluk*, discretionary considerations do not rate a mention and the implication is that, provided the three conditions are met, the doctrine will apply automatically.[20]

---

20   Subsequently, in yet another (un)employment insurance case, another panel of the Ontario Court of Appeal indicated its agreement with *Minott* and the existence of an overriding judicial discretion even where the three conditions are satisfied but, in exercising its discretion, was much more inclined to apply the doctrine to the administrative agency determination than Laskin J.A. had been in *Minott*: *Schweneke v. Ontario*, (2000), 47 O.R. (3d) 97 (C.A.).

Indeed, insofar as *Danyluk* might be read as denying the existence of such an overriding judicial discretion based on broad conceptions of equity and fairness, it is inconsistent not only with other authority on the application of issue estoppel to the determinations of administrative tribunals but also with the law governing its operation in the domain of findings by regular courts. Thus, in *British Columbia (Minister of Forests)* v. *Bugbusters Pest Management Ltd.*,[21] Finch J.A., in refusing to apply the doctrine in a subsequent tort action to a determination of responsibility for a fire made by the Chief Forester, stated:

> It must always be remembered that although the three requirements for issue estoppel must be satisfied before it can apply, the fact that they may be satisfied does not automatically give rise to its application. Issue estoppel is an equitable doctrine, and as can be seen from the cases, is closely related to abuse of process. The doctrine of issue estoppel is designed as an implement of justice, and a protection against injustice. It inevitably calls upon the exercise of judicial discretion to achieve fairness according to the circumstances of each case.[22]

In this instance, the court relied upon the fact that the parties to the civil litigation did not at the time of the proceedings before the Chief Forester reasonably expect that that official's decision on cause would finally resolve for all purposes the issue of responsibility for the fire. The court also noted the express legislative preservation of an action for damages.

What these judgments demonstrate graphically is that there is presently much variation in the approaches taken by various judges (even on the same court) to the extent of the application of the principles of issues estoppel to the determinations of statutory authorities and, in particular, to the scope of judicial discretion to refuse to apply the principles in the name of equity in these contexts. Presumably, it will take at least the judgment of the Supreme Court of Canada in *Danyluk* to sort this issue out.[23] In the meantime, the law in this domain is destined to remain tantalizingly unclear.

---

21 (1998), 159 D.L.R. (4th) 50 (B.C.C.A.).

22 *Ibid.* at 61.

23 An application for leave to appeal was also filed in the Supreme Court in *Minott*. However, it was discontinued shortly thereafter: [1999] S.C.C.A. No. 120 (Q.L.).

B. REMEDIES: REFUSAL ON DISCRETIONARY GROUNDS

1) General Principles and Considerations

On occasion it is said that judicial review for wrongful administrative action is available automatically, particularly in a situation involving jurisdictional error. This concept of an entitlement as of right to a remedy is also sometimes characterized by the Latin expression, *ex debito justitiae*. It is, however, abundantly clear that, even in the case of jurisdictional error, the courts have a considerable degree of discretion in determining whether a remedy should follow a wrong.

In any event, to characterize this area of judicial review simply in these terms would be to undercategorize the situations in which discretionary considerations play a role in public law litigation. Nonetheless, the instances in which courts have proceeded through the merits of an application for judicial review, decided that a basis for judicial review has been made out but then declined to remedy the wrong are in fact comparatively rare. Far more common, particularly in recent years, are cases in which courts determine at the outset of a hearing or on an interlocutory motion that discretionary reasons dictate that the case not be allowed to proceed. That may be a judgment that is based on the nature of the claim, the forum in which the proceedings have been brought, *or* the type of remedy that is being pursued. In other words, this section is in reality as much, if not more, about initial access to the courts as it concerns the availability of judicial remedies in the event of established wrongs. The discretions discussed here rank alongside standing as threshold devices limiting the pursuit of certain kinds of litigation.

In many respects, the grounds on which courts may refuse judicial review even in the face of an otherwise reviewable wrong or at the outset of proceedings correspond to the discretionary reasons that restrict the availability of private law remedies and equitable remedies in particular. Thus, undue delay (or lâches), misconduct (or unclean hands), and the availability of alternative grounds of relief (damages) parallel the bases on which specific performance, injunctions, and other equitable forms of relief are denied regularly by the superior courts in the exercise of their equitable jurisdiction. Concepts of prematurity, mootness, and general lack of utility also either exist or find analogues in private law remedial regimes. Behind the recognition of these discretionary reasons for the denial of relief in both public and private law are a number of fairly obvious policy reasons.

Among the interests at stake is that of ensuring the integrity of the judicial process by not subjecting its scarce resources to proceedings that are hypothetical, no longer of significance, or would serve no useful purpose. This concern with the integrity of the judicial process is also reflected in other ways. Where there is undue delay, the court's ability to adjudicate fully and fairly may be hampered because it will be forced to decide on the basis of a less than satisfactory evidentiary record. The same kind of possible litigation frailty arises in the case of premature and hypothetical litigation. There are frequently problems in determining legal questions in a factual vacuum. Denying relief on the basis of other remedial alternatives also speaks to a concern with the comparative substantive and remedial advantages of having the dispute tried in this rather than another proceeding and possibly also another forum. On another level, the integrity of the judicial process can be brought into question if relief is available to litigants who have not conducted themselves well in their relations with the other side or with the court itself. Similarly, if the general public perceives that courts are willing to take purely hypothetical or moot cases when brought by the powerful, this can give rise to a sense of the judicial process being manipulated by those with influence in our society at the expense of others with "real" disputes and fewer resources.

Respect for the "other side" is also a consideration in most of these reasons for denying access to the courts or to relief. Cases that compromise the integrity of the court will produce significant disadvantages to the respondent or defendant. To take just one example, delay can hamper the respondent's or defendant's abilities to marshal all of the proofs and arguments that would have been available at some earlier point to resist the applicant's or plaintiff's case. In the case of delay, there is also the possibility of an added disadvantage to the other side: the longer the delay in commencing and sometimes in prosecuting the proceeding, the more chance there is of prejudicial reliance on the state of affairs that is now being challenged.

On occasion, in private law litigation, the concern of the court will also focus on third parties whether before the court or not. To allow the litigation to proceed or to grant the remedy in question may be unfairly prejudicial to the rights and interests of such third parties. In the case of identifiable third parties not before the court, this may be because the court feels deprived of a sufficient basis for making an overall assessment of the claims being made or the consequences of taking a particular course of action or awarding a particular remedy. Where third parties are actually before the court, the court may, for example, recognize that their ability to make out a case in support of their claims has been prejudiced by undue delay in the proceedings or that they have relied justifiably on an apparent legal position such that it would now make it unjust to allow those expectations to be disturbed.

Although cases of the kind identified in this general survey can and do arise in the domain of public law, my principal purpose in this section is not to develop or elaborate on those situations where the analysis would not differ significantly whether the case is a public law or a private law one. Rather, I want to concentrate on the special public law dimensions that come into play when discretion over access to the courts' processes and remedies are a factor in public law litigation. More specifically, my concern will be with the considerations that are added to the matrix when a statutory decision maker is part of the mix either as the nominal or real defendant or respondent in judicial review proceedings or is there as a third party.

This introduction of a second institutional dimension in the case of most judicial review litigation clearly raises another set of integrity concerns. What will be the impact of allowing the case to proceed or these remedies to be granted on the functioning and imperatives of the administrative process under challenge be it a tribunal, departmental official, Minister of the Crown, Cabinet, or some other statutory body such as a municipality or a university? What are the special factors or considerations that are at stake here?

If we take once again the instance of delay in the commencement or pursuit of judicial review proceedings, it is easy to conjure up examples where delay in challenging a government program or a regulatory decision can have an impact on the integrity of the decision maker's operations. Other decisions and action may have been taken on the assumption that the original program or decision are legally beyond reproach such as to make it now inappropriate for the courts to intervene. The only difference between this and the taking into account of the same consideration in the case of essentially private law litigation will be the explicit assertion and frequent recognition of broader public interest appeals. "The dam is now half built. The ramifications for the public fisc in allowing this action to proceed would be enormous. The applicant public interest group should not have delayed in commencing these proceedings."

That this sense of an overarching public interest is part of Canadian public law is manifest in a really diverse range of situations beyond the conventional delay kind of case. Thus, as we have seen already, in the principles governing the availability of interlocutory injunctions, the Supreme Court has developed a methodology that always requires the public interest to be considered when the court is assessing the balance of convenience. Moreover, the public interest in the maintenance until trial of existing statutes and orders is frequently the single most decisive issue in such litigation. To take yet another example, in the domain of monies paid to governments under an unconstitutional law, the Supreme Court (albeit controversially) has developed special public interest–based defences that mean that the normal principles governing the recovery of money paid under mistake of fact and now law are not determinative in the instance of such "unconstitutional" overpayments.[24]

However, the terrain in which the integrity of administrative processes and decision makers is most frequently a consideration in the exercise of judicial discretion on questions of access to courts and to remedies is that of alternative remedies. Where the statute provides or an institution acting under statutory authority has created a particular regime for dealing with claims or complaints, respect for the integrity of the administrative process itself will be a consideration in determining whether the judicial review application should proceed to adjudication. Moreover, there will be the added factor or consideration of respect for or deference to legislative judgment in the case of other than court regimes established by primary legislation and perhaps also in the case of subordinate legislation. Of course, the interests of the court are also implicated in that its scarce resources will be affected by any decision that allows the case to proceed by way of judicial review rather than through the statutorily designated internal or alternative external route. Similarly, if there are any private parties adverse in interest, any advantages that will accrue to them from the internal or alternative processes may be compromised by allowing the matter to be contested by way of judicial review. In other words, in many alternative remedy situations, there will be a coalescence of four separate interests to which the court will have to have regard in determining whether the matter should be allowed to proceed by way of judicial review instead of internally or before some other external body.

Of course, in many instances where the right of appeal or review established by legislation is to the court itself, the primary concern will be respect for legislative choice particularly in cases where there is no discernible difference between the way in which the case would be conducted in judicial review or appellate proceedings. However, even in this domain, the integrity of the court's own processes can be a factor when the designated route to the court has different dimensions to those of judicial review. These same factors might also have an impact on parties adverse in interest.

---

24   See *Air Canada v. British Columbia*, [1989] 1 S.C.R. 1161 and discussed further in Chapter 21.

2) The Jurisprudence

a) Prematurity and Existence of Alternative Mechanisms for Raising of Issues

At one time, the law on prematurity and alternative remedies largely reflected the principle identified at the beginning of this section. Where issues going to jurisdiction were at stake, the courts could and would intervene in response to an application for judicial review at any point in the proceedings. More particularly, those with standing had universal access to prohibition or injunctive relief when a statutory authority was acting without or in excess of jurisdiction. Moreover, for these purposes, jurisdiction included an absence of authority in its traditional threshold sense but also a denial of procedural fairness and bias. All of that has now changed.

The most dramatic recent manifestation of the current attitude of the courts is the judgment of the Supreme Court of Canada in *Canadian Pacific Ltd.* v. *Matsqui Indian Band*.[25] There, as we have seen in other contexts, Canadian Pacific was challenging Indian Band tax assessment of the land over which their railway lines ran. It claimed that the land in question was not "in the reserve" and therefore not within the taxing domain of the bands. Instead of raising this matter before the various tribunals established under the relevant legislation to hear appeals from initial assessments and the further right of appeal to the Federal Court of Canada, the company sought immediate judicial review of the initial assessments.

All members of the Supreme Court accepted that this was a jurisdiction-conferring matter and a minority of the Court, referring to earlier Supreme Court of Canada jurisprudence, held that the company had immediate access to the Courts to raise this jurisdictional challenge. In so ruling, the minority also expressed doubts as to the capacity of the appeal tribunals to deal with this issue. In contrast, the majority of the Court (on this point[26]) were of the view that, notwithstanding the jurisdictional character of this question, the Court still had a discretion to decline to deal with it in light of the appeal route

---

25 [1995] 1 S.C.R. 3 [*Canadian Pacific*].

26 Constructing a *ratio* in *Matsqui Indian Band* is a problematic exercise in that the end result was that the company succeeded. It did so as a result of a combination of two judges who believed that it was appropriate to deal immediately with a challenge to the independence of the appeal tribunals and the three judges who were in a minority on the question of the prematurity of the issue as to jurisdiction over the company's operations.

available to the company. Lamer C.J.C., speaking for the majority on this point, then went on to hold that the first instance judge had not acted unreasonably in exercising his discretion against the company at least on this point.

His primary reason for doing so was his assessment that to allow judicial intervention at this stage, even on a jurisdictional issue, would compromise the integrity of Parliament's clear intention to place primary responsibility for the operation of the relevant taxing scheme in the hands of Indian bands. He was also of the view that the combination of appeal rights within that regime, including ultimate access to the Federal Court of Canada, represented an adequate alternative "remedy" for the company. He also noted that the question is not about whether the tribunal is a "better" forum than the courts in the sense of it having a greater capacity or expertise than the courts to deal with the matter in issue. In other words, it is not a comparative exercise but one in which the court simply assesses whether the tribunal is "an adequate forum"[27] for addressing as a matter of initial impression the matter in issue, in this case, a jurisdictional challenge.

In reaching this conclusion, Lamer C.J.C. confirmed (and, indeed, extended) at least one earlier Supreme Court authority that had been subject to much criticism and even judicial questioning and in which there was a strong dissent by Dickson J.: *Harelkin* v. *University of Regina*.[28] There, a majority of the Court had held that a student complaining of a lack of procedural fairness in the taking of a decision to require him to withdraw from an academic program should have exhausted internal appeals before coming to the court. In so doing, it accepted the institutional capacities of the university's appeal structures to address the allegations of a breach of the rules of natural justice or procedural fairness or at the very least to cure them by providing the fair hearing that the student had been denied below. In delivering the judgment of the majority in *Harelkin*, Beetz J. also emphasized that recourse to internal appeals for resolution of the problem could have saved a lot of money and time and been far less disruptive to the life of the student and the operation of the university. Where such a recourse has the potential to deal with the problem, it should generally be used, albeit that the courts might still have to be called upon at some later point.

---

27   *Canadian Pacific*, above note 25 at 29.
28   [1979] 2 S.C.R. 561.

Thus, at least in contexts where there are adequate rights of appeal (either internal or external) or other statutorily designated processes, the clear message is that pre-emptive judicial review is not normally available and that, almost invariably, those routes should be utilized instead. Moreover, for these purposes, the nature of the challenge will not normally matter. As long as the appellate body or other mechanism has the institutional capacity to deal with the issues raised, it should be given the opportunity to do so whether those issues involve the rules of procedural fairness or jurisdiction-conferring provisions.

However, as *Matsqui Indian Band* itself suggests, there may be occasions on which pre-emptive judicial review is available even where there is a statutorily designated appeal mechanism which would normally be expected to deal with the matters in issue. As well as raising the jurisdictional question of whether the land over which the lines ran was "in the reserve," Canadian Pacific was challenging the institutional independence of the tribunals established by the Indian bands for the resolution of such issues. In a sense, of course, such a challenge goes to the adequacy or competence of the statutory appeal or review mechanism and, at that level, can be seen as a necessary exception to the general principle.

Indeed, this is how two judges in the Supreme Court in effect saw the matter. When their position was joined to that of the three judges who were of the view that judicial review was available immediately because a jurisdictional issue was raised, the actual result in the case was one that vindicated Canadian Pacific's decision to seek judicial review rather than go through the band tribunal process. Nonetheless, a plurality of the Court,[29] in a judgment delivered by Sopinka J., was of the view that even the challenge based on institutional independence was premature. In particular, these four judges were of the opinion that judicial assessment of the institutional independence argument would be more informed on the basis of evidence as to how the process actually operated.

Subsequently, the Supreme Court accepted that, at least in some circumstances, Sopinka J. was correct. Where the statutory regime establishing an adjudicative process left room for choice on matters of detail relevant to the assessment of lack of independence arguments, the court should take into account the choices that had been made and how the tribunal operated in practice. However, what is also clear is that that information does not necessarily have to await the outcome of the particular matter before the tribunal. As opposed to the situation in

---

29 The three judges who held that the company had an immediate entitlement to seek judicial review on the jurisdictional issue did not rule on this issue.

Matsqui Indian Band, where the jurisdiction was one on which there was no evidence of past practice, the choices of modality will on many occasions have already been made and there will be a history of how the tribunal has actually functioned or operated in practice. This is clear from *Katz* v. *Vancouver Stock Exchange*, where the Court in a brief judgment more or less simply affirmed the judgment of the British Columbia Court of Appeal though making the one point that it approved that Court's use of evidence of how the disciplinary regime of the Exchange *had* operated in practice in what was in effect a pre-emptive strike.[30] Katz had taken his concerns to the British Columbia Securities Commission once a panel was struck to hear his case, the Commission had ruled against him, and he then appealed this decision to the British Columbia Court of Appeal.

What this suggests is that, provided that the reviewing court has an adequate factual basis on which to make a ruling on a lack of independence challenge, it may do so without requiring the affected parties first to submit to a hearing on the merits. However, as indicated by *Katz*, as part of laying the foundation for such a judicial review application, it may be necessary or at least useful for the matter to be placed before the tribunal itself for a ruling as a prelude to launching the judicial review application. Nonetheless, even in this kind of case, it is dangerous to overgeneralize and assert that provided the evidential foundation is there and the tribunal itself has ruled against the challenge, the court must take the case. There are, in fact, other dimensions to the problem.

In all cases where allegations of bias, lack of institutional independence, and, more generally, a denial of procedural fairness are raised in the context of an application to prohibit or enjoin the continuation of the proceedings, there is always a chance that the issue will be rendered moot by the affected person succeeding before the tribunal on the merits. This raises questions as to whether this is or should ever be an independent factor justifying denial of access to the courts in advance of the actual disposition of the matter by the decision-maker. Indeed, in some instances, as exemplified by *Harelkin*, the frailty of the proceedings at first instance may be cured by a full rehearing by an unbiased, independent body according procedural fairness in the context of a statutory appeal or review.

---

30   [1996] 3 S.C.R. 405, aff'g (1995), 128 D.L.R. (4th) 424 (B.C.C.A.).

More recently, this consideration, coupled with the fact that the tribunal itself (as opposed to its chair) had still to rule on a motion for disclosure of information, led the Ontario Court of Appeal in *Howe* v. *Institute of Chartered Accountants of Ontario*[31] to dismiss a judicial review application as premature. Rather than fragment the proceedings, it was preferable to await the outcome of the process and deal with all relevant issues (including ones that might arise subsequently in the course of the hearing and internal appeal) in the context of the statutory appeal to the courts provided for in the *Act*.

Indeed, even in a context where there are no appeal mechanisms (just judicial review), these considerations have weight particularly when one adds the further dimension that such pre-emptive strikes may be taken principally for tactical reasons and, in particular, to delay the process. While administrative tribunals are not obliged to adjourn their proceedings simply because a party has made a pre-emptive judicial review application, many frequently do so. Also, even if they do not, there is always the possibility of an application for an interim injunction or a stay of proceedings until such time as the pre-emptive challenge has been dealt with. It, therefore, becomes necessary to consider how a court effectively can discourage the use of pre-emptive judicial review as a tactic in delaying the administrative process.

Many of these problems are well illustrated by the facts of and the judgment of Evans J., then of the Federal Court, Trial Division in *Lorenz* v. *Air Canada*.[32] Air Canada had dismissed Lorenz and Lorenz grieved that action under the unfair dismissal provisions of the *Canada Labour Code*. Five days into the hearing, Air Canada asked the adjudicator to recuse himself on the basis of a reasonable apprehension of bias. The allegation was that he was disqualified by reason of the fact that he was at the time representing an employee of another company who was grieving dismissal under the equivalent Québec legislation. As far as could be ascertained, this particular ground was a novel one in Canadian bias jurisprudence. The adjudicator considered and rejected the challenge in a reasoned decision and the proceedings were then

31 (1994), 19 O.R. (3d) 483 (C.A.).
32 [1999] F.C.J. No. 1383 (Q.L.) (T.D.). [*Lorenz*].

stayed[33] pending judicial review of the issue by the Federal Court. For whatever reason, the hearing of Air Canada's application in the Federal Court did not occur until nearly two years later.

Evans J. identifies the two principal considerations that bear on the exercise of judicial discretion in a case such as this, a judicial discretion which he had earlier held existed even in situations where the allegation was one of bias and there was no right of appeal or review provided for in the relevant statute:

> On the one hand are the possible hardships caused to Air Canada, and the time and resources that will have been wasted, if the bias question is not determined prior to the hearing before the adjudicator. On the other hand, there are the adverse consequences of delaying the administrative process and countenancing a multiplicity of litigation.[34]

He then proceeded to evaluate these and other competing considerations in the context of this case before reaching the conclusion that the application for judicial review was premature.

There are obviously situations where to compel an affected person to await the outcome of the proceedings before being able to have an allegation of bias considered will constitute hardship to that person. In earlier jurisprudence, the Federal Court itself had identified one form of this hardship — having to submit to the "indignity" of disciplinary proceedings or other form of inquiry into one's conduct by a possibly

---

33   Though this is nowhere stated in the judgment, it appears as though this was by consent of the parties and that the issue of prematurity was not raised initially by the dismissed employee but by the intervening Attorney General of Canada. At that point, counsel for the employee supported the position of the Attorney General. This raises an interesting question as to what extent, if at all the court's determination of such issues should be affected by the position of the parties. If the party potentially most adversely affected by both the bias and the delay of the proceedings wants the issue of bias determined before the hearing proceeds any further, should this be a relevant consideration, determinative, or of absolutely no significance? Is it important that, in *Lorenz*, the Attorney General's intervention was based on transcendant institutional concerns? Would or should it have made any difference in *Lorenz* had the Attorney General (purporting to represent the concerns of the process) asserted that those administering this aspect of the legislation had a preference for bias challenges to be dealt with by the court separately and in advance of the hearing of the merits of a grievance rather than await judicial review after the final decision had been rendered?

34   *Lorenz*, above note 32 at para. 18.

biased tribunal or adjudicator.[35] These concerns are also apparent in the following statement of Lambert J.A. of the British Columbia Court of Appeal in granting a stay of further hearing of an insider trading investigation by the British Columbia Securities Commission pending the hearing of an appeal from a ruling by the Commission that an allegation of bias against one of its members was unfounded:

> There is a great deal of harm being done to the applicants by this very public hearing. It has been said by counsel that the applicants themselves may be called by the Commission to testify. Their credibility may well be challenged. Considerable prejudice may be visited on all of the applicants before any decision of the Commission is made. A decision of the Commission adverse to the applicants could cause further prejudice to them and further prejudice to many other people as well.
>
> The Superintendent of Brokers argues that the public interest requires that the hearing continue. I do not agree. There is no public interest, in my opinion, in inflicting grave prejudice on the three applicants by concluding a hearing which may turn out in the end to be void because a decision of this Court is made that there is a reasonable apprehension of bias in relation to one or more members of the panel in the carrying out of their judicial duty.[36]

There are also the monetary costs involved in having to participate in a hearing that may, after the event, be quashed on the basis of facts known at the outset or shortly thereafter. Indeed, in many instances, this will be a concern for the tribunal as well as for both the parties. Thus, in the leading bias case of *Committee for Justice and Liberty* v. *Canada (National Energy Board)*,[37] an allegation of bias was raised at the outset of a hearing process that was likely to last well over a year. In those circumstances, at least where there is some merit to the allegation, it is in the interests of everyone including the tribunal or agency to have the issue adjudicated by a court before the hearing gets underway. In the particular instance, this led to the board stating a

---

35 See, for example, *Canada (Royal Canadian Mounted Police)* v. *Malmo-Levine*, (1998), 161 F.T.R. 25, in the context of an application by RCMP officers for an interim injunction to halt hearings by the APEC Inquiry until such time as a challenge to the impartiality of the Chair of the Inquiry had been determined, the Chair having refused an adjournment for those purposes.

36 *Bennett* v. *British Columbia (Superintendent of Brokers)*, [1993] B.C.J. No. 246 (Q.L.) (B.C.C.A.).

37 [1978] 1 S.C.R. 369.

case to the Federal Court of Appeal under then section 28(4) of the *Federal Court Act*.[38]

Nonetheless, as Evans J. suggests in *Lorenz*, these are characteristics of every case in which bias allegations are raised before, at the outset of, or during the course of a hearing. Albeit that the conduct of personnel at Air Canada was in issue in these wrongful dismissal proceedings, the court was not prepared to see hardship to the company merely by reason of the fact that it had to submit to a hearing before a possibly biased adjudicator. To concede that in this case would be virtually to accept that proceedings must cease every time a serious issue as to bias was raised and that there was no discretion in the courts to postpone dealing with the issue until the hearing had concluded. Evans J. was also not prepared to attribute too much significance to the fact that there were still eighteen days of hearing scheduled, particularly when five days had already taken place. In so doing, he also drew attention to the possibility that Air Canada might in any event win on the substance of its case at that hearing.

As well, Evans J. drew attention to the usual list of countervailing considerations: that this was a novel case and, while it was certainly not a frivolous claim nor was it a "cast iron" one. As well, he emphasized with particular reference to the delays in this case, the potential weapon too ready a willingness to hear such cases on a pre-emptive basis would confer on those with an interest in delaying the administrative process. While not in fact attributing such a motive to Air Canada and its lawyers, Evans J. clearly thought the mere danger of this occurring was always a relevant consideration. There was also the further danger (noted already) of fragmentation of the court's involvement on judicial review with the particular proceedings. Wherever possible, all grounds of attack on a particular decision should be dealt with in a single judicial review application and pre-emptive strikes created the risk that, as a result of what happened at any resumed hearing, there would have to be yet another judicial review application. Finally, he made reference to the statutory context as re-enforcing these arguments. That statutory context indicated a legislative desire for a speedy, efficient mode of resolving unfair dismissal claims in non-unionized, federal workplaces with the absence of a right of appeal and the presence of a strong privative clause also bespeaking a clear intention of very restricted judicial supervision of that process.

---

38   Now s. 18.3(1). For a fuller description of how the bias allegation arose in *Committee for Justice and Liberty*, see chapter 14, note 27.

All of these considerations indicated to Evans J. that in this context

> it will be a rare case indeed when the court should determine the merits of the claim prior to the release of the adjudicator's ultimate decision, such as when the allegation reveals a very clear case of bias and the issue arises at the outset of a hearing that is scheduled to last for a significant length of time.[39]

Indeed, to the extent that the conditions identified by the court as relevant to this case are commonly found albeit in varying degrees in many administrative proceedings, any subsequent acknowledgment of this reasoning as authoritative would almost certainly mean a far greater reluctance on the part of the courts to entertain applications involving allegations of bias prior to the conclusion of the relevant hearing. It might also have an impact on the actions of decision makers themselves to the extent that they will see this kind of decision as giving them far more reason to refuse to adjourn proceedings when an allegation of bias is raised than they sometimes previously had seen themselves as having.

Whether the judgment of Evans J. will have this impact is, of course, another question. It is, in fact, consistent with the line generally taken in such matters by the Ontario courts where "exceptional circumstances"[40] are required for pre-emptive judicial intervention even where the ground is a reasonable apprehension of bias. However, courts in other jurisdictions (including the Federal Court itself) have often been somewhat more liberal in their willingness to entertain such pre-emptive applications either in the form of hearing the actual application for prohibition or injunctive relief, or granting stays of proceedings in anticipation of the hearing of such an application. Indeed, it is also worthy of note that Evans J. was prepared to accept that the making out of exceptional circumstances might be somewhat easier in bias cases to the extent that the continuation of the hearing will seldom add anything to the factual record necessary to make out such an allegation save to the extent that the actions of the impugned adjudicator might add further dimensions to the allegation. It is also an issue on which there is no room for curial deference to any tribunal assessment that it or one of its members is not biased.[41] There are also questions about the extent to

---

39   *Lorenz*, above note 32 at para. 35.
40   See *University of Toronto v. Canadian Union of Education Workers* (1988), 28 O.A.C. 295 (Div. Ct.) at 306 and *Ontario College of Art v. Ontario (Human Rights Commission)* (1992), 99 D.L.R. (4th) 738 (Ont. Div. Ct.) at 740 (both of which are cited by Evans J. (at para. 37)).
41   *Lorenz*, above note 32 at para. 38.

which "prejudice" to the person affected will continue to loom as a predominant consideration in disciplinary and related proceedings.

More generally, outside of the bias domain, there remain questions of the extent to which the concept of jurisdiction remains relevant. After all, in *Matsqui Indian Band*, there had been no ruling by a tribunal on the jurisdiction-conferring issue. If a tribunal had segmented the case and ruled first on this issue, would judicial review have been available at that point? If the answer to this question is either "Always" or "At least sometimes," will this even create an obligation on the part of a tribunal to segment its hearing in such a way as to deal with such jurisdictional issues first or in the context of preliminary motions?

In this regard, it is of some significance that, in *Howe*, a case that is in other respects very firmly against the use of pre-emptive judicial review, Finlayson J.A., delivering the judgment of the majority, conceded the availability of pre-emptive judicial review in the case of preliminary rulings by tribunals on issues that bear upon whether a tribunal "never had jurisdiction or has irretrievably lost it." As one example, he cites a case in which there was a question as to whether a requirement of timely written notice was a jurisdictional requirement of a tribunal being able to proceed with a hearing.[42] In a slightly different vein, Evans J., in *Lorenz*, echoing the implicit position of the two judges in *Matsqui Indian Band* who were prepared to deal with the lack of institutional independence argument, stated that "a reviewing court may also be more willing to intervene when the applicant alleges that the tribunal's enabling statute is constitutionally flawed."[43] All of this serves to indicate that there is no general rule, that context almost invariably matters, and that there remain many areas of uncertainty.

b) The Relevance of the Merits of the Application

In general, as exemplified by *Lorenz*, issues of prematurity, including failure to exhaust (or utilize) alternative recourses, are dealt with as preliminary or threshold issues with the actual merits of the claim playing a very limited role. The same is true of the stay of proceedings or interim injunction jurisprudence where, in general, there is a very limited initial or tentative assessment of the applicant's case. Indeed, in such cases, for the court to move on and engage in a full assessment of the substantive basis for the applicant's claim would be contradictory of the purposes being served by the existence of such discretionary

---

42   *Gage v. Ontario (A.G.)* (1992), 90 D.L.R. (4th) 537 (Ont. Div. Ct.).
43   *Lorenz*, above note 32 at para. 44.

grounds for refusing to entertain an application for judicial review: judicial preference that the substantive issues be resolved by the designated statutory authority in advance of any judicial review application.

The same is also generally true in two situations that are the other side of the prematurity coin: mootness and collateral attack. As already indicated in the earlier separate treatment of collateral forms of attack, the Supreme Court of Canada has recently established the discretionary nature of collateral attack as an administrative law remedy.[44] This was based primarily on the consideration that those affected should not be allowed to frustrate the operations of the administrative process by foregoing opportunities for direct attack and waiting in the weeds until such time as enforcement proceedings are taken and then raising for the first time in that context a challenge to the validity of the original decision on which the enforcement proceedings are based. Moreover, in that context, the Court made it clear that it did not matter that the challenge was one based on a jurisdiction-conferring provision. In other words, there is very little or no consideration of the nature of the alleged invalidity let alone the merits of any challenge.

In the domain of mootness, the nature of the grounds of attack may have some relevance in the sense of the court assessing whether this is the kind of issue that is likely to recur in other cases thereby justifying attention notwithstanding mootness in the particular circumstances. However, this in no way depends on a consideration of the merits of the challenge or its strength.

In contrast, the substantive merits of the applicant's case often play a far more significant role in any court decision to deny relief on some of the other discretionary grounds for the refusal of judicial review: undue delay, misconduct, balance of convenience, and even waiver. Frequently, the reviewing court will express the view that it cannot properly deal with one or more of these considerations without hearing the application for judicial review on the merits and indeed reaching a conclusion on whether the applicant has made out the case on the merits.

There are two separate but not necessarily connected reasons for such a stance. First, the facts pertaining to the potential discretionary grounds for the denial of relief and to the substantive merits of the applicant's case may coincide or overlap or simply not be segregated easily. Second, the decision to invoke the discretionary ground for the

---

44 R. v. *Consolidated Maybrun Mines Ltd.*, [1998] 1 S.C.R. 706 and R. v. *Al Klippert Ltd.*, [1998] 1 S.C.R. 737.

denial of judicial review may depend on the extent or gravity of any error or a full understanding of the circumstances in which it occurred.

c) Delay

The assertion of undue delay in the seeking of relief provides a useful scenario for illustrating this point. On occasion, the courts will deal with this discretionary ground for the denial of relief as a preliminary matter without direct regard for the merits of the applicant's case. In such instances, they inquire as to the extent of the delay, whether there are any cogent explanations for it, and, most significantly, whether the delay in seeking judicial review has prejudiced the position of any of the parties to the proceedings, the public interest generally, and also the effective functioning of the administrative process. On a balancing of all these various considerations, the court then decides whether to proceed to hear the merits of the application or dismiss it.[45] However, in most situations, the court will not feel capable of reaching a fully informed judgment on whether delay should be decisive against the applicant's claim without having a full sense of the nature of that claim and the impact of any error on the applicant.

A good example is provided by the judgment of the British Columbia Court of Appeal in *MacLean* v. *University of British Columbia*.[46] There, a university teacher had delayed a year in challenging a decision of an internal appeal board confirming a recommendation of the president of the university that his appointment not be renewed. He claimed that the delay had been a consequence of lack of funds. In rejecting the university's motion to strike out MacLean's petition for judicial review on the ground of prejudicial delay (someone else had been hired), the court held that, in terms of the provision with respect to delay in the *Judicial Review Procedure Act*, this at least was a case in which the motions court should not have considered the impact of delay in the context of a motion to strike out the petition for judicial review:

> In my opinion, the question of whether delays should affect the outcome of a Judicial Review Application must be made in conjunction with the merits of the Judicial Review Application itself. It is only when those merits are weighed and the prejudice to both sides has been weighed that it is possible for the chambers judge to exercise the

---

45   In the context of an application to commence judicial review proceedings outside the normal time limits, see, for example, *Breton* v. *Battlefords Union Hospital Board* (1992), 6 Admin. L.R. (2d) 11 (Sask. Q.B.).

46   (1993), 109 D.L.R. (4th) 569 (B.C.C.A.).

principled and guided discretion that is conferred on a chambers judge in relation to granting a remedy under the *Judicial Review Procedure Act*.[47]

This was so even though, for the purposes of argument, the university was prepared to concede the basis on which MacLean was seeking judicial review. Indeed, the statements of the Court can be read to amount to a statement of a general rule in such cases. However, in considering the impact of this judgment in other jurisdictions, it is probably important to keep in mind the terms of section 11 of the British Columbia *Judicial Review Procedure Act*, which can be read as creating a heavier burden on those seeking to have a proceeding struck out or dismissed on the basis of delay than is the case under common law: "Unless an enactment otherwise provides, and unless the court considers that substantial prejudice or hardship will result to any other person affected by reason of delay, an application for judicial review is not barred by effluxion of time."

d) Misconduct

Misconduct, a rare basis for the refusal of relief, provides another example particularly when the grounds of judicial review are based on the manner in which a tribunal or agency fulfilled its process obligations. This is well illustrated by *Homex Realty and Development Co. Ltd. v. Village of Wyoming*.[48] There, the allegation was a breach of the rules of natural justice by the village in passing a by-law which in effect deregistered a subdivision plan filed by the developer. The reason for this action was in order to force the issue over whether the developer had to pay for the installation of municipal services to the subdivision. This had been a matter of ongoing dispute and the passage of the by-law was the culmination of a lengthy negotiation between the parties. In the circumstances, the questions whether there had been a breach of the rules of natural justice in the passage of the by-law and whether the developer had misconducted itself in its dealing with the village to such an extent that it should not be allowed to rely on any breach of the rules of natural justice were linked evidentially. The Court needed to understand the whole sequence of events to make a sensible ruling on either issue. Moreover, in any assessment of the discretionary ground for the denial of judicial review, the nature and extent of the natural justice violation and the nature and the extent of the devel-

---

47   *Ibid.* at 572.
48   [1980] 2 S.C.R. 1011.

oper's alleged misconduct were obviously considerations that had to be balanced against one another. This is apparent from the way in which Estey J. dealt with this aspect of the case in delivering the judgment of the majority of the Court in denying relief on the basis of the developer's misconduct.[49]

e) Waiver

As already outlined in chapter 14 on bias and lack of independence, the issue of waiver arises most commonly in situations of a failure to object in a timely fashion to the participation of an adjudicator, who may be subject to disqualification on the basis of bias or lack of independence. Generally, this will cause a loss of entitlement to take that objection later and, in particular, after a matter has been heard on its merits and decided against the interests of the person now objecting.[50] However, for there to be an operative waiver, the person concerned must be aware of the facts giving rise to the likelihood of disqualification. Without that, an essential foundation of the defence is lacking — knowingly failing to assert one's rights in a timely fashion.

Waiver can also surface in other situations involving potential violation of the rules of procedural fairness as, for example, participating in proceedings without objecting to inadequate notice of the date or time of those proceedings or not asserting a claim to representation by counsel. Indeed, recent jurisprudence of the Supreme Court of Canada seems to suggest that the Court is willing to recognize that statutory employees and at least some office holders may contract out of their common law rights to procedural fairness as a prelude to effective dismissal from their positions.[51] It remains, however, a matter of great

---

49   In so doing, he also asserted that it was part of the responsibility of the court to recognize misconduct even if the argument had not been made by the parties. While that may very well be true, it certainly does not follow from that that a court should also be free to deny relief on this basis without alerting to the parties to the fact that it has this possibility in mind and providing them with an opportunity to address argument and perhaps even adduce further evidence on the issue. Indeed, it is quite remarkable that the Court was prepared to act unilaterally in this case and without any such warning given that the basis on which judicial review was sought was a breach of the rules of natural justice or procedural fairness by the municipality. The irony of this was not lost on Dickson J. in his dissenting judgment (Ritchie J. concurring). He was unusually blunt in his rejection of the majority's taking of this point.

50   *Callahan* v. *Newfoundland (Deputy Minister of Social Services)* (1993), 23 Admin. L.R. (2d) 32 (Nfl'd. S.C. T.D.).

51   See *Board of Education of the Indian Head School Division No. 19 of Saskatchewan* v. *Knight*, [1990] 1 S.C.R. 653.

uncertainty how far this recognition of contracting out of common law rights extends and whether it ever has any application when the rights in question have a constitutional foundation as in cases where the right to "life, liberty, and security of the person" as guaranteed by section 7 of the *Charter* is engaged.

More generally, it is also accepted that, while procedural rights may at least sometimes be waived, it is still the case that jurisdiction cannot be conferred by consent.[52] As a consequence, it is almost certainly not a defence to an application for judicial review based on a wrongful assumption of jurisdiction by a tribunal or the wrongful interpretation of a jurisdiction-conferring provision that the person affected consented to the tribunal's actions and waived her or his right to object subsequently. Nonetheless, to the extent that considerations of delay and a failure to commence an application for judicial review within a statutory limitation period may prevent the hearing of an application for judicial review, it is clear that the courts do not regard the opportunity to challenge on jurisdictional grounds as surviving all exigent circumstances. Nullities or void decisions will on occasion achieve legal or *de facto* recognition.[53]

f) Balance of Convenience

Under the heading of balance of convenience I include a variety of grounds for the denial of relief that are sometimes treated separately but which all seem to involve a sense that the grant of judicial review would either be of very little utility or would be contrary to some broader public interest even though a substantive basis for judicial review has been made out. With one or two notable exceptions (such as the generally accepted principles on mootness), they are also generally quite controversial as bases for the denial of relief.

Thus, for example, as already identified, it is sometimes asserted that courts should not be in the business of granting judicial review on the basis of procedural unfairness when it is abundantly clear that, irrespective of the denial of adequate procedural protections, the decision maker came to a correct decision on the merits. However, as I have already elaborated in the section on the consequences of procedural

---

52   See, for example, *Rosenfeld v. College of Physicians and Surgeons (Ontario)* (1970), 11 D.L.R. (3d) 148 (Ont. H.C.).

53   As reflected, for example, by the effect of the expiration of time limits for seeking judicial review and the recent jurisprudence refusing to allow collateral attack on decisions possibly tainted by error on a jurisdiction-conferring issue.

unfairness, since *Cardinal* v. *Director of Kent Institution*,[54] the Supreme Court has treated failure to accord procedural fairness as a "free standing" ground of judicial review. In particular, the Court has maintained that, save in truly exceptional circumstances,[55] it is simply not appropriate to speculate whether the substantive determination would have been any different had the common law's requirements of procedural fairness been met.

Futility or lack of utility is, however, a recognized ground for the denial of relief in other contexts. Thus, as noted already, if the matters in issue have become moot, the courts can refuse to proceed. Indeed, the discretion to continue with hearing the judicial review application in such instances has been constrained quite significantly by the Supreme Court and depends essentially on a determination that the case raises an issue of significant public concern or that is likely to recur in future situations and where there will likely always be impediments to timely judicial determination of the issue before it becomes moot.[56]

More controversial, however, are the admittedly infrequent cases where courts have denied relief by reference to concerns about the broader impact of the grant of a remedy.

Thus, in *Re Central Canada Potash Co. Ltd. and Minister of Mineral Resources of Saskatchewan*,[57] the Saskatchewan Court of Appeal held that, even if the minister had been legally obliged to grant the company the potash-producing licence for which it had applied, it would still have denied relief in the nature of *mandamus* on the basis that to grant it "would lead to confusion and disorder in the potash industry."[58] Whether courts should be able ever to allow such public interest considerations to supercede recognition and enforcement of legal rights is a difficult question and, even if sometimes justifiable, represents a jurisdiction that should be exercised very sparingly.

Somewhat more commonly and less controversially, courts will postpone giving effect to remedies to enable the administrative process to avoid the chaos that would ensue from the immediate grant of relief.

---

54 [1985] 2 S.C.R. 643. For an example in the case of bias, see *Newfoundland Telephone Co.* v. *Newfoundland (Board of Commissioners of Public Utilities)*, [1992] 1 S.C.R. 623.

55 See, for the only subsequent example, *Mobil Oil Canada Ltd.* v. *Canada–Newfoundland Offshore Petroleum Board*, [1994] 1 S.C.R. 202, discussed in the section on the Consequences of Procedural Unfairness.

56 *Borowski* v. *Attorney General*, [1989] 1 S.C.R. 342.

57 (1972), 32 D.L.R. (3d) 107 (Sask. C.A.), aff'd (1973) 38 D.L.R. (3d) 317 (J.C.C.).

58 *Ibid.* at 115.

In the constitutional domain, the most dramatic example of this is provided by the *Manitoba Language Rights Case*,[59] where the Court held that there was a constitutional requirement that the laws of Manitoba be enacted in both English and French. To have given immediate effect to this ruling would have meant that all the current statutes of Manitoba would have been inoperative and had no legal basis until they were re-enacted bilingually. Rather than create such a legal vacuum and bring into question potentially all actions taken under that legislation, the Court crafted a remedial order that preserved the validity of actions previously taken under all past legislation and preserved the legal effectiveness of the existing laws in order to provide the legislature with the opportunity (subject to time constraints) to rectify the situation by re-enacting the laws.

In like fashion, Rothstein J. then of the Federal Court, Trial Division, in *Sparvier* v. *Cowessess Indian Band No. 73*,[60] postponed the operation of an order quashing the decision of a biased election appeal tribunal which had set aside the election of the chief of an Indian band and ordered a new election which had produced a different outcome. Rather than restore the result of the original election by quashing the decision of the appeal tribunal with immediate effect, he held the order in abeyance until such time as a differently constituted appeal tribunal sustained the original election or the day after any new election ordered by that tribunal.

Under some modern judicial review legislation, there is an express grant of judicial discretion to deny relief in the case of a mere "defect in form or technical irregularity."[61] Such a provision was applied to deny relief in *Berg* v. *British Columbia (A.G.)*.[62] There, the court was faced with a group of landowners who had not been notified in accordance with the mandatory provisions of relevant regulations of a decision to allow logging for the purpose of combatting a beetle infestation. In denying relief, the court relied on the fact that they had been heard in any event and had, therefore, not been prejudiced by the breach. The judge also recognized the disruption that would be caused by bringing the logging to a halt at that point as well as the limited effect that it was having on the interests of the petitioning landowners not to mention the serious problem that the logging was designed to eliminate. Such a

---

59 [1985] 1 S.C.R. 721.
60 (1993), 13 Admin. L.R. (2d) 266 (F.C. T.D.).
61 See *Judicial Review Procedure Act*, R.S.B.C. 1996, c. 241, s. 9, and R.S.O. 1990, c. J.1, s. 3.
62 (1991), 48 Admin. L.R. (2d) 82 (B.C.S.C.) [*Berg*].

"program of control should not be frustrated without good cause."[63] Whether or not explicit legislative authority exists for dismissing a judicial review application in situations such as this, this does provide, at least on the facts as found by the judge, an excellent example of the limited kind of situation where strict concerns about legality should not frustrate the public interest.

3) Review of First Instance Judgments Denying Relief on Discretionary Grounds

To the extent that the decision of a first instance judge, whether on a motion to strike or on the hearing of the judicial review application itself is a discretionary determination, appellate courts will not normally substitute their judgment for that of the motions or hearing judge. Rather, interference will take place only where the first instance determination reveals an error in principle. Nonetheless, recent Supreme Court of Canada jurisprudence indicates that this still leaves appellate courts considerable room for manoeuvre.

In *Friends of the Oldman River Society* v. *Canada (Minister of Transport)*,[64] the Court was dealing with the refusal of a remedy by a first instance judge on the basis of a nineteen-month delay between the taking of the decision under attack and the filing of the motion for judicial review and fourteen months from when the Society became aware of that decision. Moreover, during that period, the building of the dam which was at the centre of the controversy had gone ahead and was 40 percent complete. Nonetheless, the Federal Court of Appeal had interfered with that exercise of discretion and the question before the Court was whether it had exceeded the permissible legal limits in so doing.

In upholding the Federal Court of Appeal, La Forest J., delivering the judgment of the majority of the Supreme Court of Canada, cited with approval the following statement from a House of Lords' judgment[65]:

> [I]f the appellate tribunal reaches the clear conclusion that there has been a wrongful exercise of discretion in that no weight, or no *sufficient* weight, has been given to relevant considerations such as urged upon us by the appellant, then the reversal of the order on appeal may be justified [emphasis added].[66]

---

63   *Ibid.* at 90.
64   [1992] 1 S.C.R. 3.
65   *Ibid.* at 76.
66   *Charles Osenton & Co.* v. *Johnston*, [1942] A.C. 130 (H.L. Eng.) at 138.

To the extent that this justifies judicial interference with the exercise of discretion on the basis of insufficiency of weight, it allows more room for intervention than the courts normally acknowledge in the case of judicial review of statutory authorities for abuse of discretion. Indeed, subsequently, in *Matsqui Indian Band*,[67] the Court assessed the first instance judge's exercise of discretion by reference to a straight reasonableness standard, as opposed to patent unreasonableness or the more testing *Wednesbury* unreasonableness test.

Applying this test in *Friends of the Oldman River Society*, La Forest J. went on to find that the first instance judge had failed to weigh certain relevant questions "adequately or at all."[68] These considerations were that, while the actual application for judicial review had been delayed, during that time, in other fora, there had been

> a concerted and sustained effort on the part of the Society to challenge the legality of the process followed by Alberta to build this dam and the acquiescence of the appellant [Federal] Ministers.[69]

As a consequence, there was an explanation for the delay. Also, the respondents were aware of the society's concerns with the legality of the process and the approvals resulting from it. Under those circumstances, continuation of the dam was a calculated risk particularly given that it was clear that the society was not about to give in "until it had exhausted all legal avenues, including an appeal to this Court."[70]

FURTHER READINGS

REID, R.E., AND P. LEAFLOOR, "Prematurity, alternative remedies and special circumstances" (1994), 3 Reid's Administrative Law 73

RUBY, P.D., "Remedial Discretion: When Should the Court Right the Wrong?" (1998), 11 Canadian Journal of Administrative Law and Practice 259

---

67 *Canadian Pacific*, above note 25. See also *Reza v. Canada*, [1994] 2 S.C.R. 394, where the Court explicitly rejected the "patently unreasonable" standard in this domain in favour of a slightly more intrusive scrutiny of the first instance judge's exercise of discretion.

68 *Berg*, above note 63 at 79.

69 *Ibid.*

70 *Ibid.*

CHAPTER 21

MONEY REMEDIES

A. INTRODUCTION

The most reliable touchstone of a legal system's commitment to the Diceyan proposition that the government should be as responsible, if not at times more responsible, for its actions than the private sector may be in the domain of civil liability. In this respect, the Canadian record is variable. Indeed, the fact that government in its various manifestations continues to possess exemptions (both legislative and common law and both procedural and substantive) from these forms of liability remains a matter of fierce contention.

Put simply, on one side of the argument are those who assert that such restrictions on liability are justified because government acts in the public good and should not be deterred from doing so by considerations of civil liability. On the other side of that fence are those who not only philosophically support the notion of equality between the state and private actors, but also contend that governments have just as much responsibility to meet normal legal standards albeit that they frequently engage in activities that have no private analogues. This is because they are in most instances well-placed to distribute losses across a broad range of the population which in general is benefiting from the work of government and should therefore be obliged to compensate the chance victims of government programs.

In between these two viewpoints, there are also many other permutations and combinations some of which are reflected at least in part in current Canadian law. For example, government liability varies with the activity, with legal responsibility more likely if the government activity in question has a private analogue. It may also depend on the drawing of distinctions between government as legislator and policy maker, on the one hand, and government in the operational sphere, on the other. Some would also contend that the level of government should make a difference. Thus municipalities, lacking the deep pockets of central government and the capacity to insure effectively against liability may be less efficient loss spreaders and should therefore have special consideration from the law, either common or statutory.

Given all this continuing controversy and the breadth of contexts in which governments operate even in the current environment of downsizing and privatization, the only effective solution may ultimately be that proposed by Hogg — that an integral part of all legislation authorizing government activity should be provisions with respect to liability.[1] Without, however, a total commitment to sorting these matters out at the time of legislative action, the common and civil law, affected on many occasions by various forms of statutory provision, will still have much work to do in this domain.

1) Damages for Administrative Action or Inaction

a) No Fault Liability

Any suggestion that there should be a form of no fault, enterprise liability for peculiarly or predominantly governmental activities suffered a perhaps irretrievable setback when in 1985 the Supreme Court of Canada, in a case coming out of the civil law jurisdiction of Québec, rejected the Continental European idea of a "theory of risk". In *Lapierre v. Québec (A.G.)*,[2] in the context of an attempt to make the provincial government liable without proof of fault for the consequences of a measles vaccination regime that it had promoted heavily, the Supreme Court refused to accept that chance victims of that program had any claim against the state. Distributing public burdens was held to be no part of the civil law of Québec and, given that the prospects for making such a claim were that much stronger in a civilian setting than at com-

---

1 Peter W. Hogg, "Compensation for Damage Caused by Government" (1995), 6 National Journal of Constitutional Law 7.

2 *Lapierre v. Québec (A.G.)*, [1985] 1 S.C.R. 241.

mon law, it can be assumed that, for the foreseeable future, the feasibility of such an action has been removed effectively from the domain of the common law as well.[3]

b) Liability for Illegal Actions

It is also clear that, under Canadian law, there is no automatic entitlement to compensation for loses caused by unlawful or illegal action. When governments act in a legislative, policy-making, or judicial or quasi-judicial role, the mere fact they have acted illegally or unlawfully does not lead to liability.[4] Indeed, subject to very limited exceptions, they are largely immune from any form of liability in those spheres. Moreover, even where they act in an administrative, operational, or implementation capacity, their liability will generally depend on the ability of a plaintiff to relate the actions or inactions to a known head of tort, extra-contractual,[5] or contractual liability.

c) Bad Faith or the Malicious Exercise of Authority

On the other hand, the Supreme Court of Canada has recognized the existence of a special regime of common law tort or extra-contractual liability to deal with egregious abuses of power by public authorities. The most dramatic manifestation of this form of liability remains the 1958 judgment of the Supreme Court of Canada in *Roncarelli* v. *Duplessis*.[6] Here, as we have seen previously, the Court held the premier of Québec civilly responsible for bad faith in the purported exercise of state power. In directing the general manager of the liquor commission to cancel forever Roncarelli's restaurant liquor licence because he was a Jehovah's Witness and stood bail for other Jehovah's Witnesses charged with various criminal and regulatory offences, Duplessis had acted maliciously in the sense of

> punish[ing] this licensee for having done what he had a right to do in a matter utterly irrelevant to the *Liquor Act* . . . [of] simply acting for a reason and purpose knowingly foreign to the administration. . . .[7]

---

3   For arguments in support of this position, see Hogg, above note 2.

4   *Welbridge Holdings Ltd.* v. *Metropolitan Corporation of Greater Winnipeg*, [1971] S.C.R. 957 at 969 (*per* Laskin J.): "Invalidity is not the test of fault and it should not be the test of liability", quoting K.C. Davis, 3 *Administrative Law Treatise* (1958) at 487 [*Wellbridge Holdings Ltd.*]

5   Previously described as "delictual" liability in the *Québec Civil Code* and now called "extra-contractuelle."

6   [1959] S.C.R. 121.

7   *Ibid.* at 141.

Later, Rand J., in delivering his classic judgment, went on to define "good faith" in the following terms:

> "Good faith" in this context . . . means carrying out the statute according to its intent and purpose; it means good faith in acting with a rational appreciation of that intent and purpose and not with an improper intent and for an alien purpose; it does not mean for the purposes of punishing a person for exercising an unchallengeable right; it does not mean arbitrarily and illegally attempting to divest a citizen of an incident of his civil status.[8]

While this case was decided by reference to the general principles of civil or delictual liability (now termed "extra-contractuelle") in what was then Article 1053 of the *Québec Civil Code*, there is now little doubt that the principles enunciated by the Court also form the basis for similar liability of statutory authorities under the common law.[9] Indeed, long before *Roncarelli* v. *Duplessis*, the Supreme Court had accepted that proof of malice defeated the traditional common law immunities of members of judicial and quasi-judicial bodies[10] from civil liability.[11] However, the common law tort is more commonly described as misfeasance in public office or abuse of public office, rather than simply "bad faith."[12]

It must, of course, be said that the occasions for the invocation of this form of liability are very infrequent. Indeed, were it not for Duplessis's frankness when testifying as to his conduct and the reasons for it, it is doubtful that Roncarelli's action would have succeeded.[13] This is confirmed not simply by the paucity of cases in which Canadian courts have found liability on the basis of the principles established in *Roncarelli* v.

---

8 *Ibid.* at 143.

9 See, for example, *Gershman* v. *Manitoba Vegetable Producers' Marketing Board* (1976), 69 D.L.R. (3d) 114 (Man. C.A.).

10 But not superior courts or those designated as having the immunities of superior courts: *Morier* v. *Rivard*, [1985] 2 S.C.R. 716.

11 See *McGillivray* v. *Kimber* (1915), 52 S.C.R. 146 (finding liability) and *Harris* v. *Law Society of Alberta*, [1936] S.C.R. 88 (recognizing immunity because of a failure on the part of the plaintiff to prove malice or bad faith).

12 See *First National Properties Ltd.* v. *Highlands (District)* (1999), 178 D.L.R. (4th) 505 (B.C.S.C.) to the effect that there is no such tort in Canada as "bad faith" [*First National Properties*].

13 See Sandra Djwa, *A Life of F.R. Scott: The Politics of the Imagination* (Vancouver: Douglas & McIntyre, 1987) at 311–12.

Duplessis,[14] but also by the restrictions identified in the chapter on abuse of discretion on requiring discovery of those suspected of bad faith and on the circumstances under which bad faith or improper motivations can even be attributed to multimember bodies such as the Cabinet or municipalities. These limitations, reaffirmed so recently by the Supreme Court of Canada in *Consortium Developments (Clearwater) Ltd.* v. *Sarnia (City)*,[15] place serious obstacles in the way of suits such as this.

Nonetheless, examples do exist particularly in the domain of government actions involving land use control and acquisition. Indeed, in a recent judgment,[16] after a full consideration of British, Commonwealth, and other Canadian authority, a judge of the Alberta Court of Queen's Bench, in finding a Cabinet Minister liable for abuse of office in a land freeze and acquisition case, held that the parameters of the tort were now wider than simply instances of "targeted" abuses of power as in *Roncarelli*. There, Marceau J., while rejecting an extension of the tort's coverage to certain types of negligence, stated that "deliberate misconduct" now embraced the following categories:

(a) an intentional illegal act, which is either [sic]:

    (a) an intentional use of statutory authority for an improper purpose; or

    (b) actual knowledge that the act (or omission) is beyond statutory authority, or

    (c) reckless indifference, or willful blindness to the lack of statutory authority for the act;

(b) intent to harm an individual or class of individual, which is satisfied by either [sic]:

    (d) an actual intention to harm; or

    (e) actual knowledge that harm will result; or

    (f) reckless indifference or willful blindness to the harm that can be foreseen to result.[17]

---

14   See H.W. Arthurs, " 'Mechanical Arts and Merchandise': Canadian Public Administration in the New Economy" (1997), 42 McGill L.J. 29 at 47, n. 31, quoting Peter Hogg, to the effect that the academic commentary applying *Roncarelli* is "more voluminous than the cases": P.W. Hogg, *Liability of the Crown*, 2nd ed. (Toronto: Carswell, 1989) at 111, n. 159.

15   [1998] 3 S.C.R. 3.

16   *Alberta (Minister of Public Works, Supply and Services)* v. *Nilsson* (1999), 46 C.C.L.T. (2d) 158 (Alta. Q.B.). See also *First National Properties*, above note 12, endorsing the approach in *Nilsson* and *Three Rivers District Council* v. *Bank of England*, [2000] H.L.J. No. 32 (H.L. Eng.) (Q.L.) (May 18, 2000) for a similar approach.

17   *Ibid.* at 198.

It is also significant that, for the purposes of this tort, the court rejected any differentiation between legislative and administrative functions at least as far as the liability of the executive was concerned.[18]

Now, it remains to be seen whether this broad conception of the reach of the tort survives Supreme Court of Canada scrutiny[19] and, if so, whether it does in fact bring about any increase in the number of successful suits.

d) Negligence Liability

In the domain of negligence liability, the Supreme Court of Canada has recognized an immunity for those exercising legislative, judicial, and quasi-judicial powers.[20] However, it remains an enthusiastic recipient[21] of the theories of Lord Wilberforce in the seminal judgment of the House of Lords in *Anns v. London Borough of Merton*.[22] This involves the drawing of a distinction between policy and operational decisions with an immunity attached to the making of policy and actions associated with that process but not to the actual implementation of policy.

Moreover, the Court has remained steadfast in its open espousal of the *Anns* doctrine notwithstanding the concerns of, first, the Privy Council[23]and, then, the House of Lords[24] that limiting the negligence liability of governments simply by reference to a distinction between policy and operational decisions was insufficiently reflective of the public interest in governments not being too readily amenable to suits in tort in the carrying out of their multifarious statutory roles. This refusal to follow the English route may be seen as indicative of a certain willingness to view governments as not too far removed from the private sector in terms of their responsibility for negligence.

Of course, there is more than one way of giving effect to such concerns. This is partially reflected by the reality that where the dividing line exists between policy decisions (which do not attract liability

---

18 *Ibid.* at 199–200.
19 In this regard, it should be noted that in *Wells v. Newfoundland*, [1999] 3 S.C.R. 199, the Court (at para. 59) reaffirmed the immunity of the legislature itself from any liability even for bad faith, while leaving unclear the possible liability of Cabinet or individual Ministers for abuse of office or misfeasance in public office in the introduction of legislation.
20 See, for example, *Welbridge Holdings Ltd.*, above note 4.
21 *City of Kamloops v. Nielsen*, [1984] 2 S.C.R. 2.
22 [1978] A.C. 728 (H.L. Eng.)
23 *Rowling v. Takaro Properties*, [1988] A.C. 473 (P.C., N.Z.) [*Rowling*].
24 Starting with *Murphy v. Brentwood District Council*, [1991] A.C. 398 (H.L. Eng.).

without proof of malice[25]) and operational decisions (where liability ensues from proof of the existence of a duty of care and negligence) is by no means a bright or red line distinction. Thus, in more recent decisions of the Supreme Court of Canada, it is possible to detect, from one perspective, the malleability of the distinction between policy and administration and, from a more instrumental standpoint, the ability of the Court, within those concepts, to reflect growing concerns with the extent to which even the adoption of the qualified form of liability espoused in *Anns* has resulted in "over-exposure" of governments in the exercise of their statutory powers to tort claims brought by citizens.

In 1989, in *Just v. British Columbia*,[26] in a judgment delivered by Cory J., the Supreme Court of Canada held the Government of British Columbia potentially responsible for the negligent operation of a system of inspection intended to prevent the fall of rocks onto highways. Just five years later, once again in judgments delivered by Cory J., accidents resulting from dangerous highway conditions did not attract liability because of the Court's decision that the "failures" in question were policy in nature. In *Brown v. British Columbia (Minister of Transportation and Highways)*,[27] the claim was rejected because of the Court's determination that the inspection failure resulted from a policy decision as to the length of the limited summer schedule for less intense checking of road conditions. On the same day, the Court also delivered judgment in *Swinamer v. Nova Scotia (A.G.)*.[28] Here, injuries had been sustained by reason of the fall of a dead tree onto a provincial highway. There had, in fact, been an inspection of the tree in question but, because of the lack of training of the inspector (he had previously been a supermarket employee),[29] its precarious state had not been detected. However, because the inspection had been conducted with a view to determining whether budgetary allocations should be made for the purpose of the removal of dead, dying, or diseased trees, the negligence alleged was in the context of moving towards the development of pol-

---

25 Though see *Ingles v. Tutkaluk Construction Ltd.*, [2000] 1 S.C.R. 298 where this is some suggestion that, on occasion at least, negligence in the development of policy may give rise to liability.

26 [1989] 2 S.C.R. 1228.

27 [1994] 1 S.C.R. 420.

28 [1994] 1 S.C.R. 445.

29 See judgment of Grant J. of the Nova Scotia Supreme Court (Trial Division): (1991), 101 N.S.R. (2d) 333. His immediate superior was also without any relevant qualifications or training.

icy and, hence, not within the ambit of liability established by *Anns* and adopted in Canada in *City of Kanloops* v. *Nielsen*.[30]

Aside from what these cases suggest about the clarity of a distinction between policy and operations, it is at least assuredly true that it was no solace to the respective plaintiffs to listen to an explanation that the reasons for non-recovery had to do with the fact that the fault in each case occurred in the context of a policy decision and that the government was, therefore, immune from liability irrespective of whether there was negligence.

Beyond the realm of personal injury suits against government, these tensions have also manifested themselves in the context of economic loss claims resulting from government regulatory failure. The trend-setting case of *Nielsen* was one involving property loss resulting from negligent inspection and, at the time, questions were raised about the appropriateness of recovery given the Supreme Court's then circumspect attitude towards the recovery of damages for purely economic loss under general tort law.[31] However, since then, the Court has expressly embraced a theory of liability for pure economic loss under general tort law,[32] and this has had an impact on the willingness of plaintiffs to bring actions for damages based on the negligent performance of licensing and other regulatory roles having economic as well as physical impacts.

Prominent in this domain are the judgments of the Federal Court of Appeal in *Brewer* v. *Canada*[33] and *Devloo* v. *Canada*,[34] in which damages were awarded against the federal government as personified by the Canadian Wheat Board for economic losses suffered as a consequence of negligent supervision of a company within the Wheat Board's jurisdiction. Also important in the overall evolution of the law in this area is another Federal Court of Appeal judgment delivered the day after both *Brewer* and *Devloo*, *Swanson Estate* v. *Canada*.[35] Here, the court, in a judgment delivered by Linden J.A., imposed liability on the Ministry of Transportation for its failure to cancel the licence of an airline that was not meeting regulatory flight safety standards. Since this was a case involving personal injury and death, it suggested that the policy defence was not one that would be entertained readily in relation to

---

30   Above note 21.
31   *Rivtow Marine Ltd.* v. *Washington Iron Works*, [1974] S.C.R. 1189.
32   See, for example, *CNR* v. *Norsk Pacific Steamship Co.*, [1992] 1 S.C.R. 1021.
33   (1991), 80 D.L.R. (4th) 321 (F.C.A.).
34   (1991), 129 N.R. 39 (F.C.A.).
35   (1991), 80 D.L.R. (4th) 741 (F.C.A.).   *ENV.*

government agency negligence in the conduct of its regulatory mandates over private sector activities.

However, in 1995, the same court, over the dissent on this occasion of Linden J.A., refused to sustain a Trial Division judgment holding a government department liable for the negligent revocation of fishing licences.[36] In so doing, one of the majority judges, Stone J.A. was, by reference to the advice of the Judicial Committee of the Privy Council in *Rowling* v. *Takaro Properties*,[37] persuaded that government exposure to liability in such cases should be confined to review by way of the prerogative writs and their modern equivalents; it was not the occasion for the visiting of tort responsibility on the government for the actions of its officials.[38] The other majority judge, Robertson J.A., in an echo of the traditional law that licensing officials acting in a judicial or quasi-judicial capacity could be liable in damages only when acting maliciously, held that the wrongful revocation of a licence did not give rise to liability in tort for the resulting financial losses. On further appeal,[39] the Supreme Court of Canada finessed these concerns by deciding the case on another basis entirely and so important aspects of the law governing liability in this domain remain unresolved.

More recently, however, the Supreme Court rendered judgment in two cases which have great potential significance for liability in an era in which governments are more and more contracting out or outsourcing responsibilities that they previously carried out internally through the use of their own personnel. *Lewis (Guardian ad litem of)* v. *British Columbia*[40] and *Mochinski* v. *Trendline Industries Ltd.*[41] both involved claims against government for the negligence of contractors hired to perform road maintenance and repair work. In each case, notwithstanding the fact that there was no proof of any negligence in the selection of the contractor, the government was held responsible for injuries resulting from the contractor's negligence. While the Court indicated that this result would not always follow, in each instance, the Court relied on what it saw as the government's continuing overall responsibilities for the management and direction of highways, responsibilities that were found in the relevant statutory provisions and the use of lan-

---

36   *Comeau's Sea Foods Ltd.* v. *Canada (Minister of Fisheries)* (1995), 123 D.L.R. (4th) 180 (F.C.A.).

37   *Rowling*, above note 23.

38   *Quaere* whether under this theory Duplessis would have escaped liability.

39   [1997] 1 S.C.R. 12.

40   [1997] 3 S.C.R. 1145.

41   [1997] 3 S.C.R. 1176.

guage such as "shall direct." This was in the nature of a "non-delega-ble" duty or responsibility.

However, what also has to be taken into account in this domain and generally is the extent to which liability can be controlled by statu-tory provision. Thus, in *Lewis* and *Mochinski*, the Court made it abun-dantly clear not only that the terms and structure of the relevant statutory provisions were crucial to the finding of liability but also that the government could exempt itself from liability by the addition of an appropriate provision to the *Act*.

That governments are quite prepared to take up this opportunity is evident from the extent to which legislatures have responded to findings of liability. Thus, in British Columbia (where *Nielsen* arose), the *Vancouver City Charter* (*inter alia*) was amended to restrict the impact of the principles of liability established in *Nielsen* as well as in other litigation respecting the nuisance and *Rylands* v. *Fletcher* liabil-ity of municipalities.[42] Even more expansively, the legislature of Alberta, by the 1991 *Safety Codes Act*,[43] acted to exempt (save in the case of bad faith) the province and accredited agencies and municipal-ities (as well as all relevant employees) from any form of tort liability in the discharge or purported discharge of a broad range of inspection and evaluative functions. This powerful alliance of a cautious judi-ciary and governments looking for easy targets in their attempts to reduce spending is clearly one that is again moving governmental lia-bility law away from parity with the situation that prevails in tort suits between private citizens.[44]

e) Nuisance and *Rylands* v. *Fletcher* Liability

Governmental authorities are liable for nuisance and for loss suffered in situations covered by the rule in *Rylands* v. *Fletcher* governing ultra-hazardous activities. In this context, the only limiting principle that has particular relevance to the liability of government authorities but which is not confined to them is the defence of statutory authorization.

---

42 R.S.B.C. 1979, c. 55 (as amended), ss. 294(8),(9).

43 S.A. 1991, S-O.5, s. 12.

44 As an antidote to this account of governments moving to reverse the impact of judicial decisions creating principles of more extensive exposure to liability, it should, however, also be recounted that, in the wake of the judgment of the Supreme Court of Canada in *Lapierre, supra*, the Québec National Assembly created a fund against which victims of the vaccination programme could claim: see S.Q. 1985, c. 23, s. 18, inserting ss. 16.1 to 16.9 in the *Public Health Protection Act*, R.S.Q., c. P-35 and section 26 specifically making that regime applicable to Lapierre and two others.

In 1989, in *Tock* v. *St. John's Metropolitan Area Board*,[45]the Supreme Court divided three ways on what precisely this defence involved and the law was left in a rather uncertain state as a consequence. Now, in *Ryan* v. *Victoria (City)*,[46] a unanimous Court has accepted one of the three formulations from *Tock*, that expressed in the solitary concurring judgment of Sopinka J. Moreover, while the defendant in *Ryan* was a private railway line and not a governmental authority, there is no reason to believe that the test is different in the case of government defendants.

Speaking for the Court, Major J. described the defence as a limited one which had traditionally been restricted to situations where an activity was authorized by statute and where the creation of the nuisance was the inevitable consequence of the exercise of the statutory power. He then rejected the formulations in *Tock* that would either have abolished the defence entirely or have restricted it to situations where the duty was mandatory or the Act laid down the precise manner in which the activity was to be performed. Rather, in pursuing a judicial policy of limiting the circumstances in which the defence was available, it was preferable to restate or elaborate the traditional rule in the terms adopted by Sopinka J. in *Tock*:

> The defendant must negative that there are alternate methods of carrying out the work. The mere fact that one is considerably less expensive will not avail. If only one method is practically feasible, it must be established that it was practically impossible to avoid the nuisance. It is insufficient for the defendant to negative negligence. The standard is a higher one. While the defence gives rise to some factual difficulties, in view of the allocation of the burden of proof they will be resolved against the defendant.[47]

Most significantly, in terms of the debate in *Tock*, the test for the defence is one that in no way depends on any differentiation between activities that are mandated by statute or merely authorized. However, as the application of the test to the facts of *Ryan* then illustrates, whether the activity is required or simply authorized, the terms in which the statute actually describes or specifies the activity in question will be relevant to the extent that statutory specification will provide a defence, whereas the carrying on of the activity in a way that is not the subject of statutory specification will not unless that in fact is the only way in which the activity could be conducted. In other words, where

---

45   [1989] 2 S.C.R. 1181 [*Tock*].
46   [1999] 1 S.C.R. 201.
47   *Tock*, above note 45 at 1226.

the mode of operating is not imperative by virtue of statutory requirement or practical necessity and where there is an element of discretion,
the defence is not available. In *Ryan*, as a matter of discretion (not
necessity), the defendant exceeded the statutory minimum size requirements for a piece of equipment that constituted a nuisance and caused
damage. It was thereby precluded from reliance on the defence.

f) The Charter as a Source of Governmental Liability Suits

The *Canadian Charter of Rights and Freedoms* not only is explicit in providing that it applies to the legislatures and governments of Canada,
the provinces and territories,[48] but also confers on courts of "competent jurisdiction" a broad remedial jurisdiction to award such remedies
for *Charter* violations which they "consider appropriate and just in the
circumstances".[49] However, notwithstanding this, the almost twenty
years since the coming into force of the *Charter* have seen little evolution of a distinct jurisprudence of *Charter* liability law.

There is some sense that part of this is the responsibility of Canadian litigators and judges who have simply been too cautious and lacking in imagination when it comes to the exploitation of the opportunities
opened up for new principles of liability when certain rights and freedoms are constitutionalized. Indeed, some credence is given to this
theory by the fact that, in what appeared to many to be a very unusual
move, a Supreme Court of Canada judge gave a speech, later published
in the Canadian Bar Review, in which he made some pretty pointed
suggestions as to how lawyers might use the *Charter* more effectively to
the advantage of their clients in the domain of tort liability for malicious prosecution.[50]

Nevertheless, what also has to be acknowledged is that the opportunities for the wholesale takeover of the principles of governmental
liability law by actions brought in the name of the *Charter* were never a
great prospect. There are some fairly obvious reasons for this. First, the
Charter does not provide any explicit protection for property rights
and thereby excludes one of the great sources of constitutional liability

---

48   S. 32(1).

49   S. 24(1).

50   See The Honourable John Sopinka, "Malicious Prosecution: Invasion of *Charter*
     Interests: Remedies: *Nelles* v. *Ontario*: *R. Jednack*: *R.* v. *Simpson*" (1995), 74 Can.
     Bar Rev. 366 (based on an address given at the Canadian Bar Association,
     Continuing Legal Education Institute, 9 Feb. 1995).

law under other constitutions.[51] Another potential source of claims against the government is on the basis of section 15's enshrining of the right not to be discriminated against on the basis of a list of enumerated and analogous grounds. However, here too, there is a major impediment in the form of human rights legislation (both federal and provincial) which designates human rights commissions and their tribunals to be the repository of complaints about the kinds of discriminatory conduct now also proscribed by the *Charter*. Prior to the advent of the *Charter*, the Supreme Court of Canada had ruled that the existence of such mechanisms precluded the evolution of a common law tort of discrimination.[52] The commissions and their tribunals were the only points of resource in such matters. While the same need not necessarily hold when the right not to be discriminated against even by government has been constitutionalized, nevertheless, the Supreme Court of Canada has made reference to the expected use of human rights commissions in discrimination cases[53] and, so far, the challenge of trying to develop a separate constitutional tort of discrimination outside that framework has still not been met.[54] Thus, two potentially fruitful sources of constitutional tort litigation may be effectively closed off from the courts. As well, one of the sections having the greatest potential for generating *Charter* damages claims, section 7 and its right to the "principles of fundamental" justice whenever "life, liberty and security of the person" is in jeopardy (along with section 15), only avails natural persons.[55]

Notwithstanding these and other significant constraints, there are, of course, several potential sources of constitutional tort liability to be found in the *Charter*. However, to the extent that many of those sources have to do with the conduct and functioning of the criminal justice system, they have counterparts in existing torts (such as false arrest and imprisonment, malicious prosecution and assault). Moreover, notwithstanding Mr. Justice Sopinka's clarion call for the use of the *Charter* rather than the common law in at least some of these

---

51 *Cf.* s. 1(a) of the *Canadian Bill of Rights* attaching a "due process" protection to "the enjoyment of property."

52 *Seneca College of Applied Arts and Technology v. Bhadauria*, [1981] 2 S.C.R. 181.

53 See *McKinney v. University of Guelph*, [1990] 3 S.C.R. 229.

54 However, there is at least one cause of action in which the existence of such liability has been held to be at least arguable. See *Perera v. Canada*, [1998] 3 F.C. 381 (C.A.), sustaining an order of Cullen J., F.C.T.D., 24 Feb. [1997] F.C.S. No. 199 (T-608-92) refusing to strike such a claim and reinstating the plaintiff's claim for a remedy to counter systemic discrimination in addition to damages resulting to him personally.

55 See, for example, *Irwin Toy v. Québec*, [1989] 1 S.C.R. 927.

domains, there are some rather large questions as to whether basing claims on the *Charter* instead of the common law in these instances would or should produce any different patterns of liability. Thus, for example, it is by no means clear that liability for denial of procedural rights in the criminal or any other process protected by the *Charter*, for that matter, should be more extensive than it is at the moment. Putting it another way, it is an open question whether there should be automatic or *per se* liability for such breaches and that traditional common law exemptions such as those belonging to administrative officials absent malice should simply disappear when the cause of action is based on the *Charter* rather than the common law.

Nevertheless, it must be acknowledged that there are possibilities here not necessarily present in the common law, such as the rights enshrined in section 10 to certain protections on arrest or detention. In this domain, there is at least some limited lower court jurisprudence holding governmental officials accountable for breach of such provisions without proof of either malice or damage.[56] More generally, there has been a lot of academic discussion[57] and limited judicial support[58] for a form of direct government liability for constitutional wrongs of this kind following in the footsteps of the Judicial Committee of the Privy Council in *Maharaj* v. *Attorney-General of Trinidad & Tobago (No. 2)*[59] by reference to the natural justice provision in the Constitution of Trinidad and Tobago.

Another domain where there have, in fact, been some hints of the availability of the *Charter* as a means of increasing governmental liability is with respect to the litigation advantages possessed by the Crown by virtue of legislation. On the one hand, the Supreme Court has rejected the proposition that litigation differentials as between the Crown and private citizens represent a species of discrimination proscribed by section 15.[60] On the other hand, by reference to section 7 and its guarantees of the "principles of fundamental justice," there have been *dicta* from the Supreme Court[61] and a ruling from the

---

56   *Crossman* v. *The Queen*, [1984] 1 F.C. 681 (T.D.).

57   See, for example, Marilyn Pilkington, "Damages as a Remedy for Infringement of the *Canadian Charter of Rights and Freedoms*" (1984), 62 *Can. Bar Rev.* 517, though *cf* Ghislaine Otis, "Constitutional Liability for the Infringement of Rights *Per Se*: A Misguided Theory" (1992), 26 *U.B.C.L.R.* 22.

58   *R.* v. *Germain* (1984), 53 A.R. 264 (Q.B.).

59   [1979] A.C. 385 (P.C. Trin. & Tob.).

60   See, for example, *Rudolph Wolff & Co.* v. *Canada*, [1990] 1 S.C.R. 695.

61   In *Nelles* v. *Ontario*, [1989] 2 S.C.R. 170.

Ontario Court of Appeal that short limitation periods and potentially broad immunities from liability possessed by the Crown in situations where "life, liberty and security of the person" are at stake can be unconstitutional.[62]

There is also the possibility that section 15 may provide a springboard for attacks on the institutional frailties of government liability regimes. Thus, for example, in a situation where human rights commissions are suffering from inadequate resources and the remedial capacities of tribunals adjudicating complaints of discrimination are limited, there may be a basis for a challenge to the legislation itself. In the wake of *Vriend* v. *Alberta*,[63] holding the Alberta *Individual Rights Protection Act* to be under-inclusive in failing to proscribe discrimination on the basis of sexual orientation, the prospect has clearly been raised of attacks on other under-inclusive aspects of the provisions of human rights codes and the resources and capacities of those given roles by those codes. Moreover, as opposed to allowing a cause of action for the constitutional tort of discrimination which would be available only against government because of section 32(1), this form of attack, if successful, would have the potential for providing a more effective remedial regime against all forms of proscribed discrimination whether the perpetrator be private or public.

In sum, while our law is a long way from a developed system of constitutional tort liability and while progress in this domain has been snail-like, nonetheless, there are pockets where the opportunity clearly still exists for making the *Charter* a vehicle for somewhat more expansive governmental liability in a selective range of situations.

2) Repayment of Monies Paid to Public Authorities under a Mistake

In the private sector, the principles of restitution provide the bases on which moneys paid under a mistake may be recovered from the payee. These same principles of restitution also apply to moneys paid under a mistake to public authorities. However, public authorities do have some immunities from the obligation to repay which do not apply in the private sector and there are also some aspects of the restitutionary principles that are particularly significant in the case of mistaken payments to public authorities.

---

62   *Prete* v. *Ontario (A.G.)* (1993), 110 D.L.R. (4th) 94 (C.A.).
63   [1998] 1 S.C.R. 493.

a) Mistake of Law and Mistake of Fact

For too long, Canadian law in both the public and private domains refused to allow recovery of monies paid under a mistake of law as opposed to a mistake of fact. However, in *Air Canada v. British Columbia*,[64] a case involving payments under an unconstitutional statute,[65] the Supreme Court finally conceded that it was inappropriate to draw such a distinction. Thereafter, monies paid under a mistake of law theoretically became recoverable in both the private and public domains.

b) The Special Case of Unconstitutional Statutes

Nonetheless, three of the four-judges of a six judge Court who dealt with this issue went on to hold that, in the case of unconstitutional statutes, there could be no recovery of monies paid save in exceptional circumstances. This restriction on recovery was said to be dictated by the need to conserve the public purse and to avoid imposing the resulting shortfall in government finances on a new generation of taxpayers.[66]

What amounted to the exceptional circumstances justifying recovery was described in terms of the collection of the tax under conditions that "are unjust and oppressive in the circumstances."[67] Later in the judgment, these exceptions seem to be given more concrete expression in the principles of "practical compulsion" and by reference to situations where the parties are not "*in pari delicto*," i.e., where there is some reason to attribute responsibility for the mistake to the government such as actual awareness or fair warning from counsel that the law was unconstitutional. However, for the latter purposes, it will not be sufficient to simply claim carelessness on the part of the government's advisers or that the government was in a better position

---

64 [1989] 1 S.C.R. 1161 [*Air Canada*].

65 Much of what is described here of the judgment is technically *dicta* since the Court held that the legislation had been validated retrospectively, thereby defeating the claim to recovery. However, in a related judgment delivered the same day, a majority of the Court allowed the recovery of taxes mistakenly applied to aircraft parts as a matter of statutory interpretation. As a consequence, it may now be taken that monies paid under a mistake of law, as well as fact, are indeed recoverable: *Air Canada, Canadian Pacific Airlines v. British Columbia*, [1989] 1 S.C.R. 1133 [*Air Canada, Canadian Pacific Airlines*].

66 There was a strong dissent from Wilson J., a dissent which subsequently attracted the approval of the House of Lords in *Woolwich Building Society v. Commissioners of Inland Revenue*, [1993] A.C. 70 (H.L. Eng.). However, in the other judgment released contemporaneously, *Air Canada, Canadian Pacific Airlines, ibid.*, Wilson J. joined the other three judges in their application of the principles they had identified in the *Air Canada* case, *supra*, note 64.

67 *Air Canada*, above note 64 at 1206–7.

to know. Also relevant to the scope of any exception is whether the government could have legally collected the relevant tax through a properly framed statute.

Subsequently, the Court has revisited some of these considerations. In particular, in *Re Eurig Estate*,[68] the Court held that the limitations on recovery were not applicable to a situation where an unconstitutional estate tax had been paid under protest. Evidently, this was so even though the state could have imposed the tax constitutionally had it done so by way of primary, rather than subordinate legislation. Also of note is *Air Canada* v. *Ontario (Liquor Control Board)*.[69] Although not willing to interfere with the first instance judge's exercise of discretion not to award punitive damages and compound interest on monies paid mistakenly under a statute, the Court emphasized that such awards were quite appropriate in cases where the authorities had collected the monies even after they had come to realize they were not legally payable.

c) Mistaken Payments Resulting from Misinterpretation or Misapplication of Law

It is also significant that, in *Air Canada* (1989) itself, the Court expressed the view that the exception should be applied only in situations where it was necessary to protect the specific concerns that would be created by allowing recovery — essentially protection of the public purse. In general, there was no such basis for the application of the rule against recovery where the mistaken payment had come about as a result of the misapplication of a valid law. Indeed, in the other judgment released that same day, *Air Canada, Canadian Pacific Airlines* v. *British Columbia*,[70] recovery was allowed for monies paid under a mistaken interpretation of the law without any reference to the normal rule against recovery in the case of unconstitutional statutes and the exceptional circumstances justifying departure from that rule.

d) Mistaken Payments under a Law which *Ultra Vires* on Basis of Administrative Law Principles

Left quite unclear in all of this, however, is whether the rule against recovery applies to mistaken payments under legislation that is not unconstitutional but *ultra vires* on administrative law grounds, as in the case of subordinate legislation (government regulations and munic-

---

68   [1998] 2 S.C.R. 565.
69   [1997] 2 S.C.R. 581.
70   *Air Canada, Canadian Pacific Airlines*, above note 65.

ipal by-laws) invalid because it is beyond the statutory authority of the promulgator of that legislation. In one of the key paragraphs in *Air Canada* (1989), La Forest J. does refer to "an otherwise constitutional or *intra vires* statute or regulation" in such a way as to suggest that the exception applies to all invalid laws irrespective of the legal basis of the invalidity. Indeed, the principles identified in favour of the exception would not seem to be affected in any way by either the source of the invalidity or the level of government. Nonetheless, a few years previously, in *Air Canada* v. *Dorval*,[71] a case involving the unlawful imposition of a tax by way of annual resolution instead of by way of a by-law, the Supreme Court allowed recovery of the mistaken payments without any reference to possible limitations in the name of conserving the municipality's fiscal position.

e) Restrictions on Recovery Based on General Restitutionary Principles: Passing on of the Burden

One of the principles governing restitutionary recovery is that not only must the payee be enriched but that that enrichment must have been at the expense of the payer. This second requirement has a particular resonance in the instance of mistaken payments of taxes. More particularly, the payment will not be recoverable where the taxpayer has "passed on" the burden of the tax. Indeed, in cases involving the recovery of taxes paid in the course of doing business, the burden is on the taxpayer to establish that the tax has not been passed on to customers of the business. What constitutes a passing on for these purposes is, however, quite problematic.

In *Air Canada* (1989),[72] gasoline tax on fuel consumed by commercial airlines was held to have been passed on in the fares paid by passengers. Thus, even if this had not been a case of an unconstitutional statute, there would have been no basis in ordinary restitutionary principles for recovery. In the related judgment delivered the same day,[73] *Air Canada, Canadian Pacific Airlines*, recovery was allowed in a misapplication case of taxes paid by airlines on their aircraft and aircraft parts but not of taxes collected on in-flight sales of alcoholic beverages. In the case of the beverage tax, recovery was denied on the basis that the airlines were simply acting as agent of the government in collecting the taxes. It could not be said that the airlines were in any sense being

---

71 [1985] 1 S.C.R. 861.
72 *Air Canada*, above note 64.
73 *Air Canada, Canada Pacific Airlines*, above note 65.

impoverished. However, the case of the tax on aircraft and aircraft parts more clearly demonstrates the problem of discerning when there has been a passing on.

While the passing on of a tax on aircraft and aircraft parts is not so immediate but rather more spread out than in the case of gasoline tax, nevertheless, it seems clear that, at some point, these taxes do find their way into the airlines' fare-pricing structure. Nonetheless, in a later British Columbia authority, *Allied Air Conditioning Inc.* v. *British Columbia*,[74] two of the judges explained the distinction between these items on the basis that "passing on" as commonly understood did not apply to "items of equipment acquired as capital assets for continuous use by the airline for the purpose of generating income."[75]

In any event, there is as yet no consensus on whether taxes paid on materials consumed in the course of a particular transaction are inevitably to be treated as having been passed on to the customer in the price paid. In the British Columbia Court of Appeal judgment just noted, the court held that there was a passing on when the company built into its tenders the tax to be paid on materials incorporated into customers' premises. In contrast, relying on the fact that building the tax into its bids actually cost the company some contracts and did not affect their securing of the contracts on which they bid successfully, the Nova Scotia Court of Appeal in *Cherubini Metal Works Ltd.* v. *Nova Scotia (A.G.)*,[76] did allow recovery of taxes mistakenly paid on structural steel supplied to building contractors. These cases appear irreconcilable save to the extent that, in one of the judgments delivered in *Allied Air Conditioning Inc.*, it does seem accepted that the result might have been different had the plaintiff proved that its "prices were established by competition with suppliers who did not have to pay the tax."[77]

Obviously, there is considerable confusion on what constitutes passing on in this domain, and definitive clarification will require further Supreme Court pronouncements.

f) Summary

At this point, the following propositions appear to be established in the case law. Payments made to a public authority under a mistake of fact or a mistake of law (including payments made as a result of a misinterpretation of the law) are recoverable subject to general restitutionary

---

74   (1994), 109 D.L.R. (4th) 463 (B.C.C.A.) [*Allied Air Conditioning*].

75   *Ibid.* at 477.

76   (1995), 137 N.S.R. (2d) 197 (C.A.).

77   *Allied Air Conditioning*, above note 74 at 477 (*per* Taylor J.A.).

principles save in the case of monies paid under unconstitutional legislation (both primary and subordinate) and perhaps also under subordinate legislation invalid for administrative law reasons. In the reserved category or categories (as the case may be), recovery will be available only in exceptional circumstances. For the exceptional circumstances to be triggered, the claimant will not only have to bring herself or himself within normal restitutionary principles but also establish that the money was paid under protest or in unfair or oppressive circumstances such as where there was practical compulsion or knowledge on the part of the collector that the demands for the money were unlawful. Of particular concern in all cases involving payments mistakenly paid in a business context which are otherwise recoverable by reference to the foregoing principles, the normal principles of restitution may prevent recovery if the burden of the tax has been passed on to a third party such as a customer. What constitutes a sufficient passing on for these purposes is a matter of some uncertainty.

FURTHER READINGS

COHEN, D., "Responding to Government Failure" (1995), 6 National Journal of Constitutional Law 23

HOGG, P.W., "Compensation for Damage Caused by Government" (1995), 6 National Journal of Constitutional Law 7

HOGG, P.W., *Liability of the Crown*, 2nd ed. (Toronto: Carswell, 1989)

KNEEBONE, S., *Tort Liability of Statutory Authorities* (Sydney: LBC Information Services, 1998)

MITCHELL, P., "Restitution, 'Passing On,'" and the Recovery of Unlawfully Demanded Taxes: Why *Air Canada* Doesn't Fly" (1995), 53 University of Toronto Faculty of Law Review 130

MOCKLE, D., "L'impact du principe d'égalité sur les privilèges et immunités de l'État" (1990), 50 Revue du Barreau 431

MULLAN, D.J., "Damages for Violation of Constitutional Rights — A False Spring?" (1995), 6 National Journal of Constitutional Law 105

OTIS, G., "Personal Liability of Public Officials for Constitutional Wrongdoing: A Neglected Issue of *Charter* Application" (1996), 24 Man. L.J. 22

PERELL, P.M., "Negligence Claims Against Public Authorities" (1994), 16 Advocates' Quarterly 48

PERELL, P.M., "Restitutionary Claims Against Government" (1995), 17 Advocates' Quarterly 71

QUINN, J.J., & MICHAEL J. TREBILCOCK, "Compensation, Transition Costs and Regulatory Change" (1982), 32 U.T.L.J. 117

CHAPTER 22

THE OMBUDSMAN

A. INTRODUCTION

Judicial review and statutory appeals are not the only ways of securing redress for unlawful administrative action. Aside from the formal and informal capacities of statutory authorities to reconsider or re-evaluate decisions that they have made, in all of the provinces except Newfoundland and Prince Edward Island, and in the Yukon Territory, there is an official appointed by and reporting to the legislature who has extensive powers to investigate allegations of maladministration.[1] In Québec, this official is known as the public protector but, in the other provinces and the Yukon Territory, the title is ombudsman, reflecting the office's Scandinavian antecedents.

The legislative objective behind the creation of such an official has been to provide a vehicle through which citizens can bring a broad range of complaints with the way in which government departments and agencies operate in dealing with the public. As specified in the relevant legislative provisions, the capacities of the ombudsman extend far beyond simply investigating allegations of illegality and are as much, if not more, concerned with lack of judgment, bad public relations, and poor or sloppy administrative practices and structures as they are with issues of unlawfulness. Nonetheless, the legislation in all

---

1   The city of Winnipeg also has an ombudsman.

provinces does make it abundantly clear that the ombudsman has the capacity to respond to complaints that a government official has acted illegally. Moreover, the history of the functioning of this office in various jurisdictions across the country (as revealed primarily in the ombudsman's annual reports) reveals that such allegations form a significant percentage of all the ombudsmen's caseloads. This supports the notion that, at least in some contexts, resort to the ombudsman may be a very attractive alternative to judicial review or statutory appeal rights, though, as will be seen below, there are some constraints on the powers of the ombudsman when a person making a complaint has access to these more traditional remedies for unlawful administrative action.

As was the case with its *Administrative Procedure Act*, Alberta in 1967 was the first province to adopt the office of the ombudsman. In so doing, it followed the 1962 precedent of New Zealand, the first common law jurisdiction in which this Scandinavian invention[2] found a home. Over the next two decades, all of the other provinces with the exception of Prince Edward Island followed suit, though Newfoundland, because of budgetary constraints, was to abolish its office in 1992. The office has also penetrated the private sector in the form of the banking ombudsman established in 1998. However, despite strong and continuing advocacy,[3] the federal government has never moved in this direction though, at the federal level, there are at least two specialized forms of ombudsman — the correctional services ombudsman and the Canadian Forces ombudsman. The federal commissioner of official languages also has many of the characteristics of an ombudsman, while, in a limited way, both federally and provincially, freedom of information and privacy commissioners as well as the auditor general or provincial auditor also play roles in checking unlawful administrative action as, of course, do human rights commissions and their tribunals when they entertain certain kinds of complaints against government and its agencies within their specialized mandates.[4]

In an era in which judicial review and statutory appeal are becoming more and more expensive and correspondingly inaccessible to ordi-

---

2   The origin of the modern institution is probably the Swedish ombudsman of 1869.

3   See, for example, "Canadian Ombudsman Association Calls for Creation of Federal Ombudsman," press release, 8 June 1999, and an associated study paper from the association, *A Federal Ombudsman for Canada*. That study paper, *inter alia*, details (in appendix 2) the history of attempts to secure the creation of a federal ombudsman.

4   In Ontario, one could add to this list the environmental commissioner, who is also an officer of the legislative assembly.

nary citizens, perhaps the single greatest advantage of the office of the ombudsman is that its services are free to those who use it. Of course, to the extent that government cutbacks in virtually all jurisdictions have had an impact on the ability of the ombudsman to serve the public adequately and, particularly, in a timely fashion, the initial advantage of free service may be offset by limitations on the ability of the ombudsman to investigate all complaints thoroughly and the time it takes to have matters resolved.[5] On the other hand, access to judicial review and statutory appeal may also be affected by the length of court lists and the resources of the person seeking redress against government.

B. JURISDICTION

The scope of the ombudsman's jurisdiction varies from province to province with the most extensive, British Columbia, covering not only provincial government departments and agencies but also colleges and universities, school and hospital boards, professional disciplinary bodies, and municipalities. In general, however, the courts and judges are excluded as well as those rendering legal advice to governments. Exceptions are also made for the deliberations of Cabinet and Cabinet committees as well as the legislature itself.

The legislation creating the office deals with the relationship between the ombudsman's jurisdiction and other forms of redress such as internal appeals and review as well as judicial review and statutory appeals in the regular courts. In Nova Scotia, the ombudsman has no jurisdiction in the face of such appeal and review rights. However, it is more common for the legislation either to provide that the ombudsman may accept jurisdiction if compelling the exercise of the other remedial avenue would be unreasonable in the circumstances, or, alternatively, that a person cannot complain to the ombudsman until statutory rights of

---

5   See, for example, the *1998/99 Report of the Ontario Ombudsman*, where the outgoing holder of that office reports (at 5):

> We have also struggled to maintain our commitment to equitable service in the face of funding cutbacks. We were forced to close four of ten regional offices and layoff more than 25% of our staff, reducing our ability to conduct outreach and public education, while making it harder to service a continuing high volume of complaints.

Later in the Report (at 12), she details the operation of the office's "managed backlog register."

appeal and judicial review entitlements have been exhausted or the time for invoking them has lapsed.

In Ontario, where the ombudsman's jurisdiction is formally postponed until exhaustion of other appeal and review rights, there has, nonetheless, been litigation involving the issue of whether or not the authority of the ombudsman extends to the process employed by and the merits of decisions made by administrative tribunals. Although the outcome has met with a mixed reception, the Ontario Court of Appeal on two separate occasions (in cases involving the Labour Relations Board[6] and the then Health Disciplines Board[7]) has held, as a matter of statutory interpretation, that the ombudsman may indeed investigate matters determined by administrative tribunals. There is also similar jurisprudence in Alberta[8] and British Columbia.[9]

This conclusion is, of course, highly significant in terms of the extent to which the ombudsman serves as a surrogate for or supplement to the courts in the exercise of their judicial review or appellate jurisdiction. Moreover, while the Ontario ombudsman's jurisdiction over such matters is also tempered by the existence of a further discretion to refuse to take a case where there is a satisfactory alternative legal remedy, it is, nonetheless, also clear from the annual reports of the Ontario ombudsman that, notwithstanding the existence of this discretion, the office has been accepting and dealing with a number of complaints involving the province's major administrative tribunals (such as the Ontario Human Rights Commission and its tribunal, the Health Disciplines Board, the Workplace Safety and Insurance Board (formerly the Workers' Compensation Board)). This has been particularly the case in the domain of procedural impropriety, often involving perceived systemic problems with the process employed by the tribunal for resolving disputes.

The key term in the Ontario legislation leading to its application to the merits of administrative tribunal decisions was the definition of the ombudsman's jurisdiction in terms of the "administration of a government agency." In other jurisdictions, the more common expression is "matter of administration." In either form, however, the expression "administration" has been defined expansively by the courts. Thus, in

---

6   *Ombudsman of Ontario v. Ontario (Labour Relations Board)* (1986), 44 D.L.R. (4th) 312 (Ont. C.A.).

7   *Ombudsman of Ontario v. Ontario (Health Disciplines Board)* (1979), 104 D.L.R. (3d) 597 (Ont. C.A.). See also *Ontario (Ombudsman) v. Board of Radiological Technicians (Ontario)* (1990), 41 Admin. L.R. 215 (Ont. Div. Ct.).

8   *Re Alberta Ombudsman Act* (1970), 10 D.L.R. (3d) 47 (Alta. S.C.T.D.).

9   *Levey v. Friedmann* (1985), 18 D.L.R. (4th) 641 (B.C.S.C.).

the cases just referred to, the Court of Appeal accepted that the *Act* did not use "administration" in contradistinction to "judicial"; rather, it was deployed in a more generic sense of the administrative process and embraced tribunals acting judicially as well as the exercise of other forms of executive and administrative powers.

Most of the impetus for this broad interpretation of this key terminology in establishing the reach of the ombudsman's jurisdiction came from the judgment of the Supreme Court of Canada in *British Columbia Development Corporation* v. *Friedmann (Ombudsman)*.[10] There, the Court was ruling on whether the ombudsman had jurisdiction over a complaint on the basis of unfairness against a decision by a British Columbia Crown corporation to not renew the lease of a long-term commercial tenant in a property it had just purchased. The Court accepted, in interpreting the British Columbia legislation, that "matter of administration" included the policy-making activities of provincial Crown corporations. It was not restricted to the domain of policy implementation.

Most commonly, the ombudsman's jurisdiction is triggered by the complaint of someone "aggrieved" or "affected" by government action or inaction. However, in some provinces, members of the legislature have the right to make a complaint and the ombudsman may, acting on her or his own initiative, investigate a matter.

As already noted, however, the fact that the ombudsman may have jurisdiction in theory does not always mean that he or she will exercise that jurisdiction. All statutes confer considerable discretion on the ombudsman to decline to investigate a complaint. In addition to focusing on the existence of adequate alternative remedies, these provisions also refer to considerations such as the interest of the complainant, and the trivial, frivolous, vexatious, or bad faith nature of the complaint, as well as containing a catchall basis for refusing to get involved, phrased in terms such as "having regard to all the circumstances of the case, any further investigation is unnecessary."[11] There may also be time limits to bring complaints though, more commonly, as under the Ontario statute, a discretion to refuse to deal with a complaint that relates to events that occurred over a year previously.

---

10   [1984] 2 S.C.R. 447.
11   See, for example, *Ombudsman Act*, R.S.O. 1990, c. O.6, s. 17(1)(b).

C. THE OMBUDSMAN IN ACTION

The ombudsman acts primarily in an investigative capacity and in private. Moreover, despite the explicit restrictions on jurisdiction already referred to, this ability to investigate a complaint applies notwithstanding privative and other forms of finality clause. For those purposes, he or she has extensive powers to compel the production of information and interview relevant personnel as well as to enter premises. These powers are subject to limited constraints such as the impeding of criminal investigations and the compromising of the confidentiality attending the deliberations of Cabinet and Cabinet committees. However, these specific exemptions aside, public interest immunity claims do not generally prevail as against the ombudsman and those interviewed are not subject to most of the normal secrecy constraints. Moreover, for the most part, those interviewed do not have testimonial immunity for material that might incriminate them — only a protection against its subsequent use against them in other proceedings.

In the exercise of this investigative role, the ombudsman is not hampered by any obligation to hold formal hearings though has a discretion to do so. Also, he or she must inform the head of any department or agency that a complaint is being investigated and, as is typical of legislation authorizing investigations, must provide any person or organization with an opportunity to make submissions in situations where there may be material in any report or recommendation that may affect adversely that person or organization.

In typical ombudsman legislation, the grounds on which the ombudsman can find maladministration cover the usual grounds of judicial review, although expressed in somewhat different language, as well as grounds that are not within the scope of judicial review. Sometimes these grounds will be within the compass of a statutory right of appeal: straight error of fact and, more significantly, on the basis that the decision is just plain "wrong." Recommendations and adverse reports may also be triggered by the ombudsman's negative views of the nature of any law (primary or subordinate) or practice of an organization covered by Act.

In this respect, section 21(1) of the Ontario *Act* provides an example. The ombudsman is entitled to intervene whenever he or she is of the opinion that "a decision, recommendation, act or omission" :

(a) appears to have been contrary to law;

(b) was unreasonable, unjust, oppressive, or improperly discriminatory, or was in accordance with a rule of law or a provision of any Act or a practice that is or may be unreasonable, unjust, oppressive, or improperly discriminatory;

(c) was based wholly or partly on a mistake of law or fact;

(d) was wrong.

Subsection 2 then goes on to provide that the section also applies to the exercise of discretionary powers for improper purposes, on irrelevant grounds, or on the basis of irrelevant considerations. As well, intervention is also permissible if the ombudsman is of the view that reasons should have been given for the exercise of any discretionary power. Thereafter, the scope of the ombudsman's powers of recommendation are conditioned by the nature of the grounds on which he or she may intervene and, not surprisingly, include the ability to recommend reconsideration, rectification, cancellation, and variation as well as a reassessment of any law or practice, the provision of reasons, and, "any other steps."

These recommendations are conveyed to the relevant decision maker and responsible minister. They may include a request that the ombudsman be informed of the disposition of the matter and also specify the time within which any action should be taken. The recommendations and processes of the ombudsman are also generally protected by privative clauses immunizing them from judicial review other than for jurisdictional error. However, unlike the decisions of most administrative tribunals and agencies and the courts on judicial review and statutory appeal, the recommendations of the ombudsman are persuasive only; they have no binding force. The ombudsman, like the auditor general or provincial auditors, is an officer of Parliament,[12] as reflected by the alternative title to the office under the New Zealand legislation: parliamentary commissioner for administration. If recommendations are not followed, the ombudsman must resort to the political arena by way of report to the premier and, thereafter, to the legislative assembly.[13] Through both press releases and annual reports, the ombudsman can make public any concerns about individual decisions and, more generally, with the functioning of government and the support provided to her or his office.

---

12 One of the ramifications of this is probably that the ombudsman, like the auditor general will have to seek the aid of the legislature, not the courts, if governmental officials fail to respond to demands based on provisions in the legislation. See *Canada (Auditor General)* v. *Canada (Minister of Energy, Mines and Resources)*, [1989] 2 S.C.R. 49.

13 See, for example,"Ombudsman Presents Four Investigation Reports," press release, 29 April 1999. Here, the Ontario Ombudsman details four investigations in which the department or agency failed to respond adequately to the Ombudsman's finding and recommendations.

It is in this latter domain, of course, that the true test of the worth of the office will become manifest. Unless the ombudsman can achieve a sufficiently high regard among the political actors or, failing that, generate effective public and constituency support through the appropriate deployment of media and other opportunities for publicity, her or his profile will suffer and departments and agencies will ignore recommendations with impunity. Indeed, as exemplified by a number of jurisdictions, without the marshalling of powerful political and public support, the effectiveness of the office can be compromised only too readily by resource constraints, particularly at the hands of governments that have been elected on a platform of downsizing. In short, the office is one of both great potential and great fragility.

D. SUMMARY OF ADVANTAGES AND DISADVANTAGES OF OMBUDSMAN'S JURISDICTION

Clearly, the ombudsman offers a number of advantages over the regular courts as a way of providing relief for unlawful administrative action. As noted already in the introduction, perhaps the most significant of those advantages is the fact that the office carries the complaint at no cost to the complainant. The ombudsman's rights of access and investigative capacities are considerable, more straightforward, and probably overall more effective than the processes of discovery in the regular courts and the obtaining of evidence for judicial review applications and statutory appeals through access to information legislation. In most jurisdictions, privative clauses are ineffective against the ombudsman while the exercise of the ombudsman's powers is itself subject to judicial scrutiny only on the basis of jurisdictional error. The ombudsman also can exercise a continuing equitable jurisdiction over complaints and has the ability through utilization of the media and drawing matters to the attention of the legislature to generate considerable adverse publicity when maladministration is uncovered and particularly when it is not rectified.

There are, however, countervailing considerations. Resource constraints may place a limit on the capacity of the ombudsman to fulfill her or his mandate effectively as may the marginalization of the ombudsman's role and office by the government in power. This latter consideration is particularly significant given the inability of the ombudsman to do anything more than make recommendations and to make a report to the legislature if those recommendations are not followed. Also, the fact that the complainant has no control over the carriage of the complaint may be a disadvantage in some circumstances but, more particularly, the various discretions that the ombudsman possesses over whether or not to take or pursue a particular complaint means, in resource-stretched situations, that many complaints will not be sufficiently compelling to attract the ombudsman's attention. In some jurisdictions, such as Ontario, the lack of any jurisdiction over colleges and universities, hospital and school boards, and municipalities also means that there are significant pockets of the administrative process not reached by this potentially very powerful instrument for correcting administrative deficiencies and wrongdoing.

FURTHER READINGS

BERZINS, C., "Reviewing the Merits of Adjudicative Decisions: The Ombudsman and Ontario's Administrative Tribunals" (1999), 21 The Advocates' Quarterly 467

MARSHALL, M.A., & L.C. REIF, "The Ombudsman: Maladministration and Alternative Dispute Resolution" (1995), 34 Alta. L Rev. 215

OWEN, S., "The Ombudsman: Essential Elements and Common Challenges" in L. Reif, M. Marshall, & C. Ferris, eds., *The Ombudsman: Diversity and Development* (Edmonton: International Ombudsman Institute, 1993) 1

PART FIVE

ADMINISTRATIVE LAW IN THE TWENTY-FIRST CENTURY

CHAPTER 23

THE FUTURE

The bulk of the jurisprudence and statutes that are the core of this book come from the last thirty years. During that time, there has been a major evolution in and refinement of the rules and principles of administrative law, as well as a significant improvement in the quality and sophistication of the delivery of administrative justice in this country.

Over the last twenty years, the Supreme Court of Canada has forged an overarching theory for judicial supervision of statutory and prerogative decision making albeit in a somewhat staccato fashion so typical of the growth of the common law. That theory is founded on the importance of respecting parliamentary choices of tribunals and officials as the primary agents for the taking of a wide range of decisions affecting individuals in their relationship with the state. It is also fuelled in part by a recognition that the ordinary courts are not the sole repositories of wisdom on the interpretation of statutes, particularly in contexts far removed from those which those courts encounter in their day-to-day work. Judicial review, especially on substantive grounds, has, in very many instances, therefore, become a sparingly exercised basis for intervention in an age in which deference is the dominant theme.

Despite often straitened circumstances, tribunals in most jurisdictions across the country merit the respect for their professionalism and expertise that they now receive regularly from the courts. Through national and regional organizations, tribunal members have developed a healthy degree of self-esteem and collegiality. This movement has at its core the missions of self-improvement, continuing education, and pro-

537

viding a lobby that keeps bringing governments face to face with the dimensions of the administrative justice system and its need for adequate resources and sufficient independence to enable it to both do its work well and instill public confidence in the quality of justice on offer.

As a consequence of statutory reforms and revisions of rules of court, the last thirty years have also seen a massive change in the nature of the issues that arise in the remedial sphere of judicial review. Largely gone, though not entirely, is judicial preoccupation with whether there are technical obstacles to the seeking and granting of the relief being sought, an inquiry that, in very many instances, was divorced totally from any sense of whether there were sufficient substantive justifications for the technical restrictions under consideration. Now, remedial issues tend to be confined to the domain of the court's discretion and the far more appropriate questions of whether judicial review is timely and whether there are alternatives to judicial review that those seeking the intervention of the courts should pursue first. This is all for the better.

All of this raises questions of where administrative law and the administrative justice system are likely to head from here. Despite downsizing, privatization, and outsourcing, it is almost certainly the case that the administrative justice system will remain the most common form of interface that Canadians will have with the law. Governments, therefore, have a major responsibility to ensure that it works properly, and that demands major resources. However, there has also been a recognition by governments that economies of scale can be achieved by the grouping and amalgamation of tribunals exercising related and, at times, overlapping jurisdictions. In general, there is nothing unhealthy about that, and it is a trend that undoubtedly will continue. In the delivery of administrative justice across the country, there is also an increasing recognition of the value of diverting as many matters as possible away from formal adjudication to various forms of alternative dispute resolution. Not only can that conserve scarce resources but, for many situations, it also provides a more effective and appropriate form of solving conflict. It is also the case that the dizzying changes in technology of recent times, particularly in the domains of communication and access to information, are affecting and will continue to affect the way in which administrative justice is being delivered. Once again, if deployed appropriately, the "information highway" cannot but help improve the quality of service.

In terms of specific institutions, two in particular merit continuing observation and assessment. Judicial review is within the range of very few. There is therefore every reason to applaud the creation of the

Québec Administrative Tribunal with its extensive, relatively informal appellate jurisdiction over a broad range of administrative decision making in that province. It will, therefore, be instructive to see whether it succeeds in its promise of greater accessibility to administrative justice and also whether the parallel creation of an administrative review council provides an effective mechanism for overall scrutiny of the operation of the administrative justice system. Even more importantly, the various offices of the ombudsman across the country, in theory, offer for most people the greatest promise for securing redress for various forms of governmental wrong, particularly in the case of decision-making within government departments and agencies. It is therefore particularly galling not only to hear of the complaints by various holders of that office of inadequate resources to fulfill their mandate effectively, but also to see the continued intransigence of the federal government to requests that it create a general federal ombudsman and to witness the legislative abolition of the post in Newfoundland.

In the world of judicial review, the recent amalgamation of review of questions of law and fact and review of exercises of discretion under the umbrella of the "pragmatic and functional" test for determining the intensity of judicial scrutiny undoubtedly will feature in lower-court decisions for some time, as the wrinkles are worked out and the matters of detail resolved. However, while some take a different position, I do not see, either as part of this exercise or otherwise, that the Supreme Court ultimately will modify its largely deferential approach to decision making by expert tribunals and those on whom the legislature has conferred broad discretions. Nonetheless, there are still a great number of issues about the extent to which the *Canadian Charter of Rights and Freedoms* impinges on and constrains the operation of the administrative process. In the purely common law domain, it is also the case that Canada lacks a modern, sophisticated law of estoppel applicable to public authorities. I, therefore, do see considerable possibilities for the evolution of limitations on administrative action based on both the *Charter* and principles of estoppel.

In the domain of procedures, it will be of interest to observe whether the pressure for enhanced opportunities for constituency and general public involvement in policy-making exercises is sustained. If it is, we might still expect to see a more general acceptance of the utility of statutory notice and comment codes. In addition or alternatively, there may be, under both common law procedural fairness and the doctrine of legitimate expectation, a re-evaluation of the extent to which current law excludes policy-making exercises from the ambit of implied procedural protections.

Of particular concern to all administrative tribunal members, there is also the growing litigation involving the independence and impartiality of decision makers. That is not likely to stop until the Supreme Court of Canada resolves how far such issues can be raised under section 7 of the *Charter* as part of the "principles of fundamental justice" and whether the preamble to *Constitution Act, 1867,* in and of itself, might be a springboard for more general assertions of an entitlement to independence for adjudicative tribunals. This issue, of course, is also one on which governments across the country could take the initiative by creating for most tribunals more transparent, qualifications-based, independent of government appointments processes, as well as dispensing with pleasure appointments and reviewing carefully by reference to appropriate standards the other terms and conditions on which members of various tribunals and agencies hold their appointments.

Of somewhat more pervasive and fundamental concern in any assessment of the future of judicial review of administrative action has to be the effects or impact of changing modes of government. At one level, there is the spectre of increasing globalization and the growing reach of international tribunals of all kinds, as exemplified by the various forms of international dispute resolution found in the North American Free Trade Agreement, mechanisms that involve the review of the decisions of domestic statutory authorities. At another level, there is the phenomenon of increasing privatization, outsourcing, and the delegation of tasks to the private sector. In this area of shared jurisdiction between governmental and non-governmental bodies for tasks that still have a significant public component, what regime of law is to operate and, to the extent that the tentacles of administrative law reach that far, what modifications, if any will be necessary? Indeed, this may very well be the most significant challenge faced by administrative law over the next few years.

One way or the other, the first years of the new millennium promise to be exciting ones for administrative law in all of its manifestations.

TABLE OF CASES

INDEX

ABOUT THE AUTHOR

David Mullan is recognized as one of Canada's foremost scholars of administrative law. He lectured at Victoria University of Wellington in New Zealand, before joining the Faculty of Law at Queen's University in 1971, where he has remained, apart from four years (1973–1977) at Dalhousie Law School. He is co-author of *Administrative Law: Cases, Text and Materials,* now in its fourth edition, written in collaboration with faculty members at Osgoode Hall Law School and the University of Toronto. He is also the author of the Administrative Law Title in the *Canadian Encyclopedia Digest.* Over the past 25 years, he has served as consultant on a number of law reform projects and is currently a panelist under Chapter 19 of the North American Free Trade Agreement. He is a part-time member of the Ontario Human Rights Code Board of Inquiry. Professor Mullan has been a recipient of the Queen's University Alumni Award for Excellence in Teaching, the Queen's University Prize for Excellence in Research, and the Canadian Association of Law Teachers' Award for Academic Excellence.